SLAVERY IN AMERICA

SLAVERY IN AMERICA

A READER AND GUIDE

Kenneth Morgan

EDINBURGH UNIVERSITY PRESS

Edinburgh University Press Ltd
22 George Square, Edinburgh

Typeset in Sabon and Gill Sans
by TechBooks, New Delhi, India, and
printed and bound in Great Britain by
Antony Rowe Ltd, Chippenham, Wilts

A CIP record for this book is available from
the British Library

ISBN 0 7486 1795 7 (hardback)
ISBN 0 7486 1796 5 (paperback)

CONTENTS

ANALYTICAL TABLE OF CONTENTS

PREFACE

Slavery in America: A Reader and Guide is designed as a core text that provides primary material and secondary readings intended for undergraduate classroom use. It is suitable for courses on American slavery and African-American history and for surveys of American history up to the Civil War. It can also be used for more specialised courses on revolutionary America, the antebellum United States and the Old South. In keeping with most undergraduate teaching, the book is intended to support a semester's work. To provide sufficient material in an important field in American history that has attracted much historical attention, I have divided up the book into twelve chapters. These cover many significant aspects of North American slavery but there was not room to include everything of potential importance. For instance, I have omitted the literature on slave medicine and diet. I would like to have included it but space constraints and the need to provide coverage for a semester's teaching meant that omissions were inevitable. The twelve topics can be assigned weekly and still leave the instructor sufficient time for an introduction to a course and for revision and examination. As there is currently no such volume in print covering the entire sweep of North American slavery, my hope is that this reader and guide will prove serviceable as a challenging teaching tool.

Each of the twelve chapters has a consistent format. An introduction discusses twenty of the leading secondary books and articles pertaining to the topic featured in a particular chapter. I highlight the main findings of these studies as succinctly as possible and also place them within the historiography of particular topics. The twenty books are listed in bibliographies appended to each chapter. This contextualises the readings in each chapter to enable a student to focus on the main issues that have attracted historical attention. I have tended to select books in preference to journal articles because undergraduates usually search out books for further consultation rather than scholarly journals. Nevertheless, some seminal articles are included on various topics. The introduction to each chapter is followed by one secondary source and three extracts from primary documents. Notes are retained for the reprinted articles – though, in some cases, they have been lightly trimmed – and only minor cuts are made in the texts. This means that students and instructors can see the evidence on which arguments are based. It also enables the intregrity of an author's analysis to be properly represented without slimming down the content. Both the secondary items and the documentary texts are introduced briefly. Several questions are appended to my introductions to the secondary readings to provide a focus for class discussion.

The selected readings seek to offer wide coverage in terms of the geography, chronology and themes connected with American slavery. I have deliberately included different historical approaches ranging from feminist and Marxist discussions to more traditional, empirically based analyses. The selections cover some of the best scholarship on American slavery written in the past thirty years. Of the twelve reprinted essays, one was published in the 1970s, four in the 1980s, three in the 1990s and four since 2000. The chosen pieces, in my experience, work well with undergraduates. Lack of space means that many fine historians and discussions of slavery are not represented, but the bibliographies should point students in the right direction for more intensive work. The documents selected for each section are pertinent to the topic under consideration. As far as possible, I have included documentary extracts that dovetail with the secondary readings. The book is prefaced by a short overview of the development of North American slavery. This does not pretend to highlight major debates; nor is it intended for instructors. Its target audience comprises undergraduates studying this field of American history without any prior knowledge. There are naturally severe limitations in trying to cover a broad and complex topic in 8,000 introductory words, but the discussion is intended to whet the appetite for more detailed consideration and reflection.

In preparing the reader and guide I have benefited from the academic advice of Christine Daniels and Michael Tadman and from the editorial input of Nicola Carr, who commissioned the book. I must also thank my family for their patience during the final stages of compilation and editing.

Kenneth Morgan
Brunel University, London

ABBREVIATIONS

AHR	*American Historical Review*
AmAS	American Antiquarian Society, Worcester, Massachusetts
BFAS	Boston Female Anti-Slavery Society
BPL	Boston Public Library
BrFAS	Brooklyn Female Anti-Slavery Society
CG	*Congressional Globe*
CSL	Connecticut State Library, Hartford
CWAL	Roy P. Basler et al. (eds), *The Collected Works of Abraham Lincoln*, 9 vols (New Brunswick, NJ, 1953–5)
CWH	*Civil War History*
DOW	Deeds, Orders, Wills
Duke	Duke University Library, Durham, North Carolina
EPI	Essex-Peabody Institute, Essex-Peabody Library, Salem, Massachusetts
GDAH	Georgia Department of Archives and History, Atlanta
Hening, *Statutes at Large*	William Waller Hening, *The Statutes at Large: Being a Collection of All the Laws of Virginia, from the First Session of the Legislature in the Year 1619*. 13 vols (Richmond, VA, 1819–23)
HNO	The Historic New Orleans Collection
HSP	Historical Society of Pennsylvania, Philadelphia
Iredell	James Iredell
JAF	*Journal of African History*
JAH	*Journal of American History*
JIH	*Journal of Interdisciplinary History*
JNH	*Journal of Negro History*
Jones	Hamilton C. Jones
JSH	*Journal of Southern History*

KSA	Kentucky State Department for Archives and History, Frankfort
LASD	Ladies Anti-Slavery Society of Dover, Massachusetts
LFAS	Lynn Female Anti-Slavery Society
LHS	Lynn Historical Society, Massachusetts
LOC	Library of Congress, Washington, DC
LSA	Louisiana Archives and Records Service, Baton Rouge
LSU	Louisiana State University, Lower Mississippi Valley Collection, Hill Memorial Library
MCGC	H. R. McIlwaine (ed.), *Minutes of the Council and General Court of Colonial Virginia*, 2nd edn (Richmond, VA, 1979)
MHS	Massachusetts Historical Society, Boston
MSA	Maryland State Archives, Annapolis
MVHR	*Mississippi Valley Historical Review*
NCDAH	North Carolina Department of Archives and History, Raleigh
NHHS	New Hampshire Historical Society, Concord
P & P	*Past & Present*
PFAS	Philadelphia Female Anti-Slavery Society
RASP	Records of Antebellum Southern Plantations on Microfilm (Kenneth M. Stampp, ed.)
Rawick (ed.), *The American Slave*	George P. Rawick (ed.), *The American Slave: A Composite Autobiography*, 19 vols (Westport, CT, 1972–)
Rich.	J. S. G. Richardson
RSDB	Runaway Slave Database
RVC	Susan Kingsbury (ed.), *Records of the Virginia Company*, 4 vols (Washington, DC, 1930–5)
SAL	*United States Statutes at Large*
SC	Schweninger Collection
SCDAH	South Carolina Department of Archives and History, Columbia
SFAS	Salem Female Anti-Slavery Society
SQR	*Southern Quarterly Review*
Statutes at Large	US, *Statutes at Large, Treaties, and Proclamations of the United States of America*, 17 vols (Boston, 1850–73)
TSLA	Tennessee State Library and Archives, Nashville

UMC	University of Missouri, Western Historical Collection, Elmer Ellis Memorial Library
UNC	University of North Carolina, Chapel Hill
UNO	University of New Orleans, Supreme Court of Louisiana Collection, Archives and Special Collections, Earl K. Long Library
VMHB	*Virginia Magazine of History and Biography*
VSL	Virginia State Library, Richmond
WMQ	*William and Mary Quarterly*
WRHS	Western Reserve Historical Society, Cleveland, OH

INTRODUCTION: SLAVERY
IN NORTH AMERICA

Slavery as an institution lasted for over two-and-a-half centuries in North America. The first black Africans to leave a trace in the documentary record can be found in the 1610s in Virginia, a few years before the traditionally accepted arrival of twenty-odd negroes in that colony in 1619. Slavery grew slowly at first but then inexorably once the plantation system became established in the American South. Though the work of abolitionists and the manumission of slaves chipped away at the margins of slavery, most black people remained slaves in the United States until, embroiled in the bloodiest conflict on North American soil, they were freed by Abraham Lincoln in the final Emancipation Proclamation of 1 January 1863. Racism and exploitation of black Americans long outlasted the American Civil War and it was not until the Civil Rights campaigns of the 1950s and 1960s that the biracial divide began to be broken down in public in the United States. The articles and documentary extracts included in this volume, however, concentrate on the era of slavery. How slavery emerged in what became the USA and how it developed and eventually came to a demise is outlined here as an introduction to a broad topic that has had as lasting an effect on modern American society as any other single theme one might choose to analyse.[1]

The initial choices available to seventeenth-century English settlers to work the land in North America consisted either in using white workers or in engaging or coercing Indian labour. White indentured servants provided only a temporary solution because they served short-term contacts of between four and seven years and thereafter seeped out into the free labour force. They had legal rights, which meant they had recourse to courts if masters tried to abuse their position over their labour. They came in significant numbers when wages were depressed in England and when job opportunities were poor; but their supply diminished after better conditions for lower-class workers became available in England in the last third of the seventeenth century.[2] Indian ways of settlement and land cultivation proved inimical for the sort of agricultural production needed by whites in the Chesapeake. They were totally unused to the sort of labour required on plantations. Their knowledge of the terrain made them difficult to contain under such a system of land and crop cultivation. Moreover, epidemics occurred from time to time in which large numbers of Indians were killed by tuberculosis, pneumonia, influenza and other diseases that partly resulted from contact with people from a different disease environment.[3]

The eventual solution to the labour supply for North American plantations lay via the Atlantic slave trade. Modern historians suggest that something in the region of 10 million Africans crossed the Atlantic during the entire period of the slave trade (c. 1440–1880).[4] This massive flow of people constituted the largest inter-continental migration of men and women, whether free or enforced, in the early modern era. The British colonies in North America were thus the recipients of large numbers of people who were primarily bought as workers. They followed in the footsteps of what other European powers had already begun to exploit in the Americas for generations. After the restoration of the Stuart monarchy, the slave trade burgeoned. Over the entire period from 1662 to 1807, when Britain abolished its slave trade, about 3.4 million slaves were exported from west Africa to different parts of the British Empire.[5] The majority of Africans taken by English slave traders ended up in the Caribbean, but the southern colonies of British North America were important secondary markets.

The large-scale adoption of slave labour owed much to the growth of the English slave trade after 1660, but it was not simply a question of more regular supply of enslaved Africans that triggered the beginning of the racial transformation of the North American population. Social and cultural reasons for enslaving Africans also assumed significance. Blackness, for Stuart Englishmen, suggested connections with the Devil. Africans were regarded as heathens, which made them seem barbaric to many western Europeans. They were feared for their lust and savagery. Africans were also singled out for their sheer difference from Europeans – in their physiognomy, gestures, languages, dress and behaviour. Together, an amalgam of negative attitudes emerged that amounted to racial prejudice towards Africans.[6] Europeans generally tolerated slavery in the seventeenth century. They knew that slavery had existed in human societies since ancient times. Various passages in the Bible condoned the existence of slave societies. The educated classes widely accepted the practice of slavery. Though some dissenting voices were troubled about the moral implications of enslaving other people, most notable European jurists and philosophers did not question the existence of slavery. Englishmen prided themselves on the fact that they were free-born Englishmen with legal rights at common law. The fact that neither serfdom nor slavery flourished on English soil meant that bonded labour at home avoided chattel status and the concomitant absence of legal rights.[7]

Englishmen's attitudes towards black Africans and slavery were important influences lying behind the acceptance of slaveholding in the seventeenth-century Chesapeake and Carolinas. Whether racial prejudice preceded slavery in North America or whether it escalated when large numbers of Africans were imported has led, however, to disagreement among historians. Some scholars consider that racial prejudice was a sufficiently ingrained trait to justify shipping millions of Africans to the New World via the Middle Passage. Yet other historians are not convinced that the various attitudes that singled out blacks for degradation are enough to explain the origins of North American slavery. They point out that the treatment of blacks and their interaction with whites and Native Americans varied considerably over time.[8]

The transition from servitude to slavery in the Chesapeake occurred in the four decades between 1680 and 1720. The availability of new indentured servants tapered off significantly after 1660. Large importations of slaves to the Chesapeake only began in the 1680s but it was not until the first decade of the eighteenth century that the supply of Africans to Virginia and Maryland was regular. Thus the rise of slavery in the Chesapeake was a consequence, not a cause, of the decrease in the availability of white bonded labour.[9] The transition from servitude to slavery in South Carolina occurred rapidly after rice production began to dominate the colony's economy after 1690. South Carolina planters quickly purchased Africans for their plantations. The growth in planting rice as a staple crop coincided with a regular supply of 'new negroes' and a sporadic supply of indentured servants. Africans had an additional attraction for buyers: namely their familiarity with rice cultivation. Some slave arrivals were familiar with growing rice in paddies along river banks in west Africa and were experienced in cultivating the crop.[10]

Slave labour was found in all the British North American colonies from Maine to South Carolina in the late seventeenth century, but it was more important in some than others. Broadly speaking, the proportion of African-Americans in a colony's population increased as one moved from north to south, with most slaves clustered south of Pennsylvania. In 1750, for instance, 210,400 (86.9 per cent) of the 242,100 slaves in North America lived in the Chesapeake and Lower South. During the eighteenth century less than 3 per cent of the New England population and less than 8 per cent of the Middle colonies' population was black.[11] Most North American slaves in 1700 were imported Africans but by 1776 creoles made up

80 per cent of the slaves in the thirteen colonies. More balanced sex ratios in the slave population, the greater fertility of creole slave women rather than Africans, and the emergence of slave families accounts for the growth of the African-American population from the mid-eighteenth century onwards. These factors meant that a self-sustained black population was already in place throughout most of North America before the founding of the United States of America.[12]

Productive work for white masters was the chief *raison d'être* for importing and employing enslaved Africans in the New World. On six days of the week most slaves spent their time toiling for their owners without any wages. In the North American context, slave work varied over time and according to regional economic demands. In New England and the Middle colonies and states there were no staple crops that required a plantation labour force. Moreover, reliance on family labour in many rural households – especially in New England, where good reproduction rates among whites produced sizeable families – meant that recruiting workers from outside the household was a secondary option. Nevertheless, blacks could be found working in a wide range of agricultural and industrial tasks and trades in the North. In port cities such as New York and Philadelphia, slaves worked in the maritime trades as sailmakers, coopers and dock workers; they assisted artisans and tradesmen in shops and workshops; and female slaves found a niche as domestic servants. Middling craftsmen and artisans in New York and Philadelphia increasingly employed one or two slaves after 1750, finding them a useful source of labour when indentured servants were unavailable or wage labourers proved too costly to hire.[13]

Slaves also worked in the rural agriculture of the northern colonies and states. Farmers were increasingly replacing servants with slaves in Pennsylvania, New Jersey and New York during the first half of the eighteenth century. They mainly held slaves in ones or twos. In the Narragansett Bay area of Rhode Island slaves could be found in larger numbers, with some stock-rearing farms employing up to twenty slaves. The other extensive rural form of employment for slaves in the northern colonies and states consisted of ironworks, situated especially in New Jersey and Pennsylvania. In the northern colonies, African-Americans' labour was regarded as interchangeable with that of various free and unfree white workers and they worked as individuals or in small groups. Supervisory arrangements, as a result, tended to be flexible, especially where blacks were working in masters' households.[14]

The situation in the South was fundamentally different: though domestic slaves were employed and some blacks were assigned artisan tasks, the majority of slaves toiled on plantations producing staple crops for export. Tobacco cultivation involved regular, monotonous work over a seasonal cycle that lasted from the beginning of the year until the autumn. Gang labour characterised most of the work done on Chesapeake tobacco plantations. Under this system, slaves worked in units of commonly nine to twelve workers. Their pace of work was determined by the leader of the gang, a black foreman, under the watchful eye of a white overseer. Gang labour maximised productivity for planters. Slave work on the Lowcountry rice plantations followed a different pattern. The normal method of work on South Carolina and Georgia estates consisted of tasks supervised by a white overseer or a black foreman, known as a driver, or both. Task work was followed at each stage of rice production. For slaves, it had several benefits. They could carry out their allocated daily portion of work at their own pace. Industrious workers could hope to complete their tasks by early afternoon. Slaves were supervised less directly than in the gang system, allowing them to become self-reliant at work and able to adapt their work practices without too much direct interference.[15]

Because of their chattel status, slaves' behaviour was strictly controlled by law. Legal codes reflected the repression involved in relations between masters and slaves. Certainly, the legislation on slavery enacted by colonial legislatures after 1660 and the range of punishments that whites could mete out to blacks appear to support this sombre view of master–slave relations. Virginia's first major slave code was passed in 1680 and strengthened in 1705. South Carolina had a series of slave codes, including detailed legislation enacted in 1712 that was tightened up in 1740 after the Stono Rebellion, led by Congolese rebel slaves, had alarmed the Lowcountry planter class. A statutory law of race and slavery existed in all thirteen British North American colonies by the middle of the eighteenth century. These acts singled out slaves as a caste. On paper they were draconian, allowing for a wide range of physical punishments including branding on the cheek or thumbs, amputation of body limbs, splitting noses, castration and the death penalty, each one applied according to the nature of wrongdoing by slaves. Under these laws, slaves lacked various rights – the right to marry, the right to testify in court, the right to challenge the hereditary nature of slavery. Examples abound of how these vehicles of white dominance were inflicted on slaves.[16]

Despite powerful instruments of coercion and compulsion, however, master–slave relations were not as unremittingly bleak or as harsh as the above paragraph suggests. One major reason why this was so lay in the spread of patriarchy as the ideological underpinning of slave control during the eighteenth century. Patriarchy meant acting towards slaves as a father figure, recognising that black workers were part of an extended household. Good work and behaviour by slaves would be rewarded by patriarchs with gifts and possibly promotion to skilled tasks or positions in the master's household. But opposition, recalcitrance, absconding would bring down on the slave the punishments that a dutiful father felt was appropriate to control his charges. During the eighteenth century, patriarchy on the American plantations modulated into paternalism. This was a complex process, not occurring everywhere at a similar time. The shift from patriarchy to paternalism – a process continued in the antebellum era – was influenced by Enlightenment concerns for benevolence towards others and progress in human society, by a greater number of creoles in the slave population, and by a gradual change in attitudes in western society about inflicting bodily pain. Patriarchal attitudes emphasised order, obedience, hierarchy and subjection; they displayed few illusions about the potential rebelliousness of slaves. Paternalistic attitudes, on the other hand, proffered a generous treatment of slaves and expected gratitude in return; they promoted the myth of the happy, contented bonded black worker.[17]

Lest we should think that the material life of slaves was cosy, the dimensions and bare furnishings of slave quarters should be remembered. Slaves usually lived in small, spartan log cabins about twelve feet by fourteen feet. The spaces between the logs were filled with mud. Slave quarters, whether on or off plantations, were near to their place of work. Despite their modest appearance, they usually enabled African-Americans to exercise control over their own domestic arrangements without too much interference from white overseers or managers.[18] Slave quarters afforded little privacy because they were huddled together and often arranged around a communal yard. But they were the site of much of the community and cultural life of slaves. By the late eighteenth century, a rich set of family networks was common in North America. African-Americans used the base of family obligations, love and affection and shared beliefs about the nature of kinship to sustain their spirit and wellbeing.[19]

Slave customs and cultural beliefs testify to a rich blend of African practices and adjustments to life on a new continent. They provided a focal point for black communities. Slaves enjoyed music and dance, playing a wide range of musical instruments ranging from fiddles to horns and percussion. They sang at work to ease the boredom and rigours of the labouring routine. Slaves told folk stories often linked with memories handed down from African traditions. Festivals and parades at Christmas, the New Year, Easter and after the crop harvest were times for slave celebrations. Spiritual values were an essential part of slave communities. A belief in spirits often seemed mere superstition to white observers; but it was bound up with a commonly held black belief that spirits cast spells that could harm or cure, something that was linked to medicinal treatments for ailments by the use of herbs. Though African beliefs that filtered through to America had many variations, they all acknowledged the existence of a supreme being and invoked the spirits of nature and ancestors. Life's major staging posts – birth, marriage, death – were all steeped in spiritual significance for slaves. Funerals, in particular, were observed with a high degree of ritual and ceremony because many blacks believed that death marked a return to Africa.[20]

Efforts to Christianise North American slaves were carried out from the beginning of the eighteenth century, but it was not until the 'Great

Awakening' of the 1740s and the religious revivalism that swept parts of the South in the 1750s and 1760s that large numbers of slaves were converted to Christianity. These evangelical stirrings of the soul were associated largely with the Presbyterians, Methodists and Baptists, who favoured itinerancy, extempore preaching, conversion as a result of God's saving grace, open-air gatherings, fervent hymn singing, and the prospect for all who joined the Christian faith and maintained their faith to live in the hope of everlasting peace in the life hereafter. Doctrinal differences were kept to a minimum by white preachers proselytising the gospels to blacks. Such evangelical exhortation had a widespread appeal to blacks as well as the ordinary white population.[21] The growth of Christianity among the American black population became more pronounced after the War of Independence, however, as African-Americans, especially in the northern states, began to form their own churches and chapels.[22]

Despite the richness of slaves' inner lives, they remained under white legal and social control. Resistance to bondage by slaves therefore occurred frequently. The form that resistance took varied. Opportunities existed to damage a master's property, to steal food and to interrupt seasonal work routines. Resistance did not necessarily have a political content; in fact, usually this was not present in acts of defiance. The most common type of slave resistance was probably flight from a master's purview.[23] Slave revolts in North America, however, did not have the impact one might suppose. There were, in fact, more aborted risings than actual revolts; more conspiracy scares than conspiracies undertaken; and not a single slave revolt that proved successful. Throughout the plantation Americas the only slave rebellion that resulted in the overthrow of white power occurred in Saint-Domingue in 1791, where 400,000 blacks, inspired by the French Revolution's ideals, overthrew their white overlords and created a black republic. The new regime lasted until Napoleon Bonaparte restored French white rule in 1804. The Saint-Domingue revolt remained an iconic moment of triumph for all subsequent generations of slaves, but it was never replicated in North America. A number of revolts and conspiracies did occur such as Bacon's Rebellion in Virginia (1676), the Stono revolt in South Carolina (1739), Gabriel Prosser's conspiracy in Virginia (1800) and Nat Turner's revolt in Virginia (1831). All occurred when white internal divisions were apparent. But they each followed a different course and each ended in failure.[24]

Antislavery ideas had begun to make headway in North America by 1776 and their impact escalated in the following quarter century. Before the 1750s, most theologians, lawyers and philosophers condoned slavery uncritically. Increasingly, however, a corpus of antislavery ideas gained currency. Influenced by the ideas of the French philosophe Montesquieu and Scottish Enlightenment thinkers, many intellectuals took up the antislavery mantle in the 1750s and 1760s by arguing that slavery was an unsatisfactory condition that denied a certain category of people the right to political and civil happiness.[25] Among religious groups, condemnation of slaveholding increased. Methodists such as John Wesley and Francis Asbury exhorted against the immorality of slaveholding.[26] Quakers denounced slavery and the slave trade as wicked.[27]

Many antislavery ideas emanated in the first place from Europe rather than America, but they were widely discussed and circulated throughout the transatlantic world via correspondence, the spread of printed literature, visits to North America, speeches, sermons and lectures. The Quakers, in particular, played a crucial role in spreading the antislavery message through their firm transatlantic links. Prominent American Friends such as Anthony Benezet and John Woolman publicised the cause both at home and on visits to Britain. The Religious Society of Friends believed in pacifism and condemned warfare; they opposed the capture of slaves in tribal conflicts in west Africa. They believed that all people were equal in the eyes of God, whatever their skin colour and worldly status. Quakers banned their members from engaging in the slave trade and disapproved of Friends owning slaves. Yet even for the Quakers the crusade against slaveholding did not come easily. In the American heartland of Quakerism – Pennsylvania and New Jersey – Friends strived for generations until about 1770 before it was accepted that slaveholding among their members should be banned.[28]

The sea change in approaches to slavery that gathered apace after 1750 stood to make some impact on the Declaration of Independence. But the relationship of slavery to that founding script of American nationhood reveals some of the ambiguities of tackling slavery publicly in the new United States of America. 'We hold these Truths to be self-evident', the document stated, 'that all Men are created equal, that they are endowed by their Creator with certain unalienable Rights, that among these are Life, Liberty, and the Pursuit of Happiness'. Behind the seemingly progressive language, however, the broad concepts espoused had a more limited meaning for contemporaries. 'Men', in the political discourse of the time, referred to adult white males. 'Unalienable Rights' meant natural rights for white men. 'Liberty' was to be reserved to those enjoying 'the Pursuit of Happiness' – white, propertied males. Blacks had an inferior position in the pyramid of human societies; they were consequently disqualified from membership in the political world.[29]

Perhaps the most telling aspect of slave behaviour during the war was the sheer numbers who used opportunities to quit slavery. Some estimates reckon that the total scale of the flight of blacks from the United States during the war amounted to between 80,000 and 100,000 people. The blacks who fled North America found new homes in Britain, west Africa and parts of the British Empire (with Nova Scotia and some of the Caribbean islands being favoured destinations).[30] If the revolutionary war achieved little in improving the situation of those who remained slaves in the United States, the ferment of libertarian ideas and the prolonged military conflict emphasised that expectations were high among blacks and antislavery supporters for moves towards black freedom. At the legislative level, little happened. True, in 1778 the Virginia House of Delegates banned the further importation of African slaves. But this, far from being a humanitarian gesture, was designed to protect Virginia from an over-supply of new slaves in a context where demographic growth among creole slaves in Virginia was flourishing.[31]

The ambiguous role of the Founding Fathers towards African-Americans illustrates the problems associated with decisions about the legitimacy of slavery in the new republic. Various historians have investigated Washington's and Madison's views on slavery.[32] But of all the Founding Fathers, Thomas Jefferson displayed the most complex reactions on this issue. His relationship to slavery has proved controversial among historians. In his *Notes on the State of Virginia* (1784), Jefferson wrote about the intellectual inferiority of black people and expressed his fears about miscegenation and the potential for violence by blacks against whites. Jefferson's solution to the continuation of slavery in the early republic was that slaves should be freed and sent back to settle in Africa. Jefferson did not envisage a harmonious social setting in the South between whites and freed slaves; he also did not regard free blacks as voters or citizens because he thought they would endanger the republic. Jefferson's famous statement about slavery in 1820 expressed his inability to act to resolve the paradox of slavery and freedom in a land of liberty: 'We have the wolf by the ears, and we can neither hold him, nor safely let him go. Justice is in one scale, and self-preservation in the other'.[33] Jefferson's words now carry more irony than intended because of recent DNA proof that he fathered the last child of Sally Hemings, a black mulatto living in his household; but his comment on the tensions that slavery caused in the public sphere summed up the thoughts of many of his white American contemporaries.[34]

While the young American Republic remained a loose conglomeration of states, little could be decided at national level about the future of slavery and the slave trade. The Articles of Confederation, agreed by the Continental Congress in 1781, had one accomplishment relating to slavery and its jurisdiction: namely the Northwest Ordinance of 1787. This law established the Northwest Territory and was mainly concerned with laying down the stages for setting up states in that domain; but it also forbade slavery legal protection inside its boundaries. Given that in 1784 Jefferson's proposal to prohibit slavery in all western territories after 1800 had failed, it was an achievement to restrict the future spread of slavery in one part of the Union. But the failure of the Northwest Ordinance to include any enforcement clauses and its stipulation that fugitive slaves 'may be lawfully reclaimed and conveyed to the person claiming' them illustrated the lukewarm commitment to antislavery of the committee that passed the measure.[35]

The most significant move by the American government over slavery came with the debates held during the Constitutional Convention over the summer of 1787. The two major issues pertaining to slavery and the slave trade at the Convention were the question of how to count slaves for purposes of representation and taxation within the federal government and what to do about the future importation of slaves into the Union. The federal ratio – the notion that three slaves should be equivalent to five white people – had first been proposed by the Confederation Congress in 1783 as part of a programme for the national government to raise revenue from the states. It had not then been adopted because it failed to receive the unanimous approval of all of the states. It was now hammered out in debate as the way in which southern states could guarantee that their chattel property would be recognised for purposes of national taxation and representation in the House of Representatives, ensuring their political strength in that chamber for the foreseeable future.

The three-fifths clause was only passed when it was tied to taxation for the first time. It was incorporated into Article 1, Section 2 of the Constitution. There was bitter sectional acrimony over the foreign slave trade but a compromise was reached. This stipulated that Congress should have no power to interfere with the slave trade for twenty-one years but taxes could be levied on imported Africans. Maryland, Georgia, South Carolina and the New England states combined to secure this arrangement. The compromise became Article 1, Section 9 of the Constitution. After this clause had been agreed in principle, a fugitive slave clause – similar to the one in the Northwest Ordinance – was drafted and included in the final document without, perhaps surprisingly, any debate. This became Article 4, Section 2 of the Constitution. But though the Founding Fathers assiduously worked to create a Constitution that would preserve national unity, the ambiguity of the clauses dealing with slavery and the slave trade meant that Americans ratified a document that left many crucial issues associated with slavery unresolved.[36] The careful wording of the Constitution, never once mentioning the word 'slave', enables some historians to view it as a proslavery document and others to regard it as neutral on the matter of slavery.[37]

If the Founding Fathers' treatment of slavery leads us into a world of ambiguity and, at best, an equivocal commitment to abolitionism, a similarly complex situation characterised the regional development of black life in the revolutionary era. Legislative, judicial and constitutional action against slavery occurred in Massachusetts and New Hampshire and gradual abolition laws were passed in Pennsylvania (1780), Rhode Island (1784) and Connecticut (1784). In New York and New Jersey, where opposition to antislavery was more virulent, gradual emancipation bills did not pass the state legislatures until 1799 and 1804. Though the essential laws to free blacks were therefore set in train in the northern states in the last quarter of the eighteenth century, these moves towards black freedom were very gradual indeed: many statutes granted freedom only for future-born children of slaves at ages between twenty-one and twenty-eight.[38]

Despite slow progress over gradual abolition, the late eighteenth century saw some improvements in the condition of African-Americans. In the northern port cities, free black communities were forged between 1770 to 1800 and slavery became more of a southern rather than a national institution. The proportion of free blacks living in both New York City and Philadelphia increased in that period – a result partly of manumissions accorded to blacks already living there and partly of migration of free blacks from the Upper South. Free blacks found work in the maritime industries and as domestic servants. They began to construct their own cohesive communities based around membership of black churches, the creation of black schools and the formation of nuclear families. The black churches tended to be evangelical in their form of worship; they stemmed from the Free African societies established in the northern port cities in the late 1780s and early 1790s. As a personal riposte to their former slave status, free blacks often changed their names; they replaced African day names, classical names and place names with English and biblical names for themselves and their children.[39]

Free blacks were also a part of life in the Chesapeake by the late eighteenth century. One-third of the free blacks in the USA lived in that region by 1810. But they only flourished in certain parts of that region, more often in Maryland than in Virginia. Thus by 1810 some 20 per cent of the Maryland black population were freedmen but only 7 per cent of Virginia's.[40] The growth of a free black population in parts of the Chesapeake was accompanied by an expansion of slavery in other parts of the region as the 'peculiar institution' became a deeply entrenched southern hallmark. In 1785 a proposal to abolish slavery within Virginia was defeated in the House of Delegates. Extensive proslavery petitions were drawn up in several Virginia counties in 1785. In 1793 Virginia prohibited the immigration of free blacks into the state, and opponents of manumission in the state were vociferous. In 1806 the Assembly, worried by the impact of Gabriel's slave conspiracy in 1800, restricted manumission. Increasing number of whites became slaveholders in western Virginia in the late eighteenth century as slavery expanded into land that had previously been unsettled.[41]

In the Lower South, yet another regional pattern became consolidated among blacks after the American Revolution. Manumissions proceeded in South Carolina in the 1780s at a much greater rate than ever before. Yet this was the state with the lowest rate of manumissions in the USA. Accordingly, the free black community was small throughout South Carolina and Georgia. Two different trends emerged with regard to slavery in that region in the last three decades of the eighteenth century. On the one hand, slavery became more deeply entrenched in South Carolina and Georgia as rice production continued to flourish. The invention of Eli Whitney's cotton gin on a Georgia plantation in 1793 and the potential for cotton growing in the Lower South and in the backcountry areas to the west of existing states in the region ensured that slavery – absolutely central as an economic institution to the Lower South's economy – would not die a quick death.[42]

The six decades between the turn of the nineteenth century and the death of slavery during the American Civil War witnessed the entrenchment of slavery in the Deep South, the spread of slavery across a cotton belt moving into southwestern states, and the creation of a self-conscious southern civilisation centrally based around the preservation of slavery in the antebellum period. Those decades also saw the rise of abolitionist sentiment in the North and various attempts to expose the moral bankruptcy of slavery and the need to eradicate it as an institution from a nation founded on libertarian principles. While these features of American slavery and abolition developed, slavery and its ramifications assumed an ever-larger role in American politics. Originally this stemmed from fears about the extension of slavery into westward territories yet to become states. These anxieties burst vividly into public debate in the two years leading up to the Missouri Compromise (1819–21). But slavery again reared its head in the westward expansion of the United States into Texas in the 1840s and Kansas and Nebraska in the 1850s. Slavery became embroiled with the major political debates and parties of the late antebellum period and spilled over into secession, the creation of the Confederacy and the fighting of the American Civil War.

The staple crops grown on North American plantations by slave labour had always been linked closely to marketing opportunities in Europe. Tobacco was shipped to Britain and northern Europe to satisfy the growing nicotine habit of consumers there. Rice was shipped to the West Indies and across the Atlantic to markets in Germany, the Low countries and the Iberian peninsula as a substitute commodity for grains.[43] But cotton became the staple commodity that served European markets par excellence. The demand of the British textile industry for raw supplies of cotton for clothing manufacture reached considerable heights at a time when the United States dominated the worldwide supply of cotton. In the first half of the nineteenth century cotton became a central cog in an Atlantic economy linking ports such as London, Liverpool, New York and Mobile, Alabama. Annual cotton production rose from c. 3,000 bales in 1790 to more than 4 million bales by 1860. 'King cotton' was the spur behind the support of Lancashire cotton producers for the Confederate cause in the American Civil War.[44] Cotton production spread from Georgia and South Carolina in the early nineteenth century in a southwestern direction into newly settled states such as Arkansas, Alabama, Florida, Texas, Mississippi and Louisiana. In the latter state sugar production on plantations also took root. Cotton plantations relied on the gang labour used on tobacco plantations; overseers and drivers provided the required discipline. They drew upon an extensive internal slave trade by which slaves no longer needed in the eastern states were transferred and sold at marts such as New Orleans and Natchez.[45] By 1860 around 4 million slaves belonged to planters, and most of those bondspeople were attached to cotton plantations.

Whether the plantations were efficient units of production that maximised or rewarded slave productivity or whether they were remnants of a passing agricultural order that failed to industrialise and modernise are large issues about the economic nature of antebellum slavery that are still debated by historians. The same is true with regard to assessments of the contribution made by plantations to southern economic development.[46] But the southern attachment to slavery was not just based on the economic contribution made by plantations; a socio-cultural attachment to slavery was also important for all white southerners. Apart from certain areas such as South Carolina, where slaves outnumbered whites as early as 1710, most of the southern states held about two white people to every black person. Many white southerners owned no slaves at all, and those that did were more likely to own a handful rather than large numbers. But the 'plain folk' of the Old South were just as wedded to the continuance of slavery as the grandee cotton masters. Slavery was an embedded part of life in the South and southerners regarded it as indelibly linked to the prosperity of the region, to the right of individuals there to choose their lifestyle without federal interference, to the continuing social hierarchy of people marked by class and race. Some southern intellectuals defended the plantation world by viewing it through a nostalgic lens in which happy slaves were graciously treated by masters as familial members. Proslavery defenders in the South based their arguments on various grounds, including John C. Calhoun's notion of slavery as a public good and as an institution that was a national cause demanding national protection.[47]

Whether paternalism continued in the South among the plantocracy has not reached a historical consensus. Eugene D. Genovese's formulation of the concept in *Roll, Jordan, Roll* and other publications has been very influential. He regarded paternalism as involving a dual process of accommodation on the part of masters and their slaves: neither party could act independently because each was so inextricably bound to the other. In this formulation, slave autonomy is strictly limited.[48] Other historians have questioned this interpretation of paternalism, arguing that the masters were exploitative individuals who had little genuine regard for slave welfare. And in this view it is possible to see slaves as not coming under the influence of the master's will but also failing to achieve any meaningful autonomy.[49]

The southern defence of slavery as an institution was partly a response to the problems that might arise if the federal government were to intervene in the political decisions over slavery extension. The federal government largely set the issue of slavery to one side in the era of the Jefferson and

Madison presidencies, though in 1808 there was Congressional agreement that the importation of slaves should end, as a clause in the Constitution, according to some interpreters, had suggested it should.[50] It was during the Jefferson presidency that the vast Louisiana Territory was purchased – an omen for the future in connection with slavery because when parts of that territory eventually applied for statehood a federal decision would be necessary about whether they should hold slaves or be free havens. Public anxiety over the spread of slavery to newly settled western territories emerged during the Missouri crisis. The incorporation into the Union of Missouri as a state raised the issue of whether it should be allowed to have slaves or not. After much acrimonious discussion, a compromise was reached whereby Missouri became a slave state and other parts of the Louisiana Purchase were excluded from slavery.[51] As it happens, Missouri became a border state and only about 10 per cent of its population were slaves by 1860.[52] What mattered to Americans, however, was not the proportion of slaves in an individual state but the principle about whether slavery extension should be allowed at all.

South Carolina emerged at the forefront of the southern protection of slavery in the 1820s. Several slave conspiracies occurred in the Palmetto state during that decade, notably that by Denmark Vesey, a free black who organised a formidable conspiracy among the slaves in Charleston in 1822.[53] In each case, planters supported the view that the planned uprisings were the result of outside interference, mainly by northern abolitionists, rather than the result of deficiencies in their own slave system. Several commentators began to argue against a broad construction of the Constitution to protect the southern commitment to slavery. John C. Calhoun was the intellectual figurehead for the right of southerners to nullify federal law. He also developed a theory of the 'concurrent majority', that is, the right of a permanent minority to veto numerical majority rule. Nullification, in his view, was based on the assumption that the Constitution was a compact between individual states and individual citizens meeting in ratifying conventions, and that the partners of this compact had as much right to veto legislation as the federal government. A nullification crisis occurred in South Carolina in 1831–2 over Congress's insistence on maintaining protectionism in the tariffs of 1828 and 1832. It led immediately to an explicit defence of the institution of slavery by South Carolinians. There was now no conception of slavery in South Carolina being evil in any sense of the term. In the next three decades many other southern states followed the lead given by South Carolina.[54]

Intense sectional feeling was aroused by the developments regarding American slavery between the admittance of Missouri to the Union as a slave state and South Carolina's decision to approach the brink of withdrawing from the Union in the nullification crisis. Sectional antagonisms emerged with the divergence of southern proslavery advocates from the revival of abolitionism in the North after the launch of William Lloyd Garrison's *The Liberator* in 1831. The North and the South in the 1830s were not completely divided in their stance over slavery. In the northern states abolitionists were divided into those in favour of gradual emancipation and those who wanted immediate freedom for blacks. Many abolitionists were willing to dilute their programme for racial justice in order to make it acceptable to a broad range of Americans.[55] Abolitionists were often treated as marginal outsiders in the North during the Jacksonian era and mobs broke up their meetings.[56] Some northerners were not abolitionists at all but merely opposed to the extension of slavery across the Mississippi River. In the South, it is true, very few abolitionist sympathisers existed, but many southerners were as much concerned with issues connected with economic development, banking and tariffs as with slavery. This perhaps explains why South Carolina was always an extreme case of a state that defended slavery against all odds in the antebellum South and why secessionism did not emerge as a general movement in the South until after the Civil War broke out in 1861.[57]

The Mexican War and the annexation of Texas received criticism from many northerners who viewed James K. Polk as a southern president prepared to extend the territory of the United States into potential slaveholding areas but not willing to follow through the same policy for acquiring a northwestern Pacific territory, Oregon. A political crisis over slavery ensued. In 1846–7 the Wilmot Proviso, intended to ban slavery from any territory acquired from Mexico, passed through the House of Representatives twice before being defeated in the Senate. Every northern legislature supported the Proviso, while southerners attacked it. Intensified sectional differences over the next few years culminated in the Compromise of 1850, which, among other things, admitted California as a free state into the Union, allowed Utah and New Mexico the option to authorise slavery by territorial law, and added a stringent fugitive slave law. These events in the period 1846–50 confirmed in the minds of southerners the threat to their section seemingly raised by northern abolitionism. After 1846 a process of political and cultural sectionalism in the South emerged fully. One important aspect of southern distinctness which came to the fore was a self-conscious view of slavery as both legitimate and virtuous. Southerners became increasingly confident that slavery was a permanent feature of their society. All the ingredients for secession were in existence by 1850; only feelings of loyalty and sentimental attachment to the Union delayed secession until 1860.[58]

The crisis between North and South assumed a broader cultural dimension with the bestselling publication of Harriet Beecher Stowe's *Uncle Tom's Cabin*, which became a reference point for sectionalism in the 1850s. Stowe's novel presented a case for slavery and slaveholders being un-American and un-Christian. This judgement was widely supported in the North but vigorously contested in the South. In the furore that emerged over the success and meaning of the novel, northerners such as Thaddeus Stevens attacked not only slavery but the planter class as a violation to American democracy. George Fitzhugh and other southerners took the opposite view. They regarded the market-orientation of northern society as cruel and inhuman and argued that the personal bond between master and slave elevated southern society above northern society. Sectionalism became much more full-blooded after the publication of Stowe's novel and hardly amenable to a compromise such as that of 1850.[59]

During the 1850s American political parties were transformed largely in relation to the sectional crisis over slavery. The Democratic Party survived; the Whig Party disappeared; and a new grouping, the Republican Party, emerged. The Democratic Party had enormously diverse interests, including strong antislavery, free soil, proslavery and secessionist elements; but it won support and retained cohesion, apart from the Texas and Mexico controversies, by voting together in Congress.[60] The Whig Party, by contrast, lacked cohesion and in the early 1850s lost great leaders such as Henry Clay and Daniel Webster. It supported nativism – prejudice against foreigners, especially Catholics – but in so doing lost much immigrant support; and it seemed in danger of disintegration. It collapsed as a party during the controversy over Kansas and Nebraska (1854–6) and was replaced by the Republican Party, which held that the openness of opportunity was fundamental to American society. Until after the 1856 presidential election the Republican Party was an insurgent party fighting on one platform but by 1860 it had broadened its appeal to win votes. Its continued existence in the late 1850s was guaranteed by the continuing turmoil in Kansas and sectional bitterness, evidenced by the thrashing of Senator Charles Sumner by congressman Preston Brooks of South Carolina after Sumner had attacked the entrenched position of Brooks's state on the matter of slavery.[61]

The turmoil over slavery surfaced in the Dred Scott case, in which the Supreme Court ruled that Congress could not bar slavery from any territory. It reared its head again in the Lecompton constitution in 1857, a proslavery constitution in Kansas that was voted down after a high turnout of antislavery voters in that territory. Slavery was also crucial in the Lincoln–Douglas debates of 1858, when the future president unequivocally argued that slavery was morally, socially and politically wrong. The Dred Scott decision in effect declared the Missouri Compromise unconstitutional, but this had no impact because that compromise had been superseded in 1854. It nevertheless inflamed public opinion. So, too, did the Lecompton Convention, in which the proslavery legislature of Kansas tried to confirm a constitution that fitted their political position. Stephen A. Douglas split the Democratic Party in 1858 and campaigned in Illinois against Abraham Lincoln for the post of senator. In the Lincoln–Douglas debates of 1858, the destiny of America appeared to be at stake. Douglas tried to brand Lincoln as a radical. He thought Lincoln favoured black equality with whites whereas he himself believed that blacks were inferior and possessed no rights. Douglas championed popular sovereignty and argued that the nation should continue on its present course; there was no need for the extinction of slavery. Douglas also attacked Lincoln because he thought his Illinois rival wanted to strengthen the national government.[62]

Lincoln argued in the 1850s that the Republican Party was a national rather than a sectional party. He had a moral belief in the ideals espoused in the Declaration of Independence and the revolutionary libertarian creed. He vigorously opposed popular sovereignty in the territories because this would give Americans the freedom to choose justice or injustice; and he thought it behoved the government to remove injustice. In his 'House Divided' speech he had argued that the ultimate extinction of slavery was a legitimate aim embedded in the thought of the American Founding Fathers. He also argued against popular sovereignty because it was a policy that appeared to break down the power of the federal government. Lincoln called the United States 'the last best hope of Earth' because the Constitution implied that slavery must eventually be extinguished and that the history of America was one of progress towards a more perfect Union.[63] Lincoln constantly attacked the immorality of slavery. The ultimate extinction of that institution was fundamental to Lincoln's belief in America's progressive destiny. Lincoln believed that morality could not be divorced from politics and that in the United States the main political and moral issue to be confronted was slavery. Lincoln sought to preserve the Union: this defined him politically and defined the existence of the Republican Party.[64]

Slavery did not die an easy death, however, in the United States. After the Union attack on Fort Sumter, South Carolina, in April 1861, various southern states gradually seceded and formed the Confederacy under the leadership of Jefferson Davis. Four years of bloody civil war followed, leaving lasting scars throughout the nation. Around 607,000 Americans died on the battleground, in prison camps and elsewhere during this conflict.[65] Lincoln waited until a suitable opportunity presented itself to launch an assault on slavery in wartime. In 1862 and 1863 he framed his emancipation proclamation, believing that this was the only way to win the war and preserve the Union. Black troops were recruited into the Union army. In the South, many slaves deliberately sabotaged the plantation system.[66] In these ways the blacks can be seen as participating in the war to resolve their own status in American society. The slaves were freed on 1 January 1863 but the crisis that provoked led to the assassination of Lincoln by John Wilkes Booth, a proslavery fanatic, at Ford's Theater, Washington, DC, on 14 April 1865. A programme of Reconstruction tried to resolve the problems of the defeated Confederacy and the position of blacks in southern society, but it did so in a largely unsatisfactory, incomplete way with equivocal attention given to black rights.[67] Discrimination against free blacks continued for nearly a century afterwards, with segregation, lynching, the rise of the

Ku Klux Klan and Jim Crow legislation. All these combined to show that the legacy of slavery in the United States cast a long and dark shadow.

NOTES

1. For good outlines of North American slavery see Peter Kolchin, *American Slavery* (Harmondsworth, 1993) and Ira Berlin, *Generations of Captivity: A History of African-American Slaves* (Cambridge, MA, 2003). Historiographical debates are covered in Peter J. Parish, *Slavery: History and Historians* (New York, 1989).
2. David W. Galenson, *White Servitude in Colonial America: An Economic Analysis* (Cambridge, 1981); Russell R. Menard, 'From Servants to Slaves: The Transformation of the Chesapeake Labor System', it Southern Studies, 16 (1977), 355–90.
3. Gary B. Nash, *Red, White and Black: The Peoples of Early America*, 4th edn (Englewood Cliffs, NJ, 2000).
4. The most important works on the volume of the transatlantic slave trade are Philip D. Curtin, *The Atlantic Slave Trade: A Census* (Madison, WI, 1969) and David Eltis, Stephen D. Behrendt, David Richardson and Herbert S. Klein, *The Trans-Atlantic Slave Trade: A Database on CD-ROM* (Cambridge, 1999).
5. David Richardson, 'The British Empire and the Atlantic Slave Trade, 1660–1807' in P. J. Marshall (ed.), *The Oxford History of the British Empire vol. 2: The Eighteenth Century* (Oxford, 1998), p. 442.
6. Winthrop D. Jordan, *White over Black: American Attitudes toward the Negro, 1550–1812* (Chapel Hill, NC, 1968).
7. David Brion Davis, *The Problem of Slavery in Western Culture* (Ithaca, NY, 1966); David Eltis, *The Rise of African Slavery in the Americas* (Cambridge, 2000).
8. A review of the arguments appears in Alden T. Vaughan, *Roots of American Racism: Essays on the Colonial Experience* (Oxford, 1995), pp. 136–74.
9. Menard, 'From Servants to Slaves', 355–90.
10. Peter H. Wood, *Black Majority: Negroes in South Carolina from 1670 through the Stono Rebellion* (New York, 1974), pp. 35–62; Judith A. Carney, *Black Rice: The African Origins of Rice Cultivation in the Americas* (Cambridge, MA, 2001).
11. John J. McCusker and Russell R. Menard, *The Economy of British America, 1607–1789*, 2nd edn (Chapel Hill, NC, 1989), pp. 103, 136, 172, 203.
12. Lorena S. Walsh, 'The African American Population of the Colonial United States' in Michael R. Haines and Richard H. Steckel (eds), *A Population History of North America* (Cambridge, 2000), pp. 191–239.
13. Gary B. Nash, *The Urban Crucible: Social Change, Political Consciousness, and the Origins of the American Revolution* (Cambridge, MA, 1979), pp. 13–15, 109–10, 320.
14. Ira Berlin, *Many Thousands Gone: The First Two Centuries of Slavery in North America* (Cambridge, MA, 1998), pp. 54–8, 178–82; Rhett S. Jones, 'Plantation Slavery in the Narragansett County of Rhode Island, 1640–1790: A Preliminary Study', *Plantation Society*, 2 (1986), 157–70; Graham Russell Hodges, *Root and Branch: African Americans in New York and East Jersey, 1613–1863* (Chapel Hill, NC, 1999).
15. Philip D. Morgan, *Slave Counterpoint: Black Culture in the Eighteenth-Century Chesapeake and Lowcountry* (Chapel Hill, NC, 1998), pp. 179–203.
16. William M. Wiecek, 'The Statutory Law of Slavery and Race in the Thirteen Mainland Colonies of British America', WMQ, 34 (1977), 258–80; Thomas D. Morris, *Southern Slavery and the Law, 1619–1860* (Chapel Hill, NC, 1996).
17. Philip D. Morgan, 'Three Planters and their Slaves: Landon Carter, Henry Laurens and Thomas Thistlewood' in Winthrop D. Jordan and Sheila L. Skemp (eds), *Race and Family in the Colonial South* (Jackson, MS, 1987), pp. 37–54; Rhys Isaac, *Landon Carter's Uneasy Kingdom: Revolution and Rebellion on a Virginia Plantation* (New York, 2004).

18. Leland Ferguson, *Uncommon Ground: Archaeology and Early African America, 1650–1800* (Washington, DC, 1992).
19. Allan Kulikoff, *Tobacco and Slaves: The Development of Southern Cultures in the Chesapeake, 1680–1800* (Chapel Hill, NC, 1986), pp. 352–80; Morgan, *Slave Counterpoint*, pp. 498–658; Herbert G. Gutman, *The Black Family in Slavery and Freedom, 1750–1925* (New York, 1976).
20. Lawrence W. Levine, *Black Culture and Black Consciousness: Afro-American Folk Thought from Slavery to Freedom* (New York, 1977).
21. Frank Lambert, *Pedlar in Divinity: George Whitefield and the Transatlantic Revivals, 1737–1770* (Princeton, NJ, 1994).
22. Sylvia R. Frey and Betty Wood, *Come Shouting to Zion: African American Protestantism in the American South and British Caribbean to 1830* (Chapel Hill, NC, 1998); Albert J. Raboteau, 'The Slave Church in the Era of the American Revolution' in Ira Berlin and Ronald Hoffman (eds), *Slavery and Freedom in the Age of the American Revolution* (Urbana and Chicago, 1986), pp. 193–213.
23. Gerald W. Mullin, *Flight and Rebellion: Slave Resistance in Eighteenth-Century Virginia* (New York, 1972); Billy G. Smith, 'Runaway Slaves in the Mid-Atlantic Region during the Revolutionary Era' in Ronald Hoffman and Peter J. Albert (eds), *The Transforming Hand of Revolution: Reconsidering the American Revolution as a Social Movement* (Charlottesville, VA, 1995), pp. 199–230; Michael P. Johnson, 'Runaway Slaves and the Slave Communities in South Carolina, 1799–1830', *WMQ*, 38 (1981), 418–41.
24. Eugene D. Genovese, *From Rebellion to Revolution: Afro-American Slave Revolts in the Making of the Modern World* (Baton Rouge, LA, 1979).
25. David Brion Davis, *The Problem of Slavery in the Age of Revolution* (Ithaca, NY, 1975).
26. Dee Andrews, *The Methodists and Revolutionary America, 1760–1800: The Shaping of an Evangelical Culture* (Princeton, 2000).
27. Jean R. Soderlund, *Quakers and Slavery: A Divided Spirit* (Princeton, NJ, 1985).
28. Ibid.; Davis, *The Problem of Slavery in the Age of Revolution*, pp. 213–54.
29. Sylvia R. Frey, *Water from the Rock: Black Resistance in a Revolutionary Age* (Princeton, NJ, 1991). For discussion of these and other concepts of the revolutionary era, see Jack P. Greene and J.R. Pole (eds), *A Companion to the American Revolution* (Oxford, 2000), pp. 625–706.
30. Frey, *Water from the Rock*, p. 211.
31. Robert McColley, *Slavery and Jeffersonian Virginia*, 2nd edn (Urbana, IL, 1973), p. 165.
32. Kenneth Morgan, 'George Washington and the Problem of Slavery', *Journal of American Studies*, 34 (2000), 279–301; Dorothy Twohig, ' "That Species of Property": Washington's Role in the Controversy over Slavery' in Don Higginbotham (ed.), *George Washington Reconsidered* (Charlottesville, VA, 2001), pp. 114–38; Drew R. McCoy, 'Slavery' in Robert A. Rutland (ed.), *James Madison and the American Nation, 1751–1836: An Encyclopaedia* (New York, 1994), p. 380, and McCoy, *The Last of the Fathers: James Madison and the Republican Legacy* (Cambridge, MA, 1989), pp. 107–11, 245–7, 297–8, 308–10, 317–22.
33. Quoted in Davis, *The Problem of Slavery in the Age of Revolution*, p. 183.
34. E. A. Foster et al., 'Jefferson Fathered Slave's Last Child' and Eric S. Lander and Joseph J. Ellis, 'DNA Analysis: Founding Father', *Nature*, (5 Nov. 1998), 13, 27–8.
35. Paul S. Finkelman, 'Slavery and the Northwest Ordinance: A Study in Ambiguity', *Journal of the Early Republic*, 6 (1986), 343–70; Peter S. Onuf, *Statehood and Union: A History of the Northwest Ordinance* (Bloomington, IN, 1987), pp. 141–5.
36. Kenneth Morgan, 'Slavery and the Debate over Ratification of the United States Constitution', *Slavery and Abolition*, 22 (2001), 40–65.

37. Paul S. Finkelman, 'Slavery and the Constitutional Convention: Making a Covenant with Death' in Richard R. Beeman et al. (eds), *Beyond Confederation: Origins of the Constitution and American National Identity* (Chapel Hill, NC, 1987), pp. 188–225; William M. Wiecek, 'The Witch at the Christening: Slavery and the Constitution's Origins' in Leonard W. Levy and Dennis J. Mahoney (eds), *The Framing and Ratification of the Constitution* (London, 1987), pp. 167–84, 336–7.

38. Arthur Zilversmit, *The First Emancipation: The Abolition of Slavery in the North* (Chicago, 1967).

39. Gary B. Nash, 'Forging Freedom: The Emancipation Experience in the Northern Seaport Cities, 1775–1820' in Ira Berlin and Ronald Hoffman (eds), *Slavery and Freedom in the Age of the American Revolution* (Charlottesville, VA, 1986), pp. 24–6, 41–7.

40. Ira Berlin, *Slaves without Masters: The Free Negro in the Antebellum South* (New York, 1974).

41. Richard S. Dunn, 'Black Society in the Chesapeake, 1776–1810' in Berlin and Hoffman (eds), *Slavery and Freedom*, pp. 49–82.

42. Russell R. Menard, 'Slavery, Economic Growth, and Revolutionary Ideology in the South Carolina Lowcountry' in Ronald Hoffman, John J. McCusker, Russell R. Menard and Peter J. Albert (eds), *The Economy of Early America: The Revolutionary Period, 1763–1790* (Charlottesville, VA, 1988), pp. 244–74; Berlin, *Many Thousands Gone*, pp. 290–324.

43. McCusker and Menard, *The Economy of British America*, pp. 118–25, 130, 132, 175–80.

44. Mary Ellison, *Support for Secession: Lancashire and the American Civil War* (Chicago, 1972); Kolchin, *American Slavery*, p. 95.

45. Michael Tadman, *Speculators and Slaves: Masters, Traders, and Slaves in the Old South*, 2nd edn (Madison, WI, 1996); Walter Johnson, *Soul by Soul: Life inside the Antebellum Slave Market* (Cambridge, MA, 1999).

46. The major issues are discussed in Robert W. Fogel and Stanley L. Engerman (eds), *Time on the Cross* (Boston, 1974); Herbert G. Gutman, *Slavery and the Numbers Game: A Critique of 'Time on the Cross'* (Urbana, IL, 1975); and Mark M. Smith, *Debating American Slavery* (Cambridge, 1998).

47. Larry E. Tise. *Proslavery: A History of the Defense of Slavery in America, 1701–1840* (Athens, GA, 1987); Merrill D. Peterson, *The Great Triumvirate: Webster, Clay, Calhoun* (New York, 1987), pp. 347–8, 410–11.

48. Eugene D. Genovese, *Roll, Jordan, Roll: The World the Slaves Made* (New York, 1974), pp. 3–7, 91–3, 119–20, 135–6, 597–8. For another formulation of paternalism, see Willie Lee Rose, 'The Domestication of Domestic Slavery' in her *Slavery and Freedom*, ed. William W. Freehling (New York, 1982), pp. 18–36.

49. Tadman, *Speculators and Slaves*, pp. 217–19.

50. Matthew E. Mason, 'Slavery Overshadowed: Congress Debates Prohibiting the Atlantic Slave Trade to the United States, 1806–1807', *Journal of the Early Republic*, 20 (2000), 59–72.

51. Glover Moore, *The Missouri Controversy, 1819–1821* (Lexington, KY, 1953); Richard H. Brown , 'The Missouri Crisis, Slavery, and the Politics of Jacksonianism', *South Atlantic Quarterly*, 65 (1966), 55–72.

52. Parish, *Slavery: History and Historians*, p. 26.

53. For a recent interpretation of this event, which questions the existence of a conspiracy, see Michael P. Johnson, 'Denmark Vesey and his Co-Conspirators', *WMQ*, 58 (2001), 915–76.

54. William W. Freehling, *Prelude to Civil War: The Nullification Crisis in South Carolina, 1816–1836* (New York, 1965).

55. Martin B. Duberman, 'The Northern Response to Slavery' in Duberman (ed.),

The Antislavery Vanguard: New Essays on the Abolitionists (Princeton, NJ, 1965), pp. 395–413.

56. Leonard L. Richards, *'Gentlemen of Property and Standing': Anti-Abolition Mobs in Jacksonian America* (New York, 1975).

57. William W. Freehling, *The Road to Disunion: Secessionists at Bay, 1776–1854* (New York, 1990), pp. 213–86.

58. David M. Potter, *The South and the Sectional Conflict* (Baton Rouge, LA, 1968).

59. Richard H. Sewell, *Ballots for Freedom: Antislavery Politics in the United States, 1837–1860* (New York, 1976), pp. 234–5; James Brewer Stewart, *Holy Warriors: The Abolitionists and American Slavery* (New York, 1976), pp. 160–2.

60. Thomas B. Alexander, *Sectional Stress and Party Strength: A Study of Roll-Call Voting Patterns in the United States House of Representatives, 1836–1860* (Nashville, 1967).

61. Eric Foner, *Free Soil, Free Labor, Free Men: The Ideology of the Republican Party before the Civil War* (New York, 1970).

62. Robert W. Johannsen, *Stephen A. Douglas* (New York, 1973), pp. 664–6, 668–77.

63. Quoted in William E. Gienapp, *Abraham Lincoln and Civil War America: A Biography* (New York, 2002), p. 124.

64. A recent discussion of Lincoln's evolving attitudes about slavery can be found in Richard J. Carwardine, *Lincoln* (Harlow, 2003).

65. The best modern surveys of the war are Peter J. Parish, *The American Civil War* (New York, 1975) and James M. McPherson, *Battle Cry of Freedom: The Era of the Civil War* (New York, 1988).

66. For this interpretation, see Ira Berlin, 'The Slaves were the Primary Force behind their Emancipation' in William Dudley (ed.), *The Civil War: Opposing Viewpoints* (San Diego, 1995).

67. Eric Foner, *Reconstruction: America's Unfinished Revolution, 1863–1877* (New York, 1988), pp. 1–142.

I

THE ORIGINS OF NORTH AMERICAN SLAVERY

Introduction

Slavery in North America was an important consequence of the European colonisation of the New World. From the Columbus voyages onwards several western European powers were intent on spreading their power and prestige across the Atlantic ocean, seeking out goods that could be traded between continents and dispatching settlers to the Americas. In many colonies, especially in tropical or semitropical zones, plantations became the chief form of agricultural production and black African slaves provided the main labour force. The staple crops grown on these plantations produced profits for owners primarily through marketing opportunities to European consumers. Blackburn (1997) analyses transatlantic slavery within this overall context of European colonisation of the Americas. He traces the spread of slave plantations, primarily based on sugar production, in Spanish-American colonies, such as Cuba and New Spain, and in Portuguese Brazil. He discusses the beginnings of Dutch and French interest in setting up plantations in the first half of the seventeenth century, the Dutch being active in Surinam and the French in several West Indian territories such as Saint-Domingue, Martinique and Guadeloupe. He also shows that the British were comparatively late starters in operating slave plantations in North America and the Caribbean in the seventeenth century. This broad discussion provides helpful background for the spread of slavery throughout the early modern Atlantic world.

Klein (1999) provides an overview of the long-term development of the Atlantic slave trade over four centuries, pulling together research findings on the slave trade of individual European powers and placing them within a comparative context. Curtin's seminal synthesis (1969) collated and analysed statistics on the volume and distribution of slaves in the Americas for the various European trading powers. This was the first modern attempt to provide accurate estimates of the flow of slaves from west Africa to the New World. The book is still serviceable, though some of its findings have been modified in research articles by other historians. The latest publication dealing with the numbers involved in the slave trade is Eltis, Behrendt, Richardson and Klein (1999). Using the technology available through a CD-ROM and computer packaging, this dataset enables users to ask myriad queries about the dimensions of the slave trade. Data are included on slave ships and their owners, on crews and slaves, and on ports of departure in Europe, of embarkation in Africa and of disembarkation in the Americas across nearly four centuries from 1500 until c.1880. This is now the best source of quantitative data on the transatlantic slave trade, enabling historians to compare and contrast the British slave trade to the Americas with the slave trades operated by other European nations. Richardson (1998) summarises the main contours of the British slave trade to North America and the Caribbean from the era of the Royal African Company until the abolition of the British slave trade.

Why black Africans ended up in the Americas in their millions was not simply owing to the spread of European capitalism overseas into tropical plantations; it was also connected with European notions of freedom and bondage. Slavery, and not just black slavery, had existed in many societies throughout the world since ancient times. Davis (1966) is the major book dealing with European intellectual attitudes towards slavery across the centuries. Among other things, it shows how deeply embedded slavery was in different societies such as ancient Rome and Kievan Russia. It also explains why slavery was condoned by European intellectuals for centuries. Jordan (1968) is another magisterial study. His book deals with the construction of race in American thought. It traces the negative connotations that the blackness of Africans aroused in colonial North America: slaves were regarded as things of darkness and as heathens; their physiognomy and habits were seen as alien; they were feared for their 'otherness'. Jordan shows that little evidence exists for the Chesapeake to show how blacks were treated between 1619 and 1640, but that mounting information shows that between 1640 and 1660 some blacks were being treated as slaves. He argues that racism accompanied these changes in the treatment and status of blacks in the seventeenth-century Chesapeake.

Eltis (2000) explains the paradoxical relationship of slavery and freedom in the early modern world in relation to European overseas expansion. He looks at the reasons why Europeans were never enslaved in the Americas. For Eltis, given transportation and cost advantages, 'European slave labour would have been no more expensive and probably substantially cheaper' (p. 70) than the enslavement of Africans. The reasons why Africans rather than Europeans were used as slaves in America stems, he suggests, from different perceptions of race and ethnicity. It was therefore a matter of which people could be enslaved and which could not according to prevailing Eurocentric views. In short, the English, Dutch and French regarded all non-Europeans as eligible for enslavement; they were unwilling to extend European notions of freedom to Africans.

The status of slaves brought to the Chesapeake in the period before 1660 has long exercised the attention of historians. Did slavery precede racism, or did racism precede slavery? Supporters of either of these propositions can be found. In addition, some historians take a middle position by emphasising the mutually reinforcing nature of slavery and racism. Part 2 of Vaughan (1995) analyses cultural and racial interactions in early Virginia. He argues that a pervading racial prejudice is discernible in white attitudes towards Africans in their first decade in Virginia after 1619. Other scholars argue, on the contrary, that racism emerged later in American history. Wood (1997) shows that such debates need to be set within the context of attitudes towards freedom and bondage in the English North American colonies. Elite discourses in sixteenth-century England, she argues, suggested that freedom could not be readily extended to Native Americans or other 'foreigners' in North America. Elizabethan England had much familiarity with servility and dependent people but chattel slavery was unknown in English law and only developed after the dissemination of negative English attitudes about Africans in the seventeenth century.

Much of the literature on the origins of slavery in North America has concentrated on the labour choices available to plantation owners, on the weight that should be attached to cultural or economic explanations for slavery's beginnings, and on the timing of the transition from servitude to slavery in the plantation South. Colonial North America was a triracial society. Native Americans proved difficult to enslave permanently for several reasons. Many died through contracting diseases from white settlers; others were decimated in warfare; and those who survived had sufficient knowledge of the terrain to evade capture. Nash (1974) offers a useful overview of the interaction between the three races in early America. Axtell (1988) provides a counterfactual argument to suggest that a colonial America without Indians would have precipitated an earlier use of black slave labour in the Chesapeake. Virgin land would have been available at cheap prices, enabling settlers to buy land more easily and then purchase more Africans. There were areas of North America where Indians were involved in enslavement, notably in the Carolinas, but it proved impossible for Europeans to coerce them into permanent bondage.

Before slavery took hold on a large scale in North America, attempts were made to use bonded servants as a labour force. Galenson (1981) summarises the main characteristics of white indentured servants drawn mainly to the Chesapeake colonies in the seventeenth century. He links their migration to North America with population trends, wages and economic opportunities in the mother country. Morgan (1975) argues that servants flourished as workers on tobacco plantations until Bacon's Rebellion in 1676 made the Virginian elite wary of the potential disruption to social order posed by a landless white proletariat. In his view, the growth of the slave trade to the Chesapeake in the 1680s reflected a preference for enslaved Africans over white servants for plantation labour: changing demographic and economic circumstances played a greater role in the embedding slavery in Virginia than race or ethnicity. Breen (1973) points to the social dangers posed by the 'giddy multitude' – a combination of ex-servants and slaves – and argues that Virginia's elite in the late seventeenth century wanted to separate slaves from servants to preserve the dominance of the white elite. Wood (1974) shows that the prior knowledge of rice cultivation by Africans influenced Carolina planters in selecting blacks as the labour force for the rice industry in the swampy Lowcountry. Carney (2001) expands this interpretation by arguing that the technological skills in rice-growing brought to South Carolina by Africans were crucial for the growth of rice exports and that slave women made a particularly important contribution in the colonial rice industry.

Some historians think that socio-cultural interpretations of the transition from servitude to slavery in the Chesapeake and South Carolina neglect supply conditions and therefore fail to explain the timing of the transition from indentured servitude to slavery. In two essays dealing with Virginia (1977) and South Carolina (1987) Menard provided a supply-side explanation of the transition from servitude to slavery in British North America. He outlines the problems of recruiting sufficient servants resulting from two factors: better economic opportunities in the mother country and an increased availability of Africans for shipment across the Atlantic after England entered the slave trade on a significant scale in the 1670s. Presenting data on comparative prices for servants and slaves, he shows that slaves provided the better long-term investment. In the Chesapeake, it was only after slaves predominated among the region's bound labourers by the first decade of the eighteenth century that planters preferred slaves to servants. For the Lowcountry, Menard contends that shifts in the volume and price of white indentured labour and Indian slaves from the interior led planters to invest in Africans, drawing upon an elastic supply of slaves once the export boom in Carolina rice was underway in the 1720s.

BIBLIOGRAPHY

Axtell, James, 'Colonial America without the Indians' in his *After Columbus: Essays in the Ethnohistory of Colonial North America* (New York: Oxford University Press, 1988)

Blackburn, Robin, *The Making of New World Slavery: From the Baroque to the Modern, 1492–1800* (London: Verso, 1997)

Breen, T. H., 'A Changing Labor Force and Race Relations in Virginia, 1660–1710', *Journal of Social History*, 7 (Fall 1973), 3–25, reprinted in his *Puritans and Adventurers: Change and Persistence in Early America* (New York: Oxford University Press, 1980)

Carney, Judith A., *Black Rice: The African Origins of Rice Cultivation in the Americas* (Cambridge, MA: Harvard University Press, 2001)

Curtin, Philip D., *The Atlantic Slave Trade: A Census* (Madison, WI: University of Wisconsin Press, 1969)

Davis, David Brion, *The Problem of Slavery in Western Culture* (Ithaca, NY: Cornell University Press, 1966)

Eltis, David, *The Rise of African Slavery in the Americas* (New York: Cambridge University Press, 2000)

Eltis, David, Stephen D. Behrendt, David Richardson and Herbert S. Klein, *The Trans-Atlantic Slave Trade: A Database on CD-ROM* (Cambridge: Cambridge University Press, 1999)

Galenson, David W., *White Servitude in Colonial America: An Economic Analysis* (Cambridge: Cambridge University Press, 1981)

Jordan, Winthrop D., *White over Black: American Attitudes toward the Negro, 1550–1812* (Chapel Hill: University of North Carolina Press, 1968)

Klein, Herbert S., *The Atlantic Slave Trade* (Cambridge: Cambridge University Press, 1999)

Menard, Russell R., 'From Servants to Slaves: The Transformation of the Chesapeake Labor System', *Southern Studies*, 16 (Winter 1977), 355–90, reprinted in his *Migrants, Servants and Slaves* (Basingstoke: Ashgate Variorum, 2001)

Menard, Russell R., 'The Africanization of the Lowcountry Labor Force' in Winthrop D. Jordan and Sheila L. Skemp (eds), *Race and Family in the Colonial South* (Jackson, MS: University of Mississippi Press, 1987)

Menard, Russell R., 'Transitions to African Slavery in British America, 1630–1730: Barbados, Virginia and South Carolina', *The Indian Historical Review*, 15 (1988–9), 33–49, reprinted in his *Migrants, Servants and Slaves* (Basingstoke: Ashgate Variorum, 2001)

Morgan, Edmund S., *American Slavery, American Freedom: The Ordeal of Colonial Virginia* (New York: W. W. Norton, 1975)

Nash, Gary B., *Red, White, and Black: The Peoples of Early America* (Upper Saddle River, NJ: Prentice Hall, 1974; 4th edn, 2000)

Richardson, David, 'The British Empire and the Atlantic Slave Trade, 1660–1807' in P. J. Marshall (ed.), *The Oxford History of the British Empire: vol. 2: The Eighteenth Century* (Oxford: Oxford University Press, 1998)

Vaughan, Alden T., *Roots of American Racism: Essays on the Colonial Experience* (New York: Oxford University Press, 1995)

Wood, Betty, *The Origins of American Slavery: Freedom and Bondage in the English Colonies* (New York: Hill and Wang, 1997)

Wood, Peter H., *Black Majority: Negroes in Colonial South Carolina from 1670 through the Stono Rebellion* (New York: Alfred A. Knopf, 1974)

ESSAY: TRANSITIONS TO AFRICAN SLAVERY IN BRITISH
AMERICA, 1630–1730: BARBADOS, VIRGINIA AND
SOUTH CAROLINA

Menard's essay (1988–9) synthesises his two articles of 1977 and 1987 and adds an extra dimension by looking additionally at the emergence of slavery in Barbados. This reminds us that the transition from servitude to slavery occurred throughout the plantation colonies in the British Caribbean as well as on mainland North America. The essay concentrates on the operation of labour markets rather than on planter attitudes towards particular categories of workers. Why, according to Menard, was the entrenchment of African slavery in the Americas not inevitable? Were there merely 'local and pragmatic choices' (p. 33) in installing Africans as the main plantation labour force, or can more general patterns be discerned? Do you find the emphasis on market factors and the changing volume and price of labour satisfactory as an explanation of the rise of African slavery in the Americas? Can socio-cultural explanations of the emergence of full-scale slavery in North America, emphasising the rise in demand for African labour, be reconciled with economic explanations?

There is an air of the inevitable to the rise of African slavery in the Americas. By the middle of the eighteenth century, Africans, slavery and Europe's American colonies had become so thoroughly entwined as to seem inseparable. Much of European America consisted of Africanized slave societies. Before 1750, or even as late as 1820 or 1830, imported slaves from Africa far outnumbered settlers from Europe among migrants to America. 'From Brazil and the Caribbean to Chesapeake Bay', David Brion Davis reminds us, 'the richest and most coveted colonies – in terms of large scale capital investment, output and value of exports and imports – ultimately became dependent on black slave labour'.[1] The identification of blacks and bondage was in the end so powerful and African slavery was eventually so central a feature of American history that it takes a major effort of imagination to entertain other outcomes.

Such an effort is essential. There was nothing inevitable about the Africanization of slavery or its entrenchment in the Americas. Several well-known facts establish the point. White slavery, an old and well-established institution in much of the West, persisted into the early modern era around the Mediterranean and in Eastern Europe and did not disappear (sometimes and at places it rather flourished) with the rise of the Atlantic slave trade. Several American colonies never depended on African slaves, while some did so only briefly before turning to other peoples and other methods

---

Russell R. Menard, 'Transitions to African Slavery in British America, 1630–1730: Barbados, Virginia and South Carolina', *Indian Historical Review*, 15 (1988–9), 33–49.

of organizing labour. Finally, and most important for this essay, many colonial societies which became dependent on black slaves did so only after an initial period of experimentation with white indentured servants or with native Americans. Again, a proposition from David Davis is helpful: 'The Africanization of large parts of the New World was the result not of concerted planning, racial destiny, or immanent historical design but of innumerable local and pragmatic choices made in four continents'.[2]

This essay examines three such sets of 'local and pragmatic choices' in a search for general patterns. It focuses on transitions in the labour force in Barbados, Virginia and South Carolina, looking at shifts from white servants, Indians and (in the case of the mainland colonies) blacks from the sugar islands to Africans to understand the rise of American slave societies. Several propositions are useful in ordering the historical record. The most important of these are that transitions to African slavery can be understood if Britain's Atlantic world is thought of as a single, if imperfect and fragile, economic system and if variations in the composition of the workforce between colonies and within particular colonial regions over time are approached through a focus on the supply and demand for labour.[3]

Some historians contend that transitions to African slavery are more profitably approached through an examination of planter attitudes toward various types of workers than through an analysis of labour markets.[4] Planters, the argument runs, turned to African slaves because they thought blacks better suited to the plantation regime than whites or Indians, more vigorous, easier to control, better able to withstand the climate, diseases, or work, and so on. One finds clear expressions of such preferences in British America. In lowcountry Carolina, for example, the belief that the region 'was not capable of being cultivated by white men', that it would have 'remained a wilderness' in the absence of Africans, was central to the ideology of the great planters by the Revolutionary era. However, such attitudes appear only after the lowcountry had become a thoroughly Africanized slave society, receiving clear expression for the first time around 1740 during the debate over the introduction of slavery in Georgia.[5] Earlier in the process of Africanization, there is little evidence that planters preferred blacks to whites or Indians. Planters took what workers they could get.

This is not to say that planter attitudes played no role in the growth of slavery. Attitudes were essential in at least two ways. First, planters had to be willing to substitute Africans for whites or Indians, to treat blacks differently than whites, to subject slaves to a harsh, degrading and severe discipline. Second, planters had to be persuaded that blacks could be employed profitably, turned with success to the tasks at hand. Attitudes may explain why British Americans turned to slavery so quickly, without hesitation and with such apparent enthusiasm. Attitudes cannot account for the timing of changes in the workforce, however: that can be understood only by close attention to markets, to the supply of workers from various sources and the demand for labour.

An examination of the three major plantation societies of British America suggests that there were two distinct paths toward an Africanized workforce. In one, the Barbadian case, the shift was triggered by a sharp jump in demand for workers associated with the introduction of a new crop, sugar. In the other, the Virginia pattern, the change was gradual and unconnected to a new crop, instead reflecting a decline in the supply of workers from other sources. The Carolina lowcountry indicates the complexities of the process. There one can discern two transitions and both paths, as lowcountry planters first followed the Virginia pattern and later that of Barbados in building their own distinctive slave society.

Barbados

Africans, and perhaps African slavery, came to Barbados with the first English settler. Ten Africans, apparently captured from the Portuguese on the outward voyage, arrived with Captain Henry Powell and the initial colonists in 1627. The status of those first blacks is unknown, but English Barbadians left little 'trace of hesitation or misgivings' concerning enslavement. Any doubts were resolved in 1637, when the Governor and Council ordered 'that *Negroes* and *Indians*, that came here to be sold, should serve for life, unless a contract was before made to the contrary'.[6]

The order of 1636 settled the status of blacks before they became a major part of the island population. In 1640, they numbered only a few hundred in a total of more than 10,000. Barbadians spent the 1630s in farm building, in achieving self-sufficiency in food production, and in experimentation with a variety of crops in search of a profitable export. Tobacco and cotton, their first staples, could be cultivated successfully on small-scale farms worked by the owner alone or with the help of a few hands. In the 1630s some of those hands were black or Indian slaves, others were free white workers, but most were English indentured servants.[7]

Although the principle behind it was articulated as early as the 1580s, the Virginia Company devised indentured servitude in the late 1610s to finance the recruitment and transport of workers to the colony. There is uncertainty regarding its antecedents. While some historians see it as an entirely new development, most view the system as an adaptation of the traditional institution of apprenticeship to a novel situation. There are broad similarities between servitude and apprenticeship, but there are also major differences. Servitude was largely an agricultural institution, designed to move people into field-work, while apprenticeship was urban, aimed toward trade, crafts and professions. Servitude attracted those too poor to purchase, while apprenticeship was for those prosperous enough to pay an entry fee in exchange for training. Servants could be sold by one master to another without consent or even consultation, while apprentices could not. And, despite occasional promises that servants would be instructed in 'the mystery, art and occupation of a planter', servitude was a labour system, not an educational institution.[8]

These considerations led David Galenson to suggest quite different antecedents for indentured servitude, 'service in husbandry'. Farm servants were numerous in Stuart England, accounting for perhaps 10 to 15 per cent of the population, appearing in a quarter to a third of all households, and making up more than half of all hired, fulltime agricultural workers. Typically, they were boys and girls from poor families who left home in their early teens to work for more prosperous farmers until they married. They usually lived in their master's household, agreed to annual contracts for wages, food and lodging, and changed places frequently, often every year. Given the pervasiveness of this form of life-cycle service, it is a likely antecedent for the indenture system and a major source of recruits for American plantations.[9]

There were important differences between indentured servitude and service in husbandry, however. According to Galenson, the major distinctions followed from 'the distance the servants travelled upon leaving home'. This proved 'a sufficiently important economic difference to necessitate several modifications in the institution', all of which made 'the indenture system more rigid and formal than its English counterpart'.[10] The major changes concerned length of term, the sale of contracts and discipline. Servants in husbandry served short terms, seldom remaining with a single master for more than a few years, and usually renegotiating their contracts annually. Indentured servants served longer periods under fixed terms negotiated at departure. While four years was the usual term for servants who had reached maturity, the length of contract varied with the time needed to repay the borrowed passage fare. Greater distance and longer terms led to transferable contracts. Planters would have been less willing to lay out the substantial sum needed to purchase a servant if they had to commit themselves to that investment for the entire term without the possibility of sale, while the servant trade could not have functioned smoothly had merchants, ship captain's agents been unable to transfer contracts to colonial masters. To sell an Englishman or woman 'like a damned slave' was at first shocking to some contemporaries, but it was essential to the success of the indenture system.[11]

These changes, Galenson suggests, introduced 'a new adversary status . . . into the relationship between master and servant'.[12] Longer terms joined with the inability of servants to renegotiate contracts and change masters to produce tension and conflict, evident in the frequency with which servants ran away and were hauled before magistrates. Unlike English servants in husbandry, who were often integrated into their master's family and treated as added children or poor relations, colonial servants were simply workers and investments. While Galenson may underestimate the potential for

affection and mutual trust between master and servant, colonial servitude
was clearly a much harsher institution than its English counterpart.

There were at least four distinct forms of servitude in British America,
three of them voluntary. Under the most common, servants signed a contract or indenture in England before departure which specified conditions
of service and which was sold to a master when the servant arrived in
the colonies. Many servants arrived without written contracts, however, to
serve according to 'the custom of the country', customs gradually specified
in colonial legislation. There were systematic differences between the two
groups. Customary servants were younger: about sixteen years of age on an
average when they immigrated in contrast to servants with contracts who
were usually in their late teens or early twenties. They also served longer
terms than those who arrived with indentures, even if age is held constant,
perhaps reflecting that, from the planter's perspective at least, they were less
productive than those with written contracts. They may also have been less
often skilled, more likely to be illiterate, of lower social origins, more often
without living parents or guardians to look out for their interests, easier
marks for an unscrupulous 'crimp', and generally less sophisticated about
labour relations and opportunities in the New World.[13] The third form of
voluntary servitude appeared in the eighteenth century with the German
migration to the mid-Atlantic colonies. German redemptioners promised to
pay passage fare upon arriving in the colonies, a promise that shifted much
of the risk in the trade from merchants and shippers to the migrants. If they
proved unable to pay, they were sold as servants to satisfy the debt.[14] In
addition to these voluntary systems, penal servitude, a minor institution in
the seventeenth century, became an important source of labour later in the
colonial period.[15]

Servants played a central role in the development of British America. During the seventeenth century, roughly 250,000 indentured migrants reached
the colonies, the majority going to the West Indies and the tobacco coast.[16]
In the 1630s, servants proved adequate to the modest labour needs of
Barbadian farmers and they dominated the island workforce. Events of
the next decade changed everything.

The Barbadian sugar revolution transformed the island in the years surrounding 1650. Sugar monoculture displaced diversified farming based on
tobacco, cotton and provisions; large estates swallowed up small farms;
blacks grew in number and whites left; destructive demographic patterns
took root; the island came to depend on imported food and fuel; and the
great planters took control – all within a few decades after 1640. The critical change was the rapid growth of African slavery, and the explanation
seems straightforward. Sugar, because of its substantial scale economies and
handsome profits, greatly increased demand for labour, stretched the capacity of the servant trade to the breaking point, and forced planters to look
elsewhere for workers. African slaves, available in large quantities through

the highly developed, century-old Atlantic trade, were the most attractive alternative. Other islands in the British and French West Indies witnessed similar transformations in the labour force as sugar came to dominate their economies.[17]

In a recent essay, Bean and Thomas have rejected this account of the rise of slavery in Barbados. They argue that growing demand for labour played no role in the replacement of servants by slaves, contending instead that the transformation was entirely due to changes in the supply of workers. Specifically, they maintain that the price of slaves declined while that of servants rose, shifting returns on the two types of labour to make slaves more attractive. They imply that slaves would have become the dominant source of bound labour in Barbados around mid-century with or without sugar. In my terms, they assert that there was no distinct 'Barbadian path' toward slavery, that one process – what I have called the 'Virginia pattern' – prevailed in both the sugar islands and along the tobacco coast.[18]

As Bean and Thomas acknowledge, the arguments rest on a weak empirical foundation. Their account hinges on three pieces of evidence. They reject the role of sugar by pointing to a lag of several years between the beginning of sugar production on a large scale and the emergence of slaves as a majority of the unfree workforce. Was there such a lag? Richard Dunn's evidence, the best available on the issue, suggests not. Dunn argues that sugar production began between 1640 and 1643 and that it was accompanied by an immediate increase in the island's black population.[19]

Bean and Thomas' description of price movements is also questionable. For slave prices they rely on records of sales by the Dutch West India Company at Pernambuco between 1636 and 1645. These data describe a sharp fall in prices in north-eastern Brazil during the mid-1640s and thus support their argument. Prices for slaves in British America – the critical variable for Barbadian planters – however rose dramatically during the period, from £16.5 sterling per slave in 1640 to 20.2 in 1645, and to 27.7 in 1650.[20]

Bean and Thomas present no direct evidence on the price of servants but use as a proxy money wages for builders in southern England, which show a sharp rise from the mid-1630s to the mid-1640s. However, since servants did not receive cash payments for their services, real wages rather than money wages seem the most appropriate measure and it is not clear that real wages rose. Direct evidence on the price of servants in the Chesapeake colonies does show an increase in the 1640s, but the data are weak and difficult to interpret and the prices, if they did in fact rise, did so only over the short term, quickly falling after mid-century.[21]

The Bean and Thomas model implies a sharp decline in the number of servants brought to the West Indies as the workforce was Africanized. Was there such a decline? Yes, but only in the 1660s, after the fact of Africanization. Sugar transformed working conditions on the island, turning Barbados into 'a Land of Misery and Beggary' by curtailing opportunities for poor whites, raising mortality and morbidity rates, and introducing a rigorous and degrading work regime. Once news of those conditions reached England, fewer servants were willing to sign indentures for the islands, while those who did so demanded (and obtained) shorter terms than servants bound for the mainland. However, during the 1640s and 1650s, when Barbados became an Africanized slave society, there was no noticeable tailing off in the number of servants brought to the sugar islands.[22] The evidence suggests that a sharp rise in demand for labour brought about by the growth of sugar cultivation – and not, as Bean and Thomas would have it, a decline in the supply of servants – made Barbados a slave society.

The existence of a highly developed, large-scale Atlantic slave trade was essential to the Africanization process and to the success of the Barbadian sugar revolution. During the first half of the seventeenth century that trade delivered an average of more than 7,000 slaves a year, the bulk of them to Brazil and Spanish America. Thus, when the increased demand for labour in Barbados stretched the capacity of the servant trade, planters had an alternative: they had only to persuade someone to divert a portion of the substantial slave traffic to the island. The Dutch, those 'great encouragers of Plantacons', were eager to accommodate.[23]

In the decades following 1640, Barbados quickly became a thoroughly Africanized slave society with a unique plantation regime. Blacks became a majority of the population in the 1650s; by 1680 they accounted for nearly 70 per cent of the total. The economy concentrated on the production of sugar to such an extent that planters imported even the food to feed their slaves. The small farms of the pre-sugar era quickly disappeared, leaving the island in the hands of a small group of great planters who owned most of the land and slaves and who thoroughly dominated local politics. Ironically, the sugar magnates, in making their fortunes, transformed Barbados in ways that made it 'almost uninhabitable' by their standards. To escape to England became the 'one consuming ambition' of the big planters. Once they became big enough, the exodus began. By the early eighteenth century, 'absenteeism had become a permanent way of life for many of the Barbados gentry'.[24]

The Chesapeake Colonies

Recent studies suggest that the Chesapeake colonies of Maryland and Virginia took a different path toward slavery than that followed in Barbados and the other sugar islands. In that mainland region the transition occurred without a change in the agricultural base: tobacco was the staple export both before and after the growth of slavery. And, again in contrast to the Barbadian case, the transition was triggered by a decline in the supply of indentured servants, a decline which forced planters to look elsewhere for labour. The number of servants delivered to Maryland and Virginia rose from the 1630s to the 1660s while the prices planters paid for them, despite a short-term increase in the 1640s, remained constant and perhaps even fell. The supply levelled out in the mid-1660s, or at least grew at a slower rate, before falling off sharply about 1680. Servant prices, after reaching a low in the mid-1670s, climbed by roughly 50 percent over the next fifteen years. The price of slaves, on the other hand, at least held steady and may have fallen during the 1680s. Planters began to purchase slaves in large numbers in the 1670s; by 1690, blacks were a majority of the bound labour force.[25]

Why these changes in secular trends? Why, that is, did the number of European immigrants to the Chesapeake increase rapidly during the first half of the seventeenth century, level out or grow more slowly in the 1660s and 1670s, and then decline after 1680? Two processes seem of central importance: changes in the size of the potential migrant group and changes in the relative attractiveness of the several destinations available to Englishmen on the move. Although neither can be measured precisely, it is clear that during the seventeenth century both changed in ways that tended first to increase and later to reduce the number of servants willing to try their luck in tobacco.

The size of the potential migrant group in seventeenth-century England was a function of total population, an assertion that must be qualified by a recognition that migration was highly age, sex and probably class specific and that the propensity to migrate varied with time. Nevertheless, changes in the rate of population growth provide a rough index to changes in the size of the migrant group. The pattern of growth within England shifted near the middle of the seventeenth century. The most reliable estimates describe an average annual growth rate of 0.4 to 0.5 per cent for roughly 200 years, beginning from a base of 2.5 million in the mid-fifteenth century and reaching 5.5 million in 1650. England's total population declined slowly over the next forty years, to about 5 million, its level during the 1620s, and then began to grow again, slowly at first, more rapidly toward the middle decades of the eighteenth century.[26] If movement to the Chesapeake were a function of the size of the migrant group alone, one would expect the rate of immigration to increase during the first half of the seventeenth century and then decline.

Other processes complemented the impact of changes in the number of potential immigrants. In part, this was a function of the pattern of population growth. During the sixteenth and early seventeenth centuries, real wages in England fell as a growing number of workers competed for employment. Falling real wages lowered the opportunity costs of migration and made movement to the colonies more attractive. Relieved of the pressure of a rapidly growing workforce, real wages rose across the last half of the seventeenth century. The evidence is far from precise, but the increase seems to have occurred in two upward steps, the first in the 1650s, the second about 1680, both followed by long periods of relative stability.[27] Rising real wages increased the opportunity cost to migration and worked both to reduce the size of the migrating population and, for those who still chose to move, to increase the attractiveness of destinations within England. This hypothesis is supported by recent work reporting a decline in both the intensity and scale of migration within England during the last half of the seventeenth century: after 1660, fewer Englishmen moved than earlier, while those who did so travelled shorter distances.[28]

Within the Chesapeake colonies, the course of opportunity for ex-servants may have helped shape the pattern of immigration. The changes that a young man who completed servitude along the Bay would achieve a comfortable position were high up to about 1660 and then began to decline, a decline that was especially sharp after 1680 when former servants often left the region in search of better prospects elsewhere. Clearly, were adequate information available, the chances of success in the colonies would have encouraged immigration until shortly after mid-century and subsequently discouraged it.[29]

Perhaps more important than the course of opportunity within the Chesapeake colonies was the changing attractiveness of the tobacco coast relative to other regions of British America. During the 1630s, poor Englishmen who decided to cross the Atlantic could choose among three destinations, but after 1640 sugar and disease gave Barbados a bad reputation while the failure of New England to find a staple crop prevented the growth of a lively demand for servants. These developments narrowed the options and focused the greatest part of the English trans-Atlantic migratory stream on the tobacco coast. After 1680, the opening up of Pennsylvania and the beginning of rapid development in the Carolinas ended this near monopoly and diverted migrants away from Maryland and Virginia. In sum, changes in the size of the British-American migration stream and in the share of all migrants attracted to the Chesapeake colonies combined to first increase and later to reduce the number of servants bound for the tobacco coast.[30]

The rate of farm formation in the Chesapeake, a rough proxy for the growth in demand for labour, remained high in the last decades of the seventeenth century: from the mid-1660s to 1700, years in which the supply of servants first levelled out and then declined, the number of plantations in Maryland and Virginia grew at about 3 per cent per year. The result was falling ratios of servants to farms and a sharp increase in the price of indentured workers. During the last third of the seventeenth century, when the initial thrust toward heavy investment in slaves occurred, Chesapeake planters faced a severe labour shortage, a shortage produced by the failure of white immigrants to keep pace with the growth of farms.[31]

Planters and merchants were not passive in the face of these changes. Indeed, recruiting agents were a critical link in the process and could, by varying the intensity of their efforts, shape both the volume and direction of migration. During the seventeenth century, their efforts were often successful in the short run and, as a consequence, the supply of new servants to the Chesapeake proved highly sensitive to short term shifts in planter demand. Over the long run, shifts in the composition of the servant group suggest some more permanent adjustment in recruiting practices as merchants cast their net more widely in the search for migrants. In the middle decades of the seventeenth century, recruiters apparently focused on young men in their late teens and early twenties from the middling ranks of English families, men who possessed some occupational skills and work experience. After 1680, however, as their numbers dwindled and their opportunities at home increased, fewer such men moved to Virginia and Maryland. Recruiters attempted to meet the resulting shortfall by drawing more heavily on other groups within Britain's population – Irish, women, convicts, homeless orphans and the labouring poor.[32] Despite these efforts, it proved impossible to overcome the powerful secular processes – a stagnant English population and the pull of other destinations – tending to diminish the ability of tobacco planters to attract willing workers. During the last decades of the seventeenth century, merchants were unable to meet the growing demand for indentured labour without driving the cost of servants beyond what planters were willing to pay. The result was a major change in the composition of the Chesapeake workforce as merchants tapped new sources of indentured servants and planters turned increasingly to African slaves as their principal source of unfree labour.

During the first decades of the eighteenth century, the main features of the Chesapeake plantation regime gradually took root. Some of the characteristics of the seventeenth century persisted. In particular, tobacco remained the staple export despite a considerable economic diversification, and small, owner-worked farms continued to account for a substantial share of regional income. Still, there were striking changes. Blacks, less than 10 per cent of the population in 1690, made up nearly a quarter by 1730, by which time the slave workforce had begun to grow through reproductive increase. And the great planters, their wealth based on land and slaves, their identities shaped by shared experience and dense kinship networks, took control and started building their 'golden age', an age that brought wealth and power to a few, poverty and oppression to many.[33]

South Carolina

The Carolina lowcountry, the last of our case studies, is the most interesting because of its complexity. It combined the major elements observed elsewhere into a unique pattern. Two distinct transitions can be identified. The first, completed by the end of the seventeenth century, was a shift from indentured servants to slaves drawn from the West Indies. It paralleled the process in the Chesapeake region in that it was triggered by a decline in the supply of servants and accomplished without a change in the agricultural base of the regional economy. The second transition, a shift to slaves from

Africa, was completed by 1730. It resembled that on Barbados as it was rooted in a major expansion of exports and a great increase in the scale of agricultural operations.[34]

By the time the first permanent English settlement was established in the lowcountry in 1670, colonists were able to draw on more than a half-century of experience in developing British America. All the English colonies faced the problem of recruiting a labour force, and a variety of methods and populations had been tried. Indentured servitude represented one of the more successful and enduring responses. The Carolina promoters expected that servants would form the core of the colony's workforce and they took steps to organize their recruitment immediately.

Their timing was unfortunate, for the days when servants willingly left England in numbers sufficient to the needs of colonial planters had passed. Carolinians recruited among a diminishing supply of willing migrants and they did so in the face of increased competition from other colonial regions. Further, the lowcountry laboured under some particular disadvantages. For one thing, the colony quickly developed a reputation as a charnel-house. Reports of ill-health and high mortality must have discouraged prospective servants.[35] For another, the region lacked a large-scale, direct trade with England before the early eighteenth century. Shipping was thus irregular, passage expensive, and, most important, there was no community of Carolina merchants in England to recruit servants for lowcountry plantations. Carolina planters were poorly placed to compete for servants against the Chesapeake and the West Indies where major staple trades supported steady shipping and cheap fares and where tobacco and sugar merchants supported a large-scale recruiting network.

Still, Carolinians had some success in recruiting servants, in part because they were able to tap the migrant stream pushed out of Barbados by the sugar revolution, and indentured labourers dominated the unfree labour force during the 1670s and 1680s. That success proved temporary, however, and it is clear that Carolina would have faced a labour shortage had it relied solely on servants. Fortunately for the planters (if not for their victims), there were other groups available. One such source, free wage labour, proved even less successful than indentured servitude. South Carolina lived up to its promise as a land of opportunity for poor whites. Planters were able to entice some free workers from Barbados and to hire newly freed servants, but high wages and cheap land permitted a quick transition to yeoman status.[36]

Indians were another source. While the Indian slave trade was important in South Carolina during the seventeenth century, it only became a major source of labour later, after 1700. Initially, most Indian captives were exported, reflecting the difficulty of enslaving an indigenous population and the need to earn credits abroad. Some of those Indians were exchanged for Caribbean blacks, who soon dominated the unfree workforce. Among new arrivals in the colony, servants outnumbered slaves until the late 1680s. Thereafter, slaves outnumbered servants.

The initial transition to slavery in the lowcountry occurred at the same time as along the tobacco coast. Simultaneous timing suggests similarity in process. In the Chesapeake colonies the transition emerged out of a complex set of changes in the supply and demand for labour. Before 1680, the great majority of unfree workers along the tobacco coast and in the low country were indentured servants. As the century progressed, however, planters found it increasingly difficult to obtain enough such workers to meet their need for labour. A declining population and slowly rising real wages in England created improved opportunities at home while the continued growth of the Americas led to greater colonial competition for workers. The result was a labour shortage in both the Chesapeake and the Carolina lowcountry and a change in the composition of the workforce as planters purchased slaves to replace servants.

The first transition to slavery in the lowcountry resembled the process along the tobacco coast in still another way: it was not the product of a major change in the agricultural base of the regional economy. Some historians have asserted the contrary, contending that the lowcountry transition resembled that of Barbados. There, a shift from an agriculture based on tobacco, cotton and food crops grown on small farms to sugar produced on large plantations triggered the move toward slavery. The Barbadian sugar revolution raised demand for labour beyond the capacity of the servant trade and created work conditions and opportunities that were not attractive to British youths. The spread of rice culture did have such consequences in Carolina during the early decades of the eighteenth century. However, the lowcountry became a slave society before it developed a plantation regime, when small farms still dominated production, and while agriculture remained focused on food crops, livestock and timber for the West Indian market.[37]

While the transition to slavery in both the Chesapeake and the lowcountry was triggered by a decline in the supply of servants and a rise in their price, there was one major difference in the process. Both regions relied heavily on the sugar islands for slaves during the seventeenth century, but Chesapeake planters were able to call on shipments directly from Africa as early as the mid-1670s, perhaps thirty years before Carolinians were able to do so.[38] That difference reflects the larger market in the Chesapeake and the greater wealth of tobacco planters. Lowcountry planters offered a steady market for small shipments of West Indian blacks and they could pay for them with products much in demand on the sugar islands. However, they would have had trouble absorbing the larger cargoes handled by African slavers, they lacked exports that merchants would accept in exchange for blacks, and few of them were rich enough to command credit in England. In the seventeenth century, the lowcountry was simply not an attractive market for African slave traders.

The conditions that denied lowcountry planters direct access to the African slave trade disappeared after 1700. While it is not certain when direct trade began, it is clear that slave imports grew dramatically during the early decades of the eighteenth century. On an average, Charles Town merchants imported 275 blacks a year during the 1710s, nearly 900 in the 1720s, and over 2,000 in the 1730s. Clearly, the direct trade with Africa had become a major supplier of lowcountry workers by the second decade of the eighteenth century.[39]

The growth of the lowcountry rice industry was a key event in that process. During the seventeenth century, South Carolinians engaged in a systematic search for an agricultural staple that would command a direct European market. They tried a variety of crops, testing both the local resource base and overseas demand. The period of experimentation ended in the 1690s with the commercial cultivation of rice, the crop that quickly became 'as much their staple commodity, as Sugar is to Barbados and Jamaica, or Tobacco to Virginia and Maryland'. The industry grew rapidly over the first three decades of the eighteenth century: rice exports passed 1.5 million pounds by 1710, 6 million in 1720, and nearly 20 million in 1730.[40]

The association of the growth of African slavery with the expansion of the rice industry suggests that a dramatic increase in demand for labour was the key element in accounting for the changing composition of the lowcountry workforce. The prospect of high returns and great wealth set Carolinians off on a vicious scramble for workers, led them to take great risks not only with their estates but with the colony's survival, and produced a thorough transformation of lowcountry society that proved destructive and oppressive to its victims, frightening and unsettling to its masters. The transformation was hardly tidy and it was purchased at a great cost by sometimes savage brutality, but we can make some progress toward understanding the process by examining the several constituent groups who laboured on lowcountry plantations: whites, particularly indentured servants; native Americans; slaves from the West Indies; and African blacks.

Servants played little role in the lowcountry economy after the 1680s: only a handful appear in estate inventories taken between 1690 and 1730. Carolina planters faced the declining supply of servants that afflicted all of British America, but conditions specific to the lowcountry aggravated the shortage. In the first place, Carolina planters had relied heavily on a secondary market in servants who completed their terms in Barbados, a supply that dried up as white migration to the island dwindled. Secondly, the growth of the export sector made the lowcountry less attractive to poor British youths. Plantation agriculture brought with it a black majority, gang labour, higher mortality and diminished opportunities. Rice cultivation in particular was unpleasant, to put it mildly, a 'horrible employment not far short of digging in Potosi'.[41]

One distinguishing feature of the lowcountry labour system during the process of Africanization was the key role played by native American slaves. While Indian slaves appear in South Carolina a early as 1683, they were rare during the seventeenth century. In 1700 there were roughly 200 enslaved Indians in the lowcountry, 3 per cent of the total population and 7 per cent of the unfree workforce. During the next decade they were the most rapidly growing group in the colony. By 1710 there were 1,500 native American slaves accounting for 15 per cent of the total and 26 per cent of the bound labourers. They continued to increase in the next decade, but much less rapidly. In 1720, there were 2,000 Indians, but they made up only 11 per cent of the total and 17 per cent of the slaves. Thereafter both their numbers and their share fell sharply: in 1730 there were 500 Indian slaves in South Carolina, less than 2 per cent of the population and only 2.4 per cent of the unfree workers.

While the subject merits a detailed investigation, the pattern is consistent with an explanation based on the supply of Indians and the demand for labour. During the seventeenth century lowcountry planters met their labour needs with servants and West Indian blacks. Few Indians were turned into slaves and most of them were exported to earn foreign exchange. In this period the slave trade was a secondary activity, subordinate to the trade in deerskin and the political aims of the English and their native American allies. Indian slaves were captured almost incidentally, as a by-product of other processes. After 1700 the lowcountry export boom led to a sharp increase in demand for labour which transformed relationships between the English and the Indians. The slave trade gained in importance and was no longer subordinated to the deerskin trade or to political concerns. More Indians were captured and more of those captives were kept in the lowcountry to grow rice and supply provisions and naval stores.[42]

The intensification of the slave trade proved devastating to the Indians. It was a bloody, violent business, impossible to institutionalize, that demanded increased warfare and ever more raiding. It produced sharp population decline and the total destruction of several smaller tribes. And it led to major political changes as Indians struggled to protect themselves by forming larger and more effective federations and by elaborating a 'playoff' system in which rivalries between the English, French and Spanish were exploited in efforts to control the worst excesses of the European invasion. Population decline and political restructuring quickly lowered the supply of Indian slaves, reducing it to a mere trickle by the 1720s.[43]

It is unlikely that planter preferences for Africans played a major role in the decline of Indian slavery. True, Indians were more vulnerable to lowcountry diseases than blacks and were thus more often sick and more likely to die young. Indians also may have found escape easier, given their geographic knowledge and the presence of nearby tribes who might take them in. And it is possible that tradition and prior work experience made Indians less productive as agricultural labourers. However, such differences were compensated for by the higher prices blacks commanded: during the 1720s adult blacks were worth 40 to 50 per cent more than adult Indians. If planter preferences were responsible for the decline of Indian slavery one would expect a sharp fall in price to accompany the fall in numbers. Prices rose, rather than fell, by 50 to 100 per cent from the 1720s to the 1730s, indicating that planters would have purchased more Indian slaves had they been available.[44]

The rapid growth of the slave trade to the West Indies during the seventeenth century, long before Africans emerged as a dominant source of unfree labour in the lowcountry, played a central role in the rise of slavery in the mainland colonies. By 1660 there were 34,000 blacks in the British Caribbean and annual slave deliveries approached 3,000. During the next few decades, English slavers greatly increased the efficiency of their operations. Prices fell dramatically, reaching a low point in the 1680s. At the same time, volume rose sharply: in the final decades of the century, annual slave deliveries approached 8,000. The supply of slaves to British America improved during the seventeenth century, the larger numbers and lower prices reflecting more efficient markets, cheaper transport costs, and the exploitation of new African sources.[45]

These developments proved critical to mainland planters. For one thing, the large slave population of the islands provided a source of labour, one easily integrated into the provisions trade between the continent and the West Indies. Further, mainland planters found themselves in the fortunate position of a minor market for a rapidly expanding supply of workers. Once they were willing to pay the price, Carolina planters would be able to get all the slaves they needed.

Carolina planters relied on the West Indies for slaves from the start of settlement in the lowcountry. While demand remained low, that reliance posed few problems. West Indian markets were easily able to supply the 100 to 200 slaves a year that Carolina planters could afford before 1710. Indeed, at those levels it was probably cheaper to acquire slaves that way than through the direct trade with Africa. Lowcountry planters could take advantage of the large and efficient island slave markets; transactions were easily integrated into the provisions trade; and blacks could be purchased in small lots without driving up their price. However, the rapid growth of demand for labour fuelled by the export boom soon stretched the capacity of this secondary trade. When the lowcountry proved capable of absorbing 500 to 1,000 and more slaves each year, certainly the case by the 1720s if not earlier, the relative advantages of the island slave trade diminished and the direct trade in Africans emerged as the chief source of workers for the Carolina plantations.

By 1730 the central features of the lowcountry plantation regime were firmly established. It was clearly a slave society, its 20,000 blacks, many of them newly arrived Africans, a substantial majority of the population. Those blacks were both heavily concentrated in the hands of a few great planters and widely distributed among white householders. In addition, the region was very prosperous, its lively export sector focused on rice production capable of supporting an impressive growth rate. It remained only for the great planters to consolidate their power, to develop the sense of group consciousness, and to forge the ideology that would transform them into an effective ruling class.

Conclusion

The structure of the Atlantic labour market played a key role in shaping the plantation regimes of the sugar islands, the Chesapeake colonies and the Carolina lowcountry. The developers of British America had several options in recruiting and organizing a workforce. They could draw on free workers and indentured servants from Britain, on Indians from the vast North American interior, on slaves from other colonies and on blacks from Africa. With the exception of African slaves, those workers moved in small, localized markets characterized by sharp, unpredictable shifts in volume and price. Africans, by contrast, were trapped in a much wider net, commodities in a stable, large-scale, international labour market that made them the victims of choice in the rapidly expanding plantation colonies of European America.

NOTES

1. David Brion Davis, *Slavery and Human Progress* (New York, 1984), 51. On the relative numbers of imported African slaves and European immigrants, see David Eltis, 'Free and Coerced Transatlantic Migrations: Some Comparisons', *AHR*, 88 (1983), 278.
2. Davis, *Slavery and Human Progress*, 52. William D. Phillips, Jr, *Slavery from Roman Times to the Early Transatlantic Trade* (Minneapolis, 1985), surveys literature on slavery in the early modern Mediterranean. John J. McCusker and Russell R. Menard, *The Economy of British America, 1607–1789* (Chapel Hill, N.C., 1985) discusses the organization of labour in those English colonies which did not rely heavily on slaves.
3. A more formal presentation of the argument employed in this essay appears in Henry A. Germery and Jan S. Hogendorn, 'The Atlantic Slave Trade: A Tentative Economic Model', *JAH*, 15 (1974), 233–46, and David W. Galenson, *White Servitude in Colonial America: An Economic Analysis* (Cambridge, 1981), especially 141–9.
4. The most important work in this tradition is Winthrop D. Jordan, *White Over Black: American Attitudes Toward the Negro 1550–1812* (Chapel Hill, N.C., 1968). For a review of the debate, see William A. Green, 'Race and Slavery: Considerations on the Williams Thesis', in Barbara L. Solow and Stanley I. Engerman, eds., *British Capitalism and Caribbean Slavery: The Legacy of Eric Williams* (New York, 1987), 25–49.
5. The quotations are from Alexander Hewatt, *An Historical Account of the Rise and Progress of the Colonies of South Carolina and Georgia*, 2 vols (London, 1779), I, 120. I have discussed these attitudes in more detail in 'Slavery, Economic Growth

and Revolutionary Ideology in the South Carolina Lowcountry', in Ronald Hoffman et al., eds., *The Economy of Early America: The Revolutionary Period, 1763–1790* (Charlottesville, Va., 1988), 244–74. On the Georgia debate, see Betty Wood, *Slavery in Colonial Georgia, 1730–1775* (Athens, Ga., 1984).

6. Jordan, *White Over Black*, 64, 66.

7. The literature on early Barbados is surveyed in McCusker and Menard, *The Economy of British America*, 145–9.

8. Records of Rappahannock County, 1664–1673, p. 21, VSL, as quoted in Philip A. Bruce, *Economic History of Virginia in the Seventeenth Century* (New York, 1895), II. 2n. The debate over the relation between indentured servitude and apprenticeship is summarized in Galenson, *White Servitude in Colonial America*, 6. Abbot E. Smith, *Colonists in Bondage: White Servitude and Convict Labor in America, 1607–1776* (Chapel Hill, N.C., 1947) remains a useful study of the institution.

9. Galenson, *White Servitude in Colonial America*, 7–8. Ann Kussmaul, *Servants in Husbandry in Early Modern England* (Cambridge, 1981) is the best analysis of this type of agricultural labour in England.

10. Galenson, *White Servitude in Colonial America*, 7.

11. Thomas Best, a Virginia servant writing in 1623, as quoted in Edmund S. Morgan, *American Slavery, American Freedom: The Ordeal of Colonial Virginia* (New York, 1975), 128.

12. Galenson, *White Servitude in Colonial America*, 8.

13. On differences between customary and indentured servants, see Lorena S. Walsh, 'Servitude and Opportunity in Charles County, Maryland, 1658–1705' in Aubrey C. Land et al., eds., *Law, Society and Politics in Early Maryland* (Baltimore, 1977), 111–15, and Russell R. Menard, 'British Migration to the Chesapeake Colonies in the Seventeenth Century' in Lois Green Carr, Philip D. Morgan and Jean B. Russo, eds., *Colonial Chesapeake Society* (Chapel Hill, N.C., 1988), 126–7.

14. Recent studies of the redemptioner system include Farley Grubb, 'Immigrants and Servants in the Colony and Commonwealth of Pennsylvania: A Quantitative and Economic "Analysis"' (Ph.D. dissertation, University of Chicago, 1984), and Marianne Wokeck, 'The Flow and Composition of German Immigration to Philadelphia, 1727–1775', *Pennsylvania Magazine of History and Biography*, 105 (1981), 249–78.

15. On convicts, see A. Roger Ekirch, *Bound for America: The Transportation of British Convicts to the Colonies, 1718–1775* (New York, 1987).

16. For estimates of migration, see Henry A. Gemery, 'Emigration from the British Isles to the New World, 1630–1700: Inferences from Colonial Populations', *Research in Economic History*, 5 (1980), 179–231.

17. The literature on the Barbadian sugar revolution is summarized in McCusker and Menarc, *Economy of British America*, 149–56.

18. Richard N. Bean and Robert P. Thomas, 'The Adoption of Slave Labor in British America' in Henry A. Gemery and Jan S. Hogendorn, eds., *The Uncommon Market: Essay in the Economic History of the Atlantic Slave Trade* (New York, 1979), 377–98. See also Hilary McD. Beckles, 'The Economic Origins of Black Slavery in the British West Indies, 1640–1680: A Tentative Economic Model', *Journal of Caribbean History*, 16 (1982), 36–56.

19. Richard S. Dunn, *Sugar and Slaves: The Rise of the Planter Class in the English West Indies, 1624–1713* (Chapel Hill, N.C., 1972), 68. See also Carl and Roberta Bridenbaugh, *No Peace Beyond the Line: The English in the Caribbean, 1624–1690* (New York, 1972), 33, and Hilary McD. Beckles and Andrew Downes, 'The Economics of Transition to the Black Labor System in Barbados, 1630–1680', *Journal of Interdisciplinary History*, 18 (1987), 228.

20. US Bureau of the Census, *Historical Statistics of the United States, Colonial Times to 1970* (Washington, D.C., 1975), Series Z 166, 1174.

21. English real wages and servant prices are discussed in more detail below, in the section on the Chesapeake colonies.

22. David Galenson, 'Immigration and the Colonial Labor System: An Analysis of the Length of Indenture', *Explorations in Economic History*, 14 (1977), 360–77; Gemery, 'Emigration from the British Isles to the New World', 215.

23. Sloane MS. 3662, as quoted in Vincent T. Harlow, *A History of Barbados, 1625–1685* (Oxford, 1926), 42. On the volume of the slave trade, see Philip D. Curtin, *The Atlantic Slave Trade: A Census* (Madison, Wis., 1969), 119.

24. Dunn, *Sugar and Slaves*, xv, 103, 116.

25. This section summarizes my essay, 'From Servants to Slaves: The Transformation of the Chesapeake Labor System', *Southern Studies*, 16 (1977), 355–90.

26. E. A. Wrigley and R. S. Schofield, *The Population History of England, 1541–1871: A Reconstruction* (Cambridge, 1981).

27. On English real wages, see Henry Phelps Brown and Sheila V. Hopkins, *A Perspective of Wages and Prices* (London, 1981).

28. Peter Clark, 'Migration in England during the Late Seventeenth and Early Eighteenth Centuries', *Past and Present*, no. 83 (May 1979), 57–90.

29. Russell R. Menard, 'From Servant to Freeholder: Status Mobility and Property Accumulation in Seventeenth-Century Maryland', *WMQ*, 3rd Series, 30 (1973), 37–64.

30. Idem, 'British Migration to the Chesapeake Colonies in the Seventeenth Century', 103–15, provides more detail.

31. Idem, 'From Servant to Freeholder', 374–6.

32. Idem, 'British Migration to the Chesapeake Colonies in the Seventeenth Century', 122–31, discusses the changing composition of the servant population.

33. Allan Kulikoff, *Tobacco and Slaves: The Development of Southern Cultures in the Chesapeake, 1680–1800* (Chapel Hill, N.C., 1986) examines the structure of the plantation regime.

34. This section summarizes my essay, 'The Africanization of the Lowcountry Labor Force, 1670–1730' in Winthrop D. Jordan and Sheila L. Skemp, eds., *Race and Family in the Colonial South* (Jackson, Miss., 1987), 81–108.

35. On Carolina's reputation for poor health, see Peter H. Wood, *Black Majority: Negroes in Colonial South Carolina from 1670 through the Stono Rebellion* (New York, 1974), 63–9.

36. On opportunities in early Carolina, see Aaron M. Shatzman, 'Servants into Planters: The Origins of An American Image – Land Acquisition and Status in Seventeenth-Century South Carolina' (Stanford University Ph.D., 1981).

37. For the argument that the transition from servants to slaves in the lowcountry resembled the process in the West Indies rather than the Chesapeake, see Galenson, *White Servitude in Colonial America*, 154–6.

38. Menard, 'Servants to Slaves', 366.

39. On Charleston slave imports, see Wood, *Black Majority*, 151, and US Bureau of the Census. *Historical Statistics*, Series Z 155, 1173.

40. James Glen, *A Description of South Carolina . . .* (London, 1761), 87. The literature on the beginnings of rice cultivation is reported in McCusker and Menard, *Economy of British America*, 176fn. For export data, see US Bureau of the Census, *Historical Statistics*, Series Z 481–99, 1192–3.

41. Harry J. Carman, ed, *American Husbandry* (New York, 1939), 277. On the transformation produced by the rapid expansion of export agriculture, see McCusker and Menard, *Economy of British America*, 181–4.

42. The best study of Indian slavery in South Carolina is William Robert Snell, 'Indian Slavery in Colonial South Carolina, 1671–1795' (University of Alabama Ph.D., 1972). See also Verner W. Crane, *The Southern Frontier, 1670–1732* (Durham, N.C., 1928); John Donald Duncan, 'Servitude and Slavery in Colonial South

Carolina, 1670–1776' (Emory University Ph.D., 1972); Almon W. Lauber, *Indian Slavery in Colonial Times Within the Present Limits of the United States* (New York, 1913); and J. Leitch Wright, Jr, *The Only Land They Knew: The Tragic Story of the American Indians in the Old South* (New York, 1981), 102–50.

43. The best study of the impact of the slave trade on native peoples is Richard White, *The Roots of Dependency: Subsistence, Environment and Social Change among the Choctaws, Pawnees and Navahos* (Lincoln, Nebraska, 1983), 34–68.

44. On prices, see Snell, 'Indian Slavery', 143–7. Wood makes the case that the planters preferred blacks to Indians in *Black Majority*, 37–40.

45. David Galenson, *Traders, Planters, and Slaves: Market Behavior in Early English America* (New York, 1986) is the best introduction to the slave trade to the islands.

DOCUMENT 1: THE ARRIVAL OF THE FIRST BLACKS
IN VIRGINIA

This letter has often been cited as the earliest reference to the arrival of blacks in a North American colony. Written by the Secretary and Recorder of the Virginia colony to Sir Edwin Sandys, the letter refers to '20 and odd negroes' brought to Point Comfort, on the Virginia capes, in early January 1619/20, and suggests that the Governor of Virginia and the Cape merchant bought the cargo. What does the letter tell us about the status of these blacks? How did this cargo end up in Virginia? Recent research has shown that thirty-two Africans were recorded in a census in Virginia five months before the arrival of this cargo, and that these 'founders' of black life in North America were taken from a Portuguese vessel bound from Angola to Vera Cruz.[1]

John Rolfe to Sir Edwin Sandys,
January? 1619/20.

About the latter end of August, a Dutch man of Warr of the burden of a 160 tuñes arriued at Point-Comfort, the Commando[rs] name Capt Jope, his Pilott for the West Indies one Mr Marmaduke an Englishman. They mett wth the Trér in the West Indyes, and determyned to hold consort shipp hetherward, but in their passage lost one the other. He brought not any thing but 20. and odd Negroes, wch the Governo[r] and Cape Marchant bought for victualle (whereof he was in greate need as he p/re/tended) at the best and easyest rate they could. He hadd a lardge and ample Comyssion from his Excellency to range and to take purchase in the West Indyes.

NOTE

1. John Thornton, 'The African Experience of the "20 and Odd Negroes" arriving in Virginia in 1619', *WMQ*, 3rd series, 65 (1998), 421–34.

Susan Myra Kingsbury (ed.), *The Records of the Virginia Company of London*, 4 vols (Washington, DC: Government Printing Office, 1933), vol. 3, p. 243.

DOCUMENT 2: MARYLAND ESTABLISHES SLAVERY FOR LIFE

An extract from a Maryland statute of 1664 that established slavery for life in that colony. The phrase durante vita means 'service for life'. This extract, by its wording, indicates that slaves – not just blacks or black servants – already lived in Maryland and that the mating of white women with slave men would lead to any children being automatically designated as slaves. Does the statute imply that any degree of black skin colour should carry the stigma of slavery? What fears were engendered in public officials and the colonial white elite by the prospect of interracial sex?

An Act Concerning Negroes & Other Slaues.

Bee itt Enacted by the Right Hon[ble] the Lord Proprietary by the aduice and Consent of the upper and lower house of this present Generall Assembly That all Negroes or other slaues already within the Prouince And all Negroes and other slaues to bee hereafter imported into the Prouince shall serue Durante Vita[.] And all Children born of any Negro or other slaue shall be Slaues as their ffathers were for the terme of their liues[.] And forasmuch as divers freeborne English women forgettfull of their free Condicōn and to the disgrace of our Nation doe intermarry with Negro Slaues by which alsoe diuers suites may arise touching the Issue of such woemen and a great damage doth befall the Masters of such Negroes for preuention whereof for deterring such freeborne women from such shamefull Matches Bee itt further Enacted by the Authority advice and Consent aforesaid That whatsoever free borne woman shall inter marry with any slaue from and after the Last day of this present Assembly shall Serue the master of such slaue dureing the life of her husband And that all the Issue of such freeborne woemen soe marryed shall be Slaues as their fathers were[.] And Bee itt further Enacted that all the Issues of English or other freeborne woemen that haue already marryed Negroes shall serve the Masters of their Parents till they be Thirty yeares of age and noe longer.

William Hand Browne (ed.), *Archives of Maryland: Proceedings and Acts of the General Assembly of Maryland, January 1637/8–September 1664* (Baltimore: Maryland Historical Society, 1883), pp. 553–4.

DOCUMENT 3: MANAGEMENT OF SLAVES, 1672

This document is taken from the records of Surry county, Virginia. It shows that a county court in the Old Dominion discriminated against slaves in terms of their free movement and clothing.

(From the Records of Surry county, Va.)

Atte a courte houlden at Southwarke for ye county of Surry ye 4th day of September, 1672, Annoque Reg. Car. 2d, 24, &c.

PRESENT—The Hon'ble Coll. Tho. Swann, Esq.
Lt. Coll. Geo. Jordan.
Capt. Law. Baker,
Maj'r Wm. Browne,
Mr. Robt. Caufield,
Capt. Robt. Spencer,
Mr. Benj. Harrison,

Justices.

Mathias Marriott haveinge in Contempt of an order of y^{is} Court, grounded upon an Act of Assembly for ye restraint of serv'ts walking abrod on Sundayes or other dayes, given his negro a Note to goe abrod & haveing noe business, and alsoe renderinge scurrilous language to ye Co'rt both yesterday & to-day, ye s'd Marriot is ord'd to pay unto ye sherife for ye use of ye county two hund'd p'ds of Tob'o & Caske, w'th Costs als., exec.

Whereas information hath been given to y^{is} Court y^{at} ye too Careles and inconsiderate Liberty given to Negroes, not only in being p'mitted to mete together upon Satterdayes & Sundayes, whereby they wine opportunity to consult of unlawful p'jects & combinations to ye danger & damage of ye neighbours, as well as to theire Masters. and Also that ye apparrell comonly worne by negroes doth as well Highten theire foolish pride as induse them to steale fine Linninge & other ornaments, for ye p'vention whereof itt is hereby ord'd & published to ye Inhabitants of y^{is} county y^{at} ye Act of Assembly for p'vention of serv'ts goeing abroad be put in due execution & from hence forth Noe negro shall be allowed to weare any white Linninge, but shall weare blew shirts & shifts y^{at} y^{ey} may be herby discovered if y^{ey} steale or weare other Linninge, & if ye Master of any Negro shall p'tend y^{at} blew is not to be had for men & women Negros for theire shifts & shirts, caps or neckclothes, y^{at} he shall supply y^{at} want in Course Lockerham or Canvis, & y^{en} to be duly observed untill a by law be made to confirme ye same.

[Several persons, besides Mathias Marriott, who was a man of some prominence, were before the court at this time charged with allowing their negroes too much liberty. Act VIII, Session of 1672, the preamble to which recites 'that many negroes have lately been and now are out in rebellion in sundry parts of this country', seems to not have been carefully obeyed by the people.]

2

SLAVERY IN COLONIAL
NORTH AMERICA

Introduction

By the late seventeenth century, slave labour was found in all the British North American colonies from Maine to South Carolina, but it was more important in some than in others. Morgan (1991) helpfully distinguishes between slaveowning societies, where slaves comprised less than 20 per cent of the total population, and slave societies where Africans constituted more than 20 per cent. Slaveowning societies included northern colonies such as Massachusetts, Rhode Island, New York, Pennsylvania and New Jersey. Slave societies were all situated south of what later became the Mason–Dixon line: they were Virginia, Maryland, the Carolinas and Georgia. Plantations growing staple crops became the *raison d'être* of slave societies, whereas in slaveowning societies Africans were employed in smaller groups in urban trades, at ironworks, and in small-scale agricultural production. The debasement of slaves was particularly associated with the plantation regime. It was during the eighteenth century that a distinctive American slave culture emerged, bringing together music, language and religion, all of which were influenced by the transmission of African customs to the New World.

Far more slaves were imported to the British Caribbean than to British North America. The demographic regimes of the island and mainland colonies had considerable differences. Heavy mortality, poor reproductive capacity and a reliance on the supply of 'saltwater' slaves from Africa characterised the Caribbean slave systems before 1775 whereas North American slaves had better fertility and better reproductive rates. A discussion of the demography of North American slaves can be found in Walsh (2000), who examines patterns of nuptiality, fertility and mortality; internal migration; and biomedical studies, anthropometric measures and archaeological evidence pertaining to the African-American population. Walsh notes that our knowledge of the transatlantic migration patterns of slaves is much fuller than our understanding of the later life experiences of blacks in colonial North America.

Fogel (1989) discusses slavery in North America from its seventeenth-century origins until its demise in the American Civil War. His book includes consideration of slavery as a system in the West Indies as well as North America, and it gives due space to abolitionism. The book does not have a specific section devoted to the colonial era but interspersed among discussions of slave fertility, mortality, diet, working arrangements and culture there is much attention to long-term trends in the evolution of North American slavery. This helps to place the colonial period within the longer trajectory of slavery's growth in North America. Fogel reminds us that North America was different from other slave-importing territories because it took only a small share of the transatlantic slave trade and had only a minor part of its plantation system given over to sugar production. He views slavery as a rational form of capitalist agriculture, with the gang system deployed as an efficient form of labour organisation. His discussion of the heights of slaves argues that North American slaves were taller, hence better-fed, than European workers.

Berlin's synthesis (1998) of the development of North American slavery before 1775 discerns three periods in the creation of a black presence in North America and examines four regional areas: the northern colonies; the Chesapeake; the Lowcountry; and the Lower Mississippi Valley. First came charter generations in which Africans were a noticeable but not overwhelming presence. This phase lasted until the late seventeenth century. During this period many African-Americans were Atlantic creoles, that is, a group of Africans characterised by 'linguistic dexterity', 'cultural plasticity' and 'social agility' that flourished in many port communities around the Atlantic trading world. The second phase involved plantation generations, in which slave societies were formed. This lasted from the turn of the eighteenth century until American independence. Atlantic creole communities were destroyed in this phase and the debasement of slaves became intermeshed with the relentless rise of the plantation regime. The third phase comprised the revolutionary generations after 1775, when plantation societies entrenched their position on slavery and societies with slaves, in the north, embarked on measures for freedom. In a brief preview of his book, Berlin (1980) analysed main differences between African and creole slaves. He showed that the diversity of the black experience in colonial North America is best understood by looking at changes over time in the recruitment, deployment and treatment of Africans and by considering the evolution of black communities within their regional settings.

Many studies dealing with colonial North American slavery are based on individual colonies or regions. Piersen (1988) looks at the comparatively small presence of slaves in New England. He argues that they lived and worked under a mantle of 'family slavery' whereby masters and slaves lived in proximity. Because most New England slaves were isolated, however, family formation was difficult to achieve. Hodges (1999) offers a parallel analysis for New York and East Jersey. His book focuses on slave religion, culture and resistance in Manhattan and the surrounding Jersey countryside. From the early days of Dutch rule in New Netherland, Hodges argues, the interaction of African and European peoples had a lasting effect on African-American culture in the region. In New Jersey Africans were employed mainly as farm workers. In New York City they found work in various tasks, but many were dock workers and seafarers.

Chesapeake slavery has been studied intensively. Morgan (1975) places the growth of slavery in Virginia within the context of available labour and examines the connections between slavery and freedom in the Old Dominion. He examines labour exploitation in early Jamestown, the growth of a tobacco economy in Virginia, and the emergence of elite white prejudice against blacks based upon white notions of freedom and fears of black rebellion. Kulikoff (1986) investigates the demographic growth and cultural development of Chesapeake slavery, concentrating particularly on St George's County, Maryland. He analyses the characteristics of the Chesapeake planters, links his findings to the creation of the Old South, and shows how class, gender and race relations in the Chesapeake were founded upon gentry rule, patriarchy and racism. Sobel (1987) is more concerned with the interaction of whites and blacks in Virginia in terms of customs and culture. She describes African-American and Anglo-American attitudes towards time, work, space, the natural world, death and the afterlife. Rather than emphasising the separateness of blacks in fashioning the African heritage to their own ends, she suggests that black and white religious experience merged in the evangelical dominations that flourished in Virginia in the second half of the eighteenth century.

Slavery in early South Carolina and Georgia has attracted more attention than slavery in North Carolina. This is perhaps unsurprising given that the tarheel colony had much lower slave imports than the other two southeastern colonies. Kay and Cary (1995) cover North Carolinian slavery in the pre-revolutionary era. They describe the significant degree of cultural autonomy retained by imported Africans. In their view, the continued importance of indigenous African systems of belief provided a coherent world view for slaves. Wood (1974) was for a long time the best study of slavery in colonial North America based on a single colony. He describes the African traits that slaves brought to this particular New World setting. He argues that slavery was adopted on a large scale in South Carolina not merely because a ready supply of Africans became available in the early eighteenth century or because planters there had West Indian – especially Barbadian – antecedents for slave plantations. Rather, he suggests that the cultural familiarity of blacks with rice cultivation in Africa was crucial for the creation of a black majority in South Carolina.

Morgan (1998) has produced the only genuinely comparative study of slavery's development in two North American regions. By highlighting different characteristics of slaves in both areas, he justifies the on-going use of a regional framework for studying North American slavery. Morgan explores the role of land and labour in shaping slave culture in Virginia and South Carolina. He also includes detailed chapters on everyday contacts between masters and slaves and on slave religious and customary beliefs. Wood (1984) traces the growth of slavery in Georgia, a colony established in 1732 that deliberately eschewed slavery in the first eighteen years of its existence only to embrace it thereafter. The royal government of Georgia came into operation in late 1754 and within a decade the staple-producing culture of Carolina planters had spread widely into that colony. Because of the common bond of rice cultivation, the development of slavery had much in common throughout the Lowcountry areas of Georgia and South Carolina.

Much can be learned from studying slave societies that lay outside British imperial control in North America. Landers (1999) covers one such society in Spanish Florida, which had a distinctive, complex slave presence with flexible race relations. Blacks in Spanish Florida were property owners, homesteaders and entrepreneurs who had greater legal and social protection than slaves in England's North American colonies. For the Lower Mississippi Valley, including West Florida and French Colonial Louisiana, Usner (1992) provides a triracial study of settlers up to the end of the War of Independence. He discusses the cross-cultural interaction that brought together Indians, slaves and settlers in patterns of exchange. The diversification of the population in colonial Louisiana led to the growth of ethnic heterogeneity. Dunn (1972) has written the most accessible book on the growth of early British West Indian slavery, through to the end of the War of the Spanish Succession. His book points to similarities and contrasts with the evolution of slavery in mainland North America; it also shows the importance of Barbadian settlers in establishing slavery in South Carolina. The demographic failure of the white and black population in the early English West Indies is an important theme running throughout Dunn's book.

Most slaves lived and worked in rural settings, but some clustered in cities and others were involved in the maritime world. Nash (1979) examines the work and economic niche of slavery in Boston, New York and Philadelphia, the three largest port cities in British North America. He looks at the occupations, residence, household structure and church associations of slaves and their interaction with servant labour. He is particularly concerned with the incidence of poverty and social tension that marked the lives of all the lower orders – slave, indentured, or free – in the northern seaports. Additional essays exploring these themes are gathered together in Nash (1986), who also discusses moves towards freedom for slaves in the northern seaports in the revolutionary generation.

BIBLIOGRAPHY

Berlin, Ira, 'Time, Space, and the Evolution of Afro-American Society on British Mainland North America', *American Historical Review*, 85 (February 1980), 44–78

Berlin, Ira, *Many Thousands Gone: The First Two Centuries of Slavery in North America* (Cambridge, MA: Harvard University Press, 1998)

Brown, Kathleen M., *Good Wives, Nasty Wenches, and Anxious Patriarchs: Gender, Race, and Power in Colonial Virginia* (Chapel Hill: University of North Carolina Press, 1996)

Dunn, Richard S., *Sugar and Slaves: The Rise of the Planter Class in the English West Indies, 1624–1713* (Chapel Hill: University of North Carolina Press, 1972)

Fogel, Robert W., *Without Consent or Contract: The Rise and Fall of American Slavery* (New York: W. W. Norton, 1989)

Hodges, Graham Russell, *Root and Branch: African Americans in New York and East Jersey, 1613–1863* (Chapel Hill: University of North Carolina Press, 1999)

Kay, Marvin L. Michael and Lorin Lee Cary, *Slavery in North Carolina, 1748–1775* (Chapel Hill: University of North Carolina Press, 1995)

Kulikoff, Allan, *Tobacco and Slaves: The Development of Southern Cultures in the Chesapeake, 1680–1800* (Chapel Hill: University of North Carolina Press, 1986)

Landers, Jane, *Black Society in Spanish Florida* (Urbana-Champaign, IL: University of Illinois Press, 1999)

Morgan Edmund S., *American Slavery, American Freedom: The Ordeal of Colonial Virginia* (New York: W. W. Norton, 1975)

Morgan, Philip D., 'British Encounters with Africans and African-Americans' in Bernard Bailyn and Philip D. Morgan (eds), *Strangers within the Realm: Cultural Margins of the First British Empire* (Chapel Hill: University of North Carolina Press, 1991)

Morgan, Philip D., *Slave Counterpoint: Black Culture in the Eighteenth-Century Chesapeake and Lowcountry* (Chapel Hill: University of North Carolina Press, 1998)

Nash, Gary B., *The Urban Crucible: Social Change, Political Consciousness, and the Origins of the American Revolution* (Cambridge, MA: Harvard University Press, 1979)

Nash, Gary B., *Race, Class, and Politics: Essays on American Colonial and Revolutionary Society* (Urbana-Champaign, IL: University of Illinois Press, 1986)

Piersen, William D., *Black Yankees: The Development of an Afro-American Subculture in Eighteenth-Century New England* (Amherst, MA: University of Massachusetts Press, 1988)

Sobel, Mechal, *The World they made Together: Black and White Values in Eighteenth-Century Virginia* (Princeton: Princeton University Press, 1987)

Usner, Daniel H., *Indians, Settlers and Slaves in a Frontier Exchange Economy: The Lower Mississippi Valley before 1783* (Chapel Hill: University of North Carolina Press, 1992)

Walsh, Lorena S., 'The African American Population of the Colonial United States' in Michael R. Haines and Richard H. Steckel (eds), *A Population History of North America* (Cambridge: Cambridge University Press, 2000)

Wood, Betty, *Slavery in Colonial Georgia, 1730–1775* (Athens, GA: University of Georgia Press, 1984)

Wood, Peter H., *Black Majority: Negroes in South Carolina from 1670 through the Stono Rebellion* (W. W. Norton, 1974)

ESSAY: ENGENDERING RACIAL DIFFERENCE, 1640–1670

Brown (1996) deals with gender and racial issues in relation to North American slavery and specifically in relation to Virginia. Three broad issues are worth discussion. First, Brown argues that English perceptions of Africans altered during the course of the seventeenth century and that changed attitudes occurred because of the increasing importance of African slave labour in Virginia's economy. Do you agree with her that race is 'an ongoing historical and cultural construction' rather than 'a biological fact' (p. 109)? Second, Brown suggests that the legal, economic and social disadvantages of slave status emerged only in and after the 1660s, when slaves were beginning to assume numerical significance among Virginia's working population. What light does this analysis throw on the long-standing debate about whether slavery preceded racism or whether racism preceded slavery in Virginia? Does her analysis change the parameters of that debate? Third, Brown charts the changing status of African women in colonial Virginia compared with English women. What reasons does she cite for the subordination of African women in colonial Virginia? How did the colony's legal codes treat English servant women and African slave women in terms of reproduction, inheritance and bondage?

Thomasine Hall's Warraskoyack was also home to several Africans during the 1620s. 'Antonio a Negro' arrived in the colony the year before Powhatan's brother, Opechancanough, led the Indian attack of 1622 that ultimately brought about the demise of the Virginia Company. Surviving the ordeal, perhaps because Indian warriors spared African lives, Anthony eventually married 'Mary a Negro Woman', who had sailed to Virginia on the *Margarett and John* just months after the attack. The two earned their freedom and moved to Virginia's Eastern Shore, where they purchased property and established a family. As a free woman, the wife of a landowner, and the mother of several free-born children, Mary enjoyed a degree of prosperity and security at midcentury that distinguished her from most other African women in the colony.[1]

The unusual path by which Mary traveled from Africa to Virginia bore the imprint of centuries-old African traditions of trade and newer European mercantile rivalries. Whether traded as a result of a local surplus of female dependents or because she fell victim to an African or European raid, Mary likely began her transatlantic journey at the hands of Portuguese slavers in one of the numerous trading centers along the West African coast between the Gulf of Guinea and the Kongo-Angola region. Although the Dutch had

---

Kathleen M. Brown, *Good Wives, Nasty Wenches, and Anxious Patriarchs: Gender, Race, and Power in Colonial Virginia* (Chapel Hill: University of North Carolina Press, 1996), pp. 107–36, 405–15.

incorporated a West Indies Company in 1621 in the hopes of siphoning profits from the booming Portuguese-dominated African trade, until the 1630s their involvement in the slave trade remained sporadic and limited mainly to confiscating Portuguese and Spanish slave cargoes for resale to other vessels. Mary might have been on board one of these Dutch vessels when the *Margarett and John* stopped for water in the Caribbean. Trading provisions with Dutch mariners as it had done on previous occasions, the crew of the *Margarett and John* would have carried Mary to Virginia as a slave unless she had been able to bargain for a shorter term of service.[2]

The idiosyncratic nature of Mary's route to Virginia foretold her unusual status in a colony dominated by English men and indentured servants. Only twenty-three Africans appear on the 1625 muster for the colony, which numbered nearly twelve hundred English. The names of eight of the twenty-three – including 'Angelo', 'Antonio', 'Anthony', 'Isabell', and 'John Pedro' – suggest previous contact with the Portuguese, perhaps even Catholic baptism. Mary was one of only ten African women. In the twenty years after the muster, as these other Africans faded from colonial records, she and Anthony reemerged on Virginia's Eastern Shore. With status accruing from both his property and his responsibility for legally dependent family members – an arrangement that would have been the envy of many of his English male contemporaries – Anthony might have considered himself a successful man in both an English and African sense.[3]

Had Mary and Anthony arrived in Virginia a generation later, however, their chances of achieving freedom would have been significantly compromised by a set of laws distinguishing between the privileges and work roles of English and African women. Until the 1660s, slavery in Virginia remained legally ill-defined. It derived meaning from several sources, including the discourses of racial difference in the travel and scientific literature of the day, the de facto enslavement of Africans by European traders, and the tactics of individuals seeking to escape bondage after they arrived in the colony. The earliest slave laws in the colony built upon these implicit racial foundations. The first such measure, passed in 1643, consisted of a tithe levied on African women from which English women were exempt. This legal measure effectively made it harder for subsequent generations of Africans to do what Anthony and Mary had done earlier in the century: marry, purchase freedom, and establish families and independent households.[4]

As slavery became a more important form of labor in Virginia, eventually replacing indentured servitude, early constructions of racial difference provided the legal background for more blatant measures of legal and social discrimination between African and English women. Perpetual bondage for the children of enslaved women distinguished these mothers from their English indentured counterparts after 1662. Christianity, which had long been a theme of English discussions of Africans, also became part of the legal discourse of slavery, race, and freedom, demarcating 'Negro' people as a separate group from Christians by 1667. These legislative landmarks signified a continuing process of evaluation through which racial difference was expressed legally, incorporated into a new social order, and endowed with legal, economic, and social meaning. Rooted in planters' assumptions about English and African women's proper roles in the tobacco economy, early definitions of racial difference and the accompanying discriminatory practices resulted ultimately in a race-specific concept of womanhood.

Race and Slavery

When Mary Johnson arrived in Virginia in 1622, she was a slave in a society that lacked a legal institution of slavery but one where most colonists already had some knowledge of Africans and the transatlantic trade in slaves. Although no laws limited Mary's opportunities for procuring her own freedom, their absence also left her vulnerable to exploitation at the hands of her master. Protected by the customs and laws surrounding English master-servant relations only if they were capable of convincing English people of their applicability, enslaved Africans appear to have been subject to longer and more intense terms of service than English servants. Slaves such as Mary remained suspended in legal limbo, experiencing bondage in a highly individual manner before the 1660s, with freedom depending upon the goodwill of masters, the support of neighbors, and their own tenacious insistence upon serving for a term of years rather than for life. Legal ambiguity in the matter of slavery, however, did not mean an absence of discussion on questions of race and difference. English national and mercantile rivalries, newly forming colonial identities, and the travel accounts written by English men after 1600 all circumscribed the possibilities created by legal silences.

The task of assessing the status of Africans imported to Virginia before 1662 has fascinated historians for many years, sparking considerable debate over the nature of racism and the origins of slavery. The discussion thus far centers on the relationship between attitudes toward race and Virginia's racially based slave labor system, with some scholars claiming precedence for racism and others contending that it followed the legal codification of slavery. In general, the debate has suffered from two related problems: the tendency to begin with a view of race as a biological fact rather than as an ongoing historical and cultural construction and, second, the failure to acknowledge that competing concepts of racial difference led to uneven and occasionally contradictory developments in the history of race. When legal, literary, and mercantile discourses of race are examined along with actual practices of coerced labor, the relationship between racism and slavery becomes much more complicated, defying our efforts to designate one as a cause of the other.[5]

Many historians have assumed that race is a physiological and genetic fact, immediately perceptible to the human senses. In one of the pioneering studies of racial attitudes in early America, Winthrop D. Jordan defined race as a biological characteristic that was beyond the scrutiny of historians. 'I assumed that when Englishmen met Negroes overseas there would be "attitudes" generated', he wrote, contending that African 'blackness' was one of the most salient features of English perceptions of racial difference. Jordan exhaustively documented English writers' theories and commentaries on racial difference. Although his careful exegesis of blackness emphasized the meanings English men brought to their encounter rather than the physical appearance of Africans, Jordan never questioned that the racial differences of which English travelers wrote were real.[6]

Even when historians have examined racial attitudes as a product of struggles for power rather than as a reaction to skin color, they rarely questioned the concept of race itself. In his study of slavery in Virginia, Edmund S. Morgan found that African 'blackness' explained little about the emergence of slavery and racism in the seventeenth century. Racism became significant in Morgan's study mainly in the aftermath of hostile settler relations with Indians and class turmoil involving bound laborers. But, like Jordan, Morgan did not scrutinize race the way he did racism and race relations.[7]

Historicizing race has allowed several scholars to probe more deeply into the connections between racial discourses and power. Rather than assuming they know what race is before beginning their inquiry, they approach it as a historically produced technology of power. Examined from this perspective, the differences between interpretations as diverse as Jordan's and Morgan's appear less significant. Rooted in older Christian associations of blackness with evil, literary constructions of racial difference acquired new importance with the rise of the European slave trade in Africa and English ventures along its western shores. This was not simply the empirical response of English travelers to new experiences, however; questions of domination and power – national, mercantile, and political – always informed English literary representations of African appearance and culture. Concepts of racial difference, moreover, acquired rhetorical force as a consequence of English efforts to naturalize them by connecting them to other power relations defined as natural, like those of gender.[8]

As we have already seen, English travelers to Africa during the late sixteenth century frequently commented upon the color of Africans, but their perceptions and evaluations of African culture were not consistently focused on physical appearance. Although the Portuguese slave trade provided an important backdrop for the English encounters with Africans, possibly influencing English men's pejorative reading of African peoples and cultures from as early as the 1530s, single-minded emphases of blackness and inferiority did not begin in earnest until the late seventeenth century, after the English were themselves solidly committed to the slave trade.[9]

The imperial rivalries of the early seventeenth century briefly opened new opportunities for the English, and with those came renewed interest in Africa. Weakened by Dutch and Spanish competition, the Portuguese monopoly on the African trade began to crumble, inspiring the English to begin a fresh assault on Portuguese territories and gold routes. One such effort led by English adventurer Richard Jobson resulted in a published account in 1623 of attempts to establish a trade outpost in the Gambia. Like the chroniclers of the Gaelic Irish and Indians, Jobson described 'black men' as idlers and their wives as drudges who toiled incessantly growing and processing rice, manufacturing cheese and butter, and preparing and serving meals for their menfolk. He also embellished theories of African men's color and lasciviousness, claiming that large 'members' and sexual appetites were the legacy of Ham's punishment for seeing his father's nakedness.[10]

Although Jobson's account contained protoracial theories of difference, many of which were based on the sexual practices rather than the blackness of the native Gambia River dwellers, its message was leavened by careful observations of religious and cultural differences among Africans. Aiming to persuade his audience of the potential for profitable trade, Jobson often presented inhabitants as cooperative and loving and lavished much attention on indigenous culture. During his journey, he recounted close relationships with several West Africans, including a young Mandingo boy, a Muslim, whose circumcision ceremony upset Jobson greatly. His emotional reaction revealed an identification with the youth as a man like himself – an empathy that transcended his earlier moralism about large members and sexual appetites.[11]

On at least one occasion, Jobson raised the issue of skin color at the behest of West Africans themselves. After English explorers insisted on bathing in crocodile-infested waters, their Mandingo guides cautiously decided to join them, reasoning that 'the white man, shine more in the water, then they did, and therefore if Bumbo [crocodile] come, hee would surely take us [the English] first'. Skin color in Jobson's account thus appeared in Mandingo reactions to the English as well as in English impressions of Africans.[12]

In Jobson's complex text, African peoples were both 'black' and 'tawney', drunken and sober, overrun with flies and fastidiously clean, loving and wary, naïve in trade yet able to assess cannily the behavior of the English intruders they described as white. The very peoples Jobson depicted as enduring 'beastly living' might also display signs of civility. Although it is true that Jobson contributed to racial discourses about Africans, in the account of his journey English desires to commence a lucrative gold trade occasionally leveled the playing field between Mandingo and European. The true villains of his narrative, moreover, were, not native dwellers, but 'lurking' Portuguese rivals for the gold trade. Littered with references to other colonial relationships – those between the English and Irish, the Portuguese and the Mandingo – and contextualized by Spain's participation in the slave trade, Jobson's commentary was part of a mercantile discourse in which the skin color of Africans was but one of many topics, and by no means the most important.[13]

Even in travel accounts less even-handed than Jobson's, English writers commented on skin color sporadically and incidentally rather than systematically before 1650. Written in 1624 to attract readers rather than investment, Andrew Battell's lurid tale of eighteen years of captivity and adventure contained harsh judgments of 'beastly' and cannibalistic Africans. Like Jobson, however, Battell drew clear distinctions between African cultures and had relatively little to say about appearance.[14]

Neither Jobson's nor Battell's narrative can rightly be described as a first impression, even though both men may have been writing about their first meetings with Africans. As Jordan has persuasively argued, long-standing Christian associations of blackness with evil and classical accounts of monstrous races influenced the way in which the earliest English explorers perceived and wrote about their encounters with Africans. Even before they set foot on African soil, Jobson and Battell probably had some idea of how they would write about what they found there. More important, the circumstances under which they confronted Africans – as potential trade partners, as slaves in the transatlantic trade, or as allies or enemies of the Portuguese – influenced their judgments. Blackness was not the dominant impression of Jobson's narrative, however, even though both he and the Africans he met used the racial vocabulary of 'black' and 'white'. Even in Battell's sensational tale, blackness received less attention than European mercantile rivalries and the absence of Christianity.[15]

English racial attitudes of the early seventeenth century are perhaps best described as an increasingly coherent construction of racial difference to communicate desires for domination. Interactions between the English and Indians in Virginia contributed to these early perceptions of difference, recasting the English national identity that had emerged from contact with the Irish. During the seventeenth century, English attitudes toward Africans shifted with the growing need for African labor and the initiation of an overseas trade in slaves. Although the concepts of racial difference elaborated in the literature of the early seventeenth century did not lead inevitably to the slave labor system of the century's final quarter, they did inform the legal and intellectual framework within which slavery emerged. The establishment of slavery as the primary labor system in Virginia subsequently ushered in a new age of racism in which legal constructions of race weighed more heavily upon the social relations of Africans and English than they had previously.

The social meaning the English attached to racial difference during the 1620s and 1630s derived from and overlapped with their attitudes toward non-English nations and laboring people. The similarity between perceptions of ethnic differences and those of race appear in colonial musters of residents, with the treatment of Africans forming one end of a continuum of English discomfort with non-English peoples. Although Mary Johnson's official listing as 'Mary a Negro Woman' distinguished her from English settlers who were listed with surnames, this expression was not inherently racial. Like 'Choupouke an Indian', 'James a Frenchman', James and John, 'Irishmen', 'Anthony a Portugall', and 'Epe the Dutchman', imported Africans endured the disadvantage of non-English heritage in a colony settled by the ethnocentric English who may have been unable to spell, pronounce, or remember unfamiliar surnames. Unlike most non-English New World residents, however, the children of imported Africans continued to receive the designation 'negar', while the offspring of Dutch, French, and Irish individuals eventually lost their ethnic labels.[16]

The bound condition of imported Africans also influenced the status-conscious middling and genteel English. Men and women of England's own lower class, for example 'Mary, a maid', were sometimes identified by only first names. The combination of non-English heritage and servility created a double jeopardy for enslaved Africans who were rarely dignified with more than a first name and the tag 'negre'. The crucial element in English constructions of racial difference during the 1630s and 1640s may not have been the physical appearance of Africans, but the context in which English people witnessed that appearance: nearly all Africans were slaves when they arrived in Virginia, and, before 1644, nearly all slaves in Virginia were Africans.[17]

The development of slavery in the Caribbean affected the servile treatment of Africans in Virginia, and, to a lesser degree, may have influenced the pattern of some early slave laws. Before 1630, Africans came to the European outposts of the Caribbean incidentally and in small numbers. With Dutch entry into both the slave trade and the sugar industry of Curaçao and Brazil, sugar technology and slavery spread throughout the region. Caribbean planters turned to slavery quickly, developing slave laws piecemeal. As early as 1636, Barbadian planters may have been holding Africans and their children in perpetual bondage. In Antigua, laws discouraging sexual intimacy between Africans and Europeans appeared by 1644, whereas, in Bermuda, legislators prohibited interracial marriages in 1663. Although before 1660 there was no clear legal template for slavery in the Caribbean upon which Virginia could rely, laws restricting sexual contact and marriage between African and English laborers revealed the subordinate status of Africans in other New World colonies.[18]

Ship captains, merchants, wealthy landowners, and enslaved Africans themselves acted as vectors for African, Dutch, and Caribbean culture in Virginia, influencing a cosmopolitan notion of slavery to take root in the colony before midcentury. As early as the 1630s, ship captains traded slaves to wealthy Norfolk and York County residents, often the same men who served as justices and burgesses. Dutch vessels carrying cloth, liquor, and slaves sailed to Virginia ports at the height of their nation's dominance of the slave trade. Like other colonial commodities, slaves became international currency for Dutch merchants in the colony. Some, like Rotterdam merchant William Moseley of Norfolk, settled debts with customers through exchanges of African laborers. By the mid-1640s, even English merchants were beginning to traffic in slaves. Frequent contact with travelers from Barbados and New England brought still other Norfolk residents into slave trade networks.[19]

Despite constituting only a small proportion of the colonial population before 1660 – probably never more than 5 percent – Africans themselves had an important impact on slavery in the colony. Virginians with overseas connections enjoyed access to a small but steady supply of incoming slaves whom they hired out, sold to other colonists, or bequeathed to their children. By midcentury, enough Virginians owned slaves that it was no longer unusual for a colonist to attach the slaves of a wealthy debtor. Enslaved Africans raised cattle, shot wolves, and escorted strangers to their destinations. In Lancaster County, an African named Grasher even served as a beadle (parish official) in charge of whipping offenders, although he was not permitted to attend the court. As the international traffic in humans began to surround Virginia by the 1630s, Africans became a part of the daily lives of an English population much larger than the actual number of slaveowners.[20]

Although the foreign birth and slave status of Africans were important to English definitions of racial difference, Christianity also played a crucial role in shaping English attitudes toward Africans. Already convinced that the syncretic Catholicism of the Gaelic Irish indicated paganism, the English easily adapted this Protestant criterion for civility to reach a similar conclusion about Chesapeake Indians. Traveling among Africans who practiced totemic religions, witchcraft, and, allegedly, cannibalism, the uneasy English believed themselves surrounded by savages and barbarians. Even those Africans christened by the Portuguese before being transported across the Atlantic did not pass muster but provoked the English to denigrate papism. Christianity ultimately provided a highly adaptable means by which Europeans designated native populations – especially those whose lands, markets, and peoples they wished to appropriate – uncivilized.[21]

Slave status was not simply a symbolic brand marking Africans as outsiders. It carried with it several legal, economic, and social disadvantages that distinguished Africans and a tiny handful of captive Indians from other populations the English deemed alien. Masters who hoped to extract long (if not life) terms from African slaves were willing from as early as the 1630s to pay more for these laborers. The greater initial investment undoubtedly complicated individual African efforts to gain freedom through self-purchase, legal petition, and enforcement of indentures. In 1659, to take one instance, a Norfolk slave with Portuguese connections sued his master for his freedom, pleading that he had lived in England and should serve only as long as other servants coming from that country. The papers 'fardinando a negro' produced to back his case were written in a language the court could not decipher; justices rejected his plea and ordered him to serve for life. For Africans like Fardinando who lacked the protection afforded by English indentures and custom, appeals for freedom could be easily circumvented by masters who sought to exploit their laborers' status as outsiders.[22]

Enduring domestic ideals for English female labor also may have affected the reception of Africans in Virginia. In contrast to their plans for their own women, English settlers perceived African women as an exploitable new source of agricultural labor, an exception to the gender division of labor but compatible with the vision of domestically employed English women. English accounts of women in West Africa as heavily burdened drudges – a staple of most English colonial literature by the second quarter of the seventeenth-century – may have influenced the predominantly cosmopolitan owners of African labor to set their female slaves to work in the fields. Many English masters also may have been aware that African women were being used interchangeably with men to grow sugar in Brazil. Few paused to contemplate the dairying, meal preparation, and child care that women from several West African societies performed. That West African women themselves viewed field work, not as indicative of servility or nastiness, but as gender-appropriate labor, may only have facilitated their exploitation at the hands of English masters.[23]

African women's significance in the population of bound female laborers may have been one reason why they became the subjects of Virginia's earliest legal discriminations. By the 1660s, as Carole Shammas has shown, enslaved women slightly outnumbered English servant women in several Virginia counties. Bound African women also outnumbered their Indian servant counter-parts for most of the century. If such patterns prevailed before 1660 – and the absence of a marked shift in female slave and servant importations before that date makes such an assumption plausible – African women's demographic significance among the colony's female laborers may have contributed to the early legal focus upon them.[24]

All of these factors – English predispositions to view African women as drudges, the usefulness of English women's domesticity for colonial promoters, and the colony's peculiar demography – combined with the demands of the tobacco economy to transform the meaning of African women's labor. In a colony in which the public acknowledgement of English women's domestic traditions did not protect them from sweating in tobacco fields, African women's domestic traditions were easily ignored and quickly eroded. Bondage and legal constraints on African families similarly altered the context of African women's agricultural labor. It was this subordination of African women to the needs of English labor and family systems that ultimately provided the legal foundation for slavery and for future definitions of racial difference.

Taxing Differences

The tax levied on African women in 1643 was the earliest distinctive and clearly unfavorable treatment of African people to the enshrined in law in Virginia. Although English precedents, colonial economic pressures, and gendered definitions of productivity and citizenship all contributed to Virginia's haphazard tax practices during the seventeenth century, the critical factor leading to the categorization of African women as 'tithables' (individuals who performed taxable labor) was planter assumptions about African women's role in the colony as laborers.

In both England and Virginia, tax practices reflected a complex web of economic and military imperatives and valuations of household labor. Under English law, property owners paid taxes to the crown on all movable possessions, contributing separately to the parish in the form of a church tax or tithe. During the sixteenth century, the crown assessed taxes upon English households in proportion to the amount of property owned. By the early seventeenth century, the crown was collecting revenues in the form of small subsidies and the 'Hearth Tax', a system under which English householders paid a tax for each hearth in the house. Both systems stressed the household rather than the individual as the critical unit of production, with masters mediating the relation between the state and their dependent household members.[25]

In Virginia, the English emphasis on the household was sometimes at odds with the exigencies of life on a colonial frontier. The demands of staple crop production largely determined settlement patterns, planter investment strategies, and consumer decisions, while the threat of invasion by neighboring Indians required the maintenance of a large military force. Prime English male laborers, who set the standard for agricultural productivity and composed the pool of potential soldiers, formed the bulk of the colonial population and predominated in households. All of these conditions may have led legislators to assess taxes upon individual men rather than upon households.[26]

Driven by their need for soldiers and military fortifications, colonial legislators adopted Virginia's first tax on individual men in the aftermath of the 1622 Indian attack led by Opechancanough. The Assembly required each household head either to send a man to the military compound or to contribute five pounds of tobacco per person for himself and each of the servants (implicitly male) in his household. As an alternative to military service, Virginia's first poll (or per person) tax thus targeted only men. Throughout the 1630s and 1640s, this definition of tithable appears to have determined local decisions about the individuals liable to serve and the compensation for their lost labor.[27]

The overwhelmingly male character of the tobacco-growing population in Virginia and the lucrative potential of production for an expanding

European market also encouraged lawmakers to view each individual laboring man, rather than the household, as a taxable unit. Markets that gave each man's labor a definable monetary value in Virginia were only just beginning to transform agricultural production along London's grain-trade routes and other farm regions. Undoubtedly hoping to maximize its revenues from this predominantly male population of tobacco producers, the Governor's Council ordered all 'male hed' above the age of sixteen to contribute tobacco and corn toward the support of the minister in 1624 and defined 'tithable[s]' in 1629 to include masters of families, all free men, and people 'working the ground'.[28]

Until the late 1620s, Virginia lawmakers never seriously entertained the notion of taxing English women. Military contributions underpinning male liability for taxes traditionally did not apply to women. English women were not only exempt from military service but also classified as dependents in need of protection. Defense plans in the colony were thus devised to minimize the dangers to this vulnerable portion of the population, as they did in 1627 when the governor and Council ordered 'woemen and children and unserviceable people' to take cover at 'Mathews Mannor' while the men made a stand against the Indian enemy.[29]

The exemption of women from taxes also reflected colonial officials' expectations that English women in Virginia would eventually take up domestic work. In England, field work was not the primary responsibility of most English women. The majority spent the bulk of their time maintaining households and processing agricultural products, working only sporadically in the fields. As we have seen, Virginia's booming tobacco economy discouraged the rise of a domestic economy, however, giving English women's traditional areas of home production and agricultural processing short shrift. The demand for laborers to produce tobacco during the 1620s and 1630s and the hoe-based agriculture it required may have overwhelmed many planters' compunctions about gender conventions and encouraged them to set English women to work in tobacco fields.[30]

Despite the difficulty of sustaining domestic ideals in a colony where English women worked alongside men hoeing, weeding, worming, and cutting tobacco, Virginia's lawmakers did not scrutinize their assumptions about English women's place in the colonial economy. As early as 1629, the General Assembly's vague reference to 'people' working in tobacco production had left open the possibility that laboring English women could be taxed on the same basis as laboring men. Efforts to limit tobacco production to maintain its high market value overseas, however, may have discouraged lawmakers from reexamining assumptions about female labor. Poll taxes, militia duty, and the long-standing English tradition of subsuming individual women under the authority of male household heads also stymied legal and fiscal innovation. With strong precedents for a mediated and at least fictively dependent relation between individual women and the state,

Virginia lawmakers were unlikely to break with tradition and treat English female laborers as they did men.[31]

In 1643, the Virginia Assembly's new definition for 'tithable' created a legal distinction between English and African women for the first time and revealed very different expectations for their future roles in the colony. Tithables who were chargeable for the minister's allowance now included 'youths of sixteen years of age [and] upwards, as also for all negro women at the age of sixteen years'. In practice, this definition meant that the masters of African women were forced to contribute to the support of the colony's ministers just as they did for all the men, African and English, in their employ. By including African women in the category of male tithables, Virginia lawmakers classified them as field laborers with a productive capacity equivalent to that of men. For the first time, the divergence in planters' attitudes toward English and 'negro' laborers appeared openly, encoded in law.[32]

Hostile relations between land-coveting English settlers and neighboring Indians deteriorated into open warfare in 1644, forcing the colonial government to increase its military expenditures. Although Opechancanough's second attack was significantly less successful than his previous effort in 1622, the governor and General Assembly took no chances. They pressed their advantage against weakened Indian populations for the next ten years, exporting Indian captives and compelling several groups to leave the peninsula between the James and York Rivers. During this war, the General Assembly continued to account African women among the tithables who funded arms and provisions for the militia. In 1645, while still calling for raids against Indians affiliated with Opechancanough, the Assembly defined the tithables footing the bill as all African men and women and all other men between the ages of sixteen and sixty. It also briefly levied a tax on livestock and land in addition to the requisite twenty pounds of tobacco per tithable.[33]

African women became part of the tax base of tobacco producers who funded the militia during the military retaliation of 1645, just as they had been included in the ranks of those owing ministers' tithes two years earlier. Yet some ambiguity remained. In 1649, Virginia's General Assembly legislated to prevent masters from falsifying the ages of male servants but said nothing about African women.[34]

Faced with imprecise laws, county courts appear to have come up with their own interpretations. In the Eastern Shore county of Northampton, some free African families found it necessary to request exemptions from the tax on women in their households during the 1640s and 1650s. Anthony and Mary Johnson employed a male and a female servant during the 1640s and paid tithes for both. The Johnsons also paid tithes for themselves and for each of their sons and daughters as they came of age. After a fire destroyed much of the Johnsons' estate in 1653, Anthony Johnson requested relief from the Northampton court for payments he customarily made for his wife and daughters. Johnson's status as a landowner, a married man with a family, and a longtime resident of the county held him in good stead with the justices. They exempted the women of the Johnson family from tithes because of Mary and Anthony's 'hard labours and knowne service performed ... in this country for the obtayneing of their livelyhood'.[35]

In Lancaster County, as in Northampton, African women seem to have been regularly included in the list of tithables from 1651, when the county was formed, until 1657. In that year, however, Lancaster justices decided that 'sev[er]all psons in this Countie have beene for many yers past ov[e]rcharged by retorneinge their Negroe woemen in the list'. To redress the wrong, they agreed to rebate the taxes of those individuals who had been paying too much.[36]

The Lancaster justices appear to have been slightly out of step with the rest of the colony. By midcentury, most African women were considered tithable by law and taxed in practice by their counties. When legislation of 1658 listed 'all negroes imported whether male or female ... being sixteen' as among the tithables, it spelled out clearly for the first time what seems already to have been standard practice in many counties for more than ten years. Northampton County went a step further than the rest of the colony, taxing the native-born children of imported African women (Mary Johnson's daughters, for example) when they came of age at midcentury. When counties such as Northampton applied the legal criteria and financial burden of tithes to the Virginia-born daughters of African women, they began to transform ethnic distinctions, based on place of birth, into racial ones.[37]

The laws defining tithability divided laborers into two groups. English women, servant and free, children, and old men were deemed too weak to produce as much as prime male hands and were categorized as dependents. Productive laborers – English men, African men, and African women – were judged capable of making their own living based on the market value of the tobacco they cultivated. The distinction between English and African women created a legal fiction about their different capacities for performing agricultural labor. Linking the productive capability of African women to that of all male laborers, lawmakers assumed that the English gender division of labor – the one they continued to hope would take hold in the colony – did not and need not apply to Africans. Although West African women's own traditions of agricultural labor may have had some influence upon English colonists' assessments of their economic value, from the English perspective such work roles connoted low social position and an absence of civility.

Productivity and Dependence

'Imperfections' continued to plague tithable collections after midcentury. Not only did the demands of a tobacco economy strain English concepts of women's proper work, but local residents and county justices often crafted their own solutions to problems of legal status and identity. Three questions faced county courts and the colonial Assembly. First, should English women who produced tobacco continue to be tax-exempt? Second, how should free African women be classified? As enslaved women or as English women? Third, by what criteria should female tithables be considered exempt? In revising the tithable laws, Virginia's planter-lawmakers developed a more coherent set of criteria to distinguish between 'negro' and English women. As legal discourse became more consistent, county courts and local residents applied the law with fewer idiosyncrasies and discrepancies.

The General Assembly tried to deal with the problem of women servants 'whose common imployment' is working 'in the ground' by declaring them tithable in December 1662, thus removing the incentive to masters to avoid levies by hiring English women to work in the fields. The law required all masters to include female servants in their list of tithables or suffer the penalty for concealment.[38]

Significantly, although the law cracked down on the masters of female servants who produced tobacco, it said nothing about wives and daughters engaged in similar labor. The omission appears to have been a deliberate effort to distinguish between different classes of English women and to acknowledge the patriarchal claims of husbands and fathers to the labor of female dependents. Women of better quality – John Hammond's good wives and their daughters – might be less likely to work regularly in tobacco fields than a newly arrived indentured servant. If they did perform such labor, however, husbands and fathers did not need to pay any taxes on them. Classification of English women as tax-exempt depended, therefore, on their status as free women and on the existence of a father's or husband's claim to the fruits of their labor.[39]

Legislators left the responsibility of enforcing the 1662 law to county courts, where justices, the sheriffs who collected taxes, and neighborhood informants determined the tax status of women servants on an individual basis. During the November 1678 assessment of taxes in Lancaster County, for example, William Lemuell petitioned the court for tax relief on a female servant of unknown birth who had died the previous July. Noting that the servant had been 'sickly' even before Lemuell had listed her, the court agreed to remove her from Lemuell's assessment. Significantly, this appears to be the only instance in which a master requested an exemption for a female servant who might have been English.[40]

In the case of Lemuell's unfortunate servant, health rather than work ultimately determined her status. In most instances, however, courts heard cases of concealment in which a neighbor's accusation or a master's decision to omit a tithable servant from his list usually revolved around questions of labor. Although the county courts handled many such cases during the late seventeenth and early eighteenth centuries, very few involved English women. Most appear to have concerned English male servants, male relatives, or African men and women. Testimony from the few cases that do exist reveals the difficulty of proving that an English woman worked primarily in the fields. Stephen Chilton, for example, was successfully convicted of concealing two female tithables on the basis of information provided by his neighbor, Nicholas George. After the court's decision, Chilton warned George publicly that he and his wife and children were 'not to set foot on any part of his plantation', suggesting the lengths to which informants might go to prove the 'common employment' of their neighbors' servants.[41]

It was more common for concealment suits involving female servants to be dismissed than upheld, owing in part to the resilience of assumptions that English women's primary responsibilities were domestic and the difficulties of producing convincing evidence to the contrary. John Barbar of Charles City County successfully defended himself against the charge of concealment in 1678 by proving that his woman servant (presumably English) was rarely employed in the ground 'unless for the tearing corn[,] housing tob[acc]o or such like'. The tasks Barbar detailed as those of his servant were seasonal and sporadic, suggesting her occasional presence in corn and tobacco fields during the harvest of each crop. Since she was not 'constantly working the ground', the court decided she was exempt.[42] Crafting individual definitions of tithability based on labor performed rather than on the sex of the laborer, the General Assembly sought to keep masters from profiting unfairly from the labor of female servants. The people charged with making the individual decisions at the county level, however, seemed to find it nearly impossible to summon sufficient empirical evidence to counter the strong presumptions of English women's household labor.

Ultimately, universal confusion about the discrepancy between English women's work and their tax status may have made the 1662 statute unenforceable. Many masters, including justices themselves, may have preferred not to jeopardize their own use of a cheap and easily exploited source of female field labor by pointing fingers at their neighbors. Individuals who wished to profit from their neighbors' tax evasion could more easily collect the informant's reward of one thousand pounds of tobacco by reporting the concealment of male tithables. During the last quarter of the seventeenth century, suits involving English female tithables were much less common than the population of female servants warranted. The last challenge to the tax status of an English female servant residing in one of the three counties in this study occurred in 1702 and was soon dismissed.[43]

Lawmakers addressed the second of their three tax problems – that posed by the tiny but potentially significant population of free African women – by replacing fading distinctions of birth and status with the legal brand of race in 1668. If they escaped slavery, African and Afro-Virginian women entered a liminal zone between the privileges of freedom enjoyed by English women and the nascent racialism that demeaned the labor of all African slaves. The reasoning behind the 1668 statute was, according to lawmakers, a need for a concept of difference that would transcend shifts in status from slavery to freedom:

> Whereas some doubts, have arisen whether negro women set free were still to be accompted tithable according to a former act, *It is declared by this grand assembly* that negro women, though permitted to enjoy their freedome yet ought not in all respects to be admitted to a full fruition of the exemptions and impunities of the English, and are still lyable to payment of taxes.[44]

The 1668 statute was an important event in the creation of a distinctive legal meaning for 'negro'. Denying English 'exemptions and impunities' to free African women, lawmakers gave those privileges an explicitly racial meaning. Freedom no longer overcame all of the legal disabilities of slavery for African women, even though the category 'negro' continued to lack precise definition. When used to describe women, 'negro' connoted servile labor, a status that persisted even after one became free and regardless of the work one performed. In contrast, 'English' signified a set of privileges in which womanhood, dependence, and domesticity were intertwined so closely that county courts found it difficult to enforce legal distinctions between free and servant English women.

Significantly, in the text of the 1668 law, lawmakers contrasted 'negro women' to a gender-neutral population of English people, a telling admission that male as well as female privileges were actually being protected. Few English women actually benefited from their own tax exemptions. Even when single, they often lived in households of masters or fathers who owned their labor and paid their taxes. English women's privileges usually translated into gains for men who benefited from female labor.

The tax burden on free black women remained in place for seventy-seven of the next ninety-five years. In 1705, colonial legislators experimented briefly with defining tithables as 'all male persons, of the age of sixteen years, and upwards, and all negro, mulatto, and Indian women, of the age of sixteen years, and upwards, *not being free*'. Some counties, such as Northampton, remitted the taxes of the free black women in their jurisdiction to the dismay of white residents who complained that 'the great number of free Negroes inhabiting within this county are a great grievance more particularly because the Negro women pay no taxes'. It is unclear whether they were upset by black women's continued tobacco production, the loss of revenue, or the blurring of racial distinctions. By 1723, however, free black women had been written back into the definition of tithable, and county courts appear to have resumed collecting taxes from them. The 1723 statute went one step further than its 1668 predecessor, however, by including the 'wives of negroes, mullattoes, or indians' as tithable women, regardless of their race.[45]

Predictably, the emerging racial discourse of the tax statutes had important consequences for the definition of exemption and informed planters' efforts to avoid tax payments for their laborers. Masters seeking exemptions made very little distinction between male tithables and African women. All were considered producers of tobacco, deemed by law to have the same capacity for work. From the late seventeenth to the mid-eighteenth century, petitions for or by black women and those presented for or by men reflected similar criteria for exemption. Citing a range of reasons to justify their requests, petitioners claimed that they or their aged slaves were 'past labor', meaning old age had made profitable labor nearly impossible. Lameness, general 'decrepitude', and bouts of 'indisposition' were also commonly mentioned. The pattern of reasons reflects, in part, the guidelines first set by the Assembly in 1643 that county justices could use their own discretion in exempting the aged, the sick, and the infirm. Although planters may have judged their male and female slaves to have different strengths and weaknesses, these differences did not shape the language of petitions, nor did they become part of the public legal discourse of black gender. Gender appears to have entered very little into the politics of procuring tax exemptions for enslaved people (see Table 1).[46]

Table 1. Successful Tax-Exemption Petitions, Norfolk, Lancaster, and York Counties

Reasons	White Men	Black Women		Black Men		Slaves
		Slave	Free	Slave	Free	(no sex given)
			1680–1699			
Age	11	1	0	0	0	
Debility	14	2	0	0	0	
Poverty	0	0	0	0	0	
Combination	11	0	0	0	0	
No reason	2	0	0	0	0	
Total	38	3	0	0	0	
			1730–1749			
Age	10	3	0	1	0	2
Debility	17	3	1	1	0	0
Poverty	3	0	0	0	0	1
Combination	15	0	1	0	0	1
No reason	24	3	0	5	0	0
Total	69	9	2	7	0	4

Note: Petitions with two or more reasons cited were classified as 'combination'. There were no petitions on behalf of white women during the periods represented in this table. Rejected petitions constituted less than 2% of total petitions.
Sources: Norfolk Orders, 1680–1699, 1730–1749; Lancaster Orders, 1680–1699, 1730–1749; York DOW, 1680–1699, 1730–1749.

Although throughout the seventeenth and eighteenth centuries the majority of those receiving exemptions were white men, all petitioners offered roughly comparable excuses. In Norfolk County between 1719 and 1750 – a period considerably later than that under discussion in this chapter, but in which seventeenth-century exemption patterns appear to have continued – most white petitioners listing reasons claimed physical disability or an inability to make a living. White men who cited old age usually also mentioned other factors, describing themselves as 'poore' as well as 'ancient'. Petitioners seeking exemptions for male slaves provided similar excuses, claiming that they should not pay taxes for blind, lame, or elderly slaves. Although slaveowners sought more exemptions for enslaved women than for enslaved men, they provided similar reasons – age and disability – in their petitions.[47]

Exemption petitions by free women of African descent presented courts with a more complicated situation. In such cases, county courts occasionally accepted pleas of poverty as grounds for exemption, much as they would have for a white male head of household. Poverty, like illness and age, signified dependent status and often qualified white people for protection or aid from the parish. To qualify on the grounds of poverty, however, free black female petitioners needed to prove that a physical disability impaired their ability to make a living by their labor, thereby threatening to render them economically dependent on the parish. In 1670, the General Court thus exempted Margaret Cornish, a black woman, owing to her poverty and age. In June 1678, a 'poor negro woman very anciene' presented a similar petition to the Charles City County Court to be levy-free. The justices accepted the request in consideration of the petitioner's 'I[m]potency'. Just a year earlier in the same county, a free black woman named Susannah was less successful. Justices rejected her petition after being informed of her 'strength and ability'. Her failure to prove physical disability led the justices to deny her request for tax exemption.[48]

To enjoy the privileges of English women, a free black woman needed to demonstrate dependent status by proving her physical disability. County court justices presumed she had a capacity for strenuous work unless shown evidence to the contrary. Only when a black woman was potentially valueless as a tobacco producer would the state relinquish its claim to tax her labor. The contrast to the treatment of English women was striking. Increasingly during the late seventeenth century, such women were categorized in legal discourse with the physically weak and economically dependent, regardless of their particular strengths or the work they performed.

The distinctions made under tithable law not only affected the fortunes of individual women but also reconfigured the marital, familial, and servile relationships in which women's labor became a type of property. Under the law of coverture, married women could not own property and had no right to control the fruits of their labor. Although deeds of gift and prenuptial contracts (both of which were prevalent in Virginia) allowed many women to circumvent the common law, they usually did not acquire lifetime or permanent rights to estates or dower property until they became widows. English women in the colony who remained single, while retaining a right to own property in their own names, were rarely heads of their own households in actual practice. They lived in the homes of relatives or as servants in a nonfamilial household. As nontithables, these women contributed to the household economy without incurring any additional tax expense, a fact the General Assembly had recognized as early as 1629. The beneficiaries of this legal arrangement were husbands, fathers, and masters, who had a right to this tax-free female labor.[49]

African women in the colony lived under a different set of constraints, in which rights to their labor were configured legally in much the same way as rights to the labor of a male household member. The masters of enslaved women paid tithes upon them as they did for male indentured servants and slaves. The expense of the labor of *free* black women, in contrast, was borne by the women themselves, or by those men who could afford it least: free black husbands and fathers who were struggling to establish a foothold in the world of white planters. Even on the Eastern Shore, where conditions were more favorable for free black people than anywhere else in Virginia during the seventeenth century, free men struggled to profit from land they leased, raising livestock in addition to tobacco. The two free black landowners of the Eastern Shore, Anthony Johnson and Anthony Longo, were occasionally compelled to turn to the courts to help them during times of extreme financial hardship. In 1653, Johnson petitioned for tax relief after a fire destroyed much of his estate. Longo, who was unable to support his three children, wrote to Governor Berkeley directly for assistance in 1669.[50] For these men, the taxes paid for a wife's labor were not inconsiderable.

Tithable laws not only imposed a significant financial burden upon free black families but stigmatized female agricultural labor that would have been highly valued in the West African context. Most West Africans in Virginia had a stronger tradition of female field labor than did their English counterparts. Throughout the regions from which these Africans hailed – the Kongo, Angola, and the Guinea coast – women were the primary agriculturalists. Many would have been familiar with the hoe agriculture used in Virginia's tobacco fields. Along with the ability to produce new dependents, women's value as laborers was one of the reasons that many West African rulers preferred to retain female slaves rather than allow them to enter the transatlantic trade. In Virginia, however, free Africans lived among English planters for whom female field work connoted servility and low status. This stigma, in combination with the genuine financial hardship created by taxes, possibly may have decreased a free black woman's chances of marriage and membership in the kin networks that enhanced social and economic status.[51]

Forced to pay extra taxes for an African wife, a free man might have thought twice about marrying her. Perhaps that was why so many free African men on the Eastern Shore married English women even though a nearly equal sex ratio would have allowed them to find African wives. Of the ten black male householders in Northampton between 1664 and 1677, five appear to have been married to women of English descent. Richard Johnson, son of Anthony, fathered four children by his white wife Susan. Richard's son also married a white woman in the 1680s. Francis Payne married Amye, a white woman, soon after securing the freedom of his children and first wife in 1655. Emmanuel Driggus fathered a child by a woman named Elizabeth, whom he married in 1661. Philip Mongan married a white widow named Martha Merris in 1651. Likewise, Anthony Longo's first wife, Hannah, seems to have been white.[52]

Some African men may have believed that white partners would enhance their ability to function within a predominantly white society, while others may have married these women because nothing stood in their way. In Northampton County, white residents whose racial attitudes had been shaped by the presence of a small but relatively successful group of free black men voiced little public dissent against interracial relationships until later in the century. Still other free black men may have chosen white mates because free black women were themselves involved in interracial unions and unavailable for marriage. For women like Ann Skiper, the black wife of white Norfolk County resident Francis Skiper, marriage to a man of English descent offered opportunities to join white planter social and economic networks.[53]

Throughout the seventeenth century, marriage provided opportunities for white men to become respected members of their communities and may similarly have enhanced the lives of free black men. No matter what his race, a married man who headed a household in Virginia was expected to rule over his dependents. The authority of being a husband, father, and master brought social and political advantages and material benefits to the lives of planters, including recognition as an adult, the ability to persist in one locale, and networks of kin and friends. In addition, white planters who married may have improved their chances of being considered for local offices. Although as a free black man, Johnson likely would not have been eligible for such political advantages, his good fortune in being a married man in the 1630s undoubtedly contributed to his success, making him remarkable, not just in the community of free Africans but in the larger pool of immigrant males scrambling to find wives among the women they outnumbered by three or four to one.[54]

The significance of marriage for community standing and security, however, was not simply a feature of New World settlements or English culture. Most Africans arriving in the colony came from societies in which marriage was one means of creating long-standing lineages, community ties, and wealth. Although marriage in West Africa took a very different form from its counterpart in Virginia, it still conveyed power and status. Obstacles impeding free black people from forming unions thus impinged upon their abilities to function in a colonial society, both in the Anglo-Virginian sense in which marriage offered opportunities for upward mobility and in the West African sense of constituting families, alliances, and wealth.

The difficulties many African men faced in trying to accumulate property also may have impeded their opportunities for marriage. As late as 1675, no laws *prohibited* a free black man like Anthony Johnson from owning land, livestock, or even slaves, but, realistically, his chances of amassing a comfortable estate were considerably lower than those of his white peers. Self-purchase, the key to the freedom of many of Northampton's free black residents, swallowed the small estates of several aspiring free men even before they had a chance to begin their lives outside their master's household. As open as Northampton society may have been for Africans before 1675, white men on the make occasionally stooped to harassment and chicanery to improve their own fortunes. None of these factors helped black men to attract spouses or maintain independent households.[55]

For free black women, the tithe's potential to impede marriage only compounded the mortal stigma of racial slavery and field labor. Pamphleteers such as Hammond and English women themselves continued to predicate female morality upon domestic employment and marriage. In his efforts to encourage English women to migrate to the colony, for example, Hammond suggested that a woman's failure to marry well in Virginia was usually caused by her own moral corruption rather than by other circumstances. Such reasoning was, as we have already noted, similar to many English women's own reckonings of female status in the colony. It left little doubt that an enslaved African woman would automatically be judged morally dissolute by English settlers. Even if she was lucky enough to escape the confines of slavery, moreover, an African woman faced an additional obstacle – the tax upon her labor – to achieving the status of a good wife.[56]

The tax on the labor of African and Afro-Virginian women was one of the first obstacles black people faced if they wished to achieve the patriarchal family forms that conferred social standing upon white people. These taxes similarly made the large family lineages of West Africa more costly and difficult to attain. Like the moral failings of English 'nasty wenches', detailed by Hammond, the tax liability of free black women also may have dimmed their prospects of marriage.

In responding to the three problems inherent in their ambiguously defined tax laws – English women's doing field work, the classification of free African women, and the criteria for female exemption – seventeenth-century Virginia lawmakers began to define the social meaning of racial difference by reserving the privileges of womanhood for the masters and husbands of English women. In a colony where many English women worked regularly in tobacco fields, creating a legal identity that would distinguish them from enslaved women was crucial to maintaining traditional English family roles. The legal discourse of womanhood that emerged during the seventeenth century enshrined the domesticity and economic dependence of English women, giving husbands and masters sole claim to the fruits of female labor.

The taxation of African women was the cornerstone of a concept of womanhood that became less class-specific and increasingly race-specific throughout the seventeenth century, laying the groundwork for subsequent distinctions between Afro- and Anglo-Virginian families. In contrast to English women, African women were presumed capable of and naturally suited to strenuous field work. African men, moreover, were denied the right to the tax-free labor of wives and daughters. By 1668, as questions arose about the labor of African women who had escaped slavery, racial distinction became its own goal. Lawmakers relegated all African women and their daughters to the status of 'negroes', making possible a more exclusive definition of English womanhood.[57]

Slaves by Birth

As a result of its involvement in the tobacco market, the colonial state – comprising planters, merchants, and royal officials – shared an interest in regulating the labor force that produced tobacco. After 1660, the reproductive lives of English servant women and African slaves, male and female, drew the state's attention.[58] At the same time that they experimented with a redefinition of servant women as productive tobacco workers, legislators confronted the potential conflict between enslaved women's roles as producers and reproducers.

Following English practice, Virginia regulated the reproductive lives of English servant women through sanctions that discouraged marriage and child-bearing during service. Through state control over the marriage of female servants, masters could maintain labor arrangements, and the reproduction of the English settler population could be kept within the confines of legally constituted families. Such measures were completely ineffective for women who spent their entire reproductive lives as slaves, however, compelling the state to redefine the legal context in which motherhood took place to allow reproductive work to contribute to, rather than detract from, the estates of masters.

English concepts of legal reproduction had long been defined by property-owners' uses of inheritance to maintain class position and local officials' attempts to balance parish budgets. Invoking these principles of family lineage and inheritance, William Fitzhugh wrote to fellow Virginian Robert Beverley concerning a point of law that had perplexed Beverley and for which he had found no good explanation. Citing several legal authorities, Fitzhugh quoted from one of them: 'No man can be heir to a fee simple by the common Law but he that hath sanguinem duplicatum the whole blood both of the father and of the mother so as the half blood is no blood inheritable by descent'. Fitzhugh offered as an example the situation 'where the eldest son dieth in the life of his father his issue shall inherit before the younger son ... for he doth represent the person of his father'. In conclusion, Fitzhugh explained to Beverley, 'none can be begotten but of a father and a Mother, and he must have in him two bloods[:] Blood of the father and the blood of the mother, these bloods commixed in him by lawfull Marriage, constitute and make him heir'.[59]

A respected lawyer in the colony, Fitzhugh rested his opinion on an English common law tradition in which family lineage and inheritance were traced patrilineally and recognized as legal when reproduction took place within marriage. By restricting legitimate birth to the context of marriage, the English used a social construct of paternity to determine inheritance and to invest fathers with rights over their children. Socially constructed paternity theoretically provided each child with a male, propertyowning provider to assume responsibility for raising the child. In the case of reproduction outside marriage (bastardy), the child not only lost his or her legal claim to the father's estate, but began life without a provider. In these situations, local authorities attempted to hold the biological father accountable for the cost of supporting the youth even though the family was not recognized legally or socially. According to the 1576 English Poor Law, the parish could require the offending woman to name her child's father, whom they punished with corporal punishment or jail if he failed to maintain his offspring.[60]

In the colonies, illegitimate children threatened not only the budgets of parish and county but the system of indentured labor. Early statutes forbidding secret marriages of women servants had originally been designed to protect masters from the expense of pregnancy and childrearing, but they also prevented conflicts between husbands and masters over claims to the economic services of a particular woman. Once presented to a local court by a minister or churchwarden, the offending couple was expected to appear to answer the charge against them. A mother might make another trip to court after she gave birth to declare her claim against the father. On occasion, a woman might bring the child to court with her, adding theater to the courtroom identification of the father of the 'child in her armes'. The court verified the truth of the woman servant's claim by requiring her to swear to the father's identity under oath or by summoning the midwife to testify to the mother's words during labor.[61]

Although statutes specified that the father of an illegitimate child was supposed to pay all expenses of the birth and maintenance of the child except for the lost time of the mother, justices crafted individual solutions in cases where the father was poor or in service himself. The main concern of most local courts was to ensure that the woman's master and the parish were well compensated for the expenses of her lost service, her lying-in, and the care of her child. After Joanne Ragged identified servant James Collings as the father of her child, the court ordered her to support the child until Collings became a free man and could provide for it himself. The justices also may have encouraged the couple to marry. When servant Elizabeth Tomlyn bore a child fathered by Thomas Mannaugh, the Lancaster court ordered him to leave a hogshead of tobacco with Tomlyn's master for the child's upkeep. A year later, Tomlyn requested that her child live with Roger Haris and his wife until the age of eighteen and be taught to read and write.[62]

When a master fathered a child by his servant woman, justices seem to have followed the rule of paternal responsibility as they did in all other cases where a father could be identified. Masters occasionally tried to obscure the paternity charge by consenting to their female servants' marriage to other men or by encouraging them to accuse others. Presented to the Norfolk court in 1656 for fornication commited before her marriage to William Norwood, Mary Roche, for example, named Thomas Allen, her former master, as the father of her child. The court ordered him to maintain the child 'according to the law in the case' and pay court charges. The case of Clement Theobalds and his servant Elizabeth Hall proved more complicated. Hall claimed that John Powis, son of a Norfolk minister, was the father of her child. Theobalds may have encouraged this deceit, hoping to escape the charge himself. After a married woman offered her testimony, presumably concerning Theobalds's involvement with his servant, Theobalds and Hall agreed to marry.[63]

If the father and mother could not maintain the child, the court often ordered the offending male to pay compensation to the parish. Daniel Grisley thus paid his Lancaster County parish twelve hundred pounds of tobacco in 1654 for having a child by Margaret Mealey, who apparently could not raise the infant herself. The parish sometimes placed the child in a household of a third party who was paid to keep it, an arrangement similar to that for poor or orphan children. By custom, these children served until age eighteen or marriage if they were girls and age twenty-one or twenty-two if they were boys.[64]

When Africans began appearing before the county courts charged with sexual misdemeanors, justices seem to have been guided by the principles they used in other cases of fornication. On at least one occasion, an African was required to participate in the penance ritual normally performed by English offenders. William Watts, a white man (apparently free), was ordered to do penance in a white sheet in 1649 for the sin of fornication with Mary, 'Mr. Cornelius Lloyds neger woman'. Watts was not charged with the maintenance of any child, perhaps because there was no illegitimate birth, but Mary was forced to perform a similar public penance, a punishment that would also have been required of an offending English woman.[65]

The real test for the applicability of English family law to enslaved Africans was, not interracial fornication, however, but cases where women serving life terms became pregnant. Here the usual remedy for pregnant English servants – extra time served by the mother to compensate the master for the loss of her labor and expense of giving birth – did not apply if the mother was already understood to be serving for life. The ambiguities surrounding the legal status of enslaved men and women and their relationships, moreover, forced African parents who wanted to enjoy legal rights over their children to make arrangements as if their children were illegitimate. John Graweere, an African 'servant', successfully arrived at such an agreement with his own and his enslaved lover's masters in 1641. William Evans permitted Graweere to keep hogs and half their increase, the profits from which Graweere used to pay Lieutenant Robert Sheppard, who owned the African mother of Graweere's child. Graweere wanted the child to 'be made a christian and be taught and exercised in the church of *England*, by reason whereof he the said negro did for his said child purchase its freedom'. The General Court ordered that the child should be free from Sheppard and Evans to 'remain at the disposing and education of the said *Graweere* and the child's godfather'. Agreements such as Graweere's were similar to arrangements made by the courts for bastard children, but the use of the terms 'freedom' and 'purchase' to describe the father's maintenance of the child would not have been part of an English father's settlement.[66]

In situations where the father was English and either incapable of or uninterested in keeping his child by an enslaved woman, the courts presumed as early as the 1650s that the child also belonged to the mother's master. In 1657, Thomas Twine, servant to Captain Daniel Parke, was brought before the York court for fathering a child by an African servant of Parke's. In this case, the court appears to have responded as it would have in any other fornication case, ordering Twine to perform public penance at Marston church. The court, however, specified no fine, no arrangements for the upkeep of the child, and no punishment for the African woman.[67] In cases such as Twine's, county court justices provided creative solutions for a situation that statutes had not considered: the damages suffered by a master whose pregnant slave was already serving for life. Twine's record is unclear, but the absence of any of the usual arrangements for damages or maintenance of the child points suspiciously in the direction of a different treatment of this case. The justices retained an interest in the paternity of the child, as they did in all bastardy cases involving English women, yet that knowledge seemed almost irrelevant if a man like Twine paid no damages to a master.

In Northumberland County, justices debated the question of how to classify enslaved women's children in a case involving an Afro-Virginian woman seeking freedom. Elizabeth Key, the illegitimate daughter of an enslaved woman and an English man, petitioned for her freedom in 1656 after serving two lengthy terms of service. Key claimed that she was Christian, had completed her service, and was the daughter of a free English man. The Northumberland jurors found her free, but the General Court subsequently judged her a slave after administrators of her master's estate appealed the county court's decision. Key's lawyer, an English man named William Greensted who had fathered two of her children, eventually won Key's freedom after marrying her and bringing the case to the General Assembly. The series of judgments in Key's case suggests that the colony's superior courts were already inclined to view the children of enslaved women as slaves as early as the 1650s.[68]

One case, in particular, may have spurred the colony to clarify the law concerning the children of slaves. In August 1662, Mr. Bartholomew Hoskins, the master of an African 'servant' woman, petitioned the governor to determine the status of his servant's child. Although the petition never again appeared in the records, by December of that year the General Assembly passed new legislation that effectively reversed the English practice by which children followed the condition of their father:

> Wheareas some doubts have arrisen whether children got by any Englishman upon a negro woman should be slave or free, *Be it therefore enacted and declared by this present grand assembly*, that all children borne in this country shalbe held bond or free only according to the condition of the mother, *And* that if any christian shall commit fornication with a negro man or woman, hee or shee soe offending shall pay double the fines imposed by the former act.[69]

Provoked by the interests of a small number of wealthy men whose cosmopolitan connections had gained them slave laborers, the General Assembly departed from English models of family lineage to protect the integrity of slave property. As in the case of the tithable laws, the property in question was the labor of African and Afro-Virginian women, the 'negro' women whose unions with 'christian[s]' and 'Englishm[e]n' had the potential to destabilize the still tentative legal distinctions between slave and free status. Worse still, in the absence of precise legal definitions of 'negro', the offspring of African and English people threatened to disturb the racial categories emerging in legal discourse and muddle their use in everyday life. Once again, African women were at the center of attempts to create concepts of difference.[70]

The 1662 law represented a bold attempt to naturalize the condition of slavery by making it heritable and embedding it in a concept of race. Its immediate effects were to make the paternity of children born of enslaved women virtually irrelevant in the eyes of the law. Masters of slave women did not suffer damages for time lost from a fixed period of servitude as they did with servant women. The short-term work losses and expense of lying-in, moreover, were more than adequately compensated for by the reproduction of the master's labor force. With their offspring provided for by masters, enslaved fathers lost any legal basis for authority over their children. The law similarly stripped enslaved mothers of the opportunity to do what Elizabeth Tomlyn had done for her daughter: to have some say in the arrangements made for raising and caring for their children. By realigning the relations of dependence in enslaved families, Chesapeake lawmakers diminished the already limited control most black men and women had over their children. Subsequent statutes further reduced this diminished parental influence.[71]

One can imagine the nightmarish consequences of this law for men and women in slavery. Through their dogged determination to purchase family members, men like John Graweere had already demonstrated that, even in the 1640s, 'slave' and 'servant' were terms with an actual, not just semantic, difference in meaning to them. Even before the 1662 statute, female slaves, like all bound women, had been vulnerable to the predations of white masters, neighbors, and other laborers. After 1662, however, enslaved women could no longer hope that the spectacle of naming the father in court might discourage a would-be seducer or rapist.

Most striking was the contrast between lawmakers' treatment of African women in 1662 and their new approach to English servant fornication. Even as the new irrelevance of paternity in cases of slave pregnancy made African women more vulnerable to sexual exploitation, the Assembly was busy strengthening existing fornication laws, making it more difficult for lecherous masters to take advantage of English female servants. Servant women convicted of fornication faced two additional years of service and the possibility of another half-year if their masters paid their fine instead of allowing them to be whipped. The parish would care for the child of a male servant during the father's term of service, but, once the father was free, he was expected to reimburse the parish and resume maintenance of the child himself. Addressing the issue of 'dissolute masters' who impregnated their female servants and then claimed additional service, the Assembly ordered these women to be sold by the churchwardens to serve additional time. The funds from the sale were to go to the parish rather than to the master.[72]

Rendering the condition of slavery inheritable through the mother, the 1662 statute resolved the most pressing problem from the point of view of white masters: how to balance masters' claims to the agricultural labor of enslaved women with the sometimes incapacitating or even deadly physical risks of their reproductive lives as women. There was legal precedent in Virginia for compensating masters for the lost work time of pregnant English servant women. Female servants who bore illegitimate children had traditionally served their masters for an additional year to repay them for lost labor and the expense of lying-in, the assumption being that time spent in pregnancy and childbirth was time lost to work in the tobacco fields. Even though most masters were undoubtedly pushing their pregnant servants to work as hard as possible for as long as possible, the legal equation was clear: production and reproduction could not take place at the same time, as long as it was on the master's time.[73]

Although the courts treated the pregnancy and childbirth of English women, free and servant, as serious and life-threatening events, they held enslaved women to a different standard.[74] As a consequence, masters *never* sought tax exemptions for pregnant slave women who might have been incapacitated for work during the year they gave birth. There are several possible explanations for this difference. As courts moved toward requiring greater verification of disability by the late seventeenth century, the reproductive complaints of enslaved women may have been too difficult to prove. The state was willing to uphold the authority and investment of the master by extending the service of pregnant English servants; such generosity cost them nothing. It was not willing to acknowledge losses to masters of enslaved women by waiving the annual tax on tobacco producers, however, in part because such an exemption would reduce state revenues. As long as the children of slaves remained slaves, capable of compensating masters for expenses incurred by enslaved mothers, neither the state nor the slaveowner would lose. After 1662, no legal discourse, economic motive, or cultural tradition provoked concern for the well-being of pregnant slave women. And no masters tried to use such a concern to avoid paying their taxes.

The difference in the legal treatment of English women's and enslaved women's reproduction lay primarily in the configuration of their lives as laborers, wives, and mothers. While servitude and marriage theoretically divided English women's lives into two distinct phases of economic dependence, one in which masters owned their labor and the second in which husbands owned both their labor and reproductive capacity, enslaved women found both their production and reproduction owned by the same man in perpetuity. The statute of 1662 confirmed slave women's status as productive and reproductive property, a condition that reflected significant innovations in English traditions for marriage, family, and parental authority. African women, whose reproductive capacity presented the most serious challenge to the integrity of slave property, had become the means by which that property would be sustained and increased. They had also become a means for naturalizing slave status with a concept of race. If being a slave was something one became at birth, rather than as a consequence of military defeat or indebtedness, certain groups of people could be seen as being inherently suited to slavery. The notion that enslaved women could pass their bound condition on to their children strengthened the appearance that slavery was a natural condition for people of African descent.

Slaves for their Lives

The Virginia colony's movement toward a concept of slavery in which race conferred an aura of naturalness to bondage was nowhere more apparent than in two laws of the late 1660s that limited the means of escaping servitude for life. Christianity had long been a part of the discourse of difference, appearing in the earliest English accounts of Africans, Gaelic

Irish, and Indians. It was crucial to the way the English defined themselves and legitimized their attempts to conquer, settle, and appropriate valuable commodities through trade. Throughout the seventeenth century, the word 'Christian' surfaced in the laws of Virginia when the English wanted a self-referential term to distinguish their own powers, privileges, and rights from the burdens, punishments, and legal disabilities of the peoples they hoped to dominate. It also helped them define who the 'other' people were. Difficulties arose when Africans and Indians became Christians and when English settlers were Virginia-born. By 1667, Christianity was still crucial to legal concepts of difference but no longer adequate for the purposes of slaveholding Anglo-Virginians.[75]

In that year, Virginia lawmakers restricted the legal meaning of 'Christian' to conform to the demands of slavery. Legislators decided that baptism would no longer free 'slaves by birth'. Cutting off an important avenue by which African slaves had demanded release from bondage, Virginia's lawmakers resolved the conflict between property interests and Christian mission, declaring 'the conferring of baptisme doth not alter the condition of the person as to his bondage or freedome'.[76] With this law, the colony reinforced the notion that slavery could not be renegotiated during an individual's lifetime.

Three years later, the Virginia Assembly resurrected the concept of Christianity to sharpen distinctions between English laborers and those non-English peoples who seemed most alien: Indians and Africans. Noting the difficulty of determining terms of service for Indians captured in war, the Assembly concluded that

> all servants not being christians imported into this colony by shipping shalbe slaves for their lives; but what shall come by land shall serve, if boyes or girles, untill thirty years of age, if men or women twelve yeares.[77]

This law made two crucial distinctions. The first separated Christian (English and other Europeans) and non-Christian (Indian, African, and Moorish) peoples, with the latter group forming the potential pool of slaves. The second distinguished between 'slaves' imported to the colony in ships and sold (African) and 'servants' captured during wartime (Indian). With this measure, the colony effectively refined its definitions of slavery, limiting bondage to imported Africans. Together, the two statutes culminated thirty years of legal measures defining Africans as slaves and excluding them from the family, gender, and religious privileges enjoyed by the English.

Tax laws, hereditary slavery, and attempts to refine the legal meaning of 'Christian' offered a measure of protection to Anglo-Virginian families from the radical economic and social changes threatened by women's work and female indentured servitude in the colony. The project of defining English families as Christian and white and privileging white patriarchs was intimately connected to the legal denial of English-style families to the enslaved.

These early laws were among the most important of all slave statutes in Virginia. They created a legal discourse of slavery rooted in the sexual, social, and economic lives of African laborers and effectively naturalized the condition of slavery by connecting it to a concept of race. Slavery and freedom, like race, became under colonial law conditions that could not be easily altered during one's own lifetime, or, if one was an enslaved woman, during the lifetime of one's children. Grounded in English class-based notions of women's proper role in an economy of commercial agriculture and in the family, 'womanhood' began to take on a race-specific meaning in the colony. It remained, after 1670, for white Virginians to wrestle with the issue of black masculinity, as economic and political conflicts among white men proliferated and increasing numbers of African men and women were brought forcibly to the colony.

NOTES

1. For background on Anthony and Mary, see T. H. Breen and Stephen Innes, '*Myne Owne Ground': Race and Freedom on Virginia's Eastern Shore, 1640–1676* (New York, 1980), 8–9, 116 n. 9; Joseph Douglas Deal III, 'Race and Class in Colonial Virginia: Indians, Englishmen, and Africans on the Eastern Shore during the Seventeenth Century' (University of Rochester Ph.D., 1981), 254–79; Annie Lash Jester and Martha Woodroof Hiden, eds., *Adventurers of Purse and Person, Virginia 1607–1625*, 2d ed. (Richmond, Va., 1964), 46; John Camden Hotten, ed., *The Original Lists of Persons of Quality ... and Others Who Went from Great Britain to the American Plantations, 1600–1700* (1874; reprint, Baltimore, 1986), 182.
2. See J. D. Fage, 'Slavery and the Slave Trade in the Context of West African History', *JAF*, X (1969), 393–404, and 'African Societies and the Atlantic Trade', *P&P*, no. 125 (1989), 97–115; Paul E. Lovejoy, 'The Impact of the Atlantic Slave Trade on Africa: A Review of the Literature', *JAF*, XXX (1989), 365–94; David Geggus, 'Sex Ratio and Ethnicity: A Reply to Paul E. Lovejoy', *JAF*, XXX (1989), 395–97; John Thornton, 'Sexual Demography: The Impact of the Slave Trade on Family Structure', in Claire C. Robertson and Martin A. Klein, eds., *Women and Slavery in Africa* (Madison, Wis., 1983), 39–48, and Claude Meillassoux, 'Female Slavery', 49–66. The classic study of the Atlantic trade is Philip D. Curtin, *The Atlantic Slave Trade: A Census* (Madison, Wis., 1969), 94–126.
3. Deal, 'Race and Class', 254–79; Breen and Innes, '*Myne Owne Ground*', 16–17, 68–72.
4. John Thornton, *Africa and Africans in the Making of the Atlantic World, 1400–1680* (New York, 1992), 146–7, contends that the global context of the slave trade made it probable that all Africans brought into the colonies of northern Europeans were enslaved. See also Edmund S. Morgan, *American Slavery, American Freedom: The Ordeal of Colonial Virginia* (New York, 1975), 154; Breen and Innes, '*Myne Owne Ground*', 72; Carl N. Degler, 'Slavery and the Genesis of American Race Prejudice', *Comparative Studies in Society and History*, II (1959), 49–66; Alden T. Vaughan, 'Blacks in Virginia: A Note on the First Decade', *WMQ*, 3d Ser., XXIX (1972), 469–78.
5. The literature on the origins of slavery in Virginia is immense. For the best and most recent summary of the debate, see Alden T. Vaughan, 'The Origins Debate: Slavery and Racism in Seventeenth-Century Virginia', *VMHB*, XCVII (1989), 311–54.

6. Winthrop D. Jordan, *White over Black: American Attitudes Toward the Negro, 1550–1812* (Chapel Hill, N.C., 1968), xi, 4, 583–5. Jordan claimed that the English first met Africans, not in the context of slavery, but as men (3). Yet the continuing European and African trade in slaves – even if it was not a specifically *English* trade – was undoubtedly significant to the relationships that developed between the two groups.

7. Morgan, *American Slavery, American Freedom*, 327–37.

8. For an attempt to link constructions of race and gender, see Evelyn Brooks Higginbotham, 'African-American Women's History and the Metalanguage of Race', *Signs*, XVII (1992), 251–74. See also Mary Douglas, *Purity and Danger: An Analysis of Concepts of Pollution and Taboo* (New York, 1966), which emphasizes the power inhering in systems of knowledge.

9. The classic study of English attitudes toward Africans is Jordan, *White over Black*, 3–43. Relying on English travelers' accounts and other sources that spanned the years 1550–1800, Jordan may have overemphasized the degree to which the earliest accounts focused on the blackness of Africans. Although most English writers during the late 16th and early 17th centuries mentioned the appearance of Africans, it was the exceptional pamphlet writer who dwelt on the subject of skin color before 1650. For these exceptions, see Robert Baker, 'The First Voyage of Robert Baker to Guinie . . . 1562', in Richard Hakluyt, *The Principall Navigations, Voiages, and Discoveries of the English Nation* (London, 1589), 2 vols (Cambridge, 1965), I, 130–5; Peter Martyr, *The Decades of the Newe Worlde*, trans. Richard Eden, in Edward Arber, ed., *The First Three English Books on America* (1885; reprint, New York, 1971), 338; Sir Thomas Browne, *Pseudodoxia Epidemia* (London, 1646), in Charles Sayle, ed., *The Works of Sir Thomas Browne* (Edinburgh, 1927), II, 367–95. Baker's racially charged language occurred mainly in his description of a bloody battle with native Guinea residents. Browne's carefully reasoned assessment of the causes of Africans' skin color, on the other hand, was remarkably free of judgments about savagery or physical deformity and included a long disquisition on the relative nature of beauty. Martyr assumed that the black appearance of Africans and the white appearance of the English placed them at opposite ends of the spectrum of skin hues.

10. Rawley, *Transatlantic Slave Trade*, 32–3; K. R. Andrews, *Trade, Plunder, and Settlement: Maritime Enterprise and the Genesis of the British Empire, 1480–1630* (Cambridge, 1984), 113; Richard Jobson, *The Golden Trade; or, A Discovery of the River Gambra, and the Golden Trade of the Aethiopians* (London, 1623), 2, 52, 53, 54. For 17th-century theories about Africans' skin color and character, including Jobson's contribution, see Jordan, *White over Black*, 17–20, 34–5.

11. Jobson, *Golden Trade*, 33–5, 75, 108–15. Jobson deemed the 'tawney' Fulbe to be less civilized than the black Mandingo. He had nothing but praise, however, for the blushing Fulbe matrons whose dairy production he deemed vastly cleaner than that of Irish women. For earlier English accounts of Muslim Africans that were generally more positive than those of peoples the English referred to as 'Negroes', see Emily C. Bartels, 'Imperialist Beginnings: Richard Hakluyt and the Construction of Africa', *Criticism*, XXXIV (1992), 527–32.

12. Jobson, *Golden Trade*, 18.

13. Ibid., 28–31. See Louis Montrose, 'The Work of Gender in the Discourse of Discovery', *Representations*, no. 31 (1991), 1–41, for European rivalries; Bartels, 'Imperialist Beginnings', *Criticism*, XXXIV (1992), 517–38, for depictions of Africans as changeable and unstable.

14. Andrew Battell, 'The Strange Adventure of Andrew Battell of Leigh in Essex', in Purchas, *Hakluytus Posthumus*, VI, 376, 395.

15. Ibid., 395. For Battell's comments on the Portuguese slave trade, see 403–4.

16. See Hotten, ed., *Original Lists*, 169–95, and Jester and Hiden, eds., *Adventurers*, 5–69, for the list of those living in Virginia in 1624 and 1625. Among the names are several non-African men and women who are designated by their first names

only or nationality, as were all the Africans listed. See also Lancaster Deeds Etc. 1, Oct. 24, 1653, 90, for reference to 'Epe the Dutchman', who was on occasion recorded with his full name, Epe Bonner; Norfolk Deed Book A, Sept. 6, 1641, 96, for Captain Sibsey's Portuguese servant. Throughout the early 17th century, Dutch, Italian, French, Portuguese, and Irish as well as Africans were recorded in official documents by their first names only and described by national origin. See Vaughan, 'The Origins Debate', *VMHB*, XCVII (1989), 342, for his observation that the designation 'negre' followed the children of Africans, distinguishing them from the progeny of other ethnic groups.

17. Hotten, ed., *Original Lists*, 182. Keith Wrightson, *English Society, 1580–1680* (New Brunswick, N.J., 1982), 24–6, notes that the social distinction made between gentry and non-gentry in England was based on the latter group's participation in manual labor.

18. Rawley, *Transatlantic Slave Trade*, 63; Parry and Sherlock, *Short History of the West Indies*, 1–80. For a discussion of the archaeological evidence of slavery in Barbados, see Jerome S. Handler and Frederick W. Lange, *Plantation Slavery in Barbados: An Archaeological and Historical Investigation* (Cambridge, Mass., 1978), 15–21. For a comparison of indentured servitude to slavery in Barbados that stresses the similarities between the two institutions, see Hilary McD. Beckles, *White Servitude and Black Slavery in Barbados, 1627–1715* (Knoxville, Tenn., 1989). Beckles claims that slavery was established by 1636, a point disputed by the more cautious interpretation of laws provided by Richard S. Dunn, *Sugar and Slaves: The Rise of the Planter Class in the English West Indies, 1624–1713* (Chapel Hill, N.C., 1972), 228, 238–46. For a discussion of slavery in Bermuda, see Virginia Bernhard, 'Beyond the Chesapeake: The Contrasting Status of Blacks in Bermuda, 1616–1663', *JSH*, LIV (1988), 545–64.

19. For a reference to Sir John Harvey's 1640 gift of the 'negro servant' Franke to Barkum Obert, see Lancaster Record Book 2, July 11, 1660, 379. Justices Sibsey and Thorowgood were among the earliest Norfolk residents to own slaves. Thorowgood's widow made her choice of an African woman as her share of the 'Negroes belonging to the said Captain Thorowgood's estate' (Norfolk Deed Book A, June 16, 1645, 255).

20. See Norfolk Deed Book A, Nov. 2, 1640, 53, for Thomas Keeling's claim to have transported an African in the *Captain Jonathan* in 1637. For Adam Thorowgood's sale of a 'neagor', see ibid., Jan. 10, 1638, 5. Lancaster resident Epaphroditus Lawson owned one African, one mulatto child, and two Indians when he died. See Lancaster Deeds Etc. 1, Aug. 6, 1652, 10.

21. Battell, 'Strange Adventure', in Purchas, *Hakluytus Posthumus*, VI, 382–6. See Loren E. Pennington, 'The Amerindian in English Promotional Literature, 1575–1625', in K. R. Andrews, N. P. Canny, and P. E. H. Hair, eds., *The Westward Enterprise: English Activities in Ireland, the Atlantic, and America, 1480–1650* (Detroit, 1979), 78; Nicholas P. Canny, 'The Ideology of English Colonization: From Ireland to America', *WMQ*, 3d Ser., XXV (1973), 585.

22. For the case of Fardinando, see Norfolk Wills and Deeds E, Aug. 15, 1667, 17a, and Warren M. Billings, 'The Cases of Fernando and Elizabeth Key: A Note on the Status of Blacks in Seventeenth-Century Virginia', *WMQ*, 3d Ser., XXX (1973), 467–74. Several other Africans appear to have been serving for life in Virginia before midcentury. See 'Selections from Conway Robinson's Notes and Excerpts from the Records of Colonial Virginia', in *MCGC*, 466, 467; *MCGC*, 316; Vaughan, 'Blacks in Virginia', *WMQ*, 3d Ser., XXIX (1972), 469–78; Jonathan L. Alpert, 'The Origin of Slavery in the United States – The Maryland Precedent', in Kermit L. Hall, ed., *The Law of American Slavery: Major Historical Interpretations* (New York, 1987), 5.

23. Jobson portrayed Mandingo life as brutal for women, who labored painfully beating rice in mortars and preparing meals while their men sat under shady trees playing games. 'I am sure there is no woman can be under more servitude', he

claimed, a judgment that Battell's account of Gaga women's relinquishing babies for sacrifice and being buried alive with their husbands did nothing to dispel. See Jobson, *Golden Trade*, 38, 54, and Battell, 'Strange Adventure', in Purchas, *Hakluytus Posthumus*, VI, 385–7.

24. Carole Shammas, 'Black Women's Work and the Evolution of Plantation Society in Virginia,' *Labor History*, XXVI (1985), 9.

25. Sir William Searle Holdsworth, *A History of English Law* (London, 1924), IV, 151–7; Sir Frederick Pollock and Frederic William Maitland, *The History of English Law before the Time of Edward I* (1898; reprint, London, 1968), I, 568, 615.

26. During the first 20 years of settlement, English men outnumbered English women substantially, sometimes by as much as five to one. By the mid-17th century, the ratio had improved to three to one. See Hotten, ed., *Original Lists*, 169–96, for the disproportionate number of white men to women in 1624. See also Herbert Moller, 'Sex Composition and Correlated Culture Patterns of Colonial America', *WMQ*, 3d Ser., II (1945), 113–53; Lois Green Carr and Lorena S. Walsh, 'The Planter's Wife: The Experience of White Women in Seventeenth-Century Maryland', ibid., XXXIV (1977), 542–71.

27. See *SAL*, Mar. 5, 1624, I, 127–8; Philip Alexander Bruce, *Institutional History of Virginia in the Seventeenth Century*, 2 vols (1910; reprint, Gloucester, Mass., 1964), II, 523; J. Frederick Fausz, 'The Powhatan Uprising of 1622: A Historical Study of Ethnocentrism and Cultural Conflict' (College of William and Mary Ph.D., 1977).

28. E. A. Wrigley, *People, Cities, and Wealth: The Transformation of Traditional Society* (New York, 1987); Wrightson, *English Society*; Joan Thirsk, ed., *The Agrarian History of England and Wales*, IV, *1500–1640*, in H. P. R. Finberg, gen. ed., *The Agrarian History of England and Wales* (London, 1967–); *MCGC*, 22. See also *SAL*, Oct. 16, 1629, I, 141–4; Feb. 21, 1632, I, 164; Feb. 1, 1633, I, 212.

29. *MCGC*, 135.

30. See Lois Green Carr, Russell R. Menard, and Lorena S. Walsh, *Robert Cole's World: Agriculture and Society in Early Maryland* (Chapel Hill, N.C., 1991), 444–5, for an example of a prosperous yeoman household in which English women did not perform field work.

31. *SAL*, Oct. 16, 1629, I, 141–4; Philip Alexander Bruce, *Economic History of Virginia in the Seventeenth Century* ... (New York, 1935), II, 101. In subsequent guidelines for restricting tobacco production, a strategy designed to drive up the price of the crop, the General Assembly struggled to reconcile women's and children's fiscal status as nonproducers with their actual capacity for cultivating tobacco. For the limits set on each tithable's production in 1629 and the confusing and contradictory tangle of ideas about gender, dependency, and market production that appeared in the law, see *SAL*, Oct. 16, 1629, I, 141–4.

32. *SAL*, Mar. 2, 1643, I, 242. Liability for the minister's rate was not the same as being subject to the public or county levy; it was customary at this early date, however, to collect all three taxes in a single tithe, making it quite possible that African women were among those assessed for the other levies as well. For interpretations in agreement with this analysis, see Bruce, *Institutional History*, II, 540; Carl N. Degler, 'Slavery and the Genesis of American Race Prejudice', *Comparative Studies*, II (1959), 49–66; Winthrop D. Jordan, 'Modern Tensions and the Origins of American Slavery', *JSH*, XXVII (1962), 18–30.

33. See *MCGC*, 564, appendix C, for extracts of Berkeley's 1645 policy of removing Indians. For an account of the 1644 attack and English military and political responses, see Helen C. Rountree, *Pocahontas's People: The Powhatan Indians of Virginia through Four Centuries* (Norman, Okla., 1990), 84–93. See also Bruce, *Institutional History*, II, 540. Old men temporarily joined the ranks of those not classified as productive workers in the 1645 statute. See *SAL*, Feb. 17, 1645, I, 292.

34. See *SAL*, Oct. 10, 1649, I, 361, and Morgan, *American Slavery, American Freedom*, 401–2. Morgan considers this 1649 statute evidence that African women were not included in the definition of tithable because it specified 'male servants' as liable for country levies no matter what their age. It did not, however, preclude earlier definitions that accounted Africans over the age of 16 among those paying ministers' allowances or soldiers' expenses.

35. Deal, 'Race and Class', 256–8. See also Breen and Innes, '*Myne Owne Ground*', 11, for their claim that the court's concession signified Mary Johnson's and her daughters' equality with white women.

36. Lancaster Orders, 1656–1666, Dec. 16, 1657, 36.

37. *SAL*, Mar. 13, 1658, I, 454. For a different reading of the significance of the 1658 legislation, see Morgan, *American Slavery, American Freedom*, 400–1. Morgan's cautious interpretation does not explain exemption petitions like that of Anthony Johnson. For fundamental similarities in the concepts of race and ethnicity and the problems with essentialist definitions of race, see Stuart Hall, ed., 'What Is This "Black" in Black Popular Culture'? in Gina Dent, ed., *Black Popular Culture* (Seattle, Wash., 1993), 21–33; Brooks Higginbotham, 'African-American Women's History', *Signs*, XVII (1992), 251–74; Barbara Fields, 'Ideology and Race in American History', in J. Morgan Kousser and James M. McPherson, eds., *Region, Race, and Reconstruction: Essays in Honor of C. Vann Woodward* (New York, 1982), 143–77.

38. Morgan, *American Slavery, American Freedom*, 400–1, interprets this law to mean that all women, African and English, were declared tithable at this time, a plausible reading if one is willing to believe that African women came under the rubric of 'servant' in 1662 and that the taxation of African as well as English women had proved problematic in practice. In light of the early classifications of African women as tithable, however, and, despite the confusion in Lancaster County, it seems likely that this law was aimed at the masters of English female servants. Masters of African women would have had less opportunity to avoid the tax. See *SAL*, December 1662, II, 170.

39. The class component to assumptions about women's work was clearly revealed in the special exemptions given to members of the Governor's Council, the wealthiest and most powerful men in the colony during the 17th century. See Bruce, *Institutional History*, II, 380 n. 1. See also Carr, Menard, and Walsh, *Robert Cole's World*, 44–5.

40. *SAL*, Sept. 10, 1663, II, 187; Lancaster Orders, 1666–1680, Nov. 13, 1678, 441.

41. Lancaster Orders 3, July 11, 1688, 43. This is the only conviction for tithable concealment involving an English woman that I have found in Norfolk, Lancaster, and York Counties from 1662 to 1750.

42. Charles City County Order Book, VSL microfilm, Aug. 5, 1678, 314. See York DOW 11, Nov. 24, 1691, 73, and York DOW 12, Sept. 24, 1702, 42. For examples of suits against concealed male servants, black and white, see Lancaster Orders 2, Mar. 8, 1682, 77; York DOW 11, Feb. 24, 1702, 539, 566; DOW 12, Mar. 25, 1706, 404.

43. York DOW 12, Sept. 24, 1702, 42. During the last quarter of the 17th century alone, reports of concealed English male tithables outnumbered those for concealed English female servants by more than five to one, a ratio significantly greater than the actual sex ratio of English men to women in the colony, which was closer to three to one. Even if one considers the possibility of a more skewed ratio for servants, the small number of concealment cases involving English servant women is striking. Between 1700 and 1750, suits involving concealed white men and people of African descent constituted close to 100% of the cases in which the race and sex of the tithable was identified in the record. Overall I found only four cases in which the tithable status of a white female servant was questioned. See Norfolk Orders, 1637–1750; Lancaster Orders, 1657–1750; York DOW, 1646–1750. See also Deal, 'Race and Class', 139, for his observation that the Northampton County tithable lists provide no evidence that the 1662 law was ever strictly enforced.

44. *SAL*, Sept. 23, 1668, II, 267.
45. See *SAL*, Oct. 23, 1705, III, 258 (emphasis added). Deal, 'Race and Class', 220, notes the 1722 complaint of white Northampton residents.
46. The ease of procuring exemptions for ill servants varied by county. In Henrico County, a sick servant might still be accounted tithable, but, in Lancaster County, he would not be. See Albert Ogden Porter, *County Government in Virginia: A Legislative History, 1607–1904* (New York, 1947), 82.
47. Among white male Norfolk residents, 49 received exemptions, compared to 13 enslaved women and 7 enslaved men. Of these, 17 white men claimed physical disability, 7 cited age and disability or poverty, and 24 men gave no reason. Among slaves, 5 women were described as old, 4 as disabled, and 4 gave no reason. See also Bruce, *Institutional History of Virginia*, I, 77; Porter, *County Government in Virginia*, 82; Bruce, *Economic History*, II, 103–4.
48. For successful petitions by or on the behalf of free black women, see Anthony Johnson's 1653 request for his wife's exemption in Deal, 'Race and Class', 256–8. See also Deal, 'A Constricted World: Free Blacks on Virginia's Eastern Shore, 1680–1750', in Lois Green Carr, Philip D. Morgan, and Jean B. Russo, eds., *Colonial Chesapeake Society* (Chapel Hill, N.C., 1988), 283. For examples of white people's pleas of poverty, see Norfolk Orders, 1675–86, May 10, 1677, 32, and Charles City County Order Book, VSL microfilm, June 24, 1678, 303. See also Bruce, *Institutional History*, I, 545, for the Westmoreland County condition that petitioners for tax exemption must produce a certificate from the churchwardens proving that they were already an object of charity and had received assistance. For other petitions of free black women, see *MCGC*, 225; Charles City County Order Book, VSL microfilm, June 24, 1678, 303; Charles City County Order Book, 1677–79, cited in Warren M. Billings, ed., *The Old Dominion in the Seventeenth Century: A Documentary History of Virginia, 1606–89* (Chapel Hill, N.C., 1975), 158. The later petition may have been from the same woman; both petitioners were named Susanna.
49. See Marylynn Salmon, *Women and the Law of Property in Early America* (Chapel Hill, N.C., 1986), xiii, xv, 55, for her analysis of married women's ability to bypass coverture and act as femes sole in the southern colonies.
50. Gloria L. Main, *Tobacco Colony: Life in Early Maryland, 1650–1720* (Princeton, N.J., 1982), 121. Main calculated that tenants in four Maryland counties could lease 50–100 acres of land for between 100 and 300 pounds of tobacco a year. If Paul Clemens's calculations for the productivity of Maryland families with two children are applicable for places other than the Eastern Shore, that would leave nearly 1,700 pounds of tobacco after the rent was paid. See Paul G. E. Clemens, *The Atlantic Economy and Colonial Maryland's Eastern Shore: From Tobacco to Grain* (Ithaca, N.Y., 1980), 159. Clemens himself, however, presents a less rosy picture of tenancy, arguing that it made family savings more difficult and limited opportunities for economic diversity that leaner times required (160). See also Russell Menard, 'From Servant to Freeholder: Status Mobility and Property Accumulation in Seventeenth-Century Maryland', *WMQ*, 3d Ser., XXX (1973), 37–64, esp. 52. Menard notes that even short-term tenancy or longer-term leaseholding accorded a man status as a head of household. See Deal, 'Race and Class', 258, 422, for biographies of Johnson and Longo. See also Breen and Innes, '*Myne Owne Ground*', 11, 86. Many of the free men discussed by Breen and Innes were actually tenants, and several who were not so fortunate worked as hired laborers.
51. For an introduction to the West African context, see Suzanne Miers and Igor Kopytoff, eds., *Slavery in Africa: Historical and Anthropological Perspectives* (Madison, Wis., 1977); Robertson and Klein, eds., *Women and Slavery in Africa*, esp. Robertson and Klein, 'Women's Importance in African Slave Systems', 3–19, and John Thornton, 'Sexual Demography', 39–48. Thornton, *African and Africans*, 74–89, 107, provides an excellent overview of African concepts of slavery and

wealth and notes that African rulers often retained women. Robin Law, *The Slave Coast of West Africa, 1550–1750: The Impact of the Atlantic Slave Trade on an African Society* (Oxford, 1991), 64–8, notes the similarity between women's value as wives and slaves who provided labor and conferred prestige upon men in the region of the Slave Coast. Meillasoux, 'Female Slavery', in Robertson and Klein, eds., *Women and Slavery*, 49–66, discusses the relationship between women's productive and reproductive value in West Africa. See also David Eltis, 'The Volume, Age/Sex Ratios, and African Impact of the Slave Trade: Some Refinements of Paul Lovejoy's Review of the Literature', *JAF*, XXXI (1990), 485–92, and Geggus, 'Sex Ratio and Ethnicity', *JAF*, XXX (1989), 396–7.

52. The ratio of men to women among people of African descent hovered near 1.0 in Northampton County during the mid-17th century. See Deal 'Race and Class', 204, and Breen and Innes, '*Myne Owne Ground*', 83. Breen and Innes identify 13 black householders, 10 of whom were male, between 1664 and 1677 (69). See Deal, 'Race and Class', 265, 315, 332, 385, 420, for the biographies of these men. Deal notes that the race of several of the wives of these men was never noted in the Northampton records. He conjectures that they were white on the basis of descriptions of their offspring as 'mulatto' and their absence from tithable lists.

53. Norfolk Wills and Deeds E, Apr. 15, 1673, 92. See Deal, 'Race and Class', 316, for his suggestion that marriage to white women may have been the most viable strategy available to black men who needed to be part of white networks for economic survival. Deal, Breen, and Innes all interpret the intermarriages of black men and white women at midcentury as signs of a racial fluidity that would quickly disappear after Bacon's Rebellion. I argue that it might also indicate an early devaluation of African women.

54. Several scholars have noted the importance of marriage networks for strategies of class maintenance, and a few have remarked upon the prominent role played by widows. See Morgan, *American Slavery, American Freedom*, 166, for his use of the term 'widowarchy' to describe the transmission of wealth in the colony, and my objections to it in Chapter 3, n. 49 above. See also Peter Clark, 'The Civic Leaders of Gloucester, 1580–1800', in Clark, ed., *The Transformation of English Provincial Towns, 1600–1800* (London, 1984), 316, for his observation that marriage served as a stepping stone to civic office in urban communities; Martin H. Quitt, 'Immigrant Origins of the Virginia Gentry: A Study of Cultural Transmission and Innovation', *WMQ*, 3d Ser., XLV (1988), 629–55; Michael Graham, 'Meetinghouse and Chapel: Religion and Community in Seventeenth-Century Maryland', in Carr, Morgan, and Russo, eds., *Colonial Chesapeake Society*, 273. See also John Hammond, *Leah and Rachel; or, The Two Fruitfull Sisters Virginia, and Mary-land ...* (London, 1656), 15. Moller, 'Sex Composition', *WMQ*, 3d Ser., XI (1945), 139, notes that women were disproportionately distributed among upper-class men, which points both to the status that marriage conferred upon a man and the advantages elite men enjoyed in finding a wife. Although eligibility for marriage in Virginia may have required that a man own land and perhaps servants, the simple act of marrying enhanced his status in communities of predominantly single men. Especially in the years before 1670, acquiring land might have proved less difficult than finding a wife. See Menard 'From Servant to Freeholder', *WMQ*, 3d Ser., XXX (1973), 37–64. See also Clemens, *Atlantic Economy*, 163. For the benefits of marriage for men in English communities, see Thirsk, ed., *Agrarian History of England*, IV, 724–5; Martin Ingram, *Church Courts, Sex, and Marriage in England, 1570–1640* (Cambridge, 1987), 128; Clark, 'The Civic Leaders of Gloucester' in Clark, *Transformation of English Provincial Towns*, 316.

On Anthony Johnson, see James H. Brewer, 'Negro Property Owners in Seventeenth-Century Virginia', *WMQ*, 3d Ser., XII (1955), 578–80. Brewer's use of the term 'patriarch' to describe Johnson, a nomenclature subsequently adopted by Breen and Innes, overstates the freedoms enjoyed by free African men in 17th-century Virginia.

55. See Deal, 'Race and Class', 260, 270, 349, for George and Robert Parker's attempt to hire away Anthony Johnson's slave Caser, for the county court's decision in 1670 that Johnson's land, rather than passing to his son Richard, should escheat to the crown because he was a negro and an alien (the land subsequently went to George Parker), and for Robert Candlin's attempt to trick Sarah Driggus and her family into fleeing the county in 1688.

56. Impediments to marriage also presented a potential difficulty for parishes that depended upon the institution to provide support for poor women.

57. Although black men's familial and social roles were profoundly affected by the laws defining a race-specific concept of womanhood, it was not until the 1680s that black men themselves became the targets of laws circumscribing economic mobility, potential for resistance, and male sexual behavior. I agree with Carole Shammas that the transition from servant to slave at the end of the 17th century was a male phenomenon, but, as I have tried to demonstrate, this was neither the first nor the only transition. See Shammas, 'Black Women's Work', *Labor History*, XXVI (1985), 9. The distinctions made between black and white women by the mid-17th century in many ways facilitated the 'dramatic transition' (9) at century's end that affected black men so significantly.

58. Menard, 'From Servants to Slaves', *Southern Studies*, XVI (1977), 355–90. See also Menard, 'British Migration to the Chesapeake Colonies in the Seventeenth Century,' in Carr, Morgan, and Russo, eds., *Colonial Chesapeake Society*, 99–132. Menard suggests that the numbers of these groups might have been increasing after 1660 with the decline in the population of potential young male migrants from England.

59. Richard Beale Davis, ed., *William Fitzhugh and His Chesapeake World, 1676–1701: The Fitzhugh Letters and Other Documents* (Chapel Hill, N.C., 1963), 68–9.

60. See N. E. H. Hull, *Female Felons: Women and Serious Crime in Colonial Massachusetts* (Chicago, 1987), 25, for a discussion of the Poor Law.

61. In September 1658, John Dickons was summoned to a York County Court for getting Rachell Hamond pregnant. Hamond, the servant of Dr. Francis Haddon, appeared in the October court soon after having her baby to name Dickons as the father of her child. See York DOW 3, Sept. 10, 1658, 36a; Oct. 26, 1658, 40. See also Norfolk Wills and Deeds D, Jan. 16, 1657, 52, for the case of Mary Roche; Julia Cherry Spruill, *Women's Life and Work in the Southern Colonies* (1938; reprint, New York, 1972), 314–23.

62. Norfolk Deed Book A, October 1645, 279; Norfolk Book B, Apr. 28, 1651, fol. 177; Lancaster Deeds Etc. 1, Feb. 6, 1654, 138; June 6, 1655, 198. See also Jon Kukla, ed., 'Some Acts Not in Hening's *Statutes*: The Acts of Assembly, October 1660,' *VMHB*, LXXXIII (1975), 77–95, esp. 83.

63. Norfolk Wills and Deeds D, Jan. 16, 1657, 52; Norfolk Deed Book A, Feb. 16, 1646, 312; May 15, 1646, 336; June 15, 1646, 348; Norfolk Book B, Nov. 17, 1646, 12a.

64. Lancaster Deeds Etc. 1, Feb. 6, 1654, 138. For a discussion of this issue, see Helena M. Wall, *Fierce Communion: Family and Community in Early America* (Cambridge, Mass., 1990), 87–125.

65. Norfolk Book B, Apr. 9, 1649, fol. 113a; Billings, ed., *Old Dominion*, 161.

66. 'Conway Robinson's Notes', in *MCGC*, 477. For another such situation in which the father arranged for the freedom of the child while the mother remained a slave, see the case of Mihill Gowen, William, and Prossa, York DOW 3, Jan. 26, 1658, 16.

67. York DOW 3, Oct. 26, 1657, 2.

68. Elizabeth Key may very well be the 'Mulatto held to be a slave and appeal taken' noted in 'Conway Robinson's Notes', in *MCGC*, 504. See also Billings, 'The Cases of Fernando and Elizabeth Key', *WMQ*, 3d Ser., XXX (1973), 467–74, for his description of the case; Billings, ed., *Old Dominion*, 165–9.

69. Norfolk Wills and Deeds D, Aug. 15, 1662, 350; *SAL*, December 1662, II, 170.
70. See Alpert, 'The Origin of Slavery in the United States', 21–3; Main, *Tobacco Colony*, 127. Virginia did not take this legislative step alone. In 1664, Maryland also made slavery hereditary according to the condition of the mother, stipulating that English women who married slaves became slaves. See Martha Elizabeth Hodes, *Sex across the Color Line: White Women and Black Men in the Nineteenth Century American South* (New Haven, forthcoming).
71. In Virginia, life and work on tobacco plantations with resident masters was conducive both to using female slaves and to encouraging their reproduction. But, in the Caribbean, other factors intervened: absentee slaveowners, their preference for male laborers, and their unwillingness to sacrifice the intensity of work to allow for the reproduction of the labor force. For further discussion, see Dunn, *Sugar and Slaves*, 311–25; Dunn, 'A Tale of Two Plantations: Slave Life at Mesopotamia in Jamaica and Mount Airy in Virginia, 1799 to 1828', *WMQ*, 3d Ser., XXXIV (1977), 32–65; Beckles, *White Servitude and Black Slavery*, 121; Barbara Bush, *Slave Women in Caribbean Society, 1650–1830* (Bloomington, Ind., 1990); Hilary McD. Beckles, *Natural Rebels: A Social History of Enslaved Black Women in Barbados* (New Brunswick, N.J., 1989).

   Whereas terms of service for poor white children were standardized in 1672 to end at age 18 for girls and 21 for boys, by custom mulatto or Indian children served longer terms. See *SAL*, Sept. 24, 1672, II, 298. For the treatment of illegitimate mulatto children, see James Hugo Johnston, *Race Relations in Virginia and Miscegenation in the South, 1776–1860* (Amherst, Mass., 1970), 174, from the Elizabeth City court records, 1684–1699, 83. In sharp contrast to the treatment of mulatto children, the bastard child of a servant woman of Mr. John Page's was ordered to serve for 24 years and was placed in the care of the parish of Middletowne in 1671. See *MCGC*, 248. By 1765, illegitimate mixed-race children were bound out according to the standards for white children: until age 21 for boys and 18 for girls. See Frank Forest Arness, 'The Evolution of the Virginia Antimiscegenation Laws' (Old Dominion College M.A., 1966), for a full discussion of these laws.
72. *SAL*, Mar. 23, 1662, II, 114; Dec. 23, 1662, II, 167–8.
73. *SAL*, Mar. 2, 1643, I, 252, 438; Mar. 23, 1662, II, 114.
74. The average married woman in 17th-century Middlesex lived to age 39 after bearing four to six children. Pregnant women, along with new immigrants and young children, were most susceptible to malaria, which Virginians knew as 'Fever and Ague'. See Darrett B. Rutman and Anita H. Rutman, ' "Now-Wives and Sons-in-Law": Parental Death in a Seventeenth-Century Virginia County', in Thad W. Tate and David L. Ammerman, eds., *The Chesapeake in the Seventeenth Century: Essays on Anglo-American Society* (Chapel Hill, N.C., 1979), 153–82, and Darrett B. Rutman and Anita H. Rutman, *A Place in Time: Middlesex County, Virginia, 1650–1750* (New York, 1984), 179. For examples of the court's view of childbirth, see York DOW 4, Dec. 20, 1669, 274; Norfolk Orders, 1675–1686, May 22, 1679, 90; December 1680, 130.
75. See Jordan, *White over Black*, 85–98; Canny, 'The Ideology of English Colonization', 575–98.
76. *SAL*, Sept. 23, 1667, II, 260.
77. Ibid., Oct. 3, 1670, 283.

DOCUMENT I: ANONYMOUS TESTIMONY BEFORE VIRGINIA
MAGISTRATES ABOUT A SEXUAL ASSAULT COMPLAINT
MADE BY A WHITE WOMAN AGAINST
A MULATTO MAN, 1681

*The difficulties of maintaining racial separation and the status of a
mulatto in colonial Virginia are highlighted in these depositions.
English common law and custom had no firm solution to the problem
of whether a mulatto (the offspring of one black and one white parent)
should be a slave. The sexual liaison described in the depositions was
a matter that courts concerned to avoid inter-racial intercourse would
have treated seriously.*

The examination of Katherine Watkins, the wife of Henry Watkins of
Henrico County in Virginia had and taken this 13 of September 1681 be-
fore us William Byrd and John Farrar two of his Majesties Justices of the
County aforesaid as followeth (vizt.)

The said Katherine aforesaid on her Oath and examination deposeth,
That on fryday being in the Month of August aboute five weeks since, the
said Katherine mett with John Long (a Mulatto belonging to Capt. Thomas
Cocke) at or neare the pyney slash betweene the aforesaid Cockes and
Henry Watkins house, and at the same tyme and place, the said John threw
the said Katherine downe (He starting from behinde a tree) and stopped
her Mouth with a handkerchief, and tooke up the said Katherines Coates
[i.e., petticoats], and putt his yard into her and ravished her; Upon which
she the said Katherine Cryed out (as she deposeth) and afterwards (being
rescued by another Negroe of the said Cockes named Jack White) she departed home, and the said John departed to his Masters likewise, or that
way; after which abuse she the said Katherine declares that her husband
inclinable to the quakers, and therefore did not make her complaint before she went to Lt. Col. Farrars (which was yesterday, Morning) and this
day in the Morning she went to William Randolphs' and found him not at
home, But at night met with the gentlemen Justices aforesaid at the house of
the aforesaid Cocke in Henrico County in Virginia aforesaid before whom
she hath made this complaint upon oath . . .

The deposition of John Aust aged 32 yeares or thereabouts Deposeth, That
on fryday being the twelvth of August or thereabouts he came to the house
of Mr. Thomas Cocke, and soe went into his Orchard where his servants
were a cutting downe weeds, whoe asked the deponent to stay and drinke,
soe the deponent stayed and dranke syder with them, and Jacke a Mulatto
of the said Thomas Cocke went in to draw syder, and he stay'd something

Warren M. Billings (ed.), *The Old Dominion in the Seventeenth Century: A Documentary History
of Virginia, 1606–1689* (Chapel Hill: University of North Carolina Press, 1974), pp. 161–3.

long whereupon the deponent followed him, and coming to the doore where the syder was, heard Katherine the wife of Henry Wakins say (Lord) Jacke what makes the[e] refraine our house that you come not oftner, for come when thou wilt thou shalt be as well come as any of My owne Children, and soe she tooke him about the necke and Kissed him, and Jacke went out and drawed Syder, and she said Jack wilt thou not drinke to me, who sayd yes if you will goe out where our Cupp is, and a little after she came out, where the said Thomas Cockes Negroes were a drinking and there dranke cupp for cupp with them (as others there did) and as she sett Negroe dirke passing by her she tooke up the taile of his shirt (saying) Dirke thou wilt have a good long thing, and soe did several tymes as he past [*sic*] by her; after this she went into the roome where the syder was and then came out againe, and between the two houses she mett Mulatto Jacke a going to draw more syder and putt her hand on his codpiece, at which he smil'd, and went on his way and drew syder and she came againe into the company but stay'd not long but went out to drinking with two of the said Thomas Cockes Negroes by the garden pale, And a while after she tooke Mingoe one of the said Cocke's Negroes about the Necke and fling on the bedd and Kissed him and putt her hand into his Codpeice, A while after Mulatto Jacke went into the Fish roome and she followed him, but what they did there this deponent knoweth not for it being near night this deponent left her and the Negroes together, (He thinking her to be much in drinke) and soe this deponent went home about one houre by sunn . . . .

The Deposition of William Harding aged about 35 yeares.

Deposeth,
That he came to the house of Mr. Thomas Cocke to speake with his brother, where he see Katherine the wife of Henry Watkins, and soe spoke to one there and sayd, that the said Henry Watkins wife had been a drinking; And that this deponent see the said Katherine Watkins turne up the taile of Negroe Dirks shirt, and said that he would have a good pricke, whereupon this deponent sayd is that the trick of a quaker, who made him answer, that what hast thou to say to quakers, It being acted on fryday the 12 of August or thereabouts and further saith not . . . .

The Deposition of Mary Winter aged about 22 yeares.

Deposeth,
That Mr. Thomas Cocks Negroes and others being in company with them a drinking of syder, Then came in Katherine Watkins the wife of Henry Watkins and went to drinking with them, and tooke Mulatto Jack by the hand in the outward roome and ledd him into the inward roome doore and then thrust him in before her and told him she loved him for his Fathers sake for his Father was a very hansome young Man, and afterwards the

said Mulattoe went out from her, and then she fetched him into the roome againe and hugged and kist him. And further saith not . . . .

The Deposition of Lambert Tye aged about 26 yeares.

Deposeth,

That being at Worke at Mr. Thomas Cocks on fryday being the twelvth of August or thereabouts, and coming into the house with William Hobson and the rest of Mr. Thomas Cocks servants and others in Company with them to drinke syder, and being a drinking then comes in Katherine Watkins the wife of Henry Watkins having a very high Colour in her face whereupon this deponent asked Humphrey then servant to the said Thomas Cocke; what made his Countrywoman have such a high Colour; whereupon he made this answear; That the [said] Katherine was at Old Humphrey's a drinking and he gave her a Cupp or two that had turned her braines, and soe being a drinking with their company she went into the Chimney (as this deponent thinketh) to light her pipe, and soe made a posture with her body as if she would have gone to danceing, and then afterwards coming into their company againe, she told Mulatto Jack, that she loved him for his father's sake, And then having left the Company and she together a drinking, This deponent went home to his owne house, and afterwards coming from home towards the house of the said Thomas Cocke, he mett with the said Katherine Watkins about halfe an houre by sun in the pathway homewards neare to this deponents house. And further saith not . . . .

Humphrey Smith aged 26 yeares, deposeth,

That he heard John Aust say (about September last past) what Matter is it what I swore to and likewise the deponent saw Katherine's Mouth (the wife of Henry Watkins) torne and her lipps swell'd, And the handkerchief that she said the Mulatto Stopt her Mouth with very much bloody And the deponent heard the Mulatto confess that he had beene to aske the said Watkins wife forgiveness three tymes, and likewise the Mulatto sayd that Henry Watkins (the last tyme he went) bidd him keepe of[f] his plantation or else he would shoote him and further saith not . . . .

DOCUMENT 2: REPEAL OF THE ACT EXCLUDING SLAVES
FROM GEORGIA, 1750

Georgia was chartered as a colony for English debtors in 1733. The investors in the colony specifically excluded slaves. In 1750, however, Georgia's charter was changed so that Africans could be imported as slaves. Over the next twenty years the population of Georgia increased almost sixfold; almost half of the 23,000 people living there in 1770 were African-American.

May it please Your Majesty,

The Trustees for establishing the Colony of Georgia in America in pursuance of the Powers and in Obedience to the Directions to them given by Your Majesty's most Gracious Charter humbly lay before Your Majesty the following Law Statute and Ordinance which they being for that purpose assembled have prepared as fit and necessary for the Government of the said Colony and which They most humbly present under their Common Seal to Your most Sacred Majesty in Council for your Majesty's most Gracious Approbation and Allowance.

Whereas an Act was passed by his Majesty in Council in the Eighth Year of his Reign Intituled by which Act the Importation and Use of Black Slaves or Negroes in the said Colony was absolutely prohibited and forbid under the Penalty therein mentioned and whereas at the time of passing the said Act the said Colony of Georgia being in its Infancy the Introduction of Black Slaves or Negroes would have been of dangerous Consequence but at present it may be a Benefit to the said Colony and a Convenience and Encouragement to the Inhabitants thereof to permit the Importation and Use of them into the said Colony under proper Restrictions and Regulations without Danger to the said Colony as the late War hath been happily concluded and a General Peace established. Therefore we the Trustees for establishing the Colony of Georgia in America humbly beseech Your Majesty that it may be Enacted And be it enacted That the said Act and every Clause and Article therein contained be from henceforth repealed and made void and of none Effect and be it Further Enacted that from and after the first day of January in the Year of Our Lord One thousand seven hundred and fifty it shall and may be lawful to import or bring Black Slaves or Negroes into the Province of Georgia in America and to keep and use the same therein under the Restrictions and Regulations hereinafter mentioned and directed to be observed concerning the same And for that purpose be it Further Enacted that from and after the said first day of January In the Year One thousand seven hundred and fifty it shall and may be lawful for every Person inhabiting and holding and cultivating Lands within the said Province of

Elizabeth Donnan (ed.), *Documents Illustrative of the History of the Slave Trade to America,* 4 *vols* (Washington, DC: Carnegie Institution of Washington, 1935), vol. 4, pp. 608–11.

Georgia and having and constantly keeping one white Man Servant on his own Lands capable of bearing Arms and aged between sixteen and sixty five Years to have and keep four Male Negroes or Blacks upon his Plantation there and so in bearing Arms and of such Age the aforesaid as shall be kept by every Person within the said Province And Be It Further Enacted that every person shall from and after the said first day of January in the Year of Our Lord One thousand seven hundred and fifty have and keep more than four Male Negroes or Blacks, to every such Male Servant as aforesaid contrary to the Intent and true Meaning of this Act shall forfeit the Sum of Ten pounds Sterling Money of Great Britain for every such Male Negroe or Black which he shall have and keep above the said Number and shall also forfeit the further Sum of Five pounds of like Money for each Month after during which he shall retain and keep such Male Negroe or Black the said several Sums of Ten pounds and Five pounds to be recovered and applyed in such manner as is hereinafter mentioned and be it Further Enacted that no Artificer within the said Province of Georgia (Coopers only excepted) shall take any Negroe or Black as an Apprentice nor shall any Planter or Planters within the said Providence lend or let out to any other Planter or Planters within the same any Negroe or Negroes Black or Blacks to be employed otherwise than in manuring and cultivating their Plantations in the Country . . . .

DOCUMENT 3: JOHANN MARTIN BOLZIUS ANSWERS A QUESTIONNAIRE ON CAROLINA AND GEORGIA

Johann Martin Bolzius (1703–65) was a pastor who emigrated from Halle via Rotterdam and England with the first group of Salzburgers to go to Georgia in 1733, shortly after that colony was founded. He remained there until his death, serving as a spiritual and civic leader at Ebenezer, twenty-five miles from Savannah. This extract is taken from a passage in questionnaire form found among his papers. Thirteen of the twenty-two questions given in the appendix to the questionnaire are reprinted here. The author of the questions was a friend of Bolzius from Augsburg. Bolzius's answers are based on his first-hand experience of dealing with slaves and plantations in the lower South.

Questions and Answers Concerning the Plantation Business in Carolina

1st Question. What is the price of new Negroes who have been brought over from Africa and are sold in Carolina?

Answer. A good new Negro man costs £28 to £32. A Negro woman is about £3 cheaper.

2nd Question. What is the price of such Negroes as are already used to the country or were born therein?

Answer. One who can do nothing but work on a plantation costs £28 to £36. If the Negroes know a craft, they are worth more by as much as their craft earns, e.g., a couple of sawyers are worth £4 to £6 more than a mere field Negro; a cooper costs £50 to £70. A carpenter £70 to £107. A Negro woman who is useful in the house costs £35 to £57. A Negro woman for field work £26 to £33. N.B. These are the prices for native or acclimatized Negroes at public auctions. If one wants to buy them from anyone who does not have to sell them because of need, they cost a little more. For cash one buys more cheaply. Otherwise one has to give 8 per cent interest.

3rd Question. What is the difference in price for the children who are born in Carolina and those who are brought into the land from Africa?

Answer. A native boy of 8 to 15 years costs from £14 to £35 according to whether he looks well and has good expectations. A Negro girl of 8 to 15 years, £10 to £21. A newly imported boy of 8 to 15 years is worth £10 to £25. A Negro girl of 8 to 15 years, £10 to £21. N.B. Boys and girls of 2 to 4 years are worth about up to £7. Boys and girls above 15 years are worth the price of adult Negro men and women. Little children are bought with their mothers. One does not easily buy a child under 8 years by itself.

4th Question. What is the best and safest way to buy Negroes?

Klaus G. Loewald, Beverly Starika and Paul S. Taylor, 'Johann Martin Bolzius answers a Questionnaire on Carolina and Georgia', *William and Mary Quarterly*, 3rd series, 14 (1957), 255–7.

Answer. The best way to buy acclimatized Negroes is at public auction, if a planter has to sell his slaves because of debts. If one wants to have new Negroes and a shipload arrives in the port of Charlestown, one agrees on a price with the buyer of the shipload, enters the ship and picks out which and how many one wants to have.

5th Question. From which Negro country do the best Negroes come?

Answer. The best Negroes come from the Gold Coast in Africa, namely, Gambia and Angolo. The Hipponegroes are the worst nation, stupid and bloodthirsty, and often kill themselves ...

6th Question. How are they clothed in winter and summer?

Answer. A plantation Negro man receives a bad coat and long pants out of 5 yards of white or blue Negro cloth (that is the coarsest, thickest cloth), which costs about 7s., and a pair of shoes (cost 2s. 6d.). The women are clothed with the same kind of cloth (their clothing costs about 10s.). [Every] 3 years each person receives a woolen blanket or bed cover (costs 7s.). Some give them nothing in summer, but some give the women a short skirt of coarse linen and the men a pair of pants of coarse linen and a cap or bad hat for the head, and a handkerchief for the women to cover their head. If the Negroes are skillful and industrious, they plant something for themselves after the day's work and buy trifles with the proceeds. The linen pants of the men and short skirts of the women together cost about 2s. and the labor 16d., but generally the overseer's wife makes them.

7th Question. How does one feed the men, women, and children?

Answer. From September to March their food is commonly potatoes and small unsalable rice, also at times Indian corn; but in summer corn and beans which grow on the plantation. Men, women, and children have the same food.

8th Question. How does one house them?

Answer. They live in huts, each family or 2 persons in one hut. The barn is built about 600 feet away from the house of the master and the huts of the Negroes are arrayed around the barn, at a little distance from one another so that if fire breaks out in one hut the others are more easily saved. The costs of such a Negro hut are very minor. One buys only a few nails for them.

9th Question. How much does the yearly upkeep of a Negro, be he man or woman, cost altogether?

Answer. The yearly upkeep per head costs 12s. for clothing, 2s. annual tax, 28s. for food, totals 2 guineas. Each adult slave receives $1\frac{1}{2}$ quarts or 3 pounds of grain, totals 20 bushels a year.

10th Question. How many acres of rice can a Negro man cultivate in one year?

Answer. If it is new land, a Negro man or woman can plant and cultivate 5 acres in one year. But if the field is old and grassy, not more than 3 acres.

11th Question. How much can a Negro cultivate in other crops per year?

Answer. A good slave may plant and cultivate 10 acres of corn and potatoes, if the land is new and good. But if it is old and grassy, not more than 6 acres. N.B. It is customary that each diligent slave must plant and cultivate 3 acres of rice and 4 acres of grain a year, apart from some potatoes, where the land is not too grassy.

12th Question. What is the day's work of each Negro woman?

Answer. A good Negro woman has the same day's work as the man in the planting and cultivating of the fields. The men fell the trees, and the women cut the bushes and carry them together, and thus they share their work, the man doing the hardest and the woman the easiest.

13th Question. What work do the children of male and female sex have?

Answer. The children are used for various small jobs according to their age, such as hoeing the potatoes, feeding the chickens, shooing the birds from the rice and grain.

3

SLAVERY AND THE AMERICAN REVOLUTION

Introduction

The American Revolution exposed the gulf between Americans' firm commitment to slavery and patriots' espousal of liberty, equality and natural rights. Many contemporaries recognised this dilemma. Morgan (1972) has referred to the contradiction between slavery and freedom as the central paradox – and, by implication, the central tragedy – of American history. In his formulation, the reasons why a people dedicated to liberty and equality maintained a system of racial bondage lay in the problem, expressed by Jefferson, that the freedom of slaves would have automatically created half a million poor people in the United States with little support and guidance for maintaining independence. This would have made blacks unfit members of an emerging republican society. Without the compulsion to work, African-Americans would have replicated the plight of the idle poor in Europe.

Fogleman (1998) argued that the trades in indentured servants, convicts and slaves – three forms of unfree labour – were altered by the libertarian ideals of the era. On the eve of independence, all three trades were operative. By the turn of the nineteenth century they had all virtually ceased to exist. In their place, free immigration rose, setting the pattern for virtually all future arrivals to the United States. This argument, however, needs to be qualified. Far from ending as a result of egalitarian ideology, the convict trade was simply cut off to North America because the American colonies were lost to Britain through war; indentured servitude was an institution already in decline before the War of Independence; and by early 1787 only three states – Georgia, South Carolina and North Carolina – allowed slave imports, the others having banned it for reasons connected more to their own internal economic affairs than to altruistic motives.

MacLeod (1974) delineates the headway made by antislavery ideas in North America by 1776 and the escalation of their impact over the subsequent quarter century. The growth of antislavery notions among European philosophers such as Montesquieu and Rousseau and their dissemination through Scottish enlightenment thinkers was one influential strand in the growth of transatlantic antislavery thought. The work of Quakers and evangelical Christians was another source of moral enlightenment on slavery. Davis's magisterial tome (1975) is the outstanding book dealing with the intersection between changing antislavery ideas and ideals and social action. He deals with white thought and action relating to antislavery imperatives rather than with slavery *per se*. His book casts a wide-angled lens on the broader parameters of antislavery thought, notably its relationship to economics, politics and transatlantic exchanges of ideas.

The main regional area where antislavery activity bore fruit lay in the northern states where gradual abolition bills were passed in five states between 1780 and 1804. Zilversmit (1967) and Nash (1990) show that these moves towards black freedom were very gradual indeed: many statutes granted freedom only for future-born children of slaves at ages between twenty-one and twenty-eight. Thus in most northern states freedom for most slaves did not occur until after the turn of the nineteenth century. Nash, in particular, views the slow emergence of antislavery in the North as the result of deep-seated racism and hypocrisy towards African-Americans. For him, even in the states where legislation was passed to free slaves, the slowness of the process represented a deliberate retreat from the libertarian ideals of the American Revolution. Slavery was therefore a national problem and not just a southern problem in late eighteenth-century America.

Quarles (1961) provided the first full treatment of blacks in the American War of Independence. His work has been amplified and given greater interpretative meaning by Frey (1991), who reveals the complexity of the issues at stake in attitudes towards blacks and in the treatment of slaves during the revolutionary war. That conflict opened up a wider range of active choices that enslaved blacks could pursue in search of liberty. They could flee from their masters, resist the plantation system, challenge their chattel condition, engage in conspiracies, join the British forces, or remain neutral. American blacks took each of these courses. Frey shows how the dual development of revolutionary ideology and evangelical Christianity among blacks combined to form the twin pillars of black resistance to white power. She suggests that 80,000 blacks fled from the United States during the war, but no historian has effectively established – naturally the sources are somewhat elusive – whether the exodus was really on this scale.

Robinson (1971) presents a solid account of role played by slavery in American politics from the Stamp Act crisis to the Missouri controversy. A more recent contribution of the involvement of the United States government with slavery appears in Fehrenbacher (2001), which discusses the slave trade, fugitive slaves and slavery in foreign relations up to the American Civil War. He argues that the United States Constitution was neutral on the issue of slavery but that the American government consistently followed a proslavery course up to virtually the end of the antebellum era. He vindicates the Founding Fathers' record on slavery at the federal level while showing that in the seventy years thereafter their followers moved towards a stance that protected slavery. Only the election of Abraham Lincoln as president in 1860 altered this governmental protection of the 'peculiar institution' at national level.

Slavery and its jurisdiction in the new republic came under scrutiny in the Northwest Ordinance of 1787. This law established the Northwest Territory – the future states of Ohio, Indiana, Illinois, Wisconsin and Michigan – and forbade slavery legal protection within its boundaries. Finkelman (1986) and Davis (1988) offer contrasting approaches to this topic. The Northwest Ordinance can be regarded as the first liberal measure enacted by the American government against slavery at a time when it was difficult to exclude slavery from any North American territory. On the other hand, the Northwest Ordinance failed to include any enforcement clauses and stipulated that fugitive slaves could be lawfully retaken and conveyed to the person claiming them. This could be viewed as an example of the lukewarm antislavery commitment of the committee that passed the measure.

The most significant move by the American government over slavery in the revolutionary era came with the debates held during the Constitutional Convention over the summer of 1787. Slavery assumed importance in debates over the question of how to count slaves for purposes of representation and taxation within the federal government and what to do about the future importation of slaves into the Union. In a succinct overview, Wiecek (1987) shows why historians have differed in their interpretation of slavery at the Federal Convention. Fehrenbacher (2001), as already mentioned, interpreted the framers' intention as neutral on the subject of slavery. Other historians have attacked the Constitution for its seemingly proslavery stance. Lynd (1966) argued, without conclusive evidence, that members of the Constitutional Convention joined with Congressional representatives to arrive at a sectional compromise on slavery by linking the three-fifths clause of the Constitution with the antislavery clause of the Northwest Ordinance and the fugitive slave clauses in both documents. Oakes (1996) emphasises the supposed proslavery thrust of the Constitution. This is also the theme of Finkelman (1987), who takes his cue from the Garrisonian remark that the Constitution made 'a covenant with death'. Finkelman's main argument is that the South secured concessions over slavery at the Convention without any *quid pro quo* for the North.

After the drafting of the Constitution at the Federal Convention, a long ratification process ensued in the individual states. The clauses on slavery and the slave trade were widely debated at this stage. Morgan (2001) provides the only detailed consideration of these debates. He shows that the issues raised about slavery and the slave trade during the ratification process reveal that Americans were divided over the extent to which Congress could or would legislate against trafficking in Africans in 1808, when, according to the Constitution, it could deal with this problem. The matters discussed also showed they were uncertain as to what extent slaves were to be classed as chattel or persons. By avoiding the words 'slaves' and 'slavery' in the Constitution and by use of carefully phrased brief generalisation susceptible to widely varying interpretations, nothing was decided in 1787 about the federal status of slavery. A silence hovered around slavery during the Convention and ratification process because sectional interests were predisposed to try and compromise so they would not deliberately inflame one another.

The essays in Berlin and Hoffman (1986) point to the reshaping of black society in mainland North America after the American Revolution. The essays are grouped into three main sections: the transformation of Afro-American Society in the Age of Revolution; the transformation of Afro-American Institutions in the Age of Revolution; and the impact of the American Revolution on Slave Societies and their Ideologies. Contributors highlight the diversity of black life, with emphasis on inter-regional and intra-regional differences. They point to the liberty achieved by some slaves during the American revolutionary era while stressing the concurrent development of an expanding and more deeply entrenched slaveholding system in the South. Menard (1988) argues, for the most intransigent of North American slave states, that prosperity, slavery and revolutionary politics were intertwined for South Carolina's planters. The success of the rice and indigo economies in Lowcountry South Carolina produced substantial per capita incomes for planters that outstripped the wealth of any other group on the North American mainland before the War of Independence. Menard suggests that South Carolinians opposed British policies before and during the revolutionary war because they had the self-confidence to run their own economy successfully and govern the colony according to their own needs.

BIBLIOGRAPHY

Berlin, Ira and Hoffman, Ronald (eds), *Slavery and Freedom in the Age of the American Revolution* (Charlottesville, VA: University Press of Virginia, 1986)

Davis, David Brion, *The Problem of Slavery in the Age of Revolution, 1770–1823* (Ithaca, NY: Cornell University Press, 1975)

Davis, David Brion, 'The Significance of Excluding Slavery from the Old Northwest in 1787', *Indiana Magazine of History*, 84 (1988), 75–89

Fehrenbacher, Don E., completed and ed. by Ward M. McAfee, *The Slaveholding Republic: An Account of the United States Government's Relations to Slavery* (New York: Oxford University Press, 2001)

Finkelman, Paul S., 'Slavery and the Northwest Ordinance: A Study in Ambiguity', *Journal of the Early Republic*, 6 (1986), 343–70

Finkelman, Paul, 'Slavery and the Constitutional Convention: Making a Covenant with Death' in Richard R. Beeman, Stephen Botein and Edward C. Carter II (eds), *Beyond Confederation: Origins of the Constitution and American National Identity* (Chapel Hill: University of North Carolina Press, 1987)

Fogleman, Aaron S., 'From Slaves, Convicts, and Servants to Free Passengers: The Transformation of Immigration in the Era of the American Revolution', *Journal of American History*, 85 (1998), 43–76

Frey, Sylvia R., 'Liberty, Equality, and Slavery: The Paradox of the American Revolution' in Jack P. Greene (ed.), *The American Revolution: Its Character and Limits* (New York: New York University Press, 1987)

Frey, Sylvia R., *Water from the Rock: Black Resistance in a Revolutionary Age* (Princeton: Princeton University Press, 1991)

Lynd, Staughton, 'The Compromise of 1787', *Political Science Quarterly*, 81 (1966), 225–50

MacLeod, Duncan J., *Slavery, Race and the American Revolution* (Cambridge: Cambridge University Press, 1974)

Menard, Russell R., 'Slavery, Economic Growth, and Revolutionary Ideology in the South Carolina Lowcountry' in Ronald Hoffman, John J. McCusker, Russell R. Menard and Peter J. Albert (eds), *The Economy of Early America: The Revolutionary Period, 1763–1790* (Charlottesville, VA: University Press of Virginia, 1988)

Morgan, Edmund S., 'Slavery and Freedom: The American Paradox', *Journal of American History*, 59 (1972), 5–29, reprinted in his *The Challenge of the American Revolution* (New York: W. W. Norton, 1976)

Morgan, Kenneth, 'Slavery and the Debate over Ratification of the United States Constitution', *Slavery and Abolition*, 22 (2001), 40–65

Nash, Gary B., *Race and Revolution* (Madison, WI: Madison House, 1990)

Oakes, James, ' "The Compromising Expedient": Justifying a Proslavery Constitution', *Cardozo Law Review*, 17 (1996), 2023–56

Quarles, Benjamin, *The Negro in the American Revolution* (Chapel Hill: University of North Carolina Press, 1961)

Robinson, Donald L., *Slavery in the Structure of American Politics, 1765–1820* (New York: Harcourt Brace Jovanovich, 1971)

Wiecek, William M., 'The Witch at the Christening: Slavery and the Constitution's Origins' in Leonard W. Levy and Dennis J. Mahoney (eds), *The Framing and Ratification of the Constitution* (London: Macmillan, 1987)

Zilversmit, Arthur, *The First Emancipation: The Abolition of Slavery in the North* (Chicago: University of Chicago Press, 1967)

ESSAY: LIBERTY, EQUALITY, AND SLAVERY: THE PARADOX
OF THE AMERICAN REVOLUTION

Frey (1987) outlines the economic systems that encapsulated slavery in the different regions of Colonial North America and probes the legitimacy or otherwise of slavery within a new republic based on libertarian foundations. She reveals the range of opinions on slavery which flourished in America during the revolutionary era. In particular, she relates notions of liberty, property, safety and happiness to revolutionary ideas. Why did most northern states agree with the libertarian ideology of the American Revolution on slavery but not concede the principle of equality? Why did slavery become more entrenched in the American South after the Revolution? What justification was made by theorists for the continuance of slavery in North America in the late eighteenth century? How did proslavery forces adopt revolutionary ideology to their own needs?

We hold these truths to be self-evident, that all men are created equal, that they are endowed by their Creator with certain unalienable Rights, that among these are Life, Liberty, and the pursuit of Happiness. That to secure these rights, Governments are instituted among Men, deriving their just powers from the consent of the governed.

In 1776, from his home in exile, Thomas Hutchinson, former royal governor of Massachusetts, read the Declaration of Independence with astonishment and disbelief. Determined to expose the 'false hypotheses' of that soon-to-be famous document, Hutchinson published what was neither the first nor the last challenge to the legitimacy of its premises.

'... In what sense', he demanded to know, are all men created equal, and 'how far life, liberty, and the *pursuit of happiness* may be said to be unalienable....' Addressing himself directly to the representatives of the slave states in the Continental Congress, Hutchinson squarely posed the great question that vexed the Revolutionary generation and has confused generations of scholars after them. How, he asked, do the delegates of Maryland, Virginia, and the Carolinas and their constituents '... justify the depriving more than an hundred thousand Africans of their rights to liberty, and the *pursuit of happiness,* and in some degree to their lives, if these rights are so absolutely unalienable'.[1]

The great disparity between democratic theory and the perquisites of practice has stimulated considerable scholarly debate on the subject of the

---

Sylvia R. Frey, 'Liberty, Equality, and Slavery: The Paradox of the American Revolution' in Jack P. Greene (ed.), *The American Revolution: Its Character and Limits* (New York: New York University Press, 1987), pp. 230–52.

legitimacy of slavery in a republic. Historians writing in the Civil War era, reflecting the interest of contemporaries in trying to explain the great upheaval, viewed the Revolutionary period as one of profound opposition to the institution of slavery. Predictably, the consensus of Northern writers was that at the adoption of the Constitution and during the early years of the Republic, there was no sectional disagreement. In this view both the North and the South looked on slavery as a social, political, and moral evil, evidenced by the original draft of the Declaration of Independence, which denounced the slave traffic; the Virginia law of 1777, which prohibited the slave traffic; the prohibition of slavery in the old Northwest by the Northwest Ordinance; the Constitutional abolition of the international slave trade in 1808; and the words and deeds of the Founding Fathers. The cumulative effect of this argument was to demonstrate that Southerners of the Civil War generation had deviated from the classical republican ideology of their Revolutionary forebears.[2]

A reassessment of the subject in the 1930s led scholars to the conclusion that although republican ideology contributed to the growth of the antislavery movement in the northern and middle states, its impact in the South was limited to a handful of leaders, whose commitment to principle was insignificant compared to the massive moral indifference of their contemporaries.[3] The civil rights movement of the 1960s led to a new burst of interest and a fresh analysis of the problem. Most of the excellent regional and local studies that issued from that period generally agreed that Southern antislavery leaders were atypical, although historians have sometimes taken the views of such leaders as evidence of general antislavery sentiment in the post-Revolutionary-War South.[4]

Heightened interest within the last twenty years in republicanism itself has extended much farther the lines of enquiry. Bernard Bailyn's *Ideological Origins of the American Revolution* and *The Origins of American Politics* represent the first systematic analysis of the subject. Taking the broad view, Bailyn concluded that Americans shared a common set of political and social attitudes, which inspired them in their struggle for independence and guided them through the difficult efforts to build new social and political structures in the post-Revolutionary period. The Bailyn paradigm of a single political and constitutional ideology producing a single, unified response from a substantially homogeneous colonial population was carried forward by a number of adherents. By the early 1970s, however, the consensus theory had come under heavy attack from a number of scholars, whose studies of local situations uncovered evidence of great diversity among Americans. In place of the picture of a relatively homogeneous society animated by a commonly held set of political ideas, a collage of increasingly heterogeneous communities strained by deepening social and economic cleavages and sharp ideological differences began to emerge.[5]

Literally dozens of local and regional studies have appeared over the last two decades, providing detailed pictures of the socioeconomic development of New England, the Middle Colonies, and the Chesapeake. Collectively they tell us that over the course of the eighteenth century, all thirteen of the British mainland colonies were moving toward the development of commercialized economies, but that the character and pace of change varied markedly from one region to the other. Although the proportion of slaves fluctuated according to labor needs and economic conditions, the urban, mercantile centers of New England, the staple-producing economies of the South, the commercial farm and livestock-raising centers of the Middle Colonies, were all to some degree dependent on black slave labor. Sanctioned in law, countenanced by every colonial government, condoned by every major church, slavery was everywhere an established institution that, except for the solitary protests of the Quakers, enjoyed almost universal acceptance.[6]

Inhibited somewhat by a cold climate, rocky soil, low crop yields, a finite supply of land, and the powerful traditions of a Christian commonwealth, New England's economic activity slowly changed from household production to a commercialized economy based on manufacturing and processed foods for market.[7] Although slavery existed, it was a marginal interest, central to neither the economic nor social life of the community. As a result of Puritan reliance on the Mosaic laws of bondage, which regarded slavery as a mark of personal misfortune, not as evidence of inherent inferiority, and the high premium that Puritans placed on education, blacks enjoyed a unique legal position and educational opportunities in New England not accorded them in other colonies. Moreover, because most of New England's small black population, which never exceeded 16,000, was native-born, they spoke English and shared certain white values, making their potential integration into white society possible.[8]

Lacking the geographic and religious constraints that delayed the development of a capitalist economy in New England, the Southern mainland colonies rapidly made the transition from subsistence to commercial agriculture. Beset by a high sex ratio and extraordinary morbidity in the early decades, the Chesapeake after 1720 moved rapidly to develop a staple economy, whose growth and expansion were closely tied to the procurement and maintenance of an unfree labor force based upon African imports until about 1720 and upon natural increase of the slave population thereafter.[9] In the quarter century after 1695, the frontier colony of South Carolina evolved from a mixed economy to a staple-producing economy that was increasingly dependent upon African slave imports.[10] Despite the Georgia Trustees' efforts to avoid the agricultural capitalism that had emerged in neighboring South Carolina, by the 1750s and 1760s Georgians had likewise succeeded in creating a plantation economy based upon African slave labor that closely resembled that of South Carolina.[11] Heavily concentrated in the tidewater counties of Virginia and in the lowland parishes of South Carolina and Georgia, black slaves played a crucial role in the prosperous plantation economies of the Southern colonies.

Occupying an intermediate geographic position, the Middle Colonies reproduced some of the same social patterns that existed in New England and in the South. Blessed by good soil quality, a long growing season, access to water transportation and to markets, the Middle Colonies moved more rapidly to develop a varied economic life based upon the production of naval stores, lumber, wheat, flour, and livestock in New York, and on the cultivation of grain crops, iron production, shipbuilding, and the processing of raw materials in Pennsylvania. Characterized by ethnic and religious diversity, the economy of the region relied upon a mix of white labor, including apprentices, servants, and wage workers, and unfree slave labor.[12] In parts of New York and in eastern New Jersey, where the plantation system existed on a small scale, blacks constituted up to fourteen percent of the total population and slavery was well entrenched. In Pennsylvania, where blacks accounted for only 2.5 percent of the population, slavery was, as in New England, only a marginal interest. As a result of the efforts of the Society for the Propagation of the Gospel and the Quakers in parts of New York and in Pennsylvania, blacks also enjoyed the benefits of education and of church membership. A fractional minority of the total population, they were less able to resist assimilation into white social and cultural structures.[13]

The diversely developing economic systems were attended by corresponding shifts in the patterns of social development. In New England the moderate pace of economic change produced no significant structural transformation prior to 1800. Expanding markets for manufactures and processed foods contributed to a generally rising standard of living and, in the aggregate, to stability in the distribution of wealth.[14] New England remained therefore a relatively egalitarian society, ideally suited for republican ideology, which favored a society composed of relatively homogeneous, egalitarian communities made up of free and independent individuals who shared similar physical and cultural characteristics. A similar pattern of social development evolved in the rural hinterlands of the Mid-Atlantic, although everywhere in the North a concomitant of economic change was the growth of inequality in urban areas, owing principally to the series of international wars that created opportunities for the accumulation of great wealth, and to demographic factors, including the age structure of the urban population, and the concentration in urban centers of what one scholar has called 'the mobile poor'.[15] By contrast, in the South the rapid development of commercial agriculture based upon slave labor led to a highly stratified social structure, pyramidal in shape, the apex formed by planters of great wealth, the descending face made up of yeoman farmers and an expanding body of tenant farmers, the broad supporting base resting on exploited slave labor.[16]

These socioeconomic differences contributed to the development of distinctive ideological constructs as peculiar to each region, or even subregion, as were the social and economic systems briefly described herein. In New England the social trauma of change had helped produce the period of evangelical revivalism known as the Great Awakening, which swept the region in the second quarter of the century. Although the spreading movement did not immediately yield broad theological or metaphysical arguments, its radical democratic critique of social institutions contributed to the growth of social and political consciousness and paved the way for Whig antislavery arguments.[17] In the Middle Colonies evangelical revivalism reinvigorated the Quaker antislavery tradition and led to the adoption of a tough new antislavery policy by the 1758 yearly Meeting.[18]

The religious frenzy of revivalism was also experienced in the South beginning in the 1740s, but its geographic strength was concentrated in a tier of counties in Virginia's Piedmont and in the upper Tidewater. Official hostility and popular preoccupation with matters of political concern caused the movement to falter, beginning in the 1770s. Enthusiasm among clergy and laity for the American Revolution drained off much of the energy needed for growth and the movement stalled during the war years. A disordered economy, the unsettled state of politics, and the excitement of westward migration in the postwar period, combined to delay the development of a general religious revival such as had occurred in the North. As a result, Southern republicanism in general and the antislavery movement in particular lacked the moralistic fervor that inspired it in New England and in parts of the Mid-Atlantic. By the time the religious fires of revivalism began to spread again across the South beginning in 1800, Southern society was nearly united on the issue of slavery.[19] To further evangelicalism Baptists and Methodists had to accommodate their radical racial attitudes to that reality. In place of emancipation they began to preach amelioration. Instead of condemning Southern society, they gradually came to defend it. Only the Quakers, few in numbers but united in their hostility to slavery, remained firm champions of emancipation.[20]

During the decade of public debate over America's status within the Empire, many of these religious ideas were channeled into the mainstream of American political thought, from which they emerged in the fresh, secular language of intellectual discourse.[21] In their resistance to Britain, American revolutionaries had used the guiding values of republican ideology – liberty, equality, and property – to justify resistance to colonial rule; to claim equality of American citizens with the inhabitants of Britain; to argue for self-government within the Empire.[22] Inevitably, their discussions raised questions about the legitimacy of slavery in a republic. Although the concerns of theory demanded unequivocal answers, the constraints of practice produced ambiguous replies.

Despite the resounding phrase in the Declaration of Independence that proclaimed 'All men are by nature equally free and independent', and similar phrases that resonated through the bills of rights of several state constitutions, only the Vermont constitution carried the liberty clause to its logical conclusion and abolished slavery,[23] although most of the Northern states gradually moved toward, if not beyond emancipation. Generally speaking, states with small, assimilable slave populations whose labor was not central to the social or economic life of the community, with a pre-Revolutionary history of religious opposition to slavery, and with early and widespread enthusiasm for republican ideology were the first to confront the problem of bondage in a free society.[24]

Building upon a persistent religious tradition hostile to slavery and buttressed by republican ideology, during the Revolutionary War years all of the Northern states but New York and New Jersey took steps to eradicate slavery: by judicial, legislative, or constitutional action in Massachusetts and New Hampshire, by a process of gradual abolition in Pennsylvania, Rhode Island, and Connecticut. In New York and New Jersey, where slavery was more deeply entrenched socially and economically, where the tradition of religious antislavery was weaker, proslavery forces beat back abolitionist efforts until 1799, when a gradual emancipation bill was adopted in New York, and 1804, when the New Jersey legislature approved a similar measure. In both states the acceptance of gradual emancipation was contingent upon the inclusion of abandonment clauses, called by Arthur Zilversmit 'thinly disguised schemes for compensated emancipation'.[25]

If the philosophy of natural rights had different meanings to different societies, it had also, in the words of Duncan MacLeod, 'racial limits'.[26] Although most Northern states decided that the liberty clause of the Declaration was universally applicable, they refused to concede that the equality principle was extendible to blacks. Both in theory and in practice, the postulate of equality was, from its inception, limited in scope.[27] As part of the concept of the social contract formulated by the English Whigs, it was incorporated into English constitutional theory. Whether or not, as James Kettner has recently argued, the Lockean argument that political society originated in the consent of free and equal individuals logically implied the obliteration of the formal laws that set up separate legal categories of citizenship and created invidious distinctions in political rights among them, Whig theory, as it had developed prior to the Revolution, emphatically did not call for the abolition of such distinctions. On the contrary, they remained largely unquestioned until some Americans of the Revolutionary generation began to extend Lockean contractual theory in such a way that implied the elimination of such distinctions and the establishment of political equality.[28]

Impelled by practical circumstances in the New World and by the imperial crisis of the 1760s, Americans logically deduced that since government originated in the consent of free and autonomous individuals, it necessarily followed that those same individuals should share the same political status and rights. In place of the English notion of second-class citizenship, they therefore substituted the idea of political equality, which was implicit in the Lockean theory of the contractual basis of all political obligation.[29] By and large the new republican governments that assumed responsibility for determining who was capable of membership in a republican society shared certain common assumptions about the qualifications for citizenship, among them being the conviction that only freemen possessed of a clear and conscious attachment to republican principles should be eligible to partake of the rights, privileges, and immunities of the body politic, Women, minors, aliens, Catholics, and Jews, whose natural or cultural disabilities or status as dependent persons made them incapable of independent political action, Indians, whose membership in the tribe claimed their allegiance, and blacks, whose inferior rank in the scale of nature disqualified them, were all unfit for membership in the political community.[30] Accordingly, although Northern state constitutions granted blacks legal protections they continued to deny them full political and social equality. Because neither equal political rights nor economic independence could alter the dependent and degraded status of blacks, many Northerners turned to colonization as the most pragmatic solution to the problem raised by the presence of an inferior race in a homogeneous nation of freemen.[31] By rejecting birth and legal privilege as the proper criteria for differentiating among citizens, the Revolutionary generation had succeeded in expanding the meaning of the equality principle. It would remain for later generations to enlarge its meaning further by adding race and gender to the proscribed list.[32]

Despite the limits of emancipation in the North, slavery had ceased to exist as a national institution. At the same time, however, it had become a deeply entrenched sectional institution. By the era of the American Revolution Southerners had succeeded in building a free political community that rested upon a slave economy. Although the ruthless pursuit of profit and privilege by the planter class had caused acute economic and social distress and contributed to the growth of class-consciousness among the first generations of Virginians, the development of tobacco culture and the establishment of slavery and racism led ultimately to the emergence of a political system that, on the issue of slavery, united the interests of large landowners and yeoman farmers.[33] Although the spread of the evangelical movement produced severe strains,[34] the white consensus on the issue of race was maintained and even reinforced by the experience of the American Revolution.

The war's crippling effect on the Southern economy and the heavy wartime losses in slaves convinced white planters that the full recovery of Southern prosperity and the Southern way of life was inseparably linked to the restoration of the slave labor system.[35] The pent-up demand led to the massive importation into Georgia and South Carolina of slaves from Africa and for a temporary period from neighboring states and from the Chesapeake.[36] Left by the transition from tobacco to wheat with a large surplus of slaves, planters in the Chesapeake resorted to the marketing of slaves in developing regions and to renting slaves to the growing numbers of tenants and small farmers and owners of local industries. The effect was to entrench slavery in the Lowcountry and the Tidewater, to extend it into the backcountry everywhere but in Maryland, and to disperse support for it throughout Southern society.[37]

Although it was a Virginian who formulated and articulated republican ideas on liberty in the most sublime form in the Declaration of Independence and the state of Virginia that produced in the Declaration of Rights the model for other states to follow, no genuine spirit of emancipation existed in Virginia or anywhere else in the South, except briefly during the 1780s when the Methodists and Quakers were officially pledged to end slavery,[38] and Maryland and Delaware briefly debated gradual abolition. Beginning in 1792 David Rice led a short-lived Presbyterian antislavery movement in Kentucky, and a Baptist emancipationist movement led by David Barrow also flourished briefly there. In the face of powerful opposition, however, religious antislavery faltered, forced by the pressures for survival to retreat or compromise.[39] It was fear of slave insurrections, not concern over the iniquities of the slave trade, that led Virginia in 1778 and Maryland in 1783 to prohibit slave importations.[40] Not until the frenzied pace of slave imports threatened to produce economic havoc in South Carolina did the General Assembly in 1787 temporarily suspend the slave trade. Georgia waited until 1798, after the pent-up demand for slave labor had been satisfied, before prohibiting the trade.[41] Virginia's revision of the slave code in 1782 to permit individual manumissions resulted in the freeing of some 10,000 slaves, most of them by Quakers and Methodists, but the proportion of freedmen remained small in comparison to the size of the slave population, which continued to grow numerically and expand spatially.[42]

To be sure, some Southern political leaders were troubled by the obvious contradiction between their professed belief in all men's natural and unalienable right to liberty and the existence of chattel slavery. But antislavery leaders like Thomas Jefferson, George Washington, and James Madison of Virginia, and the Laurenses and David Ramsay of South Carolina were exceptional rather than representative. In most cases, they were forced to conform or pay the political consequences[43] because the majority of Southerners came out of the war convinced that the promises of the Declaration of Independence could only be secured to them by the continuation of slavery.

Although unsuccessful, antislavery assaults on the validity and justice of slavery led to the development of the first conscious proslavery theorizing. Following in the slipstream of classical authorities and later philosophers such as Thomas Hobbes and John Locke, Southerners, in popular petitions and proslavery writings and in political debates in state assemblies and the national Congress, laid the theoretical foundations for proslavery thought. The ideas they formulated would later be utilized more systematically by another generation of Southerners.[44] It was in response to attacks by religious emancipationists, whose opposition to slavery was based principally on religious and moral grounds, that proslavery writers first began publicly to defend slavery as a moral institution. In so doing they had, as David Brion Davis has observed, 'a long tradition of justifying human bondage to draw upon'.[45] The first and most comprehensive religious justifications for slavery were written by non-Southerners: Richard Nisbet, a native of the West Indies whose proslavery tracts were, however, published in Philadelphia; Bernard Romans, a native of Holland who served as a Crown official in East Florida; and William Graham, a native of Paxton, Pennsylvania, who served as rector and principal instructor of Liberty Hall Academy in Lexington, Virginia.[46]

Slavery, these writers insisted, was already a part of the civil constitution of most countries when Christianity appeared. Instead of trying to alter the political or civil state of human relations it found, early Christianity accepted slavery as part of God's design. As the inspired word of God, the Bible offered proof for the theory of the divine ordination of slavery: as a punishment for crimes and as a consequence of war, custom, consent or birth. Just as Noah in Genesis, chapter 9, verses 25 and 27, condemned Ham, his son, to slavery for the crime he committed, so too slaves, as descendants of Ham, were visited with the crimes of their fathers. The enslavement of captives taken in war received divine approval in Joshua, chapter 9, verse 23, while Exodus, chapter 21, verse 7, and Matthew, chapter 18, verse 25, confirmed divine sanction for the parental sale of children. In vindication of the perpetuity of slavery, which distinguished black slavery in the South from ancient slave systems, proslavery writers invariably invoked Leviticus, chapter 25, verses 39–47: 'Both thy Bond Men and Bond Maids, which thou shalt have, shall be the Heathen that are round about you; of them shall ye buy Bond Men and Bond Maids. Moreover, of the Children of the Strangers that do sojourn among you, of them shall ye buy, and of their Families that are with you, which they beget in your Land, and they shall be your Possession, and ye shall take them as an Inheritance, for your Children after you, to inherit them for a Possession; they shall be your Bond-men forever'. Rather than offering a mode of emancipation, or even suggesting the propriety of it, the Holy Word, these defenders suggested, '. . . only directs [slaves] diligently and faithfully to perform the duties of their station as doing the Lord's service and therefore performing his will'.[47]

The resolution of religious uncertainties provided proslavery spokesmen with a moral framework in which to construct their defense of slavery. When James Jackson of Georgia rose in Congress in 1790 to dispute the arguments for emancipation offered in Benjamin Franklin's memorial to Congress, he invoked scriptural sanctions 'from Genesis to Revelations'.[48] William Smith of South Carolina read quotations from Greek and Roman history to prove that slavery existed 'at the time Christianity first dawned on society', and that it 'was not disapproved of by the Apostles when they went about diffusing the principles of Christianity'.[49] By degrees the presumption of divine ordination assumed the character of an axiomatic truth. Despite William Smith's efforts to prove the religious justification for slavery, some vagrant doubts appear to survive in his admission that '... if [slavery] be a moral evil, it is like many others which exist in all civilized countries and which the world quietly submit to'.[50] No such doubt remains in Georgia congressman Peter Early's candid confession to his colleagues sixteen years later that 'A large majority of the people in the Southern States do not consider slavery as a crime. They do not believe it immoral to hold human flesh in bondage. Many deprecate slavery as an evil; as a political evil ...' but 'few, very few, consider it as a crime'.[51]

With the development in the decade before the Revolution of secular antislavery, with its emphasis on natural rights arguments, proslavery forces turned increasingly to republican ideology and forged out of the ambivalence inherent in it weapons that later were to become the mainstay of Southern proslavery arguments. Republican ideology in its inception rested upon a diverse array of doctrines which lent themselves easily to semantic confusion. Conventional Whig wisdom from James Harrington and John Locke to Richard Price had proclaimed property to be a 'natural' right associated with each individual's right to life. Whatever the Whig philosopher's intention in claiming the status of natural right for all kinds of property, proslavery spokesmen fastened on the idea that the right of private property was fundamental.[52]

Above all, property in the South meant slaves. Defined by law as a capital asset,[53] slaves accounted for almost half of the total physical wealth of the region. Although half of the total wealth was owned by the richest tenth of the householders,[54] small farmers and even tenants were heavily dependent upon the labor of slaves. A half century after abandoning white contract labor in favor of black slave labor, Chesapeake planters were more than ever convinced that 'it is impossible to grow tobacco without slaves'.[55] Mindful of the connection between the commercial development of rice and the introduction of slaves from the rice-producing areas of West Africa, South Carolina planters had likewise concluded that the great export commodity could 'only be cultivated by slaves; the climate, the nature of the soil, ancient habits, forbid the whites from performing the labor.... Remove the cultivators of the soil, and the whole of the low country, all fertile rice and indigo swamps will be deserted, and become a wilderness'.[56] So inextricably linked was slave labor to agriculture, it was assumed that without slaves the Southern economy was doomed.[57]

The Southern defense of the primacy of property rights was not, however, merely a tactical or instrumental requirement but related to their fundamental understanding of republicanism. A paean to human liberty, Locke's celebrated *Treatise* nevertheless justified the holding of foreign captives as slave property. Jefferson had amended the classic Lockean triad of 'life, liberty and estate', to 'Life, Liberty, and the pursuit of Happiness', perhaps because he personally questioned the moral basis of some forms of property.[58] Southern proslavery spokesmen did not abjure the basic premises of the Declaration; what they did instead was to adhere to them as inherited dogma. Like most Americans, Southerners believed that the Revolutionary War had been a crusade to secure liberty against Britain's surreptitious assaults. By a kind of ironic paradox, however, they equated property with 'liberty' and translated 'liberty' as the freedom to own human beings. In their petition to the Virginia assembly for repeal of the private emancipation act of 1782, and for the rejection of Methodist emancipation proposals, citizens of eight Virginia counties emphasized that they had '...waded thro' Deluges of civil Blood to that unequivocal Liberty, which alone characterises the free independent Citizen....' Through the agonies of war, they had '...seald with our Blood, a Title to the full, free, and absolute Enjoyment of every Species of our Property, whensoever, or howsoever legally acquired....'[59] The same theme resonates through James Jackson's bitter denunciation of a Quaker emancipation petition in 1790. Georgia slaveowners had fought in the Revolutionary War while Quakers had opposed it: 'Why, then on their application should we injure men Who, at the risk of their lives and fortunes, secured to the community their liberty and property'.[60]

The explicit association of the right of property with liberty had another component, safety and happiness, which like property was an element of the inalienable legacy. Arguing from the Lockean premise that the right of property derives from each person's right to life, Americans of the Revolutionary generation proclaimed property the necessary foundation of happiness, without which no individual could enjoy independence or free will, the most essential component of liberty.[61] State constitutions written during the Revolutionary period invariably link the three words, liberty, property, and happiness, as though each implied the other.[62] In their defense of slavery, proslavery spokesmen used without change that political frame of reference. When, for example, William Smith of South Carolina spoke against the Quaker emancipation petitions he maintained that '...slavery was so ingrafted into the policy of the Southern States, that it could not be eradicated without tearing up the roots of their happiness, tranquility, and prosperity'.[63] Speaking of 'the almost insurmountable difficulties' surrounding the question of slavery, Henry Laurens singled out the 'great task effectually to persuade Rich Men to part willingly with the very source of their wealth &, as they suppose, tranquility'.[64] Whatever other meanings it might have had, to the Southerner tranquility meant the right to live free of the fear of slave insurrections.

More than merely the source of Southern wealth and prosperity, slavery was, in the words of William Smith, 'the palladium of the property of our country'.[65] Smith's homologue of the statue of Pallas Athena, the preservation of which was believed to ensure the safety of Troy, and the institution of slavery was singularly appropriate. As Edmund Morgan has brilliantly demonstrated, the existence of slavery had made possible the freedom espoused by republican ideology. Like Greece and Rome, Southern slave society had produced 'industry crowned with affluence, hospitality, liberality of manners ...', the 'noblest sentiments of freedom and independence',[66] a land, as Morgan writes, 'to fit the picture of republican textbooks'.[67] Although slaves were admittedly useful members of that society, they were also '...savages whose dispositions prompt[ed] them to act as savages in opposition to every principle of humanity and such persons cannot be fit for civil liberty ...', nor for that matter 'would it be safe to trust them with it'.[68]

Heightened slave rebelliousness during the era of the Revolutionary War had revived latent white fears of slave risings.[69] Acutely conscious of their own vulnerability, Southerners drew peculiar comfort and a certain specious support from another element of republican ideology, the right of self-preservation. Emancipation, they argued, would be attended with the most dire consequences, for slaves and their owners. Insisting upon the amiable fiction that slaves were more humanely treated than were the lower classes of whites in many countries,[70] most proslavery writers argued that emancipation would 'tend to make slaves wretched in the highest degree'.[71] Should they be 'thrown upon the world void of property and connections', they would, as the Maryland experience had already shown, 'turn out common pickpockets, petty larceny villains'.[72] Worse than that, emancipation would destroy Southern society by producing 'one or other of these consequences: either that a mixture of the races would degenerate the whites, without improving the blacks, or that it would create two separate classes of people in the community involved in inveterate hostility, which would terminate in the massacre and extirpation of one or the other....'[73] In the catalog of emancipation horrors were 'Want, Poverty, Distress, and Ruin to the Free Citizen; Neglect, Famine and Death to the black Infant and superannuate Parent; The Horrors of all the Rapes, Murders, and Outrages, which a vast Multitude of Unprincipled, unpropertied, revengeful, and remorseless Banditti are capable of perpetrating....'[74] Preoccupied to an almost obsessive degree by fear, proslavery spokesmen concluded that emancipation was impossible because 'the first law of self-preservation forbid it'.[75]

Despite certain elements of logical incompatibility, proslavery spokesmen had thus achieved an apparent reconciliation of slavery with the moral precepts of republican ideology. The next step was to secure the existence of slavery, which they temporarily accomplished, by relying upon constitutional guarantees. In their petition to the Virginia assembly for repeal of the manumission act of 1782, the citizens of Lunenberg County appealed to the Virginia Declaration of Rights, claiming that by it their property rights were 'so clearly defined; so fully acknowledged; and so solemnly ratified and confirmed . . . as not to admit of an equivocal Construction, nor of the smallest Alteration or Diminution, by any Power, but that which originally authorised its Establishment'.[76]

Southern representatives in Congress did not yet interpret the Constitution as an expressly proslavery document. Instead, they argued that it clearly limited the national government in the scope of its powers and in that way served as a vessel to protect slavery. They supported their position with a reliance upon contract theory and strict construction of the Constitution. In one of the seminal assertions of the doctrine of strict construction, William Smith argued that slavery was present when the union was formed: '. . . for better or for worse', he contended, 'the Northern States adopted us with our slaves, and we adopted them with their Quakers. There was then an implied compact between the Northern and Southern people, that no step should be taken to injure the property of the latter, or to disturb their tranquillity'. As the original contractors to the formation of the union the 'State Governments clearly retained all the rights of sovereignty which they had before the establishment of the Constitution, unless they were exclusively delegated to the United States. . . .'[77] The bounds thus drawn around the powers of Congress clearly protected slavery from any change by action of the national government.

The first test of that theory came in 1797 when a group of manumitted slaves from North Carolina attempted to petition Congress to review their situation. Manumitted by their Quaker owners in apparent violation of a state law prohibiting the freeing of any slaves except for 'meritorious services, acknowledged by a license of the court', some 134 former slaves were apprehended under the federal fugitive slave law of 1793 and were subsequently returned to slavery. Antislavery spokesmen, who supported their petition, argued that as freedmen they were not subject to the federal fugitive slave act and were moreover entitled to claim the protection of the House. Proslavery spokesmen on the other hand insisted that under the state law the petitioners were slaves and were accordingly subject only to state authority: 'This is a kind of property on which the House has no power to legislate', not even to receive the slaves' petition. Referred to a select committee, the committee decided that the matter was 'exclusively of judicial cognizance' and recommended that the petition be withdrawn. Although they had not expounded their principles in a comprehensive philosophical treatise, proslavery spokesmen had made it clear that slave property enjoyed so privileged a position under the Constitution that should human claims be advanced against it, the rights of property must prevail.[78]

Poles apart in moral intent and purpose, proslavery and antislavery spokesmen nevertheless drew from the same wellspring. Republican ideology, as William Freehling has observed, articulated concern for both liberty and property. For reasons peculiar to the cultural and social context from which most of them issued, antislavery spokesmen identified with the root postulate of liberty and accorded to property an instrumental or secondary character. For hard practical reasons, proslavery spokesmen presumed that the right of property was fundamental, standing as it were on an equal plane with liberty. In the beginning antislavery forces conceded, in part because as property-conscious republicans themselves, they too believed that property was *a* fundamental right, if not *the* fundamental right; in part because as Freehling has also noted, they had a passion for creating and preserving the Union, which led them to accept 'endless compromises'.[79]

In the end, the apocryphal logic employed by proslavery spokesmen could not be maintained against the moral drive and power of the antislavery forces. Challenged by the inspired humanitarianism of the Quakers, proslavery spokesmen fashioned a justification for slavery from arguments that had flowed without break from ancient slave societies and had been given enhanced force by the logic of republican ideology. Refracted through the lens of radical religion, however, republican ideology became a transformed and a transforming creed. Expropriated by the incipient abolitionists, as David Brion Davis has called them, over the next fifty years the inconsistencies inherent in it were gradually dissolved while the cluster of ideas and values were distilled into the deathless truths that have since functioned as the conscience of society.

NOTES

1. Thomas Hutchinson, *Strictures Upon the Declaration of the Congress at Philadelphia* (London, 1776), 9–10.
2. William Goodell, *Slavery and Anti-Slavery; A History of the Great Struggle in Both Hemispheres; With a View of The Slavery Question in the United States* (New York, 1852); George Livermore, *An Historical Research Respecting the Opinions of the Founding Fathers of the Republic on Negroes as Slaves, as Citizens and as Soldiers* (Boston, 1863).
3. Matthew T. Mellon, *Early American Views on Negro Slavery: From the Letters and Papers of the Founders of the Republic* (New York, 1934); William Sumner Jenkins, *Pro-Slavery Thought in the Old South* (Chapel Hill, N.C., 1935); James Hugh Johnston, *Race Relations in Virginia and Miscegenation in the South 1776–1860* (Amherst, 1937).
4. Leon F. Litwack, *North of Slavery: The Negro in the Free States, 1790–1860* (Chicago, 1961); Robert McColley, *Slavery and Jeffersonian Virginia*, 2nd edn. (Urbana, Ill., 1973); Donald L. Robinson, *Slavery in the Structure of American Politics* (New York, 1971); Duncan J. MacLeod, *Slavery, Race and the American Revolution* (Cambridge, Mass., 1974); C. Duncan Rice, *The Rise and Fall of Black Slavery* (London, 1975); Harry P. Owens, ed., *Perspective and Irony in American Slavery* (Jackson, Miss., 1976).
5. Bernard Bailyn, *The Ideological Origins of the American Revolution* (Cambridge, Mass., 1967) and *The Origins of American Politics* (New York, 1967); Gordon

S. Wood, *The Creation of the American Republic, 1776–1787* (Chapel Hill, N.C., 1969); J. G. A. Pocock, *The Machiavellian Moment: Florentine Political Thought and the Atlantic Republican Tradition* (Princeton, 1975); see also Caroline Robbins, *The Eighteenth-Century Commonwealthman: Studies in the Transmission, Development and Circumstance of English Liberal Thought from the Restoration of Charles II until the War with the Thirteen Colonies* (Cambridge, Mass., 1959).

6. David Brion Davis, *Slavery and Human Progress* (New York, 1984), contends that proslavery arguments had been almost universally accepted for centuries and that no systematic body of argument against it existed; see especially 80, 81, 107–8.

7. See for example Bruce C. Daniels, 'Economic Development in Colonial and Revolutionary Connecticut: An Overview', *WMQ*, 3rd ser., 37 (1980), 429–50; James F. Shepherd and Gary M. Walton, *Shipping, Maritime Trade, and the Economic Development of Colonial North America* (Cambridge, Mass., 1972); Darrett B. Rutman, 'Governor Winthrop's Garden Crop: The Significance of Agriculture in the Early Commerce of Massachusetts Bay', *WMQ*, 3rd ser., 20 (1963), 396–415; Bernard Bailyn, *The New England Merchants in the Seventeenth Century* (New York, 1955); Howard S. Russell, *A Long, Deep Furrow: Three Centuries of Farming in New England* (Hanover, N.H., 1976).

8. Arthur Zilversmit, *The First Emancipation: The Abolition of Slavery in the North* (Chicago, 1967), 4–5.

9. For economic developments see Jacob M. Price, *France and the Chesapeake: A History of the French Tobacco Monopoly, 1674–1791, and of Its Relationship to the British and American Tobacco Trades*, 2 vols (Ann Arbor, Mich., 1973); Carville V. Earle, *The Evolution of a Tidewater Settlement System: All Hallow's Parish, Maryland, 1650–1783* (Chicago, 1975); Paul G. E. Clemens, *The Atlantic Economy and Colonial Maryland's Eastern Shore: From Tobacco to Grain* (Ithaca, 1980); for the growth of slavery see Edmund S. Morgan, *American Slavery, American Freedom: The Ordeal of Colonial Virginia* (New York, 1975); Russell R. Menard, 'From Servants to Slaves: The Transformation of the Chesapeake Labor System', *Southern Studies*, 16 (1977), 355–90; Allan Kulikoff, 'A "Prolifick" People: Black Population Growth in the Chesapeake Colonies, 1700–1790', *Southern Studies*, XVI (1977), 392–414; Russell R. Menard, 'The Maryland Slave Population, 1658 to 1730: A Demographic Profile of Blacks in Four Counties', *WMQ*, 3rd ser., 32 (1975), 29–54.

10. Peter H. Wood, *Black Majority: Negroes in Colonial South Carolina from 1670 through the Stono Rebellion* (New York, 1975); see also Daniel C. Littlefield, *Rice and Slaves: Ethnicity and the Slave Trade in Colonial South Carolina* (Baton Rouge, La., 1981).

11. Betty Wood, *Slavery in Colonial Georgia* (Athens, Ga., 1984).

12. Thomas Elliot Norton, *The Fur Trade in Colonial New York, 1686–1776* (Madison, Wis., 1974); Sung Bok Kim, *Landlord and Tenant in Colonial New York: Manorial Society 1664–1775* (Chapel Hill, N.C., 1978); Michael Kammen, *Colonial New York: A History* (New York, 1975); James T. Lemon, *The Best Poor Man's Country: A Geographical Study of Early Southeastern Pennsylvania* (Baltimore, 1972); Duane E. Ball and Gary M. Walton, 'Agricultural Productivity Change in Eighteenth-Century Pennsylvania', *Journal of Economic History*, 36 (1976), 102–17.

13. Zilversmit, *First Emancipation*, 5, 6, 26–7.

14. James Henretta, 'Economic and Social Structure in Colonial Boston', *WMQ*, 3rd ser., 22 (1965), 75–92; Gloria L. Main, 'Inequality in Early America: The Evidence from Probate Records in Massachusetts and Maryland', *JIH*, VII (1977), 559–81, says that although gross inequality became a permanent feature of Southern life in the late seventeenth century, the same thing did not occur in Massachusetts until

the early nineteenth century. G. B. Warden, 'Inequality and Instability in Eighteenth Century Boston', *JIH*, VI (1976), 49–84, maintains that the distribution of wealth did not change between 1687 and 1772.

15. Kim, *Landlord and Tenant*; Edward Countryman, *A People in Revolution: The American Revolution and Political Society in New York, 1760–1790* (Baltimore, 1981); Lemon, *Best Poor Man's Country*; Stephanie Grauman Wolf, *Urban Village: Population, Community, and Family Structure in Germantown, Pennsylvania, 1683–1800* (Princeton, 1976); Gary B. Nash, *Urban Crucible: Social Change, Political Consciousness, and the Origins of the American Revolution* (Cambridge, Mass., 1979), 54–75; Duane E. Ball, 'Dynamics of Population and Wealth in Eighteenth-Century Chester County, Pennsylvania', *JIH*, VI (1976), 621–44.

16. Aubrey, C. Land, 'Economic Base and Social Structure: The Northern Chesapeake in the Eighteenth Century', *Journal of Economic History*, 25 (1965), 639–54; Gerald W. Mullin, *Flight and Rebellion: Slave Resistance in Eighteenth-Century Virginia* (New York, 1972); Rhys Isaac, *The Transformation of Virginia, 1740–1790: Community, Religion, and Authority* (Chapel Hill, N.C., 1982). Some recent studies, including Isaac's *Transformation of Virginia*, emphasize the rise of tensions in society. See, for example, Marvin L. Michael Kay, 'The North Carolina Regulation, 1766–1776: A Class Conflict', in *The American Revolution: Explorations in the History of American Radicalism*, Alfred F. Young, ed. (De Kalb, Ill., 1976), 71–123; Ronald Hoffman, *A Spirit of Dissension: Economics, Politics, and the Revolution in Maryland* (Baltimore, 1973); A Roger Ekrich, *'Poor Carolina': Politics and Society in Colonial North Carolina, 1729–1776* (Chapel Hill, N.C., 1981); Richard R. Beeman, 'Social Change and Cultural Conflict in Virginia: Lunenburg County, 1746 to 1774', *WMQ*, 3rd ser., 35 (1978), 455–76. For the growth of tenancy see Willard F. Bliss, 'The Rise of Tenancy in Virginia', *VMHB*, 59 (1950), 427–41.

17. Richard L. Bushman, *From Puritan to Yankee: Character and the Social Order in Connecticut, 1690–1765* (New York, 1967), 113–95; Alan Heimert, *Religion and the American Mind: From the Great Awakening to the Revolution* (Cambridge, Mass., 1966), sees the Great Awakening as the intellectual force that propelled the colonies toward revolution. His work focuses principally on New England. John M. Murrin, 'No Awakening, No Revolution? More Counterfactual Speculations', *Reviews in American History*, 11 (1983), 161–71, argues that although the Great Awakening did not create the Revolution, it contributed to its success. Nathan Hatch, 'The Christian Movement and the Demand for a Theology of the People', *JAH*, 67 (1980–81), 545–67, stresses the liberating impact of the Revolution on religion.

18. Zilversmit, *The First Emancipation*, 71–74.

19. Wesley, M. Gewehr, *The Great Awakening in Virginia, 1740–1790* (Chapel Hill, N. C., 1930), described the Great Awakening in Virginia as having three distinct phases; the last, the Methodist revival, was cut short by the Revolution. John B. Boles, 'Evangelical Protestantism in the Old South: From Religious Dissent to Cultural Dominance', in Charles Reagan Wilson, ed., *Religion in the South* (Jackson, Miss., 1985), argues that although the South experienced a series of localized revivals, it was not until 1800–1805 that general revivalism swept the area. William Parks, 'Religion and the Revolution in Virginia', in Richard A. Rutyna and Peter C. Stewart, eds., *Virginia in the American Revolution: A Collection of Essays* (Norfolk, Va., 1977), 38–56, demonstrates the geographic concentration of the movement, as does J. Stephen Kroll-Smith, 'Transmitting a Revival Culture: The Organizational Dynamics of the Baptist Movement in Colonial Virginia, 1760–1777', *JSH*, L (1984), 551–68; for postwar developments see John B. Boles, *The Great Revival in the South, 1787–1805: Origins of the Southern Evangelical Mind* (Lexington, 1972). Evidence for the proslavery consensus is extensive. See, for example, Thomas Coke, *Extracts of the Journals of the Reverend Dr. Coke's Five Visits to America*

(London, 1793), 33, 37; Jesse Lee, *A Short History of the Methodist, in the United States of America; Beginning in 1766, And Continued till 1809* (Baltimore, 1810), 120; Jesse Lee, *A Short Account of the Life and Death of the Reverend John Lee, A Methodist Minister in the United States of America* (Baltimore, 1805), 126. See also Arthur H. Shaffer, 'Between Two Worlds: David Ramsay and the Politics of Slavery', *JSH*, L (no. 2, 1984), 175–96; Larry E. Tise, 'Proslavery Ideology: A Social and Intellectual History of the Defense of Slavery in America, 1790–1840', (University of North Carolina Ph.D., 1975), xxv.

20. McColley, *Slavery and Jeffersonian Virginia*, 154.
21. Murrin, 'No Awakening, No Revolution', 161–71; Hatch, 'The Christian Movement', 545–67.
22. Willi Paul Adams, *The First American Constitutions: Republican Ideology and the Making of the State Constitutions in the Revolutionary Era* (Chapel Hill, N. C., 1980), 165, 166, 169.
23. Ibid., 156–8.
24. This is the general argument made by Zilversmit, *The First Emancipation*; see also Litwack, *North of Slavery*, 4–23, which is in general agreement.
25. Zilversmit, *The First Emancipation*, 199. The gradual emancipation bill passed by New York in 1799 freed Negro children born after July 4, 1799, but required them to serve the masters of their mothers until they were twenty-eight (males) or twenty-five (females). The bill, however, permitted owners to abandon the children a year after their birth, after which time they were considered paupers and would be bound out to service by the overseers of the poor. The state would reimburse the towns for the support of abandoned children. Since the law did not prohibit overseers from binding out children to the same masters who abandoned them, masters could receive a lucrative income.
26. MacLeod, *Slavery, Race and the American Revolution*, 47.
27. J. R. Pole, *The Pursuit of Equality in American History* (Berkeley, 1978); chaps. 6, 7, and 8 deal with equality as it bears on race.
28. James H. Kettner, *The Development of American Citizenship, 1608–1870* (Chicago, 1978), 53–4; Adams, *First American Constitutions*, 165. For a different reading of eighteenth-century insights on equality see Garry Wills, *Inventing America: Jefferson's Declaration of Independence* (Garden City, N.Y., 1978), 207–28, which argues for the influence in America of the moral-sense school represented by the Scottish Enlightenment. In recognizing the moral sense as man's highest faculty, Scottish philosophers such as Frances Hutcheson advanced the notion of a literal equality of men, which Wills believes was the formative influence on Jeffersonian thought.
29. Kettner, *Development of American Citizenship*, 213–47.
30. Jack P. Greene, *All Men Are Created Equal: Some Reflections on the Character of the American Revolution* (Oxford, 1976), 12, 15, 18, 23, 26. The classic study of the history of racism is Winthrop D. Jordan, *White Over Black: American Attitudes Toward the Negro, 1550–1812* (Chapel Hill, N.C., 1968); see also George M. Fredrickson, *The Black Image in the White Mind: The Debate on Afro-American Character and Destiny, 1817–1914* (New York, 1971).
31. Litwack, *North of Slavery*, 15, 16, 17, 22, 28; Adams, *First American Constitutions*, 184–85; David M. Streifford, 'The American Colonization Society: An Application of Republican Ideology to Early Antebellum Reform', *JSH*, XLV (1979), 201–20; Betty L. Fladeland, 'Compensated Emancipation: A Rejected Alternative', *JSH*, XLII (1976), 169–86.
32. Rowland Berthoff and John M. Murrin, 'Feudalism, Communalism, and the Yeoman Freeholder: The American Revolution Considered as a Social Accident', in Stephen G. Kurtz and James H. Hutson, eds., *Essays on the American Revolution* (Chapel Hill, N.C., 1973), 282.

33. Morgan, in *American Slavery, American Freedom*, argues for a white political consensus based at least in part on the issue of slavery.

34. Issac, in *Transformation of Virginia*, stresses the strains on Virginia society caused by the rise of religious revivalism. My own research suggests that on the issue of slavery the consensus held firm and was in fact reinforced by the Revolutionary War experience.

35. Joseph Clay to James Jackson, February 16, 1784, in Letters of Joseph Clay, Georgia Historical Society, *Collections*, VIII, 194–5; from Ralph Izard, June 10, 1785 (Enclosure 2), in Julian P. Boyd, ed., *The Papers of Thomas Jefferson* (Princeton, 1950–) VIII, 199. See also Darold D. Wax, '"New Negroes Are Always in Demand": The Slave Trade in Eighteenth-Century Georgia', *Georgia Historical Quarterly*, LXVIII (1984), 193.

36. Joseph Clay to Messrs. Scott Dover Taylor and Bell, April 15, 1783; and Clay to James Jackson, February 16, 1783, Letters of Joseph Clay, Georgia Historical Society, *Collections*, VIII, 187, 194–5; Philip D. Morgan, 'Black Society in the Lowcountry, 1760–1810', in Ira Berlin and Ronald Hoffman, eds., *Slavery and Freedom in the Age of the American Revolution* (Charlottesville, Va., 1983), 83–141; Patrick S. Brady, 'The Slave Trade and Sectionalism in South Carolina, 1787–1808', *JSH*, XXXVIII (1972), 601–20.

37. Richard S. Dunn, 'Black Society in the Chesapeake, 1776–1810', in Berlin and Hoffman, eds., *Slavery and Freedom*, 49–82; see also Allan Kulikoff, 'Uprooted Peoples: Black Migrants in the Age of the American Revolution, 1790–1820', in ibid., 143–71; Sarah S. Hughes, 'Slaves for Hire: The Allocation of Black Labor in Elizabeth City County, Virginia, 1782 to 1810', *WMQ*, 3rd ser., 35 (1978), 260–86.

38. McColley, *Slavery and Jeffersonian Virginia*, 148. The emancipation rule was suspended in 1785, ibid., 152.

39. Zilversmit, *First Emancipation*, 155. For the antislavery movement in Kentucky see John B. Boles, *Religion in Antebellum Kentucky* (Lexington, Ky., 1976), 101–22; Jeffrey Brooke Allen, 'Were Southern White Critics of Slavery Racists? Kentucky and the Upper South, 1791–1824', *JSH*, XLIV (1978), 169–90. Eugene D. Genovese has called to my attention the fact that in 1836 the Kentucky Presbyterian Synod published an antislavery manifesto. See Committee of the Synod of Kentucky, *An Address to the Presbyterians of Kentucky, Proposing a Plan for the Instruction and Emancipation of their Slaves* (Newburyport, Ky., 1836), cited in Genovese, '*Slavery Ordained of God': The Southern Slaveholders' View of Biblical History and Modern Politics*, 24th Annual Robert Fortenbaugh Memorial Lecture, Gettysburg College, 1985, n. 14, 26.

40. McColley, *Slavery and Jeffersonian Virginia*, 117.

41. Brady, 'The Slave Trade and Sectionalism', 602, n. 2.

42. Dunn, 'Black Society in the Chesapeake', 49–82.

43. McColley, *Slavery and Jeffersonian Virginia*, 114–18; Arthur H. Shaffer, 'Between Two Worlds: David Ramsay and the Politics of Slavery', *JSH*, L (1984), 175–96. Some Southerners led an effort to defeat Jefferson's bid for the presidency in 1796 because of his antislavery views. See William Loughton Smith, *The Pretensions of Thomas Jefferson to the Presidency Examined* (n.p., 1796). There is some evidence to suggest that it was not safe to publicly oppose slavery. See Albert Matthews, 'Notes on the Proposed Abolition of Slavery in Virginia in 1785', Colonial Society of Massachusetts, *Publications*, VI (1904), 373, which describes the harassment of Thomas Coke during a tour of Virginia. See also James Jackson's response to a comment made by a colleague during the Congressional debate over slavery in 1790 to the effect that 'if he was a federal judge he does not know to what length he would go in emancipating these people;' but Jackson warned, 'I believe his judgment would be of short duration in Georgia, perhaps even the existence of such a judge might be in danger', *Abridgment of the Debates of Congress* (February, 1790), I, 209.

44. Jordan, in *White Over Black*, 310–11, sees the Revolution as 'a critical turning point', because for the first time Americans became conscious of the pervasiveness of slavery, which 'mocked the ideals upon which the new republic was founded'. Fredrickson, in *Black Image in the White Mind*, 3, contends that because antislavery forces were so weak in the South and because slavery had never been seriously threatened, 'slavery in the South had survived the Revolutionary era and the rise of the natural rights philosophy without an elaborated racial defense – without, indeed, much of an intellectual defense of any kind'. Tise, in 'Proslavery Ideology', 94, sees the American Revolution as 'the first great crisis which challenged the social and moral values of a slave society'. Although I generally agree with Tise, his emphasis is on the tension between proslavery thought and the ideology of the Revolution. Although I recognize the tension, I emphasize the reliance of Southerners upon Revolutionary ideology to defend the institution of slavery; their rejection of the natural rights arguments occurred after 1800, as Tise's evidence clearly shows.

45. David Brion Davis, *The Problem of Slavery in the Age of Revolution* (Ithaca, 1975), 165 and especially chap. 34.

46. [Richard Nisbet], *Slavery Not Forbidden by Scripture* (Philadelphia, 1773); Bernard Romans, *A Concise Natural History of East and West Florida* (New York, 1775, reprint ed., 1961); David W. Robson, ed., '"An important Question Answered": William Graham's Defense of Slavery in Post-Revolutionary Virginia', *WMQ*, 3rd ser., 37 (1980), 644–52.

47. [Nisbet], *Slavery Not Forbidden*, 3, 4; Romans, *A Concise Natural History*, 76–78; 'Graham's Defense of Slavery', 650–1.

48. *Abridgment of the Debates of Congress* (February, 1790), I, 209.

49. *Annals of Congress*, 1 Cong., 2 Sess., 1506 (March 17, 1790); see also 'Early Proslavery Petitions in Virginia', Fredrika Teute Schmidt and Barbara Ripel Wilhelm, eds., *WMQ*, 3rd ser., 30 (1973), 139, 143, 149.

50. *Annals of Congress*, 1 Cong., 2 Sess., 1510 (March 17, 1790).

51. *Abridgment of the Debates of Congress* (December, 1806), III, 501.

52. William B. Scott, *In Pursuit of Happiness: American Conception of Property from the Seventeenth to the Twentieth Century* (Bloomington, Ind., 1977), 24–35.

53. For the history of colonial efforts to establish a statutory law of slavery, see A. Leon Higginbotham, Jr., *In the Matter of Color: Race and the American Legal Process: The Colonial Period* (New York, 1978); Whittington B. Johnson, 'The Origin and Nature of African Slavery in Seventeenth Century Maryland', *Maryland Historical Magazine*, 73 (1978), 236–45; M. Eugene Sirmans, 'The Legal Status of the Slave in South Carolina, 1670–1740', *JSH*, 28 (1962), 462–73; William M. Wiecek, 'The Statutory Law of Slavery and Race in the Thirteen Mainland Colonies of British America', *WMQ*, 3rd ser., 34 (1977), 258–80.

54. Alice Hanson Jones, ed., *American Colonial Wealth: Documents and Methods*, 3 vols (New York, 1978), III, 1940, 1947.

55. Jacques-Pierre Brissot de Warville, *New Travels in the United States of America* (Cambridge, Mass., 1964), 231.

56. *Annals of Congress*, 1 Cong., 2 Sess., 1510, 1513 (March 17, 1790).

57. *Abridment of the Debates of Congress* (February, 1790), I, 210. See also Romans, *A Concise Natural History*, 71.

58. Most Jefferson scholars agree that although Jefferson clearly believed that slavery was a moral evil, he also believed that the Negro was probably inferior. Jordan, *White Over Black*, 481, concludes that Jefferson's derogation of the Negro '...constituted, for all its qualifications, the most intense, extensive, and extreme formulation of anti-Negro "thought" offered by any American in the thirty years after the Revolution'. Proslavery forces in fact used Jefferson's *Notes on Virginia* to argue for Negro inferiority. See, for example, *Annals of Congress*, 1 Cong., 2 Sess., 1506 (March 17, 1790).

59. 'Early Proslavery Petitions', 140, 141. Even Southerners who opposed slavery implicitly recognized that owners had a legally vested right of property in their slaves. See McColley, *Slavery and Jeffersonian Virginia*, 158, 186; Louis Morton, *Robert Carter of Nomini Hall: A Virginia Tobacco Planter of the Eighteenth Century* (Williamsburg, Va., 1941), 60–1; Arthur Lee, *An Essay in Vindication of the Continental Colonies of America: From A Censure of Mr. Adam Smith in his Theory of Moral Sentiments* (London, 1764). Although he opposed slavery, Lee defended the legality of it, which he contended derived from the legislative power in each society, 32. For a different view of Jefferson's omission of property from the list of 'inalienable rights' see Willis, *Inventing America*, 207–39, 293–306, which argues that Jefferson's view of natural rights was more in accord with Scottish Enlightenment thought than with Lockean political principles.

60. *Annals of Congress*, 1 Cong., 1 Sess., 1229 (February 11, 1790).

61. Greene, *All Men Are Created Equal*, 18.

62. Adams, *The First American Constitutions*, especially chaps. 7, 8, and 9, which treat the three postulates separately.

63. *Annals of Congress*, 1 Cong., 2 Sess., 1508 (March 17, 1790). See also Rutland, ed., *Papers of George Mason*, III, 1065–66; 'Early Proslavery Petitions', 140, 142, 145.

64. Henry Laurens to John Laurens, September 21, 1779, 'Correspondence Between Hon. Henry Laurens and His Son, John, 1778–1780', *South Carolina Historical and Genealogical Magazine*, VI (1905), 150.

65. *Abridgment of the Debates of Congress* (February, 1790), I, 210.

66. *Annals of Congress*, 1 Cong., 2 Sess., 1511–12 (March 17, 1790).

67. Morgan, *American Slavery, American Freedom*, 377–8. I am indebted to Eugene D. Genovese for pointing out that Moses I. Finley, *Slavery in Classical Antiquity: Views and Controversies* (Cambridge, Mass., 1969), 52–72, first noted the historic relation of slavery to freedom.

68. 'Graham's Defense of Slavery', 651.

69. Jeffrey J. Crow, 'Slave Rebelliousness and Social Conflict in North Carolina, 1775 to 1802', *WMQ*, 3rd ser., 37 (1980), 79–102; Sylvia R. Frey, 'Between Slavery and Freedom: Virginia Blacks in the American Revolution', *JSH*, 49 (1983), 375–98.

70. *Abridgment of the Debates of Congress* (May, 1789), I, 74; *Annals of Congress*, 1 Cong., 2 Sess., 1502 (March 17, 1790), 1513 (March 19, 1790).

71. *Annals of Congress*, 1 Cong., 2 Sess., 1502 (March 17, 1790).

72. *Abridgment of the Debates of Congress* (May, 1789), I, 74.

73. *Annals of Congress*, 1 Cong., 2 Sess., 1508 (March 17, 1790).

74. 'Early Proslavery Petitions', 141, 146.

75. *Abridgment of the Debates of Congress* (December, 1806), III, 498.

76. 'Early Proslavery Petitions', 142.

77. *Annals of Congress*, 1 Cong., 2 Sess., 1504, 1508 (March 17, 1790). For other assertions of constitutional guarantees see *Abridgment of the Debates of Congress* (February, 1790), I, 209, 210; Smith, *The Pretensions of Thomas Jefferson*, 10.

78. *Annals of Congress*, 4 Cong., 2 Sess., 2015–24 (January 30, 1797); 5 Cong., 1 Sess., 658–70 (November, 1797); 1032–33 (February, 1798).

79. William W. Freehling, 'The Founding Fathers and Slavery', *AHR*, 77 (1972), 81–93.

DOCUMENT 1: THE NORTHWEST ORDINANCE, 1787

The Northwest Ordinance (13 July 1787) laid down a governmental structure for Congress's territory north and west of the Ohio River. It provided for a territorial stage and later statehood to be carved out of the western lands. Slavery was prohibited in the Northwest Territory under Article 6 of the Ordinance, which also included a fugitive slave clause that served as a model for a similar clause in the United States Constitution.

Article the Sixth. There shall be neither slavery nor involuntary servitude in the said territory otherwise than in punishment of crimes whereof the party shall have been duly convicted: provided always that any person escaping into the same from whom labor or service is lawfully claimed in any one of the original states, such fugitive may be lawfully reclaimed and conveyed to the person claiming his, or her labor, or service as aforesaid.

Henry S. Commager (ed.), *Documents of American History* (New York: Appleton-Century-Crofts, 1963), p. 132.

DOCUMENT 2: SLAVERY AND THE UNITED STATES
CONSTITUTION

Constitutional provisions that directly or indirectly affected slavery were debated at the Constitutional Convention, held at Independence Hall, Philadelphia, over the summer of 1787. The three most important clauses dealing with slavery that were incorporated in the Unites States Constitution are reprinted here. The three-fifths clause (Article 1, Section 2) was known as the federal ratio. It concerned the role to be played by slaves in the American republic for purposes of direct taxation and apportioning representatives from the states in Congress. Under Article I, Section 9 Congress lacked the power to prohibit the foreign slave trade into the United States before 1808. A clause in Article V precluded the possibility of any amendment to that stipulation. Article IV, Section 2 was a fugitive slave clause modelled closely on a similar clause in the Northwest Ordinance.

ARTICLE I, SECTION 2. Representatives and direct Taxes shall be apportioned among the several States which may be included within this Union, according to their respective Numbers, which shall be determined by adding to the whole Number of free Persons, including those bound to Service for a Term of Years, and excluding Indians not taxed, three fifths of all other persons.

ARTICLE I, SECTION 9. The Migration or Importation of such Persons as any of the States now existing shall think proper to admit, shall not be prohibited by the Congress prior to the Year one thousand eight hundred and eight, but a Tax or duty may be imposed on such Importation, not exceeding ten dollars for each Person.

ARTICLE V .... Provided that no Amendment which may be made prior to the Year One thousand eight hundred and eight shall in any Manner affect the first and fourth Clauses in the Ninth Section of the first Article ....

ARTICLE IV, SECTION 2. No Person held to Service or Labour in one State, under the Laws thereof, escaping into another, shall, in Consequence of any Law or Regulation therein, be discharged from such Service or Labour, but shall be delivered up on Claim of the Party to whom such Service or Labour may be due.

www.nationalcenter.org/HistoricalDocuments.html

DOCUMENT 3: PETITION FROM THE PENNSYLVANIA ABOLITION SOCIETY TO CONGRESS, 1790

The Pennsylvania Abolition Society, founded in 1775, lobbied Congress to stop the slave trade after the United States Constitution had been ratified. This petition, influenced by Quaker benevolence, was signed by the Society's president, Benjamin Franklin, and presented to the second session of the inaugural Congress in February 1790.

That from a regard for the happiness of Mankind, an Association was formed several years since in this State by a number of her Citizens, of various religious denominations for promoting the *Abolition of Slavery* & for the relief of those unlawfully held in bondage. A just and accurate Conception of the true Principles of liberty, as it spread through the land, produced accessions to their numbers, many friends to their Cause, & a legislative Co-operation with their views, which, by the blessing of Divine Providence, have been successfully directed to the *relieving from bondage a large number of their fellow Creatures of the African Race*. They have also the Satisfaction to observe, that in consequence of that Spirit of Philanthropy & genuine liberty which is generally diffusing its beneficial Influence, similar Institutions are gradually forming at home & abroad.

That mankind are all formed by the same Almighty being, alike objects of his Care & equally designed for the Enjoyment of Happiness the Christian Religion teaches us to believe, & the Political Creed of Americans fully coincides with the Position. Your Memorialists, particularly engaged in attending to the Distresses arising from Slavery, believe it their indispensable Duty to present this Subject to your notice – They have observed with great Satisfaction, that many important & salutary Powers are vested in you for 'promoting the Welfare & *securing the blessing of liberty to the People of the United States*'. And as they conceive, that these blessings ought rightfully to be administered, *without distinction of Colour*, to all descriptions of People, so they indulge themselves in the pleasing expectation, that nothing, which can be done for the relief of the unhappy objects of their care will be either omitted or delayed –

From a persuasion that equal liberty was originally the Portion, & is still the Birthright of all Men, & influenced by the strong ties of Humanity & the Principles of their Institution, your Memorialists conceive themselves *bound to use all justifiable endeavours to loosen the bands of Slavery* and promote a general Enjoyment of the blessings of Freedom. Under these Impressions they earnestly intreat your serious attention to the Subject of Slavery, that you will be pleased to countenance the *Restoration of liberty* to those unhappy Men, who alone, in this land of Freedom, are degraded into perpetual Bondage, and who, amidst the general Joy of surrounding

Gary B. Nash, *Race and Revolution* (Madison, WI: Madison House, 1990), pp. 144–5.

Freemen, are groaning in Servile Subjection, that you will devise means for removing this *Inconsistency from the Character of the American People*; that you will promote Mercy and Justice towards this distressed Race, & that you will Step to the very verge of the Powers vested in you for discouraging every Species of Traffick in the Persons of our fellow Men.

B. Franklin

Presidt. of the Society

Philadelphia, *Feby.* 3d. 1790.

4

SLAVERY AND THE FOUNDING FATHERS

INTRODUCTION

The Founding Fathers of the United States were well aware of the contradiction between their espousal of political liberty at the time of the American Revolution and the continued presence of thousands of enslaved blacks throughout the new nation. Many leading American patriots saw themselves as throwing off the yoke of slavery they associated with continued membership of the British Empire, but leading political figures were more cautious in their public and private views on slavery. During the American Revolution a major transformation occurred in creating a republic based on federalism and enduring written constitutional principles; it failed, however, to resolve the stain of slavery even though it represented the best opportunity for doing so in North American history up to that time. Indeed, some historians now emphasise the way in which the Revolution entrenched and expanded the South's commitment to slavery while pointing to the lukewarm response of many northern states towards abolitionism.

A large, complex historiography has delineated the complexity of the Founding Fathers' views on race and slavery. Freehling's two essays (1972 and 1994) provide a good introduction to the main issues. Freehling shifted his interpretative stance over the course of a quarter of a century. In the earlier piece, he tackled the long-term impact of the Founding Fathers' interaction with slavery on antebellum America. He argued that the leaders of the new nation concentrated their energies on erecting a white man's republic, maintaining property rights and preserving a fragile American Union rather than pursuing antislavery ideals. They attacked the weak parts of a thriving slave system through abolitionism in the North, the passing of the Northwest Ordinance (1787) and the abolition of the African slave trade (1808) and, by so doing, were able to confine slavery to the Deep South. This essay therefore argues that the Founding Fathers proceeded cautiously because of larger political imperatives but that their actions counted in the long drive towards antislavery in the United States. Freehling's revised essay takes a more sceptical view. He now argues that the Founding Fathers failed to achieve a social revolution because they excluded slaves from the political changes ushered in by the new American republic. They delayed emancipation legislation in the northern states and expanded slaveholder power in the Lower South. In this revised version, Freehling refers to Jefferson as a 'conditional terminator', someone who could not conceive of acting against slavery without specifying conditions that were impossible to meet.

Davis (1975) and MacLeod (1974) both deal with the broad context for the Founding Fathers' interaction with slavery from the immediate pre-revolutionary period through to the Missouri crisis of 1819–21. Davis is particularly concerned to show that ideas about slavery were related to other intellectual currents of the late eighteenth- and early nineteenth-centuries with regard to politics, economics and free society. He dissects the ideological functions of British and American antislavery and finds significant differences between them. MacLeod's book is more concerned with the impact of American revolutionary ideology upon race and slavery. In particular, it demonstrates that the ambivalent position of slavery during the course of a libertarian revolution forced northerners and southerners to try to resolve publicly their uneasiness about slavery. This unfortunately led to a heightened defence of slavery by many southerners, focusing on the supposed inferiority of the enslaved population and the rise of social, economic and scientific sources of racism. Jordan (1968) has a subtle discussion of the evasions of the Founding Fathers on slavery. He looks at their failure to reconcile their insistence on natural rights with the Lockean heritage of the sanctity of property rights. By defending natural rights negatively, the revolutionary generation could sideline action on slavery.

Much discussion of the Founding Fathers' views on slavery has focused on the role played by three prominent Virginians, George Washington, James Madison and Thomas Jefferson. All were slaveholders from a state that included 40 per cent of the entire slaves in the United States at the time of the first Federal Census in 1790. They were all in a position to influence perceptions of slavery in the revolutionary era because of their elevated public status. Washington's leadership as commander-in-chief of the Continental army in the revolutionary war and first president of the United States gave him the most prestigious military and political positions in the young American republic and vantage points of great influence where the problem of slavery had to be addressed. Madison, as co-author of the *Federalist* papers, drafter of the Bill of Rights, and later fourth president, had the public position and intellectual capacity to offer a solution to the Pandora's box of slavery. Jefferson, as author of the Declaration of Independence, governor of Virginia and third president, also had the platform in public life and through his writings, to offer a lead to the nation on slavery.

Ketcham (1971) and McCoy (1994) show that Madison was uncomfortable with slavery from his young manhood and felt repugnance at the continuation of slavery in a young republic founded on principles of natural rights. He failed to free himself from dependence on slaves in the 1780s and failed to secure a law for the gradual abolition of slavery in Virginia. Throughout his public career Madison struggled to accept the continued existence of slavery in the United States and pursued schemes that he thought would eradicate it, but these all came to nothing. Like Jefferson, Madison advocated schemes for the removal of blacks to Africa; he believed that white Americans were not ready for the racial adjustment necessary to accept free blacks on an equal footing within the United States. McCoy (1989) looks at the views of Madison on slavery in his old age. Madison wanted slavery abolished in the United States but did not know when or how this would occur. He believed (as did others) that the continued existence of slavery damaged the moral force of American republican principles. Madison believed in the gradual emancipation of slaves, but with no timescale specified. He also thought that a racially integrated society was impossible in the United States by the 1820s and 1830s.

Hirschfeld (1997) focuses on the contradictions implied by Washington's stance on slavery. He argues that Washington's thinking on slavery evolved from being that of a conventional slaveholder to that of a lukewarm abolitionist. Washington could not speak out publicly about slavery, however, without taking steps to free the slaves at his Mount Vernon property and without contradicting the goals expressed in the Declaration of Independence, the Constitution and the Bill of Rights, and so he chose to remain silent on the issue. Schwarz (2001) is a collection of six essays dealing with Washington as a slaveowner. Material is included on Washington's slave management style, on the diversification of the skills among his labour force, and on the archaeological evidence for slave life at Mount Vernon.

Jefferson's ambivalent responses to slavery in the United States have attracted voluminous commentary, with sharply divergent positions taken by historians. Approaches to Jefferson and slavery are controversial, moreover, because of allegations that he fathered a black child with a mulatto mistress, Sally Hemings. Peterson (1970) found it difficult to imagine Jefferson having a miscegenous relationship: 'such a mixture of the races, such a ruthless exploitation of the master–slave relationship, revolted his whole being' (p. 707). He dismisses the Hemings story as fiction and suggests that Jefferson bequeathed to posterity an antislavery legacy. Miller (1977) similarly discounts the Hemings connection but is more critical of Jefferson's record on slavery. He argues that Jefferson emerges with more credit on slavery if he is judged by his words rather than by his deeds. Scientific evidence, based on DNA studies done in 1998, has shown that rumours about the intimate connection of Jefferson and Hemings were correct beyond reasonable doubt (see Document 3). The contributors to Lewis and Onuf (1999) accept the DNA evidence that Jefferson fathered a child with Hemings. Their contributions are helpful in dissecting the inter-racial social world inhabited by Jefferson.

Stanton (1993) provides the best discussion of the slaves under Jefferson's care at Monticello. She notes that Jefferson was a reluctant buyer and seller of slaves but that he also tried to make efficient use of his enslaved labour force. There was a vigorous musical tradition and story-telling culture among the slaves at Monticello. Jefferson disliked physical punishment of slaves. He wanted to reform the condition of his slaves, but it is difficult to tell how far any amelioration went.

Other historians are critical of Jefferson's stance on slavery, though the thrust of their attack varies. Cohen (1969) stresses Jefferson's limited role in counteracting slavery, pointing out that the failure of the Southwest Ordinance of 1784 was Jefferson's last public attempt to end slavery; thereafter his uneasiness about slavery was mainly confined to his private correspondence. Jordan (1968) emphasises Jefferson's anti-black stance on miscegenation, black sexuality and psychological repression. He follows the traditional view that Jefferson was trapped by a system of slavery he disliked but still considered blacks an inferior race. Finkelman (1993) admits that Jefferson had complex and contradictory attitudes towards slavery and that he tried to avoid discussion of the topic in public. But he also considers that Jefferson lacked a serious commitment to slave emancipation and therefore does not deserve his antislavery reputation. He argues that Jefferson failed to transcend his economic interests and sectional background with regard to slavery; he had a deep-seated negrophobia, feared that slaves would take revenge on their masters, and procrastinated on the subject of slavery.

Zuckerman (1993) takes a similarly harsh view of Jefferson. He views Jefferson as 'the foremost racist of his era in America', someone whose revulsion of blacks was highlighted in his horrified reaction to the Saint-Domingue slave revolt of 1791, a massive slave revolt in the French Caribbean that succeeded in overturning, for more than a decade, French colonial rule there. Zuckerman does not think that Jefferson was as troubled by slavery as some historians have argued; he was essentially negrophobic. Temperley (1997) offers a less harsh appraisal but still sees Jefferson's approach to slavery as one of moral perplexity. Finkelman (1996) is a set of essays on the Founding Fathers and slavery. It includes an effective demolition of Jefferson's antislavery credentials.

BIBLIOGRAPHY

Cohen, William, 'Thomas Jefferson and the Problem of Slavery', *Journal of American History*, 56 (1969), 503–26

Davis, David Brion, *The Problem of Slavery in the Age of Revolution, 1770–1823* (Ithaca, NY: Cornell University Press, 1975)

Finkelman, Paul, 'Jefferson and Slavery: "Treason against the hopes of the World"' in Peter S. Onuf (ed.), *Jeffersonian Legacies* (Charlottesville, VA: University Press of Virginia, 1993)

Finkelman, Paul, *Slavery and the Founders: Race and Liberty in the Age of Jefferson* (Armonk, NY: M. E. Sharpe, 1996, new edn, 2001)

Freehling, William W., 'The Founding Fathers and Slavery', *American Historical Review*, 77 (February 1972), 81–93

Freehling, William W., 'The Founding Fathers, Conditional Antislavery, and the Nonradicalism of the American Revolution' in his *The Reintegration of American History: Slavery and the Civil War* (New York: Oxford University Press, 1994)

Hirschfeld, Fritz, *George Washington and Slavery: A Documentary Reader* (Columbia: University of Missouri Press, 1997)

Jordan, Winthrop D., *White over Black: American Attitudes toward the Negro, 1550–1812* (Chapel Hill: University of North Carolina Press, 1968)

Ketcham, Ralph L., *James Madison: A Biography* (London: Macmillan, 1971)

Lewis, Jan Ellen and Onuf, Peter S. (eds), *Sally Hemings and Thomas Jefferson: History, Memory, and Civic Culture* (Charlottesville, VA: University Press of Virginia, 1999)

MacLeod, Duncan J., *Slavery, Race, and the American Revolution* (Cambridge: Cambridge University Press, 1974)

McCoy, Drew R., *The Last of the Fathers: James Madison and the Republican Legacy* (Cambridge, MA: Harvard University Press, 1989)

McCoy, Drew R., 'Slavery' in Robert A. Rutland (ed.), *James Madison and the American Nation, 1751–1836: An Encyclopedia* (New York: Simon and Schuster, 1994)

Miller, John C., *The Wolf by the Ears: Thomas Jefferson and Slavery* (New York: Free Press, 1977)

Morgan, Kenneth, 'George Washington and the Problem of Slavery', *Journal of American Studies*, 34 (2000), 279–301

Peterson, Merrill D., *Thomas Jefferson and the New Nation: A Biography* (New York: Oxford University Press, 1970)

Schwarz, Philip J. (ed.), *Slavery at the Home of George Washington* (Mount Vernon, VA: Mount Vernon Ladies' Association, 2001)

Stanton, Lucia C., ' "Those who Labor for my Happiness": Thomas Jefferson and his slaves' in Peter S. Onuf (ed.), *Jeffersonian Legacies* (Charlottesville, VA: University Press of Virginia, 1993)

Temperley, Howard, 'Jefferson and Slavery: A Study in Moral Perplexity' in Gary L. McDowell and Sharon L. Noble (eds), *Reason and Republicanism: Thomas Jefferson's Legacy of Liberty* (Lanham, MD: Rowman & Littlefield, 1997)

Zuckerman, Michael, *Almost Chosen People: Oblique Biographies in the American Grain* (Berkeley and Los Angeles: University of California Press, 1993)

ESSAY: GEORGE WASHINGTON AND THE PROBLEM OF SLAVERY

Morgan's essay (2000) shows that Washington expressed much dissatisfaction with the slave system and was forced to articulate his views on slavery by having to deal with the problem of whether to arm blacks in the revolutionary war. How far did Washington's public cautiousness on the question of slavery stem from his sense of the divisive nature of slavery in the young republic? Do you agree with the article's argument that one can trace in Washington's private meetings and correspondence an increasing, if circumspect, sympathy for abolitionism from the end of the revolutionary war onwards? Washington was the only Founding Father to free a significant number of his slaves. Does this suggest that he should be given more credit in promoting freedom for slaves than Madison or Jefferson?

Slavery was not the most important issue for which George Washington is remembered; nor were his views on the institution as revealing as those of some of his fellow Founding Fathers. But Washington was a slaveowner for all of his adult life and he lived in Virginia, which was dominated by tobacco plantations based on slave labour. Slavery was central to the socio-economic life of the Old Dominion: after 1750 40 percent of the North American slave population lived there and the first United States census of 1790 showed 300,000 slaves in Virginia. The tobacco they produced was the most valuable staple crop grown in North America.[1] At his home Mount Vernon, situated on the upper Potomac river overlooking the Maryland shore, Washington created an estate, based on the latest agricultural practice, that was also a set of plantation farms centred around the work of enslaved Africans. Slavery, then, was clearly a persistent part of Washington's life and career. Because of this and his pre-eminent position in American public life, Washington's use of slave labour and his views on an important paradox of American history in the revolutionary era – the coexistence of slavery and liberty – deserve close attention. One man's dilemma in dealing with the morality of his own slaveholding was mirrored in the broader context of what the United States could or would do about the problem of slavery.

The evolution of Washington's ideas on the peculiar institution, however, was confined mainly to private remarks in his diary and in correspondence, occasional at first but fuller as he grew older and as the blight of slavery in the midst of a new republic founded upon notions of equality and natural rights theory became more apparent.[2] Washington did not write essays, tracts or memorials on slavery and made few public pronouncements on

---

Kenneth Morgan, 'George Washington and the Problem of Slavery', *Journal of American Studies*, 34 (2000), pp. 279–301.

the subject. To some extent this reflected his personal reserve: he was the least eloquent of the Founding Fathers and did not advance arguments on the problem of slavery that matched the intellectual calibre of, say, Thomas Jefferson or James Madison. On slavery, as on other issues, Washington's circumspect comments might lead us to view him as a sphinx without a riddle. Nevertheless, Washington's approach to slavery, both at Mount Vernon and more broadly in public life, changed over time, became more complex, and revealed the unresolvable problems of race relations in the era of the American Revolution and the birth of the republic. This article examines these themes in relation to the public and private arenas of Washington's life. It also compares and contrasts Washington's views on slavery with those of his fellow Virginians, including several Founding Fathers, to analyse the distinctiveness and the commonalities of his attitudes towards slavery. Such a detailed appraisal of Washington's views on slavery within the context outlined has attracted relatively little attention from historians.[3]

Mount Vernon consisted of a main tract of 2,126 acres plus a smaller separate tract of 172 acres when Washington inherited it in 1754. The acquisition of new land during Washington's lifetime increased the size of the property to at least 7,500 acres by the mid-1790s.[4] This made it a substantial agricultural estate. Washington oversaw five farms at Mount Vernon – Muddy Hole, Dogue Run, River, Ferry and Home House. Slaves were kept on each of these properties and lived on the farm where they were assigned to work rather than in family units, though they moved regularly from one farm to another.[5] Washington could not give the estate his full attention while undertaking military service in the Seven Years War and the revolutionary war, or when absent on public duties later in life. In those periods, he left the estate in the care of managers and maintained regular correspondence about the state of his crops, the behaviour of the slave workforce and the difficulties of plantation management. But from the mid-1780s onwards, in particular, he was directly involved in running the Mount Vernon estate, and it is from this period that his most illuminating comments on slavery can be found.

Washington's initial involvement in slavery arose through inheritance. His father left him about ten or a dozen slaves.[6] He inherited slaves as his share of his deceased half-brother Lawrence's will, after the death of his niece Sarah in 1754; and he also received some slaves bequeathed by Ann, Lawrence's wife, when she died in 1761. Added to this, Washington gained effective legal right to his wife's property, including her dower slaves, when he married Martha, the widow of Daniel Parke Custis, in January 1759.[7] Washington regularly recorded the number of his slaves and listed their occupations.[8] His Mount Vernon census of February 1786, for instance, referred to 216 slaves, among whom were 86 field hands plus four carpenters, three coopers, three drivers and stablers, and one gardener.[9] Washington was then the largest slaveowner in Fairfax County, Virginia, where his extensive slaveholdings were situated in the area of highest slave density and in the largest settled area of that county. He also owned extensive land tracts in other Virginian counties.[10] By 1799 Washington's slave labour force had increased significantly. It now totalled 317 people, including some 143 children.[11]

Washington's views about Mount Vernon and his slave charges were a mixture of commercial, patriarchal and paternalist attitudes. Sometimes one of these three models dominated his behaviour as a planter, but it would be simplistic to separate them into distinct modes of thought; they intermingled to make up a complex view of slavery. Washington took a commercial view of slavery as a business, wanting to make profits from tobacco and grain cultivation, oversee agricultural improvements and keep debts to a minimum. This outlook underscored the fact that the Mount Vernon slaves were his chattels. He also had patriarchal attitudes that he had absorbed from the planter culture of his youth in Virginia.[12] These manifested themselves in strict control of slaves after the manner of a father figure looking after dependants; they meant that he acted distantly and sometimes rigorously towards his slaves. But paternalistic elements also existed in his outlook: these were reflected mainly in his concern for slave families and their personal relationships and in his dislike of splitting up slaves who had established such personal and familial ties. Washington realized his control of African Americans required mutual obligations even though he did not identify emotionally with their plight. It is not surprising that each of the three models – commercial, patriarchal, paternalist – underpinned Washington's personal dealings with slaves, for all appear to have been in a state of redefinition in North America in the last quarter of the eighteenth century.[13]

Washington administered his Mount Vernon farms with a meticulous eye for detail. He wanted a productive agricultural estate but also one that ran smoothly. Setting out detailed memoranda about the costs of slaveholding, his aim, as he put it, was for 'tranquillity with a *certain* income'.[14] To maximize the use of slave labour, he sometimes shifted workers around the Mount Vernon farms; there are examples of his dower slaves being moved from Tidewater Virginia to his New Ferry farm.[15] Though he complained about the costs of slavery, the scarcity of hired labour south of Pennsylvania made the alternatives to using slaves an expensive option.[16] Moreover, the trade in indentured and convict servants from the British Isles to the Chesapeake had ended with the Revolution, cutting off the obvious alternative labour supply.[17] Over time, Washington underwrote the expense of housing a growing number of slaves, many of whom were domestic workers surplus to the requirements of field work.[18] He struggled to maintain profits at Mount Vernon and faced growing debts there towards the end of his life. Indeed, it seems that he rarely profited from slavery financially.[19] Finding his estate overstocked with slaves and needing to reduce expenses, Washington suggested in 1799 that he move some supernumerary hands from Mount Vernon to some of his tenements in Berkeley and Frederick counties. This plan did not materialize. In fact, Washington did not want his Mount Vernon property to be broken up; such a move, he felt, would be economically ruinous and, as we shall see, difficult for his slaves.[20]

Washington mainly employed white overseers at Mount Vernon, though he also tried out some black superintendents, who were either dower slaves or mulattos.[21] Some of these men turned out to be poor appointments: on one occasion Washington referred to rascally overseers taking advantage of him in his absence.[22] But he tried hard to regulate their behaviour. He instructed them to produce a good crop of tobacco and corn and requested that they treat the slaves 'with proper humanity and discretion'.[23] He wanted overseers to treat sick slaves with care and to deliver their meals regularly. On the other hand, overseers were expected to prevent slaves from running about and unnecessarily visiting each other when well.[24] Washington believed that slaves who were looked after by humane owners should not be sold or split up from their families. In this respect he had similar views to Jefferson, who also realized the importance of family bonds for his slaves.[25] Thus Washington disliked slaves being put up for auction, like cattle in a market, and he would not buy or sell slaves when personal relationships were likely to be broken up.[26] 'If these poor wretches are to be held in a state of slavery', he once remarked, 'I do not see that a change of masters will render it more irksome, provided husband and wife, and Parents and children are not separated from each other, which is not my Intentions to do'.[27] Interestingly, when Washington listed his slaves in 1799, at the end of his life, nearly all were specified as having partners, with many living as man and wife and others maintaining close relationships across the five Mount Vernon farms.[28] However, the residence of each slave was determined by the labour and production needs of the different farms; some of the married slaves did not therefore live in the same dwellings as their spouses.[29]

Washington's engrained sense of racial superiority to African Americans did not lead to expressions of negrophobia. In this respect he can be contrasted with Madison, who never expressed sentiments that blacks were inferior to whites, and with Jefferson, whose negrophobia is evident in his *Notes on the State of Virginia* and his reaction to the impact of the Saint Domingue slave rebellion on the United States.[30] Yet Washington wanted his white workers to be housed away from the blacks at Mount Vernon, believing that close racial intermixture was undesirable.[31] The blacks still needed decent treatment, however. Concerned about the welfare of his slaves, Washington criticized overseers who had an uncaring attitude, especially those who 'seem to consider a Negro more in the same light as they do the brute beasts, on the farms; and often times treat them as inhumanly'.[32] He was kind towards blacks who had assisted him personally, such as William Lee, a mulatto and a loyal personal servant throughout the late colonial and revolutionary years.[33] Visitors to Mount Vernon commented on Washington's good treatment of African Americans. A French *savant* wrote that the slaves there were 'well fed, well clothed, and required to do only a moderate amount of work'.[34] One Polish visitor, who left a detailed account of his visit to Mount Vernon, stated unequivocally that Washington treated his slaves far more humanely than his fellow Virginian citizens, most of whom 'give to their Blacks only bread, water and blows'.[35] These comments may have been somewhat exaggerated; yet the control of slaves at Mount Vernon seems to have been milder than one finds with many other planters, whether in the Chesapeake, South Carolina or the West Indies.[36] The beneficent side of Washington's treatment of slaves is illustrated in Junius Brutus Stearns' painting *Washington as a Farmer at Mount Vernon*, which depicts him paternally overseeing his slaves and his stepgrandchildren.

Though Washington's personal concern for slaves' welfare permeated many remarks in his writings, he still treated his black charges rigorously. Overseers were instructed to ensure that slaves worked hard; the blacks were to begin work as soon as daylight came and to labour diligently until darkness fell. Washington advocated a strong work ethic; he believed that 'lost labour can never be regained'.[37] In his view Mount Vernon had a plentiful supply of workers except for ditching and, apart from some seasonal work or in exceptional circumstances, there was no need to supplement the slaves' labour. To ensure productivity, overseers were instructed to stay with slaves and keep an eye on their work routines. They also had to ensure that slaves were fully occupied in winter.[38] Washington wanted his overseers to get slaves working as soon as they were fit to do so because he expected 'to reap the benefit of their labour myself'.[39] Lying behind these comments seems to have been a sense that slavery adapted itself poorly as an institution to the agricultural progress Washington wished to achieve as an innovative planter.[40]

Washington's strict control of his slave charges manifested itself in other ways. He was parsimonious in spending on clothes and bedding for his slaves, and only provided them with just enough food.[41] Overseers were expected to implement a strict meal allowance for slaves, feeding sufficiently but no more. They were also enjoined to cut down on waste at harvest time.[42] The slaves were expected to contribute to their own living expenses, for Washington commented in the revolutionary years that they 'have a just claim to their Victuals and cloaths, if they make enough to purchase them'.[43] Sometimes Washington acted as a patriarch who was not impressed by the general conduct of slaves. He disliked feigned illnesses among his workers, hated slave idleness, and found that his enslaved blacks stole corn, meat, apples and cattle frequently. He instructed overseers to whip recalcitrant slaves. This harsh treatment of slaves was not as pervasive as one finds with a Virginia planter such as Landon Carter, but it was imbued with the same disciplinary aspects of patriarchalism.[44] According to a contemporary visitor, Washington could speak to blacks in a sterner voice than he usually did, 'as differently as if he had been quite another man, or had been in anger'. This particular observer felt that Washington's skill in handling slaves derived from the regularity and methodical practices he learned during his military career.[45]

In his early years at Mount Vernon, Washington sometimes bought slaves. Between 1754 and 1768, for example, he purchased forty-three slaves partly because he needed to support his family expenses.[46] To a limited extent some of these purchases were substitutions for runaway slaves to which Washington, like other slaveowners, was prone.[47] Washington, like Jefferson, was intensely irritated by runaway slaves; sometimes he did not want them back once they had strayed. He felt that slaves who had escaped bondage could not be returned to their chattel condition and resume being passive, obedient, useful workers.[48] Over time, however, Washington realized that Mount Vernon was overstocked with black labourers. In 1778, in a cryptic aside, he noted that he had slaves 'of whom I everyday long more and more to get clear of', a comment made just after a remark about the difficulty of his estate supporting itself financially.[49] At the end of his life he had more slaves than he could use for farming. As early as the 1760s he began to transfer from tobacco cultivation to wheat, corn, rye and oat production, commodities that required less labour input than tobacco; he had abandoned tobacco cultivation by the 1780s. He admitted that he did not know what to do with his surplus slaves.[50]

It is apparent that Washington expressed a fair amount of dissatisfaction with the system of chattel slavery. Why, it must then be asked, did he not free his slaves during his lifetime? To answer this question, one needs to look at the private and public contexts of his life. The private reasons for Washington's disinclination to sell or free his slaves stemmed not so much from a commitment to running Mount Vernon profitably, for we have noted the surplus labourers there, but from his genuine difficulty about envisaging the conditions under which slaves could be freed. The two views were inextricably linked in his thinking; the agriculturist and the businessman was never disentangled from the slaveowner. Washington's commercial outlook made him conceive of slaves as chattel upon whose head a price could be calculated; and, despite his protestations about being overstocked with slaves, he did not intend to diminish or lose what to him was an important investment, unless he benefited financially. Instances can be found of Washington selling slaves to pay taxes, renting out his own slaves, and hiring them from others.[51] In 1786, Washington wrote that he never wanted to purchase another slave unless there were particular circumstances. In using a phrase that crops up several times in his letters, he referred to 'that species of property which I have no inclination to possess'.[52]

That phrase nevertheless conceals as much as it reveals. When tempted to sell slaves, Washington was reluctant to do so on personal and economic grounds. Similarly, when he advanced arguments for not buying slaves, he qualified the issue by suggesting a price that might be acceptable or keeping open the option of purchase. During the revolutionary war he calculated that if a male slave sold for £1,000, with women and children fetching a proportionate price, it would be in his interest to sell them. But he also worried that he would not achieve good prices for slaves because of depreciating wartime currency in Virginia, and so he decided not to sell.[53] In 1786 Washington stated that it was 'a great repugnance' for him to buy more slaves, but then purchased six more. Shortly afterwards he wrote that he had no predilection or call for new slaves, but then offered money for slaves he was prepared to buy.[54] The number of people involved was always in single figures; he never bought large slave parcels after the American Revolution. His surplus labourers plus the natural growth and geographical spread of the Virginian slave population made this unnecessary.[55] Washington's buying and selling of slaves occurred on a limited and strictly controlled basis. Jefferson, by contrast, bought and sold slaves with much greater freedom, even when he was president.[56]

Washington made few public pronouncements on slavery. An older historian once explained this by stating that Washington 'probably never deeply concerned himself with this phase of the subject, being content to abide by the opinions of the majority'.[57] This explanation of the first president's non-committal approach to public discussion of slavery is too simplistic, however. Washington's cautiousness was not merely temperamental but stemmed from his sense of his own leadership positions and from the divisive nature of slavery in the young republic. As Commander-in-Chief of the Continental Army during the American Revolution, chairman of the Constitutional Convention in Philadelphia in 1787, and first President of the United States of America, Washington knew that the eminence of his public positions made it imprudent for him to speak openly about slavery. At the same time his burgeoning public career gave him wider experience of travel, military action, politics and diplomacy that enabled him to appreciate the complexity of the problem of slavery in a broader context within a nation that had proclaimed as its touchstone that all men are created equal.

Washington was present at a number of public occasions where slavery could not be ignored. At the beginning of the revolutionary war, the Council of War at Cambridge, Massachusetts, at which Washington was present, rejected having slaves in the Continental Army, a position reiterated by the Continental Congress.[58] The position was different for free Negroes. On 30 December 1775 Washington wrote in his orderly book that, since a number of free blacks wished to enlist, he would bring the matter before Congress, which he felt would approve of their inclusion in the army. The desired outcome soon arose. On 16 January 1776 Congress resolved that free blacks who had served faithfully in the army at Cambridge could enlist but no others: slaves were excluded from American armies.[59]

Washington stated that he had not given much thought to the position of slaves in the War of Independence; but he was worried that arming them would cause the British forces to follow suit, and that enlisting slaves while they remained chattels would cause serious problems.[60] He came around to the view that the outcome of the war depended 'on which side can arm the Negroes the faster'.[61] As the conflict dragged on he urged that slaves be enlisted with the promise of freedom at the war's end.[62] Yet at the conclusion of hostilities Washington was adamant that blacks should not be allowed to escape with the retreating forces; he regarded this as a violation of the preliminary articles of peace signed at Paris on 30 November 1782. He also wanted any of his own slaves who were thinking of running away prevented from doing so.[63] On 6 May 1783 at Orangetown, New York, Washington held a conference with Sir Guy Carleton, the British Commander-in-Chief, to discuss the recovery of American blacks evacuated with the British towards the end of the war. At least as many as 80,000 slaves had quit the United States by this means. Washington failed to win the argument: the British view prevailed. To prevent a resumption of war, Washington and Congress accepted the loss of slaves manumitted by the British forces before the provisional peace treaty was signed, acknowledging the British desire to redeem promises made to black American troops that had fought with them.[64] Though the Americans did not gain all they wanted during the peace negotiations, the debate over the inclusion or exclusion of blacks from the Continental army challenged them to articulate their views on blacks publicly; it also served to deepen Washington's awareness of the moral complexity of changing the status of blacks.[65] At the end of the war, none the less, Washington's speeches contained no reference to slavery.

The year 1783 seems to have been a turning-point in Washington's attitude towards the future of slavery in North America. Along with other leading public figures in the United States, he did not see abolition as an extreme or forlorn hope. He signed a copy of one of the leading abolitionist tracts published in that year, the Quaker David Cooper's *A Serious Address to the Rulers of America, on the Inconsistency of their Conduct respecting Slavery . . .*, printed at Trenton, New Jersey.[66] In 1783 his friend the Marquis de Lafayette began to persuade Washington of the need for action over the plight of slaves. Lafayette suggested they should jointly purchase a small estate where they would employ only free blacks as tenant labourers, seeing this as an experiment that might set an example and be replicated in the West Indies.[67] Lafayette realized this was a madcap scheme, but he soon pressed ahead with acquiring a plantation in Cayenne on which he employed only free Negroes.[68] Washington praised this experiment but noted that the question of abolitionism had not yet generally penetrated the minds of the American people.[69] This, after all, was during the 1780s when even the British battle against the slave trade, let alone slavery itself, was only just gaining momentum; and British abolitionist sympathizers, like the Americans, saw this as a two-stage process, with abolition of the slave trade coming first, to be followed later by slave emancipation. Nor should we forget that moves towards black freedom in America's northern states were, at this time, often very gradual indeed: many statutes granted freedom only for future-born children of slaves at ages between twenty-one and twenty-eight.[70]

Evidence of Washington's increasing, if cautious, sympathy for abolitionism can be glimpsed in his private correspondence and meetings – for instance, in response to Thomas Coke and Francis Asbury's visit to Mount Vernon in 1785. The two prominent Methodists showed him their petition for slave emancipation. Though he did not sign it, Washington privately agreed with their sentiments and noted that he had conveyed his views to other leading Virginians. He agreed to send a supportive letter to the state assembly if it were to consider the petition.[71] Nothing further came of this, but lingering hopes for some form of abolitionism remained in Washington's mind. Washington confessed in a letter to Robert Morris – former superintendent of finance – that he sincerely wanted to see a plan adopted for the abolition of slavery in the United States, but that legislative authority to do so was needed.[72] He also discussed with a French visitor to Mount Vernon his desire to see slavery end, yet noted that this would not occur immediately and that 'time, patience and education' were needed.[73]

Within Virginia, the legal means were available to manumit slaves. Between 1723 and 1782 only the governor and council could free a slave in the Old Dominion, but the law was changed in 1782 to allow masters to free slaves individually or in groups.[74] Unfortunately, though many Virginians shared an uneasiness about slavery, vigorous opposition to abolition existed at legislative level: in 1785 a proposal to bring about this very situation was defeated in the House of Delegates.[75] Washington hoped the Virginia legislature would none the less abolish slavery 'by slow, sure, & imperceptable degrees'.[76] Later he wrote: 'I wish from my soul that the Legislature of this state could see the policy of a gradual Abolition of slavery; it would prev[en]t much future mischief'.[77] At the time there seemed no hope for such a policy in Virginia. Those Virginians, like Washington, who were troubled by the continuation of slavery in their midst had to bow to a political atmosphere that opposed their views – something readily apparent in the proslavery petitions drawn up in several Virginia counties in 1785.[78] Some Virginian planters, such as Washington's neighbour George Mason, despised the slave system but foresaw no possibility of an immediate end to slavery.[79]

Despite these problems, some progress towards freeing slaves occurred, but slowly and on a piecemeal basis. In the 1790s hundreds of Virginian masters began to free their slaves, but they usually manumitted only small numbers of black workers. Even exceptions to this rule, such as Robert Carter of Nomini Hall, arranged to manumit slaves over a long time span (in Carter's case some 509 blacks over twenty-two years, not all of whom were in fact eventually freed). Though the free black population grew rapidly at this time in the upper Chesapeake, the institution of slavery became an ever more deeply entrenched southern hallmark. In 1793 Virginia prohibited the immigration of free blacks into the state, and opponents of manumission in Virginia were vociferous.[80] There was no prospect of immediate abolition in the United States; even many abolitionists did not make the transition from gradualism to immediatism before the 1820s, and those who spoke of the gradual abolition of slavery before then were vague, as Washington himself was, about the timing of the process.[81]

A public opportunity for Washington to grapple with slavery came in Philadelphia in the summer of 1787, when he was one of nineteen slave-holders among the fifty-five delegates to the Constitutional Convention.[82] During proceedings, the issue of slavery delayed the work of the commit-tee and nearly caused the adjournment of that body. Securing clauses in the United States Constitution that counted slaves as three-fifths of white men for purposes of taxation and political representation, and inserting the fugitive slave clause, without even so much as mentioning the word slave, were only arrived at after much heated debate between northern and south-ern delegates.[83] There were periods during the Constitutional Convention when Washington acted as chairman and thus could not speak to the sub-ject. There were also times when he joined fellow delegates on the floor and, in theory, was entitled to debate this and other issues. Some of the extended debate about slavery at the Convention took place while he was in the chair and some while he was on the floor.[84] He chose to say nothing. Recognizing his public and symbolic role as figurehead for the revolution and the new nation, he realized that to speak out on such a sensitive issue would be foolhardy. Washington knew of his fame and of the need to pre-serve what he referred to as his 'line of conduct' for the greater good of a newly independent people.[85] In sending the final draft of the Constitution to Congress, Washington enclosed a letter that referred to 'the consolidation of our Union' as 'the greatest interest of every true American'. This Consti-tution, he contended, was 'the result of a spirit of amity, and of that mutual deference and concession which the peculiarity of our political situation rendered indispensable'.[86]

During the public debate over the Constitution, some criticisms of Washington's position were made. The chief accusation was that he had secured fame for himself while remaining a slaveholder at a time when pub-lic discourse emphasized notions of liberty. 'Oh! Washington, what a name he has had! How he has immortalized himself!' cried one contributor to the debates in the Massachusetts convention for ratification of the Consti-tution. The criticism continued: 'but he holds those in slavery who have as good a right to be free as he has – He is still for self; and in my opin-ion, his character has sunk 50 per cent'.[87] An article in the *Massachusetts Gazette* echoed these sentiments. It extolled Washington's illustrious role at the Constitutional Convention, but added: 'notwithstanding he wielded the sword in defence of American liberty, yet at the same time was, and is to this day, living upon the labours of several hundreds of miserable Africans, as freeborn as himself'.[88] There is no record of whether Washington knew of these criticisms of his conduct with regard to slavery. But they were made in places that attracted wide interest among those following the leading public issues of the day, and we know that Washington keenly followed the ratification of the Constitution at state level.[89] Even if Washington did not hear the dissenting critiques, the points made reveal the sensitivity of his continuing role as slaveholder in the new nation.

During his years as president, Washington continued to wrestle with the problem of slavery and abolition. The leading advocates of abolition in a transatlantic context in the late eighteenth century were the Quakers, who were deeply committed to this reform issue on humanitarian grounds; they believed, *inter alia*, in the equality of all men before God, and could not accept the capturing of slaves through violence or warfare. Washington considered, however, that the Quaker abolitionist crusade was rash, and that its interference with slavery south of Pennsylvania was uncalled for and likely to cause more evil than it cured.[90] In March 1790 the Quakers presented several memorials to Congress over the abolition of the slave trade, but a House of Representatives committee had resolved that Congress could not abolish the slave trade to the United States before 1808, the date already agreed at the constitutional convention. In addition, Congress could not interfere over the matter of abolitionism or the internal regulation of individual states pertaining to slavery.[91] Washington refused to discuss the Society of Friends' position when visited privately by the prominent Quaker abolitionist Warner Mifflin in 1790. Since it was an issue that might well come before him as president for an official decision, he was not disposed to discuss the matter beforehand.[92] Washington thought this abolitionist attempt by the Quakers was very poorly timed: 'The memorial of the Quakers (& a very malapropos one it was) has at length been put to sleep, from which it is not [illegible] it will awake before the year 1808'.[93] He added later that the Quaker petitions were 'not only an ill-judged piece of business, but occasioned a great waste of time. The final decision thereon, however, was as favourable as the proprietors of that species of property could well have expected considering the great dereliction to Slavery in a large part of this Union'.[94] These views were expressed privately. In public, Washington dealt with the Quakers carefully because he was then living in Philadelphia and did not want to appear to be acting against the Pennsylvania abolition statute of 1780.[95] This explains also why he surreptitiously arranged for some slaves he had taken with him to Philadelphia to be sent back to Virginia, where they would remain slaves.[96]

In his next public opportunity to display his views on slavery, Washington signed the Fugitive slave law of 1793 that enabled slaveowners to cross state lines to recapture slave runaways.[97] This is in keeping with Washington's antipathy towards slave runaways and his need to support entrenched southern interests. But the spectre of slave revolt did not elicit much commentary from him. He referred to the Saint Domingue slave rebellion of 1791, the first and only successful black slave uprising in Western history, as 'the unfortunate insurrection of the Negroes in Hispaniola' and wondered where the spirit of revolt among the black slaves would stop; but he left matters there even though he received correspondence and memorials about the event over the next two years.[98] For Washington the Haitian revolution, with its radical implications for resistance in slave societies, did not have the impact it made on Jefferson or the black community in Virginia; or, to put it differently, it did not cause him to articulate, either in private correspondence or public statements, the fears of other slaveholders.[99] When Washington gave his Farewell Address in 1796, he remained silent on slavery. No doubt he wanted to present a harmonious message in handing on his executive position, and was aware that his position as first president of the United States would earmark his words for posterity. By the time he left the presidency, of course, developments had begun to tackle the blot of slavery in an era concerned with political and humanitarian progress: there was a ban set upon the growth of slavery in the first five states of the old Northwest under the Northwest Ordinance of 1787, and the northern states had either introduced legislation to abolish slavery within their boundaries or had set in train policies that would eventually have the same effect. Washington accepted these developments without any comment. It would be wrong to conclude, however, that his public reticence on the problem of slavery meant that he was not developing ideas about the future of African Americans in the United States.

When Washington died in late 1799, he owned 124 of his own slaves plus 40 that were leased; there were also 153 dower slaves on his estate.[100] In other words, he did not own most of the Mount Vernon slaves outright. In old age he thought carefully about what to do with these people. At this stage the public and private arenas of his approach to slavery coalesced. In what can be regarded as a private document essentially concerned with personal inheritance and a public statement of his position on slavery, Washington dealt with the plight of his own slaves, and implicitly signalled his intentions for the American republic, in his last will and testament.[101] Apart from the section dealing with his wife, the longest part of his twenty-nine page will consisted of arrangements made for his slaves. In that document he decreed that his own slaves should be freed but only after his wife's death; he had no legal power over the dower slaves. Remembering that Martha's slaves and his own had conducted long-established personal relationships, he was convinced these would be broken up if he arranged for his slaves to be emancipated after his death.[102] Washington made generous provision for his faithful slave William Lee, granting him food, clothing and $30 a year for the rest of his life. He charged his executors with responsibility for the care of old and disabled slaves, arranged for lifelong support for blacks on the estate, and made special arrangements for the welfare and education of estate workers aged under twenty-five.[103]

Perhaps the most revealing indication of Washington's thoughts about slavery and his hopes for its eradication are found in a remark made in his voice by David Humphreys, who served as his military aide during the revolutionary war and who lived at Mount Vernon at Washington's invitation from 1786 to 1789. Humphreys came to know Washington well and regularly discussed his career and outlook on life with him. His unpublished life of Washington has recently been edited and published.[104] In this source Humphreys attributed these words to Washington: 'The unfortunate condition of the persons whose labour in part I employed, has been the only unavoidable subject of regret. To make the Adults among them as easy & comfortable in their circumstances as their actual state of ignorance & improvidence would admit; & to lay a foundation to prepare the rising generation for a destiny different from that in which they were born; afforded some satisfaction to my mind, & could not I hoped be displeasing to the justice of the Creator'.[105]

Washington's public positions precluded him from taking action against slavery because he was committed to the unity of the new nation and realized all too well how Federal interference with slavery would tear the nation asunder. It is also true, of course, that he genuinely did not know what to do about the problem of slavery. His need to run his Mount Vernon estate without recourse to satisfactory alternative cheap labour and his control of the African Americans he owned also made him retain his slaves. Before the War of Independence, he expressed few doubts about the morality of slavery. But the pressing problem of what to do about incorporating blacks into the continental army forced him to give the matter serious thought. Thus the revolutionary war was the crucial turning-point in his thinking about slavery. After 1783, under pressure from abolitionists and aware of the intense debates over the future of slavery in the new nation, he began to express inner tensions about the problem of slavery more frequently, though always in private and not in eloquent prose. This occurred despite the fact that in old age he noted that he did not 'like to think, much less talk' of slavery.[106] In most cases his comments on slavery occurred only after he had been asked to address the topic; this is true of his encounters with the Methodists, the Quakers and Lafayette. He did not usually volunteer opinions on slavery of his own accord. Revealingly, however, he once remarked to his one-time military aide Edmund Randolph, sometime governor of Virginia and the first US attorney general, that if slavery continued to divide America 'he had made up his mind to move and be of the northern'.[107] In public, however, he maintained a deliberate silence, on slavery, partly to help preserve the potentially fragile unity of the new nation, and partly because he seemed to have little specific notion that emancipation could come soon in Virginia or what shape or form it could take.

To many modern historians Washington appears to be a classic example of someone who vacillated over slavery; one could argue that to free one's slaves in one's will is a cowardly act because the social consequences of freedom would not be witnessed. 'President Washington profited from his slaves while living', William W. Freehling has noted, 'and then freed them in his last will and testament'.[108] According to James T. Flexner, Washington 'chose to ignore the situation Martha would find herself in when some hundred and fifty individuals eagerly awaited her death to set them free'.[109] Historians who agree with these tart remarks might add that Washington's sympathy with gradual abolition and emphasis on keeping slave families together conflicted with his continued buying and selling of slaves; and that to adopt such a contradictory position seems either hypocritical or ambiguous. The cynical might add that signalling freedom for his slaves in his will was an easy decision since he had no direct male heirs. Critics might also consider that the eminence of Washington's position in American public life was a useful excuse for him to avoid determined action over slavery, and that, even without that position, his actions might not have been significantly different. These interpretations are based, of course, on the knowledge of hindsight and some are speculative, reminding us that slavery is a perennial topic where values cannot be divorced from historical analysis.[110]

Those who criticize Washington's views on slavery should nevertheless recognize the significant development in his views on the subject over the course of forty years. His ideas on slavery evolved and became more complex over time as his dual career in public life and as a Virginian farmer progressed and his horizons expanded. He found the whole question of slavery distasteful, but could not see any labour alternative to the extensive use of slaves in the Chesapeake economy. In addition to the explanations offered above, his silence in the public domain on slavery could be interpreted in a positive light: to allow the progress that the revolutionary generation had made over manumission in the northern states to proceed without hindrance and to hope in due course that the Virginian legislature would change its position on abolition. Washington recognized that such a shift in a state that had been tied to slavery for one-and-a-half centuries would not occur overnight and that some form of gradualism would be the solution. There can be no denying that Washington's comments on slavery contained many ambiguous elements. But it should be remembered that, though some contemporary Virginians freed their slaves, Washington was the only Founding Father to make legal arrangements to free all of his slaves, most of which – with the exception of the dower slaves – were manumitted by his widow at the end of 1800, the earliest date that granting their freedom was legally possible.[111] Two other leading Founding Fathers, by contrast, had a poorer record on slavery. In his will Jefferson emancipated only 5 slaves and sent off another 200 for auction. Madison's will did not free any of his slaves. Both Jefferson and Madison could not foresee blacks living a peaceful co-existence with whites in the United States, and that is why they favoured schemes for the recolonization of American blacks overseas. However one interprets Washington's position on slavery, he did do something finally in a personal sense to assist his own slaves, and he never succumbed to these extreme solutions for dealing with the racial divide in the United States.[112]

NOTES

1. Jim Potter, 'Demographic Development and Family Structure', in Jack P. Greene and J. R. Pole, eds., *Colonial British America: Essays in the New History of the Early Modern Era* (Baltimore, 1984), 138–9.
2. Edmund S. Morgan, 'Slavery and Freedom: The American Paradox', *JAH*, 59 (1972), 5–29, reprinted in his *The Challenge of the American Revolution* (New York, 1976), 139–73.
3. Older discussions of the topic are Walter H. Mazyck, *George Washington and the Negro* (Washington, D.C., 1932) and Matthew T. Mellon, *Early American Views on Negro Slavery* (Boston, 1934), 38–85. A recent overview is Fritz Hirschfeld, *George Washington and Slavery: A Documentary Portrayal* (Columbia, Mo., 1997).
4. Donald Jackson and Dorothy Twohig, eds., *The Diaries of George Washington*, 6 vols (Charlottesville, Va., 1976–79), 1, 240–2.
5. Donald M. Sweig, 'Slavery in Fairfax County, Virginia 1750–1860: A Research Report', unpublished typescript, History and Archaeology Section, Office of Comprehensive Planning, Virginia, 1983, 23–5.
6. Paul Leland Haworth, *George Washington: Farmer* (Indianapolis, 1915), 192.
7. W. W. Abbot, Dorothy Twohig et al., eds., *The Papers of George Washington: Colonial Series*, 10 vols (hereafter cited as *GW Colonial*), (Charlottesville, Va., 1983–95), 6, 202–3, which explains the complex legal situation with regard to Washington's management of his wife's estate.
8. E.g. *GW Colonial*, 6, app. C, 'List of Artisan and Household slaves belonging to the Custis estate, *c.* 1759', 282, app. F, 'List of Dower slaves, 1760–1', 311–12.
9. Jackson and Twohig, eds., *Diaries of George Washington*, 4, 277–83.
10. Sweig 'Slavery in Fairfax County', 16, 23–5; Philander D. Chase, 'A Stake in the West: George Washington as Backcountry Surveyor and Landholder', in Warren R. Hofstra, ed., *George Washington and the Virginia Backcountry* (Madison, Wis., 1998), 159–94.
11. John E. Ferling, *The First of Men: A Life of George Washington* (Knoxville, Tenn., 1988), 176; John C. Fitzpatrick, ed., *The Writings of George Washington from the Original Manuscript Sources, 1745–1799*, 39 vols (Washington, D.C., 1931–44), 37, 256–68. This older edition is cited in cases where material has not yet appeared in the new scholarly edition of Washington's papers published by the University Press of Virginia.
12. Paul K. Longmore, *The Invention of George Washington* (Berkeley and Los Angeles, 1988), 3–4.
13. Studies of patriarchy and paternalism among eighteenth-century Virginia planters include Rhys Isaac, 'Communication and Control: Authority Metaphors and Power Contests on Colonel Landon Carter's Virginia Plantation, 1752–1778', in Sean Wilentz, ed., *Rites of Power: Symbolism, Ritual, and Politics since the Middle Ages* (Philadelphia, 1985), 275–302; Richard S. Dunn, 'Servants and Slaves: The Recruitment and Employment of Labor', in Greene and Pole, eds., *Colonial British*

America, 177–80; Philip D. Morgan, 'Three Planters and their Slaves: Perspectives on Slavery in Virginia, South Carolina, and Jamaica, 1750–1790' and Robert Middlekauff, 'The Southern Colonies: A General Perspective' in Winthrop D. Jordan and Sheila L. Skemp, eds., *Race and Family in the Colonial South* (Jackson, Miss., 1987), 37–54, 135–7.

14. George Washington to William Pearce, 20 Mar. 1796, in Fitzpatrick, ed., *Writings of George Washington*, **34**, 501–2.

15. Joseph Valentine to George Washington, 21[–23] Nov. 1770, *GW Colonial*, **8**, 400–1.

16. George Washington to Arthur Young, 18[–21] June 1792, in Fitzpatrick, ed., *Writings of George Washington*, **32**, 65–6.

17. E.g. David Galenson, *White Servitude in Colonial America: An Economic Analysis* (Cambridge, 1981); A. Roger Ekirch, *Bound for America: The Transportation of British Convicts to the Colonies, 1718–1775* (Oxford, 1987); Bernard Bailyn, *Voyagers to the West: A Passage in the Peopling of America on the Eve of the Revolution* (New York, 1986).

18. Metchie J. E. Budka, ed., Julian Ursyn Niemcewicz, *Under Their Vine and Fig Tree: Travels through America in 1797–1799, 1805 with some further account of life in New Jersey*, Collections of the New Jersey Historical Society, **14** (Elizabeth, N.J., 1965), 101.

19. Eugene E. Prussing, *The Estate of George Washington, Deceased* (Boston, 1927), 154–5; Mount Vernon Ladies Association *Report* (1979), 14–15.

20. George Washington to Robert Lewis, 7 Dec. 1799, Mount Vernon Ladies Association *Report* (1982), 28–9; George Washington to Arthur Young, 12 Dec. 1793, in Fitzpatrick, ed., *Writings of George Washington*, **33**, 180.

21. W. W. Abbot, Dorothy Twohig et al., eds., *The Papers of George Washington: Confederation Series*, 6 vols (hereafter *GW Confederation*), **3**, 407 n. 1.

22. George Washington to William Pearce, 13 July 1794, in Fitzpatrick, ed., *Writings of George Washington*, **33**, 429.

23. Agreement with Edward Violet, 5 Aug. 1762 (quotation), and agreement with Nelson Kelly, 1 Sept. 1762, *GW Colonial*, **7**, 143, 148.

24. E.g. Jackson and Twohig, eds., *Diaries of George Washington, passim*; agreement with Nelson Kelly, 1 Sept. 1762, *GW Colonial*, **7**, 148; articles of agreement with William Garner, [10 Dec. 1788] in W. W. Abbot, Dorothy Twohig et al., eds., *The Papers of George Washington: Presidential Series* (hereafter *GW Presidential*) (Charlottesville, Va., 1987–96), 6 vols so far, **1**, 172; George Washington to Anthony Whiting, 14 and 28 Oct. 1792, in Fitzpatrick, ed., *Writings of George Washington*, **32**, 184, 197.

25. Lucia C. Stanton, ' "Those Who Labor for my Happiness": Thomas Jefferson and his Slaves' in Peter S. Onuf, ed., *Jeffersonian Legacies* (Charlottesville, Va., 1993), 149–50.

26. George Washington to Alexander Spotswood, 23 Nov. 1794, to Benjamin Dulany, 15 July 1799, and to Robert Lewis, 18 Aug. 1799, in Fitzpatrick, ed., *Writings of George Washington*, **34**, 47, and **37**, 307, 338–9; George Washington to John Francis Mercer, 24 Nov. 1786, to John Lawson, 10 Apr. 1787, and to John Fowler, 2 Feb. 1788, *GW Confederation*, **4**, 394, **5**, 138, and **6**, 77.

27. George Washington to Lund Washington, 24[–26] Feb. 1779, in Fitzpatrick, ed., *Writings of George Washington*, **14**, 148.

28. James Thomas Flexner, *Washington: The Indispensable Man* (London, 1976), 392.

29. Brenda E. Stevenson, *Life in Black and White: Family and Community in the Slave South* (New York, 1996), 210–12; Donald Sweig, 'Chart of African-American families at Mount Vernon, 1799' (typescript available at the Mount Vernon Library).

30. E.g. Winthrop D. Jordan, *White over Black: American Attitudes towards the Negro, 1550–1812* (Chapel Hill, 1968), 436–40, 457–60; Drew R. McCoy,

'Slavery', in Robert A. Rutland, ed., *James Madison and the American Nation 1751–1836: An Encyclopaedia* (New York, 1994), 380; Paul Finkelman, 'Jefferson and Slavery: "Treason against the hopes of the World,"' in Onuf, ed., *Jeffersonian Legacies*, 184–5, 219 n. 109.

31. George Washington to William Pearce, 2 Nov. 1794, in Fitzpatrick, ed., *Writings of George Washington*, **34**, 13.

32. George Washington to William Pearce, 10 May 1795, ibid., **34**, 193.

33. E.g. George Washington to Clement Biddle, 28 July 1784, *GW Confederation*, **2**, 14. John Trumbull's painting of Washington and Lee together is in the collection of the Metropolitan Museum of Art, New York.

34. Durand Echeverria, ed., *J. P. Brissot de Warville, New Travels in the United States of America 1788* (Cambridge, Mass., 1964), 238.

35. Budka, ed., *Under their Vine and Fig Tree*, 101.

36. E.g. Morgan, 'Three Planters and their Slaves', 37–79; Jack P. Greene, ed., *The Diary of Landon Carter of Sabine Hall, 1752–1778*, 2 vols (Charlottesville, Va., 1965); Douglas Hall, *In Miserable Slavery: Thomas Thistlewood in Jamaica, 1750–86* (London, 1989); Robert Olwell, ' "A Reckoning of Accounts": Patriarchy, Market Relations, and Control on Henry Lauren's Lowcountry Plantations, 1762–1785', in Larry E. Hudson, Jr., ed., *Working Toward Freedom: Slave Society and Domestic Economy in the American South* (Rochester, N.Y., 1994), 33–52.

37. George Washington to John Fairfax, 1 Jan. 1789, *GW Presidential*, **1**, 223.

38. George Washington to Anthony Whiting, 14 Oct., **4**, 11 and 18 Nov. 1792, 6 Jan. 1793, in Fitzpatrick, ed., *Writings of George Washington*, **32**, 179, 202–3, 215, 227–8, 293.

39. George Washington to the overseers at Mount Vernon, 14 July 1793, ibid., **33**, 11.

40. Twohig, 'The Making of George Washington', in Hofstra, ed., *George Washington and the Virginia Backcountry*, 21.

41. Ferling, *The First of Men*, 479–80.

42. George Washington to Arthur Young, 18[–21] June 1792, in Fitzpatrick, ed., *Writings of George Washington*, **32**, 474.

43. George Washington to Lund Washington, 10 Dec. 1776, in W. W. Abbot, Dorothy Twohig et al., eds., *The Papers of George Washington: Revolutionary War Series* (hereafter cited as *GW Revolutionary*) (Charlottesville, Va., 1985–97), 7 vols so far, **7**, 290.

44. Ferling, 478; Isaac, 'Communication and Control', **297**; George Washington to Anthony Whiting, 2 June 1793, in Fitzpatrick, ed., *Writings of George Washington*, **32**, 483; Gerald W. Mullin, *Flight and Rebellion: Slave Resistance in Eighteenth-Century Virginia* (New York, 1972), 55, 60; Edmund S. Morgan, *The Meaning of Independence: John Adams, George Washington, Thomas Jefferson* (New York, 1976), 30–2.

45. Richard Parkinson, *A Tour in America, in 1798, 1799, and 1800...* (London, 1805), 420, 436.

46. Mazyck, *George Washington and the Negro*, 5. Some material on Washington's buying of slaves can be found in Worthington Chauncey Ford, *Washington as an Employer and Importer of Labor* (Brooklyn, N.Y., 1889).

47. E.g. Advertisements by Washington for runaway slaves in the *Maryland Gazette* (Annapolis), 20 Aug. 1761, reprinted in *GW Colonial*, 7, 65–6.

48. Duncan J. MacLeod, *Slavery, Race and the American Revolution* (Cambridge, 1974), 132–3; Howard Temperley, 'Jefferson and Slavery: A Study in Moral Perplexity', in Gary L. McDowell and Sharon L. Noble, eds., *Reason and Republicanism: Thomas Jefferson's Legacy of Liberty* (Lanham, Md., 1997), 91–2.

49. George Washington to Lund Washington, 15 Aug. 1778, in Fitzpatrick, ed., *Writings of George Washington*, **12**, 327.

50. George Washington to Robert Lewis, 18 Aug. 1799, ibid., **37**, 338–39; Lois Green Carr and Lorena S. Walsh, 'Economic Diversification and Labor Organization in the Chesapeake, 1650–1820', in Stephen Innes, ed., *Work and Labor in Early America* (Chapel Hill, N.C., 1988), 178–9.

51. MacLeod, *Slavery, Race and the American Revolution*, 133–4.

52. George Washington to John Francis Mercer, 9 Sept., 5 Dec. 1786 (from which the quotation is taken), *GW Confederation*, **4**, 243, 442.

53. George Washington to Lund Washington, 24[–26] Feb. 1779, in Fitzpatrick, ed., *Writings of George Washington*, **14**, 148.

54. George Washington to John Francis Mercer, 6 Nov., 19 Dec. 1786, and to Henry Lee, Jr., 4 Feb. 1787, *GW Confederation*, **4**, 336, 465, and **5**, 10.

55. This growth is analysed in Allan Kulikoff, '"A Prolifick" People: Black Population Growth in the Chesapeake Colonies, 1700–1790', *Southern Studies*, **16** (1977), 391–428, and his *Tobacco and Slaves: The Development of Southern Cultures in the Chesapeake, 1680–1800* (Chapel Hill, N.C., 1986), Ch. 8; and Richard S. Dunn, 'Black Society in the Chesapeake, 1776–1810', in Ira Berlin and Ronald Hoffman, eds., *Slavery and Freedom in the Age of the American Revolution* (Charlottesville, Va., 1983), 49–82.

56. Temperley, 'Jefferson and Slavery', 91.

57. Stephen Decatur, Jr., *Private Affairs of George Washington from the Records and Accounts of Tobian Lear, Esquire, his Secretary* (Boston, 1933), 225.

58. *GW Revolutionary*, **2**, Council of War, 8 Oct. 1775, 125, Minutes of a Conference of the Delegates of the Continental Congress, 23 Oct. 1775, 199.

59. Joseph Dillaway Sawyer, *Washington*, 2 vols. (New York, 1927), **2**, 334; General Orders, 30 Dec. 1775, *GW Revolutionary*, **2**, 620; Sylvia R. Frey, *Water from the Rock: Black Resistance in a Revolutionary Age* (Princeton, N.J., 1991), 78; Worthington C. Ford, ed., *Journals of the Continental Congress*, 34 vols. (Washington, D.C., 1904–37), **4**, 60.

60. George Washington to Henry Laurens, 20 Mar. 1779, in Fitzpatrick, ed., *Writings of George Washington*, **14**, 267.

61. Quoted in Frey, *Water from the Rock*, 78.

62. Flexner, *Washington: The Indispensable Man*, 387.

63. George Washington to Daniel Parker, 28 Apr. 1783, and entry for 6 May 1783, in Fitzpatrick, ed., *Writings of George Washington*, **26**, 364, 404–6. Some of Washington's slaves had been taken from Mount Vernon by the British during the war (ibid., **22**, 14n).

64. Frey, *Water from the Rock*, 192–3; Benjamin Quarles, *The Negro in the American Revolution* (Chapel Hill, N.C., 1961), 168–72; Donald L. Robinson, *Slavery in the Structure of American Politics 1765–1820* (New York, 1971), 125–6.

65. Mullin, *Flight and Rebellion*, 132–34; Charles Cecil Wall, *George Washington: Citizen-Soldier* (Charlottesville, Va., 1980), 62.

66. Gary B. Nash, *Race and Revolution* (Madison, Wis., 1990), **20**, 117n.

67. Louis Gottschalk, ed., *The Letters of Lafayette to Washington 1777–1799* (New York, 1944), 260.

68. Ibid., 309.

69. George Washington to the Marquis de Lafayette, 10 May 1786, *GW Confederation*, **4**, 43–4.

70. Peter Kolchin, *American Slavery 1619–1877* (Harmondsworth, 1993), 78; William W. Freehling, 'The Founding Fathers, Conditional Antislavery, and the Nonradicalism of the American Revolution', in his *The Reintegration of American History: Slavery and the Civil War* (New York, 1994), 17–18.

71. Robert McColley, *Slavery and Jeffersonian Virginia* (Champaign-Urbana, 1964), 151; John Vickers, *Thomas Coke: Apostle of Methodism* (London, 1969), 98.

72. George Washington to Robert Morris, 12 Apr. 1786, *GW Confederation*, **4**, 16.

73. Echeverria, ed., *J. P. Brissot de Warville, New Travels*, 238.
74. William Waller Hening, ed., *The Statutes at Large; Being a Collection of All the Laws of Virginia, from the First Session of the Legislature, in the Year 1619*, 13 vols (Richmond, Va., 1819–23), II, 39–40.
75. MacLeod, *Slavery, Race and the American Revolution*, 127; Richard R. Beeman, *Patrick Henry: A Biography* (New York, 1974), 97.
76. George Washington to John Francis Mercer, 9 Sept. 1786, *GW Confederation*, 4, 243.
77. George Washington to Lawrence Lewis, 4 Aug. 1797, in Dorothy Twohig, Philander D. Chase, Beverly H. Runge and W. W. Abbot, eds., *The Papers of George Washington: Retirement Series*, 2 vols so far (Charlottesville, Va., 1998–), 1, 288.
78. Sylvia R. Frey, 'Liberty, Equality, and Slavery: The Paradox of the American Revolution', in Jack P. Greene, ed., *The American Revolution: Its Character and Limits* (New York, 1987), 238; Fredrika Teute Schmidt and Barbara Ripel Wilhelm, 'Early Proslavery Petitions in Virginia', *WMQ*, 3rd ser., 30 (1973), 133–46.
79. Pamela C. Copeland and Richard K. MacMaster, *The Five George Masons: Patriots and Planters of Virginia and Maryland* (Charlottesville, Va., 1975), 162–3, 166.
80. Ira Berlin, *Slaves without Masters: The Free Negro in the Antebellum North* (New York, 1974), 92, 101, 150; Frey, 'Liberty, Equality, and Slavery', 237–8; Finkelman, 'Jefferson and Slavery', 188; Louis Morton, *Robert Carter of Nomini Hall: A Virginia Tobacco Planter of the Eighteenth Century* (1941; reprinted Charlottesville, Va., 1964), ch. 11; Peter J. Albert, 'The Protean Institution: The Geography, Economy, and Ideology of Slavery in Post-Revolutionary Virginia' (University of Maryland Ph.D., 1976). The difficulties of opposing slavery in Virginia in the early republic are highlighted in James H. Kettner, 'Persons or Property? The Pleasants Slaves in the Virginia Courts, 1792–1799', in Ronald Hoffman and Peter J. Albert, eds., *Launching the 'Extended Republic': The Federalist Era* (Charlottesville, Va., 1996), 136–55.
81. David Brion Davis, 'The Emergence of Immediatism in Antislavery Thought', *MVHR*, 49 (1962), 209–30.
82. Lathan A. Windley, *A Profile of Runaway Slaves in Virginia and South Carolina from 1739 through 1787* (New York, 1990), 141.
83. See, e.g., William M. Wiecek, 'The Witch at the Christening: Slavery and the Constitution's Origins', in Leonard W. Levy and Dennis J. Mahoney, eds., *The Framing and Ratification of the Constitution* (London, 1987).
84. Mazyck, *George Washington and the Negro*, 106, 109.
85. W. W. Abbot, 'George Washington, the West, and the Union', *Indiana Magazine of History*, 84 (1988), 9.
86. Max Farrand, ed., *The Records of the Federal Convention of 1787*, 4 vols (New Haven, Conn., 1911), 2, 666–7.
87. Quoted in John P. Kaminski, ed., *A Necessary Evil? Slavery and the Debate over the Constitution*, Constitutional Heritage Series, 2 (Madison, Wis., 1995), 89.
88. *Massachusetts Gazette*, 25 Jan. 1788, 95. There is also implied criticism of Washington's views and actions on slavery in Philadelphia's *Independent Gazetteer*, 6 May 1788, which was reprinted in at least four other North American newspapers, ibid., 153.
89. E.g. George Washington to John Jay, 8 June 1788, *GW Confederation*, 6, 318–20.
90. George Washington to Robert Morris, 12 Apr. 1786, *GW Confederation*, 4, 16. See also Paul F. Boller, Jr., 'Washington, the Quakers, and Slavery', *JNH*, 46 (1961), 83–8.
91. Warner Mifflin to George Washington, 12 Mar. 1790, and George Washington to David Stuart, 28 Mar. 1790, *GW Presidential*, 5, 222–3, 288.

92. Jackson and Twohig, eds., *George Washington Diaries*, 6, 47–48.
93. George Washington to David Stuart, 28 Mar. 1790, *GW Presidential*, 5, 288.
94. George Washington to David Stuart, 15 June 1790, *GW Presidential*, 5, 525.
95. Decatur, *Private Affairs of George Washington*, 225.
96. MacLeod, *Slavery, Race and the American Revolution*, 132.
97. Ferling, *The First of Men*, 475.
98. George Washington to Jean Baptiste Tenant, 2 Oct. 1791, and to John Vaughn, 27 Dec. 1791, in Fitzpatrick, ed., *Writings of George Washington*, 31, 380, 453; Dorothy Twohig, ed., *The Papers of George Washington: The Journal of the Proceedings of the President 1793–1797* (Charlottesville, Va., 1981), 16–17, 187.
99. William Cohen, 'Thomas Jefferson and the Problem of Slavery', *JAH*, 56 (1969), 520; Michael Zuckerman, *Almost Chosen People: Oblique Biographies in the American Grain* (Berkeley and Los Angeles, 1993), ch. 6; James Sidbury, 'Saint Domingue in Virginia: Ideology, Local Meanings, and Resistance to Slavery, 1790–1800', *JSH*, 63 (1997), 531–52; Sidbury, *Ploughshares into Swords: Race, Rebellion, and Identity in Gabriel's Virginia, 1730–1810* (Cambridge, 1997), 39–48.
100. Howarth, *George Washington: Farmer*, 217.
101. For the influence of this decision on Madison, see Drew R. McCoy, *The Last of the Fathers: James Madison and the Republican Legacy* (Cambridge, 1989), 308–18.
102. Prussing, *Estate of George Washington*, 154; Decatur, *Private Affairs of George Washington*, 33; Fitzpatrick, ed., *Writings of George Washington*, 37, 276–7.
103. Howarth, *George Washington: Farmer*, 206–9; Wall, *George Washington: Citizen-Soldier*, 63. The fate of the Mount Vernon slaves after Washington's death is discussed in Hirschfeld, *George Washington and Slavery*, 213–22.
104. Rosemarie Zagarri, ed., *David Humphreys' 'Life of General Washington' with George Washington's 'Remarks'* (Athens, Ga., 1991).
105. Quoted in Kaminski, ed., *A Necessary Evil?*, 277.
106. George Washington to Alexander Spotswood, 23 Nov. 1794, in Fitzpatrick, ed., *Writings of George Washington*, 34, 47.
107. Quoted in Kaminski, ed., *A Necessary Evil?*, 244.
108. Freehling, 'The Founding Fathers, Conditional Antislavery, and the Nonradicalism of the American Revolution', 19.
109. James Thomas Flexner, *George Washington: Anguish and Farewell, 1793–1799* (Boston, 1972), 445–6.
110. Cf. Bernard Bailyn, *Context in History*, North American Studies Bernard Bailyn Lecture No. 1: 1995 (Melbourne: La Trobe University, 1995), 16–18.
111. Paul Finkelman, *Slavery and the Founders: Race and Liberty in the Age of Jefferson* (Armonk, N.Y., 1996), 112.
112. Finkelman, 'Jefferson and Slavery'; McCoy, 'Slavery', 378–80; Cohen, 'Thomas Jefferson and the Problem of Slavery', 510, 523–4; Ralph L. Ketcham, *James Madison: A Biography* (New York, 1971), 625–9.

DOCUMENT 1: EXTRACT FROM THOMAS JEFFERSON, NOTES ON THE STATE OF VIRGINIA

In his Notes on the State of Virginia *(1784), Thomas Jefferson wrote about the intellectual inferiority of blacks and expressed fears about miscegenation and the potential for violence by blacks against whites. Blacks should not be incorporated into the state because white prejudice and black resentment 'will probably never end but in the extermination of the one or the other race'. Jefferson thought that some form of colonisation would place the slave 'beyond the reach of mixture' so that he would not stain 'the blood of his master'. It is not surprising that Jefferson did not want this racism circulated publicly, which is one reason why the* Notes *were not published in his lifetime.*

It will probably be asked, Why not retain and incorporate the blacks into the state, and thus save the expence of supplying, by importation of white settlers, the vacancies they will leave? Deep rooted prejudices entertained by the whites; ten thousand recollections, by the blacks, of the injuries they have sustained; new provocations; the real distinctions which nature has made; and many other circumstances, will divide us into parties, and produce convulsions which will probably never end but in the extermination of the one or the other race. – To these objections, which are political, may be added others, which are physical and moral. The first difference which strikes us is that of colour. Whether the black of the negro resides in the reticular membrane between the skin and scarf-skin, or in the scarf-skin itself; whether it proceeds from the colour of the blood, the colour of the bile, or from that of some other secretion, the difference is fixed in nature, and is as real as if its seat and cause were better known to us. And is this difference of no importance? Is it not the foundation of a greater or less share of beauty in the two races? Are not the fine mixtures of red and white, the expressions of every passion by greater or less suffusions of colour in the one, preferable to that eternal monotony, which reigns in the countenances, that immoveable veil of black which covers all the emotions of the other race? Add to these, flowing hair, a more elegant symmetry of form, their own judgment in favour of the whites, declared by their preference of them, as uniformly as is the preference of the Oran-ootan for the black women over those of his own species. The circumstance of superior beauty, is thought worthy attention in the propagation of our horses, dogs, and other domestic animals; why not in that of man? Besides those of colour, figure, and hair, there are other physical distinctions proving a difference of race. They have less hair on the face and body. They secrete less by the kidnies, and more by the glands of the skin, which gives them a very strong

Thomas Jefferson, *Notes on the State of Virginia*; ed. William Peden (Chapel Hill: University of North Carolina Press, 1955), pp. 138–40.

and disagreeable odour. This greater degree of transpiration renders them more tolerant of heat, and less so of cold, than the whites. Perhaps too a difference of structure in the pulmonary apparatus, which a late ingenious experimentalist has discovered to be the principal regulator of animal heat, may have disabled them from extricating, in the act of inspiration, so much of that fluid from the outer air, or obliged them in expiration, to part with more of it. They seem to require less sleep. A black, after hard labour through the day, will be induced by the slightest amusements to sit up till midnight, or later, though knowing he must be out with the first dawn of the morning. They are at least as brave, and more adventuresome. But this may perhaps proceed from a want of forethought, which prevents their seeing a danger till it be present. When present, they do not go through it with more coolness or steadiness than the whites. They are more ardent after their female: but love seems with them to be more an eager desire, than a tender delicate mixture of sentiment and sensation. Their griefs are transient. Those numberless afflictions, which render it doubtful whether heaven has given life to us in mercy or in wrath, are less felt, and sooner forgotten with them. In general, their existence appears to participate more of sensation than reflection. To this must be ascribed their disposition to sleep when abstracted from their diversions, and unemployed in labour. An animal whose body is at rest, and who does not reflect, must be disposed to sleep of course. Comparing them by their faculties of memory, reason, and imagination, it appears to me, that in memory they are equal to the whites; in reason much inferior, as I think one could scarcely be found capable of tracing and comprehending the investigations of Euclid; and that in imagination they are dull, tasteless, and anomalous. It would be unfair to follow them to Africa for this investigation. We will consider them here, on the same stage with the whites, and where the facts are not apocryphal on which a judgment is to be formed. It will be right to make great allowances for the difference of condition, of education, of conversation, of the sphere in which they move. Many millions of them have been brought to, and born in America. Most of them indeed have been confined to tillage, to their own homes, and their own society: yet many have been so situated, that they might have availed themselves of conversation of their masters; many have been brought up to the handicraft arts, and from that circumstance have always been associated with the whites. Some have been liberally educated, and all have lived in countries where the arts and sciences are cultivated to a considerable degree, and have had before their eyes samples of the best works from abroad. The Indians, with no advantages of this kind, will often carve figures on their pipes not destitute of design and merit. They will crayon out an animal, a plant, or a country, so as to prove the existence of a germ in their minds which only wants cultivation. They astonish you with strokes of the most sublime oratory; such as prove their reason and sentiment strong, their imagination glowing and elevated. But never yet could I find that a black had uttered a thought above the level of plain narration; never see even an elementary trait of painting or sculpture. In music they are more generally gifted than the whites with accurate ears for tune and time, and they have been found capable of imaging a small catch. Whether they will be equal to the composition of a more extensive run of melody, or of complicated harmony, is yet to be proved.

DOCUMENT 2: GEORGE WASHINGTON, LAST WILL AND TESTAMENT, 9 JULY 1799

An extract from Washington's will, in which he decreed that his own slaves should be freed but only after his wife's death; he had no legal power over the dower slaves owned by Martha Washington.

... Upon the decease of my wife, it is my Will and desire that all the Slaves which I hold in my own right, shall receive their freedom. To emancipate them during her life, would, tho' earnestly wished by me, be attended with such insuperable difficulties on account of their intermixture by Marriages with the Dower Negroes, as to excite the most painful sensations, if not disagreeable consequences from the latter, while both descriptions are in the occupancy of the same Proprietor; it not being in my power, under the tenure by which the Dower Negroes are held, to manumit them. And whereas among those who will receive freedom according to this devise, there may be some, who from old age or bodily infirmities, and others who on account of their infancy, that will be unable to support themselves; it is my Will and desire that all who come under the first and second description shall be comfortably cloathed and fed by my heirs while they live; and that such of the later description as have no parents living, or if living are unable, or unwilling to provide for them, shall be bound by the Court until they shall arrive at the age of twenty-five years; and in cases where no record can be produced, whereby their ages can be ascertained, the judgment of the Court upon its own view of the subject, shall be adequate and final. The Negroes thus bound, are (by their Masters or Mistresses) to be taught to read and write; and to be brought up to some useful occupation, agreeable to the Laws of the Commonwealth of Virginia, providing for the support of Orphan and other poor Children. And I do hereby expressly forbid the Sale, or transportation out of said Commonwealth, of any Slave I may die possessed of, under any pretence whatsoever. And I do moreover most pointedly, and most solemnly enjoin it upon my Executors hereafter named, or the Survivors of them, to see that this clause respecting Slaves, and every part thereof be religiously fulfilled at the Epoch at which it is directed to take place; without evation, neglect or delay, after the Crops which may then be on the ground are harvested, particularly as it respects the aged and infirm; Seeing that a regular and permanent fund be established for their Support so long as there are subjects requiring it; not trusting to the uncertain provision to be made by individuals. And to my Mulatto man William (calling himself William Lee) I give immediate freedom; or if he should prefer it (on account of the accidents which have befallen him, and which have rendered him incapable of walking or of any active employment)

John P. Kaminski (ed.), *A Necessary Evil? Slavery and the Debate over the Constitution* (Madison, WI: Madison House, 1995), pp. 277–8.

to remain in the situation he now is, it shall be optional in him to do so: In either case however, I allow him an annuity of thirty dollars during his natural life, which shall be independent of the victuals and cloaths he has been accustomed to receive, if he chuses the last alternative; but in full, with his freedom, if he prefers the first; and this I give him as a testimony of my sense of his attachment to me, and for his faithful services during the Revolutionary War.

DOCUMENT 3: DNA EVIDENCE ON THOMAS JEFFERSON AND SALLY HEMINGS

Rumours of an illicit relationship between Thomas Jefferson and his mulatto slave Sally Hemings first emerged in a Richmond, Virginia, newspaper in 1802. But for almost two centuries this presidential sex scandal could not be verified. Recently, however, geneticists have found a solution. DNA testing of Y chromosomes from modern-day male-line descendants provides strong evidence that Jefferson was the father of at least one of Hemings's children. Jefferson's haplotype perfectly matches that of Eston Hemings, born in 1808, the last son of Sally Hemings.

Jefferson Fathered Slave's Last Child

There is a long-standing historical controversy over the question of US President Thomas Jefferson's paternity of the children of Sally Hemings, one of his slaves[1–4]. To throw some scientific light on the dispute, we have compared Y-chromosomal DNA haplotypes from male-line descendants of Field Jefferson, a paternal uncle of Thomas Jefferson, with those of male-line descendants of Thomas Woodson, Sally Hemings' putative first son, and of Eston Hemings Jefferson, her last son. The molecular findings fail to support the belief that Thomas Jefferson was Thomas Woodson's father, but provide evidence that he was the biological father of Eston Hemings Jefferson.

In 1802, President Thomas Jefferson was accused of having fathered a child, Tom, by Sally Hemings[5]. Tom was said to have been born in 1790, soon after Jefferson and Sally Hemings returned from France where he had been minister. Present-day members of the African-American Woodson family believe that Thomas Jefferson was the father of Thomas Woodson, whose name comes from his later owner[6]. No known documents support this view.

Sally Hemings had at least four more children. Her last son, Eston (born in 1808), is said to have borne a striking resemblance to Thomas Jefferson, and entered white society in Madison, Wisconsin, as Eston Hemings Jefferson. Although Eston's descendants believe that Thomas Jefferson was Eston's father, most Jefferson scholars give more credence to the oral tradition of the descendants of Martha Jefferson Randolph, the president's daughter. They believe that Sally Hemings' later children, including Eston, were fathered by either Samuel or Peter Carr, sons of Jefferson's sister, which would explain their resemblance to the president.

Because most of the Y chromosome is passed unchanged from father to son, apart from occasional mutations, DNA analysis of the Y chromosome

Lander, Eric S. and Joseph J. Ellis, 'DNA Analysis: Founding Father' and Eugene A. Foster et al., 'Jefferson Fathered Slave's Last Child', *Nature*, vol. 396 (5 November 1998), pp. 13–14, 27–8.

can reveal whether or not individuals are likely to be male-line relatives. We therefore analysed DNA from the Y chromosomes of: five male-line descendants of two sons of the president's paternal uncle, Field Jefferson; five male-line descendants of two sons of Thomas Woodson; one male-line descendant of Eston Hemings Jefferson; and three male-line descendants of three sons of John Carr, grandfather of Samuel and Peter Carr (Fig. 1a). No

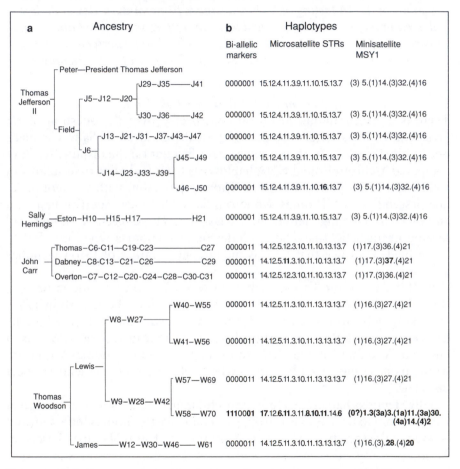

Figure 1. Male-line ancestry and haplotypes of participants. **a**, Ancestry. Numbers correspond to reference numbers and names in more detailed genealogical charts for each family. **b**, Haplotypes. Entries in bold highlight deviations from the usual patterns for the group of descendants. Bi-allelic markers. Order of loci: YAP-SRYm8299-sY81-LLY22g-Tat-92R7-SRYm1532. 0, ancestral state; 1, derived state. Microsatellite short tandem repeats (STRs). Order of loci: 19-388-389A-389B-389C-389D-390-391-392-393-dxys 156y. The number of repeats at each locus is shown. Minisatellite MSY1. Each number in brackets represents the sequence type of the repeat unit; the number after it is the number of units with this sequence type. For example, J41 has 5 units of sequence type 3, 14 units of sequence type 1, 32 units of sequence type 3, and 16 units of sequence type 4.

Y-chromosome data were available from male-line descendants of President Thomas Jefferson because he had no surviving sons.

Seven bi-allelic markers (refs 7–12), eleven microsatellites (ref. 13) and the minisatellite MSY1 (ref. 14) were analysed (Fig. 1b). Four of the five descendants of Field Jefferson shared the same haplotype at all loci, and the fifth differed by only a single unit at one microsatellite locus, probably a mutation. This haplotype is rare in the population, where the average frequency of a microsatellite haplotype is about 1.5 per cent. Indeed, it has never been observed outside the Jefferson family, and it has not been found in 670 European men (more than 1,200 worldwide) typed with the microsatellites or 308 European men (690 worldwide) typed with MSY1.

Four of the five male-line descendants of Thomas Woodson shared a haplotype (with one MSY1 variant) that was not similar to the Y chromosome of Field Jefferson but was characteristic of Europeans. The fifth Woodson descendant had an entirely different haplotype, most often seen in sub-Saharan Africans, which indicates illegitimacy in the line after individual W42. In contrast, the descendant of Eston Hemings Jefferson did have the Field Jefferson haplotype. The haplotypes of two of the descendants of John Carr were identical; the third differed by one step at one microsatellite locus and by one step in the MSY1 code. The Carr haplotypes differed markedly from those of the descendants of Field Jefferson.

The simplest and most probable explanations for our molecular findings are that Thomas Jefferson, rather than one of the Carr brothers, was the father of Eston Hemings Jefferson, and that Thomas Woodson was not Thomas Jefferson's son. The frequency of the Jefferson haplotype is less than 0.1 per cent, a result that is at least 100 times more likely if the president was the father of Eston Hemings Jefferson than if someone unrelated was the father.

We cannot completely rule out other explanations of our findings based on illegitimacy in various lines of descent. For example, a male-line descendant of Field Jefferson could possibly have illegitimately fathered an ancestor of the presumed male-line descendant of Eston. But in the absence of historical evidence to support such possibilities, we consider them to be unlikely.

Eugene A. Foster, M. A. Jobling, P. G. Taylor, P. Donnelly, P. de Knijff, Rene Mieremet, T. Zerjal, C. Tyler-Smith

NOTES

1. Peterson, M. D. *The Jefferson Image in the American Mind* 181–187 (New York, 1960).
2. Malone, D. *Jefferson the President: First Term, 1801–1805* Appendix II, 494–498 (Boston, 1970).
3. Brodie, F. M. *Thomas Jefferson: An Intimate History* (New York, 1974).
4. Ellis, J. J. *American Sphinx: The Character of Thomas Jefferson* (New York, 1997).

5. Callender, J. T. *Richmond Recorder* 1 September 1802 [Cited in: Gordon-Reed, A. *Thomas Jefferson and Sally Hemings: An American Controversy* (Charlottesville, Va., 1997)].
6. Woodson, M. S. *The Woodson Source Book* 2nd edn (Washington, 1984).
7. Hammer, M. F. *Mol. Biol. Evol.* 11, 749–761 (1994).
8. Whitfield, L. S., Sulston, J. E. & Goodfellow, P. N. *Nature* 378, 379–380 (1995).
9. Seielstad, M. T. *et al. Hum. Mol. Genet.* 3, 2159–2161 (1994).
10. Zerjal, T. *et al. Am. J. Hum. Genet.* 60, 1174–1183 (1997).
11. Mathias, N., Bayes, M. & Tyler-Smith, C. *Hum. Mol. Genet.* 3, 115–123 (1994).
12. Kwok, C. *et al. J. Med. Genet.* 33, 465–468 (1996).
13. Kayser, M. *et al. Int. J. Legal Med.* 110, 125–133 (1997).
14. Jobling, M. A., Bouzekri, N. & Taylor, P. G. *Hum. Mol. Genet.* 7, 643–653 (1998).

5

SLAVE LIFE AND WORK

INTRODUCTION

Older studies of slave life and work concentrate heavily on the slave society of the antebellum South, but this focus is now less pronounced in the historiography. Indeed, over the past four decades a plethora of fine studies have explored different aspects of slave life and work over time from the colonial period to the 1860s. Slave work has been analysed on plantations, at ironworks, and in urban and domestic settings. Particular attention has been paid to regional differences in slave labour in connection with different economic structures and the productivity achieved by black workers. Slave life has been probed with respect to demographic and family structure, religious and cultural beliefs, the personality of slaves and the medical treatment, clothing and music of slaves. There are also detailed studies of slave women and slave children. For most North American colonies and virtually all slaveholding states one can find a selection of significant monographs.

Phillips (1918) was the earliest major study of slave society in the antebellum South. Today this study is attacked for its aura of white superiority and racial bias but for forty years after publication it was the leading book on its topic. Phillips, a conservative southerner, interprets slavery as an essentially benign institution in which a paternalistic plantocracy presided over a system that saved blacks from languishing in a state of backwardness. Slaves, according to Phillips, were docile, lazy, poor workers; they reached an accommodation with their white masters. Their families were kept together rather than being broken up and sold. Stampp (1956) mounted the first major challenge to this proslavery approach. He argues that resistance was a continuing part of the slave experience; to suggest, as Phillips did, that slaves were largely contented, was erroneous. Stampp also shows that slave families could be disrupted; that the slave system was inherently cruel and brutal; and that slave culture occupied an uneasy middle position between African and white culture. Much subsequent literature has extended and modified these points but newer themes have also been explored.

Elkins (1959) follows Stampp in underscoring the degradation of American slavery. However, his work suggests that powerless slaves acquired a docile 'Sambo' personality on the plantations and that their condition resembled the plight of victims in Nazi concentration camps. Slave 'Sambos' behaved in an infantilist way because the control exercised by masters forced them to adopt such a face to the world. This view of slaves as depersonalised and degraded by their treatment provoked much controversy among historians. Many scholars consider that Elkins pushed his concentration camp analogy too far. But his book provoked other historians to explore the actions and behaviour of southern slaves and to assess how far they became actors in their own lives, creating a degree of autonomy in their work and leisure activities.

The personality and behaviour of slaves have been the focus of other major studies that offer different interpretations. Blassingame (1972) vigorously refuted the slave's purported 'Sambo' personality. In so doing, he challenged Elkins's interpretation of the slave psyche. Blassingame argued that slave behaviour was defined by the character of the antebellum plantation; but he added that the 'slave had much more freedom from restraint and more independence and autonomy than his institutionally defined role allowed' (p. 249).

Genovese (1974) draws upon the neo-Marxist thought of the Italian communist and martyr Antonio Gramsci to address the question of how slave masters maintained their stability and position by generating acquiescence among slaves. He argues that a complex process of accommodation and resistance on the part of slaves forced a similar process on to the masters. Out of the tension and interplay between the unequal forces of slaves and masters there emerged an institution based on paternalism. Slaves managed to play off masters against overseers and were therefore responsible for the amelioration of their own position. But they paid a heavy price: every concession made them more dependent on the white slaveholders. Genovese plays down the element of force in plantation slavery and so, in his interpretation, slavery becomes more normal, more 'unpeculiar' as an institution.

Fogel and Engerman's book (1974) was at least as controversial as that of Elkins. By use of quantitative techniques known as 'cliometrics' – involving testing of economic models with hard data – they produced an iconoclastic work that aimed to transform historians' views of slavery in the American South. They argue in favour of plantations being highly viable in economic terms, with efficient agricultural production achieved through the organisation of the work force into gang systems. Fogel and Engerman emphasise the positive incentives in slave work rather than the negative ones. In particular, they argue that slaves worked hard because an occupational structure existed that enabled them to work their way up to the artisan and managerial classes. This allowed for a high input of labour and helped slaves to be chosen for jobs according to their capacity. Women and children also contributed to the efficiency of slave plantation work. Fogel and Engerman consider that planters encouraged slave families rather than attempting to separate and sell them and that whipping of slaves was infrequent.

Numerous studies have attacked the methodologies and conclusions of *Time on the Cross*. Gutman and Sutch (1976) provide a detailed rebuttal of the arguments concerning slave work. They show that slaves were, in fact, given the lash frequently and that, although a hierarchy of slave jobs existed, there is insufficient evidence to argue that this acted as an incentive for slaves to work hard. Other historians have argued against Fogel and Engerman that, even in cases where slaves responded positively to incentives provided by masters, they did not absorb the white bourgeois values associated with them.

Gutman (1976) studied the impact of slavery on African-American families. He argues that slaves built up a resilient, strong family structure based on extended kinship systems that stretched beyond the nuclear family. Many familial arrangements were based upon west African traditions whose cultural legacy led most American slaves to oppose polygamy, adultery and desertion. Gutman's arguments counterpose those of Elkins: instead of slave families being crushed by an oppressive social institution, they were a lasting and positive influence on slave culture throughout the South and persisted into the post-slavery era. Gutman paints a picture of an autonomous slave culture that was distinct from that imposed by white masters. Unlike Genovese, he does not emphasise the influence of a hegemonic white master class on slave culture.

Slave life and work in colonial North America has attracted significant studies in the past thirty years. Berlin and Morgan (1993) is a fine collection of studies focusing on such themes as the work performed by Jefferson's slaves at Monticello and the contribution made by slave women to the work process. Berlin (1998) provides a nuanced synthesis of slave life and work in early American history. By organising the book into distinct slaveholding regions – the northern colonies, the Chesapeake, the Lowcountry and the Lower Mississippi Valley – and by charting changes over three broad timespans, Berlin shows how North American slavery adapted over time and differed in various regional settings.

Morgan (1998) focuses a very large study on the differences and similarities of slavery in the Chesapeake and the Carolinas over the course of the eighteenth century. Much important material is included on material life, field work, economic exchanges and social transactions between whites and blacks as well as African-American culture and family life. Wood (1995) examines the activities of bondwomen and bondmen as producers and consumers in Savannah, Georgia, and its environs from 1750 until c. 1830. This is one of the few studies of North American slavery to straddle that time period. Wood analyses the impact of Protestant Christianity and economic morality on informal slave economies and shows that Lowcountry slaves forged cohesive family and kinship ties in those economies that helped them cope with the brutality of formal slavery. Malone (1992) analyses changes over time in slave households and family life in 155 slave communities in twenty-six Louisiana parishes. She demonstrates the diversity and flexibility of slave family arrangements. Most slaves in Louisiana did not live in units of two parents and children but were more likely to do so during stable phases of development. Cecelski (2001) is a good regional study of North American slavery. Without minimising the oppressive situation in which slaves lived and worked, he charts the growth of a vital black culture among the fishermen, sailors, ferrymen and other maritime workers along the inland waters of North Carolina. He describes the skills and actions of African-Americans and their significant role in local abolitionist activity, the Civil War and Reconstruction.

Two-fifths of antebellum slaves were younger than fifteen, so scholarship on slave children focuses on a significant portion of the slave community. King (1995) traces the slave child's experience through work, play, education, resistance and the move towards freedom. Such children, she finds, were made to work from an early age. They were separated from their families and sometimes dealt with harshly. While resisting slavery, they nevertheless deferred to white authority. Schwartz (2000) looks at the life cycle of slave children in parts of Virginia, Alabama, South Carolina and Georgia. She concentrates particularly on the competing claims of owners and parents on the lives of slave children. The book makes extensive use of the Works Project Administration (WPA) slave testimonies gathered during the New Deal years.

White (1985) explores the differences between the roles assumed by slave women in the plantation South and traditional female roles in the United States. She shows how female slave work and west African traditions gave women a powerful position in the slave community. White focuses on the gender differences between black slave women and all men in the antebellum South and the autonomy of black slave women: slave women often worked in segregated units; they were sexually exploited by both black and white men; and they cultivated healing arts that enabled them to escape the values of slave masters. White shows that slave women were resourceful in dealing with an oppressive plantation world.

Fox-Genovese (1988) pursues different arguments with regard to slave women's identity. Instead of forming an autonomous culture distinct from the cultural values of their masters, as White argues, she suggests that African-American women created an identity circumscribed by the political and economic authority of their masters. Slave women in the plantation South were not free from the domination of white male heads of slaveholding households: planter hegemony was the prime determining factor that limited the choices of slave women.

Creel (1988) explores the material culture, language and folktales of the Gullah people in Lowcountry South Carolina and Georgia. She is particularly interested in the complex transmission of an African people across the Atlantic. Levine (1977) describes the vitality of slaves' internal culture, which he interprets as a response to bondage: instead of externalising their challenge to slavery through rebellions that were likely to be quashed, slaves internalised their creative impulses. Levine follows through his exploration of individual and communal black consciousness through slavery to the era of freedom and up to the 1940s. This is one of several studies that do justice to the creation of an African-American identity based upon appropriation of African cultural practices, elements absorbed from the white plantation world, and a response to the condition of enslavement.

BIBLIOGRAPHY

Berlin, Ira, *Many Thousands Gone: The First Two Centuries of Slavery in North America* (Cambridge, MA: Harvard University Press, 1998)

Berlin, Ira and Morgan, Philip D. (eds), *Cultivation and Culture: Labor and the Shaping of Slave Life in the Americas* (Charlottesville, VA: University Press of Virginia, 1993)

Blassingame, John W., *The Slave Community: Plantation Life in the Antebellum South* (New York: Oxford University Press, 1972; rev. and enlarged edn, 1979)

Cecelski, David S., *The Waterman's Song: Slavery and Freedom in Maritime North Carolina* (Chapel Hill: University of North Carolina Press, 2001)

Creel, Margaret Washington, *'A Peculiar People': Slave Religion and Community-Culture among the Gullahs* (New York: Oxford University Press, 1988)

Elkins, Stanley M., *Slavery: A Problem in American Institutional and Intellectual Life* (Chicago: University of Chicago Press, 1959; 3rd edn, 1976)

Fogel, Robert W. and Engerman, Stanley L., *Time on the Cross: The Economics of American Negro Slavery* (Boston: Little, Brown, 1974)

Fox-Genovese, Elizabeth, *Within the Plantation Household: Black and White Women of the Old South* (Chapel Hill: University of North Carolina Press, 1988)

Genovese, Eugene D., *Roll, Jordan, Roll: The World the Slaves Made* (New York: Pantheon Books, 1974)

Gutman, Herbert G., *The Black Family in Slavery and Freedom, 1750–1925* (New York: Pantheon Books, 1976)

Gutman, Herbert G. and Sutch, Richard, 'Sambo Makes Good, or Were Slaves Imbued with the Protestant Work Ethic'? in Paul A. David, Herbert G. Gutman, Richard Sutch, Peter Temin and Gavin Wright (eds), *Reckoning with Slavery: A Critical Study in the Quantitative History of American Negro Slavery* (New York: Oxford University Press, 1976)

King, Wilma, *Stolen Childhood: Slave Youth in Nineteenth Century America* (Bloomington: Indiana University Press, 1995)

Levine, Lawrence W., *Black Culture and Black Consciousness: Afro-American Folk Thought from Slavery to Freedom* (New York: Oxford University Press, 1977)

Malone, Ann Patton, *Sweet Chariot: Slave Family and Household Structure in Nineteenth-Century Louisiana* (Chapel Hill: University of North Carolina Press, 1992)

Morgan, Philip D., *Slave Counterpoint: Black Culture in the Eighteenth-Century Chesapeake and Lowcountry* (Chapel Hill: University of North Carolina Press, 1998)

Phillips, Ulrich Bonnell, *American Negro Slavery: A Survey of the Supply, Employment and Control of Negro Labor as Determined by the Plantation Regime* (New York: Appleton, 1918)

Schwartz, Marie Jenkins, *Born in Bondage: Growing Up Enslaved in the Antebellum South* (Cambridge, MA: Harvard University Press, 2000)

Stampp, Kenneth M., *The Peculiar Institution: Negro Slavery in the Ante-Bellum South* (New York: Alfred A. Knopf, 1956)

White, Deborah G., *Ar'n't I a Woman? Female Slavery in the Plantation South* (New York: W. W. Norton, 1985, rev. edn, 1999)

Wood, Betty, *Women's Work, Men's Work: The Informal Slave Economies of Lowcountry Georgia* (Athens, GA: University of Georgia Press, 1995)

ESSAY: THE GOSPEL IN THE SLAVE QUARTERS

Religion plays a central part in Genovese's dialectical analysis (1974). He explores slave religious beliefs and the impact of evangelical Christianity upon slaves. Masters spread Christianity among their slave workforce but blacks had their own religious beliefs – partly based on African customs – which made them feel morally superior to their masters. One example consists of the call-and-response pattern. Why did slaves prefer the Baptists and the Methodists among Christian denominations? How far did slaves exercise autonomy over their Christian observance? What, according to Genovese, were slave conceptions of sin and the soul? How did slaves conceive of Heaven?

Folk beliefs might not so easily have passed into the heart of black Christianity had the slaves and free Negroes of the cities not wrested some degree of control of the churches from the whites. Without that degree of autonomy within the structure of formal religion folk belief might have remained an antithesis, and the slaves might have had to make the hard choice between Christianity and an anti-Christianity. Institutional developments and the ability of preachers and the slaves themselves to take advantage of them opened the way toward the absorption of much of the folk culture into the Christian faith.

Whatever the religion of the masters, the slaves, when given a choice, overwhelmingly preferred the Baptists and secondarily the Methodists. By the 1850s the recruitment of blacks to the Episcopal Church in Virginia had virtually ceased.[1] In the South as a whole the Presbyterians had a small following, especially in the up country, and the Catholics scored some success in Louisiana. Melville J. Herskovits has advanced the provocative thesis that the slaves' preference for the Baptists reflected the continued strength of traditional West African religion. Noting the practice of total immersion, he has suggested a connection in the slaves' mind with the powerful river spirits in the West African religions; in particular, he thinks that enslaved priests from Dahomey must have provided leadership and continuity from Africa to Afro-America.[2] E. Franklin Frazier, who has led the attack on Herskovits's thesis, dismisses the argument on the grounds that enslavement and the slave trade had effectively destroyed the social basis of African religion among the blacks and that Herskovits's speculations hardly constitute evidence. He suggests, instead, that the slaves responded to the fiery style and uninhibited emotionalism of the frontier Baptist and Methodist preachers and that the Baptists had the additional advantage of a loose church structure to accommodate slaves more easily.[3] Although Frazier's views have come under withering fire for their extreme formulation of a break with the African past, he clearly has had the better of this particular argument.

Eugene D. Genovese, *Roll, Jordan, Roll: The World the Slaves Made* (New York: Pantheon Books, 1974), pp. 232–53, 721–5.

Herskovits's insistence on links between West African and Afro-American folk religion has merit, but it simply cannot be stretched to account for the slaves' preference for the Baptists. Arthur Huff Fauset has pointed out that the same blacks who chose the Baptists might have chosen the Methodists, the Baptists' hottest rivals in the plantation districts – and the Methodists' greatest fun in life was ridiculing total immersion and adult baptism.[4]

Methodism, on the face of it, hardly seems a likely candidate for the affections of a high-spirited, life-loving people. Grim, humorless, breathing the fires of damnation – notwithstanding love feasts and some joyful hymns – it was more calculated to associate Jesus with discipline and order than with love. The slaves adjusted Methodism, as they adjusted every other creed, to their own way of life, and they transformed each in the process, as the ring shout may demonstrate. Once converted, the slaves had to stop dancing, for it was sinful. Dutifully, they stopped going to dances and went to the praise-house instead. What they did there looked like dancing to the white uninitiated and still looks like dancing to those who recognize the origin of the Charleston and several other popular dances. But no: it could not have been dancing. Dancing was sinful, and these slaves had been converted. They were not dancing; they were 'shouting'. Henry George Spaulding, a white Unitarian minister who visited Port Royal, South Carolina, with the United States Sanitary Commission during the war, left us a description of the ring shout, which he insisted was the 'religious dance of the Negroes':

> Three or four, standing still, clapping their hands and beating time with their feet, commence singing in unison one of the peculiar shout melodies, while the others walk around in a ring, in single file, joining also in the song. Soon those in the ring leave off their singing, the others keeping it up the while with increased vigor, and strike into the shout step, observing most accurate time with the music . . . . They will often dance to the same song for twenty or thirty minutes . . . .[5]

Whatever Spaulding thought, the blacks convinced themselves that they did not dance the shout, for as everyone knows, you cross your feet when you dance; and since they did not tolerate crossing of feet, they clearly were not dancing.

The slaves' insistence on shouting harked back to Africa in both form and content. The style, which subsequently came to dominate American popular dancing in a variety of versions, could not have been more clearly African. The same might also be said about the insistence that the community worship God in a way that integrated the various forms of human expression – song, dance, and prayer, all with call-and-response, as parts of a single offering the beauty of which pays homage to God. This idea of beauty as deriving from the whole of human expression rather than from its separate manifestations, or even its artifacts, was not entirely new to the Christian tradition. It had originally been as much a part of Euro-Christian tradition as of African but had been lost during the Middle Ages and especially after the Reformation. Thomas Merton ends his study of the reform of the Roman Catholic liturgy: 'One thing that is certain to come out of Africa is the revival of the ancient liturgical art of *the dance*, traditionally a problem to Western Christianity'.[6]

The Methodists had in common with the Baptists certain features, beyond those mentioned by Frazier, that did appeal to the slaves. They had retained some interest in ameliorating plantation conditions; their congregations had long been racially mixed and never wholly accepted the white pressures to segregate; and above all, their preachers spoke plainly. Richard Allen, founder of the Bethel African Methodist Episcopal Church of Philadelphia and himself an ex-slave, explained: 'I was confident that no religious sect or denomination would suit the capacity of the colored people so well as the Methodists, for the plain simple gospel suits best for any people, for the unlearned can understand, and the learned are sure to understand'.[7] But the greatest advantage held by both Baptists and Methodists, with their particular strength in the countryside and in the cities respectively, was that they worked hard to reach the blacks and understood the need to enlist black preachers and 'assistants' to work with them. Emotional appeal and organizational flexibility gave the Baptists the edge, but they might have thrown it away had they not undertaken the task of conversion with the vigor they did. The organizational flexibility of the Baptists provided a particularly good opportunity for the retention of magic and folk belief despite the theological strictures against them. Excommunications for backsliding into paganism occurred, but the loose methods of organization made surveillance difficult; and the black preachers found it easy to look the other way without incurring the wrath of a watchful hierarchy.

The Baptists' efforts to proselytize among slaves and their willingness to rely on, or at least not exclude, black preachers did not prove them less racist or more deeply concerned with the secular fate of the blacks than were others. Whatever advantage they may have derived from their early hostility to slavery and later concern with amelioration faded as the several southern churches closed ranks behind the single reform formula of confirming slavery as a normal condition for blacks and urging more humane treatment. During the last three decades of the antebellum period Baptists, Methodists, Presbyterians, and others accelerated, both by design and simply by taking the path of least resistance, the long-developing trend toward racial separation within the churches.[8]

Even during the eighteenth century a double push for separation had been taking place. Hostile whites steadily tried to push the blacks into separate congregations, especially where the black population was substantial, and blacks often moved to facilitate the split, partly because they felt uncomfortable and wished to practice their religion in their own way, and partly because they resented the inferior position into which they were being thrust within the white churches. For the blacks the move to separate was thus both a positive desire for independent cultural expression and a defense against racism.[9]

The rise of the independent black churches in Philadelphia and other cities of both North and South, often under the leadership of strong personalities, did make the task of the white segregationists all the easier.[10] At the same time the trend toward separation affected the plantation belt itself in less dramatic and less formal ways. By the end of the antebellum period most southern blacks who professed Christianity called themselves Baptists, and so they were. But they had become black Baptists – a category increasingly of their own making. The division had fateful consequences. Ulrich Bonnell Phillips clearly saw the negative implications for both black and white, but especially white: 'In general, the less the cleavage of creed between master and man, the better for both, since every factor conducing to solidarity of sentiment was of advantage in promoting harmony and progress. When the planter went to sit under his rector while the slave stayed at home to hear an exhorter, just so much was lost in the sense of fellowship'.[11] What Phillips did not wish to see was that the consequences for the slaves were not entirely negative, for separation helped them to widen the degree of autonomy they were steadily carving out of their oppressors' regime.[12]

On the plantations and farms the slaves met for services apart from the whites whenever they could. Weekly services on Sunday evenings were common. Where masters were indulgent, additional meetings might take place during the week, and where they were not, they might take place anyway. Masters and overseers often accepted the Sunday meetings but not the others, for the slaves would stay up much of the night praying, singing, and dancing. The next day being a workday, the meetings were bad for business.[13]

The slaves' religious meetings would be held in secret when their masters forbade all such; or when their masters forbade all except Sunday meetings; or when rumors of rebellion or disaffection led even indulgent masters to forbid them so as to protect the people from trigger-happy patrollers; or when the slaves wanted to make sure that no white would hear them. Only during insurrection scares or tense moments occasioned by political turmoil could the laws against such meetings be enforced. Too many planters did not want them enforced. They regarded their slaves as peaceful, respected their religious sensibilities, and considered such interference dangerous to plantation morale and productivity. Others agreed that the slaves presented no threat of rising and did not care about their meetings. Had the slaves been less determined, the regime probably would have been far more stringent; but so long as they avoided conspiracies and accepted harsh punishment as the price for getting caught by patrols, they raised the price of suppression much too high to make it seem worthwhile to planters with steady nerves.[14]

When the meetings had to be held in secret, the slaves confronted a security problem. They would announce the event by such devices as that of singing 'Steal Away to Jesus' at work.[15] To protect the meeting itself, they had an infallible method. They would turn over a pot 'to catch the sound' and keep it in the cabin or immediate area of the woods. Almost infallible: 'Of course, sometimes they might happen to slip up on them on suspicion'.[16] George P. Rawick suggests that the practice of turning over a pot probably had African origins, and John F. Szwed links it to rituals designed to sanctify the ground. The slaves' belief in its efficacy gave them additional confidence to brave the risks, and their success in avoiding detection led some whites to think that there might just be something to the pot technique.[17]

The desire of the slaves for religious privacy took a limited as well as a general form. Eliza Frances Andrews went down to the plantation praise-house after dinner one night to hear the slaves sing. 'At their "praise meetings" ', she commented, 'they go through all sorts of motions in connection with their songs, but they won't give way to their wildest gesticulations or engage in their sacred dances before white people for fear of being laughed at'.[18] But the slaves had no objection to pleasing curious whites when they expected an appreciative response. They took enormous pride in their singing and in the depth of their religious expression. They resisted being laughed at, but they responded to expressions of respect. Gus Feaster, an ex-slave from Union County, South Carolina, proudly told of such instances:

> At night when the meeting done busted till next day was when the darkies really did have they freedom of spirit. As the wagon be creeping along in the late hours of moonlight, the darkies would raise a tune. Then the air soon be filled with the sweetest tune as us rid on home and sung all the old hymns that us loved. It was always some big black nigger with a deep bass voice like a frog that'd start up the tune. Then the other mens jine in, followed up by the fine little voices of the gals and the cracked voices of the old womens and the grannies. When us reach near the big house us soften down to a deep hum that the missus like! Sometimes she hist up the window and tell us sing 'Swing Low, Sweet Chariot' for her and the visiting guests. That all us want to hear. Us open up, and the niggers near the big house that hadn't been to church would wake up and come out to the cabin door and jine in the refrain. From that we'd swing on into all the old spirituals that us love so well and that us knowed how to sing. Missus often 'low that her darkies could sing with heaven's inspiration.[19]

This pride, this self-respect, this astonishing confidence in their own spiritual quality, explain the slaves' willingness to spend so much of their day of leisure at prayer meetings. Often they would hear the white preacher or the master himself on Sunday morning, but the 'real meetin' and the 'real preachin' came later, among themselves.[20] Richard Carruthers, an ex-slave from Texas, explained another feature of the concern with prayer. 'Us niggers', he said, 'used to have a prayin' ground down in the hollow and some time we come out of the field, between eleven and twelve at night, scorchin' and burnin' up with nothin' to eat, and we wants to ask the good Lord to have mercy'.[21]

The meetings gave the slaves strength derived from direct communion with God and each other. When not monitored, they allowed the message of promised deliverance to be heard. If the slaves had received false information or had been misled by the whites, they provided an opportunity for correction, as when the white preachers led them in prayers for the Confederacy, and their black preachers, in secret session, led them in prayers for the Union.[22] But above all, the meetings provided a sense of autonomy – of constituting not merely a community unto themselves but a community with leaders of their own choice.

The slaves' religious frenzy startled white onlookers, although few ever saw it fully unleashed. The more austere masters tried to curb it but usually had little success. Emoline Glasgow of South Carolina had a Methodist master who took one of his slaves to church and determined to keep him in line by bribery if necessary. He offered to give the slave a new pair of boots if he behaved himself. All went well until about the middle of the service, when the slave let go: 'Boots or no boots, I gwine to shout today'.[23] The slaves took their letting-go seriously and condemned those who simulated emotion. When the Catholic priests forbade shouting in Louisiana, Catherine Cornelius spoke for the slaves in insisting that 'the angels shout in heaven' and in doggedly proclaiming, 'The Lawd said you gotta shout if you want to be saved. That's in the Bible'. Sincerity meant everything. Emma Fraser, an ex-slave from South Carolina, talked about her singing in church in the way that others talked about shouting. 'But ef I sing an' it doan move me any, den dat a sin on de Holy Ghost; I be tell a lie on de Lord'.[24] The frenzy, as W. E. B. Du Bois called it, brought the slaves together in a special kind of communion, which brought out the most individual expressions and yet disciplined the collective. The people protected each other against the excesses of their release and encouraged each other to shed inhibitions. Everyone responded according to his own spirit but ended in a spiritual union with everyone else.[25]

Possession appeared much less often among the slaves of the Old South than among those of Saint-Domingue or Brazil, where the practice of Vodûn and the rites of the African cults ran high. Yet ecstatic seizures, however defined, appeared frequently and submit to differing interpretations. Critics have recognized in them a form of hysteria, and Frantz Fanon even speaks of a kind of madness. Roger Bastide has suggested that they are vehicles by which repressed personalities surface in symbolic form. Many anthropologists, however, have remained skeptical of psychoanalytic explanations and have pointed out that no genuine schizophrenic could possibly adjust to the firm system of control that the rituals demand. No matter how wild and disorderly they look to the uninitiated, they are in fact tightly controlled; certain things must be done and others not done. They thus require, according to Alfred Métraux, social, not psychological, explanation. Yet, schizophrenia aside, a psychoanalytic explanation is compatible with a social one. The question may be left for experts, if any. Two things are clear. First, the slaves' wildest emotionalism, even when it passed into actual possession, formed part of a system of collective behavior, which the slaves themselves controlled. The slaves may have been driven wild with ecstasy when dancing during their services, but never so wild that their feet would cross without evoking sharp rebuke. And second, the slaves' behavior brought out a determination to assert their power and the freedom of their spirit, for, as Max Weber says, ecstasy may become an instrument of salvation or self-deification.[26]

If emotional fervor alone had distinguished black religion, the usual interpretations would take on greater credibility – that no great difference existed between the religion of the slaves and that of the lower-class whites who followed the frontier Baptist and Methodist preachers. The frequently heard assertion that the blacks merely copied the whites may be left aside as unworthy of discussion. If one must choose between the two separate tendencies, the view of Dr. Du Bois, according to which the style of the poor whites has been a 'plain copy' of the style of the blacks, easily holds the field.[27] White and black responses reinforced each other, as they had to in an interracial setting. Their blending reflected a common frontier Christian character and no doubt contributed something toward bringing together two antagonistic peoples. But there were differences that illuminate the special quality of the black experience.

Neither a common body of belief – to the extent that it was in fact common – nor even common rites could guarantee a common spiritual experience. Rites reflect, and in turn reshape, the communities that practice them. Slaves and poorer rural whites (that is, small farmers and actual 'poor whites') brought fundamentally different community settings to their common rites, and they therefore brought fundamentally different spiritual needs, responses, and values.[28] When slaves from small farms shared religious meetings and churchgoing with their white yeomen and poor white neighbors, they no doubt drew closer to their inner experience, but even then some distance was inevitable. For plantation blacks, the distance had to be much greater.

The blacks did not hide their disdain for white shouters, whom they regarded, as Dr. Du Bois did later, as a plain copy of themselves. Even in the early camp meetings the blacks notoriously outshouted the whites and stayed up singing and praying long after the whites had retired. They made up their own hymns, which drew protests from orthodox whites because they were their own and because they came too close to sounding like plantation jubilee melodies.[29] Viewing a meeting in Georgia, which attracted even more blacks than whites, Olmsted observed: 'The Negroes kept their place during all the tumult; there may have been a sympathetic groan or exclamation uttered by one or two of them, but generally they expressed only the interest of curiosity.... There was generally a self-satisfied smile upon their faces; and I have no doubt they felt they could do it with a great deal more energy and abandon, if they were called upon'.[30] Beneath the similarities and differences of style lay a divergence of meanings, including some divergence in the very meaning of God.

The slaves drew their call-and-response pattern from their African heritage, however important the reinforcing elements from the Europeans. Europeans had also used something like a song-style of preaching and responding, which had somewhat different qualities. Blacks and whites in the South performed in distinct ways. The content of the white responses to a preacher – undoubtedly with many exceptions – consisted of 'Amens' and the like. The whites cheered their preacher on or let him know they were moved. The preacher needed that response, craved it, even demanded it. But the black preacher had to evoke it, not for his own satisfaction, subjectively important as that may have been, but because without it the service had no relationship to God.[31] This difference in style betrayed a difference in theological tendency. The whites were fundamentalists to the core, the blacks only apparently so. Both preached the Bible in fiery style, but as the Reverend Henry H. Mitchell suggests, the whites were fiery mad, while the blacks were fiery glad.[32] Or as Martin Ruffin, an ex-slave from Texas, said of a black preacher, Sam Jones, he 'preached Hell-fire and judgment like the white preachers'.[33]

While the religion of the slaves, as everyone saw, exhibited joy much as the religion of their African forebears had, who in his right mind would say the same thing of the religion of the whites? W. J. Cash writes of white southern religion:

> What our Southerner required ... was a faith as simple and emotional as himself. A faith to draw men together in hordes, to terrify them with Apocalyptic rhetoric, to cast them into the pit, rescue them, and at last bring them shouting back into the fold of Grace.... The God demanded was an anthropomorphic God – the Jehovah of the Old Testament: a God who might be seen, a God who *had* been seen. A passionate, whimsical tyrant to be trembled before, but whose favor was the sweeter for that. A personal God, a God for the individualist, a God whose representatives were not silken priests but preachers risen from the people themselves.
>
> What was demanded here, in other words, was the God and the faith of the Methodists and the Baptists and the Presbyterians.[34]

Cash fails to note that the blacks identified with the same churches and turned them into something rather different.

Olmsted's description of that white hellfire preacher in action before a congregation of lower-class whites says a great deal:

> The preliminary devotional exercises – a Scripture reading, singing, and painfully irreverential and meaningless harangues nominally addressed to the Deity, but really to the audience – being concluded, the sermon was commenced by reading a text, with which, however, it had, so far as I could discover, no further association. Without often being violent in his manner, the speaker nearly all the time cried aloud at the utmost stretch of his voice, as if calling to some one a long distance off; . . . and as he was gifted with a strong imagination, and possessed of a good deal of dramatic power, he kept the attention of the people very well. There was no argument upon any point that the congregation were likely to have much difference of opinion upon, nor any special connection between one sentence and another; yet there was a constant, sly, sectarian skirmishing, and a frequently recurring cannonade upon French infidelity and socialism, and several crushing charges upon Fourier, the Pope of Rome, Tom Paine, Voltaire, 'Roosu', and Jo Smith . . . . He had the habit of frequently repeating a phrase, or of bringing forward the same idea in a slightly different form, a great many times. The following passage, of which I took notes, presents an example of this, followed by one of the best instances of his dramatic talent that occurred. He was leaning far over the desk, with his arm stretched forward, gesticulating violently, yelling at the highest key, and catching breath with an effort:
> 'A—ah! why don't you come to Christ? ah! what's the reason? ah! Is it because he was of *lowly birth*? ah! Is that it? *Is it* because he was born in a manger? ah! Is it because he was of a humble origin? ah! Is it because he was lowly born? a-ha! . . . Perhaps you don't like the messenger – is that the reason? I'm the Ambassador of the great and glorious King; it's his invitation, 'taint mine. You musn't mind me. I ain't no account. Suppose a ragged, insignificant little boy should come running in here and tell you, "Mister, your house's a-fire"! would you mind the ragged, insignificant little boy, and refuse to listen to him, because he didn't look respectable'?[35]

It is not easy to imagine a black preacher's wanting to know if his slave congregation despised Jesus for being poor and not looking respectable. Time and again, the message of the black preachers turned precisely on the low earthly station of the Son of God.

Dr. Mitchell draws for us a sharp distinction between southern black and white uses of the Bible. 'A Black preacher', he notes, 'is more likely to say, "Didn't He say it"! than to be officious about what "the Word of God declares!" ' For the blacks the Bible provides an inexhaustible store of good advice for a proper life; it does not usually provide an unchanging body of doctrine, as with the white fundamentalists. Hence, biblical figures must come alive, must be present, must somehow provide a historical example for modern application. Black religion eschews bibliolatry and does not have a strong anti-intellectual bias.[36] Those who might suspect that Dr. Mitchell is being carried into romantic exaggeration might note that social scientists who have closely studied black religious behavior in the South have unearthed materials that lend firm support to his analysis.[37] At issue, therefore, are the slaves' notions of heaven, hell, sin, and soul.

White Methodist and Baptist preachers ripped each other up in theological debates all over the South and did not let up when singly preaching to the slaves. The slaves turned out to cheer them on. Olmsted, after remarking that Baptist and Methodist preachers spent much of their time denouncing each other's doctrines, added, 'The negroes are represented to have a great taste for theological controversy'.[38] Eliza Frances Andrews described a Methodist slave in Georgia who had a staunch Baptist master: 'They used to have some high old religious discussions together'.[39]

The slaves' penchant for theological disputation ought neither to be dismissed as a ridiculous spectacle nor accepted at face value. There is nothing ridiculous in the idea of illiterate field hands' trying to follow an argument about God, for He was ever-present in their lives, even if they did respond more readily to evidence of spiritual motivation in the preacher than they did to his argument. Then too, the white Baptist and Methodist preachers had learned to translate the most difficult points of theology into unadorned English for their frontier congregations. If they could not make themselves understood to the slaves, it was usually for reasons other than their inability to speak plain English. But neither should the slaves' reaction be taken straight, first, because the theological questions that most interested them were of a different order, and second, because they had too high a sense of humor not to respond to a good show when they saw one.

The Baptist churches in the South ran the gamut from Calvinism to Arminianism, but the powerful tendency, especially in the rougher terrain of the Mississippi Valley, took extreme predestinarian ground. Now, Regular Baptists who talk like John Calvin on the fate of man present something of a puzzle. The accepted and plausible, if somewhat impish, explanation is that the free-will polemics of the rough-and-tumble Methodists drove their Baptist adversaries further and further into extreme formulations of their standpoint. So far did one wing go that its famous two-seed doctrine, according to which Eve produced two seeds only one of which originated with God, has quite sensibly been classified by some scholars as thinly disguised Manichaeanism.[40] Yet, predestinarian doctrine did not appear in black religion. In part, the explanation may lie in a greater attention to preaching among the slaves by the free-will Baptists and those who glided over the issue. But the deeper reason must be sought in the slaves' own inclinations. Only rarely did orthodox Calvinism come from the mouths of black preachers, and even in those cases its uses remain in doubt. In 1793, a black preacher upset Harry Toulmin by preaching Calvinist doctrine, but the point he was making in his excellent sermon was the equality of man before God.[41] The slave quarters provided poor ground for predestinarianism. When slaves and ex-slaves insisted that God had foreordained everything, they usually meant that even slavery had an appropriate place in His eternal design. And at that, their reaction could turn bitter. In Wilkinson County, Mississippi, an old slave gravedigger, accompanied by a young helper, asked a white stranger a question:

> 'Massa, may I ask you something'?
> 'Ask what you please'.
> 'Can you 'splain how it happened in the fust place, that the white folks got the start of the black folks, so as to make dem slaves and do all de work'?
> The younger helper, fearing the white man's wrath, broke in:
> 'Uncle Pete, it's no use talking. It's fo'ordained. The Bible tells you that. The Lord fo'ordained the Nigger to work, and the white man to boss'.
> 'Dat's so. Dat's so. But if dat's so, then God's no fair man'![42]

Since predestination leaves no room for magic, its attraction for people whose religious sensibility retained the features of folk origin was almost nonexistent. No socially deprived lower class has found it easy to warm to Calvinist theology. As Keith Thomas writes:

> The doctrine of providence was always less likely to appeal to those at the bottom end of the social scale than the rival doctrine of luck. For the believer in luck can account for his misfortune without jeopardizing his self-esteem. The concept of luck explains any apparent discrepancy between merit and reward and thus helps to reconcile men to the environment in which they live.[43]

The slaves stayed close to their conjurers, and the preachers who could reach them knew enough not to force the issue.

For the slaves, salvation came through an uneasy combination of free will and faith – faith in God and faith in each other – because faith meant love. An old preacher, who had been a slave in South Carolina, remarked, 'Brother, you has to have faith in your fellow man befo' you has faith in de lawd'.[44] The spirituals vibrated with the message: God will deliver us if we have faith in Him. And they emphasized the idea of collective deliverance of the slaves as a people by their choice of such heroes as Moses, Jonah, and Daniel.[45] The slaves' attachment to the doctrine of salvation by faith, their ability to turn the most serious matters to good-humored advantage, and their inexhaustible penchant for puttin' on Ole Massa all appeared in an incident described by Olmsted. A formally pious slave was plaguing his master by his persistence in undefined immorality. The master asked a minister to intercede and try to appeal to the slave's religious nature. As Olmsted told it:

> The clergyman did so, and endeavored to bring the terrors of the law to bear upon his conscience. 'Look yeah, massa', said the back-slider, 'don't de Scriptur say, "Dem who believes an' is baptize shall be save" '? 'Certainly', the clergyman answered; and went on to explain and expound the passage: but directly the slave interrupted him again.
>
> 'Jus you tell me now, massa, don't de good book say dese word: "Dem as believes and is baptize, shall be save"; want to know dat'.
>
> 'Yes, but ... '
>
> 'Das all I want to know, sar; wat's de use o' talkin' to me. You ain't a going to make me bleve wat de blessed Lord says, ain't so, not ef you tries forever'.
>
> The clergyman again attempted to explain.... 'De Scriptur say, if a man believe and be baptize he *shall* be save. Now, massa minister, I *done* believe and I *done* baptize, an I *shall be save suah*—Dere's no use talkin', sar'.[46]

According to the scriptural defense of slavery, which commanded enormous attention throughout the white South during the forties and fifties, the enslavement of the blacks by the whites fulfilled the biblical curse on Ham, much as for the Russian landlords the curse had fallen on their serfs. Japheth's predicted dwelling in the tents of Shem accounted for the expropriation of the Indians' lands, and the enforced service of blacks to whites took care of the sons of Ham. The suggestion that in time Ethiopia would stretch out her hand to God caused some misgivings, but not many. 'Panola', as a planter from Mississippi signed himself in the agricultural journals, nicely took care of any qualms. Was Ethiopia ready to stretch out her hand to God? No. How did he know? 'Niggers are too *high* for that'.[47] The imagery extended even to militant black sources and appears, for example, although with a quite different meaning, in David Walker's famous *Appeal to the Colored Citizens of the World*.

Despite a few hints to the contrary, the slaves did not view their predicament as punishment for the collective sin of black people. No amount of white propaganda could bring them to accept such an idea. Occasionally, blacks spoke of slavery as a punishment for sin, but even then the precise meaning remained vague. The stark assertion of the white preachers that blacks suffered from the sin of Ham had few if any echoes in the quarters.

When Eli Coleman, an ex-slave from Kentucky, spoke of blacks' being under God's curse and therefore in a living hell, he insisted that their great problem was lack of higher vocational and educational skills.[48] Rarely if ever has the transition from John Calvin to Adam Smith been so tightly telescoped. Charity Moore remembered her father's interpretation of the Bible and original sin. The story is charming enough, but its finale demands attention. Adam, it seems, had been so frightened by his sin that he turned white. The rest of the story she 'disremembered'.[49] Another version, by Ezra Adams, who had been a plowhand on a South Carolina slave plantation, took a plainly secular turn: Adam sinned by taking what did not belong to him. 'If what Adam done back yonder', he explained, 'would happen now, he would be guilty of crime. Dat's how 'ciety names sin'. Thus black preachers invoked parables to demonstrate that God could make good come from evil; that there was good in the most errant brother and sister; and, by implication, that He was bringing good to His enslaved people whose conditions rather than themselves were evil.[50]

For the slaves, sin meant wrongdoing – injustice to others and violation of accepted moral codes. Their otherworldly idea of Heaven shared its place with a this-worldly idea that stressed freedom and a community of love for one's brothers and sisters; little room remained for a theology based on original sin. Hence, black theology largely ignored the one doctrine that might have reconciled the slaves to their bondage on a spiritual plane.

Original sin does not appear in African religions, and the problem of freedom and order therefore assumes radically different forms. Without such a doctrine the delicate balance between the two tips toward the claims of the collective against those of the individual. Much as the doctrine of original sin reflects the class divisions in Western society, whatever its deeper insight into human nature, it also creates greater possibilities for individual freedom, particularly since the cause of individual freedom has historically been inseparable from the use of private property. When the Christian faith took its stand on the doctrine of original sin, it constructed a defense of the individual personality on which the most secularized ideologies of liberalism came to be built. But Christianity's world-shaking achievement also rested on guilt and self-contempt, without which its doctrine of freedom could not have been theologically and socially disciplined. This particular tension between freedom and order provided the driving force of Western culture, as well as the basis for its pessimism.

The African legacy to Afro-America – that celebrated joy in life which is so often denigrated or explained away – represented a life-affirming faith that stressed shame and minimized guilt. Enslavement might be shameful and an expression of weakness, but it could not easily produce a sense of guilt – of getting what you deserved and of being punished for having offended God. Christianity might have transformed the slaves into the slavish robots of Nietzsche's polemic or the Sambos of Stanley Elkins's model, if they had not virtually reshaped it to fit their own psychic needs and their own sensibility.

The ambiguity of the slaves' Heaven and of the limitations on their idea of sin had roots in African ideas of the Soul. Again, it is not possible to know to what extent they stubbornly clung to African ideas and to what extent plantation slave conditions recreated certain patterns of thought. But, clearly, no sharp break occurred. Their life as slaves in the New World, even after conversion to Christianity, did not destroy the traditional sensibility. Newbell Niles Puckett, in his study of folk beliefs among southern blacks during the twentieth century, pointedly insists that their idea of the Soul comes close to traditional African ideas. In some cases he finds 'a definite belief in a *kra* or dream-soul', according to which a dream becomes the actual experience of the dreamer's Soul wandering into another world.[51]

A more significant question concerns the relationship of the Soul to the natural order. In the classical Christian tradition man is unique; he alone has a Soul, which establishes his claims to freedom as a matter of responsibility before God. Even in Calvinist theology, in which man's Soul is predestined to salvation or damnation, man himself chose not to obey God in the first place. African ideas place man himself and therefore his Soul within nature. Reincarnation and the return of spirits to the world of the living may occur. Man's Soul is one spirit among many, for all things are infused with spirits. Man himself is one of many material hosts. For traditional Africans, like many non-Christian peoples elsewhere, the Soul came to mean the inner life – the quintessential experience of which matter was merely the form. Thus the Soul, crystallized in a man's shadow, could be detached from his person. Hence, spirits wandered in this world.[52]

The theology of the black preachers made peace with folk ideas of the Soul when it slid over the meaning of Heaven. In so doing, it strengthened the slaves' sense of belonging to the world and of being promised deliverance through faith in Jesus Christ. The compromise was effected on Christian ground, but it necessarily had to reduce that very otherworldliness on which classical Christian individualism in general and antinomianism in particular had arisen. This adjustment entailed sacrifice of considerable revolutionary power.

The idea that the slaves' repeated references to Heaven prove their religious orientation to have been primarily otherworldly rests on a narrow reading of their complex thought. The most obvious function of a concern with Heaven among preachers to the slaves would appear to have been a determination to reconcile them to their lot and turn their attention to an ideal realm. The sermons of black preachers, not to mention white, often centered on this theme. E. S. Abdy heard a slave preacher in Kentucky in 1834 and described him and his performance: 'He was about sixty years of age – shrewd and sensible, and, as far as I could judge from some of his observations, a very religious man. What he said upon the duty of submission to his lot here, and his reliance on Divine justice hereafter would have done no discredit to the best educated white'.[53] Yet, such messages contain much ambiguity, and so did the very language and delivery of those who spoke them.

Miles Mark Fisher, in a provocative, controversial, but often strained study of the slave songs, vigorously denies that the slaves had any understanding of or interest in the immortality of the Soul. The part of his interpretation that evokes most querulousness is his insistence that Africa played the central role in slave consciousness and that references to Heaven in the spirituals should be understood as meaning Africa or other earthly places of refuge. He does not prove this part of his case, but he does suggest a deep ambiguity in the slaves' apparently otherworldly references.[54]

The slaves' concern with Heaven cannot be interpreted as escapism, especially since, as Howard Thurman and Lawrence Levine point out, a rigid separation of the sacred and the secular had no place in the slaves' view of the world.[55] The several meanings of Heaven in the spirituals must therefore be seen as one – as a necessary and intrinsic ambiguity that reflects a view of the world in which the spiritual and the material merge. No choice need be made between this-worldly and otherworldly interpretations of the song sung by slaves in Mississippi:

> But some ob dese days my time will come,
> I'll year dat bugle, I'll year dat drum,
> I'll see dem armies, marchin' along,
> I'll lif my head an' jine der song.[56]

Or of 'Didn't My Lord Deliver Daniel', or of 'Joshua Fit de Battle ob Jericho', or of 'Oh, Mary, Don't You Weep', or of 'Go Down, Moses'. They do not necessarily refer to deliverance in this world or in the other, for they might easily mean either or both. But either way or both ways, they did imply the immanence of God's justice here or hereafter, as He sees fit to bestow it. In this sense, the spirituals were, as Dr. Du Bois himself suggested, 'Sorrow Songs' that transcended their sorrow and became hymns of joy.

> Through all the sorrow of the Sorrow Songs there breathes a hope – a faith in the ultimate justice of things. The minor cadences of despair change often to triumph and calm confidence. Sometimes it is faith in life, sometimes a faith in death, sometimes assurances of boundless justice in some fair world beyond. But whichever it is, the meaning is always clear: that sometime, somewhere, men will judge men by their souls and not by their skins.[57]

The slaves' talent for improvisation, as well as their deep religious conviction, drew expressions of wonder and admiration from almost everyone who heard them sing. The boatmen of Georgia and South Carolina and of the Mississippi River received the most attention and drew the most comment, but the common field hands of the Cotton Belt did not lag far behind in performance. The words 'wild' and 'weird' recurred among white observers, from the abolitionists to the slaveholders to the merely curious. Harriet Beecher Stowe heard Sojourner Truth sing 'There Is a Holy City' and remarked, 'Sojourner, singing this hymn seemed to impersonate the fervor of Ethiopia, wild, savage, hunted of all nations, but burning after God in her tropic heart and stretching her scarred hands towards the glory to be revealed'.[58] Eliza Frances Andrews, listening to the slaves on her plantation singing at a praise-meeting, called their songs 'mostly a sort of weird chant that makes me feel all out of myself when I hear it way in the night, too far off to catch the words'.[59]

Asked how the songs originated, a black man replied:

> I'll tell you; it's dis way. My master call me up and order me a short peck of corn and a hundred lash. My friends see it and is sorry for me. When dey come to de praise meeting dat night dey sing about it. Some's very good singers and know how; and dey work it in, work it in, you know; till dey get it right; and dat's de way.[60]

In 1845, J. Kennard wrote in *Knickerbocker Magazine*:

> Who are the true rulers? The Negro poets to be sure. Do they not set the fashion, and give laws to the public taste? Let one of them, in the swamps of Carolina, compose a new song, and it no sooner reaches the ear of a white amateur, than it is written down, amended (that is, almost spoilt), printed and then put upon a course of rapid dissemination, to cease only with the utmost bounds of Anglo-Saxondom, perhaps with the world. Meanwhile, the the poor author digs away with his hoe, utterly ignorant of his greatness.[61]

T. S. Eliot observed:

> When a poet's mind is perfectly equipped for its work, it is constantly amalgamating disparate experience; the ordinary man's experience is chaotic, irregular, fragmentary. The latter falls in love, or reads Spinoza, and these two experiences have nothing to do with each other, or with the noise of the typewriter or the smell of cooking; in the mind of the poet these experiences are always forming new wholes.[62]

It is doubtful that, by this standard, the world has ever seen so many poets whose minds were 'perfectly equipped' simultaneously at work to produce so powerful a synthesis of sacred and secular themes.

Alexander K. Farrar, a planter in Adams County, Mississippi, provided an illuminating illustration of the slaves' understanding of Heaven and its worldly uses. Some slaves had committed murder and had been sentenced to hang. A public display was in order, he thought, for too many slaves believed that the punishment for murder would be transportation, and they had to be disabused. Farrar urged that the bodies be exhibited to the slaves but strongly opposed a public hanging. 'If the Negroes are brought out in public to be hung', he explained, 'and they get up and talk out that they have got religion and are ready to go home to heaven, etc. etc. – it will have a bad effect upon the other Negroes'.[63]

In its blandest and most accommodationist forms, the orientation of oppressed classes toward an afterlife contains important elements of political judgment that help to counteract the pressures for dehumanization and despair and contribute toward the formation of class consciousness. If the lower classes cannot claim to be much, the idea of Heaven, with its equality before God, gives them a strong sense of what they are destined to become. It thereby introduces a sense of worth and reduces the stature of the powerful men of the world. The emphasis on Heaven metamorphoses from the otherworldly into the inner-worldly and creates its own ground for dissent in this world.[64] The other side of this lower-class concern with Heaven is its vision of Hell – the afterlife appropriate to the oppressor. Of the Methodists' influence on the British working class, E. P. Thompson writes: 'Faith in a life to come served not only as a consolation to the poor but also as some emotional compensation for present sufferings and grievances: it was possible not only to imagine the "reward" of the humble but also to enjoy some revenge upon their oppressors, by imagining their torments to come'.[65] This sense of a revenge to come always carried with it the thrust of a political quiescence accompanied by vicarious thrills. Its positive political significance remained only a tendency. By sharpening a sense of class justice it prepared the way for explosive hostility, should circumstances present an opportunity for aggressive action.

In less dramatic ways, the slaves manipulated the idea of Heaven both defensively and offensively. It could become a vehicle for a sarcastic judgment of the masters, as it did for Andrew Moss of Georgia: 'De white folks what owned slaves thought that when dey go to Heaven de colored folks would be dere to wait on 'em'.[66] One theme that recurs is love for each other. The slaves viewed Heaven as a place of reconciliation with each other; only sometimes did they view it as a place of reconciliation with whites. Annie Laurie Broiderick, a white woman from a slaveholding family in Vicksburg, Mississippi, recalled the activities of the Methodist slaves. 'During their protracted meetings', she wrote, 'after becoming pious, they would work themselves into a frenzy, and begin their shouting by walking up to each other, taking and shaking the hand with words, "I hope to meet you in heaven .... " '[67] Anne Bell, an ex-slave from South Carolina, made the same point in her own way: 'Does I believe in 'ligion? What else good for colored folks? I ask you if dere ain't a heaven, what's colored folks got to look forward to? They can't git anywhere down here. De only joy they can have here is servin' and lovin'; us can git dat in 'ligion but dere is a limit to de nigger in everything else'.[68]

Fanny Kemble's three-year-old daughter confronted the maid: 'Mary, some persons are free and some are not'. No reply. 'I am a free person. I say, I am a free person, Mary – do you know that'? Acknowledgment: 'Yes, missus'. Relentless child: 'Some persons are free and some are not – do you know that, Mary'? Reply: 'Yes, missus, *here*; I know it is so here, in this world'.[69]

Did the slaves sing of God's Heaven and a life beyond this life? Or of a return to Africa? Or of a Heaven that was anywhere they would be free? Or of an undefined state in which they could love each other without fear? On any given occasion they did any one of these; probably, in most instances they did all at once. Men and women who dare to dream of deliverance from suffering rarely fit their dreams into neat packages.

Black eschatology emerges more clearly from the slaves' treatment of Moses and Jesus. The slaves did not draw a sharp line between them but merged them into the image of a single deliverer, at once this-worldly and otherworldly. Colonel Higginson said that their heads held a jumble of Jewish biblical history and that they associated Moses with all great historical events, including the most recent. After the war black preachers took the political stump to tell the freedmen in South Carolina that the Republican gubernatorial candidate, Franklin J. Moses, was none other than the man himself, who had come to lead them to the Promised Land. All across the South blacks insisted that they had seen Mr. Linkum visit their locality as part of his work of deliverance.

The image of Moses, the this-worldly leader of his people out of bondage, and Jesus, the otherworldly Redeemer, blended into a pervasive theme of deliverance. A former house slave, who considered himself superior to the field hands, admitted praying with them. 'Well, yes'm', he explained, 'we would pray the Lord to deliver us'. Eliza Frances Andrews waxed indignant over the freedmen's adulation for the abolitionist who had come to teach them during the Union occupation. They think he is Jesus Christ, she protested. 'Anyhow', she paraphrased them, 'he has done more for them than Jesus Christ ever did'. The Reverend C. C. Jones observed that the few remaining Muslim slaves on the Georgia coast identified Muhammed with Jesus, and he might have added, therefore with Moses too.[70]

The variety of uses to which the slaves put Moses may be glimpsed in two comments by ex-slaves. Savilla Burrell of South Carolina said:

> Young Marse Sam Still got killed in de Civil War. Old Marse live on. I went to see him in his last days and I set by him and kept de flies off while dere. I see the lines of sorrow had plowed on dat old face and I 'membered he'd been a captain on hoss back in dat war. It come into my 'membrance de song of Moses; 'de Lord had triumphed glorily and de hoss and his rider have been throwed into de sea'.[71]

And George Briggs, also from South Carolina, himself an old preacher, commented: 'Man learns right smart from Exodus 'bout how to lead.... Moses still de strongest impression dat we has as rulers. God gits His-self into de heads of men dat He wants to rule and He don't tell nobody else nothing 'bout it neither'.[72] The great heroes of the spirituals, even when Jesus' name appears, often turn out to be the deliverers of the people as a whole in this world.[73]

The slaves had a special and central place for Jesus, but a place that whites had difficulty recognizing. Julius Lester has given us, with a few short strokes, a convincing reading. The slaves, he writes, 'fashioned their own kind of Christianity, which they turned to for strength in the constant times of need. In the Old Testament story of the enslavement of the Hebrews by the Egyptians, they found their own story. In the figure of Jesus Christ, they found someone who had suffered as they suffered, someone who understood, someone who offered them rest from their suffering'.[74] Moses had become Jesus, and Jesus, Moses; and with their union the two aspects of the slaves' religious quest – collective deliverance as a people and redemption from their terrible personal sufferings – had become one through the mediation of that imaginative power so beautifully manifested in the spirituals.

NOTES

1. William K. Scarborough, ed., *The Diary of Edmund Ruffin*, 2 vols (Baton Rouge, La., 1972), Feb. 20, 1859 (I, 284).
2. Melville J. Herskovits, *The Myth of the Negro Past* (Boston, 1962), 232–4.
3. The ultimate complexity of the problem is suggested by the parallel success of fundamentalist sects among colonial peoples. See Peter Worsley, *The Trumpet Shall Sound: A Study of the 'Cargo Cults' in Melanesia* (London, 1957), 235.
4. Arthur Huff Fauset, *Black Gods of the Metropolis: Negro Religious Cults of the Urban North* (Philadelphia, 1971), 101–2.
5. Henry George Spaulding, 'Negro "Shouts" and Shout Songs', in Bernard Katz, ed., *The Social Implications of Early Negro Music in the United States* (New York, 1969), 4–5.
6. Thomas Merton, *Seasons of Celebration: Meditations on the Cycle of Liturgical Feasts* (New York, 1965), 248.
7. Richard Allen, quoted in Eileen Southern, *The Music of Black Americans: A History* (New York, 1971), 87.
8. In North Carolina the Methodists worked harder than the Baptists among the slaves and recruited more widely. See John Spencer Bassett, *Slavery in the State of North Carolina* (Baltimore, 1899), ch. 3; Everett Dick, *The Dixie Frontier: A Social History of the Southern Frontier from the First Transmontane Beginnings to the Civil War* (New York, 1964), 188; Walter B. Posey, *The Baptist Church in the Lower Mississippi Valley, 1776–1845* (Lexington, Ky., 1957), 89–93; and in general, Carter G. Woodson, *The History of the Negro Church* (Washington, D.C., 1921).
9. R. B. Semple, *History of the Rise and Progress of the Baptists in Virginia* (Richmond, Va., 1810), 101; Joseph C. Robert, *The Road from Monticello: a study of the Virginia slavery debate of 1832* (New York, 1970), 7; C. P. Patterson, *The Negro in*

Tennessee, 1790–1865: A Study in Southern Politics (Austin, 1922), 20; Joe G. Taylor, *Negro Slavery in Louisiana* (Baton Rouge, 1963), 138; William L. Richter, 'Slavery in Ante-bellum Baton Rouge, 1820–1860', *Louisiana History*, X (Spring, 1969), 125–46; Henry L. Swint, ed., *Dear Ones at Home: Letters from Contraband Camps* (Nashville, 1966), 125; Gaston Hugh Wamble, 'Negroes and Missouri Protestant Churches Before and After the Civil War', *Missouri Historical Review*, LXI (April, 1967), 321–47.

10. Richard C. Wade, *Slavery in the Cities: The South, 1820–1860* (New York, 1964), 83, 161–2, 167–8; Benjamin Elizah Mays, *The Negro's God as Reflected in His Literature* (New York, 1969), 30–65; Walter H. Brooks, 'Evolution of the Negro Baptist Church', *JNH*, VII (Jan., 1922), 11–22; Christopher Rush, *A Short History of the Rise and Progress of the African Episcopal Church in America* (New York, 1843), esp. 18, 60–1, 91, for efforts in the North and relations with white churches.

11. Ulrich B. Phillips, *American Negro Slavery: A Survey of the Supply, Employment and Control of Negro Labor as Determined by the Plantation Regime* (New York, 1918), 321.

12. See E. U. Essien-Udom, *Black Nationalism: A Search for an Identity in America* (New York, 1964), 31, 37–8.

13. Frederick Law Olmsted, *A Journey in the Back Country* (reprinted New York, 1970), 93.

14. South Carolina had as good a police system as any and also a no-nonsense tradition in matters of social control, yet the laws were enforced only during times of stress. See H. M. Henry, *The Police Control of the Slave in South Carolina* (Emory, Va., 1914), 133–41.

15. Rawick, ed., *The American Slave: Texas Narrative*, V, pt. 4, 198.

16. Fisk University, *The Unwritten History of Slavery: Autobiographical Accounts of Negro Ex-slaves* (comp. and ed. Ophelia Settle Egypt *et al.*, Washington, D.C., 1968), 87.

17. George P. Rawick, *From Sundown to Sunup: The Making of the Black Community* (Westport, Conn., 1972), 41ff.; John F. Szwed in personal correspondence. Also, Rawick, ed., *The American Slave: Indiana Narrative*, VI, pt. 2, 98.

18. Eliza F. Andrews, *The War-Time Journal of a Georgia Girl, 1864–1865* (New York, 1908), Feb. 12, 1865 (p. 89).

19. B. A. Botkin, ed., *Lay My Burden Down: A Folk History of Slavery* (Chicago, 1945), 146.

20. Norman R. Yetman, ed., *Life Under the 'Peculiar Institution': Selections from the Slave Narrative Collection* [Library of Congress] (New York, 1970), 13 (testimony of Lucretia Alexander of Arkansas).

21. Ibid., 53.

22. Rawick, ed., *Texas Narrative*, IV (1), 11; *Arkansas Narrative*, IX (4), 254; *Missouri Narrative*, XI, 305.

23. Rawick, ed., *South Carolina Narrative*, II (2), 135.

24. Lyle Saxon *et al.*, *Gumbo Ya-Ya* (Boston, 1945), 242; Rawick, ed., *South Carolina Narrative*, II (2), 87.

25. Some elite house slaves, free Negroes, and urban slaves – by no means all and probably not the majority – were quite uncomfortable in these circumstances and preferred to pray in the 'white' manner. See, e.g., Mary Sharpe to C. C. Jones, June 2, 1856, in Robert M. Myers, ed., *The Children of Pride: A True Story of Georgia and the Civil War* (New Haven, 1972); Frederick Law Olmsted, *A Journey in the Seaboard slave states, with remarks on their economy* (New York, 1859), 405.

26. Max Weber, *The Sociology of Religion* (trans. E. Fischoffs; Boston, 1964), 157. On spirit possession see Roger Bastide, *Sociologie et psychoanalyse* (Paris, 1950), 252; Georges Balandier, *Ambiguous Africa: Cultures in Collision* (trans. Helen Weaver; New York, 1965), 46–7; Worsley, *Trumpet Shall Sound*, 61.

27. W. E. B. Du Bois, *The Souls of Black Folk*, new edn. (Millwood, N. Y., 1973), 142.
28. See the illuminating discussion by E. E. Evans-Pritchard, *Theories of Primitive Religion* (Oxford, 1965), 46, and his analysis of Radin's views on 247.
29. For a good summary discussion see Southern, *Music of Black Americans*, 96.
30. Olmsted, *Seaboard*, 460.
31. On the African origins of the call-and-response pattern in the spirituals see esp. Alan Lomax, 'The Homogeneity of African–Afro-American Musical Style', in Norman E. Whitten and John F. Szwed, eds., *Afro-American Anthropology: Contemporary Perspectives on Theory and Research* (New York, 1970), ch. 9. Also John W. Work, *American Negro Songs and Spirituals* (New York, 1940), 9; John J. Szwed, 'Afro-American Musical Adaptation', *Journal of American Folklore* (Mar., 1969), 219–28; Charles W. Joyner, *Folk Song in South Carolina* (Columbia, S.C., 1971), 6, 71.
32. Henry H. Mitchell, *Black Preaching* (Philadelphia, 1970), 50.
33. Rawick, ed., *Texas Narrative*, V (3), 266.
34. W. J. Cash, *The Mind of the South* (New York, 1941), 58.
35. Olmsted, *Seaboard*, 455–7.
36. Mitchell, *Black Preaching*, 49–50, 101, 112–13, 133.
37. See, e.g., Newbell N. Puckett, *Folk Beliefs of the Southern Negro* (Chapel Hill, 1926), 535; Hortense Powdermaker, *After Freedom: A Cultural Study in the Deep South* (New York, 1939), 246, 260–1.
38. Olmsted, *Seaboard*, 123.
39. Andrews, *War-Time Journal of a Georgia Girl*, June 28, 1865 (321).
40. Posey, *Baptist Church in the Lower Mississippi Valley*, 70–1.
41. Harry Toulmin, *The Western Country in 1793: Reports on Kentucky and Virginia*, ed. Marion Tinling and Godfrey Davies (San Marino, Calif., 1948), 30.
42. See, e.g., Elizabeth Keckley, *Behind the Scenes, or Thirty years as slave and four years in the White House* (New York, 1868), xii, for a combination of these tendencies. The graveyard incident is from Charles S. Sydnor, *Slavery in Mississippi* (New York, 1933), 251–2.
43. Keith Thomas, *Religion and the Decline of Magic* (London, 1970), 111.
44. Rawick, ed., *South Carolina Narrative*, II (1), 93.
45. See the perceptive analysis of Lawrence Levine, 'Slave Songs and Slave Consciousness' in Tamara K. Hareven, ed., *Anonymous Americans: Explorations in Nineteenth-Century Social History* (Englewood Cliffs, N. J., 1971), 118–21.
46. Olmsted, *Seaboard*, 123–4.
47. For an account of the polemic over the meaning of the curse in relation to the condition of Africa, see Eugene D. Genovese, 'A Georgia Slaveholder Looks at Africa', *Georgia Historical Quarterly*, LI (June, 1967), 189.
48. Rawick, ed., *Texas Narrative*, IV (1), 239; also *Alabama Narrative*, VI (1), 5, 336.
49. Rawick, ed., *South Carolina Narrative*, III (3), 205–7.
50. Ibid., II (1), 7. For the good-from-evil preaching see J. G. Williams, '*De Ole Plantation*' (Charleston, S. C., 1895), 12; Rawick, ed., *Georgia Narrative*, XII (1), 296.
51. Puckett, *Folk Beliefs*, 110.
52. See Clifford Geertz, *The Religion of Java* (New York, 1960), 232, and Ivar Paulson, *The Old Estonian Folk Religion*, English trans. (Bloomington, Ind., 1971), 22, 166.
53. Edward Strutt Abdy, *Journal of a Residence and Tour in the United States of North America, from April 1833 to October 1834*, 3 vols, reprinted (New York, 1969), II, 292.
54. Miles Mark Fisher, *Negro Slave Songs in the United States* (Ithaca, N. Y., 1953), 71–2; also pp. 137, 146, 156.
55. Howard Thurman, *The Negro Spiritual Speaks of Life and Death* (New York, 1947), 17, 27–8, 38, 51; Levine, 'Slave Songs and Slave Consciousness', 114.
56. Vernon L. Wharton, *The Negro in Mississippi, 1865–1890* (Chapel Hill, 1947), 20.

57. Du Bois, *Souls of Black Folk*, 189; also *The Gift of Black Folk: The Negroes in the Making of America* (New York, 1970), ch. 7.
58. Harriet Beecher Stowe, quoted in Charles H. Nichols, *Many Thousand Gone: The Ex-slaves' Account of Their Bondage and Their Freedom* (Leiden, 1963), 99.
59. Andrews, *War-Time Journal of a Georgia Girl*, Feb. 12, 1865 (91).
60. James Miller McKim, 'Negro Songs' in Katz, ed., *Social Implications of Early Negro Music*, 2. See also Alvan Sanborn, ed., *Reminiscences of Richard Lathers* (New York, 1907), 5.
61. J. Kennard, quoted in Southern, *Music of Black Americans*, 103.
62. T. S. Eliot, 'The Metaphysical Poets', *Selected Essays* (London, 1936), 286–7.
63. Alexander K. Farrar to W. B. Foules, Dec. 6, 1857, in the Farrar Papers.
64. See the stimulating discussion by Weber, *Sociology of Religion*, 106–8.
65. E. P. Thompson, *Making of the English Working Class* (London, 1963), 34.
66. Yetman, ed., *Life Under the 'Peculiar Institution'*, 232.
67. Broidrick, 'A Recollection of Thirty Years Ago' (ms.).
68. Rawick, ed., *South Carolina Narrative*, II (1), 53–4.
69. Fanny Kemble, *Journal of a Residence on a Georgia plantation in 1838–1839* (New York, 1864), 22.
70. Rawick, ed., *South Carolina Narrative*, III (4), 159; Botkin, ed., *Lay My Burden Down*, 16 ff.; Fisk University, *Unwritten History of Slavery*, 112; Andrews, *War-Time Journal of a Georgia Girl*, July 21, 1865, 339.
71. Rawick, ed., *South Carolina Narrative*, II (I), 151.
72. *Ibid.*, II (1), 91, also 151.
73. See the analysis of Levine, 'Slave Songs and Slave Consciousness', 121; see also Fisher, *Negro Slave Songs*, for a different interpretation that is nonetheless compatible with Levine's.
74. Julius Lester, comp., *To Be a Slave* (New York, 1968), 79. As Powdermaker says, the slaves, deprived of their African history, seized the biblical history of the Jews and made it their own: *After Freedom*, 231–2.

DOCUMENT 1: SLAVE WORK AND LIFE IN GEORGIA

A description of slave work and life on an antebellum southern plantation by Emily Burke, a northern schoolteacher who lived in Georgia for part of the 1830s and 1840s.

Letter XVI

Agreeable to my promise in my last letter, I will now go on with my description of the buildings belonging to a Southern plantation.

In the first place there was a paling enclosing all the buildings belonging to the family and all the house servants. In the centre of this enclosure stood the principal house, the same I have already in a previous letter described. In this the father of the family and all the females lodged. The next house of importance was the one occupied by the steward of the plantation, and where all the white boys belonging to the family had their sleeping apartments. The next after this was a school house consisting of two rooms, one for a study, the other the master's dormitory. Then the cook, the washerwoman, and the milkmaid, had each their several houses, the children's nurses always sleeping upon the floor of their mistress' apartment. Then again there was the kitchen, the store-house, corn-house, stable, hen-coop, the hound's kennel, the shed for the corn mill, all these were separate little buildings within the same enclosure. Even the milk-safe stood out under one great tree, while under another the old washer woman had all her apparatus arranged; even her kettle was there suspended from a cross-pole. Then to increase the beauty of the scene, the whole establishment was completely shaded by ornamental trees, which grew at convenient distances among the buildings, and towering far above them all. The huts of the field servants formed another little cluster of dwellings at considerable distance from the master's residence, yet not beyond the sight of his watchful and jealous eye. These latter huts were arranged with a good deal of order and here each slave had his small patch of ground adjacent to his own dwelling, which he assiduously cultivated after completing his daily task. I have known the poor creatures, notwithstanding 'tired nature' longed for repose, to spend the greater part of a moonlight night on these grounds. In this way they often raise considerable crops of corn, tobacco, and potatoes, besides various kinds of garden vegetables. Their object in doing this is to have something with which to purchase tea, coffee, sugar, flour, and all such articles of diet as are not provided by their masters, also such clothing as is necessary to make them appear decent in church, but which they can not have unless they procure it by extra efforts.

From this you see the slave is obliged to work the greater part of his time, for one coarse torn garment a year, and hardly food enough of the coarsest

---

Emily P. Burke, *Reminiscences of Georgia* (n.p.: James M. Fitch, 1850), pp. 111–13, 115–17.

kind to support nature, without the least luxury that can be named. Neither can they after the fatigues of the day repose their toil worn bodies upon a comfortable bed unless they have earned it by laboring many a long, weary hour after even the beasts and the birds have retired to rest. It is a common rule to furnish every slave with one coarse blanket each, and these they always carry with them, so when night overtakes them, let it be where it may, they are not obliged to hasten home to go to rest. Poor creatures! all the home they have is where their blanket is, and this is all the slave pretends to call his own besides his dog . . . .

I found after I had been in the country a few months that the season when I first went there was the most gloomy part of the year. At this time there were but few slaves upon the plantation, many of them being let out to boatmen who at this season of the year are busily engaged in the transportation of goods and produce of all kinds up and down the rivers. The sweet singing birds, too, were all gone to their winter quarters still farther South, but when they had all returned, and the trees began to assume the freshness of summer, and the plants to put forth their blossoms, I found it was far from being a dull and gloomy place. During the greater part of the winter season the negro women are busy in picking, ginning, and packing the cotton for market.

In packing the cotton, the sack is suspended from strong spikes, and while one colored person stands in it to tread the cotton down, others throw it into the sack. I have often wondered how the cotton could be sold so cheap when it required so much labor to get it ready for the market, and certainly it could not be if all their help was hired at the rate of northern labor.

The last of January the servants began to return to the plantation to repair the fences and make ready for planting and sowing. The fences are built of poles arranged in a zigzag manner, so that the ends of one tier of poles rests upon the ends of another. In this work the women are engaged as well as the men. They all go into the woods and each woman as well as man cuts down her own pine sapling, and brings it upon her head. It certainly was a most revolting sight to see the female form scarcely covered with one old miserable garment, with no covering for the head, arms, or neck, nor shoes to protect her feet from briers and thorns, employed in conveying trees upon her head from one place to another to build fences. When I beheld such scenes I felt culpable in living in ease and enjoying the luxuries of life, while so many of my own sex were obliged to drag out such miserable existences merely to procure these luxuries enjoyed by their masters. When the fences were completed, they proceeded to prepare the ground for planting. This is done by throwing the earth up in ridges from one side of the field to the other. This work is usually executed by hand labor, the soil is so light, though sometimes to facilitate the process a light plough, drawn by a mule, is used. The ground there is reckoned by tasks instead of acres. If a person is asked the extent of a certain piece of land, he is told it contains so many tasks, accordingly so many tasks are assigned for a day's work. In hoeing corn, three tasks are considered a good day's work for a man, two for a woman and one and a half for a boy or girl fourteen or fifteen years old....

DOCUMENT 2: CRUEL TREATMENT OF A SLAVE GIRL

An extract from a manuscript written by Harriet Ann Jacobs (born c. 1813), a freed fugitive slave girl who became an activist in the abolitionist movement. It depicts her life in slavery and her struggle to gain freedom for herself and her children. Incidents in the Life of a Slave Girl *was published in 1861 but omitted the author's name; instead the well-known abolitionist Lydia Maria Child was named as editor.*

XIV
Another Link to Life

I had not returned to my master's house since the birth of my child. The old man raved to have me thus removed from his immediate power; but his wife vowed, by all that was good and great, she would kill me if I came back; and he did not doubt her word. Sometimes he would stay away for a season. Then he would come and renew the old threadbare discourse about his forbearance and my ingratitude. He labored, most unnecessarily, to convince me that I had lowered myself. The venomous old reprobate had no need of descanting on that theme. I felt humiliated enough. My unconscious babe was the ever-present witness of my shame. I listened with silent contempt when he talked about my having forfeited *his* good opinion; but I shed bitter tears that I was no longer worthy of being respected by the good and pure. Alas! slavery still held me in its poisonous grasp. There was no chance for me to be respectable. There was no prospect of being able to lead a better life.

Sometimes, when my master found that I still refused to accept what he called his kind offers, he would threaten to sell my child. 'Perhaps that will humble you', said he.

Humble *me*! Was I not already in the dust? But his threat lacerated my heart. I knew the law gave him power to fulfil it; for slaveholders have been cunning enough to enact that 'the child shall follow the condition of the *mother*', not of the *father*; thus taking care that licentiousness shall not interfere with avarice. This reflection made me clasp my innocent babe all the more firmly to my heart. Horrid visions passed through my mind when I thought of his liability to fall into the slave trader's hands. I wept over him, and said, 'O my child! perhaps they will leave you in some cold cabin to die, and then throw you into a hole, as if you were a dog'.

When Dr. Flint learned that I was again to be a mother, he was exasperated beyond measure. He rushed from the house, and returned with a pair of shears. I had a fine head of hair; and he often railed about my pride of arranging it nicely. He cut every hair close to my head, storming and swearing all the time. I replied to some of his abuse, and he struck me. Some

Jean F. Yellin (ed.), *Incidents in the Life of a Slave Girl* (Cambridge, MA: Harvard University Press, 1987), pp. 76–9.

months before, he had pitched me down stairs in a fit of passion; and the injury I received was so serious that I was unable to turn myself in bed for many days. He then said, 'Linda, I swear by God I will never raise my hand against you again'; but I knew that he would forget his promise.

After he discovered my situation, he was like a restless spirit from the pit. He came every day; and I was subjected to such insults as no pen can describe. I would not describe them if I could; they were too low, too revolting. I tried to keep them from my grandmother's knowledge as much as I could. I knew she had enough to sadden her life, without having my troubles to bear. When she saw the doctor treat me with violence, and heard him utter oaths terrible enough to palsy a man's tongue, she could not always hold her peace. It was natural and motherlike that she should try to defend me; but it only made matters worse.

When they told me my new-born babe was a girl, my heart was heavier than it had ever been before. Slavery is terrible for men; but it is far more terrible for women. Superadded to the burden common to all, *they* have wrongs, and sufferings, and mortifications peculiarly their own.

Dr. Flint had sworn that he would make me suffer, to my last day, for this new crime against *him*, as he called it; and as long as he had me in his power he kept his word. On the fourth day after the birth of my babe, he entered my room suddenly, and commanded me to rise and bring my baby to him. The nurse who took care of me had gone out of the room to prepare some nourishment, and I was alone. There was no alternative. I rose, took up my babe, and crossed the room to where he sat. 'Now stand there', said he, 'till I tell you to go back'! My child bore a strong resemblance to her father, and to the deceased Mrs. Sands, her grandmother. He noticed this; and while I stood before him, trembling with weakness, he heaped upon me and my little one every vile epithet he could think of. Even the grandmother in her grave did not escape his curses. In the midst of his vituperations I fainted at his feet. This recalled him to his senses. He took the baby from my arms, laid it on the bed, dashed cold water in my face, took me up, and shook me violently, to restore my consciousness before any one entered the room. Just then my grandmother came in, and he hurried out of the house. I suffered in consequence of this treatment; but I begged my friends to let me die, rather than send for the doctor. There was nothing I dreaded so much as his presence. My life was spared; and I was glad for the sake of my little ones. Had it not been for these ties to life, I should have been glad to be released by death, though I had lived only nineteen years.

Always it gave me a pang that my children had no lawful claim to a name. Their father offered his; but, if I had wished to accept the offer, I dared not while my master lived. Moreover, I knew it would not be accepted at their baptism. A Christian name they were at least entitled to; and we resolved to call my boy for our dear good Benjamin, who had gone far away from us.

My grandmother belonged to the church; and she was very desirous of having the children christened. I knew Dr. Flint would forbid it, and I did not venture to attempt it. But chance favored me. He was called to visit a patient out of town, and was obliged to be absent during Sunday. 'Now is the time', said my grandmother; 'we will take the children to church, and have them christened'.

When I entered the church, recollections of my mother came over me, and I felt subdued in spirit. There she had presented me for baptism, without any reason to feel ashamed. She had been married, and had such legal rights as slavery allows to a slave. The vows had at least been sacred to *her*, and she had never violated them. I was glad she was not alive, to know under what different circumstances her grandchildren were presented for baptism. Why had my lot been so different from my mother's? *Her* master had died when she was a child; and she remained with her mistress till she married. She was never in the power of any master; and thus she escaped one class of the evils that generally fall upon slaves.

When my baby was about to be christened, the former mistress of my father stepped up to me, and proposed to give it her Christian name. To this I added the surname of my father, who had himself no legal right to it; for my grandfather on the paternal side was a white gentleman. What tangled skeins are the genealogies of slavery! I loved my father; but it mortified me to be obliged to bestow his name on my children.

When we left the church, my father's old mistress invited me to go home with her. She clasped a gold chain around my baby's neck. I thanked her for this kindness; but I did not like the emblem. I wanted no chain to be fastened on my daughter, not even if its links were of gold. How earnestly I prayed that she might never feel the weight of slavery's chain, whose iron entereth into the soul!

DOCUMENT 3: SLAVE TESTIMONIES

These testimonies are taken from personal narratives dictated by ex-slaves in the 1930s to interviewers of the WPA's Federal Writer's Project.

Lucy Galloway, resident of North Gulfport, Mississippi

When the writer asked Lucy to tell her something more about the 'black girl that came from Africa', her face brightened and she said: 'We was all crazy about "Little Luce". Dat wuz what we called her, cause she wuz little, but my! she wuz strong and could whup anybody dat fooled wid her. She remembered her mother who wuz also a slave in Africy. Their master over dere wuz a black man and he wuz mean to dem; would beat 'em when dey didn't do to suit him. Luce had one tooth missing in front, which she said she lost while fighting the black boss over dere. She said dat wuz de reason dey sold because she was so bad about fightin' and bitin' – she wuz strong and could fight jes' like a cat.

'When dey wuz fixin' to sell her to de white folks, dey made her grease her long black hair and plait it in braids to hang down her neck, and to wash and grease her legs to make dem shine when she wuz dancing fer dem. De speculators sho' like to see her dance! She said all she wore wuz a full skirt dat come to her knees and a sash tied roun' her waist. She said dat she always brought big money when dey put her on de block to sell. She wuz a good-lookin' gal – jest as black and slick as a – "gutta-pucha button".

'She was sold over here to a man name Hutson, and she always go by de name of 'Lucy Hutson'.... She married Alf Hutson, one of de black men on de place. She said dat dey dressed her up and told her dat her and Alf had to "Jump over de Broom". After dey jumped over de broom. Old Masta said: "Now salute yer bride"! After dat dey had cake and feasting. Luce wuz a favorite wid all of dem. She said she always took de prize at all de dances....'

Asked about her grandmother – 'Frances', she said:

'My grandmother was a "good breeder", and dat is de reason she did not have to work as hard as some of de other slaves. She had 22 chillun. It was her job to look after all the slave chillun. She saw dat dey all got fed good. She had two big wooden trays and about four o'clock ever evin' she would fill dem trays wid somethin' to eat and call all de pick-a-ninnies, and dey would all come a-runnin. Den dey didn't git no more till mawnin' – but dey wuz round and fat as butter balls'.

Robert Edgar Conrad (ed.), *In the Hands of Strangers: Readings on Foreign and Domestic Slave Trading and the Crisis of the Union* (University Park, PA: Pennsylvania State University Press, 2001), pp. 232–4, 236–7.

*Thomas Johns of Cleburne, Texas, 90, born in
Chambers County, Alabama*

My mother was born and raised in slavery in Virginia, and she married and she and her husban' had a little girl, and my mother and de little girl wuz sol' away from her husban' and brought to Alabama.... My father's name was George and my mother's name was Nellie. My father was born in Africa. Him and two of his brothers and one sister was stole and brought to Savannah, Georgy, and sol'. Dey was de children of a chief of de Kiochi tribe (the name of the tribe is spelled phonetically by the writer from Tom's pronunciation). De way dey was stole, dey was asked to a dance on a ship which some white men had, and my aunt said it was early in de mornin' w'en dey foun' dey was away from de lan', and all dey could see was de stars and de water all 'roun'. She said she was a member of de file-tooth tribe of niggers. My father's teeth was so dat only de front ones met together when he closed his mouth. De back ones didn' set together ....

Ol' mahster never beat his slaves, and he didn't sell 'em; didn' raise none to sell neither, but some of de owners did. If a owner had a big woman slave and she had a little man for her husban' and de owner had a big man slave, or another owner had a big man slave, den dey would make the woman's little husban' leave, and dey would make de woman let de big man be with her so's dere would be big children, which dey could sell well. If de man and de woman refuse to be together dey would get whipped hard and maybe whipped to death. Course hard whippin' made a slave hard to sell, maybe couldn' be sold 'cause w'en a man went to buy a slave, he would make him strip naked and look him over for whip marks and other blemishes, jus' like dey would a horse. Course even if it did damage de sale of a slave to whip him, dey done it, 'cause dey figured kill a nigger, breed another – kill a mule, buy another.

*William Matthews, 90, resident of Galveston, Texas,
born in Franklin Parish, Louisiana.*

De quarters was back of de big white house dat de white folks live in de middle of some pine trees. De cabins didn' have no floors in 'em. Dey set plumb on de ground. Dey was build like you build a hog pen .... Dey only had 'bout fifty slaves on de place. It was big, big 'nough for a hundred more, but what they do? Dey take the good slaves an' sell em, dat's what dey do. Den dey makes de ones dat was lef' do de work. Dey never bought nobody dat I can rec'lect. Sell, sell all de time an' never buy nobody. Dat was dem.

Like I done said, de marster sol' de good slaves in Monroe. I ain' never been sol', an' I ain' seen none of 'em sol', but I know how dey done it, Dey stand 'em on blocks an' bid 'em off. Some other man git 'em. Mothers was taken 'way from dere chillun, husbands was taken 'way from dere wives, wives was taken 'way from dere husbands. You know what happen? After de War when dey was all free, dey marry who dey want to an' sometimes a long time after dat dey find out dat brothers had married dere sisters, an' mothers had married dere sons, an' things like dat. How I know? I hear 'em talk 'bout it. 'Course I don' know anybody who done it, but on places like ours where dere wasn' no marriages, how you going to know who is your brother an' who ain'?

Nobody marry in dem days. A girl go out an' take a notion for somebody an' dey make a 'greement an' take a house together if it's 'greeable to de white folks an' if she 'low me to come in, I's her husband. Course if a unhealthy nigger take up wit' a healthy stout woman, de white folks sep'rate 'em. Dey matched 'em up like dey wan' em. If a man was a big stout man, good breed, dey give him four, five women. Dat's de God's truth.

6

THE BUSINESS OF SLAVERY

INTRODUCTION

The historiography of American slavery as a business can be conveniently divided into three themes: the business of the internal slave trade; the efficiency and profitability of slavery on the plantation; and the economic impact of slavery as a system on the South. The internal slave trade flourished between the early years of the republic and the Civil War. It involved the movement of around 835,000 slaves from the eastern states to the southwest by often unscrupulous traders. Slave marts flourished at places such as Natchez, Mississippi, and New Orleans, Louisiana. The business of slavery on plantations is concerned with issues of efficiency, productivity, crop output and profitability. Discussions of the micro-economic level of slavery have also debated the extent to which slavery was a capitalist or pre-capitalist system. Studies of the profitability of slavery as a system have addressed macro-economic issues including the relationship of cotton production to industrialisation and economic development, or the lack thereof, in the South.

Bancroft (1931) provided a detailed account of the internal slave trade, with an emphasis on the cruelty of the traffic and the prevalence of family separation. Tadman's more sophisticated study (1996) analyses the scale of the overland trade in slaves, pointing out that the Chesapeake–New Orleans coastal trade was the exception to the rule. It also provides evidence to show that family separations were more common than Bancroft argued: around one-fifth of slave marriages from the exporting states were broken up and one in three children were separated from their parents. The inner workings of the New Orleans slave market are best explored in Johnson (1999), who is perceptive on the packaging and rebranding of slaves at auctions. Pritchett and Freudenbeger (1992) analyse the selection of slaves for that market.

Parish (1989) and Smith (1998) are two syntheses that offer a starting point for considering the business of slavery on the plantation and in relation to the antebellum southern economy. Woodman (1963) prefigured many themes addressed in later studies. His article is helpful in highlighting the complexity of the issues that need to be addressed in examining the profitability of slavery and the impact of that institution on southern economic development. He provides a survey of these issues from the antebellum period up to the 1960s. A methodological breakthrough came with the work of Conrad and Meyer (1964), who were among the pioneers of the 'new' economic history. They use econometric methods to estimate inputs and outputs on slave plantations. This enables broader conclusions to be drawn than had been the case with studies of individual plantations or groups of plantations. Conrad and Meyer found respectable profit rates from slavery throughout the South. They argued that these were comparable with rates of return on northern investments.

A further leap forward in the consideration of slavery as a business came with the controversial work of Fogel and Engerman (1974). Using economic theory and quantitative methods, they produced a picture of plantation slavery as highly viable in economic terms – a profitable form of enterprise. They argue that the effective organisation of the work force into gang systems allowed for high labour inputs and the allocation of slave jobs according to individual capacity. Fogel and Engerman maintain that 97 per cent of the extra efficiency of slavery stems from this. They note that a quarter of the slaves held skilled and semi-skilled jobs and were rewarded with goods and food that gave them more security than some poor northern free workers. Slave families, to continue the argument's thrust, are seen as stable units. Fogel and Engerman also argue that plantation slavery was profitable and stimulated economic growth in the South. Per capita incomes in the North in 1860 were a quarter higher than in the South, they concede, but one needs to disaggregate the northern regional economy to present a more realistic picture: thus the per capita income of the north central states was 14 per cent lower than per capita income in the southern states. Many of these conclusions are incorporated into Fogel (1989), which adds material on the height and diet of slaves. One main conclusion drawn here is that slaves were taller and better fed than many European workers. This accords with Fogel and Engerman's attempt to paint a positive picture of southern slavery.

Criticisms of *Time on the Cross* came thick and fast in the wake of its publication. Gutman's critique (1975) is concerned only with the nature of slave life; the economics of the slave system as a whole are not considered. But he charges Fogel and Engerman with underrepresenting large plantations, drawing erroneous conclusions from their quantitative data, and underestimating the fragility of slave family life. David, Gutman, Sutch, Temin and Wright (1976) offer varied criticisms of Fogel and Engerman, focusing on the work, punishment, diet and exploitation of slaves. They highlight the use of inappropriate statistics on slave whippings and slave welfare that are misleading for the interpretation of slave life and culture. Ratcliffe (1976) is a good, balanced but lesser-known critique of the findings of *Time on the Cross*.

Genovese (1965, 1974) does not focus on many of the economic measures pursued by Fogel and Engerman, yet the economics of slavery is one of his central concerns. The southern plantation system, he argues, was pre-capitalist and fundamentally different from northern liberal capitalism and industrialisation. Planters were mainly interested in maintaining slavery as part of the control of black people within a world view based on an aristocratic, leisurely, anti-bourgeois way of life. The lack of emphasis on profit-making and the fact that slaves were not wage earners had a detrimental effect upon the development of capitalism in the South. Because slaves were often treated cruelly and lacked the incentive of wages, work was often slack. Technological progress on the plantations proceeded slowly. Soil exhaustion, concentration on staple cotton agriculture and lack of internal improvements also made the plantation sector a backwater and one that was not easily susceptible to modernisation. These arguments, it goes without saying, present a very different picture of the slave South from that painted by Fogel and Engerman.

Starobin (1970) shows that southern slaves were not just confined to the plantation sector; they also undertook industrial work in manufacturing, mining, lumbering, crop processing and the construction and operation of roads, canals and railroads. He shows that most industrial entrepreneurs employing slave labour earned a satisfactory annual return of about 6 per cent on their capital investments; that industrial slaves were no less efficient than free workers in the Old South; that industrialists utilised slave capital fully by employing women and children extensively; and that slave ownership did not lessen labour mobility or stem investment in industrial enterprises. This generally favourable appraisal of industrial slavery is used to support a broader thesis that slavery was not the sole cause of industrial backwardness. Other factors unconnected with slavery, but linked with the geography, topography and climate of the southern states, were at least as important in retarding regional industrial growth.

Bateman and Weiss (1981) argue that southern industry produced good profits but that capital investment in the industrial sector was limited by conservative planters who maintained their interest in cotton production and were averse to taking risks. Wright (1978) shows that per capita dollars invested in manufacturing capital and manufacturing output by the cotton

South in 1850 and 1860 were significantly lower than in New England, the middle states or the South as a whole. While acknowledging the good economic performance of the antebellum southern cotton industry, he notes that the South was ill placed to adapt to urbanisation and industrialisation and to economic diversification. He argues that the success of the cotton plantations on the eve of the Civil War lay more in their ability to serve an apparently insatiable world demand for cotton than in labour efficiencies achieved by slaves and their masters. Kilbourne (1995) offers a microcosmic view of the southern slave economy focused on one Louisiana parish. He concentrates on the use of slaves as collateral for debt and shows that this use of credit served its purpose well until emancipation but that black freedom was a severe blow to southern credit. The internal economy created by slaves has not received as much attention as other aspects of the business of American slavery; but a helpful account, based on Louisiana's sugar plantations, is given in McDonald (1993).

BIBLIOGRAPHY

Bancroft, Fredric, *Slave Trading in the Old South* (Baltimore: J. H. Furst and Company, 1931)

Bateman, Fred and Weiss, Thomas, *A Deplorable Scarcity: The Failure of Industrialization in the Slave Economy* (Chapel Hill: University of North Carolina Press, 1981)

Conrad, Alfred H. and Meyer, John R., *The Economics of Slavery and Other Studies in Econometric History* (Chicago: Aldine, 1964)

David, Paul A., Herbert G. Gutman, Richard Sutch, Peter Temin and Gavin Wright, *Reckoning with Slavery: A Critical Study in the Quantitative History of American Negro Slavery* (New York: Oxford University Press, 1976)

Fogel, Robert W., *Without Consent or Contract: The Rise and Fall of American Slavery* (New York: W. W. Norton, 1989)

Fogel, Robert W. and Engerman, Stanley L., *Time on the Cross: The Economics of American Negro Slavery* (Boston: Little, Brown, 1974)

Genovese, Eugene D., *The Political Economy of Slavery: Studies in the Economy and Society of the Slave South* (New York: Pantheon Books, 1965)

Genovese, Eugene D., *Roll, Jordan, Roll: The World the Slaves Made* (New York: Pantheon Books, 1974)

Gutman, Herbert G., *Slavery and the Numbers Game: A Critique of 'Time on the Cross'* (Urbana-Champaign, IL: University of Illinois Press, 1975)

Johnson, Walter, *Soul by Soul: Life inside the Antebellum Slave Market* (Cambridge, MA: Harvard University Press, 1999)

Kilbourne, Richard H., *Debt, Investment, Slaves: Credit Relations in East Feliciana Parish, Louisiana, 1825–1885* (Tuscaloosa: University of Alabama Press, 1995)

McDonald, Roderick A., *The Economy and Material Conditions of Slaves: Goods and Chattels on the Sugar Plantations of Jamaica and Louisiana* (Baton Rouge, LA: Louisiana State University Press, 1993)

Parish, Peter J., *Slavery: History and Historians* (New York: Harper & Row, 1989)

Pritchett, Jonathan and Freudenberger, Herman, 'A Peculiar Sample: The Selection of Slaves for the New Orleans Market', *Journal of Economic History*, 52 (1992), 109–28

Ratcliffe, Donald J., 'The "Das Kapital" of American Negro Slavery? "Time on the Cross" after Two Years', *Durham University Journal*, 69 (1976), 103–30

Smith, Mark M., *Debating Slavery: Economy and Society in the Antebellum American South* (Cambridge: Cambridge University Press, 1998)

Starobin, Robert S., *Industrial Slavery in the Old South* (New York: Oxford University Press, 1970)

Tadman, Michael, *Speculators and Slaves: Masters, Traders, and Slaves in the Old South* (Madison, WI: University of Wisconsin Press, 1989; 2nd edn, 1996)

Woodman, Harold D., 'The Profitability of Slavery: A Historical Perennial', *Journal of Southern History*, 29 (1963), 303–25

Wright, Gavin, *The Political Economy of the Cotton South: Households, Markets and Wealth in the Nineteenth Century* (New York: W. W. Norton, 1978)

ESSAY: TURNING PEOPLE INTO PRODUCTS

Johnson provides an original interpretation of the internal slave market in New Orleans in the antebellum era. In this chapter he explores the refashioning of the bodies and identities of slaves for sale in the marketplace. He describes the rituals of preparing slaves for sale with regard to height, medical care, clothing, price and racial categories, and size of lots. Selling slaves was a carefully orchestrated phenomenon that involved different strategies by sellers, the desires and expectations of buyers, and sometimes the collusion of the slaves waiting to be sold. How far did slave traders go in 'dismantling and repackaging' slaves for sale? How did they sell slaves as commodities? How were slaves advertised and moved in the sale yards?

Slave traders were sometimes accused of selling people who were dead. J. B. Alexander, for instance, did not have time to get very far from the slave market with the slave he had just bought before a man whom he did not know walked up to him and 'remarked to him that he had bought a dead Negro'. Alexander asked the man what he meant. The man replied that he could see that 'the boy was sick', too sick to be cured – already dead. The man, it turned out, was in a position to know dead slaves when he saw them. He had been a slave trader for almost thirty years.[1] The lawyers for the hapless Dixons invoked a similar set of images in the suit brought by the couple against the slave dealer who had sold them Critty and Creasy. As the Dixons' lawyers saw it, the trader was 'an experienced jockey' who had resorted 'to all of the nostrums and arts of his profession, such as cod liver oil, stimulants, etc. to fatten and keep up these dying consumptives until he could get them off his hands'.[2] Essentially, they charged the dealer with sending the dead to market.

The imagery used by the lawyers – the imagery of forbidden nostrums and secret arts – had much more to do with the world of the occult than with the supposedly rational workings of the slave trade. But what served the lawyers for the Dixons as an accusation of improper conduct might have summoned up a vision of the perfect sale for a slave trader; an otherwise lifeless body quickened into motion by the magic of the market. By this dark magic, this necromancy, new people could be made out of the parts of old ones: slaves could be detached from their pasts and stripped of their identities, their bodies could be disciplined into order and decorated for market, their skills could be assigned, their qualities designated, their stories retold. Slaves could be remade in the image of the irresistible power of their salability—fed, medicated, beaten, dressed, hectored, and arrayed until they outwardly appeared to be no more than advertisements for themselves. The

Walter Johnson, *Soul by Soul: Life inside the Antebellum Slave Market* (Cambridge, MA: Harvard University Press, 1999), pp. 117–34, 249–54.

dead, their bodies disjointed from the past and their identities evacuated, would walk to sale.[3]

Slave Making

In the daily practice of the slave pens, slaves were treated as physical manifestations of the categories the traders used to select their slaves – No. 1, Second Rate, and so on. After gathering individuals into categories and attributing to those categories an independent existence in 'the slave market' by which they could be compared to all other categories (and all other goods), the traders turned those categories around and used them to evaluate the individuals of whom they were supposedly composed.[4] Thus could slave trader J. M. Wilson walk into a Louisiana courtroom, declare himself 'familiar with the prices of slaves in this market' (that is, with the price categories that traders used to do their business), and testify to the value of Clarissa and her family without ever having seen them. Similarly, slave trader J. W. Boazman could testify to the value of 'Negroes bought about September 1851' in supporting a slaveholder's claim that the death of a woman he owned at the hands of a careless contractor had cost him a thousand dollars. Thus could slave trader David Wise testify to the value of a human eye: 'Being asked if the girl had a filter on her eye if it would impair her value, he says it would impair its value from $25 to $40'.[5] In switching the pronoun from 'her' to 'it', Wise revealed in a word what his business was about: turning people into prices. He used the tables of aggregates which *reflected* the market valuation of people to *project* that valuation.

The price tables made traders like Boazman and Wise capable of extraordinary feats of comparison, but it was their daily business to guide the buyers beyond comparison to selection: to get them to single out the one slave especially suited to their purposes from the many nominally similar slaves available in the market. In the daily practice of the slave pens, then, real slaves had a double relation to the abstract market in the traders' imaginations. On the one hand, they were to be transformed into exemplars of the category to which they had been assigned; but once the categories of comparison had been established and embodied, the slaves were supposed to become once again visible as individuals – comparable to all of those who inhabited the same category, yet different enough to attract a buyer's eye and seal the sale. This daily dialectic of categorization and differentiation was the magic by which the traders turned people into things and then into money.

Traders began to package their slaves for market before they ever reached the slave pens. As they neared their destination, the traders removed the heavy chains and galling cuffs from their slaves' arms and legs and allowed the slaves to wash and rest and heal. The traders shaved men's beards and combed their hair, they plucked gray hairs or blackened them with dye – the 'blacking' that appears in their account books was perhaps intended for this purpose. Slave trader John White was clearer about what he did with the tallow he bought: it was 'for the girls' hair'.[6] The rituals of preparation continued once slaves had reached the market. In the slave pens the traders increased rations of bacon, milk, and butter, a fattening diet one trader referred to as 'feeding up'.[7] To keep the slaves' muscles toned, the traders set them to dancing and exercising, and to make their skin shine with the appearance of health, the traders greased the slaves' faces with 'sweet oil' or washed them in 'greasy water'.[8]

The traders also hired doctors to visit their pens regularly. 'Scarcely a day passes . . . but what I go to his establishment, it being on the road to my office', testified Dr. J. H. Lewis of J. M. Wilson's slave pen. Dr. John Carr spoke similarly of the slave yard owned by Hope H. Slatter in the 1840s: 'is generally in the habit of calling there and sitting for an hour in the afternoon . . . he usually visited all the slaves'. When Slatter's yard passed into the possession of Bernard and Walter Campbell, Carr continued as the yard's doctor: 'was the attending physician at Campbell's establishment . . . is in the habit of visiting Campbell's establishment two or three times a day'.[9] These accounts may be exaggerated, for these doctors had as much experience in the courts as they did in the slave market, and it was part of their ongoing business relation with the traders to emphasize the good care received by slaves in the pens. But even if they overstated the frequency and quality of their slave-market ministrations, it is clear that sick slaves in the pens often received professional treatment. At the time of his death and estate settlement, slave dealer Elihu Cresswell was carrying debts for having slaves' teeth pulled and providing them with medicine. In his account book John White recorded the twenty-five dollars he paid a physician to look after his slaves in 1845, and regularly noted prescriptions and treatment for slaves in the pens – chloride of lime, capsules, cupping, medicine. The New Orleans slave yards kept by Cresswell and Benjamin Screws both had separate rooms set aside for the sick. Fear of contagion more than charity might have motivated the traders' concern, but the separation of the sick was often accompanied by medical care. Frank, for example, was 'nursed' back to health from yellow fever in slave dealer Calvin Rutherford's 'private house', and Solomon Northup was treated for small pox in the hospital, as, according to an 1841 city law, all slaves suffering from infectious disease were to be.[10]

In the slave pens, however, medical treatment was a trick of the trade, nothing more. These expenditures were speculations like any others the traders made, tactical commitments to slaves' bodies that were underwritten by the hope of their sale. When that hope ran out, so seemingly did the traders' concern. John White's reckoning of his chances of curing and selling Harriet, for instance, can be tracked through the pages of his account book – capsules for Harriet on February third, cupping Harriet on the fifth, burial of her child on the fourteenth, brandy for Harriet on the sixteenth, burial for Harriet on the nineteenth, the sale of Harriet's surviving children on the twenty-first. Harriet was treated when it seemed possible to save her, comforted (or quieted) with alcohol when it did not, and buried when she died. Her children, less valuable than she had been, were not treated at all and were quickly sold when their care became the trader's responsibility and their presence in the yard a threat to his other property.[11] There was always an alternative to caring for sick slaves: selling them quickly.

Their bodies prepared, the slaves in the pens were packaged for sale. The traders' account books document their extensive daily attention to presentation: entries for dresses, shoes, stockings, and head coverings for the women; suits with undershirts, drawers, socks, boots, and sometimes a hat for the men. In October of 1857 John White bought forty identical blue suits for the men in his yard.[12] The clothes masked differences among the slaves; individual pasts and potential problems were covered over in uniform cloth. The sick and the well, those from far away and those from nearby, the eager, the unattached, and the angry – all looked alike in the trader's window-dressed version of slavery.

The clothes suggested not only comparability but also cleanliness and chastity. Eyre Crowe's famous drawing of slaves lined out for sale in New Orleans shows women with long-sleeved blouses and covered heads, men in black suits with top hats. Noting the kerchiefs tied around their heads 'in a mode peculiar to the Negress', northern writer Joseph Ingraham pronounced the women he saw in the market 'extremely neat and "tidy"'. 'Their appearance had little of the repulsiveness we are apt to associate with the slaves', wrote Robert Chambers, another northern visitor to the slave pens.[13] None of the poverty and toil that characterized the daily life of American slaves, none of the bareness that contributed so powerfully to the historical sexualization of black bodies, was immediately apparent in the slave market. These people were dressed as ideal slaves, exaggerated in the typicality of their appearance, too uniform, too healthy, too clean. Through the daily practice of the pens, individual slaves were turned into physical symbols of their own salability – nothing else about them was immediately apparent.

Except for the occasional whim or fancy. On the same page of the ledger book in which he recorded the prices of the steel rings and chain which he used to shackle the limbs of his slaves on the way south, Floyd Whitehead noted his purchases of the three gold rings and half-dozen 'plated' ones he placed on their fingers when he sent them to market. John White bought a cravat and a 'Boy's Fancy Suit' in 1857; in earlier years he had bought 'trimmings' for men's pants and a shawl for a woman he was taking to Mobile to be sold. A. J. Walker sent enslaved women to sale wearing gloves.[14] These conceits were meant to draw a buyer's eye as he scanned a line of slaves, to suggest uncommon gentility, a paternalism of the 'his-master's-clothes' variety, or an exotic fantasy. These obviously contrived appearances – self-revealing in their pretense – both perplexed the buyers' gaze and invited further investigation.

Their bodies treated and dressed, the slaves were turned out for sale divided by sex. 'Men on one side, women on the other': the phrase runs through descriptions of the slave market like a leitmotif. 'Here may be seen husbands separated from wives by only the width of the room, and children from parents, one or both', wrote John Brown, re-envisioning the family ties that were erased by the traders' practice.[15] Even when the traders kept track of family ties, they often severed them in the slave market. Of the seven slaves bracketed with the label 'Overton purchase' in John White's 'slave record' for 1846, two were sold together, one sent home as unsaleable, and the rest sold individually in Louisiana, Tennessee, and Alabama. Families were likewise carefully bracketed on the bill of lading for a shipment of slaves received by Seraphim Cucullu in the winter of 1836. But they were indiscriminately separated as Cucullu sold them over the course of the spring. Cucullu's account-book record of the buyers of his divided slaves is a testament to the commitment of his employees to his instructions 'that price might be the guide and to sell for the best of his interests'.[16] That meant selling slaves the way the buyers wanted them, according to sex-specific demand rather than according to family ties.

The lengths to which slave traders could go in dismantling and repackaging slave families in the image of the market were limited by Louisiana law. The original *Code Noire* forbade the separation by sale of children under the age of ten from their mothers, and in 1829 the law was explicitly extended to outlaw the importation of thusly separated slaves.[17] While the 1829 law should not be ignored (it is a good example of slaveholders negotiating a hard bargain with their own consciences and of the tendency of paternalism to limit its already meager promises to protection of the very young), its effect should not be overemphasized. What the law did was to give legal credence to the categories according to which slave traders did their business. Who, after all, would favor a trade in motherless children? Not the slave traders. The vast majority of family-separating sales occurred in the upper South, out of the effective reach of the law. And the vast majority of these involved the removal of the parent; slave traders, especially those who traveled long distances, had little use for small children.[18] By the 1850s, as single women became a featured category of trade, orphaned children became a recognizable portion of the population in upper South slave communities.[19] Trader John White left four of Mary Cole's children (aged two to ten) behind when he took Cole and her three older children to New Orleans in 1846. Trader J. W. Boazman explained a similar choice this way: 'servants are less valuable with children than without'. But if the traders wanted to trade in children who had been separated from their mothers, there was little to keep them from adhering to the letter of the law by making orphans rather than finding them. It is hard to read slave trader David Wise's statement that 'witness has often sold little children . . . ' without wondering about his own role in the qualification he quickly added ' . . . who had lost their mother'.[20] The 1829 law, then, provided the maximal rhetorical effect with the minimal practical disruption of the slave trade. It stripped 'the slave family' of its existing members, their history, their ties and affinities and substituted a more salable definition – a mother and a young child.

As well as packaging the slaves into saleable lots, the traders packed them into racial categories. By the time they turned their slaves out for sale, the traders had transformed the market categories they used to talk to one another into the racial categories they used to talk to the buyers. In their back-and-forth market reports the traders described slaves as Prime, No. 1, No. 2, and so on, but on ninety per cent of the Acts of Sale recorded by New Orleans notaries they used words like Negro, Griffe, Mulatto, or Quadroon.[21] These words were explicitly biological: they bespoke pasts that were not visible in the slave market by referring to parents and grandparents who had been left behind with old owners. But they did so by referring to something that the buyers would be able to see: skin color.

Brushed, dressed, and polished, divided by sex (or lamely protected by law), assigned a new history and a racial category, the people in the pens were lined out for sale by height: 'The men were arranged on one side of the room, the women on the other, the tallest were placed at the head of the row, then the next tallest, and so on in order of their respective heights', remembered Solomon Northup.[22] Around the walls of the slave pens, the slaves were arranged to reflect the traders' buyer-tracking tables. As the slaves were hectored into line at the beginning of every day, there were no husbands or wives apparent among them, no old lovers or new friends; there were only men and women, field hands and house servants, Negro, Griffe, and Mulatto, tall, medium, and short.

Having done all they could to make real people represent the constructed categories of the marketplace, the traders began to try to turn them into money. Value in the slave market emerged out of the play of similarity with difference, the choice of one slave from among many similar slaves made a sale. To sell a slave, the traders had to peel back their own representations of commodified similarity and slip beneath them a suggestion of personal distinction that would make one slave stand out to a buyer who was trying to distinguish himself from all of the other buyers in the market. The traders had to make a pitch. In the slave pens, the traders pitched their slaves by telling stories that seemed to individualize and even humanize the depersonalized slaves. They breathed the life of the market into the bodies, histories, and identities of the people they were trying to sell, by using a simulacrum of human singularity to do the work of product differentiation.

The traders' reputation for buying the sick and malign on the cheap only to sell them at premium prices made it important for the traders to explain why slaves were in the market in the first place.[23] Such as: 'Sold for no fault of their own'. This unasked-for excuse had specific variants, all of which shifted attention from slaves to their former owners. From an advertisement: 'The Owner of the following named valuable Slaves being on the eve of departure for Europe'. From Edward Sparrow's account of why he sent a man later alleged to have been alcoholic to be sold in the slave market: 'Mrs. Sparrow expressed a wish that he should be sold here where his wife was'. From the pitch made by a trader for a slave who had been once returned: 'the party to whom he was sold had no fault except that the man was too much of a French Cook'. From the explanation made by a trader about a man later alleged to have been once returned to him as a thief, drunkard, and runaway: 'Did not take him back because he was a bad Negro, but because Forbes [the first buyer] was unable to pay for him'. From a trader's account of why Jane, who was allegedly consumptive, had been returned after her first sale: 'she was not a hair dresser, the lady was not pleased with her, that is the only reason I heard . . . for not keeping the girl'.[24] These stories were neither wholly believable nor easily disproven; the former owners to whom they referred all questions were distant in time and space, unavailable to offer their own account. As a warranty the stories were useless; the traders were bound only by the stories they wrote down and signed. But as a warning to buyers, the pitches were perhaps more useful: the slaves' histories, not quite visible behind the shimmering tales told in the slave pens, belonged to the traders.

Some of the stories the traders told were quite simple, advertisements, that were put forward as qualifications, accounts of past work through which buyers could view a certain future: first-rate cotton picker, experienced drayman, cooper, carpenter, cook, nurse, and so on. And some were more detailed: in the words of a slave trader's handbill, 'Bill, Negro man, aged about 28 years, excellent servant and good pastry cook'; or, in the words of a witness to a trader's pitch, '[He] said that said slave was a first rate cook, a very good washer and could plait plain shirts very well & that Mr. Hewes would be satisfied in every respect with having purchased said Negress'.[25] However brief, these lists of skills referred to the experience and judgment of former owners, to a past distant from the slave pens. But they insinuated themselves into the present as trustworthy representations of past experience, drawing whatever authenticity they had (enough to convince Mr. Hewes) from the constant babble of talk about slaves that characterized the social life of southern slaveholders. The traders were taking hold of slaveholders' fantasies about the slave market, wrapping them around the slaves they had for sale, and selling them back to the buyers as indications of those buyers' own good fortune and discernment.

And the traders' pitches went well beyond work. They could spin a detailed fantasy out of a list of supposed skills: 'Sarah, a mulatress, aged 45 years, a good cook and accustomed to housework in general, is an excellent and faithful nurse for sick persons, and in every respect a first rate character'. Sarah, as sold, was gentility and paternalism embodied – good meals, a clean house, a companion who would wait faithfully by the bed of an ailing (vulnerable) owner. 'Dennis, her son, a mulatto, aged 24 years, a first rate cook and steward for a vessel, having been in that capacity for many years on board one of the Mobile packets; is strictly honest, temperate, and is a first rate subject'.[26] Dennis would bring with him a hint of riverboat grandeur: the plush seats and ornate surroundings; the graceful service and extensive menu; the pleasure of traveling first class.[27] And Dennis was trustworthy: he had worked on a boat but not run away; he might be hired out or given the run of the house. His purchase would make good sense; his service would be in good taste. And, though Dennis and his mother were put up for sale separately, they could be bought together by someone who cared enough to do so.

The slave traders could line their families out separately and then knit them together again in the sales pitch. They could package and sell the negation of their own way of doing business by offering the buyers a chance to rejoin families that had been sundered in the market. Slave-market paternalism thus replayed the plots of proslavery propaganda and fiction: the good-hearted slave at the side of the dying master; the slave who could be trusted to master himself; the slave-holder's saving interventions in the life of the unfortunate slave. As representations of individual slaves, the traders' pitches drew their authenticity from slaveholders' shared fantasies of gentility, reciprocity, and salvation. The traders' stories helped the buyers to mirror their shared fantasies in the individual slaves who stood before them, to imagine that they were distinguishing themselves through the purchase of the slave they chose.

There was a specific commercial variant to the slave-sale story in which the traders set aside bargaining to give the buyer some inside advice. The Virginia slave trader who sold Eden said that he was 'so pleased' with Eden that he put the slave to work in the slave pen. He continued his description of Eden's virtues (that is, salability) by saying that the slave 'always rendered a correct account to his master . . . and he was never chastised, and it is a rare case when a slave is sent six months to sell without being chastised'.[28] Those who did not trust the traders' stories were sometimes allowed to take a peek into their business practice. James Blakeny literally opened his account books – where else would a trader unmask himself but in the counting room? – in trying to sell Mary Ellen Brooks to Bruckner Payne. Blakeny 'told Payne he would sell her for $600 thereby losing her clothing and shipping costs' and exhibited a bill of lading to prove the price he had paid. Making a similar pitch, slave trader David Wise exhibited his own incentives when he told Clarissa's buyers 'that he would dispose of the girl at a low price on account of her advanced state of pregnancy'.[29] At the time Blakeny and Wise retold these slave-market stories, they were in Louisiana courtrooms being sued for knowing that the slaves they sold were mortally ill. In the courtroom, as in the slave market, the references to their own incentives were deployed by the traders to shield their motives from further scrutiny. 'Negro Driver', 'Southern Yankee', 'Southern Shylock', they were called: what better proof of a trader's sincerity than an open accounting of what they had at stake?[30]

As they played their way back and forth between the stories told about every slave and the pitches they made for any slave, the traders sometimes had to refit their shopworn pitches to specific circumstances. Apparent ills required careful narration. A cough in the slave market was evidence of a present cold or past sickness – nothing serious, nothing incipient. Other ailments were similarly explained by being explained away: Sally's loose teeth – 'they could have been pulled out with a person's finger' – were attributed to her excessive use of Calomel; the fit Henry had been seen having in the street was a result of his 'pretending to be sick all the time'; Lewis's ruined knee was described by the broker at a probate sale as a 'temporary twist received a few days previous while assisting others in covering a house'; Phillis's swollen leg was rheumatism, 'nothing...it had never interfered with her work'; the swelling beneath Seraphine's skirt, which turned out to be a very large tumor, was described by the man selling her as evidence of her pregnancy.[31] These were minor ailments – some regrettable like Henry's fake fits, some laudable like Lewis's willingness to endanger himself in helping others – but all temporary. All of these stories emphasized circumstance in explaining apparent irregularity, and all of them provided buyers with the opportunity to demonstrate their abilities in the choice of their slaves: a little treatment, a little discipline – in short, a little mastery – and these slaves would be as good as new.

The traders had to be equally ready to spin unruly evidence of slaves' inward feelings back into the comforting conventions of proslavery rhetoric. When a woman who was missing two fingers mounted the stand in Richmond, the auctioneer quickly explained that the doctor had removed the first finger for a medical reason and she had herself cut off the second because it pained her. The disquieting specter of a woman who would choose to mutilate her hand rather than be sold was brushed over with the reassuring image of a slave so stupid and imitative that she would cut off one finger because the doctor had cut off another.[32] Anton Reiff, a visitor to New Orleans, remembered seeing a woman crying on the auction stand and recorded what he was able to learn about her in his diary: 'Her master was in debt and was obliged to sell her to pay some mortgage. She had always lived with the family. She was about 35 years old. Her grief (to me) was heartrending. She wept most bitterly'.[33] The loyal slave sold for her owner's debts: whether or not the story Reiff recorded was true, it was effective. The woman's tears became part of the auctioneer's pitch, and Anton

Reiff, standing in the slave market, felt his heart rent by a convention of proslavery paternalism.

All of these stories may have been believed by the traders who told them; most of them may have been true, but their veracity is less important than their form. The traders' stories, redolent with the comforting commonplaces of slaveholding culture, guided the buyers' eyes to what they were supposed to see. The slave traders' stories suggested that the buyer of a particular slave would be a man with a sharp eye for the main chance, or a taste for the exceptional, or a singular capacity to do right. As they packaged their slaves in stories about the distant past, the traders were telegraphing suggestive accounts of the slaveholding futures that were for sale in the pens. Along with the virtues of their slaves, the traders were scripting those of their buyers.

Some of the people the traders sold were not slaves at all. Eulalie had been living as free for decades when she, her six children, and ten grandchildren were taken by force from their home in Pointe Coupeé, Louisiana, sold at auction in New Orleans, and then placed in a slave pen for 'safe keeping'. Euphémie and her seven children were held in a New Orleans slave pen, advertised for sale in the New Orleans *Bee*, and sold at public auction. She had been living as a free person for over twenty years. Though they lost years of their life to the slave traders, these women and their families had nearby friends and relatives who could help them reconstruct their histories and successfully sue to have their freedom restored on the grounds that whatever claim there was to their ownership had long since lapsed through disuse.[34] The hopes of other free people sold as slaves, however, were even more attenuated.

The shades of legality in which the traders dealt sometimes crossed into outright kidnapping. The list of those who managed to send word out of slavery must stand as a partial list of the kidnapped: John Merry, a free man from Illinois, was arrested as a slave in St. Louis and shipped to New Orleans to be sold; Solomon Northup, a free man from New York, was lured with lies to Washington, drugged, threatened with death, and put on a boat for New Orleans, where he was sold in the yard of slave dealer Theophilus Freeman; Albert Young was freed by his Alabama owner's will but nevertheless carried to New Orleans by the will's executor and sold to the New Orleans dealers McRae, Coffman & Co.; John Wesley Dunn, another free man, was charged with stealing an 'old coat' in Baltimore, jailed, sold to slave dealer Hope H. Slatter, and carried to New Orleans, where he was sold again. Messages sent by Merry and Northup reached their friends, and they were freed from slavery through the intervention of the courts. Young's suit also reached the courts, but his freedom was voided on the grounds that his emancipation was not legal under Alabama law. The letter Dunn sent for help may never have reached his father, to whom it was addressed.[35]

None of these stolen people could have been sold if their histories were known, so they were sold with new ones. These were only the most extreme cases of the creative power of the traders' market practice. Or, at least, they seem the most extreme, because lying about a slave's origins seems more abject than ignoring them, selling a person under an uncertain title seems more mendacious than selling with a clear title, and kidnapping a free person seems more shocking than selling a slave. But the extremity of these stories represents the regularity of what slave traders did every day for four hundred years, what they did hundreds of thousands of times during the antebellum period. Just as kidnapping made slaves of free people, the traders' packaging created slaves who did not previously exist out of the pieces of people who formerly did. By detaching slaves from their history and replacing human singularity with fashioned salability, the traders were doing more than selling slaves: they were making them.

Ultimately, however, the rites of the market had to be enacted by the slaves. From the time the buyers entered the yard in the morning to the time they left at night, the slaves were expected to enact carefully scripted roles. Solomon Northup remembered Theophilus Freeman hectoring his slaves to perform and 'threatening' them with beatings if they stepped out of their assigned roles. In the slave pens, wooden boards with holes drilled through them or wide leather straps attached to a handle, were substituted for the mortifying lash, because paddles raised blisters but left no permanent scars. The traders' instruments of torture enforced the story they were trying to tell without leaving a trace of its source.[36] Northup also remembered Freeman 'holding out various inducements', which left even fewer traces than beatings. Michael Tadman has discovered that slaves were sometimes promised small cash rewards 'if they would try to get homes and not do anything against the interest of their sales'. As well as the entries for calico dresses and pantaloons, slave trader John White recorded regular cash outlays to slaves to make sure that the costumes he had bought were inhabited with the right spirit. Northup remembered that Freeman used his slaves' own hopes to fund his inducements. Instructing Northup to hold up his head and look 'smart', Freeman told Northup that he 'might, perhaps, get a good master' if he 'behaved'.[37]

Throughout the day, the traders goaded the slaves into motion so that the buyers could better evaluate the way they moved. 'Now hold up your head and walk pert . . . Quick – come – pert – only there already? – pert'! the antislavery journalist James Redpath remembered hearing a slave dealer's assistant bark at a slave. Around the walls of the pens, slaves were set into motion to prove their stamina and agility. Fredrika Bremer remembered seeing 'forty or fifty' men walking up and down in front of a slave pen in Georgia. Robert Chambers remembered seeing slaves being asked to run across the sale room in Virginia. John Brown remembered slaves dancing, jumping, walking, leaping, tumbling and twisting before the buyers' eyes, showing off that they had 'no stiff joints or other physical defects'. The physician philosophers of the slave market admonished buyers to look even deeper. Juriah Harriss believed that constitutional unsoundness would become apparent as slaves were forced into motion before the buyers. Samuel Cartwright thought that slaves with 'Negro Consumption' would be unable to ascend a flight of stairs without elevating their heart rates to a hundred and thirty or forty beats per minute.[38]

The traders instructed slaves to give ages that accorded with their polished bodies and to hide pasts that might make buyers wary. Slaves who had run away or been ill were told to hide their histories. Those who were being sold for their skills were told to 'exaggerate their accomplishments'. Slaves in the pens were instructed to appear happy and active, William Wells Brown remembered, 'some were set to dancing, some to jumping, some to singing, and some to playing cards. This was done to make them seem cheerful as possible'. Solomon Northup remembered that Theophilus Freeman 'exhorted us to appear smart and lively' and provided Northup with a violin that he might give the others music to dance by. Following the conventions of antebellum racism, slaves were made to demonstrate their salability by outwardly performing their supposed emotional insensibility and physical vitality.[39]

These carefully prepared performances made it difficult for the buyers to sort representation from reality, and like other slave-importing states, Louisiana had strong warranty laws designed to rebalance the relationship between seller and buyer.[40] The asymmetry of information in the slave market had been addressed in the Louisiana *Civil Code* by the law of redhibition, or 'the avoidance of sale on account of some vice or defect in the thing sold'. As a justice of the Louisiana Supreme Court put it in 1859, these laws were 'evidently created as a matter of policy and...founded upon the difficulty which purchasers of slaves recently brought from another state experience in procuring proof of their bodily condition and the comparative ease with which the proof of that fact could be made by the vendors'.[41] Specific provisions of the *Civil Code* limited actions for redhibition to those cases in which the problem was not apparent upon 'simple inspection' and not explicitly exempted from the general warranty. The sales of slaves (and animals) could be voided for 'vices' of either body or character. Leprosy, madness, and epilepsy were considered absolute vices of body, their bare existence sufficient cause to void a sale. Other diseases were considered in proportion to the disability they caused. Vices of character, as defined by Louisiana law, were limited to cases in which it could be proven that a slave had committed a capital crime, was 'addicted to theft', or 'in the habit of running away'. A habit of running away was established by proving that a slave had run away 'twice for several days, or once for more than a month'. Warranty suits had to be preceded by an attempt at 'amicable return' of the unwanted slave(s) and filed within one year of the date of purchase. Under an 1834 addition to the law, buyers of recently imported slaves did not have to prove that the 'vice' was existent at the time of the sale if it became evident within two months (for questions of character) or two weeks (for illness or infirmity).[42]

These buyer-protection laws and presumptions could be overcome by specific declarations, which took the form of either a written statement of the maladies or 'vices' that were specifically excepted from the warranty or simply a clause voiding the standard form of warranty ('guaranteed against the vices and maladies prescribed by law'). Such provisions, however, were comparatively rare, appearing on only six per cent of the Acts of Sale notarized by buyers in the New Orleans market.[43] Most slave traders appear to have played the odds, preferring to sell risky slaves as sound ones and counting on the buyers' difficulties in returning a slave and filing a suit to make good their risk.

Returning slaves, after all, cost dissatisfied buyers even more money than they had already spent in the market: the cost of transportation for the slave, the buyer, and usually a sympathetic witness; the cost of having depositions taken or of getting people to court, including exceptional charges for expert witnesses like physicians; court costs and lawyers' fees; the possibility of losing. Indeed, the relative frequency with which buyers who lived at some distance from New Orleans appeared in court to sue slave traders suggests that the traders may have been choosing their targets carefully, identifying the out-of-town buyers for whom returning an unwanted slave would be the most difficult and steering them toward slaves about whom the traders themselves had suspicions.[44]

When dissatisfied buyers did make it back to the market, the traders sometimes raised other barriers. They refused to accept returns, which made buyers go to law; they deducted charges from the price of the slave or would take back slaves only if they were exchanged for new ones, the buyer paying a surcharge of a few hundred dollars; they temporized about whether the slaves were really unsound and put buyers off by asking them to wait until they returned for the next selling season or until slaves' diseases abated; they dodged buyers when they knew the year within which buyers had to file their suits was about to expire.[45] Again, the traders' behavior may have been influenced by the circumstances of the buyer. 'Repeat players', slave traders who hoped to develop relationships with specific buyers or reputations in a region, may have been more likely to accept returns. Wealthy Louisiana planter Thomas Pugh, who yearly bought large numbers of slaves for his sugar plantations near Donaldsonville, Louisiana, certainly had no trouble in negotiating returns and exchanges with both John White and Theophilus Freeman.[46]

Though most buyers had to take more care than a man with the slave-market stature of Thomas Pugh, those who returned slaves to the pens usually had the law on their side, and many traders accepted returns rather than risking suits. One slave salesman stated that such a practice was a matter of course in the pen where he worked: 'Mr. Slatter's instructions were never to misrepresent Negroes and to exchange them at any time rather than go to a lawsuit'.[47] It is hard to imagine the man saying anything else – that Slatter told him to lie to customers, sell them sick slaves, and refuse to take them back, for example – with a thousand dollar suit hanging in the balance. But even if accepting returned slaves was not a hard-and-fast rule, it was a practice common enough to have generated a common resolution: slaves who had been returned to the traders were often resold to other buyers, sometimes for prices higher than the traders had received the first time around.[48]

No matter what they eventually did when faced with a returned slave, traders did the daily work of preparing and selling their slaves in the shadow of the law. The representations traders made in the marketplace could be subject to subsequent legal action; vices they managed to conceal at the time of sale could later emerge as the grounds for a suit; credulous buyer could turn sedulous litigant. The traders had to consider the law when they decided who to sell to whom. John White's slave record book listed a number of slaves as 'in my hands unsold' at the end of every season. Some people the slave traders just could not sell.[49] Every year White's firm sent a few slaves back to central Missouri after unsuccessfully offering them for sale in New Orleans: five sent in 1846; six in 1851; five more in 1852.[50] No doubt those were small numbers to John White, who sold a hundred or more slaves in a season. But they were momentous decisions to the small number they affected. Slaves who could not be sold sometimes ended up in the places from which they had been taken in the first place, restored to their families and communities. 'Sent home', one of White's entries reads.

The daily practice of the pens lay at the juncture of an unknown past and a promised future. As a justice of the Louisiana Supreme Court put it when considering the necessity of the enforcement of redhibition law: 'The condition of a Negro at a trader's quarters, well dressed, well fed, unworked – in a word well cared for in every material respect for the express purpose of making a favorable impression on purchasers – is not necessarily a conclusive criterion of the future or the past condition and capability of that same Negro when undergoing the necessary hardships of ordinary slave service'. The traders' daily business was to shape the real people they had in their hands to reflect the abstract market they had in their heads, and then to punctuate their categories of comparison with the value-producing practice of differentiation: the special clothes and spatial arrangement, the articulated human connections, the singular story. In the pens the traders medicated and fed and shined and shaved and plucked and smoothed and dressed and sexualized and racialized and narrated people until even the appearance of human singularity had been saturated with the representations of salability. This was the traders' version of necromancy – the magic that could steal a person and inhabit their body with the soul of another – the forcible incorporation of a slave with the spirit of a slaveholder's fantasy.

But though they went to great lengths to replace people with packaging, the traders did not have to fool anyone. Indeed, the traders could no more force their self-revealing representations upon a skeptical buyer than they could do their deadly business without the resistant bodies of living slaves. By replacing biography with salability, the traders did not have to do anything more than shape the discussion. Under the traders' watchful eyes, visible physical coordinates replaced invisible historical identities as the most accessible means for buyers to make their comparisons. Faced with the uncertainties of the slave pens, slave buyers turned to race as the best way to do the business of slavery.

NOTES

1. *Alexander v. Hundley*, #5276, 13 La. Ann. 327 (1858), testimony of T. R. Davis, UNO.
2. *Dixon v. Chadwick*, #4388, 11 La. Ann. 215 (1856), plaintiff's brief, UNO.
3. On slavery, sale, life, and death see Orlando Patterson, *Slavery and Social Death: A Comparative Study* (Cambridge, 1982); Igor Kopytoff, 'The Cultural Biography of Things: Commoditization as Process', in Arjun Appaudurai, ed., *The Social Life of Things: Commodities in Cultural Perspective* (Cambridge, 1986), 64–91; and Akhil Gupta, 'The Reincarnation of Souls and the Rebirth of Commodities: Representations of Time in "East" and "West,"' *Cultural Critique* (Fall, 1992), 187–211.
4. For the evolution of the market from a place to a power see Jean-Christophe Agnew, *Worlds Apart: The Market and the Theater in Anglo-American Thought, 1550– 1750* (Cambridge, 1986).
5. *Coulter v. Cresswell*, #2734, 7 La. Ann. 367 (1852), testimony of J. M. Wilson and David Wise, UNO; *Peyton v. Richards*, #3523, 11 La. Ann. 63 (1856), testimony of J. W. Boazman, UNO.
6. John Brown, *Slave Life in Georgia: A Narrative of the Life, Sufferings, and Escapes of John Brown, a Fugitive Slave Now in England*, L. A. Chamerovzow, ed. (1855; reprinted Savannah, 1991), 112; William Wells Brown, *Narrative of William Wells Brown, A Fugitive Slave, Written by Himself (1847)* in Gilbert Osofsky, ed., *Puttin' on Ole Massa* (New York, 1969), 193. For 'blacking' see *Ledger of Accounts*, Tyre Glen Papers, RASP, and John White, *Day Book*, April 19, 1845, UMC; for tallow see White, *Day Book*, January 4, 1845, UMC.
7. For fattening diet see John White, *Day Book*, January 5, 29, April 12, 13, May 2, 1845, June 12, 1846, *passim*, UMC; for the quotation see A. J. McElveen to Ziba Oakes, September 8, 1856, reproduced in Edmund Drago, ed., *Broke by the War: Letters of a Slave Trader* (Columbia, S.C., 1991).
8. John Brown, *Slave Life in Georgia*, 95–96; William Wells Brown, *Narrative*, in Osofsky, ed., *Puttin' on Ole Massa*, 194; Moses Roper, *A Narrative of the Escape and Adventure of Moses Roper* (London, 1838), 62; Henry Bibb, *Narrative of the Life and Adventures of Henry Bibb, An American Slave, Written by Himself* (New York, 1845), in Osofsky, ed., *Puttin' on Ole Massa*, 115.
9. *Dohan v. Wilson*, #5368, 14 La. Ann. 353 (1859), testimony of Dr. J. H. Lewis, UNO; *Stillwell v. Slatter*, unreported Louisiana Supreme Court case #4845 (1843), testimony of Dr. John J. Carr, UNO; *Murphy v. Mutual Benefit & Fire Insurance*

Company of Louisiana #2244, 6 La. Ann. 518 (1851), testimony of Dr. John J. Carr, UNO.

10. *Succession of Cresswell*, #2423, 8 La. Ann. 122 (1853), UNO; John White, *Day Book*, 1846, *passim*, UMC; *Perkins v. Shelton*, unreported Louisiana Supreme Court case #5654 (1859), testimony of E. F. Harrot, UNO; *Lynch and Wiesman v. McRae*, unreported Louisiana Supreme Court case #270 (1859), UNO; Solomon Northup, *Twelve Years a Slave*, Joseph Logsdon and Sue Eakin, eds. (Baton Rouge, 1968), 55; ordinance XLVII, articles 2 and 3 (passed June 8, 1841), in *Digest of the Ordinances and Resolutions of the General Council of the City of New Orleans* (New Orleans, 1845), 28.

11. John White, *Day Book*, February 3, 5, 14, 16, 19, 21, 1846, UMC.

12. N. C. Folger to John White, bill for clothing purchased in New Orleans, dated October 1, 1857 (and totaling $585.25), Chinn Collection, MHS; John White, *Day Book*, *passim*, UMC; Tyre Glen account with Bragg and Stewart, 1833, Tyre Glen Papers, RASP; Whitehead and Loftus Account Book, 1835–1837, Floyd Whitehead Papers, Duke; *Succession of Cresswell*, unreported Louisiana Supreme Court case #3521 (1954), UNO.

13. Eyre Crowe, 'The Slave Market in New Orleans', *Harper's Weekly Magazine*, January 24, 1863, 197; Joseph Holt Ingraham, *The Southwest by a Yankee* (New York, 1835), II, 193, 197; Robert Chambers 'Journal', October 1853, in Frederick Law Olmsted, *The Cotton Kingdom: A Traveler's Observations on Cotton and Slavery in the American Slave States* (New York, 1862), II, 597.

14. Whitehead and Loftus Account Book, 1835–1837, Floyd Whitehead Papers, Duke; N.C. Folger to John White, bill for clothing purchased in New Orleans, November 1, 1857, Chinn Collection, MHS; John White, *Day Book*, December 17, 1844, February 28, 1844, UMC; A and A. J. Walker, *Account Book*, 69 (March 14, 1852), Walker Papers, UNC.

15. John Brown, *Slave Life in Georgia*, 100; see also Northup, *Twelve Years a Slave*, 51.

16. John White, *Slave Record*, 1846, UMC; *Gourjon v. Cucullu*, #2324, 4 La. 115 (1852), list of Negroes on board brig *Seraphim*, Compte de Vente du 94 esclaves reçu par le brick *Seraphim*, and testimony of Charles Tremot, UNO.

17. *Code Noire*, sections 8 and 9, quoted in Judith Kelleher Schafer, *Slavery, the Civil Law, and the Supreme Court of Louisiana* (Baton Rouge, 1994), 165; *Laws of Louisiana, 1829, 1st Session, 9th Legislature* reproduced in Henry J. Levoy, ed., *The Laws and General Ordinances of New Orleans* (New Orleans, 1857), 269.

18. Michael Tadman, *Speculators and Slaves: Masters, Traders, and Slaves in the Old South* (Madison, Wis., 1989), 153–4.

19. Brenda Stevenson, *Life in Black and White: Family and Community in the Slave South* (New York, 1996), 182–3, 224.

20. John White, *Slave Record*, 1846, UMC; *Coulter v. Cresswell*, #2734, 7 La. Ann. 367 (1852), testimony of J. W. Boazman and David Wise, UNO.

21. Robert Fogel and Stanley Engerman, eds., *The New Orleans Slave Sample, 1804–1862*, database available from the Inter-University Consortium for Political and Social Research.

22. Northup, *Twelve Years a Slave*, 51. See also John Brown, *Slave Life in Georgia*, 96–100.

23. For the traders' reputation see Tadman, *Speculators and Slaves*, 179–189.

24. Slave Sale Broadside, May 13, 1835, LSU; *Wright, Allen & Co. v. Railley*, #5731, 13 La. Ann. 536 (1858), testimony of Edward Sparrow, UNO. Washington, Jackson & Co. to Daniel Turnbull, October 13, 1859, Turnbull-Bowman Family Papers, LSU; *Smith v. Taylor*, #5755, 10 Rob. 133 (La. 1845), testimony of H. Cobbs; *Perkins v. Shelton*, unreported Louisiana Supreme Court case #5654 (1859), testimony of R. W. Levy, UNO.

25. 'Sale of valuable Servants', 1838, mss 44 f.86, HNO; *Hewes v. Baron*, #1641, 7 Mart. (N.S.) r34 (1828), testimony of Edward Durin, UNO.

26. Slave Sale Broadside, May 13, 1835, Lower Mississippi Valley Collection, Hill Memorial Library, LSU.

27. For the role of steamboats in shaping notions of 'the good life' see Louis C. Hunter, *Steamboats on the Western Rivers: An Economic and Technical History* (Cambridge, 1949), 390–418.

28. *Fortier v. LaBranche*, #3289, 13 La. 355 (1839), testimony of L. Labarré, UNO.

29. *White v. Slatter*, #943, 5 La. Ann. 27 (1849), testimony of Francis H. Jump, UNO; *Coulter v. Cresswell*, #2734, 7 La. Ann. 367 (1852), testimony of David Wise, UNO.

30. For these insults see D. R. Hundley, *Social Relations in our Southern States* (New York, 1860; reprinted Baton Rouge, 1960), 139–49; and Tadman, *Speculators and Slaves*, 179–92.

31. *Dixon v. Chadwick*, #4388, 11 La. Ann. 215 (1856), John W. Cole, UNO; *Hepp v. Parker*, #1788, 8 Mart. (N.S.) 473 (1830), testimony of L. A. Gaiennie, UNO; Douglas to William Hamilton, March 3, 1857, William Hamilton Papers, LSU; William D. Hennen, ed., *Digest of the Reported Decisions of the Superior Court of the Late Territory of Orleans; the Late Court of Errors and Appeals; and the Supreme Court of Louisiana* (Boston, 1852), 1409. *Hitchcock v. Hewes*, #1935, 1 La. 311 (1830), testimony of James Ervin, UNO; *Nixon v. Boazman and Bushy*, #3485, 11 La. Ann. 750 (1856), testimony of A. Celoi and T. Reddington, UNO; *White v. Hill*, #3958, 10 La. Ann. 189 (1855), testimony of G. W. Munday, UNO; *Hewes v. Baron*, #1641, 7 Mart (N.S.) 134 (1828), plaintiff's petition and testimony of J. Dupin; *Lemos v. Daubert*, #4198, 8 Rob. 224 (La. 1844), testimony of Maurice Barnett, UNO.

32. James Redpath, *The Roving Editor, or Talks with Slaves in the Southern States* (New York, 1859), 252. On race and slavishness as imitation see Ariela Gross, 'Pandora's Box: Slave Character on Trial in the Antebellum Deep South', *Yale Journal of Law and the Humanities*, 7 (1995), 283–8.

33. Anton Reiff, *Journal*, 42 (1995), 283–8.

34. *Eulalie, f.w.c. and her Children v. Long and Mabry*, #3237, 9 La. Ann. 9 (1854), testimony of Pierre Pouche, L. M. Foster, and the decision of the Supreme Court, UNO; *Euphemié, f.w.c. v. Juliet and Jourdan*, unreported Louisiana Supreme Court case #6740 (1865), plaintiff's petition, testimony of Juliette Maran, decision of the Supreme Court, UNO; see also *Eulalie, f.w.c. v. Long and Mabry*, #3979, 11 La. Ann. 463 (1856), and *Andrinette, f.w.c. and her Children v. Maran*, f.w.c., unreported Louisiana Supreme Court case #6741 (1865), UNO. The acronym 'f.w.c'. stands for 'free woman of color' and indicates the presumption of freedom which was granted under Louisiana law to anyone who appeared to be 'mulatto' and sued for their freedom. For 'f.w.c'. (and 'f.m.c'), these cases, and those of others whose suits for freedom were heard by the Louisiana Supreme Court see Schafer, *Slavery, the Civil Law, and the Supreme Court of Louisiana*, 220–49.

35. *Merry, f.m.c. v. Chexnaider*, #1877, 8 Mart. (N.S.) 699 (1830), plaintiff's petition and decision of the Supreme Court, UNO; Northup, *Twelve Years a Slave*, 12–20; *Young, f.m.c. v. Egan*, #4075, 10 La. Ann. 415 (1855); John Wesley Dunn to Charles Dunn, January 3, 1845, John Wesley Dunn Letter, 81–73-L, HNO. See also Schafer, *Slavery, the Civil Law, and the Supreme Court of Louisiana*, 250–88.

36. Northup, *Twelve Years a Slave*, 25. See also John Brown, *Slave Life in Georgia*, 97–8; Bibb, *Narrative*, in Osofsky, ed., *Puttin' on Ole Massa*, 115; Frederika Bremer, *Homes of the New World: Impressions of America*, trans. Mary Howlitt (New York, 1853), II, 535.

37. Obediah Fields, memorandum, February 11, 1828, quoted in Tadman, *Speculators and Slaves*, 101; John White, *Day Book*, December 30, 31, 1844, January 8, 1845,

passim, UMC; Northup, *Twelve Years a Slave*, 36; see also Bibb, *Narrative*, in Osofsky, ed., *Puttin' on Ole Massa*, 101.

38. Redpath, *The Roving Editor*, 248–9; Bremer, *Homes of the New World*, 373; Chambers, 'Journal' in Olmsted, *Cotton Kingdom*, II, 378–9; Brown, *Slave Life in Georgia*, 99–100; Juriah Harriss, 'What Constitutes Unsoundness in the Negro'? *Savannah Journal of Medicine*, 1 (1858), 220–1; Samuel Cartwright, 'Diseases and Peculiarities of the Negro Race', *DeBow's Review*, 11 (1851), 212.

39. L. M. Mills interview in John Blassingame, ed., *Slave Testimony: Two Centuries of Letters, Speeches, Interviews, and Autobiographies* (Baton Rouge, 1977), 503; William Wells Brown, *Narrative*, in Osofsky, ed., *Puttin' on Ole Massa*, 196; Bib, *Narrative*, in ibid., 95, 139; John Brown, *Slave Life in Georgia*, 99–100; Northup, *Twelve Years a Slave*, 36.

40. For the general point about slave-importing states see Andrew Fede, 'Legal Protection for Slave Buyers in the U.S. South: A Caveat Concerning *Caveat Emptor*', *American Journal of Legal History*, 31 (1987), 322–58. For the specifics of Louisiana law see Judith Kelleher Schafer, ' "Guaranteed against the Vices and Maladies Prescribed by Law": Consumer Protection, the Law of Slave Sales, and the Supreme Court in Antebellum Louisiana', *American Journal of Legal History*, 31 (1987), 306–21, and Schafer, *Slavery, the Civil Law, and the Supreme Court of Louisiana*, 127–79.

41. *Dohan v. Wilson*, #5368, 14 La. Ann. 353 (1859), decision of the Supreme Court, UNO.

42. Thomas Gibbes Morgan, ed., *Civil Code of the State of Louisiana* (New Orleans, 1853), articles, 2496–2508, 2512.

43. Fogel and Engerman, eds., *The New Orleans Slave Sample, 1804–1862*.

44. See, for example, *Rist v. Hagan*, #4503, 8 Rob. 106 (La. 1844); *Peterson v. Burn*, #912, 3 La. Ann. 655 (1848); *Slater v. Rutherford*, #1021, 4 La. Ann. 382 (1849); *Executors of Haggerty v. Powell*, #2215, 6 La. Ann. 533 (1851); *Coulter v. Cresswell*, #2734, 7 La. Ann. 367 (1852); *Person v. Rutherford*, #3585, 11 La. Ann. 527 (1856), UNO.

45. For forcing buyers to go to law see Bernard Kendig's statement that he 'would do nothing unless compelled to do so by law', *Buie v. Kendig*, #6356, 15 La. Ann. 440 (1860), testimony of Isaac Doyle. For deductions see *Herries v. Botts*, #3635, 14 La. 432 (1840), testimony of Dr. E. H. Barton and *Matthews v. Pascal's Executors*, #3287, 13 La. 53 (1839), testimony of William Flower: 'Pascal appeared to be satisfied that there were grounds for recision and proposed by a compromise to pay half the amount of the Negro Dempsey – alleging that he was a partner & had only half the sale'. For exchanges and surcharges see *Nixon v. Boazman and Busby*, #3485, 11 La. Ann. 750 (1856), testimony of Bernard Kendig; for traders putting buyers return requests off see *Blair v. Collins*, #6449, 15 La. Ann 683 (1860), plaintiff's petition, and *Executors of Haggerty v. Powell*, #2215, 6 La. Ann. 533 (1851), testimony of Hoyt. For dodging the day the prescription ran see *Smith v. Taylor*, #5755, 10 Rob. 133 (La. 1845), plaintiff's brief to the Supreme Court, UNO.

46. On 'repeat players' see Gross, 'Pandora's Box: Slavery, Character, and Southern Culture in the Courtroom' (Stanford University Ph.D., 1996), 245; John White, *Slave Record*, 1851, UMC; *Stewart v. Sowles*, #725, 3 La. Ann. 464 (1948), testimony of Theophilus Freeman, UNO.

47. *Kock v. Slatter*, #1748, 5 La. Ann. 734 (1850), testimony of James Blakeny, UNO.

48. For returned slaves resold see *Stewart v. Sowles*, #725, 3 La. Ann. 464 (1848); *Peterson v. Burn*, #912, 3 La. Ann. 655 (1848); *Kock v. Slatter*, #1748, 5 La. Ann. 734 (1850); *Romer v. Woods*, #1846, 6 La. Ann. 29 (1851); *Person v. Rutherford*, #3585, 11 La. Ann. 527 (1856); *Gatlin v. Kendig*, #6894, 18 La. Ann. 118 (1866). For higher prices and sale in different states see John White, *Slave Record*, 1851, *passim*, UMC. The other thing the traders did was return slaves themselves. Their

legal rights were the same as any other slaveholders, and they could sue when they were dissatisfied or call previous owners 'in warranty' when they were sued.

49. John White, *Slave Record*, *passim*.
50. John White, *Slave Record, 1846* (David Overton, Megan Wells, Esther Taylor, Runel Causey, Berry), 1851 (Mary Ellette and her five children), 1852 (Abram Godwin, Kate King, and her three children), UMC.

DOCUMENT 1: THE NEW ORLEANS SLAVE MARKET

An account of the New Orleans slave market in December 1850, as witnessed by Fredrika Bremer, a Scandinavian novelist whose visit to the United States was inspired by her desire to see the position of women in American society.

On the 31st of December I went with my kind and estimable physician to witness a slave-auction, which took place not far from my abode. It was held at one of the small auction-rooms which are found in various parts of New Orleans. The principal scene of slave-auctions is a splendid rotunda, the magnificent dome of which is worthy to resound with songs of freedom. I once went there with Mr. Lerner H., to be present at a great slave-auction; but we arrived too late.

Dr. D. and I entered a large and somewhat cold and dirty hall, on the basement story of a house, and where a great number of people were assembled. About twenty gentlemenlike men stood in a half circle around a dirty wooden platform, which for the moment was unoccupied. On each side, by the wall, stood a number of black men and women, silent and serious. The whole assembly was silent, and it seemed to me as if a heavy gray cloud rested upon it. One heard through the open door the rain falling heavily in the street. The gentlemen looked askance at me with a gloomy expression, and probably wished that they could send me to the North Pole.

Two gentlemen hastily entered; one of them, a tall, stout man, with a gay and good-tempered aspect, evidently a *bon vivant*, ascended the auction platform. I was told that he was an Englishman, and I can believe it from his blooming complexion, which was not American. He came apparently from a good breakfast, and he seemed to be actively employed in swallowing his last mouthful. He took the auctioneer's hammer in his hand, and addressed the assembly much as follows:

'The slaves which I have now to sell, for what price I can get, are a few home-slaves, all the property of one master. This gentleman having given his bond for a friend who afterward became bankrupt, has been obliged to meet his responsibilities by parting with his faithful servants. These slaves are thus sold, not in consequence of any faults which they possess, or for any deficiencies. They are all faithful and excellent servants, and nothing but hard necessity would have compelled their master to part with them. They are worth the highest price, and he who purchases them may be sure that he increases the prosperity of his family'.

After this be beckoned to a woman among the blacks to come forward, and he gave her his hand to mount upon the platform, where she remained standing beside him. She was a tall, well-grown mulatto, with a handsome

Fredrika Bremer, *The Homes of the New World: Impressions of America*, trans. Mary Howitt, 3 vols (London, 1853), vol. 3, pp. 7–11.

but sorrowful countenance, and a remarkably modest, noble demeanor. She bore on her arm a young sleeping child, upon which, during the whole auction ceremonial, she kept her eyes immovably riveted, with her head cast down. She wore a gray dress made to the throat, and a pale yellow handkerchief, checked with brown, was tied round her head.

The auctioneer now began to laud this woman's good qualities, her skill, and her abilities, to the assembly. He praised her character, her good disposition, order, fidelity; her uncommon qualifications for taking care of a house; her piety, her talents, and remarked that the child which she bore at her breast, and which was to be sold with her, also increased her value. After this he shouted with a loud voice, 'Now, gentlemen, how much for this very superior woman, this remarkable, &c., &c., and her child'?

He pointed with his outstretched arm and fore-finger from one to another of the gentlemen who stood around, and first one and then another replied to his appeal with a short silent nod, and all the while he continued in this style:

'Do you offer me five hundred dollars? Gentlemen, I am offered five hundred dollars for this superior woman and her child. It is a sum not to be thought of ! She, with her child, is worth double that money. Five hundred and fifty, six hundred, six hundred and fifty, six hundred and sixty, six hundred and seventy. My good gentlemen, why do you not at once say seven hundred dollars for this uncommonly superior woman and her child? Seven hundred dollars – it is downright robbery! She would never have been sold at that price if her master had not been so unfortunate', &c., &c.,

The hammer fell heavily; the woman and her child were sold for seven hundred dollars to one of those dark, silent figures before her. Who he was; whether he was good or bad; whether he would lead her into tolerable or intolerable slavery – of all this, the bought and sold woman and mother knew as little as I did, neither to what part of the world he would take her. And the father of her child – where was he?

With eyes still riveted upon that sleeping child, with dejected but yet submissive mien, the handsome mulatto stepped down from the auction-platform to take her stand beside the wall, but on the opposite side of the room.

Next, a very dark young negro girl stepped upon the platform. She wore a bright yellow handkerchief tied very daintily round her head, so that the two ends stood out like little wings, one on each side. Her figure was remarkably trim and neat, and her eyes glanced round the assembly both boldly and inquiringly.

The auctioneer exalted her merits likewise, and then exclaimed,

'How much for this very likely young girl'?

She was soon sold, and, if I recollect rightly, for three hundred and fifty dollars.

After her a young man took his place on the platform. 'He was a mulatto, and had a remarkably good countenance, expressive of gentleness and refinement. He had been servant in his former master's family, had been brought up by him, was greatly beloved by him, and deserved to be so – a most excellent young man'!

He sold for six hundred dollars.

After this came an elderly woman, who had also one of those good-natured, excellent countenances so common among the black population, and whose demeanor and general appearance showed that she too had been in the service of a good master, and, having been accustomed to gentle treatment, had become gentle and happy. All these slaves, as well as the young girl, who looked pert rather than good, bore the impression of having been accustomed to an affectionate family life.

And now, what was to be their future fate? How bitterly, if they fell into the hands of the wicked, would they feel the difference between then and now – how horrible would be their lot! The mother in particular, whose whole soul was centered in her child, and who, perhaps, would have soon to see that child sold away, far away from her – what would then be her state of mind!

No sermon, no anti-slavery oration could speak so powerfully against the institution of slavery as this slave-auction itself!

The master had been good, the servants good also, attached, and faithful, and yet they were sold to whoever would buy them – sold like brute beasts!

DOCUMENT 2: A SLAVE COFFLE

A description of a slave coffle by George W. Featherstonhaugh, an English author and geographer employed by the United States War Department to make geological surveys of lands west of the Great Lakes. This extract records his impressions of the internal slave traffic while travelling from Virginia through Alabama to the southwest in September 1834.

Just as we reached New River, in the early grey of the morning, we came up with a singular spectacle, the most striking one of the kind I have ever witnessed. It was a camp of negro slave-drivers, just packing up to start; they had about three hundred slaves with them, who had bivouacked the preceding night *in chains* in the woods; these they were conducting to Natchez, upon the Mississippi River, to work upon the sugar plantations in Louisiana. It resembled one of those coffles of slaves spoken of by Mungo Park, except that they had a caravan of nine waggons and single-horse carriages, for the purpose of conducting the white people, and any of the blacks that should fall lame, to which they were now putting the horses to pursue their march. The female slaves were, some of them, sitting on logs of wood, whilst others were standing, and a great many little black children were warming themselves at the fires of the bivouac. In front of them all, and prepared for the march, stood, in double files, about two hundred male slaves, *manacled and chained to each other*. I had never seen so revolting a sight before! Black men in fetters, torn from the lands where they were born, from the ties they had formed, and from the comparatively easy condition which agricultural labour affords, and driven by white men, with liberty and equality in their mouths, to a distant and unhealthy country, to perish in the sugar-mills of Louisiana, where the duration of life for a sugar-mill slave does not exceed seven years! To make this spectacle still more disgusting and hideous, some of the principal white slave-drivers, who were tolerably well dressed, and had broad-brimmed white hats on, *with black crape round them*, were standing near, laughing and smoking cigars.

Whether these sentimental speculators were, or were not – in accordance with the language of the American Declaration of Independence – in mourning 'from a decent respect for the opinions of mankind', or for their own callous inhuman lives, I could not but be struck with the monstrous absurdity of such fellows putting on any symbol of sorrow whilst engaged in the exercise of such a horrid trade; so wishing them in my heart all manner of evil to endure, as long as there was a bit of crape to be obtained, we drove on, and having forded the river in a flat-bottomed boat, drew up on

George W. Featherstonhaugh, *Excursion through the Slave States, from Washington on the Potomac to the Frontier of Mexico: with Sketches of Popular Manners and Geological Notices* (New York: Harper & Bros, 1844), pp. 36–8, 46–7, 141–2.

the road, where I persuaded the driver to wait until we had witnessed the crossing of the river by the 'gang', as it was called.

It was an interesting, but a melancholy spectacle, to see them effect the passage of the river: first, a man on horseback selected a shallow place in the ford for the males slaves; then followed a waggon and four horses, attended by another man on horseback. The other waggons contained the children and some that were lame, whilst the scows, or flat-boats, crossed the women and some of the people belonging to the caravan. There was much method and vigilance observed, for this was one of the situations where the gangs – always watchful to obtain their liberty – often show a disposition to mutiny, knowing that if one or two of them could wrench their manacles off, they could soon free the rest, and either disperse themselves or overpower and slay their sordid keepers, and fly to the Free States. The slave-drivers, aware of this disposition in the unfortanate [sic] negroes, endeavour to mitigate their discontent by feeding them well on the march, and by encouraging them to sing 'Old Virginia never tire', to the banjo.

The poor negro slave is naturally a cheerful, laughing animal, and even when driven through the wilderness in chains, if he is well fed and kindly treated, is seldom melancholy; for his thoughts have not been taught to stray to the future, and his condition is so degraded, that if the food and warmth his desires are limited to are secured to him, he is singularly docile. It is only when he is ill-treated and roused to desperation, that his vindictive and savage nature breaks out. But these gangs are accompanied by other negroes trained by the slave-dealers to drive the rest, whom they amuse by lively stories, boasting of the fine warm climate they are going to, and of the oranges and sugar which are there to be had for nothing: in proportion as they recede from the Free States, the danger of revolt diminishes, for in the Southern Slave-States all men have an interest in protecting this infernal trade of slave-driving, which, to the negro, is a greater curse than slavery itself, since it too often dissevers for ever those affecting natural ties which even a slave can form, by tearing, without an instant's notice, the husband from the wife, and the children from their parents; sending the one to the sugar plantations of Louisiana, another to the cotton-lands of Arkansas, and the rest to Texas.

DOCUMENT 3: INVENTORY OF SLAVES ON A LOUISIANA SUGAR PLANTATION

An inventory dated 1849 of the slaves owned by James Coles Bruce (1806–65) on a sugar plantation in Louisiana. Bruce was one of the largest slaveowners in the Old South. The valuations remind us that all slaves, even infants, had a market price. 'Full Hands' were adult slaves capable of undertaking heavy field work. 'Half Hands' were young children, sick or elderly slaves incapable of strenous work.

List of Negro Men & Boys, also their ages & Value

Names	Ages	Full Hands	Half Hands	Value	Remarks
Perry—Driver	40 Years	1″		$900 00	Disposed to medle with women
Old Daniel	70 Years		½	100 00	old and decriped
John Miller	28 Years	Full Hand		600 00	a Runaway
Jim Bassy	25 Years	″		600 00	Sickly
Claiborn West	28 Years	″		800 00	good Negro
Jack Page	35 Years	″		700 00	has Runaway
Claiborn Anderson	35 Years	″ 1		400 00	has runaway
Orange	28 Years	″		800 00	good Hand
Anderson M	25 Years	″		800 00	good Negro
Bob Scooner	28 Years	″		700 00	Well disposed but Sloe
Izor M	45 Years	″		500 00	African, good but Sloe
George M.	25 Years	″		600 00	a cooper, Sickly but good
Jin. Wilbot	45 Years	″		400 00	a Runaway no account
Carter Allen	23 [Years]	″		400 00	a Runaway, verry Sloe
Charles Mena	45 [Years]	″		500 00	African, verry good
Randle	45 [Years]	″		800 00	Sugar Maker, good hand
Edmond	40 [Years]	″		600 00	A great drunkard
Sam Williams	25 [Years]	″		600 00	A good hand
Gallant	45 [Years]	″		500 00	rather trifling, but will do
Old Mat M.	35 ″	″	½	300 00	Sickly consumption
Bill Kenty	45 ″	″		700 00	good hand
Fleming	45 ″	″		400 00	a runaway
Jefferson	28	″		800 00	Superior Hand
Simond (Carpenter)	45 ″	″		800 00	the greatest rascal on Plantation
Friday	40		½	350 00	Sickly Subject to fits
Milton	20 ″	″		700 00	good hand
Ezekiel	25 ″	″		800 00	good hand
John Davis	45 ″		½	400 00	Sickly, & a runaway
Jackson Tailor	28 ″	″		800 00	good hand
Sam Briggs	23 ″	″		700 00	good hand
David	44 ″	″		700 00	well disposed but sloe
John Henderson	20 ″	″		700 00	a fine hand
Richmond	23 ″	″		800 00	a good hand

Willie Lee Rose (ed.), *A Documentary History of Slavery in North America* (New York: Oxford University Press, 1976), pp. 338–44.

Names	Ages	Full Hands	Half Hands	Value	Remarks
Simond Melacha	25 [Years]	full Hand		700 00	good hand but tricky
Ned Duck	35 "	"		500 00	not much account
Granison	26 "	"		600 00	good hand
Ransom	25 "	"		800 00	good hand
Tellemark	50 "		1/2	200 00	African King, no account
Charles Sims	28 "	"		700 00	good hand
Jack Coopper	30 "	"		1000 00	Jack Cooper, good hand
Bill Pleasant	28 "	"		700 00	good hand
Bill Sprague	30 "	"		600 00	good hand
Wyatt	30 "	"		700 00	good hand
Isaac Pascal	35 "	"		700 00	verry Sloe and high tempe[red]
Bill Berry	35 "	"		700 00	Sugar Maker, a great Liar
Squire	50 "		1/2	200 00	not much account
Ceazor	50 "		1/2	200 00	well disposed but no account
Little Daniel	40 "	"		600 00	disposed to fein sickness
Patrick	50 "		1/2	200 00	gardner no account
Ephraim	30 "	"		800 00	excelent hand
Old Champ	50 "		1/4	100 00	most Blind, but well disposed
Washington	20 "	"		600 00	a Runaway
Carter M.	35 "	"		600 00	verry deceptive
John Comedy	45 "	"		600 00	a great Rascal & Runaway
Jack Allen	18 "		1/2	300 00	Sickly (Breast complaint)
Jo Blacksmith	30 "	"		1200 00	Blacksmith good hand
Old Luis	50 "		1/2	200 00	water hauler no account
Richard	15 "	"	1/2	500 00	good hand
One Leg Bob	50 "		0	000 00	no earthly use
John Robinson	16 "	"	1/2	500 00	assistant Blacksmith good
Emmanuel	45 "		1/2	100 00	criple, (in the Doct yard)
Old Charles	60 "		0	5 00	wore out, no account
General	30 "	"		800 00	No 1 hand
Little Mat M.	17 "		1/2	300 00	reumatic (but well disposed)
Little Jo	15 "		1/2	500 00	excelent Boy
Israel	20 "	"		600 00	Brick layer fair hand
Willson	22 "	"		600 00	Brick layer fair hand
Pleasant	26 "	"		1000 00	Carpenter fine Negro
Moses	27 "	"		1000 00	Engineer good Negro
Phill	10 "		1/3	300 00	wants much watching
Sandy	9 "		1/3	300 00	verry fine Boy
Jo	8 "		1/3	250 00	verry trifling
Anderson M	25 "	"		900 00	good hand
Will Shoemaker	28 "	"		800 00	good hand
Jim Wilkins	27 "	"		700 00	good hand
Little Bob	12 "		1/2	300 00	a verry good Boy
Julius	12 "		1/2	300 00	good Boy
One hand Luis	30 "		1/2	400 00	Bad Negro Runaway
Old Jake	50 "		1/2	300 00	well disposed
John Wilkins	30 "	"		600 00	verry good
Ballard Doct	12 "		1/2	300 00	good Boy but Sloe
Little Jack Doct	10 "		1/2	300 00	verry Smart Boy
William	6 "	0	0	200 00	verry good Boy

Continued

(*Continued*)

Names	Ages	Full Hands	Half Hands	Value	Remarks
Nelson	4 [Years]	0	0	150 00	rather young to Judge
Lunon	3 ″	0	0	150 00	″ ″
Maldry	4 ″	0	0	150 00	″ ″
Mose	4 ″	0	0	200 00	″ ″
Ceazor	4 ″	0	0	200 00	″ ″
George	2 ″	0	0	100 00	″ ″
Pier	5 ″	0	0	250 00	″ ″
Henry Lewis (Louisa child 9 months)	0 ″	0	0	100 00	″ ″
Prince (Araminta child 8 months) 92 Men & Boys & 44 Women & Children 136 in all	0 ″	0	0	100 00	″ ″

A List Women their ages & Value

Names	Ages	Full Hands	Half Hands	Value	Remarks
Letha	20 [Years]	″		500 00	good hand
Elmira	25 ″		½	400 00	Sickly
Eliza Ann	18 ″	″		500 00	good hand
Nanny	16 ″	″		500 00	good hand
Long Mariah	45 ″		½	200 00	not much account
Tena	40 ″	″		400 00	well disposed fair hand
Eliza	20 ″	″		400 00	fair hand
Amy	35 ″	″		400 00	fair hand
Jennette	35 ″	″		400 00	verry good cook
Peggy	30 ″	″		500 00	good hand
Fanny	18 ″	″		500 00	good hand
Nancy	16 ″	″		500 00	good hand
Harriet (Black)	25 ″	″		500 00	good hand
Olive	20 ″	″		500 00	good hand
Hager	50 ″		½	200 00	excells in telling lies
Angelina	30 ″	″		400 00	verry good hand
Mariah (Cook)	40 ″	″		300 00	all mouth. Plantation cook
Polly	40 ″	″		300 00	verry Bad woman (great temper)
Lucy	20 ″	″		500 00	good hand
Martha	35 ″	″		500 00	good hand
Lydia	25 ″	″		400 00	good hand
Yellow Harriet	18 ″		¼	100 00	verry little account sickly
Cathrine	20 ″	″		400 00	fair hand
Penelopy	60 ″		½	200 00	Plantation Nurse
Mary Jose	55 ″		½	100 00	wash woman, no account
Little Mary	14 ″		½	400 00	good Girl
Dina	40 ″	″		400 00	Hospital nurse. fair

Names	Ages	Full Hands	Half Hands	Value	Remarks
Julia	20 [Years]	"		400 00	fair hand
Vina	30 "		½	200 00	Sickly
Tamor	30 "	"		400 00	fair hand
Matilda	16 "	"		500 00	good hand
Rose	10 "		0	300 00	a great Liar (but will do)
Mary Creole	20 "	"		500 00	good hand
Hannah	45 "		½	300 00	mischief maker (all talk)
Terese	11 "		½	300 00	will Lie & Steal
Farma	30 "	"		500 00	good hand
Louisa (Doctors)	22 "	"		500 00	good hand
Araminta "	22 "	"		500 00	good hand
Micky	5 "	0	0	150 00	well disposed
Eliza	7 "	0	0	250 00	great Liar (but will do)
Rebecca 6 mo	0 "	0	0	100 00	to young to Judge
Nancy (5 months)	0 "	0	0	100 00	" " " "
Rachael (3 months)	0 "	0	0	100 00	" " " "
Delphy 2 months	0 "	0	0	100 00	" " " "

List of Negros that does not work in the field

Sawmill Hands

Mose, Anderson, Carter[,] Izor[,] Friday ($\frac{1}{2}$)[,] old Mat ($\frac{1}{2}$), Little Mat ($\frac{1}{2}$), Charles [,] Louis[,] Little Jack ($\frac{1}{2}$)

4 of which are half Hands which make 10 in number & onely 8 full Hands	10 in Number
Pleasant, Little Jo, (Anderson Wilkins) old Davy & Simond are the carpenters	5 in Number
Jack, George, & Jim Bassy are the Coopers	3 in Number
Jo Blacksmith & John Robison are the Blacksmiths	2 in Number
John Comedy [,] Ned Duck, Sandy ($\frac{1}{2}$), Phill ($\frac{1}{2}$), & Joe ($\frac{1}{2}$) are the Stable Boys	5 in Number
Dina, is Hospital Nurse	1 in Number
Penelopy is Plantation washwomen	1 in Number

Master and Man

Mary Jose is a Nurse for children	1 in Number
Mariah & Harriet are Plantation Cooks	2 in Number
Fanny is the Doct Cook	1 in Number
Polly is at Mr Knowltons House	1 in Number
Jennett is at the overseers House	1 in Number
old Bob, Old Dan, Old Champ, Old Charles, & Old Patrick, employed in various ways Such as gardening Shingle makeing Shaveing hoops &c all together will not do more than one good hand but are called $\frac{1}{2}$ Hands	5 in Number

Making in Number 37 Negros who does not work in the field except in Rooling [sugar rolling] Season and in the Said 37 Negroes their are 27 full Hands

Their are	45 men full hands in the field &
their are	25 women in the field full Hands
makeing	70 in Number for the field

Continued

(*Continued*)

&	24 full hands employed in various ways as above stated
makeing	97 full hands on the Plantation

The men & Boys are worth in the agrigate as per
inventory $47,005.00
The Women & Girls are worth   15,600.00
                                                                              $62,605.00
Off for Dr Wilkins Negros   1 800.00
                                                                              60 805.00

Average value of each $460.33 & a fraction 130 in all after deducting 6 for Dr Wilkins

7

SLAVERY AND THE LAW

The legal history of American slavery focuses on legal cases and procedures, crime and justice, and specific colonies and states. Hall (1987) reprints some seminal articles dealing with these issues. Hyman and Wiecek (1982) is a sure-footed synthesis of the historiography of American constitutional development, with much of interest on slavery, in the forty years after 1835. Watson (1989) is a brief comparative survey of manumission, restrictions on slave punishment, the criminal liability of slaves and the legal personality of slaves in Roman law and the European colonies in America. He focuses on the legal traditions that made up these laws rather than on social and economic factors that influenced the making of statutes. He shows that the Latin American colonies all received versions of Roman law on to which they grafted slave laws whereas British America was outside of the orbit of Roman law and therefore created its own slave legislation piecemeal and according to local needs. Watson also puts forward the debatable view that Roman law was less racist in its treatment of enslaved black people than the slave codes established in British America.

Sirmans (1962) discusses the changing legal status of slaves in South Carolina from the founding of the colony through to the aftermath of the Stono Rebellion. He finds considerable change over time. The first South Carolinian law relating to slavery in 1690 defined the slave as freehold property. Chattel slavery was not specified in the colony's law until the slave code of 1740. Wiecek's article (1977a) is a useful brief consideration of the statutes relating to slavery and the law throughout the British North American colonies. Colonial law defined slavery as a lifetime condition, distinguishing it from servitude and other types of unfree status. Wiecek shows that the most troublesome element for colonial legislators dealing with slavery was the legal status of slaves as property.

Higginbotham (1978) is a more extended discussion of racism, slavery and the law in colonial North America. He examines statute law and court cases in six American colonies – Massachusetts, New York, Pennsylvania, Virginia, South Carolina and Georgia. In each colony, Higginbotham argues that slaves were initially treated as somewhere between indentured servants and chattel slaves but that, over the course of the eighteenth century, they became subject to harsher legal codes and greater discrimination, especially in the South. Legal codes hardened. Enslaved blacks were usually debarred from providing testimony in court against whites. Nor were they afforded legal means to protect themselves and their families. Though Higginbotham deals thoroughly with statutes and court decisions, he is less interested in exploring the legal status of slaves outside of the statutory framework.

Schwarz (1988) provides a mass of information about the implementation of slave laws in Virginia, drawing extensively on local court records. His title arises from the notion that slaves were condemned both by their status as chattel and by the court system. Flanigan (1974) argues that southern legislatures and courts were very considerate towards slaves' procedural rights in major criminal cases. Wahl (1998) sifts through thousands of cases heard in southern courts to show how legal incentives and outcomes influenced business transactions concerning slavery. She shows, *inter alia*, that slave buyers received more protection under the law than purchasers of livestock. Her main argument is that the protection of property rights made slavery a continuing economic proposition in the South.

Morris (1996) offers the major study of slavery and the law in the southern colonies and states from the Jamestown settlement to the American Civil War. He covers the racial and legal sources of American statutes pertaining to slavery. He also investigates three other topics in depth: slaves as property, slaves as persons and manumission. His evidence, drawn from local records as well as published statutes, emphasises the immiseration of African-Americans in the system of slavery and the impact of racism on lawmaking. But he also detects limited legal developments that afforded more assistance to slaves in the late antebellum period, including taking slave testimony seriously, providing legal counsel for African-Americans and affording slaves some protection in terms of food, clothing and health care. Whether such advances in the legal treatment of slaves were intended to protect them as property or as people varied according to local conditions.

In an earlier study, Morris (1974) focused on the personal liberty laws of the North between the revolutionary era and the outbreak of the Civil War.

These laws dealing with fugitive slaves were intended to protect free blacks from being captured and to prevent runaway slaves from being returned to their owners. Morris looks at the deployment of habeas corpus and trial by jury to ensure black freedom in five selected states – Massachusetts, New York, Pennsylvania, Ohio and Wisconsin. The personal liberty laws he examines operated under the presumption of freedom and therefore served as an important basis for the fourteenth amendment, which prohibited state violation of life, liberty and property and guaranteed equal protection under the law.

Tushnet (1981) uses Marxist theory and evidence largely drawn from the period 1840–60 to show that judicial cases concerning slavery in the South often failed to distinguish carefully between slaves as human beings and as property. He argues that many judges did not have the intellectual capacity to formulate a coherent approach to slave cases that could reconcile these opposing notions of African-Americans. In many instances, common law precedents set constraints on the action of appellate judges. Looking at the same tension between slaves as people and as property in the eyes of the law, Schafer (1994) concentrates on the Supreme Court of Louisiana to show that in most cases the latter definition prevailed where this was a matter of dispute.

The constitutional doctrine of slavery is treated at length in Wiecek (1977b). He argues that until the 1830s the legal status of slaves was guaranteed under the United States Constitution: a federal consensus existed under which it was accepted that only the states could regulate slavery within their jurisdiction. A major change only occurred when the abolitionist movement split into various wings. Radical abolitionists then interpreted the Constitution's clauses as favouring antislavery: Garrisonians insisted that the Constitution was proslavery. This process occurred in the decade after 1838. It provides an exception to the rule that changes in the interpretation of the Constitution mainly arose through the judicial process. Nieman (1991) agrees that the constitutional order recognised slavery but differs from Wiecek in arguing that the Constitution was a 'malleable' and 'open-ended document' (pp. viii, 13).

Fehrenbacher (1978) investigates Chief Justice Roger B. Taney's opinion on the Dred Scott case, a cause célèbre in the legal treatment of American slaves. Dred Scott was a slave who had lived in the slave state of Missouri and was subsequently taken by his owner to live in the free state of Illinois and the Louisiana Purchase territory, where slavery was banned under the terms of the Missouri Compromise of 1820. In 1846 Dred Scott and his wife sued for their freedom in the Missouri Circuit Court of St Louis on the basis that they had lived in the Louisiana territory. Their case was stalled but was finally taken on appeal to the United States Supreme Court. Taney's verdict (1857) argued that Dred Scott was not a citizen of Missouri and therefore that the Supreme Court had no jurisdiction in this case. Two months after this decision, the Scott family were transferred to another owner who freed them. Fehrenbacher's book provides a definitive study of the legal and constitutional issues raised by the Scott case about slavery in the territories.

The legal handling of slaves travelling between the slave and free states is the subject of Finkelman's study of the doctrine of comity (1981), whereby the states exercised mutual forbearance. Covering the entire period from the Federal Convention of 1787 until the outbreak of the Civil War, this study argues that a change in the legal handling of slaves in transit with their masters occurred in the 1850s. Before that decade, southern states awarded freedom to slaves who had spent time in the North and the northern states allowed slaveowners to bring their slaves with them when visiting the free states. The sectional accommodation on this matter began to break down in the 1830s. With the intensification of the sectional controversy in the 1850s, however, most northern states emancipated slaves in their jurisdictions while southern states confirmed the slave status of slaves who had been sojourners in the North.

The first section of Ayers (1984) investigates the criminal justice system of the antebellum South, with particular reference to three Georgia counties. Criminal justice in those settings and throughout the South, in his view, combined the realities of slavery with traditional southern attitudes, such as the concept of honour. Hindus's comparative study of criminal justice in Massachusetts and South Carolina (1980) highlights the racial dimensions of crime in the Palmetto state. Slaves there were sometimes subjected to plantation trials and were forbidden from testifying against whites. On the eve of the Civil War the greatest threat to the hegemony of South Carolina's planters came from offences against property and authority by blacks. The court system in South Carolina remained weak until Reconstruction so that private means of settling disputes could be pursued. Nevertheless, during the first half of the nineteenth century at least 296 South Carolinian slaves were executed whereas only 28 executions occurred in Massachusetts among a population twice as large.

Hadden (2001) treats a long-neglected topic. Her discussion of slave patrols in Virginia and the Carolinas from the late seventeenth century through to the end of the Civil War shows how slave codes were enforced. Slave patrols were formed by county courts and state militias. They comprised a cross-section of white people, including members of respectable society and poorer folk. They searched slave quarters, broke up slave gatherings, and captured runaways. They harassed slaves, carrying whips and guns to instil terror into the black community. Sanctioned by legal codes on slavery, they indicate the ways in which southern colonies and states defended the continuance of slavery through close surveillance.

BIBLIOGRAPHY

Ayers, Edward L., *Vengeance and Justice: Crime and Punishment in the 19th-Century American South* (New York: Oxford University Press, 1984)

Fehrenbacher, Don E., *The Dred Scott Case: Its Significance in American Law and Politics* (New York: Oxford University Press, 1978)

Finkelman, Paul, *An Imperfect Union: Slavery, Federalism, and Comity* (Chapel Hill: University of North Carolina Press, 1981)

Flanigan, Daniel J., 'Criminal Procedure in Slave Trials in the Antebellum South', *Journal of Southern History*, 40 (1974), 537–64

Hadden, Sally E., *Slave Patrols: Law and Violence in Virginia and the Carolinas* (Cambridge, MA: Harvard University Press, 2001)

Hall, Kermit L. (ed.), *The Law of American Slavery: Major Interpretations* (New York: Garland, 1987)

Higginbotham, A. Leon, *In the Matter of Color: Race and the American Legal Process* (New York: Oxford University Press, 1978)

Hindus, Michael Stephen, *Prison and Plantation: Crime, Justice, and Authority in Massachusetts and South Carolina, 1767–1878* (Chapel Hill: University of North Carolina Press, 1980)

Hyman, Harold M. and William M. Wiecek, *Equal Justice under Law: Constitutional Development, 1835–1875* (New York: Harper, 1982)

Morris, Thomas D., *Free Men All: The Personal Liberty Laws of the North, 1780–1861* (Baltimore, MD: Johns Hopkins University Press, 1974)

Morris, Thomas D., *Southern Slavery and the Law, 1619–1860* (Chapel Hill: University of North Carolina Press, 1996)

Nieman, Donald G., *Promises to Keep: African-Americans and the Constitutional Order, 1776 to the Present* (New York: Oxford University Press, 1991)

Schafer, Judith Kelleher, *Slavery, the Civil Law, and the Supreme Court of Louisiana* (Baton Rouge: Louisiana State University Press, 1994)

Schwarz, Philip J., *Twice Condemned: Slaves and the Criminal Laws of Virginia, 1705–1865* (Baton Rouge: Louisiana State University Press, 1988)

Sirmans, M. Eugene, The Legal Status of the Slave in South Carolina, 1670–1740', *Journal of Southern History*, 28 (1962), 462–73

Tushnet, Mark V., *The American Law of Slavery, 1810–1860: Considerations of Humanity and Interest* (Princeton, NJ: Princeton University Press, 1981)

Wahl, Jenny Bourne, *The Bondsman's Burden: An Economic Analysis of the Common Law of Southern Slavery* (New York: Cambridge University Press, 1998)

Watson, Alan, *Slave Law in the Americas* (Athens, GA: University of Georgia Press, 1989)

Wiecek, William M., 'The Statutory Law of Slavery and Race in the Thirteen Mainland Colonies of British America', *William and Mary Quarterly*, 34 (1977a), 258–80

Wiecek, William M., *The Sources of Antislavery Constitutionalism in America, 1760–1848* (Ithaca, NY: Cornell University Press, 1977b)

ESSAY: SLAVE PROPERTY CRIMES AND THE LAW
IN THE SOUTH

Morris (1996) looks at the legal treatment of slave crimes against property in the American South. Arson, larceny and burglary receive detailed treatment. Morris refers to the English common law practices that underpinned much American legislation on slave crime. He also shows that most colonial and state laws against slaves involved considerable differences in punishment from one jurisdiction to another. Should slave crimes against property be seen as acts of accommodation or of resistance? What factors influenced sentencing practices throughout the southern states? What does the enforcement of laws against theft and burning show about the treatment of slaves?

> The morality of free society could have no application to slave society.
> Frederick Douglass, *My Bondage and My Freedom* (1855)

E. P. Thompson's notion that criminal acts are often efforts to establish a 'moral economy' by oppressed lower-class people has informed some efforts to find meaning in slave crimes against property. Alex Lichtenstein, for instance, saw them as attempts to 'redefine and extend the bounds of paternalism' and as 'incipient class-conflict over the forms the slave economy would take and the claims to its profits'. Slaves, he believed, 'used theft to reject, not accommodate to, their condition of slavery'.[1] The views of slaves and the recollections of ex-slaves are filled with discussions of thefts. They were often justified as a 'taking' rather than stealing. As Frederick Law Olmsted put it, 'the agrarian notion has become a fixed point of the negro system of ethics; that the result of labour belongs of right to the labourer, and on this ground, even the religious feel justified in using "massa's" property for their own temporal benefit'. Others felt unease about stealing. One ex-slave commented: 'See old Marse and Missus give us such little rations led her slaves to stealin' .... We knowed hit was de wrong thing to do but hunger will make you do a lot of things'. There is little doubt that some felt personal degradation because of it, as the case of Frederick Douglass shows. But he ultimately rationalized thefts because the 'morality of free society could have no application to slave society'.[2]

Thefts of food from masters were not the only offenses against property committed by slaves, and petty stealing – as opposed to a crime like burglary – did not usually become a legal problem. Masters simply punished the slaves on the plantations for stealing chickens, which is why property crimes played a relatively small role in *legal* experience. This level of the struggle between masters and slaves was largely outside the public law.

Thomas D. Morris, *Southern Slavery and the Law, 1619–1860* (Chapel Hill: University of North Carolina Press, 1996), pp. 322–36, 506–10.

Law was involved only in that authority to punish was permitted to masters. As James Henry Hammond noted, 'we try, decide, and execute the sentences, in thousands of cases, which in other countries would go into the courts'.[3]

This was not the case with arson. William Faulkner caught the profound unease aroused in Southern whites by fire. The image of the burning house in *Light in August* is memorable, as is the fear Flem Snopes generated when he arrived in town with a reputation for a barn burning in *The Hamlet*. Arson was an easily concealed crime,[4] and it was often thought to be an act of resistance. As early as 1820 a Northern insurance company declined to provide fire insurance in Virginia because of a supposed tendency of a 'species of population' to use fire as revenge.[5]

Historians, however, have not always seen arson through the same lens. Stampp claimed that 'next to theft, arson was the most common slave "crime"'. Fire 'was a favorite means for aggrieved slaves to even the score with their master'. Genovese took a more circumspect approach. Arson was of a 'restricted character'. If a slave 'burned down the Big House, which few ever did, or the carriage house, or some other building of little direct economic significance, the slaves might easily sympathize with and protect them'. It was different if they burned the 'corncrib, smokehouse, or the ginhouse'. The reason was that 'destruction of food stores meant their own deprivation. Destruction of the cotton meant severe losses to their master, but this furious vengeance also threatened the sale of one or more members of the slave community, or worse, bankruptcy and the breakup of the community altogether'.[6] At the heart of these different views is the question of whether slave crimes should be seen as acts of accommodation or resistance. For Southern whites that probably was a question unasked: for them the problem was simply the 'criminal' conduct of those in bondage, not the motives or meaning underlying that conduct. The theft of chickens was surely an annoyance, but that form of 'crime' was something they could live with. Crimes like larcenies, burglaries, or arson, however, were a different matter. Larcenies of chickens from neighbors could also be grievous, as they might involve the relationships among the free, not just those among masters and slaves.

Larceny

Most slave crimes against property fell in the category of larceny. 'Simple larceny', according to Blackstone, 'is the felonious taking, and carrying away, of the personal goods of another'. A compound larceny included an element of aggravation as in a 'taking from one's house or person'. One form was robbery. As Pearson put it in *State v. John, (a slave)* (North Carolina, 1857), 'Robbery is committed by force; larceny by stealth'. Larceny from the person was not simply a crime against property. 'Open and violent larceny from the *person*,... is the felonious and forcible taking', Blackstone noted, 'from the person of another, of goods or money to any value, by putting him in fear'. The compound larceny of stealing from a house shaded off into burglary, but it could be different. Under the common law a burglary involved breaking into a house at night.[7]

There was a further breakdown between petit or petty larceny and grand larceny. Policy determined the distinction and the punishment. During the late eighteenth century Sir Matthew Hale argued that public order might require the death penalty for some thefts if they became too widespread and thereby threatened social stability. Grand larceny was a capital, but clergyable offense and occurred whenever the goods stolen were over twelve pence in value. Petit larceny, the theft of property valued under twelve pence, was punished by imprisonment or whipping at the discretion of the magistrate.[8] By the eighteenth century hanging a person for the theft of goods over twelve pence in value troubled many people, and juries would sometimes save a person by the 'pious perjury' of valuing goods below that sum no matter what the true value.[9] In the slave societies of the South the law might be bent in different ways as public order, and thus policy, could be satisfied by the justice of the plantation in some cases but not in others.

Hog stealing was one of the most frequent thefts in the South and one of the first dealt with specifically in a statute. Throughout the region hogs were relatively plentiful and formed a major part of people's diets. If a hog was valued over twelve pence, the hog stealer would be guilty of a capital offense under English law. By an act of 1699 Virginia's burgesses provided that a slave would receive thirty-nine lashes 'well laid on' for the first offense. For a second he was to stand in the pillory for two hours with both ears nailed to it, and then the ears would be cut off. By a law of 1705 a third offense was made capital without benefit of clergy, which is what it would have been under the common law for a second theft of a hog valued over twelve pence if clergy had been granted for the first crime.[10]

The treatment of sheep-stealing slaves contrasted with the practice and the statutory development for the theft of hogs. Virginians did not directly follow the English law. In England, where sheep cost more than hogs, sheep stealing was a capital offense without benefit of clergy. It remained non-clergyable in colonial Virginia in theory but not always in practice. In 1763 Cupid was burned on the hand in Westmoreland County after his conviction for sheep stealing. But two years earlier Sam was hanged in Princess Anne County for the same crime.[11]

By the nineteenth century the distinction between grand and petit larceny was collapsing, and statutory limits had been set on punishments. Any functional difference between the two larcenies was eliminated in 1822 in Mississippi, for instance. The categories remained but there was no point. Grand larceny was the theft of goods valued above $20, and petit larceny the theft of goods below that figure. The punishment, however, was identical – thirty-nine lashes.[12]

By its law of 1856 North Carolina abolished the distinction. This statute was construed by the state supreme court a year later in *State v. Harriet, (a slave)*. Nash noted that there had been a distinction at common law, but 'morally speaking, there is no difference; each is equally forbidden by the great Lawgiver'. North Carolina's lesser lawgivers agreed. They abolished the distinction and provided that the offense, unless otherwise specified, would be punished as a petit larceny in all cases. They diminished grand larceny, 'a change which the spirit of the times demanded'.[13] A major exception to this trend was a Louisiana law of 1856: 'any slave who shall be guilty of larceny, shall be punished at the discretion of the court'. Discretion was retained, but the distinction was not. One illustration of the use of this discretion is an 1831 case from St. Landry Parish. George, who had taken cash, clothes, a pocket knife, and so on from different people, was convicted of larceny. The judgment of the court was that his owner was to pay unspecified damages, the value of the property taken from one of the victims, and court costs. George himself was whipped thirty-nine times with a cow skin and had 'an Iron Collar of five pounds weight with three prongs put upon & round the neck'. He had to wear the collar for one year.[14]

Statutes sometimes retained the distinction but removed the unbridled discretion. In Alabama's 1852 law a magistrate was authorized to sentence a slave up to thirty-nine lashes for a petit larceny. If he felt that the offense warranted more, he could consult two 'respectable freeholders' and with their assent order up to one hundred lashes. Maryland was unique in that it provided prison terms for slaves convicted of grand and petit larceny.[15]

Throughout the South sentencing practices for slaves found guilty of larceny collapsed distinctions. The procedure in New Hanover County, North Carolina, for the period 1821–56 illustrates the point. There were eleven cases involving charges of grand larceny and none of petit larceny. Benefit of clergy is mentioned in several of these cases, and the sentences with guilty verdicts ranged from twenty-five lashes to thirty-nine lashes on two separate occasions.[16]

Probably the most extreme example of the older common law approach to larceny was in South Carolina, which adopted no significant statute on slave thefts, kept the common law language, and allowed the magistrate-freeholders discretion in sentencing.[17] In Anderson District sentences for simple larceny ranged from the ten lashes given Linda in 1832 for stealing to one hundred lashes given Marshele and Pleasant in 1865 for hog stealing. In 1852 Wash and Jim were involved in the theft of bacon. Wash was the principal, and Jim was found guilty of being an 'accessory before and after the fact'. Jim was sentenced to fifty-five lashes 'moderately well' laid on, whereas Wash was not tried at all. The telling reason was that Wash's owner allowed him to be flogged by the owner of the bacon and then flogged him himself, but Jim's owner refused to allow Jim to be whipped.[18]

Although the distinctions in the common law offense of simple larceny were collapsing, the same was not true of compound larceny. Robbery and 'larceny from the house', however, do not appear often. Robbery is mentioned most often in the records of the old slave societies along the Atlantic coast. Generally, when a trial for robbery ended in a guilty verdict, the slave was hanged.[19] A rare exception occurred in Chatham County, Georgia, in 1813. Elijah was found guilty of robbery but the jury recommended mercy, and he was sentenced to receive thirty-nine lashes on two separate occasions.[20]

At the opposite extreme was the treatment of Nathan, the slave of Gabriel South (South Carolina, 1851). His case involved two trials on separate charges based on the same event. Elizabeth Mitchell claimed that Nathan had assaulted her. He was choking her and released her only when she promised to give him what money she had, which was one dollar. He then left. On these facts Nathan was first tried on a charge of assault and battery with intent to rape. He was found guilty of assault and battery and was sentenced to receive fifty lashes on two separate occasions. After this was carried out he was indicted on a charge of robbery on the same facts, found guilty, and sentenced to hang. O'Neall issued a writ of prohibition because the first conviction was a bar to the second trial and because 'if there was no intent to commit a rape, the delivery of the money was without such a putting in fear, as the law requires to make the offence of robbery'. When the case was appealed to the state supreme court, O'Neall's ruling was overturned. The majority of the court held that whatever Nathan's intent, his acts that followed the assault and battery '(when explained and characterized by his previous violence,) show such a taking by putting in fear, as constitutes a case of robbery'. The justices also held that the first trial was no bar. O'Neall in dissent contended that the first trial showed that there was no assault and battery with intent to rape, and therefore the facts could not be used to prove force or fear so as to constitute the offense of robbery. 'Indeed there is no larceny: it is the delivery of a dollar without compulsion'. The rest of the court was satisfied that 'justice' would be done with the execution of Nathan for robbery. 'If the prisoner was a white man', O'Neall asked, 'and not a negro, could such a course receive the countenance of any one'?[21]

The other compound larceny, 'larceny from the house', rarely appears. Spencer was sentenced to seventy-five lashes in Chambers County, Alabama, in 1853 for this offense.[22] Cases of breaking into stores, storehouses, and meat houses, on the other hand, are numerous indeed, especially in urban communities.[23] Oddly enough, it does not clearly appear in the records for some states at all, or some cities, such as Natchez.

Burglary

A commonsense view of burglary is breaking into some building and stealing things, but this is misleading. Coke defined a burglar as 'he that by night breaketh and entereth into a mansion-house, with intent to commit a felony'.[24] Obviously, there is a property element here, but that is not all. The intention had to be to commit a 'felony', and that included more than theft.

According to Hawkins, moreover, the 'currant Opinion' in early eighteenth-century England was that the place broken into had to be a dwelling, but outbuildings, such as barns, were considered part of the dwelling unless far removed. There could be no burglary, in his opinion, in a shop or workhouse alone. In the *Historia Placitorum Coronae*, Hale noted why: burglary involved the 'habitation of man, to which the laws of this kingdom hath a special protection'. Blackstone pointed out that the reason burglary was so serious was that it created a 'midnight terror'. The 'malignity of the offence' was based on the fact that it occurred 'at the dead of night; when all the creation, except beasts of prey, are at rest; when sleep has disarmed the owner, and rendered his castle defenceless'. Burglary was not simply a crime against property, it was one of only two 'crimes against the habitation'. The other was arson.[25]

A shift in emphasis toward the more modern perception appeared in Adam Smith's *Lectures on Jurisprudence*. He treated burglary in his discussion of thefts. According to him, 'theft appears naturally not to merit a very high punishment. . . . But there is one case wherein thefts of the smallest value are punished with death both by the Scots and English law, that is, where a house is broken open in the commission of it. The security of the individuals requires here a severer and more exact punishment than in other cases. Burglary therefore is always capitally punished'.[26] The crime was essentially one involving theft. This was not a correct summary of English law, and Smith did note that the reason it was a capital offense was to protect people, not property rights. But for Smith – for whom property rights were so important, and who discussed burglary among 'thefts' – and for those influenced by his thought, it was easy to end seeing burglary as a property crime.

During the colonial period some lawmakers tinkered with the elements of common law burglary. Georgians and Carolinians left them intact, but Marylanders did not. The section of their 1729 law on burglary removed the benefit of clergy for the felonious breaking and entering of shops, storehouses, or warehouses, even though they were not used as dwellings or even contiguous, if the goods stolen were worth at least five shillings. Whereas other jurisdictions treated such crimes as larcenies, Maryland squeezed them under the rubric, 'burglary'. It shifted the emphasis toward the property element in the offense. A similar law was adopted in Virginia in 1748, except that the Maryland law applied to slaves alone, whereas the Virginia law did not.[27]

In 1719 Delawareans provided the death penalty for anyone convicted of burglary, which was defined as follows: 'a breaking and entering into the dwelling-house of another in the night time, with an intent to kill some reasonable creature, or to commit some other felony within the same house'. Later they stipulated that anyone who entered the dwelling of another, by night or day, with intent to commit a felony would be guilty of burglary. The same law made it a capital offense, without benefit of clergy, to break or enter 'any dwelling-house, out-house or other house whatsoever' in the daytime with an intent to 'kill some reasonable creature, or to commit some other felony'.[28]

Post-Revolutionary experimentation was erratic. In 1806 Georgia required the death penalty for any slave who broke open a dwelling 'or other building whatsoever'. Most of the experimentation did not concern the definition of the crime, but the punishment. But there were some changes in the nineteenth-century South. In Louisiana and Texas the emphasis shifted toward viewing burglary as a property offense. By 1856 Louisiana made it a capital offense for a slave to commit a traditional common law burglary, or to break into a 'store, or house of any kind, or who shall attempt to do so', whose purpose was to 'steal or commit any other crime'. Missouri was a state that modified burglary law in a general criminal code and created different degrees of the offense.[29] A number of states eliminated the death penalty for burglary and substituted either a prison term or severe whippings. Severity was being moderated in the wake of the campaigns against cruelty and the movement in favor of institutionalization for deviancy.[30] This did not always work to the advantage of slaves, of course.

The most intriguing modification came in Alabama and Mississippi in the 1850s. In 1852 Alabama changed the definition of dwelling: no building would be considered a dwelling 'unless some white person is in such house at the time the act is done or offence committed'. Statutory burglary was defined by race. It could not be such a 'burglary' to break into a free black's home, or into a slave cabin with the intent to commit a felony, unless, of course, a white person was there, a none too likely – although not impossible – condition. Five years later Mississippi provided the death penalty for slaves 'guilty of burglary, some white person being at the time in the house broken'.[31] The Alabama law was noted in one of the only appellate cases that involved the elements of the crime. In *Ex parte Vincent, (a slave)* (1855), Judge Goldthwaite wrote that the meaning of the 'dwelling' was narrowed because it was believed that the old law punishing all burglaries by slaves was too severe. This did not help Vincent, however: he broke into a white man's store at night when the owner and his brother were sleeping in the back room.[32]

These were the principal statutory alterations in burglary law. The tendency, outside of the old colonial states, was to reduce the punishment and to experiment with altering the various elements of the offense. Everywhere the crime increasingly was a crime against property, but the crime as one against the habitation was not wholly lost. Indictments were still brought against slaves for burglaries that did not involve theft. For instance, in 1824 in Culpeper County, Virginia, Dick was tried for burglary and felony. The burglary was breaking into the dwelling of John Wale with the intent to 'ravish Lucy Wale spinster'. He was found guilty and hanged a month after his trial.[33] There were also burglary cases involving attempted rape in, among other places, Anderson District, South Carolina, in 1830; Jessamine County, Kentucky, in 1843; and Lunenburg County, Virginia, in 1862. In Lunenburg County, moreover, the slave John was tried for burglary in 1860 for breaking into a dwelling and stabbing a slave with intent to kill.[34]

Burglary Cases

Because burglary was not as difficult to prove as arson, we might expect to see a high conviction rate, but that was not so. Although burglary was a capital offense, colonial Virginians actually convicted and executed far less than one-half of those slaves indicted. Hindus found a 60 per cent conviction rate for all crimes against property, including burglary, in the nineteenth century in Anderson and Spartanburg Districts, South Carolina. The punishments could be brutal, yet the slaves convicted of burglary in those districts were not always sentenced to death.[35] By the 1770s, according to Philip Schwarz, Virginians began to focus much more attention on burglary. His figures for the counties he examined show a notable increase in the number of cases, and the conviction rate rounded off to 65 per cent. Of those convicted of felonies, however, 42 per cent were granted benefit of clergy. In addition, a little over 9 per cent were convicted of misdemeanors rather than the felonies with which they were charged. From the 1780s on, moreover, Virginians hanged fewer slaves for property crimes: they viewed 'major stealing by slaves as less reprehensible and dangerous as time passed'.[36]

Intuitively we would guess that the greatest variations or deviations from the strict legal conception of burglary occurred in the lower – rather than the appellate – courts. This is a sound instinct; even so, it does not capture how skewed things could sometimes be, as one illustration shows. Will's road to the gallows in Charles City County was convoluted. He was tried in November 1761 for breaking and entering the stable of John Christian and stealing a horse. If the stable was adjacent to the dwelling, this would be a common law burglary. He was acquitted of the charge, but without any new indictment he was found guilty by the same court at the same trial of the theft of a gun belonging to John Johnson. His sentence was that of a slave granted benefit of clergy. In July 1762 Will was tried again. Three of the men who sat on the earlier trial were involved in this one. The charge was burglary: Will was indicted for breaking into the dwelling of Agness Parish and stealing property valued at twenty shillings. His owner testified against him, but he was found not guilty. Yet again he was confronted with new information for the same offense but in a different dwelling. Will pled guilty to stealing but denied breaking into the dwelling. He was found guilty of housebreaking and hanged. The problem, of course, was that he had already had his clergy, a fact the court noted.[37]

By the nineteenth century technical legal arguments appeared even at the trial court level, where slaves were defended by legal counsel. An example was the argument made in the case of John in Wilkinson County, Mississippi, in 1853. John was indicted for burglary and larceny. One of the points made by his counsel in a motion to quash the indictment was that it did 'not alledge, or show that the House into which the defendant is said to have burglorously entered was a dwelling'. The court sustained the motion, quashed the indictment, and remanded John for further proceedings. Two days later he was indicted on a charge of grand larceny, and two days after that he was acquitted. In 1844 in Screven County, Georgia, Guy escaped the gallows after a conviction for burglary, robbery, and assault. The 'evidence did not authorize a conviction for Burglary inasmuch as it established that there was no breaking of the house but the door was opened to him'.[38]

A variation on the theme occurred in South Carolina, where the magistrate-freeholders did not always show much regard for technical definitions, and where the right of appeal from their judgments was very limited. One case did reach the state supreme court. In *State v. Ridgell* (1831) the court granted a prohibition against the execution of the slave because the storehouse he broke into was about one hundred yards from any dwelling, was separated from the nearest dwelling by a public road, and was not used 'as a place for sleeping by any person at the time when it was broken open'. Nonetheless, the magistrate-freeholders had found the slave guilty of burglary and sentenced him to death. This, the court held, was inappropriate.[39] A rather rare exception in the records of these courts is that of the trial of Philip for burglary and larceny in Anderson District in 1854. The magistrate-freeholders found him guilty of larceny only and sentenced him to thirty-six lashes. They noted that they could not find him guilty of burglary 'from the fact that the law Requires to constitute Burglary the breaking and entry must be done in the night time & of which there was no evidence & we could not presume it was done in the night'.[40]

The actual practice varied a great deal from jurisdiction to jurisdiction and over time, with more and more formalism as time passed. In some jurisdictions the old common law definition of burglary remained firm, and in others it did not, either in practice or because of statutory modifications. One thing that the lower-court records do make clear is that we need to be careful with legal categorizations and not overly rely on statistical evidence, or we will sketch an erroneous picture of the actual historical experience. At the same time, there is no doubt that the spread of capitalism led to an increased emphasis on the offense of burglary as a crime against property.

The Use of Fire

Early seventeenth-century treatise writers sometimes discussed 'burnings' rather than 'arson'.[41] By the time Hawkins wrote a century later, the crime of arson was viewed as 'maliciously and voluntarily burning the House of another by Night or by Day'. He added that it 'seems Agreed' that 'not only a Mansion-House, and the Principal Parts thereof' but also 'any other House, and the Out-buildings, as Barns, and Stables, adjoining thereto; and also Barns full of Corn, whether they be adjoining to any House or not, are so far secured by Law, that the malicious burning of them is Arson'. Neither a 'bare intention' nor an 'actual attempt' would amount to the felony unless a part of a house were in fact burned. Blackstone defined arson as 'the malicious and wilful burning the house or out-house of another man'. Arson was especially pernicious, he believed, because 'it is an offence against that right of habitation, which is acquired by the law of nature as well as by the laws of society'.[42]

By the time of the settlements the punishment for arson was hanging. Colonials began to modify the law in the 1720s. As of 1729 a slave in Maryland would have his right hand severed, and then his body (after he was hung) would be quartered and distributed about the countryside. The punishment was not applied to the whole range of possible 'burnings'. In 1751 it became a capital offense without benefit of clergy for any slave to burn 'any house or houses' or to attempt 'to burn any dwelling-house, or out-houses contiguous thereto, or used with, any dwelling-house, or any other house wherein there shall be any person, or persons, or any goods, merchandise, tobacco, Indian corn or other grain or fodder'.[43] This law blurred the distinction Hawkins had made between an actual burning and an attempt. It also blended Blackstone's crime against the habitation with purely economic crimes against property. The specific crops covered, of course, were adjusted to correspond to those of Maryland.

The Maryland law dealt with slaves only. The law of Virginia did not. In 1730 'all and every person' could be executed who burned 'any tobacco-house, warehouse, or storehouse, or any house or place, where wheat, Indian corn, or other grain, shall then be kept, or any other houses what-soever'. The property element was uppermost in the minds of the burgesses rather than the protection of the habitation. Virginia adopted this law because 'divers wicked and evil disposed persons, intending the ruin and im-poverishing his majesty's good subjects' had resorted to burnings.[44]

South Carolina's first statute on fires was that of 1690. Among the crimes listed was the 'burning of houses'. This was repeated in 1712. By 1740 it was added that any person of color who burned 'any stack of rice, corn or other grain, of the product, growth or manufacture of this Province' or who burned 'any tar kiln, barrels of tar, turpentine or rosin, or any other the [sic] goods or commodities of the growth, produce or manufacture of this Province', would be executed without benefit of clergy.[45] These statutes

Burnings Trials

The pattern of trials and convictions under these various schemes is tangled. In the sample counties examined for Missouri, Texas, Arkansas, and Delaware there were no cases of arson or burnings. Trials occurred, but convictions were difficult to obtain in Mississippi, Alabama, Kentucky, Florida, Tennessee, and Louisiana. One conviction was won in St. Landry Parish, Louisiana, where Patrick Woods sold his slave Mary to the state in 1838 for half her value after she was found guilty of attempting to burn a house. She was sentenced to life in prison.[53] In all, there was only one clear conviction in this set of states, and it did not result in the death penalty. In the other states the trials either ended in acquittal or the disposition is unknown.

Experience in the remaining states and within given jurisdictions diverged. There were differences, for instance, between the trials in the rural and urban communities of Virginia. In Petersburg, from 1784 to 1840, thirteen indictments were brought against slaves for arson or other burnings, but only two slaves were convicted.[54] In 1793 Dennis and Isaac were indicted for setting fire to a lumber house. Dennis was acquitted, but Isaac was found guilty of an attempt to burn. He was lashed thirty-nine times and jailed until his master either entered into a bond to guarantee his good behavior for life or transported him out of Virginia. The second conviction was that of Claiborne in 1798.[55] The remaining twelve cases all ended in not guilty verdicts. Temporally, there were two cases in the 1790s, three between 1800 and 1810, one in the teens, four in the 1820s, and two in the 1830s. The only convictions came in the 1790s. The objects burned were a lumber house, the jail, a coach maker's shop, a dwelling, a store (this was also a robbery case), a house near an old shed, the home of the person to whom the slave was hired out, a smokehouse, a house used as a tobacco factory, and a tobacco factory. In the remaining cases the charge was simply arson, without specifying what was burned.

Of the six cases in Richmond, three were in 1858. The 1858 case against Frank and George charged them with burning a tobacco factory valued at $15,000 and with breaking and entering the tobacco factory. They were found guilty only on the second count and received thirty-nine lashes. The same year Victoria was discharged on an indictment for stealing and attempted arson of a building. The only exception to this pattern was in the third case from 1858 – that of Lewis, who was hanged for burning a dwelling in the city. This was common law arson.[56] The indictments in both Petersburg and Richmond were for more than simple arson – they were for stealing, or robbery, or breaking and entering, as well as for the use of fire.[57] These were instances of arson used to cover another offense rather than an outburst at enslavement or resistance to the system of oppression per se.

Outside Virginia's major urban centers the story is different. In Caroline County, for instance, Andrew and Malina were hanged in 1861, Andrew for burning the master's dwelling and Malina for setting fire to his barn, stable, corn house, and tobacco house. These slaves were clearly out to destroy everything their owner possessed, except presumably themselves. In Sussex County Lewis and Caesar were discharged on an indictment in 1801 for burning a house when no evidence was produced against them. The same did not happen in Fed's case in Charles City County in 1833. Although he was not convicted of arson, the court remained deeply suspicious, so much so that it 'doth recommend to the owner of the said Fed or the person who has charge or management of him to sell him forthwith'.[58] Among the things to note about these cases is the high proportion that included two defendants and the fact that none contained charges other than for straight burning or arson. The same conclusions can be drawn from the records of Lunenburg, Orange, and King George Counties.[59]

Burnings in the cities of Virginia differed from those in the countryside. Because the overwhelming majority of these cases ended in not guilty judgments, it is feckless to conclude that slaves burned this or that with a particular motive in mind. What the records show is the perceptions whites had of slaves and the ways they would employ the law to deal with the perceived use of fire. Arson was always difficult to establish, but the willingness of whites to acquit slaves of this horrifying offense is remarkable. After the turn of the century the overwhelming majority of convicted slaves were never executed, and in fact most were found not guilty.

Perhaps one of the more intriguing legal issues concerned intention. An example of the problem is Mary's case in 1819 in Prince William County, Virginia. She was transported because she was not really moved by malice and was not 'fully sensible' of the enormity of her crime. Because malice was an essential ingredient of arson, it is a wonder that she was convicted at all. The issue of malice also came up in one of the only arson cases to reach the appellate level, aside from those that also involved other issues such as confession. In *Jesse, (a slave), v. State* (Mississippi, 1854) the court reversed the conviction and sent the case back because the charge against the slave had not included the claim that the offense was done with malice, and the 1822 state statute 'does not dispense with the averment of malice'.[60] There were more arson or burning cases in Maryland, the Carolinas, and Georgia than outside the eastern seaboard slave communities.[61]

The story in Georgia is different again. In 1819 Rodney was hanged for burning his master's ginhouse with cotton inside. In 1821 Susan was acquitted of burning her master's home in Savannah, whereas three years later Molly was hanged on a similar charge. The oddest case was that of Adeline, who was found guilty of arson for burning a dwelling in 1849. Under the state code this was a capital offense, but her sentence was fifty lashes for three consecutive days, and then she was to be branded with an *H* on her right cheek and a *B* on her left, doubtless for 'house burner'.[62] The Georgia experience comes closer to what we would intuitively expect – a high conviction rate and arson associated with the property of masters, especially their dwellings.

There were a large number of indictments and a very high number of acquittals in North Carolina. The most striking thing about the record there is that a disproportionate number of the cases came from one county, New Hanover. The experience of masters and slaves in any given locale was different from that of slaves in another, even within the same state or region. Too often we lose sight of the fact that localism is as important as regionalism in the study of the law of slavery. The experience of masters and slaves with crime – as with much else – differed, for instance, between Texas and South Carolina and Virginia, but it also differed between Lowndes and Wilkinson Counties in Mississippi. In any event, the one North Carolina lower court that pronounced a guilty verdict was that of New Hanover in 1843. Sandy and John were indicted for arson, and Sandy alone was convicted.[63]

The final state, South Carolina, produced some interesting findings. Hindus identified twenty-six cases of arson in Spartanburg and Anderson Districts between 1818 and 1860. This amounted to 2.5 per cent of all crimes and made arson the tenth most frequent offense. The number is higher than elsewhere in the South.[64] Only one of the cases in Anderson District led to an execution. Jane was hanged in 1863 after she confessed to burning a dwelling. Five cases ended in acquittal. Finally, there was the case of John in 1855. He was charged with the burning of a carriage house, workshop, and adjacent dwelling. The magistrate-freeholders recorded that 'while many *strongly suspicious circumstances*, arise in our minds against the Prisoner, yet, the nature of the *Evidence*, does not authorise us, to found a verdict of Guilty'.[65]

The pattern in Spartanburg is not the same. Of the seven cases there, all involved only one defendant, and three ended in acquittal. In 1855 Adam was sold out of state for burning a carriage workshop, and in 1860 Alfred was hanged for burning a dwelling. Miles was executed in 1864, but he was found guilty of the murder of his master as well as arson. Finally, on April 28, 1865, George was acquitted of robbery and arson.[66]

One thing that is clear from this record is that, except for the punishments provided, the statutory changes made within these categories of property crimes were less because of an effort to accommodate the common law rules to a slave society than they were to accommodate the growth of capitalism. A clear exception is the Alabama and Mississippi burglary statutes, which required that a white person be present before a home could be a 'dwelling' at law. Many of the statutory changes would have occurred even in the absence of slavery. During the eighteenth century some of the statutes do show a particular concern with the criminality of slaves, but some also reveal a concern with the criminality of lower-class people in general, 'divers wicked' people. Lower-class people, regardless of status, would be punished severely if they tried to control the distribution of goods by stealing, for instance.

But what does the actual experience with the enforcement of these laws against thefts, burglary, and burnings shows regarding the treatment of slaves? Was there any serious effort to obtain 'justice'? Were the crimes charged examples of an attempt to claim the profits of slavery? Were they acts of accommodation or resistance to slavery? Were they efforts to establish a 'moral economy', or is it as fruitful to see them in terms of the notion that criminal law is a marginal element in a legal order? One thing we should not lose sight of is the fact that many of these offenses were handled by the 'complementary system of plantation justice' rather than in a public forum. But insofar as the public law was concerned, the answers to the above questions depend on whether the questions are addressed from the viewpoint of the slaves, or of the masters, or of whites generally. From the latter two perspectives, the most probable response would be that slaves who were charged with violating the norms of any civilized society, especially one based on a regard for property rights, were treated justly. From the viewpoint of the slaves, of course, the answers would be different. As Douglass had finally resolved, the 'morality of free society could have no application to slave society'.

NOTES

1. E. P. Thompson, 'The Moral Economy of the English Crowd in the Eighteenth Century', *P&P*, 50 (1971), 76–136; Alex Lichtenstein, ' "That Disposition to Theft, with Which They Have Been Branded": Moral Economy, Slave Management, and the Law', *Journal of Social History*, 22 (1988), 415, 433. See also Marvin L. Michael Kay and Lorin Lee Cary, ' "They Are Indeed the Constant Plague of Their Tyrants": Slave Defense of a Moral Economy in Colonial North Carolina, 1748–1772', *Science and Society*, 6 (1985), 37–8, 52.
2. Olmsted, the ex-slave, and Douglass are quoted in Edward L. Ayers, *Vengeance and Justice: Crime and Punishment in the 19th-Century American South* (New York, 1984), 127–9.
3. James Henry Hammond, 'Letter to an English Abolitionist' in Drew Gilpin Faust, ed., *The Ideology of Slavery: Proslavery Thought in the Antebellum South, 1830–1860* (Baton Rouge, 1981), 190.
4. Eugene D. Genovese, *Roll, Jordan, Roll: The World the Slaves Made* (New York, 1974), 613.
5. *Richmond Enquirer*, April 18, 1820.
6. Kenneth M. Stampp, *The Peculiar Institution: Slavery in the Ante-Bellum South* (New York, 1956), 127; Genovese, *Roll, Jordan, Roll*, 613–15.
7. William Blackstone, *Commentaries on the Laws of England*, 4 vols (Oxford, 1765–69), IV, 230, 241, 240; *State v. John, (a slave)*, 5 Jones N.C. 170–1 (1857).
8. Harold J. Berman, 'The Origins of Historical Jurisprudence: Coke, Selden, Hale', *Yale Law Journal* 103 (1994), 1710 (Hale); Blackstone, *Commentaries*, IV, 238–39.
9. Hening, *Statutes at Large*, III, 102, 179, 278.
10. Trial of Daniel, December 18, 1765, Orange County Order Book No. 7, 1763–69, VSL. Daniel was granted benefit of clergy after his conviction of stealing sheep valued at fifteen shillings.

11. Trial of Cupid, December 7, 1763, Westmoreland County Order Book, 1761–64, and Trial of Sam, October 3, 1761, Princess Anne County Minute Book, 1753–62, VSL.
12. Commonwealth v. Bob, September 6, 1831, and Commonwealth v. Granville, September 6, 1831, Charles City County Minute Book 2, 1830–37, VSL; *The Revised Code of the Laws of Mississippi* (Natchez, 1824), 381–2.
13. *State v. Harriet, (a slave)*, 4 Jones N.C. 265–6 (1857).
14. U. B. Phillips, *The Revised Statutes of Louisiana* (New Orleans, 1856), 51; Parish Court Case: Parish of St. Landry v. George, August 1831, LSA.
15. John J. Ormond, Arthur P. Bagley, and George Goldthwaite, *The Code of Alabama* (Montgomery, 1852), 595; Otho Scott and Hiram McCullough, *The Maryland Code*, 2 vols (Baltimore, 1860), 1, 230, 434. The prison term applied to 'any person'. There was a second section providing that a slave convicted of petty larceny 'may' be whipped up to forty lashes.
16. See, e.g., State v. Cesar, April 1837 (benefit of clergy granted in a grand larceny case, and the slave to be whipped thirty-nine times on two separate occasions), New Hanover Minute Docket, Superior Court, 1849–55, and State v. Alfred, Fall 1854 (thirty-nine lashes for grand larceny), New Hanover Superior Court, State Docket, 1854–67, NCDAH.
17. John Belton O'Neall, *The Negro Law of South Carolina* (Columbia, S.C., 1848), 33, 35: 'The whippings inflicted by the sentence of Courts trying slaves and free negroes, are most enormous – utterly disproportioned to offences, and should be prevented by all means in our power'. From Virginia, a clear example of where a court maintained the distinction is Commonwealth v. Paul, June 29, 1826, Lunenburg County Minute Book, 1824–28, VSL. Paul was found guilty of grand larceny (stealing $80 in silver and two tortoise shell combs). His sentence was severe: he was burned on the hand and also sentenced to fifty lashes.
18. State v. Linda, February 18, 1832, State v. Marshele and Pleasant, February 15, 1865, and State v. Jim, May 6, 1852, Anderson District Magistrate Freeholders' Trial Papers, SCDAH.
19. An example is Commonwealth v. Peter, November 27, 1799, Petersburg City Hustings Court Minute Book, 1797–1800, VSL.
20. State v. Elijah, June 18, 1813, Chatham County Inferior Court Trial Docket, 1813–27, 3, GDAH.
21. *State v. Nathan, (a slave)*, 5 Rich. 232–33 (S.C., 1851). See also *State v. Gabriel South*, 5 Rich. 489 (S.C., 1852). South was indicted for conveying Nathan away so that he could not be tried and punished. He was found guilty, and the verdict was upheld on appeal.
22. State v. Spencer, November 22, 1853, Chambers County Circuit Court Minutes, vol. 6., Chambers County Courthouse, Haynesville, Ala.
23. See, e.g., Commonwealth v. Blade Johnston, Hampton Jones, and Tom Baker, slaves, December 8, 1797, Commonwealth v. Charles, February 23, 1798, Commonwealth v. Billy, May 1, 1798, and Commonwealth v. Peter, November 29, 1799, Petersburg City Hustings Court Minute Book, 1797–1800, VSL.
24. Quoted in Michael Dalton, *The Countrey Justice, Containing the Practise of the Justices of the Peace out of Their Sessions* (London, 1622), 233–4.
25. Sir William Hawkins, *A Treatise of the Pleas of the Crown*, 2 vols (London, 1724–26), 103–4; Sir Matthew Hale, *Historia Placitorum Coronae: The History of the Pleas of the Crown*, ed. W. A. Stokes and S. Ingersoll, 2 vols (Philadelphia, 1847), 1, 546; Blackstone, *Commentaries*, IV, 220, 223–24.
26. Adam Smith, *Lectures on Jurisprudence*, ed. R. L. Meek et al. (Oxford, 1978), 127–8.
27. Virgil Maxcy, *Laws of Maryland*, 3 vols (Baltimore, 1811), 1, 190–1; Hening, *Statutes at Large*, VI, 105–6.

28. John D. Cushing, *First Laws of the State of Delaware*, 4 vols (Wilmington, 1981), 1, 68–69, 237.

29. *Session Laws of Georgia, 1806*, 335; U. B. Phillips, *Revised Statutes of Louisiana*, 50; Charles Hardin, *The Revised Statutes of the State of Missouri*, 2 vols (Columbia, Mo., 1856), II, 572–74. William C. Jones, *The Revised Statutes of the State of Missouri* (St. Louis, 1845), 356–7. Burglary was conspicuously left off the list of capital crimes in Texas, a list that included murder, rape, robbery, and arson. Williamson S. Oldham and George W. White, *A Digest of the General Statute Laws of the State of Texas* (Austin, 1859), Penal Code, Title III, ch. 1, art. 819.

30. Jones, *Revised Statutes of . . . Missouri*, 357; Oldham and White, *Digest of the . . . Laws of Texas . . .*, Penal Code, Title III, ch. 1, arts. 819, 821; Josiah Gould, *A Digest of the Statutes of Arkansas* (Little Rock, 1858), 340; *Revised Statutes of the State of Delaware* (Dover, 1852), 257; Leslie Thompson, *A Manual and Digest of the Statute Law of the State of Florida* (Boston, 1847), 538.

31. Ormond, Bagley, and Goldthwaite, *Code of Alabama*, 594; *The Revised Code of the Statute Laws of the State of Mississippi* (Jackson, 1857), 248.

32. *Ex parte Vincent, (a slave)*, 26 Ala. 153 (1855).

33. Commonwealth v. Dick, 1824, Auditor's Item 153, Box 4, VSL.

34. Commonwealth v. John, August 13, 1860 (not guilty), and Commonwealth v. Emanuel, December 8, 1862 (guilty), Lunenburg County Minute Book, 1859–66, VSL; Commonwealth v. Neat, 1843 (guilty), Circuit Court Clerk, Circuit Court Indictments, Jessamine County, Box 9, 1842–49, KSA; State v. Sam, June 1, 1830 (not guilty), Anderson District Magistrate Freeholders' Trial Papers, SCDAH.

35. Michael S. Hindus, *Prison and Plantation: Crime, Justice, and Authority in Massachusetts and South Carolina, 1767–1878* (Chapel Hill, N.C., 1980), 146.

36. Philip J. Schwarz, *Twice Condemned: Slaves and the Criminal Laws of Virginia, 1705–1865* (Baton Rouge, La., 1988), 123. The percentage of convictions was higher, but many were granted benefit of clergy. 'Slave courts', Schwarz noted, 'began to concentrate on burglary in the 1770s'. The conviction rate was 59.9 per cent from 1770 to 1774 and 55.1 per cent from 1775 to 1779; in the first period 40 per cent of those convicted were granted clergy, and in the second the percentage was 58.7. Schwarz defined burglary as 'breaking and entering with intent to steal, especially at night'. This is a common perception today, but it is not the correct definition of burglary under English law.

37. Trial of Will, November 9, 1761, July 14, 1762, Charles City County Orders, 1758–62, VSL.

38. State v. John, December 17, 1852–June 22, 1853, Wilkinson County Circuit Court Minute Book, vol. 13, 1851–56, 118, 162, 173, 184, 188, Wilkinson County Courthouse, Woodville, Miss.; State v. Guy, October 1844, Screven County, Docket for Trial of Slaves and Free Persons of Color, 1844–48, GDAH.

39. *State v. Ridgell*, 2 Bailey 560–1 (S.C., 1831).

40. State v. Phillip, May 18, 1854, Anderson District Magistrate Freeholders' Trial Papers, SCDAH.

41. Dalton, *Countrey Justice*, 245–6.

42. Hawkins, *Treatise of the Pleas of the Crown*, 105–6; Blackstone, *Commentaries*, IV, 220–1.

43. Ibid., 222; Maxcy, *Laws of Maryland*, 1, 190, 286.

44. Hening, *Statutes at Large*, III, 271.

45. Thomas Cooper and David J. McCord, *Statutes at Large of South Carolina*, 10 vols (Columbia, S.C., 1836–41), VII, 345, 354, 373, 402.

46. Trial of Phill, December 19, 1743, Caroline County Order Book, 1741–46, and Case of Cook, April 2, 1729, Princess Anne County Minute Book 4, 1728–37, VSL.

47. *Maryland Gazette*, December 23, 1762, January 6, 1763.

48. Lord Proprietary v. Abram, November 1762, and Lord Proprietary v. Tim, March Court 1763, Talbot County Court Criminal Judgments, 1761–67, MSA; Lord

Proprietary v. Adam, Lord Proprietary v. Beck, and Lord Proprietary v. Jenny and Grace, *Maryland Archives*, XXXII, 55, 125, XXVIII, 504.

49. *South Carolina Gazette*, July 30–August 15, 1741.

50. Hening, *Statutes at Large*, XIII, 31; Commonwealth v. Claiborne, November 18, 1797, January 1–13, 1798, Petersburg City Hustings Court Minute Book, 1797–1800, VSL; *The Revised Code of the Laws of Virginia*, 2 vols (Richmond, 1819), 587.

51. James L. Petigru, *Portion of the Code of Statute Law of South Carolina* (Charleston, 1860–62), 604 n.

52. Ormond, Bagley, and Goldthwaite, *Code of Alabama*, 594; Oldham and White, *Digest of the ... Laws of Texas ...*, 543; Return J. Meigs and William F. Cooper, *The Code of Tennessee* (Nashville, 1858), 509; Jones, *Revised Statutes of ... Missouri*, 354–5.

53. Trials for arson or burnings were conducted in the following sample counties for Mississippi, Alabama, Kentucky, Florida, Tennessee, and Louisiana: State v. Ann, April 21, 1863, Lowndes County File Papers, File 2200–2498, 1860–63, Case 2212, Lowndes County Department of Archives and History, Lowndes County Courthouse, Columbia, Miss.; State v. Huldy, Spring 1857, and State v. Tom, April 1861–April 1864, Chambers County Circuit Court Minutes, State Cases, vol. 9, 1856–70, 26, 51, 239, 242, 250, 257, 263–4, Chambers County Courthouse, Lafayette, Ala.; Commonwealth v. Jess, 1826, Circuit Court, Clerk, Circuit Court Indictments Box 4, 1824–26, Jessamine County, KSA; State v. Gloster, November 17–April 29, 1844, Leon County Circuit Court Minute Book, 93, 165, 196, and State v. Billy Hays alias William Hays, Slave, May 16, 1849, Leon County Circuit Court Minute Book, 1847–55, 203, Leon County Courthouse, Tallahassee, Fla.; State v. Lawson, May 2–12, 1837, Maury County Circuit Court, vol. 1834–37, 429, 434, 476, 496, State v. Simon, May 14–18, 1847, Maury County Circuit Court Minutes, 1844–51, 253, 255, 258–9, and State v. Henry, May 1854, Davidson County Circuit Court Minutes, 1852–56, TSLA; Patrick Woods to State of Louisiana, May 28, 1838, St. Landry Parish Conveyance Record (1836–41), I-1, J-1, 237, St. Landry Parish Courthouse, Opelousas, La.

54. See, e.g., Commonwealth v. Sally, January 19, 1826, Petersburg City Hustings Court Minute Books, 1827–32, and Commonwealth v. Simon, March 7, 1834, Petersburg City Hustings Court Minute Books, 1832–35, VSL.

55. Commonwealth v. Dennis and Isaac, February 22, 1793, Petersburg City Hustings Court Minute Books, 1791–97, and Commonwealth v. Claiborne, November 18, 1797–January 1–13, 1798, Petersburg City Hustings Court Minute Books, 1797–1800, VSL.

56. Commonwealth v. Frank and George, November 1858, and Commonwealth v. Victoria, November 1858, Richmond City Hustings Court Minutes No. 24, 1857–58, 134, 169–70, VSL; Commonwealth v. Lewis, March 1858, Richmond City Hustings Court Minutes No. 24, 1857–58; 341, VSL.

57. See, e.g., Commonwealth v. Reuben, July 16, 1818, Petersburg City Hustings Court Minute Book, 1816–19, VSL. Reuben was acquitted of 'robbery & arson' of a store.

58. Commonwealth v. Malinda and Andrew, January 1861, Caroline County Minute Book, 1858–61, 199, 202, 412–14; Commonwealth v. Lewis and Caesar, March 5, 1801, Sussex County Order Book, 1795–1801; Commonwealth v. Fed, April 18, 1833, Charles City County Minute Book, 1830–37, 1150 – all in VSL.

59. See, e.g., Commonwealth v. Nelson and Lewis, February 12 and 27, 1818, Lunenburg Minute Book, 1817–19; Commonwealth v. Thornton, January 23, 1854, Orange County Order Book (Minutes), 1852–56; and Commonwealth v. Sarah and Monmouth, January 11, 1808, King George County Order Book 7A, 1805–8 – all in VSL.

60. Mary's Case, August 7, 1819, Auditor's Item 153, VSL; *Jesse, (a slave), v. State*, 28 Miss. 110 (1854).

61. See, e.g., State v. Peggy Coale, May Term 1830, Frederick County, Criminal Docket, and State v. Galloway Pice, November 1854, Talbot County Criminal Judgments, 1842–57, 233, MSA.

62. State v. Susan, January 22, 1821, Chatham County Inferior Court, Trial Docket, 1813–27; State v. Rodney, February 12, 1819, Baldwin County, Ordinary Inferior Court Minutes, 1812–29; State v. Adeline, May 16–28, 1849, Hancock County, Ordinary Inferior Court Minutes, Slave Trials, 1843–50 – all in GDAH.

63. State v. Sandy and John, March 1843, New Hanover Minute Docket, Superior Court, 1843–48. Sandy was sentenced to hang after a motion for a new trial was rejected. In June 1843 the state supreme court overruled the judgment because of 'error in the record and proceedings'. *State v. Sandy, (a slave)*, 3 Iredell 570 (N.C., 1843). The opinion by Judge Ruffin is a good example of formalism.

64. Hindus, *Prison and Plantation*, 141, 144.

65. State v. Jane, May 4, 1863, State v. Thornton, George, Pete, and Phil, November 20, 1860, State v. Ellen, March 27, 1846, and State v. John, June 18, 1855, Anderson District Magistrate Freeholders' Trial Papers, SCDAH.

66. State v. Alfred, October 6, 1860, State v. Adam, April 9, 1855, State v. Miles and others, November 19, 1864 (Harriet was sentenced to 600 lashes, Sandy to 300, and no disposition was recorded in Minerva's case), and State v. George, April 28, 1865, Spartanburg District Magistrate Freedholders' Trial Papers, SCDAH.

Document 1: The Louisiana Slave Code, 1824

An extract from the Louisiana Slave Code of 1824, based on the French Code Noir *and influenced by Roman civil law.*

ART. 172.—The rules prescribing the police and conduct to be observed with respect to slaves in this State, and the punishment of their crimes and offences, are fixed by special laws of the Legislature.

ART. 173.—The slave is entirely subject to the will of his master, who may correct and chastise him, though not with unusual rigor, nor so as to maim or mutilate him, or to expose him to the danger of loss of life, or to cause his death.

ART. 174.—The slave is incapable of making any kind of contract, except those which relate to his own emancipation.

ART. 175.—All that a slave possesses, belongs to his master; he possesses nothing of his own, except his *peculium*, that is to say, the sum of money, or moveable estate, which his master chooses he should possess.

ART. 176.—They can transmit nothing by succession or otherwise; but the succession of free persons related to them which they would have inherited had they been free, may pass through them to such of their descendants as may have acquired their liberty before the succession is opened.

ART. 177.—The slave is incapable of exercising any public office, or private trust; he cannot be tutor, curator, executor nor attorney; he cannot be a witness in either civil or criminal matters, except in cases provided for by particular laws. He cannot be a party in any civil action, either as plaintiff or defendant, except when he has to claim or prove his freedom.

ART. 178.—When slaves are prosecuted in the name of the State, for offences they have committed, notice must be given to their masters.

ART. 179.—Masters are bound by the acts of their slaves done by their command, as also by their transactions and dealings with respect to the business in which they have entrusted or employed them; but in case they should not have authorised or entrusted them, they shall be answerable only for so much as they have benefitted by the transaction.

ART. 180.—The master shall be answerable for all the damages occasioned by an offence or quasi-offence committed by his slave, independent of the punishment inflicted on the slave.

ART. 181.—The master however may discharge himself from such responsibility by abandoning his slave to the person injured; in which case such person shall sell such slave at public auction in the usual form, to obtain payment of the damages and costs; and the balance, if any, shall be returned to the master of the slave, who shall be completely discharged,

---

James O. Fuqua (ed.), *Civil Code of the State of Louisiana: With the Statutory Amendments from 1825 to 1866 inclusive . . .* (New Orleans, 1867), pp. 20–33; the statutory amendments have been omitted.

although the price of the slave should not be sufficient to pay the whole amount of the damages and costs; provided that the master shall make the abandonment within three days after the judgment awarding such damages, shall, have been rendered; provided also that it shall not be proved that the crime or offence was committed by his order; for in case of such proof the master shall be answerable for all damages resulting therefrom, whatever be the amount, without being admitted to the benefit of the abandonment.

ART. 182.—Slaves cannot marry without the consent of their masters, and their marriages do not produce any of the civil effects which result from such contract.

ART. 183.—Children born of a mother then in a state of slavery, whether married or not, follow the condition of their mother; they are consequently slaves and belong to the master of their mother.

ART. 184.—A master may manumit his slave in this State, either by an act *inter vivos*[1] or by a disposition made in prospect of death, provided such manumission be made with the forms and under the conditions prescribed by law; but an enfranchisement, when made by a last will, must be express and formal, and shall not be implied by any other circumstances of the testament, such as a legacy, an institution of heir, testamentary executorship or other dispositions of this nature, which, in such case, shall be considered as if they had not been made.

ART. 185.—No one can emancipate his slave, unless the slave has attained the age of thirty years, and has behaved well at least for four years preceding his emancipation.

ART. 186.—The slave who has saved the life of his master, his master's wife, or one of his children, may be emancipated at any age.

ART. 187.—The master who wishes to emancipate his slave, is bound to make a declaration of his intentions to the judge of the parish where he resides; the judge must order notice of it to be published during forty days by advertisement posted at the door of the court house; and if, at the expiration of this delay, no opposition to made, he shall authorize the master to pass the act of emancipation.

ART. 188.—The act of emancipation imports an obligation on the part of the person granting it, to provide for the subsistence of the slave emancipated, if he should be unable to support himself.

ART. 189.—An emancipation once perfected, is irrevocable, on the part of the master or his heirs.

ART. 190.—Any enfranchisement made in fraud of creditors, or of the portion reserved by law to forced heirs is null and void; and such fraud shall be considered as proved, when it shall appear that at the moment of executing the enfranchisement, the person granting it had not sufficient property to pay his debts or to leave to his heirs the portion to them reserved by law; the same rule will apply if the slave thus manumitted, was specially mortgaged; but in this case the enfranchisement shall take effect, provided the slave or any one in his behalf shall pay the debt for which the mortgage was given.

ART. 191.—No master of slaves shall be compelled, either directly or indirectly, to enfranchise any of them, except only in cases where the enfranchisement shall be made for services rendered to the State, by virtue of an act of the Legislature of the same, and on the State satisfying to the master the appraised value of the manumitted slave.

ART. 192.—In like manner no master shall be compelled to sell his slave, but in one of two cases, to wit: the first, when being only co-proprietor of the slave, his co-proprietor demands the sale in order to make partition of the property; the second, when the master shall be convicted of cruel treatment of his slave, and the judge shall deem proper to pronounce, besides the penalty established for such cases, that the slave shall be sold at public auction, in order to place him out of the reach of the power which his master has abused.

ART. 193.—The slave who has acquired the right of being free at a future time, is from that time, capable of receiving by testament or donation. Property given or devised to him must be preserved for him, in order to be delivered to him in kind, when his emancipation shall take place. In the mean time it must be administered by a curator.

ART. 194.—The slave for years[2] cannot be transported out of the State. He can appear in court to claim the protection of the laws in cases where there are good reasons for believing that it is intended to carry him out of the State.

ART. 195.—If the slave for years dies before the time fixed for his enfranchisement, the gifts or legacies made him revert to the donor or to the heirs of the donor.

ART. 196.—The child born of a woman after she has acquired the right of being free at a future time, follows the condition of its mother, and becomes free at the time fixed for her enfranchisement, even if the mother should die before that time.

NOTES

1. Between living persons.
2. A slave *'for years'* was one whose servitude was to end at a specified age, or after a specified number of years.

DOCUMENT 2: ASSAULT AND BATTERY ON A SLAVE WOMAN

An extract from the case of the State v. John Mann, *Chowan County, North Carolina, 1829, in which Judge Thomas Ruffin, Associate Justice of the Supreme Court, reversed a decision made in a lower court that had found Mann guilty of battery and assault on a slave woman called Lydia.*

The State

v.

John Mann.

From Chowan [County].

The Master is not liable to an indictment for a battery committed upon his slave.

One who has a right to the labor of a slave, has also a right to all the means of controlling his conduct which the owner has.

Hence one who has hired a slave is not liable to an indictment for a battery on him, committed during the hiring.

But this rule does not interfere with the owner's right to damages for an injury affecting the value of the slave, which is regulated by the law of bailment.

The Defendant was indicted for an assault and battery upon *Lydia*, the slave of one *Elizabeth Jones*.

On the trial it appeared that the Defendant had hired the slave for a year – that during the term, the slave had committed some small offence, for which the Defendant undertook to chastise her – that while in the act of so doing, the slave ran off, whereupon the Defendant called upon her to stop, which being refused, he shot at and wounded her.

His honor Judge DANIEL charged the Jury, that if they believed the punishment inflicted by the Defendant was cruel and unwarrantable, and disproportionate to the offence committed by the slave, that in law the Defendant was guilty, as he had only a special property in the slave.

A verdict was returned for the State, and the Defendant appealed.

No Counsel appeared for the Defendant.

The Attorney-General contended, that no difference existed between this case and that of the *State v. Hall*, (2 *Hawks*, 582.) In this case the weapon used was one calculated to produce death. He assimilated the relation between a master and a slave, to those existing between parents and children, masters and apprentices, and tutors and scholars, and upon the limitations

Thomas P. Devereaux (ed.), *Cases Argued and Determined in the Supreme Court of North Carolina from December Term, 1828, to December Term, 1830* (Raleigh: J. Gales & Sims, 1831), vol. 2, pp. 263–8.

to the right of the superiors in these relations, he cited *Russell on Crimes*, 866.

RUFFIN, Judge. – A Judge cannot but lament, when such cases as the present are brought into judgment. It is impossible that the reasons on which they go can be appreciated, but where institutions similar to our own, exist and are thoroughly understood. The struggle, too, in the Judge's own breast between the feelings of the man, and the duty of the magistrate is a severe one, presenting strong temptation to put aside such questions, if it be possible. It is useless however, to complain of things inherent in our political state. And it is criminal in a Court to avoid any responsibility which the laws impose. With whatever reluctance therefore it is done, the Court is compelled to express an opinion upon the extent of the dominion of the master over the slave in North-Carolina.

The indictment charges a battery on *Lydia*, a slave of *Elizabeth Jones*. Upon the face of the indictment, the case is the same as the *State v. Hall*. (2 *Hawks* 582.)—No fault is found with the rule then adopted; nor would be, if it were now open. But it is not open; for the question, as it relates to a battery on a slave by a stranger, is considered as settled by that case. But the evidence makes this a different case. Here the slave had been *hired* by the Defendant, and was in his possession; and the battery was committed during the period of hiring. With the liabilities of the hirer to the general owner, for an injury permanently impairing the value of the slave, no rule now laid down is intended to interfere. That is left upon the general doctrine of bailment.[1] The enquiry here is, whether a cruel and unreasonable battery on a slave, by the hirer, is indictable. The Judge below instructed the Jury, that it is. He seems to have put it on the ground, that the Defendant had but a special property. Our laws uniformly treat the master or other person having the possession and command of the slave, as entitled to the same extent of authority. The object is the same – the services of the slave; and the same powers must be confided. In a criminal proceeding, and indeed in reference to all other persons but the general owner, the hirer and possessor of a slave, in relation to both rights and duties, is, for the time being, the owner . . . .

The power of the master must be absolute, to render the submission of the slave perfect. I most freely confess my sense of the harshness of this proposition, I feel it as deeply as any man can. And as a principle of moral right, every person in his retirement must repudiate it. But in the actual condition of things, it must be so. There is no remedy. This discipline belongs to the state of slavery. They cannot be disunited, without abrogating at once the rights of the master, and absolving the slave from his subjection. It constitutes the curse of slavery to both the bond and free portions of our population. But it is inherent in the relation of master and slave.

That there may be particular instances of cruelty and deliberate barbarity, where, in conscience the law might properly interfere, is most probable. The difficulty is to determine, where a *Court* may properly begin. Merely in the abstract it may well be asked, which power of the master accords with right. The answer will probably sweep away all of them. But we cannot look at the matter in that light. The truth is, that we are forbidden to enter upon a train of general reasoning on the subject. We cannot allow the right of the master to be brought into discussion in the Courts of Justice. The slave, to remain a slave, must be made sensible, that there is no appeal from his master; that his power is in no instance, usurped; but is conferred by the laws of man at least, if not by the law of God. The danger would be great indeed, if the tribunals of justice should be called on to graduate the punishment appropriate to every temper, and every dereliction of menial duty. No man can anticipate the many and aggravated provocations of the master, which the slave would be constantly stimulated by his own passions, or the instigation of others to give; or the consequent wrath of the master, prompting him to bloody vengeance, upon the turbulent traitor – a vengeance generally practised with impunity, by reason of its privacy. The Court therefore disclaims the power of changing the relation, in which these parts of our people stand to each other.

We are happy to see, that there is daily less and less occasion for the interposition of the Courts. The protection already afforded by several statutes, that all-powerful motive, the private interest of the owner, the benevolences towards each other, seated in the hearts of those who have been born and bred together, the frowns and deep execrations of the community upon the barbarian, who is guilty of excessive and brutal cruelty to his unprotected slave, all combined, have produced a mildness of treatment, and attention to the comforts of the unfortunate class of slaves, greatly mitigating the rigors of servitude, and ameliorating the condition of the slaves. The same causes are operating, and will continue to operate with increased action, until the disparity in numbers between the whites and blacks, shall have rendered the latter in no degree dangerous to the former, when the police now existing may be further relaxed. This result, greatly to be desired, may be much more rationally expected from the events above alluded to, and now in progress, than from any rash expositions of abstract truths, by a Judiciary tainted with a false and fanatical philanthropy, seeking to redress an acknowledged evil, by means still more wicked and appalling than even that evil.

NOTE

1. The laws of bailment are concerned with complications that may arise when one person has delivered property or goods to a second person in expectation that some service or trust will be performed.

DOCUMENT 3: EXTRACT FROM THE DRED SCOTT
DECISION, 1857

*An extract from Judge Taney's verdict in the Dred Scott case, explaining
why the Missouri Compromise, in his opinion, was unconstitutional.*

They had for more than a century before been regarded as beings of an
inferior order; and altogether unfit to associate with the white race, either
in social or political relations; and so far inferior that they had no rights
which the white man was bound to respect; and that the negro might justly
and lawfully be reduced to slavery for his benefit.... This opinion was at
that time fixed and universal in the civilized portion of the white race. It
was regarded as an axiom in morals as well as in politics, which no one
thought of disputing, or supposed to be open to dispute; and men in every
grade and position in society daily and habitually acted upon it in their
private pursuits, as well as in matters of public concern, without doubting
for a moment the correctness of this opinion....

The legislation of the different Colonies furnishes positive and undis-
putable proof of this fact....

The language of the Declaration of Independence is equally conclusive....

This state of public opinion had undergone no change when the Constitution was adopted, as is equally evident from its provisions and language....

But there are two clauses in the Constitution which point directly and
specifically to the negro race as a separate class of persons, and show clearly
that they were not regarded as a portion of the people or citizens of the
Government then formed.

One of these clauses reserves to each of the thirteen States the right to
import slaves until the year 1808, if he thinks it proper. And the importation which it thus sanctions was unquestionably of persons of the race
of which we are speaking, as the traffic in slaves in the United States had
always been confined to them. And by the other provision the States pledge
themselves to each other to maintain the right of property of the master, by
delivering up to him any slave who may have escaped from his service, and
be found within their respective territories.... And these two provisions
show, conclusively, that neither the description of persons therein referred
to, nor their descendants, were embraced in any of the other provisions of
the Constitution; for certainly these two clauses were not intended to confer
on them or their posterity the blessings of liberty, or any of the personal
rights so carefully provided for the citizen....

Indeed, when we look to the condition of this race in the several States
at the time, it is impossible to believe that these rights and privileges were
intended to be extended to them....

Henry S. Commager (ed.), *Documents of American History* (New York: Appleton-Century-Crofts,
1963), pp. 343–5.

The legislation of the States therefore shows, in a manner not to be mistaken, the inferior and subject condition of that race at the time the Constitution was adopted, and long afterwards, throughout the thirteen States by which that instrument was framed; and it is hardly consistent with the respect due to these States, to suppose that they regarded at that time, as fellow-citizens and members of the sovereignty, a class of beings whom they had thus stigmatized; ... More especially, it cannot be believed that the large slave-holding States regarded them as included in the word 'citizens', or would have consented to a constitution which might compel them to receive them in that character from another State. For if they were so received, and entitled to the privileges and immunities of citizens, it would exempt them from the operation of the special laws and from the police regulations which they considered to be necessary for their own safety.... And all of this would be done in the face of the subject race of the same color, both free and slaves, inevitably producing discontent and insubordination among them, and endangering the peace and safety of the State....

But it is said that a person may be a citizen, and entitled to that character, although he does not possess all the rights which may belong to other citizens; as, for example, the right to vote, or to hold particular offices; and that yet, when he goes into another State, he is entitled to be recognized there as a citizen, although the State may measure his rights by the rights which it allows to persons of a like character or class, resident in the State, and refuse to him the full rights of citizenship.

This argument overlooks the language of the provision in the Constitution of which we are speaking.

Undoubtedly, a person may be a citizen, that is, a member of the community who form the sovereignty, although he exercises no share of the political power, and is incapacitated from holding particular offices....

So, too, a person may be entitled to vote by the law of the State, who is not a citizen even of the State itself. And in some of the States of the Union foreigners not naturalized are allowed to vote. And the State may give the right to free negroes and mulattoes, but that does not make them citizens of the State, and still less of the United States. And the provision in the Constitution giving privileges and immunities in other States, does not apply to them.

Neither does it apply to a person who, being the citizen of a State, migrates to another State. For then he becomes subject to the laws of the State in which he lives, and he is no longer a citizen of the State from which he removed. And the State in which he resides may then, unquestionably, determine his *status* or condition, and place him among the class of persons who are not recognized as citizens, but belong to an inferior and subject race; and may deny him the privileges and immunities enjoyed by its citizens....

... But if he ranks as a citizen of the State to which he belongs, within the meaning of the Constitution of the United States, then, whenever he goes into another State, the Constitution clothes him, as to the rights of person, with all the privileges and immunities which belong to citizens of the State. And if persons of the African race are citizens of a state, and of the United States, they would be entitled to all of these privileges and immunities in every State, and the State could not restrict them; for they would hold these privileges and immunities, under the paramount authority of the Federal Government, and its courts would be bound to maintain and enforce them, the Constitution and laws of the State to the contrary notwith-standing . . . .

And upon a full and careful consideration of the subject, the court is of opinion that, upon the facts stated in the plea in abatement, Dred Scott was not a citizen of Missouri within the meaning of the Constitution of the United States, and not entitled as such to sue in its courts; and, consequently, that the Circuit Court had no jurisdiction of the case, and that the judgment on the plea in abatement is erroneous . . . .

We proceed, therefore, to inquire whether the facts relied on by the plaintiff entitled him to his freedom . . . .

In considering this part of the controversy, two questions arise: 1st. Was he, together with his family, free in Missouri by reason of the stay in the territory of the United States hereinbefore mentioned? And 2d, If they were not, is Scott himself free by reason of his removal to Rock Island, in the State of Illinois, as stated in the above admissions?

We proceed to examine the first question.

The Act of Congress, upon which the plaintiff relies, declares that slavery and involuntary servitude, except as a punishment for crime, shall be forever prohibited in all that part of the territory ceded by France, under the name of Louisiana, which lies north of thirty-six degrees thirty minutes north latitude, and not included within the limits of Missouri. And the difficulty which meets us at the threshold of this part of the inquiry is, whether Congress was authorized to pass this law under any of the powers granted to it by the Constitution; for if the authority is not given by that instrument, it is the duty of this court to declare it void and inoperative, and incapable of conferring freedom upon any one who is held as a slave under the laws of any one of the States.

The counsel for the plaintiff has laid much stress upon that article in the Constitution which confers on Congress the power 'to dispose of and make all needful rules and regulations respecting the territory or other property belonging to the United States'; but, in the judgment of the court, that provision has no bearing on the present controversy, and the power there given, whatever it may be, is confined, and was intended to be confined, to the territory which at that time belonged to, or was claimed by, the United States, and was within their boundaries as settled by the treaty with Great Britain, and can have no influence upon a territory afterwards acquired from a foreign Government. It was a special provision for a known and particular territory, and to meet a present emergency, and nothing more . . . .

If this clause is construed to extend to territory acquired by the present Government from a foreign nation, outside of the limits of any charter from the British Government to a colony, it would be difficult to say, why it was deemed necessary to give the Government the power to sell any vacant lands belonging to the sovereignty which might be found within it; and if this was necessary, why the grant of this power should precede the power to legislate over it and establish a Government there; and still more difficult to say, why it was deemed necessary so specially and particularly to grant the power to make needful rules and regulations in relation to any personal or movable property it might acquire there. For the words, *other property* necessarily, by every known rule of interpretation, must mean property of a different description from territory or land. And the difficulty would perhaps be insurmountable in endeavoring to account for the last member of the sentence, which provides that 'nothing in this Constitution shall be so construed as to prejudice any claims of the United States or any particular State', or to say how any particular State could have claims in or to a territory ceded by a foreign Government, or to account for associating this provision with the preceding provisions of the clause, with which it would appear to have no connection....

But the power of Congress over the person or property of a citizen can never be a mere discretionary power under our Constitution and form of Government. The powers of the Government and the rights and privileges of the citizen are regulated and plainly defined by the Constitution itself. And when the Territory becomes a part of the United States, the Federal Government enters into possession in the character impressed upon it by those who created it. It enters upon it with its powers over the citizen strictly defined, and limited by the Constitution, from which it derives its own existence, and by virtue of which alone it continues to exist and act as a Government and sovereignty. It has no power of any kind beyond it; and it cannot, when it enters a Territory of the United States, put off its character, and assume discretionary or despotic powers which the Constitution has denied to it. It cannot create for itself a new character separated from the citizens of the United States, and the duties it owes them under the provisions of the Constitution. The Territory being a part of the United States, the Government and the citizen both enter it under the authority of the Constitution, with their respective rights defined and marked out; and the Federal Government can exercise no power over his person or property, beyond what that instrument confers, nor lawfully deny any right which it has reserved....

The rights of private property have been guarded with equal care. Thus the rights of property are united with the rights of person, and placed on the same ground by the fifth amendment to the Constitution.... An Act of Congress which deprives a person of the United States of his liberty or property merely because he came himself or brought his property into a particular Territory of the United States, and who had committed no offense against the laws, could hardly be dignified with the name of due process of law . . . .

It seems, however, to be supposed, that there is a difference between property in a slave and other property, and that different rules may be applied to it in expounding the Constitution of the United States. And the laws and usages of nations, and the writings of eminent jurists upon the relation of master and slave and their mutual rights and duties, and the powers which governments may exercise over it, have been dwelt upon in the argument . . .

Now . . . the right of property in a slave is distinctly and expressly affirmed in the Constitution. The right to traffic in it, like an ordinary article of merchandise and property, was guaranteed to the citizens of the United States, in every State that might desire it, for twenty years. And the Government in express terms is pledged to protect it in all future time, if the slave escapes from his owner . . . . And no word can be found in the Constitution which gives Congress a greater power over slave property, or which entitles property of that kind to less protection than property of any other description. The only power conferred is the power coupled with the duty of guarding and protecting the owner in his rights.

Upon these considerations, it is the opinion of the court that the Act of Congress which prohibited a citizen from holding and owning property of this kind in the territory of the United States north of the line therein mentioned, is not warranted by the Constitution, and is therefore void; and that neither Dred Scott himself, nor any of his family, were made free by being carried into this territory; even if they had been carried there by the owner, with the intention of becoming a permanent resident . . . .

Upon the whole, therefore, it is the judgment of this court, that it appears by the record before us that the plaintiff in error is not a citizen of Missouri, in the sense in which that word is used in the Constitution; and that the Circuit Court of the United States, for that reason, had no jurisdiction in the case, and could give no judgment in it.

Its judgment for the defendant must, consequently, be reversed, and a mandate issued directing the suit to be dismissed for want of jurisdiction. WAYNE, J., NELSON, J., GRIER, J., DANIEL, J., CAMPBELL, J., AND CATRON, J., filed separate concurring opinions. McLEAN, J. and CURTIS, J. dissented.

8

SLAVE RESISTANCE

INTRODUCTION

Resistance to bondage by slaves in North America occurred frequently, as one might expect in a situation where unequal power relationships defined the position of masters and their chattel property. An unwillingness by slaves to perform work adequately, either because their condition engendered negative reactions or because they were badly treated, was a common act of resistance. This could be effected by working below the levels of expected productivity, failing to complete tasks, or sabotaging work routines. In severe cases of disenchantment or alienation from their lot, slaves downed tools and stopped work. Opportunities existed to damage a master's property, to steal food, and to interrupt seasonal work routines. Resistance did not usually have a political content; in fact, this was usually not present in acts of defiance. Nor did resistance always have ulterior aims of securing full freedom. Rather, it took the form of negotiation and renegotiation of the parameters of power and compulsion. Slaves were not docile recipients of whatever their masters doled out to them; they determined when and where cooperation should be suspended. Slaves occasionally staged revolts that had wide repercussions for their situation, but there were relatively few major slave rebellions in North America.

The most influential work on slavery in the American South in the first half of the twentieth century found little role for slave resistance. Thus Phillips (1918) viewed slaves as docile, lazy recipients of patriarchal authority. In his analysis, slaves lacked agency and there was not a great deal of discontent for them to protest about. Planters behaved decently towards their slaves; the slaves, for their part, accepted such paternalism gracefully. This complaisant view of slavery in the Old South was underpinned by Phillips's identification with the outlook of the plantocracy and his sense of black inferiority, but the work itself was solidly based on archival sources. A challenge to this prevailing view of slave inertness came from the Marxist historian Aptheker (1943) who found evidence of 250 instances of slave rebellions, rumours of revolts and acts of collective resistance in North America. He was unable to document a continuous tradition of slave revolt and many of his examples concerned putative uprisings that failed to threaten the dominance of white masters; but he showed that collective slave resistance could be found in North America in the eighteenth and nineteenth centuries.

Two books that dominated the historiography of North American slavery in the 1950s included material on slave resistance. Stampp (1956) effectively challenged the notion of slave docility propagated by Phillips. Portraying slavery in the Old South as brutal, dehumanising and profitable, he argued that slaves 'resisted bondage as much as any people could have done in their circumstances'. Slaves had to submit to their masters most of the time because of the nature of their circumstances; but they still expressed insolence and unruliness and resisted their condition by slowing down and doing careless work, damaging planters' property, exploiting overseers' weaknesses and absconding. Elkins (1959) offered a psychological reading of slavery that included an interpretation of slave accommodation to white planter dominance. He did not revive Phillips's notion of the innate docility of slaves but argued that masters rendered slaves in North America so powerless that the latter acquired passive characteristics whereby they failed to challenge their condition. Slaves, in Elkins's view, exhibited a childlike 'Sambo' personality that resulted from their conditioning in slavery.

Blassingame (1972) and Genovese (1974) provided a conceptual breakthrough in interpreting slave resistance in North America. Blassingame refuted Elkins's notion that slaves were reduced to the condition of dependent 'Sambos'. Instead, he drew upon the writings of fugitive slaves to emphasise that slave resistance was common even if open revolt was rare. Genovese stressed the pre-capitalist, paternalist attitude of masters to slaves and argued that African-Americans accommodated themselves to planter hegemony in various ways. Planters extended various privileges to slaves as a means of social control but slaves developed a repertoire of resistance that included malingering, running away and a defiant stubbornness. Nevertheless, Genovese showed that slave resistance was largely carried out individually and therefore did not directly threaten planter control.

Genovese (1980) extended his arguments to suggest that slave conditions in North America were not favourable for a large revolt. The existence of paternalism meant that relations between masters and slaves were not just a business matter. Slaveholding units in the United States were relatively small compared with the Caribbean or Brazil. Slaves generally did not live in areas where they outnumbered whites and free blacks. Nor did North American slaves have much military experience. These were the comparative reasons, Genovese contends, why North American slave rebellions were relatively sporadic and modest in scale.

Stealing away from masters was a common feature of slave society in North America. Slaves usually ran off singly or in pairs; they were often disguised; sometimes they took the tools of their trade to aid their flight. Permanent runaway communities among slaves were uncommon. Many studies have investigated patterns of slave runaways, largely drawing upon voluminous newspaper advertisements for their source material. Mullin (1972) argued that acculturated, skilled slaves fled in disproportionately large numbers in eighteenth-century Virginia and stood a good chance of remaining at large. His statistics show that between 1736 and 1801 22 per cent of the fugitive slaves in the Old Dominion were either artisans or domestics. But this argument is not persuasive because he does not estimate the proportion of skilled slaves in Virginia's population as a whole. Morgan (1998) compares and contrasts African and creole patterns of flight in eighteenth-century Virginia and South Carolina. He shows that the typical African-born slave runaway in Virginia left with one other African whereas in South Carolina half of the Africans who quit plantations left in groups of three or four. Creoles in Virginia and South Carolina generally ran away singly. Morgan finds that different patterns of slave acculturation influenced these patterns of escape.

There were a number of small slave uprisings before the American Revolution. In the northern colonies, the most serious outbreak of resistance was the 'Great Negro Plot' in New York in 1741. Linebaugh and Rediker (2000) view this as a revolutionary conspiracy that was Atlantic in scope. Irishmen, African slaves and Spanish-American sailors were among the conspirators. Popular religious enthusiasm inspired by the Great Awakening also inspired the rebels. The failure of the insurrection led to conspiracy trials and executions of those found guilty. New York's rulers attempted to clamp down on further insurrectionary possibilities by promoting the unifying advantages of white identity and by making it more difficult for waterfront workers to act in combination.

Wood (1974) analyses the Stono Rebellion, which broke out near Charleston, South Carolina, in early September 1739. This was the largest slave revolt in the history of the British North America. Caused by harsh working conditions in swampy Lowcountry rice plantations and news that the Spanish garrison of St Augustine had offered freedom to Carolinian slaves shortly before the revolt occurred, this uprising was largely put down within a day. About twenty white people and forty-four blacks died during the rising. White fears of the rebelliousness stirred up by the Stono revolt were not quelled, however, for a couple of months. Most of the rebels, including the leader, were Africans rather than creoles. Thornton (1991) shows that many of them had been dispatched from Angola and were of Congolese extraction. Their actions exhibited features of resistance associated with ethnic martial traditions in Africa. The use of banners and drums to accompany the march of the slaves was integral to fighting methods followed in west-central Africa. The decapitation of two white men mirrored the display of severed heads in African societies as trophies of military prowess.

Frey (1991) provides the leading study of black resistance during the American revolutionary era. She covers a wide range of slave challenges to white authority: fugitive slaves, maroon settlements, abortive and actual risings, petitions for freedom, and escape with the British military forces. After the Revolution, she contends, rebellious and insurrectionary activities by slaves became more prominent in areas such as coastal South Carolina and Georgia, where bands of blacks harassed planters by guerrilla attacks on their properties. The initial success of the massive Saint-Domingue slave revolt of 1791 inspired American slaves to carry out plots and risings in Virginia and North Carolina in 1792.

Mullin (1992) examines patterns of slave resistance in relation to the extent of slave acculturation in Virginia, South Carolina and the West Indies in the century culminating in Nat Turner's Revolt in Virginia (1831). He argues that slave acculturation varied according to the crop cultivated, planter attitudes, population density and the involvement of slaves in market production. Rejecting Genovese's emphasis upon paternalism in the treatment of slaves, he suggests that slaves developed their own modes of resistance that were related to increasing creole leadership after 1800, the example of external influences and the impact of Christianity on black consciousness. He singles out three phases in slave resistance: a first period based upon African ritual from the 1730s to the 1760s, a second phase from the 1760s to the early 1800s involving slaves who took few risks over revolts, and a third phase stretching to the second quarter of the nineteenth century in which acculturated slaves were drawn to open rebellion.

The first major attempted slave rebellion in the early republic – Gabriel's conspiracy – occurred near Richmond, Virginia, in the summer of 1800. This was a planned attempt by creole slaves to overthrow white hegemony and gain freedom for enslaved blacks. The leader, Gabriel Prosser, was a young, literate slave serving as a blacksmith on Thomas Prosser's plantation in Henrico County. Sidbury (1997) shows that the rebellion was planned more meticulously than the Stono outbreak but bad luck and lack of unanimity among slaves who knew of the rising in advance contributed to its swift demise. Nevertheless, whites were worried in its aftermath by the potential for further revolt by acculturated slaves. Johnson (2001) provocatively looks at the court record for the Denmark Vesey conspiracy in

Charleston (1822) and concludes that the justices intimidated slaves into confessing about a rebellion that may never have happened.

Nat Turner's revolt was the largest and bloodiest slave insurrection in the antebellum South. Organised by a slave in Southampton County, Virginia, it began on 21 August 1831. Oates (1975) offers a vivid account of this uprising in which fifty-five white people were killed. The militia restored order and killed around 100 blacks. Sixteen captured rebels were later hanged. Turner claimed to be a Baptist preacher inspired by visions of black freedom. He was hunted down after evading capture for more than a month after the insurrection failed. This revolt shocked white Virginians. The state legislature held its last debate on ending slavery in 1832. Thereafter Virginia and most other southern states passed strict laws to guard their slave populations and prevent insurrections.

In the nineteenth century, free blacks and abolitionists assisted slave runaways through an Underground Railroad, a topic covered in Gara (1961). The 'railroad' comprised assistance given by abolitionists ('conductors') to fugitive slaves travelling through the northern states usually en route to Canada to find freedom. These slaves were harboured at night in 'stations', where they remained hidden until safe journeying seemed likely. After the Fugitive Slave Act of 1850, vigilance committees in northern communities provided food and temporary shelter for escapees. The Liberty Line was a complex institution that helped blacks to escape bondage usually after they had initially escaped from their masters by their own volition. Frederick Douglass was the most famous slave to flee from bondage via the Underground Railroad.

BIBLIOGRAPHY

Aptheker, Herbert, *American Negro Slave Revolts* (New York: Columbia University Press, 1943)

Blassingame, John W., *The Slave Community: Plantation Life in the Antebellum South* (New York: Oxford University Press, 1972; rev. edn, 1979)

Elkins, Stanley M., *Slavery: A Problem in American Institutional and Intellectual Life* (Chicago: University of Chicago Press, 1959; 3rd edn, 1976)

Franklin, John Hope and Loren Schweninger, *Runaway Slaves: Rebels on the Plantation* (New York: Oxford University Press, 1999)

Frey, Sylvia R., *Water from the Rock: Black Resistance in a Revolutionary Age* (Princeton: Princeton University Press, 1991)

Gara, Larry, *The Liberty Line: The Legend of the Underground Railroad* (Lexington: University Press of Kentucky, 1961)

Genovese, Eugene D., *Roll, Jordan, Roll: The World the Slaves Made* (New York: Pantheon Books, 1974)

Genovese, Eugene D., *From Rebellion to Revolution: Afro-American Slave Revolts in the Making of the Modern World* (Baton Rouge: Louisiana State University Press, 1980)

Johnson, Michael P., 'Denmark Vesey and his Co-Conspirators', *William and Mary Quarterly*, 58 (2001), 915–76.

Linebaugh, Peter and Rediker, Marcus, *The Many-Headed Hydra: Sailors, Slaves, Commoners, and the Hidden History of the Revolutionary Atlantic* (Boston: Beacon Press, 2000)

Morgan, Philip D., *Slave Counterpoint: Black Culture in the Eighteenth Century Chesapeake and Low Country* (Chapel Hill: University of North Carolina Press, 1998)

Mullin, G. W., *Flight and Rebellion: Slave Resistance in Eighteenth Century Virginia* (New York: Oxford University Press, 1972)

Mullin, Michael, *Africa in America: Slave Acculturation and Resistance in the American South and British Caribbean, 1736–1831* (Urbana and Chicago, IL: University of Illinois Press, 1992)

Oates, Stephen B., *The Fires of Jubilee: Nat Turner's Fierce Rebellion* (New York: Harper, 1975)

Phillips, Ulrich Bonnell, *American Negro Slavery: A Survey of the Supply, Employment, and Control of Negro Labor as Determined by the Plantation Regime* (New York: Appleton, 1918)

Sidbury, James, *Ploughshares into Swords: Race, Rebellion, and Identity in Gabriel's Virginia, 1730–1810* (Cambridge: Cambridge University Press, 1997)

Stampp, Kenneth M., *The Peculiar Institution: Slavery in the Ante-Bellum South* (New York: Alfred A. Knopf, 1956)

Thornton, John K., 'African Dimensions of the Stono Rebellion', *American Historical Review*, 96 (1991), 1101–13.

Wood, Peter H., *Black Majority: Negroes in Colonial South Carolina from 1670 through the Stono Rebellion* (New York: Alfred A. Knopf, 1974)

ESSAY: PROFILE OF A RUNAWAY SLAVE

Based on advertisements in newspapers for over 2,000 slaves, this essay provides a profile of slave runaways in two periods (1790–1816 and 1838–60) for the following five states: Virginia, North Carolina, Tennessee, South Carolina and Louisiana. Why were most runaways young adult men? What accounts for the increase in mulatto runaways between 1790 and 1860? Was there a typical runaway slave?

On 25 October 1816, William W. Bell, a North Carolina farmer, placed a notice in the *North Carolina Minerva and Raleigh Advertiser* about his runaway slave. Explaining that he had purchased Frank from John Patterson of Matthews County, Virginia, Bell wrote:

> RUNAWAY, from the Subscriber, on Friday Evening last, Near Enfield Court House, a NEGRO MAN, named FRANK, pretty stout, one strait scar on his cheek passing from the under part of the ear towards the corner of the mouth, of a common dark color, something of a flat nose, a short, round chin, and a down look, about 26 or 27 years of age. Had on, brown yarn homespun Pantaloons, striped homespun waistcoat, and a white yarn round-about. TWENTY-FIVE DOLLARS reward will be given *for lodging* said runaway in any gaol in this state or TWENTY DOLLARS if in any gaol out of the state.[1]

Forty-one years later, in the fall of 1857, a South Carolina planter, E. M. Royall, published a similar notice in the *Charleston Mercury*:

> TWENTY-FIVE DOLLARS REWARD. – Ranaway from the subscriber's plantation, in Christ Church Parish, his Negro Man TONEY. Said fellow is about 5 feet 6 inches in height; stoutly built, is very black, has a broad, full face, black eyes, and when he laughs, shows a very white set of teeth. The above reward will be paid for his apprehension and delivery to the Work House in Charleston, or to the subscriber on his place.[2]

In size, build, color, gender, age, attire, reward, probable occupation, and personality – at least as perceived by whites – the 'NEGRO MAN, named FRANK' and the 'Negro Man TONEY' fit the profile of typical runaway slaves. The largest segment of the runaway army included strong, young field hands in their late teens and twenties. The two advertisements also demonstrate the continuity that existed among typical runaways from one generation to the next.

John Hope Franklin and Loren Schweninger, *Runaway Slaves: Rebels on the Plantation* (New York: Oxford University Press, 1999), pp. 209–33, 393–400.

If the typical runaway was a young, male plantation hand, runaways also included a range of other slaves, young and old, black and mulatto, healthy and infirm, female and male, skilled and unskilled, urban and rural. They absconded from farms, plantations, urban residences, town houses, job sites, and riverboats. Indeed, despite the norm, runaways were a diverse lot, and judging from the comments of slave owners, it seemed impossible to predict who might abscond.

In the sections that follow, there will be an examination of the salient characteristics of runaways resulting from a statistical examination of more than two thousand slaves advertised in newspapers in five states during two time periods: early, or 1790–1816, and late, or 1838–60. It will show that, while the profile of runaways was diverse, there was a remarkable consistency over time. Indeed, as the peculiar institution evolved and changed in unprecedented ways over more than sixty years, the profile of runaways, with few exceptions, remained virtually unchanged.

Age and Gender

As the descriptions of Frank and Toney suggest, the great majority of runaways were young men in their teens and twenties. During the early period, males constituted 81 percent of those who were advertised as runaways, and among them, 78 percent were between the ages of thirteen and twenty-nine. Exactly the same proportion of males was listed during the later period and, again, about three out of four – 74 percent – were in their teens and twenties. During both periods, these men were described as healthy, strong, and stout, and only about one out of six possessed skills as artisans or house servants. The proportion of men to women was slightly higher in Virginia and Louisiana than in North and South Carolina and Tennessee during the early period, and it was lower in Louisiana during the later period, when male runaways dropped to 71 percent, but the variations were less important than the remarkable consistency: the precise male–female percentage remaining exactly the same over a period of more than two generations.[3]

Young men ran away in greater numbers because often they had not yet married or, if they had married, had not yet begun a family. Those who married sometimes took their loved ones with them, but in most cases, they were forced to leave wives and children behind. Young man also ran away more often because they were more willing to defy overseers and owners if they felt aggrieved. Once away from the plantation, young men could better defend themselves and were willing to resist recapture. The young slave Jack of Orangeburgh District, South Carolina, had been out for some time when he was discovered in 1807 by a white farmer. In the struggle that ensued, Jack slashed the white man so severely that he remained bedridden for weeks and more than a year-and-a-half later had not fully recovered. A few years later, the slave Sampson, also of South Carolina, was confronted in a similar manner by William Villard, a white farmer in Barnwell District.

Table 1. Gender of Runaways by State, Early Period (1790–1816)

	Virginia	North Carolina	Tennessee	South Carolina	Louisiana	Total
Number of females	14	18	29	55	13	129
(percentage)	(15)	(18)	(21)	(23)	(11)	(19)
Number of males	81	82	109	185	109	566
(percentage)	(85)	(82)	(79)	(77)	(89)	(81)
Total	95	100	138	240	122	695

Sampson brandished a knife in one hand and a hatchet in the other, and as Villard approached him, he cut the white man across the forehead and swung the hatchet into his ribs. Six months later, Villard was still disabled 'from the Severe Injury he sustained in the apprehension of this desperate out Law'.[4]

Not only did young men offer fierce resistance, but many realized that if they did not make an attempt to escape time would run out. Death came early to slaves, and those who reached their twenty-first birthday could expect to live about sixteen or seventeen additional years. In some sections, yellow fever, dysentery, pneumonia, and cholera carried off many slaves still in their teens and twenties.[5] It was not difficult for those who survived to observe the small number of elderly slaves or know about the funerals that occurred so often on their own and nearby plantations. This, coupled with the energy and vitality of youth and the physical stamina it took to go on the run, prompted young men to leave in greatest numbers. Among the 424 runaway males whose approximate ages were given in the early period, the average age was twenty-five; among the 835 during the later period, the mean age was twenty-seven. The oldest runaways were in their forties and fifties, a handful in their sixties, but those forty or older represented only 5 percent in the early period and 6 percent in the later period.

Young slave women were less likely to run away because they had often begun to raise families by their late teens and early twenties. With youngsters to care for, it became difficult to contemplate either leaving them behind

Table 2. Gender of Runaways by State, Late Period (1838–1860)

	Virginia	North Carolina	Tennessee	South Carolina	Louisiana	Totals
Number of females	17	18	20	89	104	248
(percentage)	(9)	(14)	(12)	(19)	(29)	(19)
Number of males	178	114	148	369	259	1068
(percentage)	(91)	(86)	(88)	(81)	(71)	(81)
Total	195	132	168	458	363	1316

or taking them in an escape attempt. Lying out in the woods or fleeing to more distant points would only mean suffering, danger, and hardship for their children. As several historians have pointed out, although slave women desired freedom as much as slave men and were often as assertive and aggressive on the plantation as male slaves, the task of uprooting and carrying children in flight 'was onerous, time-consuming, and exhaustive'. As a result, a smaller proportion than among men decided to run away.[6]

Like their male counterparts, however, those who did abscond usually did so in their teens and twenties. These young females represented more than two-thirds of the women in both periods – 69 and 68 percent respectively – who ran off. Some took their children with them or, following a sale, attempted to find their sons and daughters, despite the difficulties of such undertakings. Others ran during pregnancy. In her twenties, Letty left her owner John J. Zollicofer of Nashville in 1814. She was a 'likely negro', her owner said, quick spoken, with 'handsome countenance'; she was about six months pregnant. Similarly, the 'American Negress *Nancy*', who ran away in New Orleans in 1828, was 'with child'. Purchased by a South Carolina man in Maryland in 1816, Sawney quickly fled from her new owner but remained out only a few months before being captured. By the time her owner claimed her, she had given birth to an infant. The North Carolina slave Delph also bore a child on the run. Angeline escaped from Richmond slave traders in 1836 to return to Greenbrier, Augusta County, Virginia, where she had been raised and had six children.[7] Angeline, too, was pregnant. Despite these desertions, women thought long and hard about the consequences for their families and themselves before making any decision to abscond.

Among both males and females, some did not fit the profile. Some pre-teenage youngsters fled. Transferred at age ten to the household of an Anne Arundel County, Maryland, woman following the distribution of an estate, Alice was about twelve when she went 'running out at night'. Catherine, a French-speaking girl in New Orleans, was also about twelve when she absconded in 1831, and Henry, a 'young mulatto', was about ten when he ran off two years later. In 1841, an eleven-year-old apprentice barber, Walter Scott, who traveled on steamboats, ran away. When Elias was arrested in 1828 in Charleston, he was advertised as being four feet nine inches tall and about twelve years old.[8]

At the other end of the age spectrum was a black man who worked in the kitchen at the Pontchartrain Hotel and as a hawker of hay in New Orleans. He had outlived several of his owners, and in 1830, at age fifty-five, he absconded. Although her exact age was not given, Nelly was 'an elderly Negro woman' who had been sold from Virginia to South Carolina. Other slaves were described as old, decrepit, elderly, gray-haired, bent, and aged. The fifty-year-old, Sumter District, South Carolina, man stooped over when walking, and was 'quite grey'. Some slaves were similarly described with physical defects and as being 'quite gray'. The Charleston carpenter Andrew was quite 'elderly looking'. Committed to the jail Orangeburg, South Carolina, in 1832, another runaway was described as being 'about eighty years old'.[9]

Color and Physical Characteristics

Most runaways were black. They were described as having dark complexion, dark skin, black complexion, being 'coal black', remarkably black, or very black. Some had 'not a very black complexion' or were 'not remarkably black' or 'nearly quite black', but others were described as 'a negro boy, perfectly black', 'jet black', with a dark complexion, 'very dark complexioned', or exceptionally dark. Abel was about sixteen years old and 'dark complected', William B. Flowers of Smyrna, Barnwell District, South Carolina, said in his 1855 notice; Abram was about twenty-eight years old, plausible and intelligent, and also very black, Z. B. Oakes of Charleston said in the same issue of the *Charleston Mercury*.[10] Although at times the precise color of the runaway was not stated and 'negro wench' or 'negro fellow' could describe a person of mixed origin, 70 percent of the runaways in the early period were either black or their skin was so dark that readers of runaway newspaper advertisements would assume they were.*

Although a minority of runaways were mulattoes, persons of mixed racial ancestry ran away in greater numbers than their proportion in the slave population would suggest. Except for the virtual elimination of African-born blacks, the increase among mulatto runaways between the early and late periods represented one of the most significant changes that occurred in the profile of runaways. The precise proportion of mulattoes in the slave population for the early period is not known, but due to the importation of Africans at least until 1808, it was surely smaller than during the late antebellum era, when it reached 10 percent. The nearly one-third mixed blood among runaways during the early period was therefore at least three times larger than would be expected in the general population. By the later period, the proportion of advertised mulattoes had risen to 43 percent, more than four times what would be expected. Even if mixed blood slaves were more readily advertised – and there is evidence that they were – this large percentage was remarkable.[11]

Persons with light skin possessed certain advantages as runaways. The prejudices against them were generally less than against those of darker hue. They were more likely to be able to pass as free persons since the proportion of mulattoes in the free Negro group was much higher than

---

* In the RSDB, if 'negro' was used with no additional information on color, the runaway was considered black; if no color was indicated, the runaway was also cited as black. Since owners were quick to point out those of mixed racial origin even when they used the term 'negro' (i.e., 'negro mulatto'), this method, which gives a color designation to all slaves in the RSDB, is probably relatively accurate.

in the slave population. The proportion of mulatto runaways in the slave population during the late period (561 of 1,316, or 43 percent) was almost exactly the same as the 41 percent of mixed racial origin in the free black population.

Sometimes they could pass as white. This was the case when the Georgia slave Coleman left his owner during a trip the two men took on the Western Atlantic Railroad in October 1839. Coleman was in his mid-twenties, with a very smooth face, straight sandy hair, blue eyes, and was 'very white to be a slave'. Bonaparte, a Virginia slave, possessed the physical appearance of a white man: very light skin and straight hair. A Georgia runaway named Guy would 'no doubt endeavor to pass himself off as a white man', and the Haywood County, Tennessee, runaway John, was described as 'a bright red Mulatto' with straight hair and fashionable attire. He would certainly attempt to pass, either 'for a free fellow, or perhaps a white man'. Other owners described their slaves as 'very nearly white', could easily pass for white, a 'white mulatto boy', three-fourths white and 'shows the negro blood but very little', 'remarkably white for a slave', could easily 'pass for a white man'. 'Stop Mabin!!' read the advertisement of Georgia planter Zachariah Booth in 1833, 'He will pass for a white man where he is not known'. Apparently, Mabin did pass, as he was still at large seven years later.[12]

Mulatto slaves were often given positions as house servants, maids, cooks, tailors, waiters, and barbers. With such skills, they could more easily attempt to pass as free blacks. Given their often privileged position as slaves, runaway mulattoes found it less difficult to affect the manners, habits, and general demeanor of free persons of color. During the later period, they were twice as likely to be literate as black runaways and more often carried freedom papers or passes. Even during the early period, when the literacy rate among runaways was only between 1 and 2 percent, nearly 10 percent of mulatto runaways possessed forged papers, compared with 6 percent among blacks.

The diversity among runaways was perhaps nowhere better illustrated than in the descriptions of mixed blood slaves who ran away. In South Carolina between 1822 and 1831, they were described as yellow, brown, mustee (brown), mulatto, pale yellow, 'of rather a yellow cast', Sambo (dark), and red. In Virginia during the early and late periods, they were described as tawny, nearly black, brown, mulatto, yellow, red, reddish, yellowish, dark yellow, bright yellow, 'tolerable light', 'dark mulatto', and as having 'a lighter complexion' than was 'common among negroes'. Others were a 'little light complected' or 'tolerably bright complected', 'more of a bright mulatto than otherwise', and of a 'dark ginger color'. A Richmond owner said his carriage driver was of a 'dark copper complexion', and other Virginia masters said their slaves were 'light copper or mulatto', 'pumpkin color', or 'light bacon color'.[13]

Louisiana owners advertised their runaways as bright yellow, very brown, 'a negro, but not of the blackest cast', 'a light colored black', 'of a light dark color', pale yellow, rather red, and 'rather light'. They described their slaves also as 'a dirty mulatto color', 'copper colored negro man', bright mulatto, light mulatto, bright yellow mulatto', 'dark freckled mulatto negro', 'not very black', 'dark copper color'. In New Orleans, the term 'griff', or 'griffe', changed from a noun to an adjective. Used in the Caribbean to denote the offspring of a black and mulatto, in New Orleans it became a color to describe runaways. 'Ranaway from the subscriber, about three weeks ago', one master said, 'a griffe colored slave named Joe'.[14]

Other physical characteristics of runaways also revealed their diversity. Owners rarely gave specific weight information, but they did suggest size and build – slight, average, heavy, stout – in about one-third of the notices. For men and women in the early period, the largest proportion was described as 'stout', meaning strong, sturdy, fleshy, large – (39 percent of the females and 41 percent of the males); in the later period, this category was still prominent although there was wider distribution among groups. With regard to height, the data on females are sketchy, although it does appear that they were shorter than what was considered 'average' at the time they absconded. The information for males is much better, and in more than 55 percent of the cases owners provided specific height data. Among the 314 males age thirteen and over during the early period, half were five feet seven inches or taller, a third were five feet ten inches or taller, and 12 percent were six feet or more. Among the 637 runaways males in the same category during the later period, the figures were almost exactly the same. In the early period, the average height of between five feet seven inches and five feet eight inches for runaways was as tall as the average white male height.[15] In both periods, many were tall, strong, young men. There is little doubt that physical strength, stamina, and size played a role in determining who was likely to flee.

A significant segment of the runaway population was identifiable by marks, scars, and disfigurements. The list was very long, including facial mark, cheek mark, unusual forehead mark, upper arm mark, finger deformity, missing finger, limp, unusual gait, leg deformity, unusual feet, missing toes, lame arm, lame hand, smallpox scars, missing ear[s], and scars from whipping and branding. It was not usually stated how, where, or when runaways lost their fingers, toes, limbs, or acquired their marks and brands. In the early period, African-born slaves often acquired tribal marks before their journey to the New World, and even in the later period some of the physical problems described were the result of accidents or disease. Such was probably the case for those described with 'white swelling', 'very remarkable lumps', a foot 'deformed and nearly half off', 'a web on one of his eyes', missing 'one-half of her right foot', 'lame in the left knee', 'diseased in his left thigh'. The frequent mention of missing teeth might also be the result of natural causes.[16]

It was clear, however, that for a number of slaves there was a direct connection between deformities and prior punishment. The Virginia slave Reuben of Culpepper County, who 'eloped' in 1807, had

> a scar on the right side of his neck below the ear; another on the left, lower on his neck; he has also a scar on the right leg a little below his knee, occasioned by a burn; his back has many scars on it from flogging he has received which he justly merited.

The 'mark of a whip' could be seen on the arms of Celia, a fifteen-year-old girl who ran from her master in Rutherford County, Tennessee, in 1814. Fond of drinking, swearing, and fighting, the runaway Dennis had his back 'very much cut with the cow-hide'. Slaves had scars on their backs, shoulders, arms, legs, sides, and faces, 'occasioned by the whip'. Neither the young nor old were spared. Fourteen-year-old Mary, who had a 'quick and lively air', had two marks on her cheek inflicted with 'a cow hide'. An elderly Virginia slave, transferred to South Carolina, had several marks between her shoulders caused by the lash. In 1826, the sheriff of Pointe Coupee Parish, Louisiana, described a captured slave as having 'around his neck an Iron collar with three prongs extending upwards' and 'many scars on his back and shoulders from the whip'.[17]

In some cases it was almost possible to trace a slave's history by the various scars. By the time he reached age twenty in 1839, William had been sold from Virginia, to New Orleans, to Vicksburg, Mississippi, and finally to a plantation on Bayou Sara, near Woodville, Mississippi. '[H]e ranaway about the 1st of April', his Mississippi owner said, 'was caught and put in jail in Woodville'. He falsely gave the name of another man as his owner. Now he was out again, but could be recognized by a scar just above his left eye, a scar above his left thumb, and when 'stripped, many scars may be seen on his back, caused from a severe whipping with a cowskin (as he says) at the time of the Southampton insurrection'.[18]

The notices contain ample evidence that branding and cropping of ears continued well into the nineteenth century, especially to punish the most obdurate runaways. The Virginia slave Archie was branded on both cheeks, and the facial scars were much darker than his normal skin color. A Georgia slave had also been branded before he ran away in 1808. It was unclear whether the 'R' on each cheek stood for 'Runaway' or 'Richard Thurmond', the Oconee River planter who claimed Joe as his slave. One Kentucky master described a runaway in 1815 as having 'a black streak on his nose, which is very plain, it extends on his left cheek near the size of one little finger'. 'I filed several notches between several of his upper fore teeth, which I expect is also very plain', he added; 'I also branded him on each cheek...about twelve months ago, which is not very perceivable'.[19]

Similarly, advertisements in the *New Orleans Bee* during the 1820s and 1830s describe runaways with brands on their backs, hands, breasts, and faces. He 'made two trips to Louisville the last time he ranaway', one notice in 1833 read. He was about thirty years old, had sunken cheeks, sulky looks, and should be easy to spot: he had a brand on his forehead of an inch-high cross, a brand on his cheek of the letter 'O', and a brand on his back of the word 'Orleans'. He also had 'the mark of the whip' on his back. The French-speaking slave Dio worked on a plantation of P. B. Marmillion, located in Orleans Parish. When he departed with two other slaves in a skiff, Marmillion warned the public to beware of Dio's 'pleasing countenance' and added that the slave would be easy to recognize. 'He is stamped on the forehead and on the breast', the owner commented, 'with the large letters P.M'. A slave who left Andry Boudousque's plantation stooped when he walked, had lost part of a thumb, and was branded 'with the letter B on the left side of his breast'.[20]

The scars from whippings, beatings, and branding, described by slave owners themselves, bore witness to the harsh realities of slavery. Yet there were many runaways whose marks and scars were never advertised in the newspapers. London was 'neither the best nor the worst Kind of a negroe', his overseer in Natchitoches Parish, Louisiana, said; rather he was 'a middling hand', or a 'Very Good Second rate Negroe'. London, however, ran away on numerous occasions and bore marks 'of Very Violent Punishment'. In August 1835, after a severe whipping, a physician wrote:

> his face was sufficiently full and round as past but on seeing the other parts of the body which were extremely poor it [his face] seemed to be swollen, that the skin on his posteriors was lank and wrinkled and that his bones protruded in such a way as to resemble more a skeleton than a living person, that not satisfied with this examination he introduced his finger into the fundament around which the[re] were a number of small flatulent Blisters that having intruded his finger as far as the intestines he found them very hard and Extremely sensitive and felt some very hard tumours & that on withdrawing his finger it was coated with putrid Matter on his finger that from the appearance of this matter that there must have been internal Tumours or Fistulaes.

A short time after the doctor's visit, London died.[21]

Among the 695 slaves listed in the runaway notices for the early period, 54 (7.8 percent) showed scars from whipping, beatings, cropping, torture, and other forms of severe violence. Among the 1,316 slaves listed for the later period, 76 (5.8 percent) showed the same types of scars. Only 6 slaves in the early period were obviously branded by their owners, but the 6 represented nearly 1 percent of the total, and only 15 had one or both ears cut off (a punishment usually reserved for runaways), but they represented 2.2 percent of the total. While the number of those branded by their owners in the later period dropped to 4, and those with cropped ears to 12, the fact that 1 out of 13 and 1 out of 17 fugitives (early and late periods) were identified by scars resulting from extreme forms of punishment reveals much about the peculiar institution.*

Appearance

It is doubtful that many runaways branded on the face or disfigured from the violent retribution of their masters made it to freedom. But others could and did hide their scars by wearing shirts, pants, and jackets, and the great majority of runaways, at least as indicated in the advertisements, could not be readily identified by the results of severe whipping or other violence. They could be recognized, their owners believed, by other means, and often this included a description of their clothes.

Most runaways fled in the clothing that their owners had issued them. Field hands were generally provided with a least one coarse suit of clothes per year – shirts and pants for men, dresses for women, long shirts for children. During the early period, the clothing was often homespun by black women on the plantation or sewn by them from 'Negro cloth' purchased by their owners from retailers in the North. The attire of a Louisiana hand was typical: in 1830 his clothing consisted of a gray jacket, straw hat, blue striped 'drilling' pantaloons, and work trousers made from 'coarse cotton cloth'. During the later period, hands sometimes wore ready-made clothes provided them by their masters and made or acquired special shirts, trousers, and dresses for holidays and church services.[22]

Given their limited wardrobes, what is striking about the appearance of runaways was the remarkable variety of clothing they took with them at the time of their departure. Some stole extra apparel, others made special clothes for their flight, and still others simply accumulated a selection of different garments. Even those who left wearing homespun often took other items. In 1814, the Tennessee slave Celia had a yellow calico frock, a blue calico frock, a white cambric dress, and two 'homespun coarse' dresses, a pair of red morocco-eyed slippers tied with a yellow ribbon, and a 'checkered gingham bonnet (or scoop)'. The runaway Solomon wore a blue Lindsey coat with yellow metal buttons, an old fur hat, and a worn yellow waistcoat; he carried with him a buffalo robe, two or three pairs of homespun cotton pantaloons, and 'several other articles of clothing'. A South Carolina slave wore a 'blue negro cloth round jacket with new yellow buttons, and blue pantaloons, a grey waistcoat with black velvet on the pockets, new boots, and grey worsted stockings'. Another South Carolina runaway wore homespun shirt and pants and an old cloak, but carried 'a large stock of Clothing'. Myal, a

---

* This discussion excludes slaves who had missing toes, fingers, a leg, arm, or hand, as well as those with various marks and scars, unless it was explicitly stated or obvious that these deformities were the result of severe punishment.

Tennessee runaway, wore plantation made pants, a cotton shirt, and a wool roundabout. He also had an extra pair of white woolen trousers, blue jeans, and a black fur hat. 'The latter clothes are missing', the master confided, and Myal probably took them when he left.[23]

Other plantation slaves discarded their homespun altogether. The Virginia slave Laban fled with a grey lamb's skin coat, white trousers, a double-breasted grey coat, a black cape, and 'sundry other clothes'. A Kentucky field hand wore a cashmere coat, nice pants, shoes, stockings, and a fur hat, taking along a cotton waistcoat and three extra pairs of cotton trousers. 'She is very fond of dress', one South Carolina owner said of his twenty-year-old black Hannah 'and carried three or four changes of clothes with her'. When he ran away from the plantation of Andre Deslondes in St. John the Baptist Parish, Louisiana, Alexander took two suits of clothes, two pairs of trousers – one dark cloth, the other striped woolen – a blue-and-white-striped jacket, shoes, and a 'drab colored hat'. The Mississippi plantation hand Patrick dressed 'very fine' and had a 'fine stock of clothes'. Six feet tall, with gold rings on his fingers, Patrick was 'a very fine looking negro'. Else would 'appear in a black Silk or white Muslin gown', her Virginia owner wrote in 1805, 'as she had many very good clothes, and is fond of dress'. The young North Carolina field hand Oba ran away wearing cotton trousers and a short coat 'napped with black wool and cotton, wove plain'. He also had two pairs of 'buff casimere breeches', a grey waistcoat, a white waistcoat, a pair of ribbed, woolen stockings, and a double-breasted, grey broadcloth coat.[24]

The wardrobes of urban slaves often included a larger selection than was available to plantation hands. Those who worked as waiters, house servants, stewards, seamstresses, tailors, and barbers possessed several suits, dresses, shirts, trousers, jackets, and hats. The Richmond house servant Claiborne took with him 'a great variety of wearing apparel, all of excellent quality', his master said, 'much better than is usually given to servants'. Despite being employed as a carpenter and railroad hand, Jackson maintained a 'general assortment of good clothes', his New Orleans owner said, and would no doubt assume 'the appearance of a dandy'. When the slave Willis boarded a steamboat in New Orleans in 1832, he wore a white shirt, brown linen pants, a blue cloth frock coat, and a black hat. He also took with him a bundle of clothing wrapped in a sheet. The Charleston slave George left his owner in July 1804 wearing a brown jacket, brown calico waistcoat, and brown linen pants with suspenders. George 'is very fond of wearing a Neckcloth with a large Pad in it', his owner said, and although hatless, he would probably buy one along the way. Twenty-year-old Walley, also of Charleston, wore a blue cloth coat with yellow buttons, thin black pants, and a black fur hat when he left in January 1828 but carried an extra jacket and two pairs of wool pants wrapped in a carpet.[25]

Other city slaves took large wardrobes. One New Orleans owner did not describe the dress of his slave, a waiter at the St. Charles Hotel, but noted he was 'genteel, and little on the dandy order'. In 1832, the twenty-six-year-old personal servant of Kinsey Burden of Charleston left wearing a black hat, grey wool pants, a striped gingham jacket, and a black bombazette frock coat. In addition, he carried along a black sealskin cap, two extra suits, two extra waistcoats – one black cassimere and one striped gingham, two pairs of white trousers, and a worn, light blue, broadcloth frock coat. When he left his owner in New Orleans, Nelson had on a tarpaulin hat, blue cotton calico shirt, and cotton pants, but he also possessed 'an array of clothing' and might be dressed with 'a white silk hat, blue dress coat, and cloth pantaloons'. George W. Prescott's petite slave Lucy in Charleston wore a handkerchief on her head and a calico gown with wide ornamental ruffles, but, he warned, she 'may change her dress as she carried her trunk'. Others took 'an abundance of clothing', 'an array of clothing', 'a bundle of clothing'. Several owners echoed the sentiments of a New Orleans man who complained that his slave had taken with him so many articles of clothing that 'it is hard to tell what he might wear'.[26]

There were practical as well as stylistic reasons for taking many articles of apparel, as the fur or beaver hats and store-bought suits indicated. But principally they took along changes of clothing to use for disguise. Some slaves were best known in their communities because of their dress – Charleston and Christ Church Parish residents knew Cyrus, a coachman, for example, by his brown frock coat and black beaver hat – and when these slaves donned new outfits, they could more readily slip away, as did Cyrus. 'She will of course appear in different dresses', a Johns Island, South Carolina, planter said of his runaway in 1822. She would be in a variety of colors because shortly before leaving she was observed dyeing a number of white dresses.[27]

Jim was well-known around Beaufort, South Carolina, and its vicinity not for his clothing, but as 'a noted thief and runaway'. He frequently disguised himself as a woman and took the name Sally Turner, his master said, 'having once been apprehended in women's apparel'. In 1828, he had made it as far as Savannah but was captured and brought back. A short time later he ran away again. The owner believed he would again disguise himself as a woman. Just the reverse was true for the 'dark griffe' Crescent City woman Mariah, who would try to pass as a boy. She frequently 'dressed herself in boy's clothes, and has her hair cut short for the purpose'.[28]

Color, age, gender, distinctive marks, size, and clothing were all part of the profile of runaways. So, too, were hair styles. What is striking in comparing the early and late periods is the similarity of these styles. In both periods, very few runaways were described by their hair style. Persons of mixed racial origin were far more likely to have their hair described than persons who were described as black. In the early period, among 695 slaves, only

38 (5.5 percent) were described as having unusual or distinctive hair; mulattoes were three times more likely than blacks to have their hair described (24 of 207 mulattoes, or 12 percent, compared with 14 of 488 blacks, or 3 percent). It was rare for a male slave to have his hair described as bushy, plaited, or standing high on his head. In the later period, among 1,316 slaves, only 97 (7 percent) were described by their hair style, and persons of mixed origin were nearly five times more likely than blacks to have their hair described. The most important change involved the proportion of women who were described as having unusual hair. In the early period only 1 percent of the female runaways were described by their hair style, compared with 5 percent of the males; in the later period, each group represented 7 percent of their respective totals.[29]

The similarities and differences between the two periods are reflected in newspaper advertisements. First, owners in both periods were more likely to see straight hair as distinctive; second, with the growth of the mulatto population among runaways, this distinction became more common; third, in the later period, slave women of mixed origin may well have not worn the traditional head scarves in order to advertise their straight hair; and fourth, even in the early period, bushy or long hair among male runaways was rare. These changes were more than stylistic. They pointed to cultural changes among slaves as they made the transition from Africans to African Americans.

Personality Traits and Countenance

Runaways possessed many similar personality traits. Here, too, there was diversity, but most runaways demonstrated self-confidence, self-assurance, self-possession, determination, and self-reliance. They were resourceful, willful, focused, and purposeful. A number were quickwitted, wily, and intelligent, while most were deceptive and calculating, and not a few were duplicitous and scheming when it came to dealing with whites. Perhaps the most salient characteristic, however, was courage, especially for those who ran away more than once despite severe punishments. Very few among them appeared surly, morose, or sullen. Indeed, such qualities would have exposed their deep hatred of bondage and made them, in their owner's eyes, troublemakers and potential runaways.

Among the most significant characteristics of runaways was their intelligence. Masters warned the public to beware of black persons who were able to provide credible excuses as to why they were traveling in the area. In 1804, one Virginia owner, W. Gatewood, said that his 'likely negro man by the name of TOM', alias Tom Smith, alias Smith, was a 'proud, artful, cunning fellow' who had a 'very smooth dissembling tongue'. The Georgia mulatto Sam was 'a keen shrewd fellow' who would 'attempt to pass for a free man, and will doubtless make for a free state'. She was very 'artful and talks very properly, and is capable of deceiving any person', the owner of Maria, a 'fine tall mulatto' woman, about thirty years of age, explained. Her husband was literate and had probably written her a pass, and it was 'therefore requested that if she should produce a pass to examine it very particularly, as she has none from me'. The mulatto carpenter George was 'very plausible when spoken to, and well calculated to deceive'. The black cooper who left a plantation near Georgetown, South Carolina, in 1828 was 'very credible' and often affected a 'pleasant but bold smile'. Other runaways were described in the same manner: they would change their names, produce false passes, wear fraudulent badges, profess to be free, lie about their owner, feign an illness. In short, as one master put it, they were 'very smart and well calculated to deceive'.[30]

In order to deceive, runaways assumed a friendly and polite countenance when dealing with whites. This was especially true for older runaways, who were often described as amicable, cordial, and congenial. The fifty-year-old Kentucky slave who was sent to Richmond, Virginia, as a hireling was remarkably polite, often repeating 'master', and 'making bows almost to the ground'. When he absconded, the man who hired him said he was 'a very artful fellow' and was probably attempting to secure a berth aboard a sailing vessel as a free man. It was also true for domestic servants and waiters who were often described in the same manner. At age twenty-two or twenty-three, Moses, the 'waiting-man' for Theodore Gaillard, a Charleston gentleman, was described as pleasant, amiable, and congenial.[31]

The speech habits of runaways came under close scrutiny in the newspaper notices. About 7 and 8 percent of slaves were said to speak slowly or to a have a downcast look when they were addressed by whites. He has rather 'slow speech', he speaks slowly and has 'Rather a down look', she 'is slow of speech', or in the words of a Louisiana master, he has 'a smiling and downcast look when spoken to'. Among this group were a few African-born slaves who experienced difficulty pronouncing English words. By 1833, Luck had been in the United States many years, but he still pronounced words with 'difficulty as is generally the case', an observer said, 'with all the Congo negroes'. Others spoke in Gullah, 'Savannah dialect', a Charleston dialect, or 'a brogue different from Negroes raised in Eastern Virginia'. Among those who spoke slowly, only a tiny number stuttered or had speech impediments. In the early period, they numbered only five; and in the later period, only twelve.[32]

Indeed, as many slaves were fluent in at least three languages as those who stuttered. Slaves in Louisiana during the 1820s and 1830s were often bilingual, and some spoke French, Spanish, and English. Advertised runaways were described as speaking English and French, English and Spanish, and as was the case of 'creole *Negress* named CELESTINE', English, French, and Spanish. Others spoke English, French, and a little Spanish or French with 'broken English'. When masters in the region described slaves as 'American creole', 'American mulatto', 'American negro', they were pointing not only to their American birth but to English as their principal language. In the upper states, including Maryland, Virginia, and North Carolina, a few runaways were bilingual in German and English, especially in sections where German settlers made up a significant portion of the population. Henry Kring of Rockingham County, Virginia, said that his Negro man Hons, who ran away in 1807, 'speaks generally the German language'.[33]

Whatever their dialect, accent, or language, runaways were generally articulate and well-spoken. They were often described as fluent and smooth with words and quick with speech. Forty-year-old Charles, who called himself Charles Wood, spoke 'smooth language and will no doubt tell a good story to pass'. The Mississippi slave Anthony, who absconded from Natchez in July 1803, spoke French and English 'tolerably well' and was 'artful in telling stories'. Forty-five-year-old Tom, who eloped from Soldier's Rest, Davidson County, Tennessee, was remarkably fluent in speech and when addressed would always respond without hesitation. A man who ran away from Nashville 'speaks bold and sensible'. The New Orleans slave Sam spoke 'very quick, and from the top of the tongue'. The South Carolina slave Jacob, who was sold to Louisiana in 1834, spoke 'quickly, and is rather abrupt in his manner'. One twenty-two-year-old black man was 'smart and active and speaks very bold in conversation'. The griffe man Sam was 'soft and smooth in conversation'. Sixteen-year-old Frances was quick with words and 'very intelligent'. A runaway railroad worker spoke in 'an impudent, self-confident way', while a Virginia runaway possessed 'very good language indeed for a slave'.[34]

The personality traits attributed to slaves by their owners and by other whites in newspaper advertisements presented only part of the picture. Though they did note that some slaves were active, bold, surly, and nervous, they rarely described them as defiant, overtly resistant, violent. Nor did they admit that they were sometimes afraid of their slaves. Runaways often demonstrated all of these traits, and owners and overseers were sometimes timid in dealing with such runaways. In their owners' opinion, these slaves were 'quarrelsome', 'disorderly', and 'disobedient'; they were vicious, turbulent, and violent. Whites admitted that they were unable to control such slaves. As one master said, his man was 'utterly disobedient and ungovernable' and despite every 'admonition and threat continued to disobey him and runaway'. Since this owner refused to use chains or other restraints, the only solution was a sale. When a fifteen-year-old Maryland girl named Eliza absconded, was captured, brought back, and threatened with sale to Georgia, she replied that she would 'as leave go to Georgia as any where else'. She ran away the next day. The owner went to Annapolis, looked up a business associate who knew Eliza's mother, and went to the associate's office. After being there a few minutes, he related, 'the door opened and in walked Eliza'. The master said he was glad to see her. She replied, '"I want nothing to do with you"'. ' She might be forcibly taken back, she added,

Table 3. Countenance of Slaves as Described in Runaway Advertisements

Description	Early Period, 1790–1816		Late Period, 1838–1860	
	Number	Percentage	Number	Percentage
Intelligent/Artful	81	12	142	11
Friendly/Polite	81	12	131	10
Cunning	52	8	51	4
Looks Down/Slow Speech	46	7	108	8
Active	46	7	79	6
Bold	27	4	34	3
Surly	20	3	37	3
Nervous	17	2	39	3

Source: Computed from RSDB; since some slaves were listed in more than one category, totals are not included.

'but she would not stay with him'. The owner sent her to jail and arranged for her sale.[35]

Such defiance was not uncommon among runaways. They were described as displaying 'bad and vicious habits', refusing to obey orders, refusing to work, and refusing to 'perform services required'. Like Eliza, they vowed not to live on their owners' farm or plantation, threatened owners and overseers, and asserted that no amount of punishment would make them change their attitudes. The owner Cosmore Robinson said that his slave was 'surly, morose and discontented', a man who was obviously 'greatly dissatisfied with his state of servitude'. Others were noted for their open defiance, 'violent and determined temper', refusal to submit, and their threats against the master's family. When the owner of one runaway decided to sell him, he arranged for the sheriff to put him in jail. He was familiar with the slave's 'Character and disposition to do harm' and believed that if the slave knew he was going to be sold the owner's family 'would be in great danger'.[36]

Three case studies – from South Carolina, Texas, and Maryland – illustrate this aspect of the profile of a runaway. Owned by Mary Cobb of Columbia, South Carolina, Leely ran away on numerous occasions. On one occasion when Leely was out, Cobb, who knew she was 'concealed and lurking' about town, hired her out, if the hirer would 'take the risk and trouble of finding and getting possession of said slave'. After finding Leely, the hirer offered to purchase her, but Cobb would not sell because the black woman 'was very evil disposed towards her', if 'sold to any person in Columbia, she might do her mischief'. A few months later, Leely insulted a member of Mary Cobb's family in the street and was arrested and publicly whipped.[37]

The testimony of a Texas overseer concerning the slave Miles, who worked on a farm in San Augustine County, suggests that runaways were often openly defiant. When a visitor arrived at the farm in 1852 searching for stolen goods, Gilbert B. McIver, the overseer, sent a slave to the field where Miles was plowing to procure the key to his locked cabin door. He refused to give it up. When this was repeated a second time, McIver broke down Miles's door but found nothing. Miles became angry and told McIver that he 'was the first Man that ever sent for *his* Keys, or that broke into his house'. The overseer explained:

> In the day after the occurrence of the matter about the Key, of his, I went into the field where he was ploughing, and he had a hatchet, or Hand axe, tied and swung to his Plough: and I thought at the time, that he had it for the purpose, in case he was attacked by me, or if I went to Correct him, to resist me with it. I did not go near him at the time to attempt to Correct him, but just let him plough on, as I was unarmed, and had nothing to defend myself with at the time.

Miles refused to 'mind, or give obedience to his overseer', and if he were to be corrected 'he would fight; he might, if he had the opportunity, run', but in any event he would resist. He was 'disposed to have his own way, and if a manager ordered him to do a task he would grouse and sometimes not perform the work if he were so inclined'. When a few days later, armed with a gun and accompanied by a neighbor and his dogs, McIver went to the fields where Miles was plowing to correct him, Miles darted into the woods carrying his hatchet.[38]

Such defiance was also demonstrated by 'a negro slave named Peter', whose owner was regarded as kind and benevolent. The owner, John Wood of Frederick County, Maryland, had provided for the future freedom of his slaves, including Peter, who was to be manumitted when he reached age thirty. By age twenty, in 1838, however, Peter had become extremely restive. Hired out to a farmer in the area, he ran away, then ran away again, and then, on a number of different occasions, absented himself without permission. After being jailed, Peter threatened his owner's family, vowed he would never return to his owner, and asserted that being put in jail would never break his spirit. He became his owner said, unruly, insubordinate, and disobedient. Incarceration had 'no effect on his bearing or his insurrectionary spirit'. Indeed, even in jail Peter boasted 'of his freedom from all fear or restraint'.[39]

How and When Slaves Absconded

Although the spectacular escapes depicted in slave narratives and abolitionist literature were not without their basis in fact, the great majority of runaways left neither dramatically nor in the end successfully. Rather, they sneaked off at night, on Saturday afternoon or Sunday, or during holidays; they stowed away on sailing vessels and steamboats, crawled into the back of wagons, concealed themselves in barns, outbuildings, or abandoned houses; they camped out in the woods and swamps. A few rode off on their owners' horses or with their wagons or gigs. By the 1840s and 1850s, some slipped aboard trains or attempted to purchase tickets as free persons.[40]

Despite the unique circumstances surrounding each flight, slaves confronted a number of choices about whether they should run away alone, with members of their families, or in groups; whether they should attempt to use written passes, don a disguise, seek assistance from whites or free blacks, leave at a certain time; and whether or not they should strike out for a city, a remote area near the plantation, or to some distant land. Even in the early period, certain patterns emerged with regard to how and when slaves absconded. By then, the number of African- and West Indian-born slaves in the South had declined significantly, and American-born slaves, now second and third generation, were dominant. As in other aspects of the runaway's profile, there were only modest changes between the early and the later periods, and those that did occur were a result of virtual elimination of African-born blacks in the slave population.

In both periods, a large proportion of runaways set out alone. In the early period, nearly 80 percent in Virginia were alone, 71 percent in North Carolina, and between 51 and 57 percent in Tennessee, South Carolina, and Louisiana; the average in the five states was 60 percent. In the Lower South and Tennessee, there were eighty-eighty African-born slaves, compared with none in Virginia and two in North Carolina. Africans were twice as likely as creoles to leave in groups, and their presence pulled the individual runaway percentages down in South Carolina, Louisiana, and Tennessee to slightly more than half. By the late period, the proportion of slaves who absconded alone in the five states had risen to 72 percent. This ranged from slightly more than 60 percent for Tennessee, to two-thirds in Virginia and North Carolina, to 73 percent in South Carolina and 82 percent in Louisiana. By then, those who ran away in groups were more likely to abscond with one or two others, and those in groups of five or more represented a meager 5 percent of the runaway population.[41] In short, by the 1840s and 1850s, the vast majority of runaways – 95 percent – struck out on their own or with one or two others.

The 'others' included slaves living on the same plantation, belonging to the same owner, working on the same projects, or hired out in the same industries. They also included slaves belonging to the same estate, to the same deceased owner, or the same new owner. Blacks absconded together after committing crimes in collusion with one another or when they were about to be sold, occasionally after plotting with fellow slaves on a neighboring plantation. The largest group of 'others' in the runaway population included slaves belonging to the same owner or to members of the same family. Various family members comprised about one out of three of the 'others' in the early period, and about one out of four in the late period.

Similarly, only small changes occurred in the profile among hired and skilled runaways, those who obtained false papers, or who were literate. In both periods, between 2 and 4 percent of the runaways were hired slaves and 15 percent possessed special skills as house servants, artisans, tailors, seamstresses, cooks, barbers, waiters, butlers, laundresses, or vendors. In both periods, 7 percent of the runaways were believed to be carrying forged freedom papers or owners' passes, while the literacy rate among absconders between the early and late periods rose from about 2 percent to 4 percent. It appears that the proportion of hired runaways was somewhat smaller than the proportion of hirelings in the general slave population, while the percentage of runaways who were literature was about the same, and those with special skills slightly higher than in the general population.[42]

As suggested by the small percentage who carried – or were believed to carry – false papers, it was not easy to obtain forged papers. The problem was further exacerbated if a recipient were illiterate, as most were, and his or her explanation did not coincide with what was written on the forged documents. Occasionally field hands did obtain counterfeit certificates, but it was usually city slaves who obtained papers and attempted to pose either as self-hired slaves or free blacks. The New Orleans mulatto Robert, who ran away in August 1839, produced papers saying he had permission to hire himself out. Another Crescent City slave, Lewis, secured a pass to visit his wife, and since that time, his master noted, 'I have not seen him'. The Charleston drayman Frank posed as a free person of color and wore a fake badge 'as a protection against being committed'.[43]

Slaves who obtained passes or wrote them for themselves were described as intelligent, artful, and 'plausible' men and women who appeared 'to be very truthful'. Virginia master Hopewell Parsons told readers that his slave Eve possessed a 'signed' document saying that she was Henry Cooper's emancipated slave Sally Cole. Eve used the document to her advantage, remaining at large for nearly a year. A Tennessee owner said his slave obtained a pass 'from some person in the neighborhood' and was heading for Ohio or Virginia. The owner of Georgia carpenter Jacob said his slave obtained 'a sealed pass, endorsed "a pass for Jacob from Oglethorpe County Georgia, to the State of Delaware"'. It said that he should be permitted to ride any stage coach. He was last seen on the main road heading north out of Columbia, South Carolina.[44]

Literate slaves sometimes wrote their own passes. Kitt was a 'very likely fellow', could read and write, and would probably 'furnish himself with a pass', one New London, Virginia, owner wrote in 1805. 'He is very intelligent', one advertisement said of a slave who escaped from a private jail in Richmond. The runaway could read and write very well; there was little doubt he would 'have in his possession Forged Papers and Passes'. The mulatto Charleston tailor Joshua, who belonged to the estate of Sabina Hall, could read and write and 'may attempt to pass by forged papers as free'. 'There can be little doubt of his attempting to pass as a free man', the owner of Richmond slave Samuel Barker said in 1805, 'as a forged certificate of his freedom was found the day after he went off'.[45]

The effective use of papers is illustrated by the field hand Levi, who escaped in 1850 from a plantation near Goldsboro, North Carolina. He stole the manumission deeds of Luke and Ned Hall, free blacks in the neighborhood. Attempting to use Luke Hall's papers to board a train, he was detected and the papers confiscated. But Levi escaped, and with a second set of papers, he journeyed to the hamlet of Black Creek, about twenty miles from Goldsboro in Wayne County, where he inquired of a station master how he could get to Raleigh. This was probably a ploy, Levi's owner James G. Edwards explained, and 'it is suspected that he may still be lurking somewhere in this region'.[46]

The moment in time chosen by slaves to run away was in part determined by individual circumstances – sale of a child, punishment of a wife or husband, a severe whipping, the decision of a master to move, the death of an owner – but a number were biding their time until they were sure that their absence would not be immediately detected or that the weather would not be a hindrance. Among the runaways whose exact departure time could be determined from newspaper notices (611 of 695 in the early period, 1,073 of 1,316 in the late period), there were similar seasonal trends. In both periods, the number of runaways in the autumn months dropped, when harvesting made surveillance close. Between 17 and 18 percent of runaways left between late September and late December. In the winter-spring-summer, the numbers increased. Although there were variations among states, by the later period the numbers of runaways by season, excluding autumn, were almost identical: 296 in the winter, 289 in the spring, and 295 in the summer, about 27 percent per season.

African-born Runaways

In many ways, then, there was a remarkable continuity over a period of seventy years in the profile of runaways. The largest single disparity involved African-born runaways. In the late period, there were only three among the entire population, but in the early period, as indicated previously, there were 90 runaways among the 695, or 13 percent, who were Africans. As would be expected, their profile is unique. Indeed, many of the differences between the two periods were the result of the Africans, who made up a small but significant group of the early runaways.[47]

Even more than the American-born, African-born runaways were predominantly male (88 percent) and described as black or very black (90 percent), but their age groupings were not unlike other runaways, being mostly in their teens and twenties. There were none, however, who were beyond their thirties, and the proportion of those twelve or under was several times that of the American-born, as African-born parents more often took their children with them during flight. None was literate, one was said to have a pass, and one out of eight was said to be bilingual. Besides these differences, among African-born slaves nearly two-thirds (58 of 90) ran away in groups of two or more, and one-third (30 of 90) in groups of five or more; while among American-born slaves, one-third (223 of 605) ran away in groups of two or more and 14 percent (84 of 605) in groups of five or more. Among the African-born to an even greater extent than among creole slaves, those setting off together were members of the same families or kinship groups.

The physical characteristics of African-born slaves were more obvious than for any group of runaways. Described as Mandingo, Ebo, 'Congo', 'Guinea', or African, in most cases, their appearance was not unlike Nuncanna, a slave who lived on a farm in Tennessee. Absconding with two other African-born slaves in 1815, Nuncanna was about thirty years old, with 'very long fore-teeth, appearing sharp as if the ends of them had been filed'. He spoke 'very bad English' and was marked 'by the African mark'. Other African-born runaways also had filed teeth and had marks of their 'nation' on their cheeks, noses, forehead, and chins. The 'Guinea negress' Rosalie in Louisiana, for example, had 'marks of her country' on both sides of her face; while the Congo black Carloe had tattoos 'from the ears to the eyes'.[48]

Even in the 1820s and 1830s, the physical appearance of African-born slaves, now very few in number, had not changed significantly. Rosalia, alias Felicite, a forty-two-year-old woman, was owned by a New Orleans physician. Her master spoke disparagingly of her: she had 'a stupid countenance', spoke almost no English and only 'broken French', and had 'marks of her country' on her cheeks. Despite her owner's remarks, in 1834 she left her employer, crossed the Mississippi River, journeyed to the suburb of Lafayette, then traveled to the various plantations where she had 'many acquaintances'. During her journey, she told anyone who questioned her that she had her owner's permission to seek a new owner. The few who spoke English or had in various ways adjusted to their new environment were still identified by their homeland: Congo-born Rose of Louisiana, who spoke French, English, and Spanish; the 'African negro' Antoine who ran away from auctioneers in New Orleans; and 'African' Billy who ran from a plantation in South Carolina.[49]

Thus, the profile of a runaway reveals a diversity in origin, appearance, language, skills, color, physique, gender, and age. There were African-born blacks, slaves who spoke only French or Spanish, slaves who were highly skilled and privileged, others who worked in the fields. There were young boys and girls, and elderly men and women. There were some who began absconding at age eight and ten; there was a fourteen-year-old youngster who stood four feet seven and a half inches tall; and there were old men described as feeble, scared, crippled, and 'quite grey'.[50]

Yet, there was remarkable continuity over time and in different states in the profile of a runaway. It would probably be difficult to find any group in the United States that changed less over a period of seventy years. When one considers the expansion of slavery across the Appalachians, the growth and expanding economic base of free blacks, and the increase of the slaveholding class, the similarities among runaways – in gender, age, color, physical characteristics, appearance, personality traits, and methods of absconding – seem all the more remarkable. The persistence was not because those who ran away were successful or even because the young men who left in greatest numbers could best endure punishment following capture. Rather, it revealed the nature of slave resistance: those who could best defy the system with even a remote chance of success – young, strong, healthy, intelligent men – continued to do so relentlessly from one generation to the next.

NOTES

1. *North Carolina Minerva and Raleigh Advertiser*, 25 October 1816, in *Stealing a Little Freedom: Advertisements for Slave Runaways in North Carolina, 1791–1840*, ed. Freddie L. Parker (New York, 1994), 120.
2. *Charleston Mercury*, 18, 21, 25 November 1857, 9, 16, 19 December 1857.
3. The statistics here and for the remainder of this chapter are computed from RSDB. The gender delineations are comparable to those found in secondary sources. See Betty Wood, *Women's Work, Men's Work: The Informal Slave Economies of Lowcountry Georgia* (Athens, Ga., 1995), 110; Freddie L. Parker, *Running for Freedom: Slave Runaways in North Carolina, 1775–1840* (New York, 1993), 70. Among 4,265 runaways in the South Carolina and Georgia low country between the 1730s and 1805, Michael Mullin found 867 female slaves, or 20 percent. Michael Mullin, *Africa in America: Slave Acculturation and Resistance in the American South and the British Caribbean, 1736–1831* (Champaign-Urbana, Ill. 1992), 289–91.
4. Records of the General Assembly, Petition of William Fairy to the South Carolina Senate, 1 November 1808, #37, SCDAH. Jack was later tried for assaulting a white man and executed. Records of the General Assembly, Petition of William Villard to the South Carolina Senate, 23 November 1813, #107, SCDAH. The incident occurred in 1812.
5. Jeffrey R. Young, 'Ideology and Death on a Savannah River Rice Planation, 1833–1867: Paternalism amidst "a Good Supply of Disease and Pain,"' *JSH* 59 (November 1993), 681.
6. Parker, *Running for Freedom*, 71; Deborah White, 'Female Slaves: Sex Roles and Status in the Antebellum Plantation South', *Journal of Family History* 8 (Fall 1983), 251; and *Ar'n't I a Woman? Female Slaves in the Plantation South* (New York, 1985), 70–6; Eugene D. Genovese, *Roll, Jordan, Roll: The World the Slaves Made* (New York, 1974), 649; Stanley W. Campbell, 'Runaway Slaves', in *Dictionary of Afro-American Slavery*, ed. Randall M. Miller and John David Smith (New York, 1988), 650; Judith Kelleher Schafer, 'New Orleans Slavery in 1850 as Seen in Advertisements', *JSH* 47 (February 1981), 43–4.
7. Records for Letty can be found in *Nashville Whig*, 6, 13 December 1814; for Nancy in *New Orleans Bee*, 23 September 1828. The advertisement ran through 12 November 1828. Information on Sawney in Records of the General Assembly, Petition of Samuel Linton, Sr., to the South Carolina General Assembly, 1817, #136, SCDAH; on Delph in Records of the General Assembly, Petition of Joseph Wardlaw to the South Carolina House of Representatives, 21 March 1817, #105, SCDAH. Wardlaw sought permission to bring Delph into the state following the passage of

a law prohibiting the importation of slaves for sale and speculation. Discussion of Angeline in *Richmond Enquirer*, 5 August 1836, cited by Herbert Gutman in *The Black Family in Slavery and Freedom, 1750–1925* (New York, 1976), 264.

8. For advertisements concerning black youngsters, see *Tennessee Republican Banner* [Nashville], 13 March 1838, 27 December 1839; *Alexandria Gazette, Commercial and Political*, 30 March 1815, in *Advertisements for Runaway Slaves in Virginia, 1801–1820*, ed. Daniel Meaders (New York, 1997), 230; *Richmond Enquirer*, 13 April 1816, in Meaders, ed., *Advertisements for Runaway Slaves in Virginia*, 292; also see Wilma King, *Stolen Childhood: Slave Youth in Nineteenth Century America* (Bloomington, 1995), 120. Alice is described in Baltimore City Register of Wills (Petitions), Petition of John Ven Ness Philip to the Orphans Court of Baltimore City, 5 September 1860, reel M-11,026, SC, MSA; Affidavit of Henrietta Johnson, 4 September 1860, with ibid. Catherine and Henry in *New Orleans Bee*, 16 March 1831; *New Orleans Bee*, 3 July 1833, with the latter notice running continuously through 30 September 1833. Water Scott in *New Orleans Bee*, 8 April 1841; Elias in *Charleston Mercury*, 15 December 1828.

9. *New Orleans Bee*, 12 August 1830; *Charleston Mercury and Morning Advertiser*, 29 December 1823; *Charleston Mercury*, 9 August 1828; notice running through 6 September 1828; *Charleston Mercury*, 7 June 1832; *Richmond Enquirer*, 14 May 1850; *Charleston Mercury*, 21 August 1832; *Charleston Mercury*, 11 December 1832.

10. *Richmond Enquirer*, 15 September 1804, 10 October 1804, 13, 15, 20 December 1804, 22 February 1805, 19 April 1805, 3 May 1805, 4 June 1805, 28 January 1806, 4, 11, 13, 15, 25, February 1806, 8 April 1806. Descriptions of the less black in *Richmond Enquirer*, 4 February 1808; of the very black in *Richmond Enquirer*, 15 May 1807; *New Orleans Picayune*, 4 February 1838, 30 June 1838, 14 July 1838, 7, 16, 19 June 1839, 3 July 1839, 10, 11, 31 August 1839, 3 October 1839, 5, 11, 13 December 1839, 2 January 1840, 13 March 1840; of Abel and Abram in *Charleston Mercury*, 11 January 1855.

11. For the census breakdown of blacks and mulattoes in 1850 in the United States, see Joel Williamson, *New People: Miscegenation and Mulattoes in the United States* (New York, 1980), 24–33; also see Edward Byron Reuter, *The Mulatto in the United States: Including a Study of the Role of Mixed-Blood Races. Throughout the World* (Boston, 1918).

12. Description of Coleman in *Tennessee Republican Banner*, 22, 24, 25, 26 February 1840; of Bonaparte in *Richmond Enquirer*, 20 June 1851; of Guy in *Tennessee Republican Banner*, 22 August 1842; of John in *Tennessee Republican Banner*, 25 May 1839; *Richmond Enquirer*, 26 March 1805, 12 December 1805, 7, 14 January 1806; *Tennessee Gazette*, 31 March 1802; *Nashville Whig*, 27 April 1814, 3, 11 May 1814; *New Orleans Picayune*, 7 April 1839; *Richmond Enquirer*, 20 February 1855. In his travels in the South, F. L. Olmsted said he read about one hundred advertisements for runaways who were 'so white they might be mistaken for white persons'. Frederick Law Olmsted, *A Journey in the Seaboard Slave State, With Remarks on Their Economy* (New York, 1856), 640–1. Discussion of Mabin in *Columbus Enquirer*, 9 February 1833, cited in William G. Proctor, Jr., 'Slavery in Southwest Georgia', *Georgia Historical Quarterly* 49 (March 1965), 6.

13. South Carolina descriptions in *Charleston Mercury and Morning Advertiser*, 4 April 1822, 25 October 1822, 26 November 1823, 29 December 1823, 27 January 1824, 30 September 1824, 18, 28 April 1825, 3 May 1825; *Charleston Mercury*, 1 July 1828, 20 February 1830, 17 July 1830, 14 January 1831, 27 May 1831. Virginia ones in *Richmond Enquirer*, 28 January 1806; *Richmond Enquirer*, 4 February 1808; *Richmond Enquirer*, 23 November 1852, 14 January 1853; *Richmond Enquirer*, 15 September 1804, 10 October 1804, 13, 15, 20 December 1804,

Estimated Heights Among Runaways: Early Period

	Number of Females	Percent in Category	Number of Males	Percent in Category
Short	21	53	71	20
Average	13	32	136	39
Tall	6	15	142	41
Total	40	100	349	100

Estimated Heights Among Runaways: Late Period

	Number of Females	Percent in Category	Number of Males	Percent in Category
Short	77	51	153	22
Average	58	38	275	39
Tall	17	11	275	39
Total	152	100	703	100

22 February 1805, 19 April 1805, 3 May 1805, 4 June 1805, 28 January 1806, 4, 11, 13, 15, 25 February 1806, 8 April 1806; *Richmond Enquirer*, 21 February 1806, 11 March 1806; *Richmond Enquirer*, 27 May 1806; *Richmond Enquirer*, 26 July 1808; *Richmond Enquirer*, 20 February 1852; *Richmond Enquirer*, 11 February 1853; *Richmond Enquirer*, 20 July 1849; *Richmond Enquirer*, 10 August 1849.

14. *New Orleans Bee*, 16, 18 October 1834, 14, 29 November 1834, 10 February 1835, 7 March 1835, 11, 14 May 1835, 8, 20, 23 June 1835, 1 July 1835, 21 August 1835, 6, 12 January 1836, 12 March 1836. Use of 'griff' in *New Orleans Picayune*, 4 February 1838, 30 June 1838, 14 July 1838, 7, 16, 19 June 1839, 3 July 1839, 10, 11, 31 August 1839, 3 October 1839, 5, 11, 13 December 1839, 2 January 1840, 13 March 1840; *New Orleans Bee*, 8 April 1841; quote about Joe in *New Orleans Bee*, 19 March 1835.

15. Slave owners sometimes used general terms to describe the height of runaways: short, medium size, tall; when these are combined with specific estimates, height categories include the following:

In 1857, an Edisto Island, South Carolina, planter described his slave Joe as 'short – say five feet six inches'. *Charleston Mercury*, 19 September 1857, 1, 6, 8, 10 October 1857. Also see the 27 September 1856 edition for a comment on height. A Virginia master described his six-foot runaway as a man of 'remarkable' height. *Richmond Enquirer*, 20 July 1852.

16. Quote of 'very remarkable lumps' in *Virginia Herald*, 8 January [1805], with Legislative Petitons, Petition of Mary Bussell to the Virginia General Assembly, 14 December 1812, Stafford County, Oversize, VSL; 'white swelling' in *Richmond Enquirer*, 15 May 1807; *Tennessee Gazette* [Nashville], 12, 19, 26 May 1802, 9, 16 June 1802; quote about deformed foot in *Nashville Whig*, 27 December 1814, 4, 10, 17 January 1815; *Nashville Whig*, 12 December 1815; 'web on one of his eyes' in *New Orleans Bee*, 17 November 1834; 'lame in the left knee' in *Charleston Mercury and Morning Advertiser*, 4 April 1822; 'one-half of her right foot' in *Charleston Mercury and Morning Advertiser*, 2 June 1825; quote about diseased left thigh in *Charleston Mercury*, 29 May 1830; *New Orleans Picayune*, 17 July 1840, 1 August 1840.

17. *Richmond Enquirer*, 13 June 1807; *Nashville Whig*, 27 April 1814, 3, 11 May 1814; *Nashville Whig*, 22 November 1814, 6 December 1814; *New Orleans Bee*, 28 November 1832; *New Orleans Bee*, 14 November 1834; *Charleston Mercury and Morning Advertiser*, 29 December 1823; *Louisiana Journal* [St. Francisville], 26 November 1826, in *A Documentary History of American Industrial Society*, ed. Ulrich B. Phillips (Cleveland, Ohio, 1910), 2:88.

18. *Richmond Enquirer*, 13 January 1857; quotes about William in *New Orleans Picayune*, 7 June 1839.

19. *Richmond Enquirer*, 30 December 1807; *Georgia Express* [Athens], 17 December 1808, in Phillips, ed., *A Documentary History*, 2, 92–3; *Nashville Whig*, 8, 15 August 1815.

20. *New Orleans Bee*, 21 October 1833; *New Orleans Bee*, 2 May 1835; *New Orleans Bee*, 11 November 1835. See also *New Orleans Bee*, 11–29 February 1828, 1–31 March 1828, 1–30 April 1828, 1–24 May 1828, 24 June 1831, 28 November 1832, 1 December 1832, 7 January 1833, 28 August 1833, 4 September 1833, 29 January 1834, 22 April 1834, 13 May 1834, 5–20 June 1834, 14 November 1834, 3–31 December 1834, 3–15 January 1835, 2 May 1835, 8 June 1835, 11 November 1835.

21. Records of the District Court, Natchitoches Parish, Louisiana, William H. Strong vs. Clement Rachal, 12 November 1836, #1,474, Parish Court House, Natchitoches, Louisiana.

22. *New Orleans Bee*, 21 October 1830; Peter Kolchin, *American Slavery, 1619–1877* (New York, 1993), 114; *Richmond Enquirer*, 26 March 1805, 12 December 1805; *Nashville Whig*, 4, 11, 25 January 1814, 28 June 1814; *New Orleans Bee*, 1 May 1841, 24 March 1841.

23. *Charleston Mercury and Morning Advertiser*, 4 October 1824, 10 November 1825; *Charleston Mercury*, 14 September 1829. Description of Celia in *Nashville Whig*, 27 April 1814, 3, 11 May 1814; Solomon in *Nashville Whig*, 15 August 1815, 5 September 1815; quote of 'negro cloth round jacket' in *Charleston Mercury and Morning Advertiser*, 27 January 1824; 'large stock of Clothing' in *Charleston Mercury*, 14 January 1831. 'Myal probably took them' in *Tennessee Republican Banner*, 7 April 1838.

24. *Virginia Herald*, 8 January [1805], with Legislative Petitions, Petition of Mary Bussell to the Virginia General Assembly, 14 December 1812, Stafford County, Oversize, VSA; *Nashville Whig*, 8, 15 August, 1815; *Charleston Mercury*, 11 October 1830; *New Orleans Bee*, 14 May 1835; *New Orleans Picayune*, 30 April 1839; *Richmond Enquirer*, 13 August 1805; *Richmond Enquirer*, 12 September 1806.

25. *Richmond Enquirer*, 13 December 1804; *New Orleans Bee*, 25 May 1832; *New Orleans Bee*, 30 August 1832; *Richmond Enquirer*, 13 October 1804; *Charleston Mercury*, 14 January 1828.

26. Mention of large wardrobe in *New Orleans Bee*, 13 December 1832; *New Orleans Picayune*, 28 August 1839; *Charleston Mercury*, 27 September 1832; *New Orleans Picayune*, 5 December 1839; *Charleston Mercury*, 28 November 1827. For the dress of slave women in New Orleans, see *New Orleans Bee*, 22 April 1834, 21 January 1841. Quotes about what others took in *Charleston Mercury and Morning Advertiser*, 3 May 1825; *New Orleans Picayune*, 5 December 1839; *New Orleans Bee*, 30 August 1832; of New Orleans man in *New Orleans Bee*, 8 October 1834. The notice ran continuously through 9 December 1834.

27. *Richmond Enquirer*, 13 October 1804; *Richmond Enquirer*, 13 December 1804, 13 August 1805; *Nashville Whig*, 15 August 1815, 5 September 1815; *Charleston Mercury and Morning Advertiser*, 24 December 1822; description of Cyrus in *Charleston Mercury*, 18 March 1828; quote about Johns Island slave in *Charleston Mercury and Morning Advertiser*, 24 December 1822. She ran away 'about the middle of November' and the notice appeared through 17 May 1823.

28. *Charleston Mercury*, 5 December 1829; *New Orleans Picayune*, 28 April 1837. The notice ran continuously through 28 August 1837. The $500 reward was almost certainly a misprint.

29. For a comparison with the pre-Revolutionary generation of runaways, see Shane White and Graham White, 'Slave Hair and African American Culture in the Eighteenth and Nineteenth Centuries', *JSH* 61 (February 1995), 66. In the mid-eighteenth century, a number of male slaves boasted 'large bushy' heads of hair, hair worn 'remarkable high', or 'a large quantity of long wool'; female slaves also had 'long black Hair', remarkably long hair, bushy heads of hair. Descriptions of male hair in *Richmond Enquirer*, 22 November 1805, 19 May 1807, 18 May 1807, 10 June 1807. In the early period, among 695 slaves advertised, 4 women and 34 men were described as having unusual hair. In the later period, among 1,316 slaves advertised, 18 women and 79 men were similarly described.

30. *Richmond Enquirer*, 13 December 1804; *Tennessee Republican Banner*, 21 August 1839; *Charleston Mercury*, 1 July 1828; *Charleston Mercury*, 29 August 1828; descriptions of other runaways in *Richmond Enquirer*, 4 March 1808; *Charleston Mercury*, 3 October 1831, 25 July 1832; *Richmond Enquirer*, 29 September 1854, 13 October 1854; *Tennessee Gazette*, 31 May 1806; *Tennessee Republican Banner*, 27 February 1840, 31 July 1851; *New Orleans Bee*, 29 March 1831, 4, 5, 6, 7, 8 April 1831, 27 May 1831, 9 August 1831, 19 July 1832, 23–30 March 1833, 1–13 April 1833; New *Orleans Picayune*, 7 June 1839; *Charleston Mercury*, 17 September 1832. Quote of 'very smart and well calculated' in *Richmond Enquirer*, 13 October 1854.

31. *Richmond Enquirer*, 21 October 1806; *Charleston Mercury*, 14 June 1826.

32. Notices for slow speakers in *Richmond Enquirer*, 23 December 1853. Quotes cited in *New Orleans Bee*, 25 April 1834, 19 March 1835; *New Orleans Picayune*, 2 August 1838. See also *Charleston Mercury and Morning Advertiser*, 20 October 1824; *Charleston Mercury*, 12 April 1832, 7 May 1832, 29 June 1832, 27 October 1832; *New Orleans Bee*, 25 April 1834, 19 March 1835, 15 July 1835; *New Orleans Picayune*, 2 August 1838; 30 July 1838. Quotes about Luck in *New Orleans Bee*, 30 September 1833; the 'Savannah dialect' is mentioned in New Orleans Bee, 17 February 1836; the 'accent of a negress' is noted in *New Orleans Picayune*, 7 April 1839; the Virginia 'brogue' is found in *Richmond Enquirer*, 31 May 1853.

33. Description of Celestine in *New Orleans Bee*, 11 February 1828, 9 April 1828; also see *New Orleans Bee*, 11 January 1831, 10, 19, 28, 29 March 1831. Descriptions of multilingual slave in *New Orleans Bee*, 21 October 1828; with the advertisement running until 12 November 1828; of American slaves in *New Orleans Bee*, 11 January 1831, 10, 19, 28, 29 March 1831; of Hons in *Staunton Eagle*, 19 November 1807.

34. *Tennessee Gazette*, 20 July 1803; *Tennessee Gazette*, 24, 31 August 1803, 7, 14, 21 September 1803; *Nashville Whig*, 2, 9 August 1814; *Nashville Whig*, 27 December 1814, 4, 10, 17 January 1815; *New Orleans Bee*, 28 August 1830; *New Orleans Bee*, 28 April 1834; *New Orleans Picayune*, 15 May 1839, 28 May 1840; *Richmond Enquirer*, 8 September 1854.

35. A few owners also described their runaways as having 'rather dull countenance', 'a broad dull face', 'a downcast, stupid look'. *Richmond Enquirer*, 22 February 1805; *Charleston Mercury and Morning Advertiser*, 4 April 1822; *Charleston Mercury*, 29 May 1830.

Maryland law required owners of term slaves to obtain court permission to sell them out of the state. The attitudes of owners toward rebellious slaves are therefore revealed in some detail. See, e.g., Frederick County Court (Petitions), Petition of Henry Kemp to the County Court, 8 March 1836, reel 11,024, SC, MSA; Howard County Register of Wills (Petitions), Petition of A. L. Mackey to the Orphans Court, 1854, reel M-11,024, SC, MSA; Howard County Register of Wills (Petitions),

Petition of George Richardson to the Orphans Court, 7 August 1855, reel M-11,024, SC.

Quotes about 'utterly disobedient' slave in Anne Arundel County Register of Wills (Petitions and Orders) 1851–60, 458–60, Petition of James S. Wilson to the Orphans Court, 16 April 1858, reel #CR 63,128–1, MSA; about Eliza in Anne Arundel County Register of Wills (Petitions and Orders) 1851–60, 122–3, Petition of Charles R. Steward to the Orphans Court, 24 October 1854, reel #CR 63,128–1, MSA.

36. The 'violent and determined temper' quote is found in Baltimore County Register of Wills (Petitions and Orders), Petition of Richard Hutchens to the Orphans Court, 22 June 1853, reel M-11,020, SC, MSA.

37. Records of the Equity Court, Richland District, South Carolina, Mary Cobb vs. Ann Reynolds, 13 January 1819, microfilm reel #153, SCDAH.

38. Records of the District Court, San Augustine County, Texas, Charles W. Brady vs. Tempe Price, 16 October 1856, Case #1,132, East Texas Research Center, Stephen F. Austin University, Nacogdoches, Texas; Testimony of Gilbert B. McIver, 13 September 1856. The testimony about the earlier incident was allowed in a case involving another overseer, Charles W. Brady, who killed Miles and then sued the slave owner for back salary.

39. Frederick County Court (Petitions), Petition of John Wood to the County Court, 31 October 1838, reel M-11,024, SC, MSA. Wood received permission to sell Peter's unexpired term 'to any person within or without this State', but the court required that Peter be furnished with a copy of his manumission deed. Order of the Court, October Term 1838, with ibid.

40. Discussion of spectacular escapes in Richard J. M. Blackett, *Beating Against the Barriers: Biographical Essays in Nineteenth-Century Afro-American History* (Baton Rouge, 1986), 87–90; Larry Gara, *The Liberty Line: The Legend of the Underground Railroad* (Lexington, 1961), 49–50. For slaves on trains, see Jenny Bourne Wahl, 'The Bondsman's Burden: An Economic Analysis of the Jurisprudence of Slaves and Common Carriers', *Journal of Economic History* 53 (September 1993), 511–15.

41. Excluding the thirty runaways in the early period who were either stolen or absconded from Amelia Island, East Florida, and advertised in the *Nashville Whig*, 7 December 1813, the proportion of runaways in the category of four or more slaves would narrow between the two periods. Nonetheless, 17 percent in the early period and 5 percent in the later period were in this category.

42. As previously noted, according to one estimate, 6 percent of rural slaves and 31 percent of urban slaves were on hire in 1860. In addition, about three-fourths of adult slaves were field hands, and by the 1850s in the deep South, with the intense labor shortage, increasing numbers of skilled slaves were pressed into field labor. Thus, the 15 percent skilled runaways was probably slightly higher than the percentage of skilled slaves in the general population. About 5 percent of slaves were probably literate or semi-literate. See Kolchin, *American Slavery*, 105, 110, 142.

43. Legislative Petitions, Petition of Nathaniel Wilkinson to the Virginia General Assembly, 7 December 1795, Henrico County, VSA.

44. Quotes about appearance of slaves with fake passes in *Charleston Mercury*, 12 September 1828; *Richmond Enquirer*, 5 September 1806. Eve absconded on 15 October 1805. Forging papers for slaves was a serious offense, but it was rarely prosecuted. In the first thirty-eight years of the nineteenth century, in the entire state of Virginia, only one person went to the penitentiary for furnishing a slave with false papers. Philip J. Schwarz, *Twice Condemned, Slaves and the Criminal Laws of Virginia, 1705–1865* (Baton Rouge, 1988), 302–4.

Other quotes in *Nashville Whig*, 27 April 1814, 3, 11 May 1814; *Charleston Mercury and Morning Advertiser*, 26 June 1822.

45. Quotes about literate slaves in *Richmond Enquirer*, 24 May 1805; *Richmond Enquirer*, 12 August 1853, with the notice running continuously through 2 December 1853; *Charleston Mercury*, 27 February 1830; *Richmond Enquirer*, 22 February 1805.

46. *Richmond Enquirer*, 27 August 1850. Levi absconded on 29 June 1850; the notice ran through 18 October 1850.

47. For roughly comparable evidence from the Chesapeake Bay region and the Carolina low country during the eighteenth century, see Michael Mullin, *Africa in America: Slave Acculturation and Resistance in the American South and the British Caribbean, 1736–1831* (Champaign-Urbana, Ill., 1992), 289–91.

48. The male stonecutter named June, who spoke 'tolerable English', for example, was described only as 'a native of Africa'. *Alexandria Daily Advertiser, Commercial and Political*, 23 October 1804, in Meaders, ed., *Advertisements for Runaway Slaves in Virginia*, 41. Quotes about Nuncanna in *Nashville Whig*, 29 November 1815, 12, 19 December 1815, 9, 16, 23 January 1816, 7, 27 February 1816, 5, 12 March 1816, 4, 25 June 1816, 2 July 1816. There were twenty-eight slaves in the RSDB for the early period who were not born in the United States. Their origins included various islands in the Caribbean, South America (one was cited as Portuguese), and not known. Because of their small number and diverse origins, they were excluded. Descriptions of other Africans in *New Orleans Bee*, 12 August 1830; *New Orleans Bee*, 25 April 1834; *New Orleans Bee*, 17 March 1835.

49. Quotes about Rosalia in *New Orleans Bee*, 21 July 1834. Identification of Africans in *New Orleans Bee*, 16 April 1835; *New Orleans Bee*, 7 January 1836, Antoine ran away on the 20 November 1835 and the notice continued until 14 January 1836; *Charleston Mercury*, 6 June 1827.

50. Descriptions by height in *Charleston Mercury and Morning Advertiser*, 3 December 1824; *Charleston Mercury*, 7 June 1832; *Richmond Enquirer*, 14 May 1850.

DOCUMENT 1: RUNAWAY SLAVE ADVERTISEMENTS

Examples of newspaper advertisements, the main source of information about runaway slaves. These notices typically give information about the appearance, clothes, gestures and supposed whereabouts of fugitive slaves.

Virginia Gazette *(Purdie & Dixon), August 12, 1773*

RUN away from the Subscriber, in Sussex County, the 5th of July last, a Negro Man named QUOMONY, about twenty three Years of Age, five Feet nine or ten Inches high, very black, and well made. He had the Misfortune some Time ago to cut one of his Feet near the Joint of his great Toe, with an Axe, which occasions a large Scar, and was not well when he went away. He has two Lumps on his left Shoulder Blade; occasioned by a whip, and one on his right Shoulder. As I am apprehensive that he will endeavour to get on Board some Vessel, and make his Escape out of the Colony, all Masters of Vessels are forewarned from entertaining or harbouring the said Runaway, at their Peril. To any Person that brings him home I will give 20 s. if taken over 20 Miles, if 30 Miles 30 s. and if farther, in Proportion to the Distance; but if it should not be convenient to bring him home, if he is secured in any Jail, and intelligence given to me, I will reward the Taker up for his Trouble, besides what the Law allows.

THOMAS PEEBLES.

Charleston South-Carolina Gazette and Country Journal, *June 28, 1774*

SIXTY POUNDS REWARD.

RUN AWAY the 20th instant, four negro men, viz. SIMON and NED, carpenters; Simon is a well made black fellow about 5 feet 10 inches high, and about 28 years of age, one of his feet has been split with an ax, and is grown up with a ridge: Ned, is a short well made fellow, of the Angola country, about 5 feet 4 inches high and about 27 years of age; he has several scars on his head. I do hereby promise a reward of TWENTY POUNDS for each of the above negroes, to any person that will deliver them to me at my plantation at Horse-Savannah: They carried their carpenters tools with them, in order to deceive people who may meet them. The other two negroes are sawyers; the one named BOB is a well set fellow, near 6 feet high, his knees pretty close, and walks battle hamm'd, has very large feet, and a scar on his face, this country born, about 24 years of age: ABEL, is about 5 feet 8 inches high, this country born, has weak eyes, and is well shaped. I will give a reward of TEN POUNDS currency, for each of the two last mentioned negroes, besides all reasonable charges, to any person that

Lathan A. Windley, *Runaway Slave Advertisements: A Documentary History from the 1730s to 1790*, 4 vols (Westport, CT: Greenwood Press, 1983), vol. 1, p. 138, vol. 3, pp. 694–5.

will apprehend and deliver them to me at my plantation aforesaid; and do hereby offer a further reward of FIFTY POUNDS, to any person or persons, that will give me certain information of their being harboured by any white person or persons, and TEN POUNDS if harboured by a negro, on their being convicted.

SAMUEL WAINWRIGHT.

June 24, 1774.

Document 2: Petition about a Slave Runaway

This petition to the Baltimore County Orphans Court, Maryland, in 1861 provides details of an inveterate runaway slave boy.

Petition to The Baltimore County Orphans Court, 1861 Petision

To the Oneable orpants court of Baltimore county your pertisiner bought a prentis negro boy isaac smuthers of Joshwa Zimmerman of Bal Co. may 20th 1858 and ratified by the said court the said negro boy has runway from our pertisiner 7 Seven different times as follows No 1 first time in november 1858 and was gone some four weeks and was taken up by one of the police of Baltimore No 2 second time in april 1859 and was gone some seven or eight days, and taken up by Mr Sheckels of annarundle county no 3 third time in june 1859 and was gone 6 days and taken up by Edward Bauldwin of annarandle county and brought home No 4 fourth time in april 1860, and was gone two months, and taken up by your petisioner in Baltimore

No 5 fifth time the said boy runaway the 3th day after he was brought home and your pertisioner sent after him and overtook him on his to road to Baltimor[e] No sixth time in december 1860 and was gone 4 weeks and was taken up by his [petitioner's] father in Baltimore, and was taken sick from a heavy could [cold] that he got by laying out of nights during the time he was runaway and some three of four moths before the said boy was able to worke

No 7 seventh time runaway was gone 5 or Six days and was taken up by an officer of annarundle county and brought home chargeing a fee of Six dollars the said negro boy Isaac has cost your pertisiner great deal of trouble and lost time your pertisioner asks of the Oneable Court for and extension of time cirvice of the said negro boy isaac as will pay for loss of time runing way and sick by runing way, the absent time of the said negro 3 months & 18 days excluson of the 4 months Sick and unable to worke

William Burtons bill taken up negro 6.00 Your pertisioners 4 diferent times going to Baltimore after the said negro boy wich is 24 miles each way, for the court to say what it is worth the court will please notice that this negro boy is verey small at his age, his cirvices are but small

Yours respectfuly
James S. Wilson

[Source: Baltimore County Register of Wills (Petitions and Order) James Wilson vs. Isaac Smithers, 30 October 1861, reel M-11,020, Schweninger Collection, MSA. Smithers's term of service was extended twelve months.]

John Hope Franklin and Loren Schweninger, *Runaway Slaves: Rebels on the Plantation* (New York: Oxford University Press, 1999), pp. 313–14.

DOCUMENT 3: AFFIDAVIT OF A TENNESSEE FUGITIVE SLAVE

During the Civil War, civil officers continued to enforce Tennessee's slave code until September 1864 when Governor Andrew Johnson ordered that slaves should henceforth be regarded as free people of colour. Before then Tennessee slaves claimed freedom at great risk because they lacked protection from the Emancipation Act. This affidavit was made by a fugitive slave who found himself in those difficult circumstances.

[Knoxville, Tenn, March 30, 1864] *Statement of*
'Jim' Heiskell

My name is Jim; I have been living on Bull run, with a man by the name of Pierce; they called him Cromwell Pierce. I run off from him nearly two months ago, because he treated me so mean: he half starved and whipped me. I was whipped three or four times a week, sometimes with a cowhide, and sometimes with a hickory. He put so much work on me, I could not do it; chopping & hauling wood and lumber logs. I am about thirteen years old. I got a pretty good meal at dinner, but he only gave us a half pint of milk for breakfast and supper, with cornbread. I ran away to town; I had a brother 'Bob' living in Knoxville, and other boys I knew. I would have staid on the plantation if I had been well used. I wanted also to see some pleasure in town. I hired myself to Capt. Smith as a servant, and went to work as a waiter in Quarter Master Winslow's office as a waiter for the mess. After Capt. Winslow went home, I went to live with Bob, helping him.

Last Friday just after dinner, I saw Pierce Mr. Heiskell's overseer. He caught me on Gay street, he ran after me, and carried me down Cumberl and street to Mr. Heiskell's house. Mr. Heiskell, his wife and two sons, and a daughter were in the house. Mr. Heiskell, his wife and two sons, and a daughter were in the house. Mr. Heiskell asked me what made me run away; he grabbed me by the back of the ears, and jerked me down on the floor on my face; Mr Pierce held me & Mr. Heiskell put irons on my legs. Mr. Heiskell took me by the hair of my head, and Mr. Pierce took me around my body, they carried me upstairs, and then Mr. Heiskell dragged me into a room by my hair. They made me stand up, and then they laid me down on my belly & pulled off my breeches as far as they could, and turned my shirt and jacket up over my head. (I heard Mr Heiskell ask for the cowhide before he started with me upstairs.) Mr. Pierce held my legs, and Mr. Heiskell got a straddle of me, and whipped me with the rawhide on my back & legs. Mr Pierce is a large man, and very strong. Mr. Heiskell rested two or three times, and begun again. I hollowed – 'O, Lord' all the time. They whipped me, it seemed to me, half an hour. They then told me to get up and dress,

Ira Berlin, Barbara J. Fields, Thavolia Glymph, Joseph P. Reidy, Leslie S. Rowland (eds), *Freedom: A Documentary History of Emancipation, 1861–1867. Series 1. Volume 1. The Destruction of Slavery* (Cambridge: Cambridge University Press, 1985), pp. 320–2.

and said if I did'nt behave myself up there they would come up again and whip me again at night. The irons were left on my legs. Mr. Heiskell came up at dark and asked me what that 'yallow nigger was talking to me about'. He meant my brother Bob, who had been talking to me opposite the house. I was standing up and when he (Mr. Heiskell) asked me about the 'yaller nigger', he kicked me with his right foot on my hip and knocked me over on the floor, as the irons were on my feet, I could not catch myself. I knew my brother Bob was around the house trying to get me out. About one hour by sun two soldiers came to the house, one staid & the other went away. I saw them through the window. They had sabres. I thought they had come to guard me to keep Bob from getting me. I heard Bob whisling, and I went to the window and looked through the curtain. Bob told me to hoist the window, put something under it & swing out of the window. I did as my brother told me, and hung by my hands. Bob said 'Drop', but I said I was afraid I would hurt myself. Bob said 'Wait a minute and I will get a ladder'. He brought a ladder and put it against the house, under the window. I got halfway down before they hoisted the window; I fell & Bob caught me and run off with me in his arms. I saw Mr. Pierce sitting at the window, he had a double-barreled gun in his hands. By the time I could count three I heard a gun fired two or three times, quick, I heard Mr. Pierce call 'Jim' 'Jim' and the guards hollered 'halt; halt'! I had no hat or shoes on. We both hid, and laid flat on the ground. I saw the guard, running around there hunting for us. After lying there until the guards had gone away, we got up and Bob carried me to a friend's house. I had the irons on my legs. I got some supper and staid there until next day. My irons were taken off by a colored man, who carried me to the hospital. I am now employed working in the hospital N⁰ 1.

his
– signed – Jim × Heiskell –

9

PLANTERS AND PROSLAVERY

INTRODUCTION

Slavery in the United States lasted until 1865 largely because it was central to the economy, society and culture of the South, the natural home for most proslavery advocates. Modern studies have emphasised the variegated nature of white society south of the Mason–Dixon line. Large planters and small planters lived side by side with plain folk who were not slaveholders. Generalising from the study of one Texas county, Campbell (1987) has suggested that southern white society should be divided into five classes: large planters holding more than twenty slaves, small planters with ten to nineteen slaves, yeoman farmers, poor whites and non-farmers. All these groups came to regard slavery as essential to their regional identity. Many southern whites regarded the preservation of slavery as worth the price of secession in 1860 and the establishment of a Confederacy to fight for their cause. But exactly why southern whites fiercely argued for the preservation of slavery has caused continuing historical debate. Smith (1998) provides a brief, clear introduction to the main areas of dispute. Chapter 7 of Parish (1989) considers the historiographical state of play on planter dominance and southern white democracy.

Collins (1985) provides a useful overview of the main features of white society in the antebellum South. In thematic chapters dealing with cotton, Indians, blacks, mobility, government and so forth, he emphasises the variety found in the South but also the social bonds that drew white southerners together. Boles (1983) treats the southern states as a biracial society.

He focuses on the humanity and continuing African heritage of slaves but also gives attention to the plantation world. Large slaveholding was concentrated among a small minority of the white population there. Moderate and large-scale slaveholders controlled a disproportionate share of the wealth and political offices in the South. The white population was bound together by its sense of racial superiority. 'Racial fears, not planter hegemony', in Boles's view, 'were at the forefront of the southern determination to maintain slavery in the face of northern opposition' (p. 78). Interestingly, however, most leading proslavery advocates of the 1840s and 1850s played down the racial factor in their dissection of slavery.

Oakes (1982) points out that most slaveholders in the South owned five slaves or less, but he argues that they were as imbued with the right to hold chattel property as the leading planters. He underscores the vitality of slavery in the 1840s and 1850s, decades when slaveholders believed their prosperity was divinely inspired. The widespread incidence of Evangelical Protestantism throughout the southern states was central to this belief. Freedom seemed impossible to southern whites without slavery. The territorial claims they pressed for the expansion of slavery in mid-century showed their belief in hoping to secure the continuance of the 'peculiar institution' through westward expansion.

In a broader study of the Old South, Oakes (1990) examines how power and freedom – or the denial thereof – infused nearly every aspect of antebellum southern life. He also explores the connections between the growth of European capitalism and American slavery, placing the southern United States within a larger framework of exchange and consumption. A more explicit link between the values of the slaveholding class and the political culture of the Old South is the main theme addressed in Greenberg (1985), who sees slavery as inextricably linked with a distinct set of political values and practices. The political culture of slavery, Greenberg contends, helped to shape the form and content of the conflict with the North. Wherever planters congregated, especially in the Deep South, the political culture of slavery pervaded their ideas and actions.

For over thirty years, Genovese (1969, 1992) has been at the forefront of studies dealing with the paternalistic nature of slaveowners in the South. His Marxist analyses, influenced by Gramscian notions of hegemony, have argued in favour of a dual process of accommodation by planters and resistance by slaves. In the former study he argues that proslavery thought served as an ideological basis for the hegemony of a master class that held power in a pre-bourgeois southern society. In the latter, he highlights the contradiction between the slaveholders' commitment to material progress and greater freedom while upholding the attachment to slavery as an essential part of the southern social order. Genovese's work emphasises the paternalism of the planter class. Some historians dissent from this interpretative position. Tadman (1996), for example, reconsiders the nature of planter paternalism. He finds this an inappropriate term for master–slave relations in the Old South because of a sharp divide between the planters' self-image and their behaviour towards slaves. For Tadman, slaves rejected many aspects of planter paternalism; accommodation to their values was strictly limited.

Many broad themes about the society and culture of the South need to be tested with detailed local studies. Harris (1985) offers one of the best available. His focus is the region in Georgia and South Carolina around the hub of Augusta. He shows that the main cohesion found among the whites in that region, who had wide inequalities in wealth and social position, was an ideological one. This was not simply racial prejudice but rather the fusion of a commitment to racial slavery with a type of conservative republicanism that justified the existing social order to whites. To preserve white southern culture, it was essential to resist the assaults of northern abolitionists and free soil advocates. Such an ideology rested on the notion, also claimed for revolutionary Virginia, that white liberty and republican virtue depended on black enslavement. The crucial value that these whites defended was personal independence.

Wayne (1990) also argues in favour of white southerners forging a consensus that the continuance of slavery was essential for their own liberty and equality. This ideological stance depended on the view that blacks were innately suited to slavery. Wayne shows that this consensus emerged in the 1830s and continued through to the Civil War. The plantocracy could persuade less affluent southerners that this racial polarity was also in their interest because of a broad distribution of landownership among whites and by propagating the view that blacks needed to remain enslaved because they needed strict control and moral guidance. Access to land and the racial justification of slavery allowed planters to persuade the plain folk of the Old South that it lay in all white southerners' interests to allow planters to act as spokesmen for the preserving the duality in social relations. Shore (1986) is also concerned with the ways in which the planter elite justified and maintained their social status in the South, but he focuses on their cultivation of a leisured, refined southern civilisation in a positive light based on the thriving agricultural economy associated with slavery.

Dusinberre (2003) provides a detailed study of President James K. Polk as one of a new breed of professional politicians who was also a cotton planter. Polk was an absentee slaveowner, with plantations in Tennessee and Mississippi. He took a harsh view of the treatment of slaves even though he preferred to present himself as a paternalist. Dusinberre argues that Polk's views on the national position of slavery were close to the extreme southern rights position of John C. Calhoun, and that Polk supported the move of slavery into territories west of the Mississippi. Polk and his Democratic colleague failed to signal a commitment to slavery's extension, an issue that could have won them greater support among most northerners.

The justification for keeping slaves in the South is illuminated by comparative studies with non-American groups and institutions. Kolchin (1980) examines the similarity of the arguments used to defend unfree labour in Russia and the United States. Common arguments in these two countries transcended cultural, economic and regional differences. But one crucial difference lay in the comparative standing of the respective landowning classes: American slaveholders were independent, autonomous and dominant in their regional society whereas Russian owners of serfs operated in a more dependent way as part of a society embedded in a peasant world. It was therefore easier, and more important, for southerners to develop a sophisticated proslavery ideology to protect their position of independence and control over their property than for Russian owners of serfs to propagate their position. Bowman (1993) takes Prussian Junkers as his comparative example. His argument is that southern planters and Prussian landowners shared an agrarian capitalism oriented towards systematic production for the world market and a conservative commitment to maintain the status quo. These commonalities are interesting, but the presence of slavery in the United States and its absence in Germany only gives the comparison some validity.

The proslavery ideology of the planters has attracted renewed attention after many decades of neglect. Tise (1987) traces the origins of American proslavery thought back to the colonial period and finds it articulated not just in the southern colonies but in New England. He argues that proslavery was longer in its incidence and genesis than most historians have conceded and that, far from being an aberration from the norm, promoters of such a view expressed many of the social, moral and cultural values present in American society in the first half of the nineteenth century. For the antebellum period, Faust (1981) offers an anthology with substantial extracts from proslavery writers that include scriptural justifications for enslavement and homilies upon the happy state of slaves within a familial household structure.

Frederickson (1971) detects a harsher form of proslavery thought emerging after c. 1840 in the southwestern states. This stemmed partly from southern attempts to justify the continuation of slavery in the light of abolitionist pressure for racial equality. Based on the notion of white supremacy and buttressed by scientific theories of black inferiority, this racist proslavery strain was propagated to many southern whites. Frederickson refers to this viewpoint as 'hierarchical biracialism', emphasising the divide between whites and blacks. The paternalism of the slaveholders fitted this pattern of white racial thought. The increasing emphasis by some proslavery advocates on black inferiority led racist white southerners to insist that slaves were unsuited to economic and political freedom. Wyatt-Brown (1982) singles out Christian patriarchalism as the cornerstone of proslavery thought. He notes that one major objective of such arguments lay in persuading the

Christian elite of the northern states that the South was acting honourably and benevolently in maintaining the system of slavery.

BIBLIOGRAPHY

Boles, John B., *Black Southerners. 1619–1869* (Lexington: University of Kentucky Press, 1983)

Bowman, Shearer Davis, *Masters and Lords: Mid-19th-Century US Planters and Prussian Junkers* (New York: Oxford University Press, 1993)

Campbell, Randolph B., 'Planters and Plain Folk: The Social Structure of the Antebellum South' in John B. Boles and Evelyn Thomas Nolen (eds), *Interpreting Southern History: Historiographical Essays in Honor of Sanford W. Higginbotham* (Baton Rouge: Louisiana State University Press, 1987)

Collins, Bruce, *White Society in the Antebellum South* (Harlow: Longman, 1985)

Dusinberre, William, *Slavemaster President: The Double Career of James Polk* (New York: Oxford University Press, 2003)

Faust, Drew Gilpin (ed.), *The Ideology of Slavery: Proslavery Thought in the Antebellum South, 1830–1860* (Baton Rouge: Louisiana State University Press, 1981)

Frederickson, George M., *The Black Image in the White Mind: The Debate on Afro-American Character and Destiny, 1817–1914* (New York: Harper & Row, 1971)

Genovese, Eugene D., *The World the Slaveholders Made: Two Essays in Interpretation* (New York: Pantheon Books, 1969)

Genovese, Eugene D., *The Slaveholders' Dilemma: Freedom and Progress in Southern Conservative Thought, 1820–1860* (Columbia: University of South Carolina Press, 1992)

Greenberg, Kenneth S., *Masters and Statesmen: The Political Culture of American Slavery* (Baltimore, MD: Johns Hopkins University Press, 1985)

Harris, J. William, *Plain Folk and Gentry in a Slave Society: White Liberty and Black Slavery in Augusta's Hinterlands* (Middletown, CT: Wesleyan University Press, 1985)

Kolchin, Peter, 'In Defense of Servitude: American Proslavery and Russian Proserfdom Arguments, 1760–1860', *American Historical Review*, 85 (1980), 809–27

Oakes, James, *The Ruling Race: A History of American Slaveholders* (New York: Alfred A. Knopf, 1982)

Oakes, James, *Slavery and Freedom: An Interpretation of the Old South* (New York: Alfred A. Knopf, 1990)

Parish, Peter J., *Slavery: History and Historians* (New York: Harper & Row, 1989)

Shore, Laurence, *Southern Capitalists: The Ideological Leadership of an Elite, 1832–1885* (Chapel Hill: University of North Carolina Press, 1986)

Smith, Mark M., *Debating Slavery: Economy and Society in the Antebellum American South* (Cambridge: Cambridge University Press, 1998)

Tadman, Michael, *Speculators and Slaves: Masters, Traders, and Slaves in the Old South* (Madison: University of Wisconsin Press, 1989; rev. edn, 1996)

Tise, Larry E., *Proslavery: A History of the Defense of Slavery in America, 1701–1840* (Athens, GA: University of Georgia Press, 1987)

Wayne, Michael, 'An Old South Morality Play: Reconsidering the Social Underpinnings of Proslavery Ideology', *Journal of American History*, 77 (1990), 838–63

Wyatt-Brown, Bertram, 'Modernizing Southern Slavery: The Proslavery Argument Reinterpreted' in J. Morgan Kousser and James M. McPherson (eds), *Region, Race and Reconstruction: Essays in Honor of C. Vann Woodward* (New York: Oxford University Press, 1982)

ESSAY: PROSLAVERY THOUGHT

Faust (1981) provides an excellent historiographical context for considering proslavery views in the Old South. She points to psychological and sociological explanations lying behind proslavery advocacy and the Federalist social influences on those writing in favour of slavery in the antebellum era. How does proslavery thought illuminate broader patterns of belief and values in the South? How far were proslavery writings directed at other southerners? Did these writings make a national impact? Did the claims of science and of the Scriptures help to unify proslavery ideology, or did they provide conflicting and irreconcilable views on slavery?

The controversy over slavery in the antebellum United States did not end with abolition of the South's peculiar institution. In the century that has followed Appomattox, historians have debated the sources and meaning of the slavery agitation nearly as vigorously as early nineteenth-century Americans argued about human bondage itself. But a disproportionate amount of this scholarly attention has been devoted to antislavery movements and ideologies. Whereas studies of abolitionism have established it as both a product and an index of fundamental aspects of nineteenth-century culture, historical treatment of proslavery has emphasized its aberrant qualities, identifying it as the evanescent product of the unique civilization that flourished in the South during the last three decades before the Civil War. Many scholars have felt uncomfortable contending with zealous defenses of a social system that the twentieth century judges abhorrent, and, like David Donald, they have found the proslavery movement 'astonishing'.[1]

In recent years, however, interpretations of proslavery thought have shifted. Perhaps more accustomed to the notion of a timeless and geographically extensive American racism, scholars have begun to place proslavery within a wider context, to regard it as more than simply a distasteful manifestation of a collective paranoia gripping the South in the years before the Civil War. Historians have come to view the proslavery argument less as evidence of moral failure and more as a key to wider patterns of beliefs and values. The defense of human bondage, they recognize, was perhaps more important as an effort to construct a coherent southern social philosophy than as a political weapon of short-lived usefulness during the height of sectional conflict. In defending what they repeatedly referred to as the 'cornerstone' of their social order, slavery's apologists were offering posterity an unusual opportunity to examine the world view of articulate southerners, their sources of social legitimation, and their self-conscious definition of themselves.[2] Slavery became a vehicle for the discussion of fundamental social issues – the

---

Drew Gilpin Faust (ed.), *The Ideology of Slavery: Proslavery Thought in the Antebellum South* (Baton Rouge: Louisiana State University Press, 1981), pp. 1–20.

meaning of natural law, the conflicting desires for freedom and order, the re-lationship between tradition and progress, the respective roles of liberty and equality, dependence and autonomy. 'The question of negro slavery', one apologist recognized in 1856, 'is implicated with all the great social prob-lems of the current age'.[3] Addressing topics of deepest import to Americans North and South, the proslavery argument embodied the South's particular perspective on those philosophical, moral, and social dilemmas confronting the nation as a whole. 'Proslavery thought', as one recent scholar has re-marked, 'was nothing more or less than thought about society'.[4]

A significant aspect of the reorientation of modern scholarship toward a widening interpretation of proslavery's significance has been a growing interest in its persistence over time. Although a few scholars of the 1930s and 1940s noted proslavery's early origins,[5] most historians continued to associate the defense of slavery with a movement of the South away from Jeffersonian liberalism in the late 1820s and 1830s. After abolitionist William Lloyd Garrison began to denounce slavery in *The Liberator* in 1831, these scholars explained, the South rapidly abandoned its Revolu-tionary American heritage and took up the almost polar opposite position of proslavery reactionism.[6]

Recent work, however, has revised this chronology, exploring in new detail the significance of proslavery doctrines during the colonial period.[7] Acknowledging a brief period of quiescence during the egalitarian ferment of the Revolutionary years, this interpretation chronicles a reemergence as early as 1808 of a proslavery literature that grew steadily in volume and ve-hemence throughout the remainder of the antebellum period. This writing, moreover, was not restricted to the South. One of the earliest slavery de-bates took place in colonial Massachusetts;[8] northerners continued publicly to defend slavery in significant numbers through the time of the Civil War. Britons in England and the West Indies also justified slavery throughout the eighteenth and early nineteenth centuries, and these arguments served as useful sources for American advocates of human bondage.[9]

This broadened chronology and geography of proslavery contains im-portant implications for the understanding of the movement and of the Old South itself. Some scholars in the past have tended to regard the defense of slavery as a product of southern guilt, an effort by slaveholders to as-suage consciences riddled with shame about violations of America's demo-cratic creed. Recent attention to the colonial origins and wide extension of proslavery views suggests the existence of a strong alternative tradition of social and even moral legitimation upon which antebellum southerners might draw. Less philosophically and morally isolated than Charles Sellers and W. J. Cash would have us think, southerners may have felt far less guilty and ambivalent as well.[10]

But emphasis on the extensiveness of proslavery thought through time and space has not diminished scholarly interest in the role of the argument in the South during the last three decades of the antebellum period. Even historians insisting upon its early origins and wide diffusion recognize its increased significance in these years. During this era, the slavery controversy not only became a matter of survival for the southern way of life; it served for Americans generally as a means of reassessing the profoundest assumptions on which their world was built.

Although proslavery thought demonstrated remarkable consistency from the seventeenth century on, it became in the South of the 1830s, forties, and fifties more systematic and self-conscious; it took on the characteristics of a formal ideology with its resulting social movement. The intensification of proslavery argumentation produced an increase in conceptual organization and coherence within the treatises themselves, which sought methodically to enumerate all possible foundations for human bondage – 'a *discussion on Slavery in all its bearings*', as one southern apologist explained, 'in the lights of History, Political Economy, Moral Philosophy, Political Science, Theology, Social Life, Ethnology and International Law'.[11] At the same time, more structured arrangements developed among the apologists and their publishers for the production and distribution of these tracts. Southerners united to call upon the region's finest minds for defenses of slavery, to discuss with one another the appropriate contents and goals for their writings, and to arrange their wide dissemination in newspapers, pamphlets, and even book-sized collections of previously printed favorites. One publisher explained his intention of producing an anthology of arguments on fine paper 'fit to take its place in the Library or Drawing Room, and to serve as a Text Book on the subject, so that every one in our community may have at hand good strong arguments ... coming in a respectable shape and in good style it will attract much more attention than if simply sent in pamphlet form'.[12] The need for a vigorous southern publishing industry became particularly obvious as a result of these efforts to diffuse proslavery views, and the defense of the peculiar institution had an important impact upon southern letters. 'We shall be indebted', one southern intellectual and proslavery essayist proclaimed, 'to the continuance and asperity of this controversy for the creation of a genuine Southern literature .... For out of this slavery agitation has sprung not merely essays on slavery, valuable and suggestive as these have been, but also the literary activity, and the literary movement which have lately characterized the intellect of the South'.[13]

Whereas earlier proslavery writers had attracted little attention, the South now rewarded her defenders with acclaim. Francis Lieber, a German emigré with little sympathy for the peculiar institution of his adopted South, remarked bitterly that 'nothing would give me greater renown than a pamphlet written ... in favor of slavery'.[14] After a long and unrewarding career as an agricultural essayist, Edmund Ruffin found that 'I have had more notice taken of my late pamphlet [on slavery] than of anything I ever wrote before'.[15]

Current scholarship regards the change in southern writings about slavery in the 1830s as more one of style and tone than of substance. Southerners did not move from an anti-to a proslavery position. Slaveholders were less troubled about *whether* slavery was right than precisely *why* it was right and how its justice could best be demonstrated. Unsympathetic to the Perfectionism embraced by many of their abolitionist counterparts, proslavery advocates always saw evils in slavery, as they were sure they would in any terrestrial system of society and government. All earthly arrangements, they believed, necessarily required men to cope as best they could with sin; it was the relative merits of social systems, their comparative success in dealing with inherent evil, that should be discussed. As William Harper explained in his *Memoir on Slavery*, 'the condition of our whole existence is but to struggle with evils – to compare them – to choose between them, and so far as we can, to mitigate them. To say that there is evil in any institution, is only to say that it is human'. With the intensification of the slavery controversy, however, apologists began to acknowledge the institution's shortcomings less openly and to consider only the positive aspects of the system. 'I see great evils in slavery', George Fitzhugh confessed to a friend, 'but I think in a controversial work I ought not to admit them'.[16]

Antebellum southerners themselves recognized and justified their heightened involvement in slavery's defense in the years after 1830. In spite of 'speculative doubts by which the slave-owners were troubled', a Virginian observed in 1856, 'the general sentiment among them . . . had always tenaciously maintained the sanctity and inviolability of slavery, but they have not arrived at a clear comprehension of the reasons by which slavery is justified and proved to be right and expedient, without the aid of the . . . treatises which the controversy still raging has called forth'. Southerners, Mississippian Henry Hughes agreed, could successfully defend slavery only when they learned 'to give the reasons for it'. 'Few of our own people', a South Carolinian advocate similarly complained, 'understand it in its philosophical and economical bearing'. These explanations suggest, as historian Ralph Morrow argued in 1961, that proslavery writings were directed primarily at other southerners. 'We think it hardly to be expected', one apologist candidly admitted in 1843, 'that anything which can be said at this late date will at all diminish the wrongheaded fanaticism and perverse intolerance of the Northern abolitionists'. Northern antislavery had progressed 'past the cure of argument'.[17]

This concern with the sources and impact of proslavery writing within the South has generated new interest in the authors of proslavery tracts and in the nature of their lives within the southern social order. The psychological 'guiltomania' interpretations of Sellers and Cash represent one aspect of this trend. David Donald offered a somewhat different but related perspective, combining sociological with psychological explanation by exploring the particular social locations of a group of slavery's southern defenders. 'All', he found, were 'unhappy men'. But their 'personal problems' had a social dimension and were even a direct result of 'their place in southern society'. Frustrated by their own failure to rise to positions of prominence in the South, slavery's apologists sought to compensate for their relegation to the 'fringes of society'; they 'looked back with longing to an earlier day of the Republic when men like themselves – their own ancestors – had been leaders in the South'.[18]

Since Donald presented his ideas in a brief 1970 presidential address to the Southern Historical Association, other scholars have inquired more closely into the biographical questions he raised. Larry Edward Tise associated proslavery with the clergy in a study of 275 proslavery ministers and explored as well the institutions and experiences that exposed these men to the Federalist influences so evident in their writings. Although Federalism as a political force disappeared well before the 1830s, many of its conservative principles and hierarchical social assumptions, Tise noted, were perpetuated in the proslavery argument. The relationship of proslavery and social role has also been examined by Drew Gilpin Faust, who has suggested that the argument served as a vehicle for expression of alienation by the South's neglected intellectuals. The logic by which these advocates justified the right of whites to hold blacks in bondage, she argued, inevitably implied the social superiority of intellectuals as well. In taking up the public defense of the peculiar institution, the southern thinker thus sought to advance his particular values and to define for himself a respected social role within a culture known for its inhospitality to letters.[19]

These studies assumed a significant relationship between social role and the particular details of the ideology invoked to legitimate it, and consequently undertook to reassess the contents of proslavery thought in light of these new sociological concerns. William Sumner Jenkins' pioneering study of proslavery in 1935 had definitively classified and explored the most familiar species of arguments. As late as 1971, David Donald still found that 'the substance of the proslavery argument has little interest'. Nevertheless, changing conceptions about the relationship of society and ideology arising in part from the impact of Eugene Genovese's Marxism and in part from shifting concerns of intellectual history have prompted a renewed interest in the contents and symbolic structure of the arguments themselves and in the nature of their development in the three decades before the Civil War.[20]

Many scholars have long acknowledged Thomas Roderick Dew's *Review of the Debate in the Virginia Legislature* as a herald of this new post-1830 era in proslavery ideology. Prompted by legislative discussion of emancipation in the winter of 1831–32, Dew's essay sought to establish the impracticality of the antislavery sentiments that had swept the state after Nat Turner's slave uprising left more than sixty whites dead in Virginia's Southside. Dew himself proclaimed his argument to be a new departure in proslavery writing, and his pragmatic tone was to serve as the inspiration for the inductive mode of almost all proslavery tracts henceforth. Rejecting the deductive principles of the Lockean contractual social theory that had influenced the Founding Fathers, Dew embraced the conservative organic view of social order that had been implicit in proslavery thought from its earliest beginnings. Social institutions and arrangements evolved slowly over time, he believed, and could not be beneficially altered by abrupt human intervention. Like the proslavery advocates that followed him, Dew called upon his audience to study society as it had existed through the ages and to derive social principles and bases for action from these empirical observations. Theoretical notions of equality could not controvert the striking differences in men's capacities evident to any impartial observer. Idealized conceptions of justice – such as those of the abolitionists – could never serve as reliable bases for social organization. It was all very well, Dew counseled his fellow Virginians, to admit the abstract evils of slavery, but the relative dangers of the alternatives – abolition with or without colonization – were far greater.[21]

Dew called upon southerners to recognize the implications of their own social order and to assume responsibility for it. 'One generation', as historian Eugene Genovese has remarked about the South in the years after the Revolution, 'might be able to oppose slavery and favor everything it made possible, but the next had to choose sides'.[22] Dew was important because he demonstrated the implausibility of straddling the issue any longer, of maintaining the stance of relativism that many southerners had found so comfortable during the Revolutionary era and its aftermath. As antislavery sentiment began to strengthen in the years after the Missouri debates of 1818–20, it was impossible any longer to endeavor to reconcile the North to the existence of the peculiar institution by conceding slavery's shortcomings. Once the issue was joined, Dew proclaimed, the South must acknowledge her commitment to her way of life and come out firmly on the proslavery side; the South must recognize that her superficial flirtation with the Revolutionary ideology of liberty and equality could be no more than just that.

Although Dew inaugurated a new era in proslavery, a flood of defenses did not appear at once. Only when northern abolitionists in 1835 inundated the South with antislavery propaganda sent through the federal mails did southerners respond in force, exhibiting a new vehemence in their defenses of their way of life. The attack from the North made southern mobilization an immediate necessity, and latent proslavery feeling was quickly translated into action.

In the course of the next decade, slavery's apologists would, in their collective oeuvre, develop a comprehensive defense of the peculiar institution that invoked the most important sources of authority in their intellectual culture and associated slavery with the fundamental values of their civilization. Their specific arguments showed striking continuity with earlier proslavery positions, elaborating rather than contradicting existing writing. The defenses of slavery of this period were, in addition, remarkably consistent with one another. While one advocate might specialize in religious arguments and another in the details of political economy, most acknowledged, accepted, and sometimes repeated the conclusions of their fellow apologists. The high level of conformity within proslavery thought was not accidental. Consistency was seen as the mark of strength and the emblem of truth. 'Earlier and later writers', the editor of a collection of proslavery classics remarked proudly in 1860, 'stood on substantially the same ground, and take the same general views of the institution'.[23]

To ensure this uniformity, slavery's apologists articulated a series of what we might regard as rules guiding the post-1835 proslavery movement. Endeavoring to avoid the 'domain of sectional controversy and political warfare', the defenders of slavery sought broader arguments and wider appeal.[24] Basing their essays in 'sober and cautious reflection' upon 'purely scientific principles' with 'no appeal to passion or to sordid interest', the South's proslavery theorists hoped to attract those who 'wished for argument instead of abuse'. Many of the South's apologists communicated with one another about their essays and ideas, so that the mature proslavery argument might well be seen as a community product.[25]

As a result of this group criticism and evaluation, there emerged what could be considered a proslavery mainstream. The Bible served as the core of this defense. In the face of abolitionist claims that slavery violated the principles of Christianity, southerners demonstrated with ever more elaborate detail that both Old and New Testaments sanctioned human bondage. God's Chosen People had been slaveholders; Christ had made no attack on the institution; his disciple Paul had demonstrated a commitment to maintaining it.[26]

But for an age increasingly enamored of the vocabulary and methods of natural science, biblical guidance was not enough. The accepted foundations for truth were changing in European and American thought, as intellectuals sought to apply the rigor of science to the study of society and morality, as well as the natural world. The proslavery argument accordingly called not only upon divine revelation, the traditional source and arbiter of truth, but sought at the same time to embrace the positivistic standards increasingly accepted for the assessment of all social problems. Man could and must, these authors contended, determine his social and moral duties scientifically, through the examination of God's will revealed in nature and in history. A subspecies of general social thought, the defense of slavery assumed the methods and arguments of broader social theories and reflected an intellectual perspective that in these years first began to regard 'social science' as a discrete and legitimate domain of human learning. Reverend Thornton Stringfellow would devise a proslavery theory designed to be at once 'Scriptural and Statistical'; George Fitzhugh would write a *Sociology for the South*; Henry Hughes's proslavery tract would appear in the guise of *A Treatise on Sociology* in which the author's striving for relevance and legitimacy beyond the confines of the Old South even led him to replace the term *slavery* with that of *warranteeism*.[27]

But most advocates did not go so far. Sociology was not yet the academic discipline it has since become; moral science – from which sociology would later emerge – still remained the central framework for social analysis in colleges and among the educated both North and South. Thus the mainstream of proslavery argument sought to imbed the peculiar institution within the legitimating context of nineteenth-century moral philosophy, with its emphasis on man's duties and responsibilities and its invocation of historical precedent as guide for future action.[28]

Turning to the past as a catalog of social experiments, slavery's defenders discovered that from the time of Greece and Rome, human bondage had produced the world's greatest civilizations. The peculiar institution, they argued, was not so very peculiar, but had provided the social foundation for man's greatest achievements. Moreover, the experience of the ages showed the fundamental principles of the American Revolution to be sadly misguided. Social law as revealed in history demonstrated that men had not in reality been created equal and free, as Jefferson had asserted; this was a mistaken view arising from erroneous modes of abstract and deductive thought. Nature produced individuals strikingly unequal in both qualities and circumstances. 'Scientific' truths demonstrated through empirical study prescribed a hierarchically structured society reproducing nature's orderly differentiations. The Revolutionary concepts of natural law were thus replaced by the tenets of social organicism; the prestige of modern science served to legitimate tradition and conservatism in a manner that held implications far wider than the boundaries of the slavery controversy.[29]

Such an approach to social order stressed the importance of man's duties rather than his rights. And for rhetorical purposes, it was often the duties of masters, rather than those of slaves, that apologists chose to emphasize. Within the organic community of a slave society, they argued, the master could not ignore the human obligation to care for his bondsman. 'Fed, clothed, protected', the slave was far better off, William J. Grayson proclaimed, than the northern factory worker whose employer had no interest in his health or even his survival. 'Free but in name', northern laborers had liberty only to starve. As William Harper argued, there existed 'some form of slavery in all ages and countries'.[30] It was always necessary, Abel Upshur explained, 'that one portion of mankind shall live upon the labor of another portion'. Every civilization needed what James Henry Hammond dubbed a 'mud-sill' class to do the menial labor of society.[31] The southern system of human bondage, they argued, simply organized this interdependence and inequality in accordance with principles of morality and Christianity.

The humanitarian arrangements of slavery, the southerners proclaimed, contrasted favorably with the avaricious materialism of the 'miscalled' free society of the North. Whereas the Yankees cared only about the wealth that their operatives might produce, southerners accepted costly responsibility for the human beings whom God had 'entrusted' to them. A number of defenders even maintained, like Harper, that 'slave labor can never be so cheap as what is called free labor'. Nevertheless, Hammond piously advised, slavery's moral purposes dictated that 'we must...content ourselves with...the consoling reflection that what is lost to us is gained to humanity'. The proslavery argument asserted its opposition to the growing materialism of the age and offered the model of evangelical stewardship as the best representation of its labor system. The master was God's surrogate on earth; the southern system institutionalized the Christian duties of charity in the master and humility in the slave. 'You have been chosen', Nathaniel Beverley Tucker declared to his fellow slaveholders, 'as the instrument, in the hand of God, for accomplishing the great purpose of his benevolence'.[32] The nineteenth-century concern with philanthropy, defenders of slavery argued, was most successfully realized in the South's system of human bondage. Reflecting the lessons of human experience through the ages, as well as the prescriptions of both divine and natural order, slavery seemed unassailable. The truths of science, religion, and history united to offer proslavery southerners ready support for their position.

But by the 1850s, challenges to the unity of proslavery ideology had begun to appear. In large part, these emerging rifts mirrored wider intellectual currents. Forms of knowledge and legitimation long assumed to be necessarily compatible were everywhere displaying nagging contradictions. Most significant was an increasingly unavoidable conflict between the claims of science and those of the Scriptures. Rather than supporting and amplifying the truths of biblical revelation, science seemed to many midcentury thinkers already a threat to the conclusions of other modes of knowledge; challenges had begun to appear to the nineteenth century's holistic conception of truth.[33]

But in the proslavery argument, as in patterns of American thought more generally, these inconsistencies were to remain largely dormant; comparatively little overt strife between religion and science appeared before the Civil War, for most Americans voiced confidence that the achievement of greater understanding would eventually reveal an underlying compatibility. So, too, southerners defending slavery sought to minimize the impact of philosophical contradictions in order to maintain the strength that derived from proslavery unity. 'There is no forked tongue in the language of learned men – whether physician or divine', one proslavery scientist insisted. 'Truth is the same whether uttered by one or the other – the phraseology may differ but truth is an unit'.[34]

By the end of the antebellum period, however, even those recognizing necessity for unity and consistency sometimes found it difficult to make their views conform to the moral-philosophical mainstream of proslavery thought. The emergence of ethnology by the late 1840s as a recognized science of racial differences was to pose inevitable difficulties for the Fundamentalist bases on which the proslavery movement had been built. On the other hand, scientific validation of Negro inferiority offered an alluring and seemingly irrefutable argument to those favoring the social subordination of blacks in slavery. 'The mission of Ethnology', as one southern proponent declared, 'is to vindicate the great truths on which the institutions of the South are founded'.[35] Yet theories that urged the existence of two permanently separate and unequal races of men directly challenged Genesis and its assertion that all humans were descended from a single set of common parents. The dilemma implicit in this conflict of knowledge and values was neatly illustrated in the personal dilemma of Josiah Nott. A leading southern spokesman for racial science, he was anxious to deemphasize challenges to religious orthodoxy, yet equally desirous of establishing the validity of his own field. The pressure for unity in the proslavery movement influenced Nott to suppress overt antagonism toward religion, and as a result the Alabama physician dotted his writings with protestations of his devotion to sacred truth. 'No one can have more positive distaste than myself for religious or any other controversy', Nott proclaimed, insisting that he used his 'best efforts to avoid unpleasant collisions'. Science and revealed religion, he asserted, would necessarily be consistent if their truths were properly ascertained. 'The works of God form one great chain, of which revealed religion is but a link; and while the Bible, on one hand, has shed a flood of light on Ethnology, this in turn has afforded immense aid to Biblical criticism'.[36]

Ultimately, however, Nott was unable to fulfill the expectations for conformity held by the proslavery mainstream. Irascible and somewhat belligerent, Nott translated a latent hostility toward religion in general into an open assault upon the clergy as the purveyors of false doctrines. While he piously proclaimed his devotion to revelation, he mercilessly attacked its clerical interpreters. Such a position, he thought, would offer the possibility of establishing scientific principles without directly undermining religion; conflicts between ethnology and the Bible could be reconciled without challenging the unity of all truth. Science and religion were consistent, he maintained, but ministers were clearly fallible and in challenging science misinterpreted the divine word.

For the most part, Nott's audience did not perceive his subtle distinction between anticlericalism and antireligionism. Nott provoked violent controversy, and clerical defenders of slavery moved to affirm the unity of the human race and of proslavery ideology by disproving his polygenist theories. To many, Nott seemed to be causing altogether unnecessary difficulties.

He and his associate George Gliddon, one critic remarked, had 'involved their cause with the discussion of the inspiration, authenticity, authorship & translation of Scripture, to such an extent that their work looks more like a labored attempt to annihilate that volume than to discuss mooted questions in ethnology'.[37]

Most defenders of slavery sought to use the scientific prestige of ethnology to enhance their position without becoming ensnared by the difficulties it presented; they were eager to sidestep the problems Nott addressed head-on. George Frederick Holmes, long sympathetic to the notion of race as a major determinant of human civilization, nevertheless advised fellow southerners that the truths of ethnology remained 'enveloped ... in all the mist of obscurity. I should steer a cautious middle course between the extreme views on this subject'. Edmund Ruffin found that despite great potential value, ethnology offered 'more amusement than reliable information', and George Fitzhugh bluntly declared that if forced to choose between the Bible and ethnology, southerners had best stick to the Holy Writ.[38] Although most proslavery advocates did not admit the inherent conflict so openly, in practice they followed Fitzhugh's advice. Racial arguments had been a part of proslavery thought since its earliest manifestations in the colonial period. The impact of ethnology was chiefly to enlarge and systematize this facet of the argument and to offer a variety of skull measurements, geological and anthropological 'facts' as incontrovertible evidence for the mainstream position. Nature was invoked to provide additional support for the moral justifications that remained the core of the proslavery argument.[39]

The intricacies of racial and ethnological arguments were not the only difficulties confronting the mainstream of proslavery thinkers. Conformity and unanimity within the movement were occasionally threatened by departures from the prescribed style, as well as the substance of proslavery tracts. In their effort to present the defense of slavery as a part of the transcendent truths of religion and science, many apologists believed that a tone of dispassionate inquiry was an absolute necessity. Polemics would injure rather than advance the ultimate goals of the proslavery cause. 'Christian candor and fairness of argument', one apologist insisted, were the emblems of 'the search after truth'.[40] When Josiah Nott replied angrily to attacks upon his ethnological assertions, the *Southern Quarterly Review* was quick to chastise him, proclaiming the tone of his work 'unfortunate'.[41] But the most vigorous criticism from the proslavery mainstream was directed against George Fitzhugh, whose 'extravagant heresies' sparked an outburst of protests from other apologists.[42]

A Virginian who began publishing well after the main lines of proslavery theory had been defined, Fitzhugh proclaimed himself the first true defender of slavery, the first to have 'vindicated slavery in the abstract'. He was the only southerner vigorously to advocate slavery as the most desirable arrangement for white as well as black labor, and the only apologist to transform the discussion of slavery into an unremitting attack on free labor and capital. But while presented in extreme form, his arguments were basically derived from those of the theorists who had preceded him and had been developing a general defense of slavery for decades. Fitzhugh's assault upon northern and British wage slavery and his discussion of the sorry plight of free workers, for example, had been a popular argument since Robert Walsh's comparison of southern slavery and European free labor in 1819. But it was Fitzhugh's outspoken tone and aggressive style that drew even more attention than the substance of his essays. His contemporaries regarded him as something of a crackpot.[43]

Fitzhugh candidly acknowledged that his involvement in proslavery was far from dispassionate or disinterested. 'Confessing myself the greatest egoist in the world', Fitzhugh hoped to attract attention and promote book sales by self-consciously making his work 'odd, eccentric, extravagant, and disorderly'.[44] Southerners reviewing his books deplored their 'utter recklessness of both statement and expression'. George Frederick Holmes, whom Fitzhugh admired as the proslavery advocate with views closest to his own, found his discussions 'incendiary and dangerous', and Edmund Ruffin pronounced Fitzhugh's views 'absurd'.[45]

Never included in the anthologies of proslavery classics of his own era, Fitzhugh's work has been often reprinted in ours, and he has attracted lavish attention from present-day historians. This modern interest in Fitzhugh may in part be a result of his very unrepresentativeness. In their perception of the proslavery argument as aberrant and 'astonishing',[46] historians have turned to its most extreme, provocative, and even outrageous presentation. Many politically motivated northerners of the mid-nineteenth century chose a similar course, pointing to Fitzhugh's arguments as proof of the impassable gulf separating North and South. There is even evidence that Abraham Lincoln himself turned to Fitzhugh's writing for the portrait of intersectional opposition that led him to conclude that the nation was a 'house divided'.[47] It was much easier for nineteenth-century northerners, as it is for modern Americans as well, to discount an argument that is 'odd, extravagant and disorderly' than to confront the ways in which the mainstream proslavery position drew upon basic values of Western civilization shared by the North and the South to justify human bondage.

Yet Eugene Genovese has argued persuasively for Fitzhugh's importance as a 'ruthless and critical theorist who spelled out the logical outcome of slaveholders' philosophy and laid bare its essence'.[48] Fitzhugh's attacks upon capitalism and free labor, he has asserted, were necessary corollaries to the defense of slavery. Because Fitzhugh was extreme, he was able to articulate the unspoken – and even unrecognized – assumptions on which proslavery rested.

Genovese was careful not to argue for Fitzhugh's representativeness. Indeed, other southerners and other proslavery advocates endeavored to refute what Genovese has called the 'logical outcome' of their own philosophy. As they sought to avoid the implicit conflicts of religion and ethnology, so too they eschewed Fitzhugh's all-out attack upon civilization as it was developing in the nineteenth-century capitalist West. Fitzhugh's 'opposition to interest or capital' one defender summarily dismissed as 'foolish'.[49] In hoping to save southern civilization as they knew it, southerners sought to perpetuate rather than resolve the inconsistencies between their prebourgeois labor system and the bourgeois world market in which it flourished. The mainstream of the South's defenders had to dissociate themselves from Fitzhugh, for he showed them to be caught in a paradox at a time when they could ill afford the luxury of the self-examination and questioning necessary for its resolution. Yet this was a paradox that did not envelop the South alone. The paternalism of much of the North's industry, the ideas of evangelical stewardship underlying its widespread reform movements, indeed the strength of northern proslavery sentiment itself bespoke the existence of a similar conflict above the Mason-Dixon line between antimaterialist, prebourgeois values and the 'cash-nexus' at the center of the modern civilization fast emerging.[50] The paradoxes that the proslavery argument encountered and unwittingly exposed – conflicts of tradition and modernity, of human and material values, of science with religion – were but further evidence of the argument's centrality within nineteenth-century American culture. These were problems in social philosophy and values confronting all Americans of this era, and unassailable solutions were as scarce in the North as in the South.

While we can continue to abhor the system of human bondage that flourished in the Old South, there is much we can learn from a more dispassionate examination of the arguments used to defend it. We have sought to distance the slaveholders and their creed, to define them as very unlike ourselves. Yet their processes of rationalization and self-justification were not so very different from our own, or from those of any civilization of human actors. The persistence of modern racism is but one forceful reminder of the ways that human beings always view the world in terms of inherited systems of belief and explanation that only partially reflect the reality they are meant to describe. By understanding how others have fashioned and maintained their systems of meaning, we shall be better equipped to evaluate, criticize, and perhaps even change our own.

NOTES

1. David Donald, 'The Proslavery Argument Reconsidered', *JSH*, XXXVII (1971), 3. For a useful summary of the extensive literature on abolition, see James Brewer Stewart, *Holy Warriors: The Abolitionists and American Slavery* (New York, 1976), and Ronald G. Walters, *The Antislavery Appeal: American Abolitionism After 1830* (Baltimore, 1976).
2. The reference to slavery as the 'cornerstone' of the southern social order has most frequently been attributed to an 1861 speech of Alexander Stephens, but contemporary

southerners recognized the origin of the phrase in a speech by George McDuffie of 1836. See James Henry Hammond to M. C. M. Hammond, July 23, 1859, in James Henry Hammond Papers, LOC. For other examples of the use of this concept, see Hammond, 'Hammond's Letters on Slavery', in *The Pro-Slavery Argument as Maintained by the Most Distinguished Writers of the Southern States* (Charleston, 1852), 111; George Frederick Holmes, 'Slavery and Freedom', *SQR*, I (1856), 87, 92; Edmund Ruffin, *The Political Economy of Slavery* (Washington, D.C., 1857), 5, 23.

3. Holmes, 'Slavery and Freedom', 95.
4. Larry Edward Tise, 'Proslavery Ideology: A Social and Intellectual History of the Defense of Slavery in America, 1790–1840' (University of North Carolina Ph.D., 1975), 57.
5. See especially William Sumner Jenkins, *Pro-Slavery Thought in the Old South* (1935; reprint ed., Gloucester, Mass., 1960); William B. Hesseltine, 'Some New Aspects of the Pro-Slavery Argument', *JNH*, XXI (1936), 1–15; Kenneth M. Stampp, 'An Analysis of T. R. Dew's *Review of the Debate in the Virginia Legislature*', *JNH*, XXVII (1942), 380–7.
6. See Charles A. and Mary R. Beard, *The Rise of American Civilization* (New York, 1927); Albert Bushnell Hart, *Slavery and Abolition, 1831–1841* (New York, 1906); Clement Eaton, *The Growth of Southern Civilization, 1790–1860* (New York, 1961).
7. See Tise, 'Proslavery Ideology'; Larry Morrison, 'The Proslavery Argument in the Early Republic, 1790–1830' (University of Virginia Ph.D., 1975); Robert McColley, *Slavery in Jeffersonian Virginia* (Champaign-Urbana, 1964); Frederika Teute Schmidt and Barbara Ripel Wilhelm, 'Early Proslavery Petitions in Virginia', *WMQ*, 3rd. ser., XXX (1973), 133–46; Rena Vassar, 'William Knox's Defense of Slavery [1768]', *Proceedings of the American Philosophical Society*, CXIV (1970), 310–26; Anne C. Loveland, 'Richard Furman's "Questions on Slavery"', *Baptist History and Heritage*, X (1975), 177–81; Stephen J. Stein, 'George Whitfield on Slavery: Some New Evidence', *Church History*, XLII (1973), 243–56; Joseph C. Burke, 'The Proslavery Argument and the First Congress', *Duquesne Review*, XIV (1969), 3–15; Peter Joseph Albert, 'The Protean Institution: The Geography, Economy, and Ideology of Slavery in Post-Revolutionary Virginia' (University of Maryland Ph.D., 1976). Winthrop D. Jordan also treats the early appearance of racist ideas in particular in *White over Black: American Attitudes Toward the Negro, 1550–1812* (Chapel Hill, 1968).
8. John Saffin, *A Brief and Candid Answer to a late printed sheet, entitled The Selling of Joseph* . . . . (Boston, n.p., 1701).
9. Many scholars have noted northern manifestations of proslavery thought, but this aspect of the argument has not been given much consideration in general treatments until recently. See Adelaide Avery Lyons, 'The Religious Defense of Slavery in the North', *Trinity College Historical Society Papers*, XIII (1919), 5–34; Henry Clyde Hubbart, 'Pro-Southern Influence in the Free West, 1840–1865', *MVHR*, XX (1933), 45–62; Howard C. Perkins, 'The Defense of Slavery in the Northern Press on the Eve of the Civil War', *JSH*, IX (1943), 501–31; Joel H. Silbey, 'Pro-Slavery Sentiment in Iowa, 1836–1861', *Iowa Journal of History*, LV (1957), 289–318; Larry E. Tise, 'The Interregional Appeal of Proslavery Thought: An Ideological Profile of the Antebellum American Clergy', *Plantation Society*, I (1979), 58–72. See Tise, 'Proslavery Ideology', for discussion of the proslavery argument in Britain and the West Indies. For an interesting new comparative perspective, see Peter Kolchin, 'In Defense of Servitude: American Proslavery and Russian Proserfdom Arguments, 1760–1860', *AHR*, 85, No. 4 (October, 1980), 809–27.
10. Wilbur J. Cash, *The Mind of the South* (New York, 1941); Charles G. Sellers, Jr., 'The Travail of Slavery', in Sellers (ed.), *The Southerner as American* (Chapel Hill,

1960), 40–71. See also William W. Freehling, *Prelude to Civil War: The Nullification Controversy in South Carolina, 1816–1836* (New York, 1966), and Ralph E. Morrow, 'The Proslavery Argument Revisited', *MVHR*, XLVII (1961), 79–94.

11. E. N. Elliott to James Henry Hammond, September 15, 1859, in Hammond Papers, LOC. Elliott was the editor of *Cotton Is King and Pro-Slavery Arguments* (Augusta, 1860), a collection of proslavery classics.

12. Joseph Walker to James Henry Hammond, May 20, 1848, in Hammond Papers, LOC. Walker published *The Pro-Slavery Argument*, which the Charleston *Courier* (May 26, 1853) greeted as a 'thesaurus of facts and arguments' on the slavery question.

13. George Frederick Holmes, 'Bledsoe on Liberty and Slavery', *De Bow's Review*, XXI (1856), 133.

14. Francis Lieber, quoted in Daniel Walker Hollis, *University of South Carolina College: South Carolina* (Columbia, S.C., 1951), 183.

15. Edmund Ruffin, Diary, January 29, 1859, in Edmund Ruffin Papers, LOC.

16. William Harper, *Memoir on Slavery, read before the Society for the Advancement of Learning at its annual meeting in Columbia, 1837* (Charleston, 1838), 8; George Fitzhugh to George Frederick Holmes, 1855, in George Frederick Holmes Papers, Manuscript Division, Duke.

17. George Frederick Holmes, 'Slavery and Freedom', 132; Henry Hughes, 'New Duties of the South', *Southern Reveille*, November 18, 1854, clipping in Henry Hughes Scrapbook, Mississippi Department of Archives and History, Jackson, Mississippi. This quotation was kindly provided me by Bertram Wyatt-Brown. William J. Grayson, to James Henry Hammond, November 3, 1849, in Hammond Papers, LOC; George Frederick Holmes, 'On Slavery and Christianity', *SQR*, III (1843), 252.

18. Donald, 'The Proslavery Argument Reconsidered', 12, 11, 12.

19. Tise, 'Proslavery Ideology', and 'The Interregional Appeal of Proslavery Thought'. On proslavery clergy, see also Jack P. Maddex, Jr., 'Proslavery Millennialism: Social Eschatology in Antebellum Southern Calvinism', *American Quarterly*, XXXI (1979), 46–62, and Jack P. Maddex, Jr., ' "The Southern Apostasy" Revisited: The Significance of Proslavery Christianity', *Marxist Perspectives*, II (Fall, 1979), 132–41. See also Drew Gilpin Faust, 'A Southern Stewardship: The Intellectual and the Proslavery Argument', *American Quarterly*, XXXI (1979), 63–80; Drew Gilpin Faust, *A Sacred Circle: The Dilemma of the Intellectual in the Old South, 1840–1860* (Baltimore, 1977).

20. Jenkins, *The Proslavery Argument in the Old South*; Donald, 'The Proslavery Argument Reconsidered', 4; Eugene Genovese, *The World the Slaveholders Made: Two Essays in Interpretation* (New York, 1969), Genovese's concern with planter 'hegemony' has focused fresh interest on ideology in the Old South. Other historians have been influenced by anthropological studies of belief systems to regard ideology in new ways. Anthropologist Clifford Geertz has been especially influential. In the realm of proslavery historiography specifically, see Tise, 'Proslavery Ideology'; Faust, *A Sacred Circle*; Kenneth Greenberg, 'Revolutionary Ideology and the Proslavery Argument: The Abolition of Slavery in Antebellum South Carolina', *JSH*, XLII (1976), 365–84.

21. Thomas R. Dew, *Review of the Debate in the Virginia Legislature of 1831 and 1832* (Richmond, Va., 1832). This essay was an expansion of 'Abolition of Negro Slavery', *American Quarterly Review*, XII (1832), 189–265, and was later reprinted in *The Pro-Slavery Argument*, 287–490.

22. Genovese, *The World the Slaveholders Made*, 133.

23. E. N. Elliott, 'Introduction', in *Cotton Is King*, xii.

24. George Frederick Holmes, 'The Failure of Free Societies', *Southern Literary Messenger*, XXI (1855), 129.

25. *Ibid.*; Albert Taylor Bledsoe, 'Liberty and Slavery; or, Slavery in the Light of Political Philosophy', in *Cotton Is King*, 274; Charleston *Courier*, May 26, 1853. See chart of personal interactions among slavery's defenders in Faust, 'A Southern Stewardship', 68.

26. A. B. Longstreet, *Letters on the Epistle of Paul to Philemon* (Charleston, 1845); Howell Cobb, *A Scriptural Examination of the Institution of Slavery in the United States* (Perry, Ga., 1856); Thornton Stringfellow, 'The Bible Argument, or Slavery in the Light of Divine Revelation', in *Cotton Is King*, 461–546.

27. For the impact of the emergence of 'social science' upon the career of one of slavery's defenders, see Neal C. Gillespie, *The Collapse of Orthodoxy: The Intellectual Ordeal of George Frederick Holmes* (Charlottesville, Va., 1972). See also H. G. and Winnie Leach Duncan, 'The Development of Sociology in the Old South', *American Journal of Sociology*, XXXIX (1934), 649–56. Thornton Stringfellow, *Scriptural and Statistical Views in Favor of Slavery* (Richmond, Va., 1856); George Fitzhugh, *Sociology for the South or the Failure of Free Society* (Richmond, Va., 1854); Henry Hughes, *Treatise on Sociology: Theoretical and Practical* (Philadelphia, 1854).

28. On the emergence of social science from moral philosophy, see Gladys Bryson, 'The Emergence of Social Sciences from Moral Philosophy', *International Journal of Ethics*, XLII (1932), 304–23; on moral science, see Donald H. Meyer, *The Instructed Conscience: The Shaping of the American National Ethic* (Philadelphia, 1972).

29. See Thomas Cooper, 'Slavery', *Southern Literary Journal*, I (1835), 188; James Henry Hammond, 'Law of Nature – Natural Rights – Slavery', MS in Tucker-Coleman Papers, Manuscript Department, Earl Gregg Swem Memorial Library, College of William and Mary, Williamsburg, Virginia; J. P. Holcombe, 'Is Slavery Consistent with Natural Law?' *Southern Literary Messenger*, XXVII (1858), 408.

30. William J. Grayson, 'The Hireling and the Slave', in Eric L. McKitrick (ed.), *Slavery Defended: The Views of the Old South* (Englewood Cliffs, N.J., 1963), 66, 68. On the notion of rights and duties, see W. T. Hamilton, D.D., *The Duties of Masters and Slaves Respectively: Or Domestic Servitude as Sanctioned by the Bible* (Mobile, 1845), and James Henley Thornwell, *The Rights and Duties of Masters: A Sermon Preached at the Dedication of a Church Erected in Charleston for the Benefit and Instruction of the Coloured Population* (Charleston, 1850). On social organicism, see Theodore Dwight Bozeman, 'Joseph LeConte: Organic Science and a "Sociology for the South" ', *JSH*, XXXIX (1973), 565–82.

31. Abel P. Upshur, 'Domestic Slavery', *Southern Literary Messenger*, V (1839), 685; James Henry Hammond, Speech in the Senate, March 4, 1858, *Congressional Globe*, 35th Cong., 1st Sess., App., 71.

32. Harper, 'Slavery in the Light of Social Ethics', 569; Hammond, 'Hammond's Letters', 122; Nathaniel Beverley Tucker, *A Series of Lectures on the Science of Government Intended to Prepare the Student for the Study of the Constitution of the United States* (Philadelphia, 1845), 349.

33. On these changes, see Charles C. Gillespie, *Genesis and Geology* (Cambridge, 1951); Theodore Dwight Bozeman, *Protestants in an Age of Science: The Baconian Ideal and Antebellum American Religious Thought* (Chapel Hill, 1977); Charles E. Rosenberg, *No Other Gods: On Science and Social Thought in America* (Baltimore, 1976).

34. Samuel Cartwright to William S. Forwood, March 24, 1858, in William S. Forwood Papers, Trent Collection, Duke Medical Library, Duke University.

35. Samuel Cartwright to William S. Forwood, February 13, 1861, in *ibid.*

36. Josiah C. Nott, *Two Lectures on the Connection Between the Biblical and Physical History of Man* (1849; reprint ed., New York, 1969), 7, 14.

37. S. W. Butler to W. S. Forwood, June 26, 1857, in Forwood Papers. Like many of Nott's nineteenth-century readers, William Stanton also failed to distinguish

between Nott's anticlericalism and antireligionism and greatly overstated the level of conflict between religion and science in the 1850s. Nevertheless, Stanton's study of the rise of ethnology is the most complete to date. See *The Leopard's Spots: Scientific Attitudes Toward Race in America, 1815–1859* (Chicago, 1960). For the attack upon Nott, see Moses Ashley Curtis, 'The Unity of the Races', *SQR*, VII (1845), 372–448, and John Bachman, *The Doctrine of the Unity of the Human Race Examined on the Principles of Science* (Charleston, 1850). Note that Bachman, a Lutheran clergyman, invoked the 'principles of science'.

38. George Frederick Holmes to Daniel Whitaker, September 25, 1844, in George Frederick Holmes Letterbook, Holmes Papers; Edmund Ruffin, January 10, 1864, in Diary, Ruffin Papers; George Fitzhugh, 'Southern Thought', *De Bow's Review*, XXIII (1857), 347.

39. In a recent reassessment of proslavery thought, historian George Fredrickson has portrayed the role of racial defenses quite differently, proclaiming the existence of significant opposition between racial and moral-philosophical rationalizations for the South's system of human bondage. Instead of proslavery unity, he found two distinct proslavery arguments, one in the aristocratic seaboard South and one in the more democratic Southwest. These latter egalitarian areas, he asserted, were unsympathetic to the hierarchical views of slavery's moral-philosophical defenders; racial arguments could provide the only convincing foundation for human bondage within the Old Southwest's 'herrenvolk democracy'. There is little evidence for these geographical differences in proslavery sentiment. A best-selling collection of defenses of slavery edited by E. N. Elliott of Mississippi included the most famous hierarchical arguments and emphasized the consistency of all proslavery thought; eastern apologists devoted considerable attention to racial justifications in their own tracts; seaboard and southwestern defenders exchanged pamphlets and essays and eagerly sought each other's advice. Fredrickson may err in regarding the mainstream proslavery position as uncongenial to the more democratic Southwest. As early as 1936, William B. Hesseltine made a convincing case that proslavery was motivated in large part by a desire to promote the loyalty of nonslaveholding whites, and he contended that all proslavery theories were designed to be attractive to these common folk. Even though the arguments 'carried but little promise to the lower classes', he remarked, they 'sufficed to draw a line of demarkation between the exploited groups of the South'. The complex factors that kept the southern yeoman loyal to the region's master class may also have attracted them to the proslavery argument. Slavery, its defenders insisted, made republicanism and white freedom possible. Because blacks served as the necessary 'mud-sill' class, whites all enjoyed enhanced liberty. George M. Fredrickson, *The Black Image in the White Mind: The Debate on Afro-American Character and Destiny, 1817–1914* (New York, 1971); William B. Hesseltine, 'Some New Aspects of the Pro-Slavery Argument', 11. On the position of the yeoman, see Eugene Genovese, 'Yeoman Farmers in a Slaveholders Democracy', *Agricultural History*, XLIX (1975), 331–42.

40. E. N. Elliott, 'Concluding Remarks', in *Cotton Is King*, 897.

41. 'Critical Notices', *SQR*, XVI (1849), 265.

42. Holmes, 'Slavery and Freedom', 65.

43. George Fitzhugh to George Frederick Holmes, March 27, 1855, in Holmes Papers; Robert Walsh, *An Appeal from the Judgments of Great Britain Respecting the United States of America* (Philadelphia, 1819).

44. George Fitzhugh to George Frederick Holmes, 1855, in Holmes Papers.

45. George Frederick Holmes, February 21, 1857, in Diary, Holmes Papers; Edmund Ruffin, October 26, 1858, in Diary, Ruffin Papers.

46. Donald, 'The Proslavery Argument Reconsidered', 3.

47. Arthur C. Cole presents evidence for the direct influence of Fitzhugh on Lincoln's 'house divided' speech. See Cole, *Lincoln's House Divided Speech* (Chicago, 1923).

48. Genovese, *The World the Slaveholders Made*, 129. Part of Genovese's attraction to Fitzhugh arises, of course, from the hostility to capitalism that this Marxist historian shares with the nineteenth-century southerner.
49. Edmund Ruffin, October 21, 1858, in Diary, Ruffin Papers.
50. The nature of this conflict between tradition and modernity has been a central concern in the extensive historical literature on the nineteenth-century North, and especially on evangelicalism and reform. For two examples, see Marvin Meyers, *The Jacksonian Persuasion* (Stanford, 1960), and Clifford S. Griffin, *Their Brothers Keepers: Moral Stewardship in the United States, 1800–1865* (New Brunswick, 1960).

DOCUMENT 1: LETTER TO AN ENGLISH ABOLITIONIST

An excerpt from the first of two letters that James Henry Hammond (1807–64), a South Carolinian, published in the Columbia South Carolinian *in 1845. Hammond summarises some of the core arguments of the proslavery position, emphasising the strength of slavery as a core republican institution in the South.*

I endorse without reserve the much abused sentiment of Governor M'Duffie, that 'Slavery is the corner-stone of our republican edifice'; while I repudiate, as ridiculously absurd, that much lauded but nowhere accredited dogma of Mr. Jefferson, that 'all men are born equal'. No society has ever yet existed, and I have already incidentally quoted the highest authority to show that none ever will exist, without a natural variety of classes. The most marked of these must, in a country like ours, be the rich and the poor, the educated and the ignorant. It will scarcely be disputed that the very poor have less leisure to prepare themselves for the proper discharge of public duties than the rich; and that the ignorant are wholly unfit for them at all. In all countries save ours, these two classes, or the poor rather, who are presumed to be necessarily ignorant, are by law expressly excluded from all participation in the management of public affairs. In a Republican Government this cannot be done. Universal suffrage, though not essential in theory, seems to be in fact a necessary appendage to a republican system. Where universal suffrage obtains, it is obvious that the government is in the hands of a numerical majority; and it is hardly necessary to say that in every part of the world more than half the people are ignorant and poor. Though no one can look upon poverty as a crime, and we do not here generally regard it as any objection to a man in his individual capacity, still it must be admitted that it is a wretched and insecure government which is administered by its most ignorant citizens, and those who have the least at stake under it. Though intelligence and wealth have great influence here, as everywhere, in keeping in check reckless and unenlightened numbers, yet it is evident to close observers, if not to all, that these are rapidly usurping all power in the non-slaveholding States, and threaten a fearful crisis in republican institutions there at no remote period. In the slaveholding States, however, nearly one-half of the whole population, and those the poorest and most ignorant, have no political influence whatever, because they are slaves. Of the other half, a large proportion are both educated and independent in their circumstances, while those who unfortunately are not so, being still elevated far above the mass, are higher toned and more deeply interested in preserving a stable and well ordered government, than the same class in

Drew Gilpin Faust (ed.), *The Ideology of Slavery: Proslavery Thought in the Antebellum South* (Baton Rouge: Louisiana State University Press, 1981), pp. 176–9.

any other country. Hence, Slavery is truly the 'corner-stone' and foundation of every well-designed and durable 'republican edifice'.

With us every citizen is concerned in the maintenance of order, and in promoting honesty and industry among those of the lowest class who are our slaves; and our habitual vigilance renders standing armies, whether of soldiers or policemen, entirely unnecessary. Small guards in our cities, and occasional patrols in the country, ensure us a repose and security known no where else. You cannot be ignorant that, excepting the United States, there is no country in the world whose existing government would not be over-turned in a month, but for its standing armies, maintained at an enormous and destructive cost to those whom they are destined to overawe – so rampant and combative is the spirit of discontent wherever nominal free labor prevails, with its ostensive privileges and its dismal servitude. Nor will it be long before the '*free States*' of this Union will be compelled to introduce the same expensive machinery, to preserve order among their 'free and equal' citizens. Already has Philadelphia organized a permanent battalion for this purpose; New-York, Boston and Cincinnati will soon follow her example; and then the smaller towns and densely populated counties. The intervention of their militia to repress violations of the peace is becoming a daily affair. A strong government, after some of the old fashions – though probably with a new name – sustained by the force of armed mercenaries, is the ultimate destiny of the non-slave-holding section of this confederacy, and one which may not be very distant.

It is a great mistake to suppose, as is generally done abroad, that in case of war slavery would be a source of weakness. It did not weaken Rome, nor Athens, nor Sparta, though their slaves were comparatively far more numerous than ours, of the same color for the most part with themselves, and large numbers of them familiar with the use of arms. I have no apprehension that our slaves would seize such an opportunity to revolt. The present generation of them, born among us, would never think of such a thing at any time, unless instigated to it by others. Against such instigations we are always on our guard. In time of war we should be more watchful and better prepared to put down insurrections than at any other periods. Should any foreign nation be so lost to every sentiment of civilized humanity, as to attempt to erect among us the standard of revolt, or to invade us with black troops, for the base and barbarous purpose of stirring up servile war, their efforts would be signally rebuked. Our slaves could not be easily seduced, nor would any thing delight them more than to assist in stripping Cuffee of his regimentals to put him in the cotton-field, which would be the fate of most black invaders, without any very prolix form of 'apprenticeship'. If, as I am satisfied would be the case, our slaves remained peaceful on our plantations, and cultivated them in time of war under the superintendence of a limited number of our citizens, it is obvious that we could put forth more strength in such an emergency, at less sacrifice, than any other people of the same numbers. And thus we should in every point of view, 'out of this nettle danger, pluck the flower safety'.

How far Slavery may be an advantage or disadvantage to those not owning slaves, yet united with us in political association, is a question for their sole consideration. It is true that our representation in Congress is increased by it. But so are our taxes; and the non slave-holding States, being the majority, divide among themselves far the greater portion of the amount levied by the Federal Government. And I doubt not that, when it comes to a close calculation, they will not be slow in finding out that the balance of profit arising from the connection is vastly in their favor.

In a social point of view the abolitionists pronounce Slavery to be a monstrous evil. If it was so, it would be our own peculiar concern, and superfluous benevolence in them to lament over it. Seeing their bitter hostility to us, they might leave us to cope with our own calamities. But they make war upon us out of excess of charity, and attempt to purify by covering us with calumny. You have read and assisted to circulate a great deal about affrays, duels and murders, occurring here, and all attributed to the terrible demoralization of Slavery. Not a single event of this sort takes place among us, but it is caught up by the abolitionists, and paraded over the world, with endless comments, variations and exaggerations. You should not take what reaches you as a mere sample, and infer that there is a vast deal more you never hear. You hear all, and more than all, the truth.

DOCUMENT 2: GEORGE FITZHUGH AND
PROSLAVERY THOUGHT

George Fitzhugh (1804–81) was a self-taught Virginian lawyer who grew up on the family plantation. He was a prolific writer, notably on slavery. This extract is taken from 'Southern Thought', two articles that appeared in De Bow's Review *in 1857. These articles summarise his proslavery position. Fitzhugh argued that human bondage provided subsistence for all and eliminated the poverty and suffering experienced by British industrial labourers.*

We differ from what are called the extremists of the South; but would not shoot down the sentinels of our camp. If not the wisest, most far-seeing, and most prudent, they are the most zealous friends of the South. They believe, that eventually, the aggressions of Northern abolition will force disunion upon us, and look to disunion as probably the only ultimate redress for the wrongs inflicted on us. We think a victory may yet, perhaps, be won by the South, not by arms, but by Southern thought and European necessities. Thought, by means of the press and the mail, has now become almost omnipotent. It rules the world. Thought, with hunger and nakedness to prompt, stimulate, and direct it, will prove irresistible. That thought has commenced and begotten a counter-current in Europe, that impels France to renew the slave-trade under a new form, and induced a debate in the British Parliament which evinces a universal change of opinion as to abolition and squints most obviously towards the renewal of the slave-trade. Revolutions of opinion do not go backwards, nor do they stand still in a half-way course. England sees, admits, and deplores the error of West India emancipation. This admission is but a step in a chain of argument, which must ultimately carry her further from abolition, and bring her nearer to slavery. For a while, she will try to maintain some middle ground between emancipation and slavery, and substitute coolies, and African apprentices, for negro slaves. But there are two reasons why she cannot long occupy this ground. First, its falsity and hypocrisy are too obvious; and secondly, coolies and apprentices do not answer the purpose of slaves. Her necessities will compel her to reinstate African slavery in its old and mildest form. Thus will Southern thought triumph, Southern morality be vindicated, and Southern wisdom, prudence, and foresight, be rendered apparent. The crusades lasted for a century. Those who conducted them had stronger convictions, and a clearer sense of duty, than modern abolitionists, for they laid down their lives by the million in the cause, whilst modern abolitionists, from Wilberforce to Greely, have not evinced the slightest taste for martyrdom. All Europe then believed the crusades a righteous and holy undertaking. Abolition has never

Drew Gilpin Faust (ed.), *The Ideology of Slavery: Proslavery Thought in the Antebellum South* (Baton Rouge: Louisiana State University Press, 1981), pp. 284–7.

commanded such universal assent, nor such self-denying sacrifices. So far from marching a thousand or more miles to fight for their cause, they have not been willing to give up a cup of coffee, an ounce of sugar, or a pound of cotton, to speed it; no, they have been encouraging slavery, whilst abusing it, by consuming slave products. Europe and the North can any day abolish slavery by disusing slave products. They should try the experiment, for should they succeed in abolishing it, they will have none of those products thereafter – Jamaica and Hayti prove this.

The crusades lasted for a century, and their signal failure opened men's eyes to the folly and wickedness of such expeditions; and soon men began to wonder at the infatuation of their crusading ancestry. So it will be with abolition. It has lasted nearly a hundred years. It has failed as signally as the crusades, and brought hunger and nakedness on its votaries, or at least on the laboring poor at their doors. As in the case of the crusades, abolition will soon be considered a mad infatuation – for want, brought on by it, combines with failure, to open men's eyes.

Southern thought must be a distinct thought – not a half thought, but a whole thought. Domestic slavery must be vindicated in the abstract, and in the general, as a normal, natural, and, *in general*, necessitous element of civilized society, without regard to race or color.

This argument about races is an infidel procedure, and we had better give up the negroes than the Bible. It is a double assertion of the falsity of the Bible – first, as it maintains that mankind have not sprang from a common parentage; and, secondly, as it contends that it is morally wrong to enslave white men, who, the Bible informs us, were enslaved by the express command of God. But it is also utterly falsified by history. The little States of Greece, in their intestine wars, made slaves of their prisoners, and there was no complaint that they did not make good slaves; whilst the Macedonians, an inferior race, were proverbially unfit for slavery. The Georgians and Circassians, the most beautiful of the human family, make excellent slaves, whilst the Bedouin Arab and American Indian are as unfit for slavery as the Bengal tiger, or those tribes in Palestine whom God commanded Moses and Joshua to put to the sword without discrimination or mercy.

Again: to defend and justify mere negro slavery, and condemn other forms of slavery, is to give up expressly the whole cause of the South – for mulattoes, quadroons, and men with as white skins as any of us, may legally be, and in fact are, held in slavery in every State of the South. The abolitionists well know this, for almost the whole interest of Mrs. Stowe's Uncle Tom's Cabin, arises from the fact, that a man and woman, with fair complexion, are held as slaves.

We are all in the habit of maintaining that our slaves are far better off than the common laborers of Europe, and that those laborers were infinitely better situated as feudal serfs or slaves than as freemen, or rather as slaves to capital. Now, we stultify ourselves if we maintain it would be wrong to remit them back to domestic slavery, which we always argue is much milder and protective than that slavery to capital, to which emancipation has subjected them. They have been wronged and injured by emancipation, would we not restore them to slavery? Or are we, too, to become Socialists, and coop them up in Greely's Free-Love phalansteries? There are no other alternative.

Again: every Southern man in defending slavery, habitually appeals to the almost universal usages of civilized man, and argues that slavery must be natural to man, and intended by Providence as the condition of the larger portion of the race, else it could not have been so universal. What a ridiculous and absurd figure does the defender of mere negro slavery cut, who uses this argument, when the abolitionist turns round on him and says – 'why, you have just admitted that white slavery was wrong, and this universal usage which you speak of has been white, not black slavery. The latter is a very recent affair'.

We must defend the principle of slavery as part of the constitution of man's nature. The defence of mere negro slavery, will, nay, has involved us in a thousand absurdities and contradictions. We must take high philosophical, biblical, and historical grounds, and soar beyond the little time and space around us to the earliest records of time, and the farthest verge of civilization. Let us quit the narrow boundaries of the rice, the sugar and the cotton field, and invite the abolitionists to accompany us in our flight to the tent of Abraham, to the fields of Judea, to the halls of David and of Solomon, to the palaces and the farms of Athens and of Rome, and to the castles of the grim Barons of medieval time. Let us point to their daily routine of domestic life. Then, not till then, may we triumphantly defend negro slavery. 'You see slavery everywhere, and throughout all times: you see men subjected to it by express command or by permission of God, with skins as white and intellects as good as yours. Can it be wrong to enslave the poor negro, who needs a master more than any of these'? Less than this is inconsiderate assertion, not Southern thought; nay, not thought at all.

The temptation to confine the defence of slavery to mere negro slavery is very strong, for it is obvious that they require masters under all circumstances, whilst the whites need them only under peculiar circumstances, and those circumstances such as we can hardly realize the existence of in America. May the day never arrive when our lands shall be so closely monopolized, and our population become so dense, that the poor would find slavery a happy refuge from the oppression of capital.

In the South, there is another and a stronger reason for the feeling of indignation at the bare suggestion of white slavery – that is pride of caste. No man loves liberty and hates slavery so cordially as the Southerner. Liberty is with him a privilege, or distinction, belonging to all white men. Slavery a badge of disgrace attached to an inferior race. Accustomed from childhood to connect the idea of slavery with the negro, and of liberty with the white man, it shocks his sensibilities barely to mention white slavery. 'Tis vain to talk to him of the usages of mankind, for his prejudices and prepossessions were formed long before he heard of history, and they are too strong to be reasoned away.

DOCUMENT 3: JUSTIFICATION FOR SLAVERY

An excerpt from William Harper's Memoir on Slavery, *an oration delivered to the South Carolina Society for the Advancement of Learning in Columbia in 1837 and printed as a pamphlet in the following year. Harper (1790–1847) compares the lot of American slaves favourably to other workers. He also argues in favour of the inferiority of black Americans.*

What is the essential character of *Slavery*, and in what does it differ from the *servitude* of other countries? If I should venture on a definition, I should say that where a man is compelled to labor at the will of another, and to give him much the greater portion of the product of his labor, there *Slavery* exists; and it is immaterial by what sort of compulsion the will of the laborer is subdued. It is what no human being would do without some sort of compulsion. He cannot be compelled to labor by blows. No – but what difference does it make, if you can inflict any other sort of torture which will be equally effectual in subduing the will? If you can starve him, or alarm him for the subsistence of himself or his family? And is it not under this compulsion that the *freeman* labors? I do not mean in every particular case, but in the general. Will any one be hardy enough to say that he is at his own disposal, or has the government of himself? True, he may change his employer if he is dissatisfied with his conduct towards him; but this is a privilege he would in the majority of cases gladly abandon, and render the connexion between them indissoluble. There is far less of the interest and attachment in his relation to his employer, which so often exists between the master and the slave, and mitigates the condition of the latter. An intelligent English traveller has characterized as the most miserable and degraded of all beings, 'a masterless slave'. And is not the condition of the laboring poor of other countries too often that of masterless slaves? ...

That they are called free, undoubtedly aggravates the sufferings of the slaves of other regions. They see the enormous inequality which exists, and feel their own misery, and can hardly conceive otherwise, than that there is some injustice in the institutions of society to occasion these. They regard the apparently more fortunate class as oppressors, and it adds bitterness, that they should be of the same name and race. They feel indignity more acutely, and more of discontent and evil passion is excited; they feel that it is mockery that calls them free. Men do not so much hate and envy those who are separated from them by a wide distance, and some apparently impassible barrier, as those who approach nearer to their own condition, and with whom they habitually bring themselves into comparison. The slave with us is not tantalized with the name of freedom, to which his whole

Drew Gilpin Faust (ed.), *The Ideology of Slavery: Proslavery Thought in the Antebellum South* (Baton Rouge: Louisiana State University Press, 1981), pp. 112–14.

condition gives the lie, and would do so if he were emancipated to-morrow. The African slave sees that nature herself has marked him as a separate – and if left to himself, I have no doubt he would feel it to be an inferior – race, and interposed a barrier almost insuperable to his becoming a member of the same society, standing on the same footing of right and privilege with his master.

That the African negro is an inferior variety of the human race, is, I think, now generally admitted, and his distinguishing characteristics are such as peculiarly mark him out for the situation which he occupies among us. And these are no less marked in their original country, than as we have daily occasion to observe them. The most remarkable is their indifference to personal liberty. In this they have followed their instincts since we have any knowledge of their continent, by enslaving each other; but contrary to the experience of every other race, the possession of slaves has no material effect in raising the character, and promoting the civilization of the master. Another trait is the want of domestic affections, and insensibility to the ties of kindred. In the travels of the Landers, after speaking of a single exception, in the person of a woman who betrayed some transient emotion in passing by the country from which she had been torn as a slave, the authors add: 'that Africans, generally speaking, betray the most perfect indifference on losing their liberty, and being deprived of their relatives, while love of country is equally a stranger to their breasts, as social tenderness or domestic affection'. 'Marriage is celebrated by the nations as unconcernedly as possible; a man thinks as little of taking a wife, as of cutting an ear of corn – affection is altogether out of the question'. They are, however, very submissive to authority, and seem to entertain great reverence for chiefs, priests, and masters. No greater indignity can be offered an individual, than to throw opprobrium on his parents. On this point of their character, I think I have remarked, that, contrary to the instinct of nature in other races, they entertain less regard for children than for parents, to whose authority they have been accustomed to submit. Their character is thus summed up by the travellers quoted, 'the few opportunities we have had of studying their characters, induce us to believe that they are a simple, honest, inoffensive, but weak, timid, and cowardly race. They seem to have no social tenderness, very few of those amiable private virtues which could win our affections, and none of those public qualities that claim respect or command admiration. The love of country is not strong enough in their bosoms to incite them to defend it against a despicable foe; and of the active energy, noble sentiments, and contempt of danger which distinguishes the North American tribes and other savages, no traces are to be found among this slothful people. Regardless of the past, as reckless of the future, the present alone influences their actions. In this respect, they approach nearer to the nature of the brute creation, than perhaps any other people on the face of the globe'. Let me ask if this people do not furnish the very material out of which slaves ought to be made, and whether it be not an improving of their condition to make them the slaves of civilized masters. There is a variety in the character of the tribes. Some are brutally, and savagely ferocious and bloody, whom it would be mercy to enslave. From the travellers' account, it seems not unlikely that the negro race is tending to extermination, being daily encroached on, and overrun by the superior Arab race. It may be, that when they shall have been lost from their native seats, they may be found numerous, and in no unhappy condition, on the continent to which they have been transplanted.

10

THE ANTISLAVERY STRUGGLE

INTRODUCTION

In North America and throughout Europe the abolition of slavery found few advocates before 1750. Most intellectuals, lawyers, clergymen and other educated people condoned slavery. Many of them accepted Thomas Hobbes's notion of the power struggle endemic in human societies and believed in a hierarchical, vertical society in which some people were naturally found at the bottom of the social order and likely to experience forms of involuntary labour and slavery. The growth of antislavery ideas emerged fully in the middle of the eighteenth century and was marked by Enlightenment philosophers placing emphasis on liberty and the moral bankruptcy of slavery as a social system. Propagated by French and Scottish moral philosophers, and later influenced by Christian notions of benevolence, God's Providence and the impact of American revolutionary ideas, antislavery had built up a considerable transatlantic constituency by 1776. Davis (1975) charts the growth of early antislavery ideas in Britain and North America in this period, ranging widely in an important, sustained analysis. Soderlund (1985) shows, however, that even the Quakers, who were at the forefront of abolitionism before the War of Independence, took many decades before reaching universal agreement in condemning slavery in their heartlands of Pennsylvania and New Jersey.

Libertarian ideas advanced during the American revolutionary era led to the first wave of abolitionism in the United States, which largely consisted of gradual emancipation laws passed in the northern states. Legislative, judicial and constitutional action occurred in Massachusetts and New Hampshire and gradual abolition laws were passed in Pennsylvania (1780), Rhode Island (1784) and Connecticut (1784). In New York and New Jersey, where opposition to antislavery was more virulent, gradual emancipation bills did not pass the state legislatures until 1799 and 1804. These moves towards black freedom in the northern states were often very gradual indeed: many statutes granted liberty only to future born children of slaves at ages between twenty-one and twenty-eight. Zilversmit (1967) is a solid overview of these developments. He underscores the gradualism prevailing among American abolitionists until around the 1820s. Nash (1990) investigates the role of abolitionists in the political debates of revolutionary America and the early Republic. He takes a critical view of abolitionist tactics and strategies. In his interpretation, abolitionists failed to grasp the opportunity offered them by the emphasis on freedom found in revolutionary rhetoric. Even where conditions seemed favourable to antislavery, change occurred gradually and often grudgingly. The title of Nash and Soderlund's book (1990) encapsulates the slow, piecemeal granting of freedom to blacks in Pennsylvania, a state traditionally seen as in the vanguard of the antislavery struggle.

American abolitionism is often analysed in two further phases: the decades leading from the aftermath of the American Revolution up to 1831, when William Lloyd Garrison began publishing his radical antislavery newspaper *The Liberator*, and the subsequent three decades culminating in the American Civil War. Newman (2002) is the best overview of the first phase. His discussion traces the continuity in abolitionist activity in the United States from the era of the Constitution to the emergence of Garrison as a national campaigner. Newman shows how women and African-American abolitionists joined forces with white reformers during that half century to transform the antislavery battle. White elite reformers were assisted by those from lower echelons on the social scale who campaigned, especially in Massachusetts, for immediate emancipation. These newcomers to abolitionism organised effectively at grassroots level, lectured widely and published compelling accounts of slavery's immorality.

Walters (1976) regards abolitionism after 1830 as a phenomenon that was an integral part of antebellum American society rather than as a disparate group of reformers whose activities lay on the fringes of mainstream political life. Internal divisions beset abolitionist groups, to be sure, and those groups dissented from the southern proslavery emphasis upon a social, racial and sexual hierarchy that elevated whites above blacks. Nevertheless, as Walters shows, abolitionists, northern anti-abolitionists and proslavery advocates often espoused a common concern with the moral direction of American society and the need for orderly change. A good general supplement to Walters's book can be found in Stewart (1976), which is

especially helpful in treating the twin themes of moral suasion and immediatism among American antislavery campaigners after 1833.

Two collections of essays throw much light on American abolitionism.
Duberman's volume (1965) contains sixteen contributions that range from
the composition of the abolitionists to their critique of the United States
Constitution, from studies of individual abolitionists such as Wendell
Phillips and Frederick Douglass to the antislavery crusade of the Republican Party, and from a comparison of British and American abolitionists to
the utopian dimensions of abolitionism. Duberman's contribution explains
why northerners were generally more committed to stopping the extension of slavery rather than to becoming abolitionists. Yellin and Van Horne
(1994) include fifteen essays dealing with female antislavery societies, the
role of black women in the political culture of reform, and the strategies
and tactics of female antislavery groups. The contributors chart the efflores-
cence of women's antislavery activity, showing how this provided a political
focus before the first women's rights convention at Seneca Falls, New York,
in 1848. Antislavery women organised fund-raising fairs, wrote pamphlets
and giftbooks, circulated petitions and gave public speeches in pursuit of
their cause. The various essays indicate the different contexts in which these
women worked and show the contribution of the abolitionist sisterhood to
political culture and to the nascent movement for women's rights.

Kraditor (1969) includes an exploratory chapter on the role of women in
American abolitionism, but her book ranges more widely to provide an intellectual history of the goals, strategy and tactics of the abolitionists in the
1830s and 1840s. The different strands of abolitionism are clearly delineated. Kraditor finds, in particular, a struggle between radical abolitionists
and more respectable reformers. She treats Garrison's place in abolitionism
more sympathetically than several other historians. Garrison took a moral,
authoritarian view of slavery and its sinfulness and advocated immediate
emancipation. He thought the northern states should leave the Union rather
than continue to exist in a polity that included slavery. He favoured a broad
constituency for abolitionist activity from people with varying social, religious and political views. Perhaps his major legacy was to shift public
opinion in the northern states to an active antislavery stance by the 1850s.

Other books focusing on individual antislavery leaders also illumine
broader themes in American abolitionism. Wyatt-Brown (1969) provides an
overview of the evangelical wing of antislavery by focusing on Lewis Tappan
and his supporters. Tappan was a wealthy Presbyterian New York merchant
who worked actively for various philanthropic and religious causes. He was
a conservative antislavery campaigner who broke away from Garrison over
the latter's espousal of various reform causes, notably women's rights, which
were viewed as straying from the abolitionist goal. Stewart (1986) views
Wendell Phillips, a Boston elite reformer, with his fiery oratory and sense

of morality and liberty, as an antislavery campaigner who believed he was following the libertarian path of American republicanism. Phillips saw the antislavery cause as a religious enterprise and as a logical outcome of the idealism of the American revolutionary tradition. Unlike Garrison, whose abolitionist commitment faded after the end of the Civil War, he continued to campaign on behalf of blacks, especially in relation to the suffrage, until the fifteenth constitutional amendment was passed.

The majority of the abolitionist leaders of the 1820s and 1830s had some formal connection with revivalism or a group of churches. Abolitionist propaganda often possessed a fire-and-brimstone quality; the violent imagery of abolitionist speeches became a commonplace in antebellum America. Some historians have consequently portrayed the abolitionists as abnormal men agitating for the sake of agitation and their own selfish ends. In this portrayal, they were branded as fanatics and irrational campaigners. This theme is developed in Donald (1956). But there is an alternative perspective. Sorin (1971) argues that New York abolitionists were not abnormal; rather they were people who tended to share in the general prosperity of the period and in public office, who were better educated than the population as a whole but only marginally better educated than any other leadership group. More work is needed on the social bases of antislavery but Magdol (1986) shows that labouring men and women, small businessmen and artisans were among the main signatories to abolitionist petitions in Massachusetts and upstate New York in the 1830s.

The contribution of free blacks to the antislavery crusade is treated in narrative manner by Quarles (1969). Jacobs (1993) includes essays that explore the interaction between black abolitionists and white reformers in Boston. Cooperation existed in a common cause across the racial divide but African-American reformers followed some distinctive courses of action. Friedman (1982) teases out the complexity and differences in outlook between prominent antislavery groups in New York City, upstate New York and Boston. Members of these groups, whatever their other characteristics, felt tension between their personal piety and adherence to a wider cause. Friedman is concerned with the connections between self and community among the first generation of immediate abolitionists. Among other issues, he shows that members of the Tappan group came to see their brand of abolitionism as indelibly tied to America's churches. In so doing, they decried abolitionists who focused their activities on parties and electoral politics.

BIBLIOGRAPHY

Davis, David Brion, *The Problem of Slavery in the Age of Revolution, 1770–1823* (Ithaca, NY: Cornell University Press, 1975)

Donald, David H., *Lincoln Reconsidered: Essays on the Civil War Era* (New York: Alfred A. Knopf, 1956; 2nd edn, 1961)

Duberman, Martin (ed.), *The Antislavery Vanguard: New Essays on the Abolitionists* (Princeton: Princeton University Press, 1965)

Friedman, Lawrence J., *Gregarious Saints: Self and Community in American Abolitionism, 1830–1870* (Cambridge: Cambridge University Press, 1982)

Jacobs, Donald M. (ed.), *Courage and Conscience: Black and White Abolitionists in Boston* (Bloomington: Indiana University Press, 1993)

Jeffrey, Julie Roy, *The Great Silent Army of Abolitionism: Ordinary Women in the Antislavery Movement* (Chapel Hill: University of North Carolina Press, 1998)

Kraditor, Aileen S., *Means and Ends in American Abolitionism: Garrison and his critics on Strategy and Tactics, 1834–1850* (New York: Pantheon Books, 1969)

Magdol, Edward, *The Antislavery Rank and File: A Social Profile of the Abolitionists' Constituency* (Westport, CT: Greenwood, 1986)

Nash, Gary B., *Race and Revolution* (Madison, WI: Madison House, 1990)

Nash, Gary B. and Jean R. Soderlund, *Freedom by Degrees: Emancipation and its Aftermath in Pennsylvania* (New York: Oxford University Press, 1990)

Newman, Richard S., *The Transformation of American Abolitionism: Fighting Slavery in the Early Republic* (Chapel Hill: University of North Carolina Press, 2002)

Quarles, Benjamin, *Black Abolitionists* (Oxford: Oxford University Press, 1969)

Soderlund, Jean R., *Quakers and Slavery: A Divided Spirit* (Princeton: Princeton University Press, 1985)

Sorin, Gerald, *The New York Abolitionists: A Case Study of Political Radicalism* (Westport, CT: Greenwood, 1971)

Stewart, James Brewer, *Holy Warriors: The Abolitionists and American Slavery* (New York: Hill and Wang, 1976; rev. edn, 1997)

Stewart, James Brewer, *Wendell Phillips: Liberty's Hero* (Baton Rouge: Louisiana State University Press, 1986)

Walters, Ronald G., *The Antislavery Appeal: American Abolitionism after 1830* (Baltimore, MD: Johns Hopkins University Press, 1976)

Wyatt-Brown, *Lewis Tappan and the Evangelical War against Slavery* (Cleveland, OH: Case Western University Press, 1969)

Yellin, Jean Fagan and Van Horne, John C. (eds), *The Abolitionist Sisterhood: Women's Political Culture in Antebellum America* (Ithaca, NY: Cornell University Press, 1994)

Zilversmit, Arthur, *First Emancipation: The Abolition of Slavery in the North* (Chicago: University of Chicago Press, 1967)

ESSAY: ORDINARY WOMEN IN THE
ANTISLAVERY MOVEMENT

This extract focuses on the ordinary women who formed part of the grassroots female army that helped to fight slavery. Jeffrey brings out the diversity of the female contribution to abolitionism. What contribution did ordinary women make to antislavery propaganda? How did they raise funds? Why was petitioning such an important female antislavery activity?

Antislavery societies offered women more than the opportunity to support emancipation. They created opportunities for friendship, conviviality, and emotional support and a worthwhile pastime outside of the home. Efforts to foster an organizational culture encouraged the acquisition of skills and attitudes valued in the larger world. Educational activities informed women about public events and encouraged them to think about and discuss them. Although not all women would follow the logic of organized abolitionism to its conclusion, associational life provided women with the information, skills, and confidence needed for active citizenship and participation in public life.

In 1836, urging more emphasis on helping free blacks in the North, Theodore Weld suggested the importance of work for organizational vitality. Work gave abolitionists something to do and thus kept them *'from shrivelling'*. Devising and carrying out projects animated association life, and the individual projects, while often modest in character, collectively lent important assistance to abolitionism. During the 1830s, women circulated abolitionist literature, secured subscriptions to newspapers, collected money, hired lecturers, sewed for and otherwise assisted needy African Americans, mounted fairs that brought in substantial sums, and were active in petition campaigns. Many of these projects demanded verbal skills and techniques that proved to be useful to women recruiting for their own societies, and they encouraged women to use these talents in a variety of settings, far from the privacy of their homes. As they worked for abolitionism, members of female antislavery societies moved closer to the conception of the woman abolitionist they had created.[1]

Some examples of projects undertaken by members of antislavery associations give an idea of the range of work in which women participated and their personal responses to doing it. Many of the activities female societies sponsored fall under the general category of propaganda. As one correspondent to the *Liberator* pointed out, an important part of publicizing the cause involved 'the circulation of anti-slavery tracts, papers, documents, &c. among those, who if not opposed, are not known to be friendly to

Julie Roy Jeffrey, *The Great Silent Army of Abolitionism: Ordinary Women in the Antislavery Movement* (Chapel Hill: University of North Carolina Press, 1998), pp. 80–95.

our views'. Not all societies aggressively sought out those unsympathetic to the cause, however. Some, like the Brooklyn Female Anti-Slavery Society, collected materials to lend 'to all who have a desire to read'. At least one society, in Plymouth, Massachusetts, had a reading room that they considered 'invaluable in spreading information where it would not otherwise reach'. The society allowed the curious to take the initiative.[2]

But other societies were willing to venture out into their communities to solicit readers. As Grace Williams pointed out, this involved 'much effort'. In Nantucket, the women's society to which she belonged visited every family on the island with the *Anti-Slavery Almanac*. When the women of the Amesbury and Salisbury (Massachusetts) Female Anti-Slavery Society declared that their most important work was the support for and circulation of Garrison's 'pioneer paper', they may well have visualized this sort of commitment. In order to circulate another antislavery paper *The Cradle of Liberty*, members of antislavery societies were instructed to spend two of three days scouring their communities, stopping at every household. In Maine, recognizing the effectiveness of women in this kind of work, the editor of the *Advocate of Freedom* commended the efforts of two women who had obtained seventy-four subscribers to that paper and encouraged others to imitate their success.[3]

None of this work was easy. People had all kinds of excuses not to read. 'So many [publications] come.... they cannot read nor hear of such cruelties', Experience Billings explained, while 'others are engaged for the heathen and have nothing for the slave'. Sarah Plummer, who received the *Liberator* as a gift from the Boston Female Anti-Slavery Society (knowing that the cost of the paper limited its usefulness, the Boston Female Anti-Slavery Society had voted to have the *Liberator* delivered free throughout the state), spoke of her 'unwearied effort' to circulate the paper. She had to 'prevail' upon people, as she did with one Bangor gentleman who was determined not to patronize Garrison. Unwilling to let the matter politely drop, Sarah badgered him until he finally agreed to try the paper. Her letter hinted at the psychic costs of her work. When she met with indifference, she confessed, 'My spirit is stirred within me, and my soul is in agony, as a burning fire shut up in my bones – then it is, that I flee to my closet, and I find if the ear of *man* is closed, that of the great Jehovah is ever open'.[4]

Women also created their own propaganda. While the contributions of women like Maria Child and the Grimké sisters are well known, associations and members of associations also voiced their opinions in print. Only a few months after the formation of their female antislavery society, women in Uxbridge, Massachusetts, drafted a letter to 'Professing Christian Women of Kentucky' and had it published in the *Philanthropist*, Appealing to the southern women as mothers, sisters, and daughters, the letter 'affectionately' urged them to overthrow slavery and warned them of the consequences of inaction. Annual reports were another means to bolster membership and to make the abolitionist case before the indifferent public. While much of this sort of propaganda has not survived or appeared in antislavery newspapers without attribution, there are enough references to women's contributions to suggest how important they were. Certainly lecturer Marius Robinson, who described the efforts of the president of the Cadiz (Ohio) Female Anti-Slavery Society, recognized their impact. This woman, unwilling to let the local Presbyterian clergyman's defense of colonization go unchallenged, wrote an article for publication that, in Robinson's opinion, 'annihilated' the cleric's speech.[5]

Female societies also paid for the publication of effective antislavery materials. On several occasions, the PFAS thought that an invited lecturer had made such a powerful case for abolitionism that his or her remarks should be published. On other occasions, societies picked up the bill for tracts and pamphlets.[6]

When the Lynn women reviewed their work at their second annual meeting, they concluded that publications and individual exertion had all been important for winning adherents to the cause (and to the association). But 'more than from any other cause', they stated, 'through the influence of the lecture we have received a considerable accession of members within the last few months'. Antislavery societies not only sponsored lectures in their own communities but also hired agents to take the message elsewhere. In Salem in 1839, the association engaged Mrs. Abigail Ordway to serve as their agent in Essex County. She found her progress slow, reporting to the board that 'the disagreeables far exceed the agreeables on such a route; and there is nothing which can sustain or console the sinking spirits, but the idea of the good eventually to be accomplished'.[7]

For many, if not most, white women's organizations, the goal of improving the situation of freed blacks was of secondary importance to abolition, partly because there were so few free blacks in their communities. In cities like Boston, Philadelphia, and New York, however, the substantial black presence shaped organizations' responses to the freedperson's plight. In these places and in others like Salem, Massachusetts, white women followed Theodore Weld's advice and undertook a variety of projects aimed at assisting the black community. Guided by the same sorts of assumptions that initially limited association membership to white women, women's associations, like men's, were certainly not free of prejudice, paternalism, or middle-class values. The decision of a group of women in the Portland Female Anti-Slavery Society to meet twice a week to instruct 'the female colored population in knitting, mending, and various kinds of needle work' in order to elevate 'the character of an unjustly degraded race', and their later expenditures for clothing and books for children in the 'colored school' exhibit all the limitations of the abolitionist approach. Blacks needed to live up to white standards if they were to overcome negative stereotypes and discriminatory treatment. Yet it is important to remember that in the context of the racism of the North, such efforts were risky to one's reputation and that women abolitionists were unusually free of the prejudices of the day. Projects aimed to provide African-Americans with the middle-class skills and values that whites believed they lacked often proved useful and even profitable for those who were involved. Furthermore, black women's organizations during the 1830s also endorsed many of the same improvement strategies as the means of overcoming prejudice.[8]

Both all-black organizations and some integrated organizations undertook projects aimed at improving education for blacks. The most ambitious effort that surviving records reveal was undertaken by the PFAS in its early years. Quakers had been pioneers in black education in Pennsylvania, and given the prominence of Hicksites in the PFAS and that black women members were from the city's most elite families, an interest in education was predictable. Both groups believed that if blacks were properly educated, they would be more successful in life. In turn, their success would undermine white prejudice. Visits to black schools to evaluate the quality of education there, gifts of educational materials, and financial support for Sarah Douglass's school for girls demonstrated this organization's commitment during the 1830s. Other educational projects included a series of scientific lectures for blacks and sewing classes for women unacquainted with this 'important branch of domestic industry'. Despite the importance of the work, however, the efforts petered out. Perhaps because the 'field of labor [proved] too extensive' for the size of the organization, it was difficult to get women to complete their assignments. Too many were 'negligent', and eventually the society turned most of its energy toward fund-raising activities.[9]

The major fund-raising device for the PFAS and other female antislavery associations was the fair, but associations took on many other, more modest efforts. The American Anti-Slavery Society, as well as abolitionist newspaper editors, lecturers, and agents were often in financial straits. Garrison himself was often short of cash and the recipient of gifts from female societies. And Garrison was not the only impecunious abolitionist leader. The Boston Female Anti-Slavery Society paid part of Samuel J. May's salary and raised money to ensure that Maria Child had access to the Boston Athenæum library. Maria Child herself wrote letters begging for money, selecting persons who were not abolitionists, because abolitionists 'have very limited means [and]...what they give to collateral objects [in this case, to help out the black Bostonian Susan Paul] must generally be deducted from their annual donation to the Anti-Slavery cause'.[10]

Societies tried a variety of schemes to raise money. In 1838, the *Liberator* was pressing women to establish cent-a-week societies, which the paper claimed were having astonishing success. 'Many little bands of female collectors are thus raising from $50 to $100 a year, places where little would be done by any other plan'. Black women's groups undertook similar work to support black papers, which were more economically vulnerable than mainstream papers like the *Liberator*.[11]

Women did not need to be reminded about the importance of money, nor did they need suggestions about how to raise it. Even the Bangor Juvenile Anti-Slavery Society, composed of about twenty-five 'misses', concluded 'that *money* is of great importance' and 'resolved to do our utmost to cast in our mite for this purpose'. Dover, New Hampshire, women, in order to work more 'efficiently', came up with the idea of appointing eight women who belonged to the town's various religious societies to canvass for donations. At the time of their reorganization in 1840, they also decided to invite men as honorary – but dues-paying – members. As the Dedham Female Anti-Slavery Society made clear, it was determined to 'raise all we could to send in with our cent a week's money'.[12]

While the sums any one society was able to raise may have been small, collectively abolitionist organizations provided important assistance to a reform movement that often was short of cash. Samuel J. May acknowledged the financial debt the antislavery movement owed to women, even as he minimized the tedious nature of the task of fund-raising. 'Often were they our self-appointed committees of ways and means, and by fairs and other pleasant devices raised much money to sustain our lecturers and periodicals', he recalled. Given the fact that most women did not have their own sources of income, the financial commitments they undertook assume an importance greater than the money itself.[13]

A few examples illustrate the frustrations women faced in fund-raising Frances Drake, after a day and a half of soliciting in response to a circular from the Massachusetts Anti-Slavery Society, had only collected $2.25, despite the fact that 'every person I called on was an avowed abolitionist, and what is more, were all persons of standing, and *much* property'. In Fitchburg, Eliza Gill's efforts to get male and female abolitionists to agree on a contribution plan proved abortive. Despite holding 'meeting after meeting', nothing was resolved. Finally, 'seeing clearly that if anything was done for the contribution plan it must be done by the women – we concluded to hold six meetings of our Soc. in districts and when we have met, I have made a point of getting as many boxes as we could. As yet I cannot speak of success but think it the best plan for us at present'.[14]

Fund-raising, even when the sums collected were tiny, demanded that women carry the abolitionist message and the financial requirements of the movement to others. Sometimes, as was the case in Fitchburg, the audience and the place were familiar and friendly, even if contributions were not forthcoming. But in other cases, solicitations were made in more public and less sympathetic environments. Women's experience with indifference and hostility in the work of fund-raising was good preparation for petitioning.

The massive petition drives undertaken by female abolitionist societies after 1835 constituted women's most extensive grassroots work during that decade. In 1837, from Concord, New Hampshire, Mary Clark reported to the Boston Female Anti-Slavery Society that, with 'great unanimity and earnestness', her society had voted to have a petition and circular prepared. That same year, at its annual meeting, the Lynn Society agreed that petitioning was 'one of the most efficient [means] that we can employ'. Unlike other petition efforts, like the one Hicksite Quakers put forth during the 1835 Genesee Yearly Meeting in New York, this work brought women like Mary Clark into 'direct ... [contact] with the classes of the community – with the pro-slavery, with the indifferent, with those who are as much as ourselves opposed to slavery, *but*' were reluctant to sign a petition. The personal interactions that collecting signatures required, Rochester women suggested, caused 'many who would not otherwise think about it ... to give it a little place in their minds'.[15]

The experience of collecting signatures and the controversy this effort generated forced many women to confront the tensions between their newly constructed identity as female abolitionists and more conservative definitions of woman. The ambitious scope of women's petitioning activities represented their entry into the world of mass democratic politics and implicitly signified their rejection of quiet influence at the hearth for a voice in the civic sphere. While some women would back away once they understood the implications of an identity that was now stretched to include political activism, others would become more radical in their assault on convention, and still others would be comfortable in living with contradiction. But whatever the individual responses to the controversies petition work sparked, the effort did pull many women into political action, most probably for the first time in their lives, and expanded ideas about the meaning of women's citizenship.[16]

In 1832, when Garrison was feeling his way to defining a role for women in abolitionism, he sensed that women might play a modest role in petitioning work: 'I cannot see the slightest force in the argument, that because women can have no part in the final decision, they ought not to take any part in helping the subject towards that decision'. For Garrison, it was clear that 'they do not ... petition, they only try to call the attention of the men of the acquaintance or neighborhood to facts that may induce them to take the step of petitioning'.[17]

This limited conception of the female role in petitioning disappeared as abolitionists made this activity one of their main strategies. In 1835, hoping to force the discussion of slavery in the halls of Congress and in the parlors of American citizens, the American Anti-Slavery Society initiated a petition drive. When Congress passed the Gag Law in 1836, which tabled abolitionist petitions, the issue broadened beyond slavery to include the highly charged and very political question of free speech. If legislators hoped to stem the flow of petitions by their actions, they must have been disappointed, for abolitionist petitioning persisted. In 1838, the American Anti-Slavery Society forwarded to Washington petitions bearing 400,000 signatures. Two years later, an astonishing number of Americans, more than two million, had signed abolitionist petitions.[18]

Encouraged by male antislavery organizations to participate in the drive, female societies responded enthusiastically. A member of the Boston Female Anti-Slavery Society described petitioning as 'a magnificent plan'. In 1836, the Boston, Philadelphia, and New York female societies coordinated campaigns that reached into country towns and villages as well as into their own communities. The free black women of Connecticut undertook a petition drive aimed especially at other free women. Women proved to be enormously successful at collecting signatures, especially those of other women. Various studies suggest that women were, in fact, far more success-ful than men at this work. One scholar points out that women's involve-ment 'immediately tripled the number of petition names secured previously by paid male agents'.[19]

While women's petitions adopted a humble posture initially, the modest pose did not prevent accusations that women were meddling in politics. During the Second Anti-Slavery Convention of American Women in 1838, Angelina Grimké took on the critics and folded the new activity into an expanded definition of female duty. 'Men may settle these and other ques-tions at the ballot box', she declared, 'but you have no such right. It is only through our petitions that you can reach the Legislature. It is, therefore peculiarly your duty to petition'.[20]

Petition campaigns touched individuals and antislavery organizations in multiple ways. For societies like Boston, Philadelphia, and New York, which coordinated the work of local groups, the project demanded time, energy, skill, and the ability to direct and supervise effectively. When Caroline Weston was a member of the Boston society's petition committee, she admitted to an acquaintance in Franklin County, 'I hardly know what steps to take'. Although she was to organize Franklin County, she had no idea to whom she should send requests for assistance and names of people 'to whom it would be proper or politic to correspond'. While organizers could count on the assistance of female antislavery societies where they existed (although each would have to be contacted), as Caroline's letter suggested, they had to extend the antislavery network and engage newcomers in the work. Anti-slavery newspapers urged participation, while circulars sent through the mail gave the call. The *Advocate of Freedom* instructed its readers in 1838 to 'circulate your petitions! Give every individual an opportunity to *sign* them, or to *refuse*. Don't wait for others – *go yourself* – *you*, reader – *man* or *woman*. Delay is dangerous'. Societies undertook a considerable amount of correspondence. Julianna Tappan, corresponding secretary of the Ladies' New-York City Anti-Slavery Society, apologizing for her hastily written letter, explained that she was so busy writing societies about petitioning that she had no time to write decently.[21]

Those who were directing the drives provided general instructions and advice for the less knowledgeable. Although Mary Clark and her Concord society had decided to participate in the work, Mary did not know how to draw up a petition about Texas. She requested either a form or written suggestions about how to proceed. Once the petitions had been completed, local societies sometimes forwarded them on so that they could be prepared to be sent to Congress. Mary Weston described working with 248 petitions from Weymouth and 130 from Braintree: 'I labored like a dog to get them [ready]'. In some cases, women copied their petitions over, which perhaps explains the comment of one woman who remarked, 'Having to send both to House & Senate makes the work no little job'.[22]

In addition to directing the petition work of local groups, city antislavery organizations also canvassed in their own communities. They established committees to divide up the city into manageable sections and to recruit volunteers to do the petitioning. As a member of the Lynn Female Anti-Slavery Society explained, because the 'highly important' work was 'one of much labor, requiring prompt attention and perseverance', it needed workers 'who have *warm hearts* and *willing minds*'. Suggesting what qualities were needed to be effective, Mary Grew mused, 'Is it not strange, that an *argument*, nay, a *train of reasoning*, should even be necessary to convince a human mind'.[23]

When Mary Clark wrote on behalf of the Concord Female Anti-Slavery Society, she sought concrete advice, but she also wished to convey her association's willingness to bear the expenses of having the petition sent to every town in New Hampshire. A committee had been formed to oversee the printing and mailing of the materials. Her association's project shows that, while individual female societies might not have the same duties as a Boston or Philadelphia organization, they still were responsible for coordinating local effort and sometimes even more than local efforts.[24]

Canvassing with petitions was done door to door, in the same way that women sometimes circulated papers, almanacs, and other antislavery material. One woman might be responsible for several streets and would have to call at every house and repeat her calls if no one was at home. In one week in 1840, Deborah Weston estimated that she had walked twenty-one miles in her pursuit of signatures. No wonder some women remarked after a stint of work, 'I wore myself out'. As Deborah herself had commented in 1836, 'I shall be thankful when it is over with, for it is hard work and takes up more time than I can spare'.[25]

Deborah occasionally referred to her efforts as amusing. Others found 'a victory' when their 'arguments find a lodgement in the mind or our expostulations arouse the sympathies of the heart'. Few were so positive. Most found canvassing difficult, tiring, and frustrating. Presenting an unpopular cause was embarrassing for some and humiliating for others. Sarah Rugg, after commenting that the work was 'humbling', remarked that nothing but duty would induce her to take it on. Maria Child summed up the feelings of most women: Petitioning was 'the most odious of all tasks'.[26]

What made it so odious? Both the demanding character of the work and the response it evoked made women uncomfortable. The *Advocate of Freedom* urged women to plead the cause with their friends of both sexes. The paper assured women who took its advice that 'from deference to your sex you will be heard when your companion would be hushed into silence. You will not be accused of partyism, of aspiring for office, or of being a spoke in the wheel of political machinery'. The assurances were comforting but false.[27]

Canvassing every household in a neighborhood brought women, as the Lynn society had pointed out, into contact with all classes and types of people. Women in Fall River, Massachusetts, for example, called on factory workers, some of them Irish. One woman described 'finding our way through crooked and dark entries, up steep and winding stair-cases' of tenement buildings. Although women did not often reveal their feelings about entering into households quite different from their own, there are hints that the experience of encountering unfamiliar class settings might not be congenial. Julianna Tappan's assignment, visiting elite women, seems at first glance as if it should have proved less awkward than canvassing in working-class areas. Julianna did not find it so. Her letter exudes the embarrassment she felt in elegant surroundings, 'the splendidly furnished drawing-rooms of wealthy citizens in Hudson Square'. Although she tried to cover her embarrassment with scorn for the ill-educated women with whom she spoke, her fervent statement that she was willing 'to be *any thing, do any thing . . .* to honor Him' suggests that she had done just that.[28]

In some cases, as records show, women collected signatures of other women only. Since their strategy was to visit households during the day, men must often have been out at work. But women also ended up soliciting signatures from men. In Nantucket, Charlotte Austin reported leaving petitions in shops frequented by men for their signatures. This technique was perhaps more acceptable than what Miss Smith did. In her visits to almost every house in Glastonbury, Connecticut, the young woman presented her case to and argued with men. It was 'the men, generally who needed "free discussion" ', she discovered, for 'the women would not act contrary to the ideas of the male part of their families'.[29]

After a January afternoon spent on the 'petition business', Lucy Chase reported feeling dispirited by a task that was 'disagreeable because so few are willing to sign'. Other women spoke of almost being thrown out of people's houses, of uncivil treatment, and of accusations of behaving in an unwomanly fashion and of meddling in male matters. Louisa Phillips, for one, was told to go home and mind her own business. But there were even graver insults. Some people suggested that petitioners were trollops, linking their behavior with sexual and racial deviance. And one woman told Deborah Weston, 'She hoped all the young ladies who interest themselves in the matter would get what she supposed they were after[,] namely nigger husbands'. Such comments were uttered in person and sometimes repeated in the newspapers.[30]

Anna Cook, who was circulating two petitions in Hadley, Massachusetts, described her reception: kindness from some, 'by some cold neglect & by others open abuse, without any regard to my feelings personally, or for the slave'. The rudeness that women encountered questioned their claim to middle-class respectability. Incivility made it clear that some parts of the community had determined that if abolitionists did not adhere to norms, if they did not act like 'ladies' in public (inconspicuously), they would not be treated like ladies. There was little question about how many Americans interpreted the meaning of women's work in petition drives.[31]

Beyond the possibility of an uncertain reception, fatigue came from the repetition of the task. Wrote Sarah Rugg, 'I have just circulated two petitions, & sent them on, I thought I had got through this unpleasant part of the business for a while; but lo & behold another is forthcoming; so we must make up our minds to keep at the work .... You know my sister what humbling work it is, to circulate petitions, & repeat them so often'. Each petition representing one aspect of the antislavery campaign needed its own rationale, even when a woman was carrying two or three at the same time. Lists of petitions sent from the same town show different numbers signing each, revealing that a signature on one did not automatically lead to a signature on another.[32]

Women's petitioning activities continued right up to and through the Civil War. An 1842 circular, for instance, rallied women to take up the arduous work once again despite the sense that results were not 'proportionate' to their efforts. Petitioning, they were reminded, represented the 'only means of direct political action ... which we can exert upon our Legislatures'. Women repeatedly sent petitions to Congress and to their state legislatures. Women in Massachusetts, for example, mounted a campaign to overturn laws forbidding interracial marriage. The massive drive finally put enough pressure on state legislators that they repealed the offensive legislation. In 1847, Illinois women were less successful in using the petition as an instrument to eliminate that state's black code.[33]

Petitioning was the one task that demanded that women be at their most articulate. Petitions had different objectives, all of which had to be explained as persuasively as possible. Why should Texas be barred from the Union? Why did Congress have the ability to abolish slavery in the District of Columbia? Why should racial intermarriage be allowed in Massachusetts? What was the problem with the resolution adopted by the House of Representatives on December 21, 1837, in relation to slavery? No wonder that Louisa Phillips found that she had to study 'a long time to become thoroughly acquainted with ... [the] arguments'.[34]

The actual situations that women encountered demonstrated their need for a wide range of information about slavery and 'the affairs of our country'. They had to mount arguments as well as counter what the Lynn society called 'misapprehensions' and 'fears'. (Was it fear that led at least one woman to sign a petition and then to scratch off her name?) They had to be flexible and able to decide what approach might work best in each encounter. Sometimes it was not facts, figures, and arguments that were needed but a basic appeal to 'feelings of compassion'. Women collecting signatures found themselves explaining the need for immediate emancipation, the evils of slavery, the pertinence of political action, the character of the Union, and the character of female duty and appealing to the heart.[35]

A few of the comments women reported hearing while petitioning give some idea of the kinds of responses that were called for. 'One woman said "no I dont want' em free, I dont want to have nothing to do with' em, for niggers will be niggers let' em be where they will" '; ' "I'm willing to put my name down' t'wont do any good or any harm" ' ; 'Said she would not sign for the world, she wished she had slaves etc.'; ' "This going about Petitions is doing more harm than anything she knew of, it will dissolve the Union" '; from an Irishman, ' "No ... we wish to be liberated ourselves first; wait till you treat us as you ought, before you ask us to help you about the negroes" '; ' "thought the men perfectly capable of managing the government without their help." ' Anna Clark, who, like other petitioners, took along antislavery almanacs when she went to collect signatures, found that some of her purchasers' husbands reviled her, threatening to burn the almanacs and thundering that she was helping to dissolve the Union.[36]

Rachel Stearn's description of canvassing in Springfield, Massachusetts, in 1842 captures the experience. 'As you very well know', she began, petitioning 'is a task requiring more than ordinary patience'. With 'one person after another', she had to 'begin at the Anti-slavery Alphabet, and go through the first principles with every one; to answer the question *"who is* Latimer"? 50 times over. But there is one comfort, that 50 people know who Latimer is, that last week did not know. In one house, where they did not know ... we got *10 names*, in another that and occasional assistance from others has swelled our list considerably. Mother and I have spent all the time we could command possibly'. She estimated that she spent about half an hour at each household debating questions.[37]

As women carried out their various responsibilities as members of female antislavery societies and confronted the varying responses to their activism, they experienced a range of emotions from despair to elation, at the money raised, the signatures secured, the sense of duty well done. Despite the complex feelings they expressed during the 1830s, many women expected their cause to triumph. When it did, they would know how much they had done to bring about the sweet moment of victory. Some women even went so far as to suggest that women's societies were more central to the cause of emancipation than men's groups. What would happen if all female societies were dissolved, Dorchester women were asked during their first annual meeting. Sin and infidelity would triumph, they were told, 'in spite of all our brethren could do'.[38]

In seeking to understand their place in the world, some women moved beyond religious rationales to place their activities within a historical context. Abolitionist women were the daughters of pilgrims, or even more saliently, the descendants of the Revolutionary generation. As one woman in a long letter to the *Liberator* reminded readers, during the Revolution women had not confined themselves to their domestic duties. 'Facts innumerable show the ardor and zeal with which they were inspired. Look back and see the societies that were formed to supply the destitute with clothing!' Her conclusion sweepingly rejected criticism. 'Let not the fear of man's ridicule, or his pretended anxiety for the supposed welfare of our sex, deter you from using all proper influence which you possess against sin'.[39]

The boldness and pride this woman exhibited were widespread and were reflected in the proceedings of the three Anti-Slavery Conventions of American Women that took place at the end of the decade. These events highlighted women's importance to the movement and marked their coming of age in abolitionism. The first, held in 1837 in New York during the week that other benevolent and moral reform groups were also meeting, drew about 200 women, both black and white, from nine states. One delegate from New England pointed out the unprecedented nature of this public gathering. 'To attend a Female Convention!' she exclaimed. 'Once I should have blushed at the thought'. At the end of the three-day affair, which, as the *Liberator* pointed out, had been 'conducted with dignity and talent', the women had condemned racial prejudice, decried the indifference of American churches to the sin of slavery, exhorted females to accept petitioning as a yearly duty, and insisted that it was 'the province of woman ... to do all that she can by her voice, and her pen, and her purse ... to overthrow the horrible system of American Slavery'. Angelina Grimké also urged American women to reject 'the circumscribed limits with which corrupt custom and a perverted application of Scripture have encircled her'. And although not all of those attending were willing to go so far as Angelina Grimké in ignoring convention, the debate caused by her resolution was 'animated and interesting'.[40]

The following year, many more women (about 300) were in attendance at the second convention, this time in Philadelphia. The success of grassroots female organizing was apparent in the financial aid promised by antislavery societies located in small communities in Maine, Rhode Island, Massachusetts, Pennsylvania, and New Hampshire. Meeting in the luxurious new Pennsylvania Hall, which also housed a free produce store and the offices of the abolitionist newspaper, the *Pennsylvania Freeman*, the women debated whether to invite men to their evening session. The Grimkés had already aroused clerical anger by addressing mixed audiences in their speaking tour in Massachusetts, and some delegates were unwilling to overstep the boundaries of propriety at their national convention. As a result, men were urged to attend a public but not officially sponsored session. Meanwhile, a mob in Philadelphia, perhaps 10,000 strong, made its disapproval clear in its efforts to disrupt the evening gathering. The next day, the mob destroyed Pennsylvania Hall. The women persevered, though, finishing their convention business elsewhere. As one abolitionist made clear, despite the violence and destruction, 'The women have done nobly today. They have held their convention to finish their business in the midst of the fearful agitation. Their moral daring and heroism are beyond all praise. They are worthy to plead the cause of peace and universal liberty'.[41]

The shocking events in Philadelphia illuminated the women's moral courage, the mob's intolerance, and problems beginning to divide abolitionists from one another. Organizers of the following year's meeting in Philadelphia had difficulty finding any space for the convention. In the end, the convention was held not in a luxurious hall, spacious meetinghouse, or church, but in a riding school. And it was the last meeting of the Anti-Slavery Convention of American Women.[42]

By the late 1830s, the controversies over women's participation in the work of antislavery societies, the difficulties inherent in efforts to abolish slavery, and conflict within the ranks of abolitionists all challenged individual and collective commitment to the cause. Some women dropped out altogether; others formed new societies or took up new forms of work. Still others labored along, feeling isolated and often discouraged. Aroline Chase, a member of the Lynn Female Anti-Slavery Society, wrote her friend Abby Kelley in 1843, 'I feel that I can not contend much longer unless renewed.... Every professed friend of the poor slave, turn on another track – our society I *suppose* has a name to live, but it is dead'. Although she was proud of the part she had played in the petition drive that eventually persuaded Massachusetts legislators to repeal laws against interracial marriage, she wondered about the future. 'You say I must not give up until 50', she reminded her friend. 'I am 30 now [and] I feel as though I stand alone'. The next decade would sorely test the ties of loyalty and commitment of women like Aroline who had labored so hard for the cause in the 1830s.[43]

NOTES

1. Gilbert H. Barnes and Dwight L. Dumond, eds., *Letters of Theodore Dwight Weld, Angelina Grimké Weld and Sarah Grimké, 1822–1844* (New York, c.1934), vol. 1, 263.
2. *Liberator*, October 17, 1835; BrFAS Records, June 13, 1837, CSL; letter from Lucia Russell to Maria Chapman, 1840, Chapman-Weston Papers, BPL.

3. Letter from Grace Williams to Maria Chapman, April 10, 1839, and letter from Charlotte Austin to Maria Chapman, October 9, 1840, both in Chapman-Weston Papers, BPL; *Liberator*, March 22, 1839; letter from Anne Weston to Deborah Weston, January 16, 1837, and printed letter to 'Dear Friend', March 25, 1839, both in Chapman-Weston Papers, BPL; *Advocate of Freedom*, April 13, 1838.

4. Letter from Experience Billings to Maria Chapman, April 22, 1839, and letter from Sarah Plummer to Anne Weston, March 31, 1838, both in Chapman-Weston Papers, BPL.

5. *Liberator*, August 27, 1836; letter from Marius Robinson to Emily Robinson, February 7, 1837, Robinson Papers, WRHS.

6. Minutes of the PFAS, December 4, 1834, September 8, November 11, 1836, PFAS Records, HSP.

7. LFAS Records, June 21, 1837, LHS; letter from A. B. Ordway to the Board, August 25, 1839, Correspondence 1839, SFAS Records, EPI, Mrs. Ordway was a milliner. Debra Gold Hansen, 'The Boston Female Anti-Slavery Society and the Limits of Gender Politics', in Jean Fagan Yellin and John C. Van Horne, eds., *The Abolitionist Sisterhood: Women's Political Culture in Antebellum America* (Ithaca, N. Y., 1994), 61.

8. *Liberator*, May 10, 1834, December 17, 1836. See also *Advocate of Freedom*, September 13, 1838, which notes continued expenditures for the black community in Portland. C. Peter Ripley, ed., *The Black Abolitionist Papers* (Chapel Hill, N. C., 1991), vol. 3, 14–18.

9. Minutes of the PFAS, June 9, 1834, February 11, 1836, February 9, 1837, January 4, March 8, 1836, April 12, 1838, July 11, 1839, January 1, 1840, PFAS Records, HSP.

10. Letter from L. L. Dodge to Garrison, January 4, 1838, SFAS Records, EPI; letter from Caroline Weston to Mrs. L. R. G. Hammatt, August 1, 1835, and letter from Deborah Weston to 'Mother', May 8, 1835, both in Chapman-Weston Papers, BPL. Milton Meltzer and Patricia G. Holland, eds., *Lydia Maria Child: Selected Letters, 1817–1880* (Amherst, Mass., 1982), 69–70.

11. The January 25, 1839, issue of the *Liberator*, included a letter from Salem's corresponding secretary, informing Garrison of the $100 gift the society had voted to give him. Another reference to the work appears in the April 13, 1838, issue. See also *Advocate of Freedom*, July 19, 1838.

12. *Advocate of Freedom*, December 6, 1838; LASD Records, July 4, 1837, 1840, NHHS; letter from A. M. Houghton to Maria Chapman, April 15, 1839, Chapman-Weston Papers, BPL.

13. Samuel J. May, *Some Recollections of Our Antislavery Conflict* (Miami, 1969), 231.

14. Letter from Frances Drake to Maria Chapman, August 6, 1841, and letter from Eliza Gill to Maria Chapman, September 2, 1840, both in Chapman-Weston Papers, BPL.

15. Letter from Mary Clark to Anne Weston, June 3, 1837, Chapman-Weston Papers, BPL; LFAS Records, June 21, 1837, LHS; Nancy A. Hewitt, *Women's Activism and Social Change: Rochester, New York, 1822–1872* (Ithaca, N. Y., 1987), 82.

16. Anne M. Boylan, 'Women and Politics in the Era before Seneca Falls', *Journal of the Early Republic*, 10 (1990), 364; Stephanie McCurry, 'The Two Faces of Republicanism: Gender and Proslavery Politics in Antebellum South Carolina', *JAH*, 78 (1992), 1245; Gerda Lerner, *The Majority Finds Its Past: Placing Women in History* (New York, 1979), 114; Deborah Bingham Van Broeckhoven, ' "Let Your Names Be Enrolled" ', in Yellin and Van Horne, eds., *Abolitionist Sisterhood*, 193.

17. *Liberator*, June 2, 1832.

18. Lerner, *Majority Finds Its Past*, 114–15; Edward Magdol, 'A Window on the Abolitionist Constituency: Antislavery Petitions, 1836–1839', in Alan M. Kraut, ed., *Crusaders and Compromisers: Essays on the Relationship of the Antislavery Struggle to the Antebellum Party System* (Westport, Conn., 1993), 45–6;

Lori D. Ginzberg, *Women and the Work of Benevolence: Morality, Politics and Class in the Nineteenth-Century United States* (New Haven, 1990), 82.

19. Letter of Caroline Weston to [?], July 14, 1835, Chapman-Weston Papers, BPL. For analyses of women's greater effectiveness, see Lerner, *Majority Finds Its, Past*, 117–23, and Van Broeckhoven, ' "Let Your Names Be Enrolled" ', 187–93.

20. Van Broeckhoven, ' "Let Your Names Be Enrolled" ', 179; Black Abolitionist Papers, reel 3, no. 291, LOC.

21. Letter from Caroline Weston to 'Dear Sir', 1836, Chapman-Weston Papers, BPL; *Advocate of Freedom*, November 8, 1838; letter from Julianna Tappan to Anne Weston, May 24, 1837, Chapman-Weston Papers, BPL.

22. Letters from Mary Clark to Anne Weston, June 3, 1837, from Mary Weston to Deborah Weston, January 22, 1837, from Charlotte Austin to Maria Chapman, July 26, 1839, and from Anne Weston to Deborah Weston, September 19, 1837, all in Chapman-Weston Papers, BPL.

23. LFAS Records, June 21, 1837, LHS; letter from Mary Grew to the BrFAS, March 17, 1837, CSL.

24. Letter from Mary Clark to Anne Weston, June 13 1837, Chapman-Weston Papers, BPL.

25. Letters from Deborah Weston to Anne Weston, February 18, 1840, from Anne Weston to Deborah Weston, September 15, 1837, from Deborah Weston to Mary Weston, November 6, 1836, all in Chapman-Weston Papers, BPL.

26. Letters from Deborah Weston to Mary Weston, October 19, 1836, from Caroline Weston to Deborah Weston, March 3, 1837, from Sarah Rugg to Anne Weston, February 16, 1838, all in Chapman-Weston Papers, BPL; Minutes of the PFAS, January 4, 1838, PFAS Records, HSP. Meltzer and Holland, eds., *Lydia Maria Child*, 93.

27. *Advocate of Freedom*, January 31, 1839.

28. *Liberator*, May 24, 1839; letter from Julianna Tappan to Anne Weston, July 21, 1837, Chapman-Weston Papers, BPL.

29. Letter from Charlotte Austin to Maria Chapman, July 26, 1839, Chapman-Weston Papers, BPL; letter from Hannah Smith to Abby Kelley, July 25, 1839, Kelley-Foster Papers, AmAS.

30. For a few examples, see letters from Deborah Weston to Mary Weston, October 19, 1836, from Anne Weston to Deborah Weston, November 19, 1836, and from Louisa Phillips to Maria Weston, August 6, 1837, all in Chapman-Weston Papers, BPL. Lucy Chase, diary fragments, January 27, no year, Chase Papers, AmAS.

31. Letter from Anna Cook to Maria Chapman, December 25, 1839, Chapman-Weston Papers, BPL. John Kasson, in *Rudeness and Civility: Manners in Nineteenth-Century Urban America* (New York, 1990), 112–21, makes the point about the importance of being inconspicuous in public. Mary P. Ryan, *Women in Public: Between Banners and Ballots, 1825–1880* (Baltimore, 1990), 3.

32. A list of petitions that was presented to Congress and reported in the *Liberator*, March 2, 1838, for example, shows that in the village of Lockport, New York, 371 women signed a petition asking Congress not to admit any new state into the Union if its constitution recognized slavery, 234 signed a petition against admitting Texas to the Union, while 405 signed the petition asking Congress to abolish slavery in the territories. Letter from Sarah Rugg to Anne Weston, February 16, 1838, Chapman-Weston Papers, BPL.

33. Hermann R. Muelder, *Fighters for Freedom: The History of Anti-Slavery Activities of Men and Women Associated with Knox College* (New York, 1959), 182; '1842 Circular of the Anti-Slavery Convention of American Women', Chapman-Weston Papers, BPL.

34. LFAS Records, June 21, 1837, LHS; *Liberator*, March 2, 1838; letter from Louisa Phillips to Maria Chapman, August 6, 1838, Chapman-Weston Papers, BPL.

35. Letter from Julianna Tappan to Anne Weston, July 21, 1837, Chapman-Weston Papers, BPL; LFAS Records, June 21, 1837, LHS; letter from Anna Cook to Maria Chapman, December 25, 1839, Chapman-Weston Papers, BPL. In *Old Anti-Slavery Days: Proceedings of the Commemorative Meeting Held by the Danvers Historical Society, April 26, 1893* (Danvers, Mass., 1893), 42, Abby Diaz, former secretary of the Plymouth Juvenile Anti-Slavery Society, recalled how she and her friends circulated petitions on their way to and from school. Schoolgirls, she pointed out, 'had become skillful in anti-slavery argument'.

36. Dorothy Sterling, *Ahead of Her Time: Abby Kelley and the Politics of Antislavery* (New York, 1991), 78–79; letter from Anne Weston to Deborah Weston, January 6, 1837, letter from Deborah Weston to Mary Weston, November 6, 1836, letters from Louisa Phillips to Maria Chapman, July 31, 1837, and August 6, 1836, letter from Anne Weston to Deborah Weston, December 15, 1839, and letter from Anna Clark to Maria Chapman, December 25, 1839, all in Chapman-Weston Papers, BPL; *Liberator*, May 24, 1839.

37. Letter from Rachel Stearns to Maria Chapman, December 18, 1842, Chapman-Weston Papers, BPL.

38. *First Annual Report of the Dorchester Female Anti-Slavery Society*, 11, Dorchester Female Anti-Slavery Society, miscellaneous papers, AmAS.

39. Letter from Anne Weston to the Concord Female Anti-Slavery Society, July 22, 1835, BFAS Records, MHS; *Liberator*, September 15, 1837. For another reference to the American Revolution and the role of women, see the *Liberator*, December 17, 1836.

40. Sterling, *Ahead of Her Time*, 43–9; quotes on 44, 48, 49; Yellin and Van Horne, eds., *Abolitionist Sisterhood*, 10–15.

41. Sterling, *Ahead of Her Time*, 62–66; Yellin and Van Horne, eds., *Abolitionist Sisterhood*, 16–17, and Margaret Hope Bacon, 'By Moral Force Alone: The Antislavery Women and Nonresistance', in ibid., 285–8, quote on 288.

42. Bacon, 'By Moral Force Alone', 289–91.

43. Letter from Aroline Chase to Abby Kelley, May or June 1843, Kelley-Foster Papers, AmAS.

DOCUMENT 1: THE GERMANTOWN PROTEST, 1688

This is the first recorded written protest against slavery in North America. Written by a congregation of Mennonite Quakers in Germantown, Pennsylvania, this statement indicates why the existence of slavery is inconsistent with the precepts of Christianity.

This is to the monthly monthly meeting held at Richard Worrell's:

These are the reasons why we are against the traffic of men-body, as followeth: 'Is there any that would be done or handled at this manner' viz., to be sold or made a slave for all the time of his life? How fearful and faint-hearted are many at sea, when they see a strange vessel, being afraid it should be a Turk, and they should be taken, and sold for slaves into Turkey. Now, what is this better done, than Turks do? Yea, rather it is worse for them, which say they are Christians; for we hear that the most part of such negers are brought hither against their will and consent, and that many of them are stolen. Now, though they are black, we cannot conceive there is more liberty to have them slaves, as it is to have other white ones. There is a saying, that we should do to all men like as we will be done ourselves; making no difference of what generation, descent, or colour they are. And those who steal or rob men, and those who buy or purchase them, are they not all alike? Here is liberty of conscience, which is right and reasonable; here ought to be likewise liberty of the body, except of evil-doers, which is another case. But to bring men hither, or to rob and sell them against their will, we stand against. In Europe there are many oppressed for conscience-sake; and here there are those oppressed which are of a black colour. And we who know that men must not commit adultery – some do commit adultery in others, separating wives from their husbands, and giving them to others: and some sell the children of these poor creatures to other men. Ah! do consider well this thing, you who do it, if you would be done at this manner – and if it is done according to Christianity! You surpass Holland and Germany in this thing, This makes an ill report in all those countries of Europe, where they hear of [it], that the Quakers do here handel men as they handel there the cattle. And for that reason some have no mind or inclination to come hither. And who shall maintain this your cause, or plead for it? Truly, we cannot do so, except you shall inform us better hereof, viz.: that Christians have liberty to practice these things. Pray, what thing in the world can be done worse towards us, than if men should rob or steal us away, and sell us for slaves to strange countries; separating husbands from their wives and children. Being now this is not done in the manner we would be done at; therefore, we contradict, and are against this traffic of men-body. And we who profess that it is not lawful to steal,

Henry S. Commager (ed.), *Documents of American History* (New York: Appleton-Century-Crofts, 1963), pp. 37–8.

must, likewise, avoid to purchase such things as are stolen, but rather help to stop this robbing and stealing, if possible. And such men ought to be delivered out of the hands of the robbers, and set free as in Europe. Then is Pennsylvania to have a good report, instead, it hath now a bad one, for this sake, in other countries; Especially whereas the Europeans are desirous to know in what manner the Quakers do rule in their province; and most of them do look upon us with an envious eye. But if this is done well, what shall we say is done evil?

If once these slaves (which they say are so wicked and stubborn men,) should join themselves – fight for their freedom, and handel their masters and mistresses, as they did handel them before; will these masters and mistresses take the sword at hand and war against these poor slaves, like, as we are able to believe, some will not refuse to do? Or, have these poor negers not as much right to fight for their freedom, as you have to keep them slaves?

Now consider well this thing, if it is good or bad. And in case you find it to be good to handel these blacks in that manner, we desire and require you hereby lovingly, that you may inform us herein, which at this time never was done, viz., that Christians have such a liberty to do so. To the end we shall be satisfied on this point, and satisfy likewise our good friends and acquaintances in our native country, to whom it is a terror, or fearful thing, that men should be handelled so in Pennsylvania.

This is from our meeting at Germantown held ye 18th of the 2d month, 1688, to be delivered to the monthly meeting at Richard Worrell's.

Garret Henderich,
Derick op de Graeff,
Francis Daniel Pastorius,
Abram op de Graeff.

DOCUMENT 2: A SLAVE PETITION FOR FREEDOM DURING THE REVOLUTIONARY ERA

The emphasis upon liberty in the pre-revolutionary era encouraged some slaves to petition colonial legislatures for their freedom. This is a petition from a slave called Felix to the Massachusetts legislature to consider the possibility of manumission.

Province of the Massachusetts Bay To His Excellency Thomas Hutchinson, Esq; Governor; To The Honorable His Majesty's Council, and To the Honorable House of Representatives in General Court assembled at Boston, the 6th Day of January, 1773.

The humble PETITION of many Slaves, living in the Town of Boston, and other Towns in the Province is this, namely

That your Excellency and Honors, and the Honorable the Representatives would be pleased to take their unhappy State and Condition under your wise and just Consideration.

We desire to bless God, who loves Mankind, who sent his Son to die for their Salvation, and who is no respecter of Persons; that he hath lately put it into the Hearts of Multitudes on both Sides of the Water, to bear our Burthens, some of whom are Men of great Note and Influence; who have pleaded our Cause with Arguments which we hope will have their weight with this Honorable Court.

We presume not to dictate to your Excellency and Honors, being willing to rest our Cause on your Humanity and justice; yet would beg Leave to say a Word or two on the Subject.

Although some of the Negroes are vicious, (who doubtless may be punished and restrained by the same Laws which are in Force against other of the King's Subjects) there are many others of a quite different Character, and who, if made free, would soon be able as well as willing to bear a Part in the Public Charges; many of them of good natural Parts, are discreet, sober, honest, and industrious; and may it not be said of many, that they are virtuous and religious, although their Condition is in itself so unfriendly to Religion, and every moral Virtue except Patience. How many of that Number have there been, and now are in this Province, who have had every Day of their Lives embittered with this most intollerable Reflection, That, let their Behaviour be what it will, neither they, nor their Children to all Generations, shall ever be able to do, or to possess and enjoy any Thing, no, not even Life itself, but in a Manner as the Beasts that perish.

We have no Property! We have no Wives! No Children! We have no City! No Country! But we have a Father in Heaven, and we are determined, as far

Herbert Aptheker (ed.), 'Slaves Petition for Freedom during the Revolution, 1773–1779' in *A Documentary History of the Negro People in the United States* (New York: Carol Publishing Group, 1951), vol. 1, pp. 6–7.

as his Grace shall enable us, and as far as our degraded contemptuous Life will admit, to keep all his Commandments: Especially will we be obedient to our Masters, so long as God in his sovereign Providence shall suffer us to be holden in Bondage.

It would be impudent, if not presumptuous in us, to suggest to your Excellency and Honors any Law or Laws proper to be made, in relation to our unhappy State, which, although our greatest Unhappiness, is not our Fault; and this gives us great Encouragement to pray and hope for such Relief as is consistent with your Wisdom, justice, and Goodness.

We think Ourselves very happy, that we may thus address the Great and General Court of this Province, which great and good Court is to us, the best judge, under God, of what is wise, just – and good.

We humbly beg Leave to add but this one Thing more: We pray for such Relief only, which by no Possibility can ever be productive of the least Wrong or Injury to Masters; but to us will be as Life from the dead.

Signed,

FELIX

DOCUMENT 3: EXTRACT FROM *THE LIBERATOR*, 1831

An extract from an editorial in the first issue of The Liberator, *the most successful abolitionist weekly in the United States. The statement illustrates William Lloyd Garrison's rhetorical vigour.*

In the month of August, I issued proposals for publishing *The Liberator* in Washington city; but the enterprise, though hailed in different sections of the country, was palsied by public indifference. Since that time, the removal of the *Genius of Universal Emancipation* to the Seat of Government has renderd less imperious the establishment of a similar periodical in that quarter.

During my recent tour for the purpose of exciting the minds of the people by a series of discourses on the subject of slavery, every place that I visited gave fresh evidence of the fact, that a greater revolution in public sentiment was to be effected in the free states – and particularly in *New-England* – than at the south. I found contempt more bitter, opposition more active, detraction more relentless, prejudice more stubborn, and apathy more frozen, than among the slave owners themselves. Of course, there were individual exceptions to the contrary. This state of things afflicted, but did not dishearten me. I determined, at every hazard, to lift up the standard of emancipation in the eyes of the nation, *within sight of Bunker Hill and in the birth place of liberty*. That standard is now unfurled; and long may it float, unhurt by the spoliations of time or the missiles of a desperate foe yea, till every chain be broken, and every bondman set free! Let southern oppressors tremble – let their secret abettors tremble – let their northern apologists tremble – let all the enemies of the persecuted blacks tremble.

I deem the publication of my original Prospectus unnecessary, as it has obtained a wide circulation. The principles therein inculcated will be steadily pursued in this paper, excepting that I shall not array myself as the political partisan of any man. In defending the great cause of human rights, I wish to derive the assistance of all religions and of all parties.

Assenting to the 'self-evident truth' maintained in the American Declaration of Independence, 'that all men are created equal, and endowed by their Creator with certain inalienable rights – among which are life, liberty and the pursuit of happiness', I shall strenuously contend for the immediate enfranchisement of our slave population. In Park-street Church, on the Fourth of July, 1829, in an address on slavery, I unreflectingly assented to the popular but pernicious doctrine of gradual abolition. I seize this opportunity to make a full and unequivocal recantation, and thus publicly to ask pardon of my God, of my country, and of my brethren the poor slaves, for having uttered a sentiment so full of timidity, injustice and absurdity. A

William Lloyd Garrison, '*The Liberator*, Vol. 1, No. 1, January 1, 1831' in Henry S. Commager (ed.), *Documents of American History* (New York: Appleton-Century-Crofts, 1963), pp. 277–8.

similar recantation, from my pen, was published in the *Genius of Universal Emancipation* at Baltimore, in September, 1829. My conscience is now satisfied.

I am aware that many object to the severity of my language; but is there not cause for severity? I *will* be as harsh as truth, and as uncompromising as justice. On this subject, I do not wish to think, or speak, or write, with moderation. No! no! Tell a man whose house is on fire, to give a moderate alarm; tell him to moderately rescue his wife from the hands of the ravisher; tell the mother to gradually extricate her babe from the fire into which it has fallen;—but urge me not to use moderation in a cause like the present. I am in earnest – I will not equivocate I will not excuse – I will not retreat a single inch – AND I WILL BE HEARD. The apathy of the people is enough to make every statue leap from its pedestal, and to hasten the resurrection of the dead.

It is pretended, that I am retarding the cause of emancipation, by the coarseness of my invective, and the precipitancy of my measures. *The charge is not* true. On this question my influence, – humble as it is, – is felt at this moment to a considerable extent, and shall be felt in coming years – not perniciously, but beneficially – not as a curse, but as a blessing; and posterity will bear testimony that I was right. I desire to thank God, that he enables me to disregard 'the fear of man which bringeth a snare', and to speak his truth in its simplicity and power.

> And here I close with this fresh dedication:
> 'Oppression! I have seen thee, face to face,
> And met thy cruel eye and cloudy brow;
> But thy soul-withering glance I fear not now—
> For dread to prouder feelings doth give place
> Of deep abhorrence! Scorning the disgrace
> Of slavish knees that at thy footstool bow,
> I also kneel—but with far other bow
> Do hail thee and thy herd of hirelings base:—
> I swear, while life-blood warms my throbbing veins,
> Still to oppose and thwart, with heart and hand,
> Thy brutalizing sway—'till Afric's chains
> Are burst, and Freedom rules the rescued land,—
> Trampling Oppression and his iron rod:
> *Such is the vow I* take—SO HELP ME GOD'!

11

SLAVERY AND POLITICS

INTRODUCTION

The expansion of slavery westwards into the territories heightened the sectional political tension in the forty years between the Missouri controversy and the outbreak of the Civil War. During that period the North and the South became more distinct sections in American life. Political parties were also directly affected by the arguments raised by slavery extension. Ultimately, the bitter divisions over slavery led to the secession of a phalanx of southern states and the onset of four years of bloodshed. Two good overviews of the entire sweep of these momentous decades in American social and political life appear in Kolchin (1993) and Levine (1991). Kolchin stresses southern distinctiveness while recognising that southerners had much in common with other Americans. He regards slavery as the main fault line that divided the North and the South and emphasises the way in which plantation slavery contributed to the lack of urbanization and to the backwardness of the antebellum southern economy. Levine also places primary emphasis on slavery and race as causes of the Civil War. He contrasts the economic and social differences of each section and outlines the many Congressional manoeuvres over the extension or containment of slavery. For Levine, the Civil War was a conflict in which slave emancipation completed the American Revolution begun in 1775.

Freehling (1990) offers a wide-ranging survey of slavery in the South and of slavery's impact on white southerners' commitment to the Union. He is attuned to the diversity of attitudes within the antebellum South, whether intellectual, social, economic, cultural or political. He shows why secessionists were in a minority in that section before the mid-1850s and why their extremism was contained. He notes that without the federal ratio – the three-fifths clause of the Constitution – the Missouri Compromise, the 'gag' rule and the Kansas–Nebraska Act (1854) would not have occurred. Freehling's book is helpful in depicting the variety of ways slavery was tested in the South and how issues there were reflected in the American political nation as a whole.

Fehrenbacher (2001) is the leading book dealing with the United States government handling of slavery from the Revolution to the Civil War. He analyses slavery in American foreign relations, the African slave trade, the fugitive slave problem, and slavery in the federal territories. Fehrenbacher argues that the United States Constitution was neutral on the issue of slavery. He shows that the apparent protection of slavery under the Constitution was fiercely debated in the antebellum period and that governmental policy towards slavery in that era was consistently proslavery. The end to this domination came with the election of Lincoln in 1860 and the drift towards war over the next year.

The Missouri crisis alarmed so many people not so much because of its terms – though many were disturbed by them – but because it raised the issue of slavery in territories applying for statehood. Many Americans felt the Constitution was becoming compromised without proper process of amendment. Moore (1953) remains the main source of information on the Congressional measures passed in 1820 and 1821 which determined the admission of slave and free states to the Union. Moore should be read critically, however, because his analysis is pro-southern. Brown (1966) is a well-known short interpretative essay that shows how the uproar over Missouri contributed to an attack on southern dominance of the federal government and to the rise of the second-party system. This is a good brief overview of the impact of the Missouri crisis on antebellum politics.

Slavery again became a national political problem during the nullification crisis of 1831–2 in South Carolina. Freehling (1965) analyses this important turning point in the southern commitment to slavery. Arising from an extensive attempt by northern manufacturers to obtain protective tariff measures in 1828 and 1832, the nullification crisis revolved around South Carolina's attempt to reject federal laws. John C. Calhoun provided the intellectual justification for nullification with his theory of the 'concurrent majority' – that is, the right of a permanent minority to veto numerical majority rule. In the 1831–2 elections in South Carolina the nullifiers gained a large majority because of the fusion of the tariff issue and slavery. Freehling shows that nullification pushed South Carolina into positive proslavery action. South Carolinians no longer had any conception of slavery being a moral evil. In the next thirty years many other southerners followed the lead of the Palmetto state.

Numerous studies deal with the sectional nature of southern politics in relation to slavery and nationalism. Sydnor (1948) is a helpful discussion of the South as a self-conscious region. He singles out the Missouri crisis as a pivotal turning point in the political attitudes of southerners. Fehrenbacher (1980) lucidly discusses three sectional crises: the Missouri controversy of 1819–21, the period from the Wilmot Proviso of 1846 to the Compromise of 1850, and the tumultuous years from the Kansas–Nebraska Act to the election of Lincoln as president (1854–60). He looks at the southern defence of slavery as part of its distinctive economy and culture. He analyses southern roll-call votes in Congress to show that the South had a commitment to the permanence of slavery by 1821, to avowal of secessionism by 1850, and to secession itself in 1860–1. Fehrenbacher underscores the fact that sectionalism and secessionism could be contained while political disputes between North and South were played out in Congress, but that the electoral victories of the Republican Party in 1856 and 1860 brought the sectional conflict into the electoral arena and gave separatists an opportunity to stake their claims for secession.

Cooper (1978) focuses on the eleven states that formed the Confederacy. He illustrates the ways in which southerners gave allegiance to political parties that would uphold the region's commitment to slavery, which he views as inextricably intertwined with the values of southern white society. In the period he covers, the era of the second-party system, the Whigs and the Democrats in the South agreed on the defence of slavery. Cooper is concerned mainly with disputes over slavery within and between parties in the South; though he does not deny that economic or other issues were important politically to southerners, his analysis emphasises the primacy of slavery for southern political debates.

Ashworth (1995) concentrates on slavery and sectionalism in federal and state politics in the late 1840s. He looks at how the annexation of Texas and Mexico to the United States brought the problem of slavery in the territories to the forefront of American political debate. Morrison (1997) also assesses the importance of the western territories in the national debate over slavery in the 1840s and 1850s. Focusing on Congress, political parties and political ideology, he argues that political reactions to the westward expansion of the United States metamorphosed from emphasis on the spread of sovereignty to concern over the merits and drawbacks of slavery extension. He charts the political disagreements of the North and the South over slavery while being alert to different stances on this issue in each section. But he does not extend his analysis to argue that a fundamental disagreement over capitalism existed in both sections. Morrison's book includes useful material on the doctrine of popular sovereignty, the moral approach to slavery, different constitutional interpretations of slavery extension, and the ideals of liberty and equality in American political life.

Foner (1970) investigates the ideological position of the Republican Party in the 1850s. He argues that the Republicans were an antislavery group committed to free labour on moral and material grounds and that they opposed slavery for similar reasons. Disagreements were widespread in the Republican Party on many issues of national importance, but radical and conservative Republicans were convinced by the late 1850s that slavery should be eradicated from American soil if the libertarian destiny of the United States was to be achieved. The North had already developed an expanding capitalist society by the time of the Civil War. The Republican coalition was committed to free labour for blacks and whites despite limits in articulating rights for black people.

The antislavery context from which the Republican Party emerged is discussed in Sewell (1976), who also examines the abolitionist Liberty Party and the free soil coalition. Stampp (1990) offers a portrait of a single critical year, when the Dred Scott decision and the Lecompton constitution dominated American politics. He shows how President James Buchanan badly handled issues that lay at the forefront of the sectional divide over slavery. The bungle over the Lecompton constitution divided the Democratic Party and paved the way for the Republican triumph under Abraham Lincoln and the onset of civil war. Zerefsky (1990) looks at the seven encounters between Lincoln and Stephen A. Douglas in the summer and autumn of 1858. He includes separate chapters on the legal, moral and historical arguments in the Lincoln–Douglas debates and relates them to the language, culture and values of American society.

The interconnection of slavery and politics in nineteenth-century America is further illuminated by studies dealing with individual states. Cooper Guasco (2001) examines the debate in Illinois over calling a constitutional convention to legalise slavery in the state. She finds that the opponents of slavery argued in favour of a combination of free soil and white labour. Moore (1989) describes the cotton-slave regime of Mississippi in the late antebellum period. Thornton (1978) uncovers the complexity of the white political world in Alabama during the antebellum era. He explains the fanaticism that arose there in the 1850s in opposition to northern abolitionism. Particular attention is paid to William Lowndes Yancey and his followers in their attacks upon the Republican Party.

BIBLIOGRAPHY

Ashworth, John, *Slavery, Capitalism, and Politics in the Antebellum Republic: vol. 1: Commerce and Compromise* (Cambridge: Cambridge University Press, 1995)

Brown, Richard H., 'The Missouri Crisis, Slavery, and the Politics of Jacksonianism', *South Atlantic Quarterly*, 65 (Winter 1966), 55–72

Cooper, William, Jr, *The South and the Politics of Slavery, 1828–1856* (Baton Rouge: Louisiana State University Press, 1978)

Cooper Guasco, Susan, ' "The Deadly Influence of Negro Capitalists": Southern Yeomen and Resistance to the Expansion of Slavery in Illinois', *Civil War History*, 47 (2001), 7–29

Fehrenbacher, Don E., *The South and Three Sectional Crises* (Baton Rouge: Louisiana State University Press, 1980)

Fehrenbacher, Don E., completed and ed. Ward M. McAfee, *The Slaveholding Republic: An Account of the United States Government's Relations to Slavery* (New York: Oxford University Press, 2001)

Foner, Eric, *Free Soil, Free Labor, Free Men: The Ideology of the Republican Party before the Civil War* (New York: Oxford University Press, 1970)

Foner, Eric, 'Politics, Ideology and the Origins of the American Civil War', in George M. Frederikson (ed.), *A Nation Divided: Problems and Issues of the Civil War and Reconstruction* (Minneapolis: Burgess Publishing Company, 1975).

Freehling, William W., *Prelude to Civil War: The Nullification Crisis in South Carolina, 1816–1836* (New York: W. W. Norton, 1965)

Freehling, William W., *The Road to Disunion: Secessionists at Bay, 1776–1854* (New York: Oxford University Press, 1990)

Kolchin, Peter, *American Slavery, 1619–1877* (New York: Hill and Wang, 1993)

Levine, Bruce, *Half Slave and Half Free: The Roots of Civil War* (New York: Hill and Wang, 1991)

Moore, Glover, *The Missouri Controversy, 1819–1821* (Lexington: University of Kentucky Press, 1953)

Moore, John Hebron, *The Emergence of the Cotton Kingdom in the Old Southwest: Mississippi, 1770–1860* (Baton Rouge: Louisiana State University Press, 1989)

Morrison, Michael A., *Slavery and the American West: The Eclipse of Manifest Destiny and the Coming of the Civil War* (Chapel Hill: University of North Carolina Press, 1997)

Sewell, Richard H., *Ballots for Freedom: Antislavery Politics in the United States, 1837–1860* (New York: Oxford University Press, 1976)

Stampp, Kenneth M., *America in 1857: A Nation on the Brink* (New York: Oxford University Press, 1990)

Sydnor, Charles S., *The Development of Southern Sectionalism, 1819–1848* (Baton Rouge: Louisiana State University Press, 1948)

Thornton, J. Mills, *Politics and Power in a Slave Society: Alabama, 1800–1860* (Baton Rouge: Louisiana State University Press, 1978)

Zerefsky, David, *Lincoln, Douglas, and Slavery: In the Crucible of Public Debate* (Chicago: University of Chicago Press, 1990)

ESSAY: POLITICS, IDEOLOGY, AND THE ORIGINS OF THE AMERICAN CIVIL WAR

Foner (1980) offers a broad view of slavery, sectionalism, political ideology and parties in the coming of the Civil War. How did the Missouri crisis indicate how the extension of slavery would be handled by Congress in the future? Why did the 1830s witness 'the closing of Southern society in defence of slavery'? Why and how did the question of slavery and its extension intrude upon political parties in the 1840s? How did Abraham Lincoln and Stephen A. Douglas differ over the politics of slavery and its extension?

It has long been an axiom of political science that political parties help to hold together diverse, heterogeneous societies like our own. Since most major parties in American history have tried, in Seymour Lipset's phrase, to 'appear as plausible representatives of the whole society', they have been broad coalitions cutting across lines of class, race, religion, and section. And although party competition requires that there be differences between the major parties, these differences usually have not been along sharp ideological lines. In fact, the very diversity of American society has inhibited the formation of ideological parties, for such parties assume the existence of a single line of social division along which a majority of the electorate can be mobilized. In a large, heterogeneous society, such a line rarely exists. There are, therefore, strong reasons why, in a two-party system, a major party – or a party aspiring to become 'major' – will eschew ideology, for the statement of a coherent ideology will set limits to the groups in the electorate to which the party can hope to appeal. Under most circumstances, in other words, the party's role as a carrier of a coherent ideology will conflict with its role as an electoral machine bent on winning the largest possible number of votes.[1]

For much of the seventy years preceding the Civil War, the American political system functioned as a mechanism for relieving social tensions, ordering group conflict, and integrating the society. The existence of national political parties, increasingly focused on the contest for the Presidency, necessitated alliances between political elites in various sections of the country. A recent study of early American politics notes that 'political nationalization was far ahead of economic, cultural, and social nationalization' – that is, that the national political system was itself a major bond of union in a diverse, growing society.[2] But as North and South increasingly took different paths of economic and social development and as, from the 1830s onward, antagonistic value systems and ideologies grounded in the question of slavery emerged in these sections, the political system inevitably came under

Foner, Eric, 'Politics, Ideology and the Origins of the American Civil War', in George M. Frederikson (ed.), *A Nation Divided: Problems and Issues of the Civil War and Reconstruction* (Minneapolis: Burgess Publishing Company, 1975), pp. 15–34.

severe disruptive pressures. Because they brought into play basic values and moral judgments, the competing sectional ideologies could not be defused by the normal processes of political compromise, nor could they be contained within the existing inter-sectional political system. Once parties began to reorient themselves on sectional lines, a fundamental necessity of democratic politics – that each party look upon the other as a legitimate alternative government – was destroyed.

When we consider the causes of the sectional conflict, we must ask ourselves not only why civil war came when it did, but why it did not come sooner. How did a divided nation manage to hold itself together for as long as it did? In part, the answer lies in the unifying effects of inter-sectional political parties. On the level of politics, the coming of the Civil War is the story of the intrusion of sectional ideology into the political system, despite the efforts of political leaders of both parties to keep it out. Once this happened, political competition worked to exacerbate, rather than to solve, social and sectional conflicts.

'Parties in this country', wrote a conservative northern Whig in 1855, 'heretofore have helped, not delayed, the slow and difficult growth of a consummated nationality'. Rufus Choate was lamenting the passing of a bygone era, a time when 'our allies were everywhere...there were no Alleghenies nor Mississippi rivers in our politics'.[3] Party organization and the nature of political conflict had taken on new and unprecedented forms in the 1850s. It is no accident that the breakup of the last major inter-sectional party preceded by less than a year the breakup of the Union or that the final crisis was precipitated not by any 'overt act', but by a presidential election.

From the beginning of national government, of course, differences of opinion over slavery constituted an important obstacle to the formation of a national community. 'The great danger to our general government', as Madison remarked at the Constitutional Convention, 'is the great southern and northern interests of the continent, being opposed to each other'. 'The institution of slavery and its consequences', according to him, was the main 'line of discrimination' in convention disputes. As far as slavery was concerned, the Constitution amply fulfilled Lord Acton's dictum that it was an effort to avoid settling basic questions. Aside from the Atlantic slave trade, Congress was given no power to regulate slavery in anyway – the framers' main intention seems to have been to place slavery completely outside the national political arena. The only basis on which a national politics could exist – the avoidance of sectional issues – was thus defined at the outset.[4]

Although the slavery question was never completely excluded from political debate in the 1790s, and there was considerable Federalist grumbling about the three-fifths clause of the Constitution after 1800, the first full demonstration of the political possibilities inherent in a sectional attack on slavery occurred in the Missouri controversy of 1819–21. These debates established a number of precedents which forecast the future course of the slavery extension issue in Congress. Most important was the fact that the issue was able for a time to completely obliterate party lines. In the first votes on slavery in Missouri, virtually every northerner, regardless of party, voted against expansion. It was not surprising, of course, that northern Federalists would try to make political capital out of the issue. What was unexpected was that northern Republicans, many of whom were aggrieved by Virginia's long dominance of the Presidency and by the Monroe administration's tariff and internal improvements policies, would unite with the Federalists. As John Quincy Adams observed, the debate 'disclosed a secret: it revealed the basis for a new organization of parties.... Here was a new party really formed... terrible to the whole Union, but portentously terrible to the South'. But the final compromise set another important precedent: enough northern Republicans became convinced that the Federalists were making political gains from the debates and that the Union was seriously endangered to break with the sectional bloc and support a compromise which a majority of northern Congressmen – Republicans and Federalists – opposed. As for the Monroe administration, its semiofficial spokesman, the *National Intelligencer*, pleaded for a return to the policy of avoiding sectional issues, even to the extent of refusing to publish letters which dealt in any way with the subject of slavery.[5]

The Missouri controversy and the election of 1824, in which four candidates contested the Presidency, largely drawing support from their home sections, revealed that in the absence of two-party competition, sectional loyalties would constitute the lines of political division. No one recognized this more clearly than the architect of the second party system, Martin Van Buren. In his well-known letter to Thomas Ritchie of Virginia, Van Buren explained the need for a revival of national two-party politics on precisely this ground: 'Party attachment in former times furnished a complete antidote for sectional prejudices by producing counteracting feelings. It was not until that defense had been broken down that the clamor against Southern Influence and African Slavery could be made effectual in the North'. Van Buren and many of his generation of politicians had been genuinely frightened by the threats of disunion which echoed through Congress in 1820; they saw national two-party competition as the alternative to sectional conflict and eventual disunion. Ironically, as Richard McCormick has made clear, the creation of the second party system owed as much to sectionalism as to national loyalties. The South, for example, only developed an organized, competitive Whig party in 1835 and 1836 when it became apparent that Jackson, the southern President, had chosen Van Buren, a northerner, as his successor. Once party divisions had emerged, however, they stuck, and by 1840, for one of the very few times in American history, two truly intersectional parties, each united behind a single candidate, competed for the Presidency.[6]

The 1830s witnessed a vast expansion of political loyalties and aware-ness and the creation of party mechanisms to channel voter participation in politics. But the new mass sense of identification with politics had omi-nous implications for the sectional antagonisms which the party system sought to suppress. The historian of the Missouri Compromise has ob-served that 'if there had been a civil war in 1819–1821 it would have been between the members of Congress, with the rest of the country looking on in amazement'.[7] The mass, non-ideological politics of the Jackson era created the desperately needed link between governors and governed. But this very link made possible the emergence of two kinds of sectional agi-tators: the abolitionists, who stood outside of politics and hoped to force public opinion – and through it, politicians – to confront the slavery issue, and political agitators, who used politics as a way of heightening sectional self-consciousness and antagonism in the populace at large.

Because of the rise of mass politics and the emergence of these sectional agitators, the 1830s was the decade in which long-standing, latent sec-tional divisions were suddenly activated, and previously unrelated patterns of derogatory sectional imagery began to emerge into full-blown sectional ideology. Many of the anti-slavery arguments which gained wide currency in the 1830s had roots stretching back into the eighteenth century. The idea that slavery degraded white labor and retarded economic development, for example, had been voiced by Benjamin Franklin. After 1800, the Federal-ists, increasingly localized in New England, had developed a fairly coherent critique, not only of the social and economic effects of slavery, but of what Harrison Gray Otis called the divergence of 'manners, habits, customs, principles, and ways of thinking' which separated northerners and south-erners. And, during the Missouri debates, almost every economic, political, and moral argument against slavery that would be used in the later sec-tional debate was voiced. In fact, one recurring argument was not picked up later – the warning of northern Congressmen that the South faced the danger of slave rebellion if steps were not taken toward abolition. (As far as I know, only Thaddeus Stevens of Republican spokesmen in the 1850s would explicitly use this line of argument.)[8]

The similarity between Federalist attacks on the South and later aboli-tionist and Republican arguments, coupled with the fact that many abolitionists – including Garrison, Phillips, the Tappans, and others – came from Federalist backgrounds, has led James Banner to describe abolitionism as 'the Massachusetts Federalist ideology come back to life'. Yet there was a long road to be traveled from Harrison Gray Otis to William H. Seward, just as there was from Thomas Jefferson to George Fitzhugh. For one thing, the Federalist distrust of democracy, social competition, and the Jeffersonian cry of 'equal rights', their commitment to social inequality, hierarchy, tradition, and order prevented them from pushing their anti-slavery views to their logical conclusion. And New England Federalists were inhibited by the requirements of national party organization and competition from voicing anti-slavery views. In the 1790s, they maintained close ties with southern Federalists, and after 1800 hope of reviving their strength in the South never completely died. Only a party which embraced social mobility and competitive individualism, rejected the permanent subordination of any 'rank' in society, and was unburdened by a southern wing could develop a fully coherent anti-slavery ideology.[9]

An equally important reason why the Federalists did not develop a consistent sectional ideology was that the South in the early part of the nineteenth century shared many of the Federalists' reservations about slavery. The growth of an anti-slavery ideology, in other words, depended in large measure on the growth of pro-slavery thought, and, by the same token, it was the abolitionist assault which brought into being the coherent defense of slavery. The opening years of the 1830s, of course, were ones of crisis for the South. The emergence of militant abolitionism, Nat Turner's rebellion, the Virginia debates on slavery, and the nullification crisis suddenly presented assaults to the institution of slavery from within and outside the South. The reaction was the closing of southern society in defense of slavery, 'the most thorough-going repression of free thought, free speech, and a free press ever witnessed in an American community'. At the same time, southerners increasingly abandoned their previous, highly qualified defenses of slavery and embarked on the formulation of the pro-slavery argument. By 1837, as is well known, John C. Calhoun could thank the abolitionists on precisely this ground:[10]

> This agitation has produced one happy effect at least; it has compelled us at the South to look into the nature and character of this great institution, and to correct many false impressions that even we had entertained in relation to it. Many in the South once believed that it was a moral and political evil; that folly and delusion are gone; we see it now in its true light, and regard it as the most safe and stable basis for free institutions in the world.

The South, of course, was hardly as united as Calhoun asserted. But the progressive rejection of the Jeffersonian tradition, the suppression of civil liberties, and the increasing stridency of the defense of slavery all pushed the South further and further out of the inter-sectional mainstream, setting it increasingly apart from the rest of the country. Coupled with the Gag Rule and the mobs which broke up abolitionist presses and meetings, the growth of pro-slavery thought was vital to a new anti-slavery formulation which emerged in the late 1830s and which had been absent from both the Federalist attacks on slavery and the Missouri debates – the idea of the Slave Power. The Slave Power replaced the three-fifths clause as the symbol of southern power, and it was a far more sophisticated and complex formulation. Abolitionists could now argue that slavery was not only morally repugnant, it was incompatible with the basic democratic values and liberties of white Americans. As one abolitionist declared, 'We commenced the present struggle to obtain the freedom of the slave; we are compelled to continue it to preserve our own'. In other words, a process of ideological expansion had begun, fed in large measure by the sequence of response and counter-response between the competing sectional outlooks.[11] Once this process had begun, it had an internal dynamic which made it extremely difficult to stop. This was especially true because of the emergence of agitators whose avowed purpose was to sharpen sectional conflict, polarize public opinion, and develop sectional ideologies to their logical extremes.

As the 1840s opened, most political leaders still clung to the traditional basis of politics, but the sectional, ideological political agitators formed growing minorities in each section. In the South, there was a small group of outright secessionists and a larger group, led by Calhoun, who were firmly committed to the Union but who viewed sectional organization and self-defense, not the traditional reliance on inter-sectional political parties, as the surest means of protecting southern interests within the Union. In the North, a small radical group gathered in Congress around John Quincy Adams and Congressmen like Joshua Giddings, William Slade, and Seth Gates – men who represented areas of the most intense abolitionist agitation and whose presence confirmed Garrison's belief that, once public opinion was aroused on the slavery issue, politicians would have to follow step. These radicals were determined to force slavery into every congressional debate. They were continually frustrated but never suppressed, and the reelection of Giddings in 1842 after his censure and resignation from the House proved that in some districts party discipline was no longer able to control the slavery issue.[12]

The northern political agitators, both Congressmen and Liberty party leaders, also performed the function of developing and popularizing a political rhetoric, especially focused on fear of the Slave Power, which could be seized upon by traditional politicians and large masses of voters if slavery ever entered the center of political conflict.

In the 1840s, this is precisely what happened. As one politician later recalled, 'Slavery upon which by common consent no party issue had been made was then obtruded upon the field of party action'. It is significant that John Tyler and John C. Calhoun, the two men most responsible for this intrusion, were political outsiders, men without places in the national party structure. Both of their careers were blocked by the major parties but might be advanced if tied to the slavery question in the form of Texas annexation. Once introduced into politics, slavery was there to stay. The Wilmot Proviso, introduced in 1846, had precisely the same effect as the proposal two decades earlier to restrict slavery in Missouri – it completely fractured the major parties along sectional lines. As in 1820, opposition to the expansion of slavery became the way in which a diverse group of northerners expressed their various resentments against a southern-dominated administration. And, as in 1821, a small group of northern Democrats eventually broke with their section, reaffirmed their primary loyalty to the party, and joined with the South to kill the Proviso in 1847. In the same year, enough southerners rejected Calhoun's call for united sectional action to doom his personal and sectional ambitions.[13]

But the slavery extension debates of the 1840s had far greater effects on the political system than the Missouri controversy had had. Within each party, they created a significant group of sectional politicians – men whose careers were linked to the slavery question and who would therefore resist its exclusion from future politics. And in the North, the 1840s witnessed the expansion of sectional political rhetoric – as more and more northerners became familiar with the 'aggressions' of the Slave Power and the need to resist them. At the same time, as anti-slavery ideas expanded, unpopular and divisive elements were weeded out, especially the old alliance of anti-slavery with demands for the rights of free blacks. Opposition to slavery was already coming to focus on its lowest common denominators – free soil, opposition to the Slave Power, and the union.[14]

The political system reacted to the intrusion of the slavery question in the traditional ways. At first, it tried to suppress it. This is the meaning of the famous letters opposing the immediate annexation of Texas issued by Clay and Van Buren on the same spring day in 1844, probably after consultation on the subject. It was an agreement that slavery was too explosive a question for either party to try to take partisan advantage of it. The agreement, of course, was torpedoed by the defeat of Van Buren for the Democratic nomination, a defeat caused in part by the willingness of his Democratic opponents to use the Texas and slavery questions to discredit Van Buren – thereby violating the previously established rules of political conduct. In the North from 1844 onward, both parties, particularly the Whigs, tried to defuse the slavery issue and minimize defection to the Liberty party by adopting anti-southern rhetoric. This tended to prevent defections to third parties, but it had the effect of nurturing and legitimating anti-southern sentiment within the ranks of the major parties themselves. After the 1848 election in which northern Whigs and Democrats vied for title of 'free soil' to minimize the impact of the Free Soil party, William H. Seward commented, 'Antislavery is at length a respectable element in politics'.[15]

Both parties also attempted to devise formulas for compromising the divisive issue. For the Whigs, it was 'no territory' – an end to expansion would end the question of the spread of slavery. The Democratic answer, first announced by Vice President Dallas in 1847 and picked up by Lewis Cass, was popular sovereignty or non-intervention: giving to the people of each territory the right to decide on slavery. As has often been pointed out, popular sovereignty was an exceedingly vague and ambiguous doctrine. It was never precisely clear what the powers of a territorial legislature were to be or at what point the question of slavery was to be decided.[16] But politically such ambiguity was essential (and intentional) if popular sovereignty were to serve as a means of settling the slavery issue on the traditional basis – by removing it from national politics and transferring the battleground from Congress to the territories.[17] Popular sovereignty formed one basis of the compromise of 1850, the last attempt of the political system to expel the disease of sectional ideology by finally settling all the points at which slavery and national politics intersected.

That compromise was possible in 1850 was testimony to the resiliency of the political system and the continuing ability of party loyalty to compete with sectional commitments. But the very method of passage revealed how deeply sectional divisions were embedded in party politics. Because only a small group of Congressmen – mostly northwestern Democrats and southern Whigs – were committed to compromise on every issue, the 'omnibus' compromise measure could not pass. The compromise had to be enacted serially with the small compromise bloc, led by Stephen A. Douglas of Illinois, aligned with first one sectional bloc, then the other, to pass the individual measures.[18]

His role in the passage of the compromise announced the emergence of Douglas as the last of the great Unionist, compromising politicians, the heir of Clay, Webster, and other spokesmen for the center. And his career, like Webster's, showed that it was no longer possible to win the confidence of both sections with a combination of extreme nationalism and the calculated suppression of the slavery issue in national politics. Like his predecessors, Douglas called for a policy of 'entire silence on the slavery question', and throughout the 1850s, as Robert Johannsen has written, his aim was to restore 'order and stability to American politics through the agency of a national, conservative Democratic party'. Ultimately, Douglas failed – a traditional career for the Union was simply not possible in the 1850s – but it is equally true that in 1860 he was the only presidential candidate to draw significant support in all parts of the country.[19]

It is, of course, highly ironic that it was Douglas's attempt to extend the principle of popular sovereignty to territory already guaranteed to free labor by the Missouri Compromise which finally shattered the second party system. We can date exactly the final collapse of that system – February 15, 1854 – the day a caucus of southern Whig Congressmen and Senators decided to support Douglas's Nebraska bill, despite the fact that they could have united with northern Whigs in opposition both to the repeal of the Missouri Compromise and the revival of sectional agitation.[20] But in spite of the sectionalization of politics which occurred after 1854, Douglas continued his attempt to maintain a national basis of party competition. In fact, from one angle of vision, whether politics was to be national or sectional was the basic issue of the Lincoln-Douglas debates of 1858. The Little Giant presented local autonomy – popular sovereignty for states and territories – as the only 'national' solution to the slavery question, while Lincoln attempted to destroy this middle ground and force a single, sectional solution on the entire Union. There is a common critique of Douglas's politics, expressed perhaps most persuasively by Allan Nevins, which argues that, as a man with no moral feelings about slavery, Douglas was incapable of recognizing that this moral issue affected millions of northern voters.[21] This, in my opinion, is a serious misunderstanding of Douglas's politics. What he insisted was not that there was no moral question involved in slavery but that it was not the function of the politician to deal in moral judgments. To Lincoln's prediction that the nation could not exist half slave and half free, Douglas replied that it had so existed for seventy years and could continue to do so if northerners stopped trying to impose their own brand of morality upon the South.

Douglas's insistence on the separation of politics and morality was expressed in his oft-quoted statement that – in his role as a politician – he did not care if the people of a territory voted slavery 'up or down'. As he explained in his Chicago speech of July 1858, just before the opening of the great debates:

> I deny the right of Congress to force a slave-holding state upon an unwilling people. I deny their right to force a free state upon an unwilling people. I deny their right to force a good thing upon a people who are unwilling to receive it .... It is no answer to this argument to say that slavery is an evil and hence should not be tolerated. You must allow the people to decide for themselves whether it is a good or an evil.

When Lincoln, therefore, said the real purpose of popular sovereignty was 'to educate and mould public opinion, at least northern public opinion, to not care whether slavery is voted down or up', he was, of course, right. For Douglas recognized that moral categories, being essentially uncompromisable, are unassimilable in politics. The only solution to the slavery issue was local autonomy. Whatever a majority of a state or territory wished to do about slavery was right – or at least should not be tampered with by politicians from other areas. To this, Lincoln's only possible reply was the one formulated in the debates – the will of the majority must be tempered by considerations of morality. Slavery was not, he declared, an 'ordinary matter of domestic concern in the states and territories'. Because of its essential immorality, it tainted the entire nation, and its disposition in the territories, and eventually in the entire nation, was a matter of national concern to be decided by a national, not a local, majority. As the debates continued, Lincoln increasingly moved to this moral level of the slavery argument: 'Everything that emanates from [Douglas] or his coadjutors, carefully excludes the thought that there is anything wrong with slavery. All their arguments, if you will consider them, will be seen to exclude the thought .... If you do admit that it is wrong, Judge Douglas can't logically say that he don't care whether a wrong is voted up or down'.[22]

In order to press home the moral argument, moreover, Lincoln had to insist throughout the debates on the basic humanity of the black; while Douglas, by the same token, logically had to define blacks as subhuman, or at least, as the Dred Scott decision had insisted, not part of the American 'people' included in the Declaration of Independence and the Constitution. Douglas's view of the black, Lincoln declared, conveyed 'no vivid impression that the Negro is a human, and consequently has no idea that there can be any moral question in legislating about him'.[23] Of course, the standard of morality which Lincoln felt the nation should adopt regarding slavery and the black was the sectional morality of the Republican party.

By 1860, Douglas's local majoritarianism was no more acceptable to southern political leaders than Lincoln's national and moral majoritarianism. The principle of state rights and minority self-determination had always been the first line of defense of slavery from northern interference, but southerners now coupled it with the demand that Congress intervene to establish and guarantee slavery in the territories. The Lecompton fight had clearly demonstrated that southerners would no longer be satisfied with what Douglas hoped the territories would become – free, Democratic states. And the refusal of the Douglas Democrats to accede to southern demands was the culmination of a long history of resentment on the part of northern Democrats, stretching back into the 1840s, at the impossible political dilemma of being caught between increasingly anti-southern constituency pressure and loyalty to an increasingly pro-southern national party. For their part, southern Democrats viewed their northern allies as too weak at home and too tainted with anti-southernism after the Lecompton battle to be relied on to protect southern interests any longer.[24]

As for the Republicans, by the late 1850s they had succeeded in developing a coherent ideology which, despite internal ambiguities and contradictions, incorporated the fundamental values, hopes, and fears of a majority of northerners. As I have argued elsewhere, it rested on a commitment to the northern social order, founded on the dignity and opportunities of free labor, and to social mobility, enterprise, and 'progress'. It gloried in the same qualities of northern life – materialism, social fluidity, and the dominance of the self-made man – which twenty years earlier had been the source of widespread anxiety and fear in Jacksonian America. And it defined the South as a backward, stagnant, aristocratic society, totally alien in values and social order to the middle-class capitalism of the North.[25]

Some elements of the Republican ideology had roots stretching back into the eighteenth century. Others, especially the Republican emphasis on the threat of the Slave Power, were relatively new. Northern politics and thought were permeated by the Slave Power idea in the 1850s. The effect can perhaps be gauged by a brief look at the career of the leading Republican spokesman of the 1850s, William H. Seward. As a political child of upstate New York's burned-over district and anti-masonic crusade, Seward had long believed that the Whig party's main political liability was its image as the spokesman of the wealthy and aristocratic. Firmly committed to egalitarian democracy, Seward had attempted to reorient the New York State Whigs into a reformist, egalitarian party, friendly to immigrants and embracing political and economic democracy, but he was always defeated by the party's downstate conservative wing. In the 1840s, he became convinced that the only way for the party to counteract the Democrats' monopoly of the rhetoric of democracy and equality was for the Whigs to embrace anti-slavery as a party platform.[26]

The Slave Power idea gave the Republicans the anti-aristocratic appeal with which men like Seward had long wished to be associated politically. By fusing older anti-slavery arguments with the idea that slavery posed a threat to northern free labor and democratic values, it enabled the Republicans to tap the egalitarian outlook which lay at the heart of northern society. At the same time, it enabled Republicans to present anti-slavery as an essentially conservative reform, an attempt to reestablish the anti-slavery principles of the founding fathers and rescue the federal government from southern usurpation. And, of course, the Slave Power idea had a far greater appeal to northern self-interest than arguments based on the plight of black slaves in the South. As the black abolitionist Frederick Douglass noted, 'The cry of Free Men was raised, not for the extension of liberty to the black man, but for the protection of the liberty of the white'.[27]

By the late 1850s, it had become a standard part of Republican rhetoric to accuse the Slave Power of a long series of transgressions against northern rights and liberties and to predict that, unless halted by effective political action, the ultimate aim of the conspiracy – the complete subordination of the national government to slavery and the suppression of northern liberties – would be accomplished. Like other conspiracy theories, the Slave Power idea was a way of ordering and interpreting history, assigning clear causes to otherwise inexplicable events, from the Gag Rule to Bleeding Kansas and the Dred Scott decision. It also provided a convenient symbol through which a host of anxieties about the future could be expressed. At the same time, the notion of a black Republican conspiracy to overthrow slavery and southern society had taken hold in the South. These competing conspiratorial outlooks were reflections, not merely of sectional 'paranoia', but of the fact that the nation was every day growing apart and into two societies whose ultimate interests were diametrically opposed. The South's fear of black Republicans, despite its exaggerated rhetoric, was based on the realistic assessment that at the heart of Republican aspirations for the nation's future was the restriction and eventual eradication of slavery. And the Slave Power expressed northerners' conviction, not only that slavery was incompatible with basic democratic values, but that to protect slavery, southerners were determined to control the federal government and use it to foster the expansion of slavery. In summary, the Slave Power idea was the ideological glue of the Republican party – it enabled them to elect in 1860 a man conservative enough to sweep to victory in every northern state, yet radical enough to trigger the secession crisis.

Did the election of Lincoln pose any real danger to the institution of slavery? In my view, it is only possible to argue that it did not if one takes a completely static – and therefore ahistorical – view of the slavery issue. The expansion of slavery was not simply an issue; it was a fact. By 1860, over half the slaves lived in areas outside the original slave states. At the same time, however, the South had become a permanent and shrinking minority within the nation. And in the majority section, anti-slavery sentiment had expanded at a phenomenal rate. Within one generation, it had moved from the commitment of a small minority of northerners to the motive force behind a victorious party. That sentiment now demanded the exclusion of slavery from the territories. Who could tell what its demands would be in ten or twenty years? The incoming President had often declared his commitment to the 'ultimate extinction' of slavery. In Alton, Illinois, in the heart of the most pro-slavery area of the North, he had condemned Douglas because 'he looks to no end of the institution of slavery'.[28] A Lincoln administration seemed likely to be only the beginning of a prolonged period of Republican hegemony. And the succession of generally weak, one-term Presidents between 1836 and 1860 did not obscure the great expansion in the potential power of the Presidency which had taken place during the administration of Andrew Jackson. Old Hickory had clearly shown that a strong-willed President, backed by a united political party, had tremendous power to shape the affairs of government and to transform into policy his version of majority will.

What was at stake in 1860, as in the entire sectional conflict, was the character of the nation's future. This was one reason Republicans had placed so much stress on the question of the expansion of slavery. Not only was this the most available issue concerning slavery constitutionally open to them, but it involved the nation's future in the most direct way. In the West, the future was tabula rasa, and the future course of western development would gravely affect the direction of the entire nation. Now that the territorial issue was settled by Lincoln's election, it seemed likely that the slavery controversy would be transferred back into the southern states themselves. Secessionists, as William Freehling has argued, feared that slavery was weak and vulnerable in the border states, even in Virginia.[29] They feared Republican efforts to encourage the formation of Republican organizations in these areas and the renewal of the long-suppressed internal debate on slavery in the South itself. And, lurking behind these anxieties, may have been fear of anti-slavery debate reaching the slave quarters, of an undermining of the masters' authority, and, ultimately, of slave rebellion itself. The slaveholders knew, despite the great economic strength of King Cotton, that the existence of slavery as a local institution in a larger free economy demanded an inter-sectional community consensus, real or enforced. It was this consensus which Lincoln's election seemed to undermine, which is why the secession convention of South Carolina declared, 'Experience has proved that slaveholding states cannot be safe in subjection to non-slaveholding states'.[30]

More than seventy years before the secession crisis, James Madison had laid down the principles by which a central government and individual and minority liberties could coexist in a large and heterogeneous Union. The very diversity of interests in the nation, he argued in the Federalist papers, was the security for the rights of minorities, for it ensured that no one interest would ever gain control of the government.[31] In the 1830s, John C. Calhoun recognized the danger which abolitionism posed to the South – it threatened to rally the North in the way Madison had said would not happen – in terms of one commitment hostile to the interests of the minority South. Moreover, Calhoun recognized, when a majority interest is organized into an effective political party, it can seize control of all the branches of government, overturning the system of constitutional checks and balances which supposedly protected minority rights. Only the principle of the concurrent majority – a veto which each major interest could exercise over policies directly affecting it – could reestablish this constitutional balance.

At the outset of the abolitionist crusade, Calhoun had been convinced that, while emancipation must be 'resisted at all costs', the South should avoid hasty action until it was 'certain that it is the real object, not by a few, but by a very large portion of the non-slaveholding states'. By 1850, Calhoun was convinced that 'Every portion of the North entertains views more or less hostile to slavery'. And by 1860, the election returns demonstrated that this anti-slavery sentiment, contrary to Madison's expectations, had united in an interest capable of electing a President, despite the fact that it had not the slightest support from the sectional minority. The character of Lincoln's election, in other words, completely overturned the ground rules which were supposed to govern American politics. The South Carolina secession convention expressed secessionists' reaction when it declared that once the sectional Republican party, founded on hostility to southern values and interests, took over control of the federal government, 'the guarantees of the Constitution will then no longer exist'.[32]

Thus the South came face to face with a conflict between its loyalty to the nation and loyalty to the South – that is, to slavery, which, more than anything else, made the South distinct. David Potter has pointed out that the principle of majority rule implies the existence of a coherent, clearly recognizable body of which more than half may be legitimately considered as a majority of the whole. For the South to accept majority rule in 1860, in other words, would have been an affirmation of a common nationality with the North. Certainly, it is true that in terms of ethnicity, language, religion – many of the usual components of nationality – Americans, North and South, were still quite close. On the other hand, one important element, community of interest, was not present. And perhaps most important, the preceding decades had witnessed an escalation of distrust – an erosion of the reciprocal currents of good will so essential for national harmony. 'We are not one people', declared the New York *Tribune* in 1855. 'We are two peoples. We are a people for Freedom and a people for Slavery. Between the two, conflict is inevitable'.[33] We can paraphrase John Adams's famous comment on the American Revolution and apply it to the coming of the Civil War – the separation was complete, in the minds of the people, before the war began. In a sense, the Constitution and national political system had failed in the difficult task of creating a nation – only the Civil War itself would accomplish it.

NOTES

1. Seymour M. Lipset, *The First New Nation* (New York, 1963), 308–11; Frank J. Sorauf, *Political Parties in the American System* (Boston, 1964), 60–5. Distinctions between American political parties, to borrow Marvin Meyers's apt phrase, have usually been along lines of 'persuasion', rather than ideology.
2. Donald L. Robinson, *Slavery and the Structure of American Politics 1765–1820* (New York, 1971), 175. See also William N. Chambers and Walter Dean Burnham, eds., *The American Party Systems* (New York, 1967), 3–32, 56–89.
3. *National Intelligencer*, Oct. 6, 1855.
4. Staughton Lynd, *Class Conflict, Slavery, and the United States Constitution* (Indianapolis, 1967), 161; Robinson, *Slavery and the Structure of Politics*, viii, 244.
5. James M. Banner, *To the Hartford Convention* (New York, 1970), 99–103; Glover Moore, *The Missouri Controversy 1819–1821* (Lexington, Ky., 1953), *passim*; Charles Francis Adams, ed., *Memoirs of John Quincy Adams* (12 vols; Philadelphia, 1874–77), IV, 529; William E. Ames, *A History of the National Intelligencer* (Chapel Hill, N.C., 1972), 121–2.
6. Paul Nagel, 'The Election of 1824: Reconsideration Based on Newspaper Opinion', *JSH*, XXVI (Aug. 1960), 315–29; Richard H. Brown, 'The Missouri Crisis, Slavery, and the Politics of Jacksonianism', *South Atlantic Quarterly*, LXV (Winter 1966), 55–72; Robert V. Remini, *Martin Van Buren and the Making of the Democratic Party* (New York, 1959), 125–32; Richard P. McCormick, *The Second American Party System* (Chapel Hill, 1966), 338–42; Chambers and Burnham, eds., *The American Party Systems*, 21, 97–101.
7. Moore, *Missouri Controversy*, 175.
8. Robinson, *Slavery and the Structure of Politics*, 72; Linda K. Kerber, *Federalists in Dissent* (Ithaca, 1970), 24–44; Banner, *To the Hartford Convention*, 104–9; Theophilus Parsons, Jr., 'A Mirror of Men's Minds: The Missouri Compromise and the Development of an Antislavery Ideology' (unpublished seminar paper, Columbia University, 1971); *Congressional Globe*, 31 Congress, 1 Session, Appendix, 1030; 36 Congress, 2 Session, 624. C. Vann Woodward observes that patterns of derogatory sectional imagery existed far earlier than most historians have assumed. C. Vann Woodward, *American Counterpoint: Slavery and Racism in the North-South Dialogue* (Boston, 1971), 6.
9. Banner, *To the Hartford Convention*, 108–9; Kerber, *Federalists in Dissent* 50, 59–63. After the transformation of their party from a national to a regional one,

New England Federalists did express their latent anti-southern feelings more openly. Richard Buel, Jr., *Securing the Revolution: Ideology in American Politics, 1789–1815* (Ithaca, 1972), 235.

10. Stanley Elkins, 'Slavery and Ideology', in Ann Lane, ed., *The Debate over Slavery* (Urbana, 1971), 376n.; William W. Freehling, *Prelude to Civil War: the Nullification Crisis in South Carolina, 1816–1836* (New York, 1966), ch. 9, esp. 333, 358; *Congressional Globe*, 25 Congress, 2 Session, Appendix, 62.

11. Alice Felt Tyler, *Freedom's Ferment* (New York, 1962 ed.), 511; Elkins, 'Slavery and Ideology', 374–7; Eric Foner, *Free Soil, Free Labor, Free Men: The Ideology of the Republican Party before the Civil War* (New York, 1970), 87–102.

12. Gilbert H. Barnes, *The Anti-Slavery Impulse* (New York, 1964 ed.), 188–90, 195–7; James B. Stewart, *Joshua R. Giddings and the Tactics of Radical Politics* (Cleveland, 1970), ch. 4.

13. Preston King to Gideon Welles, Sept. 16, 1858, Gideon Welles Papers, LOC; Eric Foner, 'The Wilmot Proviso Revisited', *JAH*, LVI (Sept. 1969), 262–70; Chaplain W. Morrison, *Democratic Politics and Sectionalism* (Chapel Hill, 1967), 34–41.

14. Morrison, *Democratic Politics*, 45–51; Eric Foner, 'Racial Attitudes of the New York Free Soilers' [essay V in Foner, *Politics and Ideology in the Age of the Civil War* (New York, 1980)].

15. Avery O. Craven, *The Coming of the Civil War* (Chicago, 1942), 197; Ronald P. Formisano, *The Birth of Mass Political Parties* (Princeton, 1971), 195, 205–6; Joseph G. Rayback, *Free Soil* (Lexington, 1970), 309; Frederick W. Seward, *Seward at Washington*, 2 vols. (New York 1891), I, 71.

16. Foner, *Free Soil, Free Labor, Free Men*, 188; Morrison, *Democratic Politics*, 87–91; Damon Wells, *Stephen Douglas, The Last Years, 1857–1861* (Austin, 1971), 61–7.

17. For the intentional nature of the ambiguities in popular sovereignty, see Robert W. Johannsen, *Stephen A. Douglas* (New York, 1973), 427, 440, 525.

18. Holman Hamilton, *Prologue to Conflict* (Lexington, 1964).

19. Johannsen, *Douglas*, 347, 483. For Webster's efforts to create a national consensus by compromising and suppressing the slavery issue, see Robert F. Dalzell, Jr., *Daniel Webster and the Trial of American Nationalism* (Boston, 1973), *passim*, and Major L. Wilson, 'Of Time and the Union: Webster and His Critics in the Crisis of 1850', *CWH*, XIV (Dec. 1968), 293–306.

20. Foner, *Free Soil, Free Labor, Free Men*, 194. Of course, on the local level, the Whigs had already been eroding under the impact of such divisive issues as temperance and nativism.

21. Allan Nevins, *Ordeal of the Union*, 2 vols (New York, 1947), II, 107. Cf. Wells, *Douglas*, 64.

22. Paul M. Angle, ed., *Created Equal? The Complete Lincoln-Douglas Debates of 1858* (Chicago, 1958), 5, 17, 18, 35, 70, 202, 303, 332–4, 351. Cf. Harry Jaffa, *Crisis of the House Divided* (Garden City, 1959); Wells, *Douglas*, 110–11.

23. Angle, ed., *Created Equal?*, 22–23, 62–3; Jaffa, *Crisis*, 36. Lincoln declared that the trouble with popular sovereignty was that Douglas 'looks upon all this matter of slavery as an exceedingly little thing – this matter of keeping one-sixth of the population of the whole country in a state of oppression and tyranny unequalled in the world'. Angle, ed., *Created Equal?*, 35. It is hard to imagine Douglas including the slaves in any way as part of 'the population of the whole country'.

24. Roy F. Nichols, *The Disruption of American Democracy* (New York, 1948), esp. ch. 15. For Douglas's intentions for the territories and his expectation that popular sovereignty would result in the creation of free states in the West, see Jaffa, *Crisis*, 48; Johannsen, *Douglas*, 276, 279–80, 565; Edward L. and Frederick H. Schapsmeir, 'Lincoln and Douglas: Their Versions of the West', *Journal of the West*, VII (Oct. 1968), 546. Lee Benson argues that the entrance of free western states into the Union was not a cause of concern for the South, since these new states, like

California and Oregon in the 1850s, would likely be Democratic and pro-southern. But the 1850s clearly showed that free, Democratic states could quickly become Republican, and the Lecompton fight demonstrated that free, Democratic states were no longer acceptable to southern leaders, who insisted that Kansas be Democratic *and* slave. Lee Benson, *Toward the Scientific Study of History* (Philadelphia, 1972), 269.

25. Foner, *Free Soil, Free Labor, Free Men*, esp. chs. 1–2.
26. Glyndon G. Van Deusen, *William Henry Seward* (New York, 1969), ch. 9; Elliot R. Barkan, 'The Emergence of a Whig Persuasion: Conservatism, Democratism, and the New York State Whigs', *New York History*, LII (Oct. 1971), 370–86; Seward to James Bowen, Nov. 3, 1844, William Henry Seward Papers, University of Michigan Library; Seward to Weed, Aug. 3, 1846, Thurlow Weed Papers, University of Rochester.
27. Formisano, *Birth of Mass Political Parties*, 329; Foner, *Free Soil, Free Labor, Free Men*, 87–102; Larry Gara, 'Slavery and the Slave Power: A Crucial Distinction', *CWH*, XV (Mar. 1969), 5–18.
28. Angle, ed., *Created Equal?*, 393.
29. William W. Freehling, 'The Editorial Revolution, Virginia, and the Coming of the Civil War: A Review Essay', *CWH*, XVI (Mar. 1970), 68–71.
30. Robert Brent Toplin, 'The Specter of Crisis: Slaveholder Reactions to Abolitionism in the United States and Brazil', *CWH*, XVIII (June 1972), 129–38; John Amasa May and Joan Reynolds Faust, *South Carolina Secedes* (Columbia, 1960), 88.
31. Benjamin F. Wright, ed., *The Federalist* (Cambridge, 1961), 132–4, 357–9. Or, as C. B. MacPherson writes, the American federal theory of politics rests on the assumption 'that the politically important demands of each individual are diverse and are shared with varied and shifting combinations of other individuals, none of which combinations can be expected to be a numerical majority of the electorate'. MacPherson, *Democratic Theory: Essays in Retrieval* (Oxford, 1973), 190.
32. William W. Freehling, 'Spoilsmen and Interests in the Thought and Career of John C. Calhoun', *JAH*, LII (June 1965), 25–6; Charles M. Wiltse, *John C. Calhoun*, 3 vols (Indianapolis, 1944–51), II, 114, 195, 199, 255, 268–70; III, 416–19, 462–63; May and Faust, *South Carolina Secedes*, 81.
33. David M. Potter, *The South and the Sectional Conflict* (Baton Rouge, 1968), 44, 58; New York *Tribune*, Apr. 12, 1855.

DOCUMENT 1: THE FUGITIVE SLAVE ACT, 1850

The Fugitive Slave Act was enacted as part of the Compromise of 1850. It was an unpopular measure throughout the northern states. Many northern abolitionists took part in the Underground Railroad to assist fugitives from the South to escape the provisions of this legislation.

Section 1

Be it enacted by the Senate and House of Representatives of the United States of America in Congress assembled, That the persons who have been, or may hereafter be, appointed commissioners, in virtue of any act of Congress, by the Circuit Courts of the United States, and Who, in consequence of such appointment, are authorized to exercise the powers that any justice of the peace, or other magistrate of any of the United States, may exercise in respect to offenders for any crime or offense against the United States, by arresting, imprisoning, or bailing the same under and by the virtue of the thirty-third section of the act of the twenty-fourth of September seventeen hundred and eighty-nine, entitled 'An Act to establish the judicial courts of the United States' shall be, and are hereby, authorized and required to exercise and discharge all the powers and duties conferred by this act.

Section 2

And be it further enacted, That the Superior Court of each organized Territory of the United States shall have the same power to appoint commissioners to take acknowledgments of bail and affidavits, and to take depositions of witnesses in civil causes, which is now possessed by the Circuit Court of the United States; and all commissioners who shall hereafter be appointed for such purposes by the Superior Court of any organized Territory of the United States, shall possess all the powers, and exercise all the duties, conferred by law upon the commissioners appointed by the Circuit Courts of the United States for similar purposes, and shall moreover exercise and discharge all the powers and duties conferred by this act.

Section 3

And be it further enacted, That the Circuit Courts of the United States shall from time to time enlarge the number of the commissioners, with a view to afford reasonable facilities to reclaim fugitives from labor, and to the prompt discharge of the duties imposed by this act.

Section 4

And be it further enacted, That the commissioners above named shall have concurrent jurisdiction with the judges of the Circuit and District Courts of

---

www.nationalcenter.org/HistoricalDocuments.html

the United States, in their respective circuits and districts within the several States, and the judges of the Superior Courts of the Territories, severally and collectively, in term-time and vacation; shall grant certificates to such claimants, upon satisfactory proof being made, with authority to take and remove such fugitives from service or labor, under the restrictions herein contained, to the State or Territory from which such persons may have escaped or fled.

Section 5

And be it further enacted, That it shall be the duty of all marshals and deputy marshals to obey and execute all warrants and precepts issued under the provisions of this act, when to them directed; and should any marshal or deputy marshal refuse to receive such warrant, or other process, when tendered, or to use all proper means diligently to execute the same, he shall, on conviction thereof, be fined in the sum of one thousand dollars, to the use of such claimant, on the motion of such claimant, by the Circuit or District Court for the district of such marshal; and after arrest of such fugitive, by such marshal or his deputy, or whilst at any time in his custody under the provisions of this act, should such fugitive escape, whether with or without the assent of such marshal or his deputy, such marshal shall be liable, on his official bond, to be prosecuted for the benefit of such claimant, for the full value of the service or labor of said fugitive in the State, Territory, or District whence he escaped: and the better to enable the said commissioners, when thus appointed, to execute their duties faithfully and efficiently, in conformity with the requirements of the Constitution of the United States and of this act, they are hereby authorized and empowered, within their counties respectively, to appoint, in writing under their hands, any one or more suitable persons, from time to time, to execute all such warrants and other process as may be issued by them in the lawful performance of their respective duties; with authority to such commissioners, or the persons to be appointed by them, to execute process as aforesaid, to summon and call to their aid the bystanders, or posse comitatus [those called to assist a law officer] the proper county, when necessary to ensure a faithful observance of the clause of the Constitution referred to, in conformity with the provisions of this act; and all good citizens are hereby commanded to aid and assist in the prompt and efficient execution of this law, whenever their services may be required, as aforesaid, for that purpose; and said warrants shall run, and be executed by said officers, any where in the State within which they are issued.

Section 6

And be it further enacted, That when a person held to service or labor in any State or Territory of the United States, has here to fore or shall hereafter escape into another State or Territory of the United States, the person or persons to whom such service or labor may be due, or his, her, or their agent or attorney, duly authorized, by power of attorney, in writing, acknowledged and certified under the seal of some legal officer or court of the State or Territory in which the same may be executed, may pursue and reclaim such fugitive person, either by procuring a warrant from some one of the courts, judges, or commissioners aforesaid, of the proper circuit, district, or county, for the apprehension of such fugitive from service or labor, or by seizing and arresting such fugitive, where the same can be done without process, and by taking, or causing such person to be taken, forthwith before such court, judge, or commissioner, whose duty it shall be to hear and determine the case of such claimant in a summary manner; and upon satisfactory proof being made, by deposition or affidavit, in writing, to be taken and certified by such court, judge, or commissioner, or by other satisfactory testimony, duly taken and certified by some court, magistrate, justice of the peace, or other legal officer authorized to administer an oath and take depositions under the laws of the State or Territory from which such person owing service or labor may have escaped, with a certificate of such magistracy or other authority, as aforesaid, with the seal of the proper court or officer thereto attached, which seal shall be sufficient to establish the competency of the proof, and with proof, also by affidavit, of the identity of the person whose service or labor is claimed to be due as aforesaid, that the person so arrested does in fact owe service or labor to the person or persons claiming him or her, in the State or Territory from which such fugitive may have escaped as aforesaid, and that said person escaped, to make out and deliver to such claimant, his or her agent or attorney, a certificate setting forth the substantial facts as to the service or labor due from such fugitive to the claimant, and of his or her escape from the State or Territory in which he or she was arrested, with authority to such claimant, or his or her agent or attorney, to use such reasonable force and restraint as may be necessary, under the circumstances of the case, to take and remove such fugitive person back to the State or Territory whence he or she may have escaped as aforesaid. In no trial or hearing under this act shall the testimony of such alleged fugitive be admitted in evidence; and the certificates in this and the first [fourth] section mentioned, shall be conclusive of the right of the person or persons in whose favor granted, to remove such fugitive to the State or Territory from which he escaped, and shall prevent all molestation of such person or persons by any process issued by any court, judge, magistrate, or other person whomsoever.

Section 7

And be it further enacted, That any person who shall knowingly and willingly obstruct, hinder, or prevent such claimant, his agent or attorney, or any person or persons lawfully assisting him, her, or them, from arresting such a fugitive from service or labor, either with or without process as aforesaid, or shall rescue, or attempt to rescue, such fugitive from service or labor, from the custody of such claimant, his or her agent or attorney, or other person or persons lawfully assisting as aforesaid, when so arrested, pursuant to the authority herein given and declared; or shall aid, abet, or assist such person so owing service or labor as aforesaid, directly or indirectly, to escape from such claimant, his agent or attorney, or other person or persons legally authorized as aforesaid; or shall harbor or conceal such fugitive, so as to prevent the discovery and arrest of such person, after notice or knowledge of the fact that such person was a fugitive from service or labor as aforesaid, shall, for either of said offences, be subject to a fine not exceeding one thousand dollars, and imprisonment not exceeding six months, by indictment and conviction before the District Court of the United States for the district in which such offence may have been committed, or before the proper court of criminal jurisdiction, if committed within any one of the organized Territories of the United States; and shall moreover forfeit and pay, by way of civil damages to the party injured by such illegal conduct, the sum of one thousand dollars for each fugitive so lost as aforesaid, to be recovered by action of debt, in any of the District or Territorial Courts aforesaid, within whose jurisdiction the said offence may have been committed.

Section 8

And be it further enacted, That the marshals, their deputies, and the clerks of the said District and Territorial Courts, shall be paid, for their services, the like fees as may be allowed for similar services in other cases; and where such services are rendered exclusively in the arrest, custody, and delivery of the fugitive to the claimant, his or her agent or attorney, or where such supposed fugitive may be discharged out of custody for the want of sufficient proof as aforesaid, then such fees are to be paid in whole by such claimant, his or her agent or attorney; and in all cases where the proceedings are before a commissioner, he shall be entitled to a fee of ten dollars in full for his services in each case, upon the delivery of the said certificate to the claimant, his agent or attorney; or a fee of five dollars in cases where the proof shall not, in the opinion of such commissioner, warrant such certificate and delivery, inclusive of all services incident to such arrest and examination, to be paid, in either case, by the claimant, his or her agent or attorney. The person or persons authorized to execute the process to be issued by such commissioner for the arrest and detention of fugitives from service or labor as aforesaid, shall also be entitled to a fee of five dollars each for each person he or they may arrest, and take before any commissioner as aforesaid, at the instance and request of such claimant, with such other fees as may be deemed reasonable by such commissioner for such other additional services as may be necessarily performed by him or them; such as attending at the examination, keeping the fugitive in custody, and providing him with food and lodging during his detention, and until the final determination of such commissioners; and, in general, for performing such other duties as may be required by such claimant, his or her attorney or agent, or commissioner in the premises, such fees to be made up in conformity with the fees usually charged by the officers of the courts of justice within the proper district or county, as near as may be practicable, and paid by such claimants, their agents or attorneys, whether such supposed fugitives from service or labor be ordered to be delivered to such claimant by the final determination of such commissioner or not.

Section 9

And be it further enacted, That, upon affidavit made by the claimant of such fugitive, his agent or attorney, after such certificate has been issued, that he has reason to apprehend that such fugitive will be rescued by force from his or their possession before he can be taken beyond the limits of the State in which the arrest is made, it shall be the duty of the officer making the arrest to retain such fugitive in his custody, and to remove him to the State whence he fled, and there to deliver him to said claimant, his agent, or attorney. And to this end, the officer aforesaid is hereby authorized and required to employ so many persons as he may deem necessary to overcome such force, and to retain them in his service so long as circumstances may require. The said officer and his assistants, while so employed, to receive the same compensation, and to be allowed the same expenses, as are now allowed by law for transportation of criminals, to be certified by the judge of the district within which the arrest is made, and paid out of the treasury of the United States.

Section 10

And be it further enacted, That when any person held to service or labor in any State or Territory, or in the District of Columbia, shall escape therefrom, the party to whom such service or labor shall be due, his, her, or their agent or attorney, may apply to any court of record therein, or judge thereof in vacation, and make satisfactory proof to such court, or judge in vacation, of the escape aforesaid, and that the person escaping owed service or labor to such party. Whereupon the court shall cause a record to be made of the matters so proved, and also a general description of the person so escaping, with such convenient certainty as may be; and a transcript of such record, authenticated by the attestation of the clerk and of the seal of the said court, being produced in any other State, Territory, or district in which the person so escaping may be found, and being exhibited to any judge, commissioner, or other officer authorized by the law of the United States to cause persons escaping from service or labor to be delivered up, shall be held and taken to be full and conclusive evidence of the fact of escape, and that the service or labor of the person escaping is due to the party in such record mentioned. And upon the production by the said party of other and further evidence if necessary, either oral or by affidavit, in addition to what is contained in the said record of the identity of the person escaping, he or she shall be delivered up to the claimant. And the said court, commissioner, judge, or other person authorized by this act to grant certificates to claimants or fugitives, shall, upon the production of the record and other evidences aforesaid, grant to such claimant a certificate of his right to take any such person identified and proved to be owing service or labor as aforesaid, which certificate shall authorize such claimant to seize or arrest and transport such person to the State or Territory from which he escaped: Provided, That nothing herein contained shall be construed as requiring the production of a transcript of such record as evidence as aforesaid. But in its absence the claim shall be heard and determined upon other satisfactory proofs, competent in law.

Approved, September 18, 1850.

Source: U.S. Congress, Fugitive Slave Act (1850; www.nationalcenter.org/HistoricalDocuments.html)

DOCUMENT 2: APPEAL OF THE INDEPENDENT
DEMOCRATS, 1854

*Outlines the views of the Independent Democrats with regard to the
Kansas–Nebraska Act and the issue of slavery's expansion into the
territories.*

As Senators and Representatives in the Congress of the United States it is
our duty to warn our constituents, whenever imminent danger menaces the
freedom of our institutions or the permanency of the Union.

Such danger, as we firmly believe, now impends, and we earnestly solicit
your prompt attention to it.

At the last session of Congress a bill for the organization of the Territory of Nebraska passed the House of Representatives by an overwhelming
majority. That bill was based on the principle of excluding slavery from
the new Territory. It was not taken up for consideration in the Senate and
consequently failed to become a law.

At the present session a new Nebraska bill has been reported by the Senate
Committee on Territories, which, should it unhappily receive the sanction
of Congress, will open all the unorganized Territories of the Union to the
ingress of slavery.

We arraign this bill as a gross violation of a sacred pledge; as a criminal
betrayal of precious rights; as part and parcel of an atrocious plot to exclude from a vast unoccupied region immigrants from the Old World and
free laborers from our own States, and convert it into a dreary region of
despotism, inhabited by masters and slaves.

Take your maps, fellow citizens, we entreat you, and see what country it is which this bill gratuitously and recklessly proposes to open to
slavery....

This immense region, occupying the very heart of the North American
Continent, and larger, by thirty-three thousand square miles, than all the
existing free States – including California...this immense region the bill
now before the Senate, without reason and without excuse, but in flagrant
disregard of sound policy and sacred faith, purposes to open to slavery.

We beg your attention, fellow-citizens, to a few historical facts:

The original settled policy of the United States, clearly indicated by the
Jefferson proviso of 1784 and the Ordinance of 1787, was non-extension
of slavery.

In 1803 Louisiana was acquired by purchase from France....

In 1818,...the inhabitants of the Territory of Missouri applied to
Congress for authority to form a State constitution, and for admission into

Henry S. Commager (ed.), *Documents of American History* (New York: Appleton-Century-Crofts,
1963), pp. 329–31.

the Union. There were, at that time, in the whole territory acquired from France, outside of the State of Louisiana, not three thousand slaves.

There was no apology, in the circumstances of the country, for the continuance of slavery. The original national policy was against it, and not less the plain language of the treaty under which the territory had been acquired from France.

It was proposed, therefore, to incorporate in the bill authorizing the formation of a State government, a provision requiring that the constitution of the new State should contain an article providing for the abolition of existing slavery, and prohibiting the further introduction of slaves.

This provision was vehemently and pertinaciously opposed, but finally prevailed in the House of Representatives by a decided vote. In the Senate it was rejected, and – in consequence of the disagreement between the two Houses – the bill was lost.

At the next session of Congress, the controversy was renewed with increased violence. It was terminated at length by a compromise. Missouri was allowed to come into the Union with slavery; but a section was inserted in the act authorizing her admission, excluding slavery forever from all the territory acquired from France, not included in the new State, lying north of 36° 30′ ....

The question of the constitutionality of this prohibition was submitted by President Monroe to his cabinet. John Quincy Adams was then Secretary of State; John C. Calhoun was Secretary of War; William H. Crawford was Secretary of the Treasury; and William Wirt was Attorney-General. Each of these eminent gentlemen – three of them being from the slave states – gave a written opinion, affirming its constitutionality, and thereupon the act received the sanction of the President himself, also from a slave State.

Nothing is more certain in history than the fact that Missouri could not have been admitted as a slave State had not certain members from the free States been reconciled to the measure by the incorporation of this prohibition into the act of admission. Nothing is more certain than that this prohibition has been regarded and accepted by the whole country as a solemn compact against the extension of slavery into any part of the territory acquired from France lying north of 36° 30′, and not included in the new State of Missouri. The same act let it be ever remembered – which authorized the formation of a constitution by the State, without a clause forbidding slavery, consecrated, beyond question and beyond honest recall, the whole remainder of the Territory to freedom and free institutions forever. For more than thirty years – during more than half our national existence under our present Constitution – this compact has been universally regarded and acted upon as inviolable American law. In conformity with it, Iowa was admitted as a free State and Minnesota has been organized as a free Territory.

It is a strange and ominous fact, well calculated to awaken the worst apprehensions and the most fearful forebodings of future calamities, that it is now deliberately proposed to repeal this prohibition, by implication or directly – the latter certainly the manlier way – and thus to subvert the compact, and allow slavery in all the yet unorganized territory.

We cannot, in this address, review the various pretenses under which it is attempted to cloak this monstrous wrong, but we must not altogether omit to notice one.

It is said that Nebraska sustains the same relations to slavery as did the territory acquired from Mexico prior to 1850, and that the pro-slavery clauses of the bill are necessary to carry into effect the compromise of that year.

No assertion could be more groundless....

The statesmen whose powerful support carried the Utah and New Mexico acts never dreamed that their provisions would be ever applied to Nebraska....

Here is proof beyond controversy that the principle of the Missouri act prohibiting slavery north of 36° 30′, far from being abrogated by the Compromise Acts, is expressly affirmed; and that the proposed repeal of this prohibition, instead of being an affirmation of the Compromise Acts, is a repeal of a very prominent provision of the most important act of the series. It is solemnly declared in the very Compromise Acts 'that nothing herein contained shall be construed to impair or qualify' the prohibition of slavery north of 36° 30′; and yet in the face of this declaration, that sacred prohibition is said to be overthrown. Can presumption further go? To all who, in any way, lean upon these compromises, we commend this exposition.

These pretenses, therefore, that the territory covered by the positive prohibition of 1820, sustains a similar relation to slavery with that acquired from Mexico, covered by no prohibition except that of disputed constitutional or Mexican law, and that the Compromises of 1850 require the incorporation of the pro-slavery clauses of the Utah and New Mexico Bill in the Nebraska act, are mere inventions, designed to cover from public reprehension meditated bad faith.

Were he living now, no one would be more forward, more eloquent, or more indignant in his denunciation of that bad faith, than Henry Clay, the foremost champion of both compromises....

We confess our total inability properly to delineate the character or describe the consequences of this measure. Language fails to express the sentiments of indignation and abhorrence which it inspires; and no vision less penetrating and comprehensive than that of the All-Seeing can reach its evil issues....

We appeal to the people. We warn you that the dearest interests of freedom and the Union are in imminent peril. Demagogues may tell you that the Union can be maintained only by submitting to the demands of slavery.

We tell you that the Union can only be maintained by the full recognition of the just claims of freedom and man. The Union was formed to establish justice and secure the blessings of liberty. When it fails to accomplish these ends it will be worthless, and when it becomes worthless it cannot long endure.

We entreat you to be mindful of that fundamental maxim of Democracy – EQUAL RIGHTS AND EXACT JUSTICE FOR ALL MEN. Do not submit to become agents in extending legalized oppression and systematized injustice over a vast territory yet exempt from these terrible evils.

We implore Christians and Christian ministers to interpose. Their divine religion requires them to behold in every man a brother, and to labor for the advancement and regeneration of the human race.

Whatever apologies may be offered for the toleration of slavery in the States, none can be offered for its extension into Territories where it does not exist, and where that extension involves the repeal of ancient law and the violation of solemn compact. Let all protest, earnestly and emphatically, by correspondence, through the press, by memorials, by resolutions of public meetings and legislative bodies, and in whatever other mode may seem expedient, against this enormous crime.

For ourselves, we shall resist it by speech and vote, and with all the abilities which God has given us. Even if overcome in the impending struggle, we shall not submit. We shall go home to our constituents, erect anew the standard of freedom, and call on the people to come to the rescue of the country from the domination of slavery. We will not despair; for the cause of human freedom is the cause of God.

S. P. Chase

Charles Sumner

J. R. Giddings

Edward Wade

Gerritt Smith

Alexander De Witt

DOCUMENT 3: ABRAHAM LINCOLN'S 'HOUSE DIVIDED' SPEECH

One of Lincoln's famous statements on slavery, delivered to the delegates of the state Republican convention in Illinois in August 1858. The thrust of the speech is that a conspiracy existed among Democratic leaders to make slavery a national institution.

Mr. President and Gentlemen of the Convention.

If we could first know where we are, and whither we are tending, we could then better judge what to do, and how to do it.

We are now far into the fifth year, since a policy was initiated, with the avowed object, and confident promise, of putting an end to slavery agitation.

Under the operation of that policy, that agitation has not only, not ceased, but has constantly augmented.

In my opinion, it will not cease, until a crisis shall have been reached, and passed.

'A house divided against itself cannot stand'.

I believe this government cannot endure, permanently half slave and half free.

I do not expect the Union to be dissolved – I do not expect the house to fall – but I do expect it will cease to be divided.

It will become all one thing, or all the other.

Either the opponents of slavery, will arrest the further spread of it, and place it where the public mind shall rest in the belief that it is in course of ultimate extinction; or its advocates will push it forward, till it shall become alike lawful in all the States, old as well as new – North as well as South.

Have we no tendency to the latter condition?

Let any one who doubts, carefully contemplate that now almost complete legal combination – piece of machinery so to speak – compounded of the Nebraska doctrine, and the Dred Scott decision. Let him consider not only what work the machinery is adapted to do, and how well adapted; but also, let him study the history of its construction, and trace, if he can, or rather fail, if he can, to trace the evidences of design, and concert of action, among its chief bosses, from the beginning.

But, so far, Congress only, had acted; and an indorsement by the people, real or apparent, was indispensable, to save the point already gained, and give chance for more.

The new year of 1854 found slavery excluded from more than half the States by State Constitutions, and from most of the national territory by Congressional prohibition.

www.nationalcenter.org/HistoricalDocuments.html

Four days later, commenced the struggle, which ended in repealing that Congressional prohibition.

This opened all the national territory to slavery; and was the first point gained.

This necessity had not been overlooked; but had been provided for, as well as might be, in the notable argument of 'squatter sovereignty', otherwise called 'sacred right of self government', which latter phrase, though expressive of the only rightful basis of, any government, was so perverted in this attempted use of it as to amount to just this: That if any one man choose to enslave another, no third man shall be allowed to object.

That argument was incorporated into the Nebraska bill itself, in the language which follows: 'It being the true intent and meaning of this act not to legislate slavery into any Territory or state, not exclude it therefrom; but to leave the people thereof perfectly free to form and regulate their domestic institutions in their own way, subject only to the Constitution of the United States'.

Then opened the roar of loose declamation in favor of 'Squatter Sovereignty', and 'Sacred right of self government'.

'But', said opposition members, 'let us be more specific – let us amend the bill so as to expressly declare that the people of the territory may exclude slavery'. 'Not we', said the friends of the measure; and down they voted the amendment.

While the Nebraska bill was passing through congress, a law case, involving the question of a negroe's freedom, by reason of his owner having voluntarily taken him first into a free state and then a territory covered by the congressional prohibition, and held him as a slave, for a long time in each, was passing through the U.S. Circuit Court for the District of Missouri; and both Nebraska bill and law suit were brought to a decision in the same month of May, 1854. The negroe's name was 'Dred Scott', which name now designates the decision finally made in the case.

Before the then next Presidential election, the law case came to, and was argued in the Supreme Court of the United States; but the decision of it was deferred until after the election. Still, before the election, Senator Trumbull, on the floor of the Senate, requests the leading advocate of the Nebraska bill to state his opinion whether the people of a territory can constitutionally exclude slavery from their limits; and the latter answers, 'That is a question for the Supreme Court'.

The election came. Mr. Buchanan was elected, and the endorsement, such as it was, secured. That was the second point gained. The endorsement, however, fell short of a clear popular majority by nearly four hundred thousand votes, and so, perhaps, was not overwhelmingly reliable and satisfactory.

The outgoing President, in his last annual message, as impressively as possible echoed back upon the people the weight and authority of the indorsement.

The Supreme Court met again; did not announce their decision, but ordered a re-argument.

The Presidential inauguration came, and still no decision of the court; but the incoming President, in his inaugural address, fervently exhorted the people to abide by the forthcoming decision, whatever it might be.

Then, in a few days, came the decision.

The reputed author of the Nebraska bill finds an early occasion to make a speech at this capitol endorsing the Dred Scott Decision, and vehemently denouncing all opposition to it.

The new President, too, seizes the early occasion of the Silliman letter to indorse and strongly construe that decision, and to express his astonishment that any different view had ever been entertained.

At length a squabble springs up between the President and the author of the Nebraska bill, on the mere question of fact, whether the Lecompton constitution was or was not, in any just sense, made by the people of Kansas; and in that squabble the latter declares that all he wants is a fair vote for the people, and that he cares not whether slavery be voted down or voted up. I do not understand his declaration that he cares not whether slavery be voted down or voted up, to be intended by him other than as an apt definition of the policy he would impress upon the public mind – the principle for which he declares he has suffered much, and is ready to suffer to the end.

And well may he cling to that principle. If he has any parental feeling, well may he cling to it. That principle, is the only shred left of his original Nebraska doctrine. Under the Dred Scott decision, 'squatter sovereignty' squatted out of existence, tumbled down like temporary scaffolding – like the mould at the foundry served through one blast and fell back into loose sand – helped to carry an election, and then was kicked to the winds. His late joint struggle with the Republicans, against the Lecompton Constitution, involves nothing of the original Nebraska doctrine. That struggle was made on a point, the right of a people to make their own constitution, upon which he and the Republicans have never differed.

The several points of the Dred Scott decision, in connection with Senator Douglas' 'care not' policy, constitute the piece of machinery, in its present state of advancement. This was the third point gained.

The working points of that machinery are:

First, that no negro slave, imported as such from Africa, and no descendant of such slave can ever be a citizen of any State, in the sense of that term as used in the Constitution of the United States.

This point is made in order to deprive the negro, in every possible event, of the benefit of this provision of the United States Constitution, which declares, that –

'The citizens of each State shall be entitled to all privileges and immunities of citizens in the several States'.

Secondly, that 'subject to the Constitution of the United States', neither Congress nor a Territorial Legislature can exclude slavery from any United States territory.

This point is made in order that individual men may fill up the territories with slaves, without danger of losing them as property, and thus to enhance the chances of permanency to the institution through all the future.

Thirdly, that whether the holding a negro in actual slavery in a free State, makes him free, as against the holder, the United States courts will not decide, but will leave to be decided by the courts of any slave State the negro may be forced into by the master.

This point is made, not to be pressed immediately; but, if acquiesced in for a while, and apparently indorsed by the people at an election, then to sustain the logical conclusion that what Dred Scott's master might lawfully do with Dred Scott, in the free State of Illinois, every other master may lawfully do with any other one, or one thousand slaves, in Illinois, or in any other free State.

Auxiliary to all this, and working hand in hand with it, the Nebraska doctrine, or what is left of it, is to educate and mould public opinion, at least Northern public opinion, to not care whether slavery is voted down or voted up.

This shows exactly where we now are, and partially also, whither we are tending.

It will throw additional light on the latter, to go back, and run the, mind over the string of historical facts already stated. Several things will now appear less dark and mysterious than they did when they were transpiring. The people were to be left 'perfectly free' 'subject only to the Constitution'. What the Constitution had to do with it, outsiders could not then see. Plainly enough now, it was an exactly fitted niche, for the Dred Scott decision to afterwards come in, and declare the perfect freedom of the people, to be just no freedom at all.

Why was the amendment, expressly declaring the right of the people to exclude slavery, voted down? Plainly enough now, the adoption of it, would have spoiled the niche for the Dred Scott decision.

Why was the court decision held up? Why, even a Senator's individual opinion withheld, till after the Presidential election? Plainly enough now, the speaking out then would have damaged the 'perfectly free' argument upon which the election was to be carried.

Why the outgoing President's felicitation on the indorsement? Why the delay of a reargument? Why the incoming President's advance exhortation in favor of the decision?

These things look like the cautious patting and petting a spirited horse, preparatory to mounting him, when it is dreaded that he may give the rider a fall.

And why the hasty after endorsements of the decision by the President and others?

We can not absolutely know that all these exact adaptations are the result of preconcert. But when we see a lot of framed timbers, different portions of which we know have been gotten out at different times and places and by different workmen – Stephen, Franklin, Roger and James, for instance – and when we see these timbers joined together, and see they exactly make the frame of a house or a mill, all the tenons and mortices exactly fitting, and all the lengths and proportions of the different pieces exactly adapted to their respective places, and not a piece too many or too few – not omitting even scaffolding – or, if a single piece be lacking, we can see the place in the frame exactly fitted and prepared to yet bring such piece in – in such a case, we find it impossible to not believe that Stephen and Franklin and Roger and James all understood one another from the beginning, and all worked upon a common plan or draft drawn up before the first lick was struck.

It should not be overlooked that, by the Nebraska bill, the people of a State as well as Territory, were to be left 'perfectly free' 'subject only to the Constitution'.

Why mention a State? They were legislating for territories, and not for or about States. Certainly the people of a State are and ought to be subject to the Constitution of the United States; but why is mention of this lugged into this merely territorial law? Why are the people of a territory and the people of a state therein lumped together, and their relation to the Constitution therein treated as being precisely the same?

While the opinion of the Court, by Chief Justice Taney, in the Dred Scott case, and the separate opinions of all the concurring Judges, expressly declare that the Constitution of the United States neither permits Congress nor a Territorial legislature to exclude slavery from any United States territory, they all omit to declare whether or not the same Constitution permits a state, or the people of a State, to exclude it.

Possibly, this was a mere omission; but who can be quite sure, if McLean or Curtis had sought to get into the opinion a declaration of unlimited power in the people of a state to exclude slavery from their limits, just as Chase and Macy sought to get such declaration, in behalf of the people of a territory, into the Nebraska bill – I ask, who can be quite sure that it would not have been voted down, in the one case, as it had been in the other.

The nearest approach to the point of declaring the power of a State over slavery, is made by Judge Nelson. He approaches it more than once, using the precise idea, and almost the language too, of the Nebraska act. On one occasion his exact language is, 'except in cases where the power is restrained by the Constitution of the United States, the law of the State is supreme over the subject of slavery within its jurisdiction'.

In what cases the power of the states is so restrained by the U.S. Constitution, is left an open question, precisely as the same question, as to the restraint on the power of the territories was left open in the Nebraska act. Put that and that together, and we have another nice little niche, which we may, ere long, see filled with another Supreme Court decision, declaring that the Constitution of the United States does not permit a state to exclude slavery from its limits.

And this may especially be expected if the doctrine of 'care not whether slavery be voted down or voted up', shall gain upon the public mind sufficiently to give promise that such a decision can be maintained when made.

Such a decision is all that slavery now lacks of being alike lawful in all the States.

Welcome or unwelcome, such [a] decision is probably coming, and will soon be upon us, unless the power of the present political dynasty shall be met and overthrown.

We shall lie down pleasantly dreaming that the people of Missouri are on the verge of making their State free; and we shall awake to the reality, instead, that the Supreme Court has made Illinois a slave State.

To meet and overthrow the power of that dynasty, is the work now before all those who would prevent that consummation.

That is what we have to do.

But how can we best do it?

There are those who denounce us openly to their own friends, and yet whisper us softly, that Senator Douglas is the aptest instrument there is, with which to effect that object. They do not tell us, nor has he told us, that he wishes any such object to be effected. They wish us to infer all, from the facts, that he now has a little quarrel with the present head of the dynasty; and that he has regularly voted with us, on a single point, upon which, he and we, have never differed.

They remind us that he is a very great man, and that the largest of us are very small ones. Let this be granted. But 'a living dog is better than a dead lion'. Judge Douglas, if not a dead lion for this work, is at least a caged and toothless one. How can he oppose the advances of slavery? He don't care anything about it. His avowed mission is impressing the 'public heart' to care nothing about it.

A leading Douglas Democratic newspaper thinks Douglas' superior talent will be needed to resist the revival of the African slave trade.

Does Douglas believe an effort to revive that trade is approaching? He has not said so. Does he really think so? But if it is, how can he resist it? For years he has labored to prove it is a sacred right of white men to take negro slaves into the new territories. Can he possibly show that it is less a sacred right to buy them where they can be bought cheapest? And, unquestionably they can be bought cheaper in Africa than in Virginia.

He has done all in his power to reduce the whole question of slavery to one of a mere right of property; and as such, how can he oppose the foreign slave trade – how can he refuse that trade in that 'property' shall be 'perfectly free' – unless he does it as a protection to the home production? And as the home producers will probably not ask the protection, he will be wholly without a ground of opposition.

Senator Douglas holds, we know, that a man may rightfully be wiser to-day than he was yesterday – that he may rightfully change when he finds himself wrong.

But, can we for that reason, run ahead, and infer that he will make any particular change, of which he, himself, has given no intimation? Can we safely base our action upon any such vague inference?

Now, as ever, I wish to not misrepresent Judge Douglas' position, question his motives, or do ought that can be personally offensive to him.

Whenever, if ever, he and we can come together on principle so that our great cause may have assistance from his great ability, I hope to have interposed no adventitious obstacle.

But clearly, he is not now with us – he does not pretend to be – he does not promise to ever be.

Our cause, then, must be intrusted to, and conducted by its own un-doubted friends – those whose hands are free, whose hearts are in the work – who do care for the result.

Two years ago the Republicans of the nation mustered over thirteen hundred thousand strong.

We did this under the single impulse of resistance to a common danger, with every external circumstance against us.

Of strange, discordant, and even, hostile elements, we gathered from the four winds, and formed and fought the battle through, under the constant hot fire of a disciplined, proud, and pampered enemy.

Did we brave all then, to falter now? – now – when that same enemy is wavering, dissevered and belligerent?

The result is not doubtful. We shall not fail – if we stand firm, we shall not fail.

Wise councils may accelerate or mistakes delay it, but, sooner or later the victory is sure to come.

12

EMANCIPATION AND THE CIVIL WAR

INTRODUCTION

Slavery played a crucial role in the sectionalism that divided North and South in the late antebellum decades. Issues of slavery extension, popular sovereignty and abolitionism kept slavery firmly within the political orbit of national politics in the United States from the mid-1840s to secession and the outbreak of the Civil War. General accounts of the events of that era and their relationship with slavery, sectionalism and politics are legion. Potter (1976) is one such study. The strength of this work lies in its lucid disentangling of political manoeuvring in the 1850s. For Potter, slavery and its extension into the territories was the torch that lit the fire in the deep sectional divide between the northern and southern states, leading to the Lower South's decision to espouse their own sense of nationalism. McPherson's detailed narrative of the American Civil War and its impact on the black population (1988) unfolds the many twists and turns in wartime strategy and tactics. He shows how black troops and freed slaves played an important part in their own destiny. Barney's survey of the Civil War and Reconstruction era (1990) also emphasises the plight of African-Americans. Collins (1981), Sewell (1988) and Cook (2003) cover the central themes and issues relating to slave emancipation and the Civil War.

Lincoln played a crucial role in political debates and actions concerning slavery and emancipation. Recognising the humanity of American black people, Lincoln was morally opposed to slavery while not being enthusiastic about white and black equality in the United States. Historians have long debated the extent to which his moral qualms over slavery influenced his actions consistently and the degree to which his dealings with slavery bespeak political pragmatism: the two views are naturally not mutually exclusive. Donald's biography (1995) highlights the pragmatic nature of Lincoln's decisions in the face of tumultuous events. Thus the emancipation proclamations of 1862–3 are seen as the calculating decisions of a practical politician acting to free slaves in the interests of preserving the nation. Cox (1981) offers a different view of Lincoln's attitude towards African-Americans. Concentrating on Louisiana during the Civil War, she argues that Lincoln was at one with radical Republicans in advocating emancipation and limited black rights. According to this interpretation, Lincoln was a forceful president who worked steadily towards the goal of black freedom despite the distractions and contingencies of wartime leadership. Vorenberg (2001) provides a detailed examination of the process of emancipation between 1863 and 1865. He focuses on the political evolution of freedom within the context of the ending of the Civil War.

Abolitionism during the Civil War is covered in McPherson (1964) and Huggins (1980). McPherson looks at the work carried out by northern abolitionists attached to radical Republicanism. He shows that they campaigned for economic, social and educational opportunities for freedmen and did not lose sight of these goals amidst the turmoil of war and Reconstruction. Huggins's biography of the leading black abolitionist is useful on his career as an agitator and spokesman for African-Americans. Drawing on the three autobiographies written by Douglass and synthesising earlier studies, Huggins presents a readable portrait of a self-made man and former slave without providing revealing insights into his subject's inner world.

Planters caught up in the throes of the Civil War and Reconstruction found their world changing rapidly as their mastery over slaves became transformed into dealings with freedmen. Roark (1977) covers the traumas experienced by planters as they searched for a viable substitute for slave labour. Mohr (1986) looks at the same process for Georgia, showing how the strains of the Confederacy and the collapse of slavery led blacks and whites into an uncertain future where their respective roles within southern culture were shifting but were yet to find a new niche. The final years of slavery in Georgia saw planters modifying their brutality and harshness towards slaves. As Mohr puts it, 'whites concealed their loss of mastery beneath a cloak of greater permissiveness' (p. 236).

Litwack (1979) covers the African-American experience between 1861 and 1868. This is a thorough discussion of how blacks perceived and experienced their condition and future in relation to their family lives, religious beliefs, social conditions and educational and political opportunities. Litwack illuminates the individual experiences of ex-slaves, selecting apt contemporary quotations to illustrate their situations. He is less successful in offering general arguments about the aspirations and actions of freedmen and in showing how different socio-economic contexts, on farms, plantations and cities, fragmented the choices available for African-Americans. Berlin, Fields, Miller, Reidy and Rowland (1992) offer three essays that emphasise slave agency. They argue that the actions of black people during the Civil War shaped their destiny and helped to drive radical Republicans towards planning for black freedom. Their emphasis lies not on Lincoln as an emancipator but on the actions taken by slaves to secure their own liberty.

Ransom (1989) offers little by way of social or cultural explanations for the demise of slavery during the American Civil War. His book is useful, however, for integrating into his analysis many findings of quantifiers in the 'new' political and economic history into his analysis. Ransom shows that the sectional conflict came to a head with the election of Lincoln as president and that the transition from slavery to freedom in the South sapped the Confederacy's war effort after the Emancipation proclamations of 1862–3. He covers the increased racism that stymied efforts made to reconstruct the South. He discusses the stagnant economy of the postbellum South and the industrial expansion made possible in the North by the Union victory in the Civil War. Ransom also looks at the economics of slavery, with good discussions of land, slave and cotton prices and the westward expansion of slavery before the Civil War.

Donald (1965) includes much material on black Americans in his investigation of the early political history of Reconstruction. Foner's large-scale work on Reconstruction (1988) includes extensive material on the African-American search for autonomy and civil and political rights. The agency of black Americans in working towards this goal is stressed. Despite the limits of Reconstruction policy, the author argues that the political gains made by freedpeople were greater than can be found in any other country where slaves were emancipated. Foner (1983) presages some of the themes found in his larger study of Reconstruction. He argues that freed blacks in Haiti and the British Caribbean lacked the political resources to make much of their freedom whereas in the United States African-Americans gained political rights, repealed the Black Codes designed to reduce them to penury, and managed to establish sharecropping as a halfway house between independent farming and free labour. Thus American blacks could demand better work conditions and wrest better concessions from planters than their counterparts in Haiti and the British West Indies.

BIBLIOGRAPHY

Barney, William L., *Battleground for the Union: The Era of the Civil War and Reconstruction, 1848–1877* (Englewood Cliffs, NJ: Prentice Hall, 1990)

Berlin, Ira, Barbara J. Fields, Steven F. Miller, Joseph P. Reidy, and Leslie S. Rowland, *Slaves no More: Three Essays on Emancipation and the Civil War* (Cambridge: Cambridge University Press, 1992)

Collins, Bruce, *The Origins of America's Civil War* (London: Edward Arnold, 1981)

Cook, Robert, *Civil War America: Making a Nation, 1848–1877* (Harlow: Longman, 2003)

Cox, LaWanda, *Lincoln and Black Freedom: A Study in Presidential Leadership* (Urbana-Champaign, IL: University of Illinois Press, 1981)

Donald, David H., *The Politics of Reconstruction, 1863–1867* (Baton Rouge: Louisiana State University Press, 1965)

Donald, David H., *Lincoln* (New York: Simon & Schuster, 1995)

Fehrenbacher, Don E., completed and ed. by Ward M. McAfee, *The Slaveholding Republic: An Account of the United States Government's Relations to Slavery* (New York: Oxford University Press, 2001)

Foner, Eric, *Nothing but Freedom: Emancipation and its Legacy* (Baton Rouge: Louisiana State University Press, 1983)

Foner, Eric, *Reconstruction: America's Unfinished Revolution, 1863–1877* (New York: Harper, 1988)

Huggins, Nathan Irvin, *Slave and Citizen: The Life of Frederick Douglass* (Boston: Little, Brown, 1980)

Litwack, Leon F., *Been in the Storm so Long: The Aftermath of Slavery* (New York: Vantage Books, 1979)

McPherson, James M., *The Struggle for Equality: Abolitionists and the Negro in the Civil War and Reconstruction* (Princeton: Princeton University Press, 1964)

McPherson, James M., *Battle Cry of Freedom: The Era of the Civil War* (New York: Oxford University Press, 1988)

Mohr, Clarence L., *On the Threshold of Freedom: Masters and Slaves in Civil War Georgia* (Athens, GA: University of Georgia Press, 1986)

Potter, David M., *The Impending Crisis, 1848–1861*, completed by Don E. Fehrenbacher (New York: Harper & Row, 1976)

Ransom, Roger L., *Conflict and Compromise: The Political Economy of Slavery, Emancipation, and the American Civil War* (New York: Cambridge University Press, 1989)

Roark, James L., *Masters without Slaves: Southern Planters in the Civil War and Reconstruction* (New York: W.W. Norton, 1977)

Sewell, Richard H., *The House Divided: Sectionalism and the Civil War, 1848–1865* (Baltimore, MD: Johns Hopkins University Press, 1988)

Vorenberg, Michael, *Final Freedom: The Civil War, the Abolition of Slavery, and the Thirteenth Amendment* (Cambridge: Cambridge University Press, 2001)

ESSAY: LINCOLN AND SLAVE EMANCIPATION

Fehrenbacher (2001) seeks to steer a course between adulation of Lincoln as 'the Great Emancipator' and Lincoln as a political opportunist who freed the slaves for ulterior personal and national considerations. What were the stages through which Lincoln moved towards an emancipation policy? Do they show that Lincoln was led by events? Can one identify a prime mover in bringing about freedom for slaves during the Civil War? How did Lincoln's Christian beliefs influence his views on slavery and freedom? How far was Lincoln committed to racial equality?

In recent years, some historians have exaggerated a portrait of an overly conservative Abraham Lincoln, waging war solely to restore a disintegrating empire, ordering generals in the field to halt their unilateral liberation of slaves, and vainly pursuing an antiquated policy of compensated emancipation for owners and colonization for any slaves thus liberated.[1] To a degree, this portrait is a legitimate corrective of Lincoln's long-standing mythological image as the 'Great Emancipator' that is even more overblown. In addition, it cannot be denied that much of the interpretation made by Lincoln's critics is founded upon solid evidence.[2] But it is as false to portray Lincoln as one caring nothing about the slavery issue as it is to make him into the premier humanitarian of his age. In fact, Lincoln was a politician first and foremost. He was devoted to certain long-range principles that consistently guided his course, but concurrently he obeyed the necessity of balancing diverse and often conflicting political interests.

It is important to understand what 'saving the Union' meant to Lincoln. It did not mean mere preservation of national empire, which might have been the case if, for example, Stephen A. Douglas had been president during the Civil War. For Lincoln, saving the Union was not separate from the eventual elimination of slavery from American life. For him, any Union worth preserving had as a prerequisite that slavery should first be restricted and ultimately be eliminated. Even before the war, secessionists had accurately sensed this about the meaning of this first Republican national administration. And William Lloyd Garrison agreed. A month before the election, Garrison wrote to a friend that Lincoln's victory would signify a sharp shift in national policy, 'which, in process of time, must ripen into . . . decisive action'.[3] Eventually, all who lived through the conflagration became equally appreciative of this fact.

'Communication and inspiration', James M. McPherson has aptly written, 'are two of the most important functions of a president in times of

---

Don E. Fehrenbacher, completed and edited by Ward M. McAfee, *The Slaveholding Republic: An Account of the United States Government's Relations to Slavery* (New York: Oxford University Press, 2001), pp. 312–28, 442–7.

crisis'.[4] More than any other person who has ever occupied the presidency, Lincoln had both an ability to define and articulate the meaning of the American national experiment and politically negotiate a deeply divided people toward progressive change. Out of a deep respect for Lincoln's leadership abilities, a distinguished southern historian once speculated that the Union would have lost the war if Jefferson Davis had been president of the United States and Lincoln had led the Confederacy.[5] Of course, such counterfactual musings are ultimately meaningless. Jefferson Davis would never have led the nation in an antislavery direction. Also, Lincoln would never have defended a permanent maintenance of slavery as called for in the Confederate constitution. In the final analysis, neither man can be divorced from the distinct ideological position that each represented.

In recent decades, historians have argued that less adulation should be given to Lincoln's leadership abilities and more to the thousands of anonymous slaves, who by escaping southern captivity during the war, eventually forced Lincoln to support a formal emancipation policy. 'Slaves set others in motion. Slaves were the prime movers in the emancipation drama', Ira Berlin has written. 'It does no disservice to Lincoln – or to anyone else – to say that his claim to greatness rests upon his willingness to act when the moment was right'.[6] A close review of the movement of Lincoln toward an emancipation policy reveals that the antislavery president was often passive, tardy, and at times discouraging of moving in this direction on his own accord. That which pressed him to act ultimately was indeed a de facto emancipation being initiated by the slaves themselves.

It was General Benjamin Butler, not Lincoln, who in May 1861 began the policy of treating runaway slaves as 'contraband' of war.[7] In this action, involving both risk-taking African Americans and a politically entrepreneurial general, the president remained essentially passive.[8] Likewise, the important role played by slaves in building Confederate military fortifications pushed Congress to take a first step beyond the tight focus of the Crittenden-Johnson Resolutions. The result became the Confiscation Act of August 6, 1861, which Republicans supported overwhelmingly and Democrats opposed. The bill, which Lincoln signed reluctantly, emancipated any slaves serving the needs of the Confederate military.[9]

Fear of alienating loyal border-state slaveholders explained Lincoln's cautious attitude, as he believed that the secession of Kentucky might lose the war for the North. Indeed, the president seemed to take the initiative in matters concerning slavery only to protect the institution in the border states, such as when he countermanded General Frémont's military emancipation in Missouri.[10] Lincoln also expressed concern when Republicans began to renounce the Crittenden-Johnson Resolutions, for fear that more radical war aims might lose essential border-state support.[11] At one point, for the same reason, he also chastised his secretary of war for endorsing the idea of arming runaway slaves.[12]

In April 1862, when Congress emancipated slaves in the District of Columbia, the most that Lincoln said in support was that it met his criteria of "expediency". He also praised the bill for including both provisions for compensating owners and colonizing the freedmen.[13] Three weeks earlier, he had written Horace Greeley that he was 'a little uneasy' about liberating the District's slaves.[14] Meanwhile, Lincoln continued countermanding generals who issued unauthorized emancipation policies and pleaded with border-state slaveholders to accept a compensated emancipation plan.[15] While modern Lincoln critics have argued that justice would have been 'better served by compensating slaves for their long years in bondage', some of these scholars grudgingly acknowledge that his persistence with the compensation idea subtly helped advance the concept of a governmentally administered emancipation.[16]

In the summer of 1862, the political momentum for emancipation began to outstrip Lincoln's political management of the issue. In June, Congress abolished slavery in all U.S. territories without any provision for either compensation or colonization.[17] In July, Congress enacted a Second Confiscation Act, emancipating the slaves of all rebels. Lincoln accepted this only after he had exacted concessions from Congress to provide funds to finance a voluntary colonization of the freedmen involved. He also let it be known that he did not like Congress contradicting his earlier emphasis that the Constitution did not allow congressional interference with slavery within the states.[18]

This step-by-step history of Lincoln's behavior during his first year in office shows him seemingly being led by events. But, from another perspective, it also shows him keeping diverse elements working together as the circumstances emphasized by Professor Berlin made increasing headway. Lincoln negotiated with abolitionist generals who thought that he was going too slowly and with proslavery generals who threatened to resign if abolition ever became an official war aim. Some states were eager to destroy slavery, whereas others pursued a bitter-end policy to preserve slavery. Most importantly, Lincoln sought to keep both abolitionist and proslavery voters backing the war effort. But in the summer of 1862, the president concluded that to maximize his effectiveness in leading this chaotic mix of conflicting interests he had to move closer to the abolitionist position. Two years later, he explained this shift to a Kentucky newspaper editor. He recalled that during his first year, he had kept Kentucky uppermost on his mind. Then, as the pace of events began to indicate that some form of emancipation was coming, he vainly tried to persuade border-state slaveholders to adjust to the emerging reality with the idea of compensated emancipation. Eventually, because of their rejection of this generous solution, he was forced to shift his strategy and move out in front of emancipation's advancing columns.[19]

Congress's Second Confiscation Act was inadequate as a practical mechanism for a general emancipation, as individual legal determinations of whether or not owners were loyal would have to occur in each instance of *de jure* liberation.[20] In any case, the act's real significance was in forcing Lincoln's decision to lead the political emancipation struggle. On July 22, he presented his cabinet members with a draft of a presidential emancipation proclamation. He also discussed with them the enlisting of African Americans in the army. Postmaster General Montgomery Blair predicted a harsh political backlash, which Lincoln was willing to absorb. The president was influenced more by Secretary of State Seward, who warned that both at home and abroad an emancipation proclamation at that moment would probably be interpreted as an act of desperation. Given a string of Union military defeats resulting from General George B. McClellan's ineffectual campaign in Virginia, Great Britain and France might even intervene to stop the mass butchery in America. Fearing that Seward was right, Lincoln decided to keep his new policy under wraps until a victory in the field occurred. Then, he determined, would be the proper moment to act.[21] As ever, the art of political timing dictated Lincoln's course.

While waiting, Lincoln put on his best poker face. No good could come from rumors of a dramatic shift in policy before the proper moment of public announcement. On August 4, he told a group of Indiana visitors that nothing had changed. They asked him to reconsider his opposition to enlisting African Americans in the army, and he dutifully repeated his old saw about how changing that policy might result in the loss of Kentucky.[22] Not only did Lincoln make public statements as conservative as any that he had given; while waiting for a significant military victory he also portrayed himself as more conservative than ever before. On August 14, he met with a faction of African Americans about a federal colonization of their race outside of the United States. He told them that he had determined that colonization in Liberia was impractical, given the costs of transporting America's black population back to Africa, and deemed a mass migration to Central America more feasible.[23] Reports of this meeting drove abolitionists into a collective rage.[24] Perhaps this effect was intended by Lincoln. In the weeks preceding issuance of his emancipation policy, Lincoln deliberately widened the distance between himself and the humanitarian reformers who had long fought for black liberation. Abraham Lincoln was preparing the political ground.

There is a slim possibility that Lincoln was informed in advance that Horace Greeley of the *New York Tribune* was going to blast his policy in his editorial columns.[25] In any case, when the blow came, in two blistering editorials on August 19 and 22, Lincoln took full advantage of the situation. He replied to Greeley in language that modern Lincoln critics are fond of quoting out of context: 'My paramount object in this struggle is to save the Union, and is not either to save or destroy slavery. If I could save the Union without freeing any slave, I would do it . . . . . What I do about slavery and the colored race, I do because I believe it helps to save this Union'.[26] With that, conservatives were assured that Lincoln would never adopt any war aim other than saving the Union. Cleverly concealing his future emancipation policy within a package of unalloyed nationalism, he sought to guarantee its ultimate acceptance by a white racist nation.

What can be made of Lincoln's apparent fixation with the idea of colonization? It was an idea that attracted more than just Lincoln. Harriet Beecher Stowe's *Uncle Tom's Cabin* (1852), a novel that worked to convert the North to antislavery, closed with a white racist fantasy that America's blacks would eventually return to their 'homeland' in Africa.[27] The colonization idea certainly revealed a blind spot in the vision of both white America in general and Abraham Lincoln in particular. Yet, given Lincoln's analytical mind, it is hard to believe that he ever thought that such an idea could ever be carried out, given the overwhelming logistical problems involved even in settling former slaves in the nearby Caribbean area. He knew that African Americans overwhelmingly had no desire to leave their true homeland, the place of their birth and collective heritage. Likewise, as he never proposed anything other than voluntary colonization, one can wonder why he expended so much public energy on the subject. The obvious answer lies in remembering that this man was a consummate politician. He knew what corollaries were necessary to prepare his white countrymen to tolerate a policy of emancipation.[28]

The tone of his reply to Greeley also made excellent political propaganda. Certainly, if 'Honest Abe' does not deserve the appellation 'The Great Emancipator', he should be appreciated as a most skillful dissimulator. Charles Sumner, the abolitionist senator from Massachusetts, practiced a far more open, honest, and transparent form of politics. Throughout the Civil War, he regularly butted heads with the president over the latter's apparent insensitivity and slowness of movement. Yet in 1868, when later reflecting upon the political style that regularly bears the best results, Sumner wrote: 'Every man must have certain theories, principles by which governments should be conducted. But where we undertake to apply them to practical problems, there are many difficulties to be overcome, many concessions which must be made in order to accomplish the desired result. The old proverb has it "the shortest way across is often the longest way round," and nowhere is this truer than in legislation. It is not every Gordian knot that can be cut: some must be patiently untied'.[29] Interestingly, while Lincoln lived, Sumner regularly chastised him for not simply cutting Gordian knots.

In Lincoln's annual address for 1862, made several months after finally revealing his emancipation policy but still on the eve of actually initiating it, the president again returned to the idea of colonization. In his remarks, again one can see him placating white racism, which he knew would show itself more viciously once the walls of slavery were broken. Then, abruptly, he turned from the colonization idea to urge white America to greet black emancipation with as much grace as it could muster. 'In times like the present', he reported, 'men should utter nothing for which they would not willingly be responsible through time and in eternity'. His following commentary revealed that he did not believe that a mass black migration out of the country would ever really occur. Turning toward advocating a more practical racial accommodation at home, he never mentioned colonization publicly again.[30]

Searching for a 'prime mover' in the historical drama of emancipation is ultimately a futile enterprise. The prime mover certainly was not Lincoln. But was it the runaway slaves collectively, as Professor Berlin has suggested? Historian Mark Voss-Hubbard has challenged that position by emphasizing that generations of abolitionists 'furnished the conceptual legacies necessary for justifying emancipation during and after the war'.[31] Does this fact make them the prime movers? In fact, many contributed to general emancipation. Of all the participants, Lincoln regularly played an often distasteful, but nonetheless essential, political role.[32] On September 13, which unknown to him at that time was only a week before his own unveiling of presidential emancipation, Lincoln met with a two-man religious delegation from Chicago. Similar to so many other well-meaning people, they told him that they knew that God wanted immediate emancipation. Frustrated at the long wait for news of a victorious battle, the president shot back that it would help if God revealed himself 'directly' 'on a point so connected with my duty'.[33] The men then tried to persuade him that a presidential emancipation policy would energize the people of the North: 'No one', one of them said, 'can tell the power of the right word from the right man to develop the latent fire and enthusiasm of the masses'. All that Lincoln could reply was, 'I know it'.[34] In this one brief conversation were all of the elements of the national vision that Lincoln had framed at the outset of his presidency – a people inspired by God to lift burdens from the shoulders of oppressed humanity.

Four days later, near Sharpsburg, Maryland, along a creek called Antietam, God's 'terrible swift sword' created the war's bloodiest day. Decimated, Lee's army retreated back into Virginia. McClellan's Army of the Potomac had also been wounded, but seeing the hand of Divine Providence at work, Lincoln politically proclaimed the victory for which he had been waiting for two months. Five days after the battle, he issued the Preliminary Emancipation Proclamation.[35] In the eyes of some, it did not constitute the inspiring declaration of freedom for which they had hoped.[36] Indeed, Lincoln the politician deliberately crafted the statement to be as boring as possible. There would be time enough later for thrilling words, after his new policy was securely established. Frederick Douglass commented at that historic moment that the president's political style had at least one virtue: 'Abraham Lincoln . . . , in his own peculiar, cautious, forebearing and hesitating way, slow, but we hope sure, has, while the loyal heart was near breaking with despair, proclaimed [emancipation] . . . . The careful, and we think, the slothful deliberation which he has observed in reaching this obvious policy, is a guarantee against retraction'.[37] Lincoln had taken the old proverb's 'longest way round'.

Accounts of Lincoln's political vacillation on the issue of emancipation often leaves a false impression. James M. McPherson has played a leading role in trying to set the record straight. He rightly claims that for all of the president's temporary and tactical stalling on the matter, Lincoln resolutely and skillfully navigated by a 'lodestar that never moved'. McPherson emphasizes that before the war, Lincoln was easily characterized as a 'one-issue man' tightly focused on restricting the spread of slavery. At the outset of his presidency, Lincoln remained steadily on course, defining a national vision, which on an abstract level included putting slavery on the course of ultimate extinction. Importantly, in 1861 he refused to compromise either on the expansion of slavery or on holding Fort Sumter, when others in his party wavered. In the final analysis, Lincoln preferred war to compromising the slavery issue. McPherson reminds us that 'without the war, the door to freedom would have remained closed for an indeterminate length of time'.[38] Steadily, over the course of his four years in office, Lincoln fulfilled his vision, transforming noble, abstract principles into an emancipation policy that eventually took root. Working within a context of conflicting passions on fundamental questions, Lincoln needed all of the patience and skill inherent within him to bring about ultimate success.

Ironically, McPherson's portrayal of Lincoln as an active, purposeful leader appears to be undermined by Lincoln's own words. In a letter to Albert G. Hodges of Kentucky, written in 1864, Lincoln stated: 'I aver that, to this day, I have done no official act in mere deference to my abstract judgment and feeding on slavery . . . . I claim not to have controlled events, but confess plainly that events have controlled me'.[39] Yet when one places this frequently quoted comment in the context of the complete letter, the impression of an essentially passive leader is dispelled. Lincoln concluded the letter with remarks that suggested that God, not he, was in control and that he as president was operating as the Almighty's principal negotiator in the American political arena: 'Now, at the end of three years struggle the nation's condition is not what either party, or any man devised or expected. God alone can claim it. Whither it is tending seems plain. If God now wills the removal of a great wrong, and wills also that we of the North as well as you of the South, shall pay fairly for our complicity in that wrong, impartial history will find therein new cause to attest and revere the justice and goodness of God'.[40]

Lincoln was not a conventional Christian believer.[41] He belonged to no church. At times, he was regarded by some as a skeptic. Indeed, his unsentimental habit of plumbing issues to bedrock depths did not encourage any simplistic acceptance of biblical teachings. Yet both the personal tragedies of his household and the collective festering wound of civil war, which he knew his own decisions had helped bring about, drove him to discover a mysterious God directing not only bloody events on numerous American battlefields but his own will as well. As such, Lincoln's admission to Hodges of not being in control was essentially a religious confession. The deepening personal conviction that it represented proved to be 'the only adequate counterweight for a burden of responsibility too heavy to carry alone'.[42]

The America of Lincoln's day was more attuned to the notion of God controlling the nation's destiny than is so today.[43] The philosophies of history that most attracted thinkers throughout all of western civilization at that time agreed that history followed an inevitable progressive course. Many of them held that history was directed by a Divine purpose. In accepting these views, Lincoln was simply accepting the leading philosophical assumptions of his age. Similar to portrayals of Providence appearing in the philosophies of Kant and Hegel, Lincoln's God was not a traditional Christian deity paying scant attention to a material pursuit of happiness. Bearing a close resemblance to the deity of ancient Hebrew belief, Lincoln's image of God was very much focused upon this world. As it took shape during his presidency, Lincoln's belief, while modern in some ways, was not the rather impersonal godhead that was typical of Enlightenment thinkers. Rather, it was a most personal God of Wrath. In his Second Inaugural Address, Lincoln elaborated upon this theme, which had appeared earlier in the Hodges letter:

> The Almighty has His own purposes . . . . He now wills to remove [slavery], and . . . . He gives to both North and South, this terrible war, as the woe due to those by whom the offense came . . . . Fondly do we hope – fervently do we pray – that this mightly scourge of war may speedily pass away. Yet, if God wills that it continue, until all the wealth piled by the bond-man's two hundred and fifty years of unrequited toil shall be sunk, and until every drop of blood drawn with the lash, shall be paid by another drawn with the sword, as was said three thousand years ago, so still it must be said 'the judgments of the Lord, are true and righteous altogether'.[44]

Lincoln was most proud of this speech and regarded it as possibly his best rhetorical work, outshining even the Gettysburg Address.[45] In the Second Inaugural, he revealed his most deeply held convictions to a national audience in a way that no other president has done throughout all of American history. In this religious belief, Lincoln had found strength to persevere, and at the time of his Second Inaugural when it was apparent that the Union cause would eventually be won, he publicly acknowledged its tenet that the final outcome had been foreordained all along. It must be emphasized that this view had not bred within Lincoln any passivity or Hamlet-like indecisiveness; rather, just the opposite. The Marxist historical philosopher

Georgi Plekhanov has written that a belief in the inevitability of ultimate historical results, instead of encouraging noncommitment in the face of events presumably beyond human control, steels the will and encourages historical actors to 'display the most indomitable energy . . . [and] perform the most astonishing feats'. This, wrote Plekhanov, was the shared psychology of Muhammad and Oliver Cromwell, as well as Martin Luther, when he proclaimed, 'Here I stand, I can do no other'.[46] Lincoln exhibited a similar resolve throughout the Civil War.

While Lincoln often described God's purposes as mysterious, he appears to have had little doubt that he as president discerned the mind and will of the Almighty. In his 1863 Proclamation of Thanksgiving, which officially inaugurated the national holiday, Lincoln interpreted the war as 'the most high God . . . dealing with us in anger for our sins'. While slavery was nowhere specifically mentioned in the proclamation, there can be little doubt how Lincoln himself regarded what he termed 'our national perverseness and disobedience'.[47] Years before, he had initially gained fame preaching to political rallies that the nation's founders had intended to put slavery on the course of ultimate extinction. In the midst of the Civil War, he emphasized that God as well intended that result. In a letter to Eliza P. Gurney, written immediately after his darkest days of doubt during the entire war, Lincoln emphasized that God intended 'some great good to follow this mighty convulsion, which no mortal could make, and no mortal could stay'.[48] Likewise, in his Second Inaugural, he revealed his own belief that God intended to keep the nation at war until emancipation was a guaranteed result, something that was not completed even at that late date.[49] Days later, in writing to Thurlow Weed, Lincoln commented: 'Men are not flattered by being shown that there has been a difference of purpose between the Almighty and them. To deny it, however, in this case, is to deny that there is a God governing the world'.[50]

Lincoln reportedly once said that his mind was like a piece of steel, 'very hard to scratch anything on it and almost impossible after you get it there to rub it out'.[51] Once that he determined that he knew the truth about anything, he typically repeated it over and over again in speeches and letters until it achieved its highest statement in some piece of polished rhetoric. This habit of mind bred within him an ultimate certainty that God had forced the nation to go through an unavoidable bloodbath for the sole purpose of redeeming the Union from its generations-long experiment as a slaveholding republic. For Lincoln, American history up to that point had mocked the nation's Providential role as a beacon for liberty and material progress available to all. While he often played the role of a humble public servant, who never let his private antislavery views affect public policy, he occasionally revealed that the truth was otherwise. In his own mind, he was God's holy instrument carrying out a Divine mandate of liberty and justice for all. On March 4, 1865, in his Second Inaugural, he shared this view with his countrymen. A month later, this interpretation was exalted by his own martyred death on Good Friday. In crafting the inexorable logic of his Second Inaugural, Lincoln ironically played a part in the subsequent development of his own mythological persona that almost immediately proved irresistible.[52] Lincoln's transfiguration into an American statesman of Christ-like proportions was also encouraged by a whole genre of contemporary popular literature, epitomized in Julia Ward Howe's widely popular poem, 'The Battle Hymn of the Republic'.[53]

It is not clear exactly when Lincoln determined that the war would continue until slavery was completely destroyed. Immediately before the war, he had done no more than hold firm against any compromise that might allow its extension into the territories. During the first year of the war, Lincoln apparently had hoped that the conflict might end without the social revolution that immediate emancipation was likely to bring in its wake. Even following the Battle of Antietam, at the time of issuing the Preliminary Emancipation Proclamation, Lincoln appreciated the tentativeness of his new policy. Exercising untested presidential war powers,[54] Lincoln threatened states and districts in active rebellion that unless they ceased all resistance before the beginning of the new year, slaves residing therein would be regarded by the national authority as free. In the preliminary proclamation, Lincoln also promised to begin the constitutional amending processes to end slavery throughout the nation at large, a reform that he eventually revealed two and a half months later in his Annual Message.[55] The first and the last of three constitutional amendments that he then proposed called for a gradual emancipation that would compensate former owners and colonize liberated slaves outside the nation. These indications of presidential purpose apparently were primarily intended only to demonstrate that Lincoln was not going to employ merely a temporary wartime policy that could be reversed once the war was over. Indeed, the second proposed amendment addressed this issue directly. 'All slaves who shall have enjoyed actual freedom by the chances of war', the proposal read, 'shall be forever free'.[56]

On January 1, 1863, Lincoln delivered the real Emancipation Proclamation, declaring free 'all persons held as slaves' within the Confederacy. The military was ordered to 'recognize and maintain the freedom of said persons' as the Confederacy gradually fell before the progress of Union arms.[57] In this decree, the death knell of the slaveholding republic was broadcast throughout the land. 'Thus ended one of the strangest paradoxes in human history', Dwight L. Dumond noted one hundred years later at a ceremony commemorating the event. 'The President of the United States pronounced the death sentence upon slavery in a country which had been dedicated to freedom eighty-seven years before'.[58]

The proclamation also called for the active recruitment of African Americans into the armed services.[59] The employment of black soldiers had actually been inaugurated by Congress as early as July 17, 1862, but

Lincoln had delayed implementation. In the late summer and fall of 1862, the president made a first step by authorizing the organization of several black regiments in South Carolina's captured sea islands.[60] Following the Emancipation Proclamation, black recruitment for military service was vastly expanded, with much publicity given to the organization of Robert Gould Shaw's Fifty-fourth Massachusetts Volunteers.[61] In the months that followed, Lincoln placed a great emphasis upon African American recruitment, which he viewed as significant not only for its potential to fill the army's insatiable manpower needs but also as a means whereby his emancipation policy could gain a greater acceptance among whites.[62] The president wrote eloquently of 'black men . . . with clenched teeth, and steady eye, and well poised bayonet' fighting to preserve a Union dedicated to the principle that all men are created equal.[63] Nonetheless, Lincoln condoned a policy of racial discrimination within the military. Blacks were required to be led by whites. African American troops were not paid at the same rates as white soldiers. Lincoln the politician knew that real equality had to come piecemeal if at all. He was fond of using the comparison of an egg not being a chicken but on the way to becoming one. He used this same metaphor differently in describing his freeing of some blacks, while leaving others within loyal districts temporarily enslaved. 'Broken eggs cannot be mended', he wrote concerning his emancipation policy.[64] He knew that some Democrats viewed even his incomplete emancipation program as grounds for impeachment.[65] Accordingly, he moved cautiously to bring northern Democrats gradually to accept the inevitability of emancipation and its consequences. Some of his contemporaries and many modern observers have found Lincoln's penchant to adopt half measures most frustrating. In this case, he approved and encouraged black enlistment while allowing racial discrimination within the ranks. In Lincoln's mind, he wanted whites to accept black enlistment before pressing for equal treatment. In the words of LaWanda Cox, this was simply 'his way of placing first things first'.[66]

Simultaneous with pursuing an emancipation program, Lincoln began to think about returning captured Confederate states to their normal place in the Union. In 1862, he began trying to convince whites in portions of such areas to begin the process of forming loyal state governments.[67] In the following year, these initial efforts evolved and by the end of the year Lincoln revealed his presidential Reconstruction policy. Utilizing his constitutional pardoning power, he decreed that whenever 10 percent of the white voters in any Confederate state swore to be loyal in the future, they could create a loyal state government. He suggested a specific loyalty oath that included acceptance of his emancipation policy, but tactfully added that he was open to discuss possible alternate oaths.[68] Essentially, he was trying to engage those who had opposed his presidency by force of arms to begin a conversation with him that would lead to their renunciation of the Confederacy. While firmly wedded to his emancipation policy, he nonetheless knew that chickens must be hatched from delicately formed eggs. Balancing one desire to further black freedom with another to wean southern whites from secessionism, he merely suggested to Michael Hahn, the governor of the presidentially reconstructed state of Louisiana, that some blacks be allowed to vote under the new order.[69] Lincoln believed that a gradual local white acceptance of black civil rights, beginning with a small minority operating under his Ten Percent Plan, would be more effective than having both emancipation and black suffrage forced upon a defeated enemy. As long as the war raged, his approach had to appear somewhat reasonable to southern whites, whom he wanted to convince to quit the fight.[70] Accordingly, he pursued a policy designed to maximize what he regarded as latent white unionist sentiment in the South rather than fulfilling African American desires for immediate and full equality.

At the outset, Charles Sumner and other Radicals in Congress accepted Lincoln's Ten Percent Plan, as they liked its apparent prerequisite that emancipation be supported as part of the pledge of future loyalty.[71] But soon they were complaining about General Nathaniel Banks's policy of working with conservative Unionists in Louisiana rather than with local Radicals who were calling for black suffrage as part of any meaningful Reconstruction.[72] Ultimately, Lincoln clarified his conservative Louisiana policy with language that had come to characterize his approach to virtually all problems: 'Concede that the new government of Louisiana is only to what it should be as the egg is to the fowl, we shall sooner have the fowl by hatching the egg than by smashing it'.[73]

Republicans in Congress feared that if opportunities for reform were not grasped boldly, they might be lost forever. Land reform was one of their major concerns, which they knew that a conservative regime in Louisiana would never allow. Banks and Lincoln, at least for the time being, seemed willing to settle for African American labor contracts, which left freedmen landless and stuck in a 'halfway house between slavery and freedom'.[74] In early July 1864, Congress enacted the Wade-Davis bill, in a bold move to direct Reconstruction policy. The measure did not require black voting but insured that the entire Reconstruction process would be put on hold until 50 percent of a state's white voters pledged their future loyalty. In fact, this was not likely to occur until the war was over and the Confederacy was no more. However, as soon as that condition was met, and as soon as 10 percent of white voters could swear to past as well as future loyalty, then the latter cohort would be allowed to create a loyal state government, one more likely to be dominated by persons willing to enact radical reforms than the president's model, which was actively welcoming the inclusion of former rebels.[75] Lincoln pocket vetoed the measure on the grounds that he had had no time to study the issue closely and that he was as yet unprepared to commit to a fixed Reconstruction policy.[76] In point of fact, the president never did commit himself to any Reconstruction concept not closely tied to his short-term goal of persuading rebels to quit the fight.

Radicals in Congress temporarily exploded in anger over the president's refusal to accept congressional direction, but soon the politics of the presidential reelection campaign dampened their rage. While Lincoln had radical challengers to his office, none could muster sufficient support to prevent the president's renomination. With the alternatives of Lincoln or the Democratic candidate, Radicals swung into line behind their president, especially as the people at large were expressing dissatisfaction with high casualty rates and few victories to show for the profligate expenditure of Union lives and treasure.

By late August, a dejected Lincoln was convinced that George McClellan, his likely Democratic challenger, would be elected in November.[77] Believing that the Union cause, which included emancipation, was supported by Providence, Lincoln nonetheless was tempted to consider a ploy whereby he would portray himself to wavering voters as willing to abandon emancipation in exchange for a simple restoration of the Union. The plan was this: Lincoln would propose to Jefferson Davis a restoration of the Union without emancipation being a prerequisite, the assumption being that Davis would immediately reject the offer, as it called for an abandonment of southern independence. The idea was proposed as political propaganda to sway Democrats friendly to the war effort to back Lincoln rather than the Democratic candidate, who would be running on a peace platform calling for a negotiated settlement that would likely result in the survival of the Confederacy.[78] In the end, Lincoln rejected the idea, probably because it would have involved the appearance of betraying African Americans on a massive scale, which certainly would have impacted negatively upon both black enlistments and fighting spirit. Putting the plan into operation would also have probably led to a complete break between Lincoln and the Radicals, who were already in a sour mood over the demise of the Wade-Davis bill. Meanwhile, McClellan's backers exulted that Lincoln's political life was almost over and that 'Old Abra'm' was 'gliding over the dam'.[79]

In tight moments before, Lincoln had left important decisions to Providence. Gideon Welles, Lincoln's secretary of the navy, wrote in his diary that following the Battle of Antietam, Lincoln had confessed to the entire cabinet that before the battle he had 'made a vow, a covenant, that if God gave us the victory in the approaching battle, he would consider it an indication of Divine will, and that it was his duty to move forward in the cause of emancipation'. Welles added that in the past the president 'had in this way submitted the disposal of matters when the way was not clear to his mind what he should do'.[80] Apparently, before the Battle of Gettysburg, a little over nine months later, Lincoln again left the war in God's hands, vowing to be emancipation's faithful instrument if a victory was granted.[81] As his letter to Albert G. Hodges amply revealed, Lincoln saw God pushing the war for a Divine purpose of emancipation.[82] Accordingly, Lincoln left the outcome of the presidential election, which all knew would determine the outcome of the war itself, in God's hands. In this moment of ultimate testing, he refused to compromise his emancipation policy for temporary political advantage. Deliverance quickly came in William T. Sherman's capture of Atlanta and in Phil Sheridan's successes in the Shenandoah Valley. With victories in the field, Lincoln's confidence returned, together with an even deeper certainty that he was God's holy instrument to complete a Providential design of African American emancipation, a conviction that was underwritten by a landslide victory at the polls in November.

Sherman's unobstructed march from Atlanta to the sea in late November put the Confederacy on notice that Lee's army was eventually to be crushed in a vice between Sherman's force moving northward from Savannah and Grant's Army of the Potomac holding Lee in place for a final engagement in Virginia. With the advantage of time completely on Lincoln's side, he lobbied House Democrats to join Republicans in completing the congressional role in the ratification of the Thirteenth Amendment, which called for the end of slavery nationwide. On January 31, 1865, with the help of presidential favors and promises of patronage, Lincoln's effort succeeded, and the antislavery amendment was sent on to the states for final approval.[83] Days later, Lincoln and Secretary of State Seward met with Confederate delegates to discuss conditions for peace. Attempting to engage these representatives in a discussion about the possibilities for a Confederate surrender, Lincoln made appearances of being willing to talk about a restoration of the Union without emancipation as a necessary prerequisite. Lincoln biographer David Donald concludes that this only revealed Lincoln playing a politics of misinformation with the enemy in preliminary discussions and not indicating any presidential change of policy. Even this ploy, however, did not succeed in getting these high-taking officials to consider the possibility of renouncing southern independence.[84]

After nearly four years of war, Lincoln was desperate to break the Confederate will to resist by almost any means necessary. A week after his failed negotiations with Confederate leaders, Lincoln proposed to his cabinet that possibly an offer of compensated emancipation might end the southern resolve to continue the fighting.[85] He also schemed to manipulate the Confederate Virginia legislature to surrender independently, but that too came to naught.[86] On the eve of Lee's surrender at Appomattox, Lincoln was concerned lest the war conclude formally only to devolve rapidly into an ugly unending guerrilla struggle combining rebel obstinacy with simple banditry.[87] Accordingly, in the weeks leading to his Second Inaugural Address, which would define the nation as in the grasp of Divine purposes, Lincoln talked of the heightened need for 'Christian Charity'.[88] In this time of war's end, the clearest implication that Lincoln made about the shape of his future Reconstruction policy was that his administration would not engage in a peace of vengeance and retribution.[89]

During the last months of his life, Abraham Lincoln seemed overeager to win over his defeated foe by means of generous treatment. Nevertheless, he never forgot that justice for the freedmen was equally a necessary part of charity for all. His overtures to the Confederates had never seriously considered abandoning African Americans on an altar of sectional reunification. At the time of his assassination on April 14, 1865, the requisite number of states had not yet ratified the Thirteenth Amendment, an event that would not occur until eight months later. In early 1865, emancipation as part of the Constitution was a probability but not yet a certainty. Given this ambiguity, Lincoln emphasized that he personally would never abandon the cause of emancipation. He conceded that the Thirteenth Amendment might yet be defeated. He acknowledged that even his wartime emancipation policy might someday be overturned. But he stated in unambiguous language that he personally would never collaborate with any such ignominious conclusion to the Civil War and would resign his office if necessary: 'If the people should, by whatever mode or means, make it an Executive duty to re-enslave such persons', he told the nation in his last Annual Message of December 1864, 'another, and not I, must be their instrument to perform it'.[90]

While Lincoln often waxed eloquently about the sovereign will of the majority and a government of, by, and for the people, ultimately, in his own mind, he was not the people's agent. Instead, he was a determined but presumably humble instrument of a Divine will driving the United States to fulfill its original promise of being a harbinger of universal human rights. Lincoln's portrait painter, who observed the president frequently in 1864, later wrote of a visiting clergyman who told Lincoln that he hoped that God was on the Union side. Lincoln reportedly replied: 'I know that the Lord is *always* on the side of *right*. But', he added, 'it is my constant anxiety and prayer that I and this *nation* should be on the Lord's *side*'.[91] This is what Lincoln possibly intended when he spontaneously injected into his delivery of the Gettysburg Address that the nation's 'new birth of freedom' would necessarily have to be 'under God'.[92] Conformity to Divine purposes was Lincoln's lodestar. This understanding provided greater power to his own purposes than would have been possible without it, revealing a style of leadership that inspired millions and eventually led to his canonization in a national civil religion tightly connected to an emancipation struggle that continues to this day.[93]

NOTES

1. Lerone Bennett, Jr., 'Lincoln, a White Supremacist', in *The Leadership of Abraham Lincoln*, ed. Don E. Fehrenbacher (New York, 1970), 129–40; Nathan Irvin Huggins, *Slave and Citizen: The Life of Frederick Douglass* (Boston, 1980),

77–86. For a discussion of this tendency within modern popular portrayals of Lincoln, see Stephen B. Oates, *Abraham Lincoln: The Man Behind the Myths* (New York, 1984), 25–30.

2. For example, see *CWAL*, IV:506–7, 517–18, 531–32; ibid., V:29–31, 144–6, 169, 192, 222–3, 317–19, 324.

3. William Lloyd Garrison to a 'friend', October 11, 1860, in William E. Cain, ed., *William Lloyd Garrison and the Fight Against Slavery: Selections from The Liberator* (Boston, 1995), 161.

4. James M. McPherson, *Abraham Lincoln and the Second American Revolution* (New York, 1991), 112.

5. David M. Potter, 'If the Union and the Confederacy Had Exchanged Presidents', in *The Leadership of Abraham Lincoln*, ed. Fehrenbacher, 63; Waldo W. Braden, *Abraham Lincoln, Public Speaker* (Baton Rouge, 1988).

6. Ira Berlin, 'The Slaves Were The Primary Force Behind Their Emancipation' in *The Civil War: Opposing Viewpoints*, ed. William Dudley (San Diego, 1995), 280, 283. Also see Leon F. Litwack, *Been In The Storm So Long: The Aftermath of Slavery* (New York, 1980), 118, 177, 180, 181, 182, 186, 187.

7. Benjamin Butler to Simon Cameron, July 30, 1861, in Frank Moore, ed., *The Rebellion Record: A Diary of American Events, With Documents . . .*, 11 vols (New York, 1861–68), II, 437–8; Benjamin F. Butler to Winfield Scott, May 24, 1861, in *Private and Official Correspondence of Gen. Benjamin F. Butler, During the Period of the Civil War*, ed. Jessie Ames Marshall, 5 vols (Norwood, Mass., 1917), I, 102–8. John B. Cary to Benjamin F. Butler, March 9, 1891, ibid.

8. David H. Donald, *Lincoln* (New York, 1995), 343.

9. *CG*, 37 Cong., 1 sess., 219, 434; ed., Moore, *Rebellion Record*, II, 475–6; *SAL*, XII:319; Donald, *Lincoln*, 314.

10. Abraham Lincoln to John C. Frémont, September 2 and 11, 1861; *Lincoln, Speeches and Writings*, Fehrenbacher, comp. 266–70; Abraham Lincoln to David Hunter, September 9, 1861, ibid., Abraham Lincoln to Orville H. Browning, September 22, 1861, ibid.

11. *CWAL*, V, 49.

12. Phillip Shaw Paludan, *The Presidency of Abraham Lincoln* (Lawrence, Ks., 1994), 103.

13. *CWAL*, V, 192; *CG*, 37 Cong., 2 sess., 347–8; Edward McPherson, *The Political History of the United States of America During the Great Rebellion . . .* (Washington, D.C., 1882), 211–12; Michael J. Kurtz, 'Emancipation in the Federal City', *CWH* 24 (1978), 250–67.

14. *CWAL*, V, 169.

15. Ibid., 22–3, 317–19.

16. Ira Berlin et al., *Slaves No More: Three Essays on Emancipation and the Civil War* (Cambridge, 1992), 29–30.

17. *SAL*, XII, 432; E. McPherson, *Political History of the Rebellion*, 254–5.

18. E. McPherson, *Political History of the Rebellion*, 197–8; Don E. Fehrenbacher and Virginia Fehrenbacher, eds., *Recollected Words of Abraham Lincoln* (Stanford, Calif., 1996), 64–5.

19. Abraham Lincoln to Albert G. Hodges, April 4, 1864, *Lincoln, Speeches and Writings*. Fehrenbacher, comp., 585–6.

20. *SAL*, XII, 589–92; Harold M. Hyman and William M. Wiecek, *Equal Justice Under Law: Constitutional Development, 1835–1875* (New York, 1982), 252.

21. Entry for July 22, 1862, in ed., David Donald *Inside Lincoln's Cabinet, The Civil War Diaries of Salmon P. Chase* (New York, 1954), 97–100; John T. Morse, Jr., introduction to *Diary of Gideon Welles*, 3 vols (Boston, 1911), I, 70–71; William Ernest Smith, *The Francis Preston Blair Family in Politics*, 2 vols (New York, 1933), II, 203.

22. *New York Tribune*, August 5, 1862.

23. *CWAL*, V, 370–5; George B. Vashon to Abraham Lincoln, September 1862, C. Peter Ripley et al., eds. *The Black Abolitionist Papers*, 5 vols (Chapel Hill, 1985–92) V, 152–5.

24. *Boston Liberator*, August 22, 1862. William Lloyd Garrison's editorial described Lincoln's comments to the African American delegation as 'puerile, absurd, illogical, impertinent, untimely'. Also see Frederick Douglass to Gerrit Smith, September 8, 1862, *The Life and Writings of Frederick Douglass*, ed. Philip S. Foner, 4 vols (New York, 1950–55), III, 260–70. 'The Spirit of Colonization', September 1862, ibid. 'The President and His Speeches', September 1862 ibid. Tellingly, Douglass commented at this time: 'The President of the United States seems to possess *an ever increasing passion* for making himself appear silly and ridiculous, if nothing worse'. Ibid., 266.

25. James R. Gilmore, *Personal Recollections of Abraham Lincoln and the Civil War* (Boston, 1898), 81–3; Harlan Hoyt Horner, *Lincoln and Greeley* (n.p., 1953), 246–8, 263. There is reason to doubt the claim made by Gilmore that Lincoln knew of Greeley's plans in advance. See Fehrenbacher and Fehrenbacher, eds., *Recollected Words*, 526 n.

26. Abraham Lincoln to Horace Greeley, August 22, 1862, Fehrenbacher, comp., *Lincoln, Speeches and Writings*, 357–8.

27. Harriet Beecher Stowe, *Uncle Tom's Cabin, or, Life Among the Lowly* (1881; reprint, New York, 1962), 494–7.

28. Don E. Fehrenbacher, 'Only His Stepchildren: Lincoln and the Negro', *CWH* 20 (1974), 306.

29. Charles Sumner to John Wolcott Phelps, April 18, 1868, in Beverly Wilson Palmer, ed., *The Selected Letters of Charles Sumner*, 2 vols (Boston, 1990), II, 424.

30. *CWAL*, V, 534–6; Fehrenbacher, 'Only His Stepchildren', 308.

31. Mark Voss-Hubbard, 'The Political Culture of Emancipation: Morality, Politics, and the State in Garrisonian Abolitionism, 1854–1863', *Journal of American Studies* 29 (1995), 160.

32. Jeffrey Rogers Hummel, *Emancipating Slaves, Enslaving Free Men: A History of the American Civil War* (Peru, Ill., 1996), 352–3, 355, claims that Lincoln's role in destroying slavery was not essential. He writes that slavery was inevitably doomed, even had Lincoln 'permitted the small Gulf Coast Confederacy to depart in peace'. Hummel imagines that slaves escaping to what was left of the United States would have eventually undermined the entire slave system. This thesis harmonizes with Berlin's self-emancipation theme, but does this counterfactual musing have merit? We do know [to borrow Hummel's words] that 'State violence directed from the top down' actually destroyed slavery in the United States. We also know that despite this bloody, organized, national sacrifice, an ideology of white supremacy and enslavement of 'inferior' peoples almost succeeded on a global scale under the leadership of Adolf Hitler eight decades later. Reason suggests that slavery's chances to survive and flourish into the twentieth century and beyond could only have been enhanced if Lincoln had not resisted southern secession with military force. For counterfactional imaginings diametrically opposed to those of Hummel, see Robert W. Fogel, *Without Consent or Contract: The Rise and Fall of American Slavery* (New York, 1989), 411–17.

33. 'Reply to Chicago Emancipation Memorial, Washington, D.C.'., Fehrenbacher, comp., *Lincoln, Speeches and Writings*, 361, 740 n.

34. Ibid., 366–7.

35. Moore, ed., *Rebellion Record*, V, 479–80.

36. William Lloyd Garrison to Fanny Garrison, September 25, 1862, Walter M. Merrill, et al., eds., *The Letters of William Lloyd Garrison*, 6 vols. (Cambridge, Mass., 1997–81), V, 114–15. One modern version of the standard complaint against the

Emancipation Proclamation can be found in Richard Hofstadter, *American Political Tradition* (1948; reprint, New York, 1960), 132.

37. Frederick Douglass, 'Emancipation Proclaimed', September 1862, in Foner, ed., *Life and Writings of Douglass*, III, 273–7.

38. J. McPherson, *Lincoln and the Second American Revolution*, 114, 125; James M. McPherson, 'Lincoln Freed the Slaves' in *The Civil War: Opposing Viewpoints*, ed. William Dudley (San Diego, Calif., 1995), 267, 269–70.

39. Abraham Lincoln to Albert G. Hodges, April 4, 1864, in *Lincoln, Speeches and Writings*, Fehrenbacher, comp., 585–6.

40. Ibid., 186.

41. Fehrenbacher and Fehrenbacher, eds., *Recollected Words*, 110–11, 191, 245, 372–4, 436–7.

42. Don E. Fehrenbacher, 'The Weight of Responsibility', in his *Lincoln in Text and Context* (Stanford, Calif., 1987), 161; also see Richard N. Current, 'The Instrument of God', *The Lincoln Nobody Knows* (New York, 1958), 51–75; Ronald C. White, Jr., 'Lincoln's Sermon on the Mount: The Second Inaugural', in *Religion and the American Civil War*, ed. Randall M. Miller et al. (New York, 1998), 208–25.

43. Charles Reagan Wilson, 'Religion and the American Civil War in Comparative Perspective', in *Religion and the Civil War*, ed. Miller et al., 396, 402.

44. 'Second Inaugural Address', March 4, 1865, Fehrenbacher, comp., *Lincoln, Speeches and Writings*, 687.

45. Abraham Lincoln to Thurlow Weed, March 15, 1865, Ibid., 689; McPherson, *Abraham Lincoln and the Second American Revolution*, 111–12.

46. George Plekhanov, *The Role of the Individual in History* (New York, 1940), 12.

47. 'Proclamation of Thanksgiving, By the President of the United States', Fehrenbacher, comp., *Lincoln, Speeches and Writings*, 520–1.

48. Abraham Lincoln to Eliza P. Gurney, September 4, 1864, ibid., 627.

49. 'Second Inaugural Address', ibid., 686–7.

50. Abraham Lincoln to Thurlow Weed, March 15, 1865, ibid., 689.

51. Fehrenbacher and Fehrenbacher, eds., *Recollected Words*, 413.

52. For examples of later popular literature portraying Lincoln in an almost mythological way, see John Wesley Hill, *Abraham Lincoln: Man of God* (New York, 1920); Ralph G. Lindstrom, *Lincoln Finds God* (New York, 1958).

53. Elizabeth Fox-Genovese, 'Days of Judgment, Days of Wrath: The Civil War and the Religious Imagination of Women Writers', Miller et al., eds., *Religion and the Civil War*, 236.

54. Joel Parker, 'Constitutional Law', *North American Review* 94 (1862), 449–54; William Lloyd Garrison, *The Abolition of Slavery: The Right of the Government Under the War Power* (Boston, 1862), 6–12; Grosvenor Porter Lowrey, *The Commander-In-Chief; A Defense Upon Legal Grounds of The Proclamation of Emancipation* . . . (New York, 1863), 7–34.

55. CWAL, V, 433–4.

56. Ibid., 530.

57. Ibid., VI, 28–30.

58. Dwight Lowell Dumond, *The Emancipation Proclamation: Freedom in the Fullness of Time* (Ann Arbor, 1963), 1.

59. CWAL, VI, 28–30.

60. James M. McPherson, *The Struggle for Equality: Abolitionists and the Negro in the Civil War and Reconstruction* (Princeton, N.J., 1964), 196–8.

61. Ibid., 202–3; CG, 37 Cong., 3 sess., App., 72–86, 103–6.

62. Herman Belz, *Emancipation and Equal Rights: Politics and Constitutionalism in the Civil War Era* (New York, 1967), 53; LaWanda Cox, *Lincoln and Black Freedom: A Study in Presidential Leadership* (Columbia, S. C., 1981) 23.

63. Abraham Lincoln to James C. Conkling, August 26, 1863, in Fehrenbacher, comp., *Lincoln, Speeches and Writings*, 499.
64. Abraham Lincoln to John A. McClernand, January 8, 1863, ibid., 428.
65. *CG*, 37 Cong., 3 sess., 15, 92.
66. Cox, *Lincoln and Black Freedom*, 35.
67. *CWAL*, V, 303, 445, 462–63, 504–5; *HR*, 37 Cong., 3 sess., No. 22, No. 23., No. 46; *CG*, 37 Cong., 3 sess., 832–3.
68. 'Proclamation of Amnesty and Reconstruction, By the President of the United States of America', December 8, 1863, Fehrenbacher, comp., *Lincoln, Speeches and Writings, 555–58*; Abraham Lincoln to Nathaniel P. Banks, January 31, 1864, ibid., 570–1.
69. Abraham Lincoln to Michael Hahn, March 13, 1864, ibid., 579.
70. Hyman and Wiecek, *Equal Justice Under Law*, 270; Eric Foner, *Reconstruction: America's Unfinished Revolution, 1863–1877* (New York, 1988), 36; William B. Hesseltine, *Lincoln's Plan of Reconstruction* (Tuscaloosa, Ala., 1960), 19–21.
71. Peyton McCrary, 'The Party of Revolution: Republican Ideas About Politics and Social Change, 1862–1867', *CWH* 30 (1984), 341–42.
72. Ibid., 342; Wendell Phillips to Edward Gilbert, May 27, 1864; E. McPherson, *Political History of the Rebellion*, 412.
73. 'Speech on Reconstruction, Washington, D.C'., April 11, 1865, Fehrenbacher, comp., *Lincoln, Speeches and Writings*, 700.
74. McCrary, 'The Party of Revolution', 339. LaWanda Cox emphasizes that Lincoln's intent in Louisiana and elsewhere was that the freedmen ultimately be provided with real opportunities to become landowners. In her estimation, Andrew Johnson almost single-handedly prevented the implementation of a modest land reform program after the war. See Cox, *Lincoln and Black Freedom*, 178–9, 190 n–191 n. For a racist argument against land reform that helped shape the political landscape of the time, see Samuel F. B. Morse et al., *Emancipation and Its Results* (New York, 1863), 15, 18–19, 23–4, 30–2.
75. E. McPherson, *Political History of the Rebellion*, 317–18; *CG*, 38 Cong., 1 sess., 2107–8, 3518; Herman Belz, *Reconstructing the Union: Theory and Policy During the Civil War* (Ithaca, N.Y., 1969), 210; Belz, *Emancipation and Equal Rights*, 91–3.
76. 'Proclamation Concerning Reconstruction, By the President of the United States', in Fehrenbacher, comp., *Lincoln, Speeches and Writings*, 605.
77. 'Memorandum on Probable Failure of Re-election', August 23, 1864, ibid., 624.
78. Abraham Lincoln to Charles D. Robinson, August 17, 1864, ibid. Abraham Lincoln to Henry J. Raymond, August 24, 1864, ibid., 620–2, 625, 754 n; Donald, *Lincoln*, 526–9, 553; Paludan, *Presidency of Lincoln*, 284; Cox, *Lincoln and Black Freedom*, 17.
79. 'We're Bound to Beat Old Abe', *Little Mac: Campaign Songster* (New York, 1864), 11.
80. Welles, *Diary*, 1:142–43.
81. William J. Wolf, *The Almost Chosen People: A Study of the Wartime Religion of Abraham Lincoln* (Garden City, N.Y., 1959), 124–6; Fehrenbacher and Fehrenbacher, eds., *Recollected Words*, 387–8.
82. Lincoln to Hodges, April 4, 1864, Fehrenbacher, comp., *Lincoln, Speeches and Writings*, 586.
83. Oates, *Lincoln: Man Behind the Myths*, 116–17.
84. Donald, *Lincoln*, 552, 559–60.
85. Ibid., 560–1.
86. Ibid., 589–90.
87. Abraham Lincoln to Thomas C. Fletcher, February 20, 1865, Fehrenbacher, comp., *Lincoln, Speeches and Writings*, 684.
88. Ibid.

89. 'Second Inaugural Address', in Fehrenbacher, comp., *Lincoln, Speeches and Writings*, 687.
90. 'Annual Message to Congress', December 6, 1864, ibid., 661.
91. Francis B. Carpenter, *Six Months at the White House With Abraham Lincoln: The Story of a Picture* (New York, 1866), 282; emphases are Carpenter's.
92. The qualification 'under God' was not in Lincoln's written text at Gettysburg but the two words were apparently spontaneously added in the act of delivery, as newspaper accounts reported the president as having said them. See *CWAL*, VII, 19, 19 n–20 n, 21 n, 23. Garry Wills in his *Lincoln at Gettysburg: The Words That Remade America* (New York, 1992), 194, speculates that it would have been 'uncharacteristic' of Lincoln to alter the text in the act of delivery 'in front of a huge audience'. Nonetheless, Wills notes that the newspaper accounts placed the words 'under God' awkwardly in the text, which is suggestive of a literal reporting of a spontaneous presidential inclusion. Ibid., 198. In the final text, used for historical publication, the words 'under God' were included in such a way to satisfy critics of presidential syntax. Wills also notes that Lincoln himself later endorsed inclusion of the two words into the speech. Ibid., 202–3, 263.
93. Richard N. Current, 'Lincoln, the Civil War, and the American Mission' in *The Public and the Private Lincoln: Contemporary Perspectives*, ed. Cullom Davis et al. (Carbondale, Ill., 1979), 145–46; Phillip Shaw Paludan, '*A People's Contest': The Union and the Civil War, 1861–1865* (New York, 1988), 372–4; Fehrenbacher, 'The Death of Lincoln', *Lincoln in Text and Context*, 175–7. In our own time, Martin Luther King, Jr., has acquired a similar status in this ongoing national civil religion.

DOCUMENT 1: THE EMANCIPATION PROCLAMATION, 1863

One of the most important documents in United States history, the Emancipation Proclamation was issued by Lincoln in the middle of the Civil War. It altered the moral dimension of that conflict.

By the President of the United States of America:
A PROCLAMATION

Whereas on the 22nd day of September, A.D. 1862, a proclamation was issued by the President of the United States, containing, among other things, the following, to wit:

That on the 1st day of January, A.D. 1863, all persons held as slaves within any State or designated part of a State the people whereof shall then be in rebellion against the United States shall be then, thenceforward, and forever free; and the executive government of the United States, including the military and naval authority thereof, will recognize and maintain the freedom of such persons and will do no act or acts to repress such persons, or any of them, in any efforts they may make for their actual freedom.

That the executive will on the 1st day of January aforesaid, by proclamation, designate the States and parts of States, if any, in which the people thereof, respectively, shall then be in rebellion against the United States; and the fact that any State or the people thereof shall on that day be in good faith represented in the Congress of the United States by members chosen thereto at elections wherein a majority of the qualified voters of such States shall have participated shall, in the absence of strong countervailing testimony, be deemed conclusive evidence that such State and the people thereof are not then in rebellion against the United States.

Now, therefore, I, Abraham Lincoln, President of the United States, by virtue of the power in me vested as Commander-In-Chief of the Army and Navy of the United States in time of actual armed rebellion against the authority and government of the United States, and as a fit and necessary war measure for suppressing said rebellion, do, on this 1st day of January, A.D. 1863, and in accordance with my purpose so to do, publicly proclaimed for the full period of one hundred days from the first day above mentioned, order and designate as the States and parts of States wherein the people thereof, respectively, are this day in rebellion against the United States the following, to wit:

Arkansas, Texas, Louisiana (except the parishes of St. Bernard, Plaquemines, Jefferson, St. John, St. Charles, St. James, Ascension, Assumption, Terrebonne, Lafourche, St. Mary, St. Martin, and Orleans, including the city of New Orleans), Mississippi, Alabama, Florida, Georgia, South

Henry S. Commager (ed.), *Documents of American History* (New York: Appleton-Century-Crofts, 1963), pp. 420–1.

Carolina, North Carolina, and Virginia (except the forty-eight counties designated as West Virginia, and also the counties of Berkeley, Accomac, Northampton, Elizabeth City, York, Princess Anne, and Norfolk, including the cities of Norfolk and Portsmouth), and which excepted parts are for the present left precisely as if this proclamation were not issued.

And by virtue of the power and for the purpose aforesaid, I do order and declare that all persons held as slaves within said designated States and parts of States are, and henceforward shall be, free; and that the Executive Government of the United States, including the military and naval authorities thereof, will recognize and maintain the freedom of said persons.

And I hereby enjoin upon the people so declared to be free to abstain from all violence, unless in necessary self-defense; and I recommend to them that, in all cases when allowed, they labor faithfully for reasonable wages.

And I further declare and make known that such persons of suitable condition will be received into the armed service of the United States to garrison forts, positions, stations, and other places, and to man vessels of all sorts in said service.

And upon this act, sincerely believed to be an act of justice, warranted by the Constitution upon military necessity, I invoke the considerate judgment of mankind and the gracious favor of Almighty God.

DOCUMENT 2: KENTUCKY, UNIONISM AND SLAVERY

Full-scale military enlistment doomed slavery in Kentucky during the Civil War. The slaveholders were indignant. Lincoln placed the state under martial law in July 1864. This letter from the governor of Kentucky underscores the bitterness felt by many citizens in the state as a result of military restrictions.

Governor of Kentucky to the President

Frankfort [Ky.] Sept 3rd 1864

Sir: Kentucky is and ever has been loyal as a State and people. Her people have triumphantly passed through the severest ordeal, and borne without yielding the severest tests ever applied to the loyalty of any people. Yet we are dealt with as though Kentucky was a rebellious and conquered province, instead of being as they are a brave and loyal people. –

Without any occasion for such measures the State has by special Executive edict been declared under Martial law; and this just preceding the elections.

Without rebuke the Military Commandant issued an order directly interfering with the most important election then depending; and in open Conflict with the Constitution and laws of the State, and in dereliction of the most sacred rights of a free and loyal people.

The ordinary and necessary trade of the State is now by Military trade regulations subjected to restrictions, which harrass the citizen without any compensating public good; and which wear more the phase of subjecting the citizens to odious political tests, than looking to the public good. I send herewith a copy of a permit, with the test questions as appended, the original I retain as a specimen and memorial of the military follies and harrassments [sic] to which Kentuckians are subjected.

The citizens of Western Kentucky have for a long while been the subjects of insult, oppression, and plunder by officers who have been placed to defend and protect them.

Having on yesterday stated the conduct of Genl Payne & his accomplices & heretofore Communicated in reference to Cunningham who is now overshadowed by Genl Payne, I will not again state it. –

The Military Authorities throughout the State assume at pleasure to make assessments upon the citizens and enforce the payment of heavy fines without a hearing. And yet the laws of Kentucky are ample and the Courts open for redress of every just grievance, without any such military judgements.

I send herewith a copy of one of those orders assessing a citizen – merely as a specimen of what is of daily occurrence.

Extract from Ira Berlin, Barbara J. Fields, Thavolia Glymph, Joseph P. Reidy, Leslie S. Rowland (eds), *Freedom: A Documentary History of Emancipation, 1861–1867. Series 1. Volume 1: The Destruction of Slavery* (Cambridge: Cambridge University Press, 1985), pp. 604–6.

That these measures with others of kindred nature have been urged by the Counsels of a class of men who represent the *evil genius* of loyalty, I am well assured[.]

No one who has a love for our Country and a desire to preserve our Government, if possessed of ordinary intellect and a common inteligence with a knowledge of our people, would advise such measures. My hope is that in the multifarious affairs of State, your attention has not been caught to these matters, and that by my drawing your attention to them your sense of justice and what is due to a loyal people will prompt you to order a revocation of those orders and a correction of these evils. The course pursued by many of those entrusted with Federal authority in Kentucky, has made to your Administration and re-election, thousands of bitter and irreconcilable opponents, where a wise and just policy and action would more easily have made friends.

Extreme measures by which they sought to break the just pride and subdue the free spirit of the people; and which would only have fitted them for enslavement, have aroused the determined opposition to your re-election of at least three fourths of the people of Kentucky; when a different and just policy might have made them friends. You will pardon me for speaking thus plainly, for I assure you it is done in the kindest spirit; although I am opposed to your re-election, and regard a change of policy as essential to the salvation of our Country.

In common with the loyal masses of Kentucky *my Unionism is unconditional*. We are for preserving the rights and liberties of our own race – and upholding the character and dignity of our position. We are not willing to sacrifice a single life, or imperil the smallest right of free white men for the sake of the negro. We repudiate the Counsels of those who say the Government must be restored *with Slavery*, or that it must be restored *without Slavery, as a condition of their Unionism*. We are for the restoration of our Government throughout our entire limits regardless of what may happen to the negro. We reject as spurious, the Unionism of all who make the Status of the negro a sine qua non to peace and unity. We are not willing to imperil the life liberty and happiness of our own race and people for the freedom or enslavement of the negro. To permit the question of the freedom or slavery of the negro, to obstruct the restoration of National authority and unity is a blood stained sin. Those whose sons are involved in this strife demand, as they have the right to do, *that the negro be ignored in all questions of settlement, and not make his condition* – whether it shall be free or slave, *an obstacle to the restoration of national unity & peace*. Such are the sentiments of the loyal masses of Kentucky. Why therefore are unequal burdens laid upon the people of Kentucky? Is it not unwise, not to say unjust that this is done[?]

Surely the appealing blood of her sons, which crimsons the battlefields, sufficiently attests the loyalty of Kentucky and her people, to entitle the State to be freed from those Military manacles, which fetter her noble limbs, and chafe the free spirit of her loyal people.

It cannot surely be the purpose of any to ascertain by actual experiment how much a brave and manly people will bear rather than revolt against their Government.

And yet some of the measures adopted wear much the aspect of such an experiment.

May the God of our Fathers speedily give to us deliverance, by a restoration of our Government in unity and peace[.]
ALS

Respectfully
Thos E. Bramlette

DOCUMENT 3: THE CIVIL WAR AMENDMENTS TO THE UNITED STATES CONSTITUTION

The thirteenth, fourteenth and fifteenth amendments to the US Constitution, ratified in 1865, 1868 and 1870, abolished slavery in the United States and granted free blacks civil liberties and voting rights.

Amendment XIII (1865)

SECTION 1. Neither slavery nor involuntary servitude, except as a punishment for crime whereof the party shall have been duly convicted, shall exist within the United States, or any place subject to their jurisdiction.

SECTION 2. Congress shall have power to enforce this article by appropriate legislation.

Amendment XIV (1868)

SECTION 1. All persons born or naturalized in the United States, and subject to the jurisdiction thereof, are citizens of the United States and of the State wherein they reside. No State shall make or enforce any law which shall abridge the privileges or immunities of citizens of the United States; nor shall any State deprive any person of life, liberty, or property, without due process of law; nor deny to any person within its jurisdiction the equal protection of the laws.

SECTION 2. Representatives shall be apportioned among the several States according to their respective numbers, counting the whole number of persons in each State, excluding Indians not taxed. But when the right to vote at any election for the choice of electors for President and Vice-President of the United States, Representatives in Congress, the Executive and Judicial officers of a State, or the members of the Legislature thereof, is denied to any of the male inhabitants of such State, being twenty-one years of age, and citizens of the United States, or in any way abridged, except for participation in rebellion, or other crime, the basis of representation therein shall be reduced in the proportion which the number of such male citizens shall bear to the whole number of male citizens twenty-one years of age in such State.

SECTION 3. No person shall be a Senator or Representative in Congress, or elector of President and Vice President, or hold any office, civil or military, under the United States, or under any State, who, having previously taken an oath, as a member of Congress, or as an officer of the United States, or as a member of any State legislature, or as an executive or judicial officer of any State, to support the Constitution of the United States, shall have engaged

Henry S. Commager (ed.), *Documents of American History* (New York: Appleton-Century-Crofts, 1963), p. 501.

in insurrection or rebellion against the same, or given aid or comfort to the enemies thereof. But Congress may by a vote of two-thirds of each House, remove such disability.

SECTION 4. The validity of the public debt of the United States, authorized by law, including debts incurred for payment of pensions and bounties for services in suppressing insurrection or rebellion, shall not be questioned. But neither the United States nor any State shall assume or pay any debt or obligation incurred in aid of insurrection or rebellion against the United States, or any claim for the loss or emancipation of any slave; but all such debts, obligations, and claims shall be held illegal and void.

SECTION 5. The Congress shall have the power to enforce, by appropriate legislation, the provisions of this article.

Amendment XV (1870)

SECTION 1. The right of citizens of the United States to vote shall not be denied or abridged by the United States or by any State on account of race, color, or previous condition of servitude –

SECTION 2. The Congress shall have power to enforce this article by appropriate legislation.

COPYRIGHT ACKNOWLEDGEMENTS

Grateful acknowledgement is made to the following sources for permission to reproduce material in this book previously published elsewhere. Every effort has been made to trace copyright holders, but if any have been inadvertently overlooked the publisher will be pleased to make the necessary arrangement at the first opportunity.

'Transitions to African Slavery in British America, 1630–1730: Barbados, Virginia and South Carolina' by Russell R. Menard from *Indian Historical Review*, 15, 1988–9. Reproduced with the permission of the author.

'Engendering Racial Difference, 1640–1670' from *Good Wives, Nasty Wenches, and Anxious Patriarchs: Gender, Race, and Power in Colonial Virginia* by Kathleen M. Brown. Published for the Omohundro Institute of Early American History and Culture. Copyright © 1996 by the University of North Carolina Press. Reproduced with the permission of the publisher.

'Anonymous testimony before Virginia magistrates about a sexual assault complaint made by a white woman against a mulatto man, 1681' from *The Old Dominion in the Seventeenth Century: A Documentary History of Virginia, 1606–1689* by Warren M. Billings. Published for the Omohundro Institute of Early American History and Culture. Copyright © 1974 by the University of North Carolina Press. Reproduced with the permission of the publisher.

'Repeal of the Act Excluding Slaves from Georgia, 1750' from *Documents Illustrative of the History of the Slave Trade to America, Volume 4* edited by Elizabeth Donnan, Carnegie Institution of Washington, 1935. Reproduced with the permission of the publisher.

'George Fitzhugh and Proslavery Thought' from *The Ideology of Slavery: Proslavery Thought in the Antebellum South* edited by Drew Gilpin Faust, Louisiana State University Press, 1981. Reproduced with the permission of the publisher.

'Justification for Slavery' from *The Ideology of Slavery: Proslavery Thought in the Antebellum South* edited by Drew Gilpin Faust, Louisiana State University Press, 1981. Reproduced with the permission of the publisher.

'Antislavery Societies' from *The Great Silent Army of Abolitionism: Ordinary Women in the Antislavery Movement* by Julie Roy Jeffrey. Copyright © 1998 by the University of North Carolina Press. Reproduced with the permission of the publisher.

'Slaves Petition for Freedom during the Revolution, 1773–1779' from *A Documentary History of the Negro People in the United States* edited by Herbert Aptheker, Carol Publishing Group, 1951. Reproduced with the permission of Herbert Aptheker's Literary Estate.

'Politics, Ideology, and the Origins of the American Civil War' by Eric Foner from *A Nation Divided: Problems and Issues of the Civil War and Reconstruction* edited by George M. Frederickson, Burgess Publishing Company, 1975. Reproduced with the permission of the author.

Extracts from *The Slaveholding Republic: An Account of the United States Government's Relations to Slavery* by Don E. Fehrenbacher and edited by Ward M. McAfee, Oxford University Press, Inc. Copyright © 2001 by Oxford University Press, Inc. Reproduced with the permission of the publisher.

INDEX